C000000368

THE HISTORY OF
SEAFARING

1. Reefing the Foresail by John Stobart, 1991

USED BY PERMISSION OF DUTTON, A DIVISION OF PENGUIN GROUP (USA) INC

THE HISTORY OF
SEAFARING
NAVIGATING THE WORLD'S OCEANS

DONALD S. JOHNSON
JUHA NURMINEN

JOHN NURMINEN FOUNDATION
CONWAY MARITIME PRESS

CONWAY

MAIN AUTHOR
Donald S. Johnson

OTHER AUTHORS
Tapio Markkanen, Juha Nurminen and Pär-Henrik Sjöström

CHIEF EDITOR
Juha Nurminen

TEXT EDITOR
Nicki Marshall and Nicholas Tracy

EXECUTIVE COMMITTEE
Peter Barber, Head of Map Collections, The British Library
Ulla Ehrensvärd, Professor, Stockholm
Juhani Kaskeala, Admiral, Chief of Defence, Finland
Peter Tamm, Professor, Wissenschaftliches
Institut für Schiffahrts- und Marinegeschichte, Hamburg
Edward L. Widmer, Director and Librarian,
The John Carter Brown Library, U.S.A.

PICTURE EDITORS
Maria Grönroos and Kaarina Pohjola

GRAPHIC DESIGNER AND LAYOUT
Olavi Hankimo

ILLUSTRATIVE PICTURES AND MAPS
Stewart Gray and Jari Patanen

MAIN PHOTOGRAPHER
Rauno Träskelin

TRANSLATION FINNISH-ENGLISH
Erik Miller

PICTURE MANIPULATION
Art-Print Oy

Art-Print Oy
Helsinki, Finland 2007

© John Nurminen Foundation 2007

This edition first published in Great Britain in 2007 by
Conway
An imprint of Anova Books Company Ltd
10 Southcombe Street
London W14 0RA
www.anovabooks.com

Donald S. Johnson and Juha Nurminen have asserted their moral
right to be identified as the authors of this work.

All rights reserved. No part of this publication may be
reproduced, stored in a retrieval system, or transmitted in any
form or by any means electronic, mechanical, photocopying,
recording or otherwise, without prior written permission of the
publishers.

British Library Cataloguing in Publication Data
A record for this book is available from the British Library

ISBN 9781844860401

Paper supplied by

LumiSilk 150 g/m²

INTRODUCTION

On a sweltering day in July 2002, the American yachtsman and author, Donald S. Johnson, tied up his boat to the jetty of our fishing cottage in the eastern Gulf of Finland. My wife and I watched with admiration as a small 28-foot schooner arrived with a smiling, grey-bearded man standing on deck. He explained that he had crossed the Atlantic and was on his way to St. Petersburg, Russia, but wanted to meet the Finnish maritime author who had recently published a book on northern explorations. He was referring to the book *Ultima Thule* by John Nurminen Foundation, in which I had mentioned his book *Phantom Islands of the Atlantic*.

This was the beginning of our friendship, and in the soft heat of our seaside sauna, the idea of a book on the history of navigation emerged almost by itself. We had a clear division of labour from the very beginning. Don, who is an experienced seaman and author, would be the principal writer of the book, and I would take on the responsibilities of chief editor and publisher. We would attract an eager and competent editorial board from Finland to supplement the book with selected Info boxes. After nearly five years of work and adventure, the book *The History of Seafaring: Navigating the World's Oceans* is finally ready.

Our project combines Don's exceptionally broad experience in traditional navigation without modern tools or the help of GPS technology, with my interest in cartography and publishing. Don has sailed and navigated five times across the Atlantic in his small schooner, *Nakomis*, which he built himself, using traditional methods. My own fascination with ancient maps, and the history of discovery and exploration, began thirty years ago. I have had the opportunity to make use of it in several other book projects; the *The History of Seafaring* has been one of my greatest and most interesting personal challenges.

Since innumerable interesting books have been written on the history of seafaring, we felt it was important to choose a well-defined topic from the vast subject matter, and to focus on it. In our book, we concentrate on the history of seafaring from the perspective of navigation. Our principal interest is the history of European navigation and the development of European navigational skill. Merchant shipping, naval wars, overseas settlement, fishing and whaling, seamanship and sailing, are all interesting topics and merit books on their own, but since they are not immediately relevant to navigation we exclude them from our account. Above all, the *The History of Seafaring* deals with finding your destination when sailing on the open sea, and with how the knowledge, skill, and tools of navigation have evolved over the centuries. We also deal with the motives, such as religion,

2. Frontispiece of *Les Premières oeuvres* by Jacques de Vaulx, 1583
BIBLIOTHÈQUE NATIONALE DE FRANCE, PARIS

warfare, power and politics, which have inspired and driven people in different periods of history to traverse the world's seas. The greatest driving force to seafaring, however, was trade. The risks involved in the voyages of discovery were enormous, but success brought immense profit.

Every mariner who set forth upon the open sea contributed in some manner to the history of navigation; their numbers are legion. We chose to chronicle here those who led the way, whose endeavours contributed 'keystones' in the building of navigation knowledge.

Although our main perspective on the history of navigation is European, we also discuss Pacific traditions of seafaring and the history of Arab seafarers on the Indian Ocean and the waters of southeastern Asia. We cover a period of 3500

years from the first documented voyages by the Egyptians to A.E. Nordenskiöld's scientific explorations in the late nineteenth century. Our story ends with the emerging domination of steamships around the world, when the main navigational devices were still the compass, the octant or the sextant, the chronometer, nautical almanac and nautical charts.

Navigation is a multidisciplinary art, and our account discusses the history of the sciences that have contributed to it; without doubt the most important subjects are geography, astronomy and cartography. We also feel it essential to discuss navigation from the standpoint of the seafarer. To this end, we include Info boxes in the book and group them under three special themes: the natural phenomena encountered by navigating seafarers; navigational tools used at sea; and ships, the principal aspects of their development. There are some thirty Info boxes in all.

Captain James Cook's encounter with the Tahitian navigator, Tupaia, in the Pacific Ocean in the eighteenth century introduces an overview in the first chapter on the seafaring traditions of the people of Oceania. This places the European seafaring heritage in a more global context. Voyages of thousands of miles were made across the open sea, using only extremely simple tools and vessels, and sufficient knowledge of the stars, waves, winds, sea currents, and the behaviour of animals, such as seabirds.

In the second chapter we take a closer look at the 'playing field' of seafaring and discuss in more detail the natural challenges seafarers have faced for millennia. The chronological discussion of the progress of navigation begins in chapter three. The emphasis is on the European perspective.

We discuss navigation as both a skill and a science. The Phoenicians, Pacific seafarers, and the Vikings had highly advanced navigational skills. Their skills were passed on by oral tradition, and only a very few were initiated in them. Today, these traditions have for the most part been lost. As a science, navigation developed in Europe and the Muslim world of the Near East, with its roots in Greek astronomy, geography, cartography, an understanding of the shape of the Earth, and movement of the Sun, planets, and stars in the sky. The ancient Greeks were the first to conjecture about these matters, and their theories formed the basis for future European navigation.

Our chronological story begins in the eastern Mediterranean, where the Egyptians, and Phoenicians, and later the Greeks and Romans, set off to ever more remote destinations. This was the earliest high point of European seafaring, and it lasted for nearly two millennia, from 1500 BC to AD 400. The Phoenicians had already headed far to the west from the eastern end of the Mediterranean Sea, reaching the Straits of Gibraltar. They are known to have sailed as far as the British Isles in search of tin.

In the early Middle Ages, after the fall of the West Roman Empire in the fifth century, it was increasingly Arab, rather than European navigators, who led the revolution in seafaring. The Arabs embraced the science of the ancient Greeks and applied their expertise in astronomy and geography to navigation. By the ninth century they developed the planispheric astrolabe into a fine instrument for astronomical computations. Introduced into Latin Europe at the very end of the eleventh, or beginning of the twelfth century, it was simplified in form to become the mariner's, or sea astrolabe, used by mariners in Western Europe from the end of the fifteenth century onward. Arabs extended their voyages to India and Asia. They dominated trade between the Far East and Europe for a long period of time, until Europeans reached the same waters.

As Arabs developed trade routes in the Indian Ocean, groups of brave sailors left Scandinavia in the ninth century to sail the stormy Atlantic. They reached Iceland, Greenland, and even North America. They were the Vikings and, like the Pacific seafarers, their navigation was based on knowledge of natural phenomena. Charts and the magnetic compass were unknown to them.

From the twelfth to the fifteenth century, Hanseatic seafarers in their cogs traded throughout an ever larger area in the Baltic and North Seas, while in the Mediterranean the emerging city-states of Italy took over the trade in goods coming from the east. During the Renaissance (roughly from the fourteenth through the sixteenth century), Spanish and Portuguese royal courts took an interest in seafaring and the riches of the Far East, challenging Italy's city-states and the maritime hegemony of the Arabs. Iberian monarchs sent many expeditions to search for maritime routes to India, China and the Spice Islands. In these voyages, the tools they used for navigation were the magnetic compass, quadrant and the astrolabe, with which they could set their course and determine latitude. By the tenth century, or perhaps even earlier, Arab seafarers were using the magnetic compass, gained from their trade voyages to China, and by the end of the twelfth century it was introduced to European navigators. From the Age of Discovery onwards, the magnetic compass was commonly used on all voyages across open sea.

Since antiquity, Mediterranean sailors had entered important sailing instructions in pilot books. These books (known by their Greek name *peripli*) were the basis of the later portolan charts. We pay special attention to the Mediterranean portolans because these masterpieces of cartography played a vital role in the history of navigation. It is interesting how the portolan tradition with its rather realistic maps, developed within the seafaring community, evolved so differently from the *mappamundi* tradition of schematic world-view maps, developed for the Church.

3. An English Ship in a Gale Trying to Claw off a Lee Shore by Willem van de Velde, the Younger, 1672

NATIONAL MARITIME MUSEUM, LONDON

8

The Renaissance witnessed an explosion of the dissemination of knowledge and a change in the humanities and arts. It also included major advances in the science of navigation, and great discoveries in the voyages of exploration. Spain and Portugal created institutions of navigation based on a solid foundation of scientific progress. Astronomers devised tables and calendars for navigators that made possible much more accurate determination of a ship's position at sea. Later, the knowledge, skills and theoretical expertise of the Iberian navigators spread north to France, England and the Netherlands.

Printed nautical charts intended for seafarers were developed in the Netherlands, where the best charts and atlases of the sixteenth and seventeenth centuries were produced. Crafted by the great names of nautical cartography, including Waghenaer, Blaeu and van Keulen, these works owed more to the portolan tradition and to hydrographic records than to the Ptolemaic world-view of antiquity.

The finding of sea routes to southeastern Asia, and especially to the fabled Spice Islands, enormously broadened the European view of the world. And westward voyages of Christopher Columbus, Amerigo Vespucci, Ferdinand Magellan, and many others, showed that a vast new continent existed between the Atlantic Ocean and the South Seas. The concept of the Ptolemaic world, which comprised a single continent, could no longer be accepted. After Vasco da Gama proved that a sea route to India was possible by sailing around the southern tip of Africa (Cape of Good Hope) and across the Indian Ocean, the Portuguese extended their voyages to the sources of spices and riches in Ceylon and the Molucca Islands. They charted the seaways and navigable passages in the regions of India and southeastern Asia. At the same time, British and Dutch seafarers sought Arctic routes to Japan, China and the Spice Islands.

The Dutch made use of Portuguese navigational expertise and knowledge, and later replaced them on the southern routes. These tough new Dutch merchants eventually challenged all other seafaring powers on the Indian Ocean and in the southeastern Asian archipelago. The Dutch fleet became the most powerful in the world, backed by navigational skill based on the latest achievements in astronomy and geography. The most accomplished scientist was the Flemish-born cartographer, Gerard Mercator, who revolutionized cartography and navigation. He occupies a special place in this book. Later, in the eighteenth and nineteenth centuries, the British achieved naval supremacy, and their fleets and merchant ships dominated nearly all seas.

The great discoveries opened sea routes to new generations of seafarers who extended their voyages around the globe.

The progress of navigation is viewed here as a kind of dialogue between the theoretical and scientific advances on land and practical experience at sea. Dry theory meets salty action at sea in the towering achievements of men such as Francis Drake, Willem Schouten, William Dampier, George Anson, Louis-Antoine de Bougainville and James Cook.

The determination of longitude remained for millennia the great unsolvable dilemma of navigation. Although there is ample recent literature on the topic, the fascinating story of the clockmaker, John Harrison, is retold here, for he developed the chronometer that finally made it possible to calculate longitude at sea.

Arguably, James Cook, who charted numerous Pacific Islands, including New Zealand, and finally determined the position of the Bering Strait in the late eighteenth century, was the last great discoverer. In the history of navigation, Cook was without question the most important figure of the modern age, and initiated the era of scientific exploration. His charts were so accurate and reliable that they were still used for comparison in the hydrographic exploration of the Pacific Ocean in the nineteenth century. During the final voyages in the age of sailing ships, the great navigators made substantial progress in the theory of magnetic phenomena, meteorology, hydrography and natural history.

In the nineteenth century, numerous expeditions left Europe to open the seaways of the Arctic. Roald Amundsen eventually succeeded in navigating the Northwest Passage, and A. E. Nordenskiöld the Northeast Passage. The key objectives in exploration also shifted to the gathering of scientific information. The last chapter in our history of navigation concludes with Nordenskiöld, the scientist, explorer and the first historian of cartography. He was leading the *Vega* expedition when Captain Louis Palander navigated the ship through the Northeast Passage and when Eurasia was circumnavigated for the first time.

European navigational achievements did more than change our geographical view of the world. By the time of the great discoveries, they irrevocably changed the entire world. They altered how Europeans saw themselves and the people with whom they came into contact. While such contact was often violent, it also served the interests of both parties at certain times and in certain places. Without the progress in navigation and shipbuilding, combined with scientific advances, the world today would be a different one culturally, politically and economically.

Juha Nurminen

FOREWORD

As mentioned in the introduction, *The History of Seafaring: Navigating the World's Oceans*, published by the John Nurminen Foundation, deals with the progress of navigation and the voyages of discovery in a chronological order. However, the book sometimes discusses events out of order or omits others, and there are even some chronological inconsistencies. It was not always possible to follow a strict sequence of time. We have followed some topics from beginning to end in their entirety to provide the reader with a better idea of the main trends.

This book is an abridged presentation of more than 2000 years of history. We may have been somewhat subjective on which events merited detailed discussion, but we have not intentionally sought to alter the course of history. Until the fifteenth century, history was considered a part of rhetoric. Speakers used their oratorical skills and high-flown talk to influence their listeners. Cicero himself said that to support his claims, an orator is allowed to embellish his speech.

We have not passed over any major source in order to promote our own opinions. I do doubt we have not committed errors, however. In the preface to his 1627 *Sea Grammar*, Captain John Smith wrote: 'If any will bestow the paines [to point them out], I shall think him my friend, and honor his endeavours. In the interim accept them as they are, and ponder errours in the balance of good will'.

Juha Nurminen Donald S. Johnson
Chief editor *Author*

4. Maidens lighthouse by Alpo Tuurnala, 2006

DONALD S. JOHNSON

GLI AR- GONAUTI

PLUS ULTRA

ACKNOWLEDGEMENTS

I had been thinking about publishing a book on the history of navigation for quite some time when I met Donald S. Johnson in 2002 and my dream started to take shape. Don Johnson took on the task of writing the principal text of the book and also contributed a third of the info boxes.

I have great respect for the dedication Don demonstrated during the five years that we worked on this book. His research was exhaustive and he never tired of going to sources for information. His mastery of traditional sailing was also of great help to us.

We discussed the structure and content of the book endlessly. After long debates, we generally reached agreement or at least a compromise. On several occasions during the making of this book, Don Johnson came to Finland – in summer, we often worked on the Baltic Sea coast in the country. We also went on a sailing pilgrimage on the Mediterranean, visiting the oldest monument of navigation, the Tower of winds in Athens. I want to express my deepest gratitude to Don Johnson for his constructive and very pleasant collaboration and tireless writing during our project. We take pride in the result.

A large number of people contributed to *The History of Seafaring: Navigating the World's Oceans* published by the John Nurminen Foundation. The editorial board itself included some twenty people. It was a great pleasure to be the chief editor, with the support of such a committed and inspired team, without which this book would not have been possible. I want to thank everyone who took part in our project from the bottom of my heart.

In addition to Don Johnson, texts were contributed by Tapio Markkanen, who wrote the info boxes that deal with astronomy. He was also our scientific advisor in matters that related to his field of expertise. The wonderful presentations of different ship types were written by Pär-Henrik Sjöström.

Our book will be published in English and in Finnish. The source material was in several languages – Greek, Latin, French, English, Swedish and Finnish. Our translators were Ed Jordan, Burton Van-Name Edwards, Renne Nikupaavola, Anne Sjöström, Ilkka Karttunen and Erik Miller.

The English text was edited by Nicholas Tracy and Nicki Marshall. Finnish texts were edited by Marketta Klinge, Tuula Talasmaa-Lainema, Ilkka Karttunen, Tuula Nurmilaukas, Riikka Sainio, Nana Smulovitz-Mulyana and Pirita Hannula. Matti Lainema and Marjo Nurminen also helped in this work.

I would like to thank Ulla Ehrensvärd for her expertise especially in cartographical matters and for checking names, dates and other facts.

The History of Seafaring: Navigating the World's Oceans is richly illustrated to complement the articles and other texts. Most of the pictures are from the Foundation's or my personal collection. Our photographer was Rauno Träskelin. In addition, the book includes drawings by Stewart Gray and maps by Jari Patanen. The editorial team for illustrations included Maria Grönroos and Kaarina Pohjola.

We also received material from our partners. I wish to express my gratitude to Hélène Richard, Monique Cohen and Thierry Delcourt of the Bibliothèque nationale de France and Peter Barber of the British Library for their collaboration. I am also grateful to Francis Herbert of the Royal Geographical Society.

I am especially grateful to Olavi Hankimo, our graphic designer. He designed a remarkably fine-looking book.

The paper for our book was donated by Stora Enso Group. The book was printed by Art-Print Oy who did a stunning job. I am deeply grateful to both.

I also want to thank the Foundation's Secretary General Erik Båsk, who was in charge of publishing, and the Foundation's staff for finalising the book for printing.

This book has been a large project which has required flexibility from everyone who took part in it, including their families. I wish to express my warmest thanks to the families, including mine, for the patience they have shown.

I hope that the readers of *The History of Seafaring: Navigating the World's Oceans* will experience enjoyable moments in the eventful world of maritime history. The book brings forth in chronological order all the brave and courageous scientists and seafarers who for centuries have been moulding the developing image of our world.

JuhaNurminen
Chief Editor
Chairman of the Board, John Nurminen Foundation

5. Frontispiece of *Gli argonauti pro ultra* by Vincenzo Maria Coronelli, 17th century

JUHA NURMINEN COLLECTION

CONTENTS

**6. Terrestrial globe by J. & G. Cary from
the beginning of the 19th century**

JUHA NURMINEN COLLECTION

THE DAWN OF NAVIGATION

SEAFARERS OF OCEANIA

A little-known historic event took place in the Pacific Ocean in 1769 that proved to be of great importance to navigation and of great symbolic significance. This event was the encounter of two top navigators of the time and it occurred in the Tahiti archipelago.

One person was the British navigator and explorer, Captain James Cook (1728–1779), who had rounded the world in *Endeavour* in search of an unknown southern continent, and as part of a scientific programme to take precise astronomical observations of the transit of Venus. Cook used the most advanced navigational technology available to Europeans: the magnetic compass, the octant, the earliest chronometers, charts and special astronomical tables prepared for navigation. The person who met Cook was Tupaia (c. 1725–1770), a Polynesian religious leader and navigator from the island of Raiatea, who could sail hundreds of miles out of sight of land without any technical aids. The only 'tools' Tupaia used was the information he gleaned from nature: from the sky, the sea, and the motion of a vessel caused by ocean swells. Both came from two completely different traditions of navigation.

Cook became interested in Tupaia's exceptional abilities in navigation and the geographic knowledge of his surroundings. The officers of the *Endeavour* tested Tupaia's knowledge and drew a map based on what he told them. The map proved that this Polynesian was familiar with an astonishingly wide region, larger than the continental United States. Tupaia had been taught to navigate by his father who had sailed long distances, perhaps all the way to New Zealand. Tupaia had precise knowledge of the bearings of nearby islands that were unknown to the captain.

Cook asked the Polynesian to be his guide. From Tahiti, Tupaia piloted Cook's expedition to nearby islands, which later became established on European sea charts. The expedition continued to New Zealand, and thence along the eastern coast of Australia. The *Endeavour* was shipwrecked in the Great Barrier Reef and had to be sailed to Batavia (present-day Jakarta) to be dry-docked. Cook and Tupaia were never again to sail together. Like many other members of the crew, Tupaia died of a tropical disease while in Batavia. Throughout the long journey in the Southern Seas, and despite the fact that the *Endeavour* visited numerous islands and changed course hundreds of times, Tupaia was always able to indicate the cor-

7. HMS *Resolution* and *Adventure* with Fishing Craft in Matavi Bay by William Hodges, 1776

The British Admiralty appointed William Hodges to record the places discovered by Captain James Cook during his second voyage of 1772–75. In this painting of Matavi Bay in the island of Otaheite (Tahiti), there are many layers of information. Among them is the documentation of the encounter between two completely different cultures; above all, it portrayed to the European public the glorious appearance of this tropical paradise.

NATIONAL MARITIME MUSEUM, LONDON

rect direction to Tahiti. This astonished the Europeans, who on the open sea depended completely on their instruments and observations. Cook checked Tupaia's bearings with compass and calculations: they proved that Tupaia never failed.

James Cook was the first European to understand and appreciate the seafaring traditions of the first people of the Pacific, and while he may not have fully understood the basis of these skills, he certainly recognized how advanced they were. He also understood their significance for the settlement of Oceania. Before Cook, Spanish mariners had charted Oceania and they believed that its people had arrived at their islands along southern continental routes or that they had simply been created there. Cook understood that all the Pacific peoples, who inhabited a vast region from the Easter Islands to New Zealand, had a common origin and that they had settled their islands by sailing from one to another using only Stone-Age technology.

After Cook, although European seafarers occasionally studied the disappearing navigation tradition of Oceania, the first systematic study did not take place until the 1970s, when David Lewis published his book *We, the Navigators*. Lewis's extensive research, in which he tested in practice the navigational systems of Oceania, did much to change our understanding of voyages in the Pacific Ocean and the navigational skills of its seafarers.

The Start of Seafaring

The encounter between Tupaia and Cook was an encounter between two completely different traditions of seafaring which, nevertheless, had similar origins. People had learned to use rudimentary boats in the Stone-Age, but in order to make longer voyages they needed to develop a vessel suitable for crossing a sea and use an appropriate mode of propulsion. Indeed, the development of boats or ships that could be used to make long voyages to distant places can well be considered one of the most significant human achievements. Like harnessing the horse or the invention of the wheel, boats and ships revolutionized the way people moved about. But to be able to make long voyages, another invention was needed – the sail – which made use of the wind as a mode of propulsion. Before the sail, paddles and oars were used to move the boat short distances, but with the sail, long voyages could be made across open water.

Although the circumstances surrounding the first sails are not known exactly, they were already in existence around 3000 BC when the Egyptians plied the Nile and later extended their trading voyages to the eastern parts of the Mediterranean. Mariners sailed down the Red Sea to the Indian Ocean as early as 1500 BC, and it is very likely that sails were used on the Indian Ocean well before the birth of Christ. Traders regularly sailed from the Arabian Peninsula to the Indian subcontinent before 1000 BC, and the seafarers of the time knew how to navigate across the open Indian Ocean.

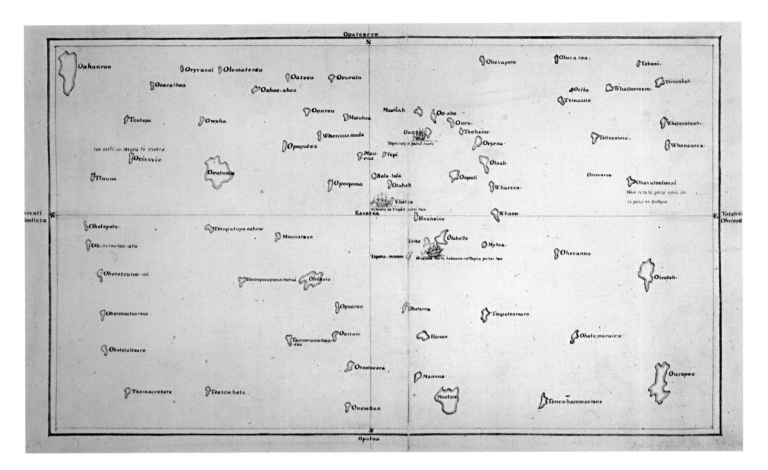

8. The Society Islands by James Cook, 1769

Guided by the stars and pattern of ocean swells, the native guide, Tupaia, navigated Captain James Cook through the Society Islands of the South Pacific. Cook gave them this name in 1769 after England's Royal Society for science. Tupaia's knowledge of the archipelago allowed Cook to produce this reasonably accurate map.

THE BRITISH LIBRARY, LONDON

Before 1000 BC, the Phoenicians also sailed from their home waters in the eastern Mediterranean to their western colonies in North Africa and the Iberian Peninsula. Later, they sailed as far as the British Isles to procure tin, which was needed to make bronze. In contrast, sails were not used in the Baltic Sea until the early Middle Ages, despite trade contacts with the Mediterranean that dated back to the Roman period.

Well before the first millennium, sails were common in various types of boats, including the small two-hulled canoes used in the archipelago of modern Indonesia and the China Sea. From this region, Pacific seafarers took navigation skills to the far reaches of the vast Pacific Ocean, which was settled in its entirety by the beginning of the ninth century. In the Indian Ocean, these seafarers extended their journeys westward (as well as eastward) as far as Madagascar. The geographic location of the Indonesian archipelago made its mariners a natural link between the navigation traditions of the Indian and Pacific Oceans.

The indigenous peoples of the Americas did not make long-distant voyages over the sea; their ventures were mostly confined to coastal travels. In the northern Arctic regions, the Eskimos used leather boats and kayaks for their fishing, hunting and trading voyages. It was not until a mere 500 years ago that Europeans introduced the sail and maritime navigating skills to the indigenous peoples of the north.

The first Europeans to cross an ocean were the Vikings. They were exceptionally good boat builders, and they were also the last seafarers not to use technical aids or charts in navigation. Like their Pacific counterparts, they used only the stars, the Sun, and natural phenomena, such as prevailing winds, waves, ocean currents, the colour of the water, and the behaviour of birds, to guide them to their destination.

The Boats of Oceania

Before Tupaia's ancestors could find their way to southeastern Asia to the islands of the vast Pacific area they had had to develop suitable vessels to make their journeys. The first Europeans to encounter the various boat-types of Oceania were the early explorers of the sixteenth century. Antonio Pigafetta (c. 1491–1534), the Spanish scribe who accompanied Ferdinand Magellan (c. 1480–1521) on his legendary voyage, described the canoes used by the local inhabitants, mainly in the vicinity of the Philippines. These canoes were equipped with an ingenious outrigger hull to balance the main hull. The Dutchman Abel Tasman (c. 1603–1659) met the same type of double-hulled canoes when he first visited Australia in 1642. At the time, the

Europeans used rather large carracks and galleons and were astonished by how swift and manoeuvrable these canoes were.

In the late eighteenth century, Louis-Antoine de Bougainville (1729–1811) and Cook also encountered Polynesian canoes with two or more hulls which could carry dozens of passengers and their provisions on long voyages. Tahitians even covered their large boats with weatherproof cabin-like structures. All Pacific vessels fit for the open sea had one or more sails, the shapes of which varied regionally. The basic shape, however, was a triangle, and its sailing characteristics and handling were somewhat similar to those of the lateen sail used in the Mediterranean Sea and the Indian Ocean. Around Tahiti the typical sail type was reminiscent of a crab's claw. The hulls of these boats were generally cut from large logs and they were steered with one or more paddles attached to the outside of the hull.

The smaller boats used in coastal waters were usually propelled with paddles; sails were used on fishing and trading voyages that ventured further. With favourable conditions, the large boats could maintain an average of six knots, and even reach as high as eight knots. But the multi-hulled canoes were not very good at sailing to windward. At best they could sail no closer than 50 degrees to the wind. In the event of a storm, the wind was usually allowed to push the boat downwind,

and the sailors tried to determine their position as best as they could, so that when the weather improved they could lay a new and proper heading to their destination.

IDEA AND ART OF PACIFIC NAVIGATION

When European sailors pictured the position and direction of their ship, they always projected it on a chart, with the sea and its islands in their appropriate places, visible to the user of the chart. Ships traversed this schematic world where position was determined with two-directional coordinates. In contrast, for the seafarers of Polynesia and Micronesia, the boat itself was the centre of the world. The islands and the surrounding world glided past it until the boat had reached its destination. The Pacific sailors were so familiar with their surroundings that they did not have to see the island to which they were travelling, or the islands that they passed, because they were able to imagine their presence, direction and distance. Charts drawn on paper seemed strange to them, whereas a mental map of their region, its islands, their bearings and the position of their boat in relation to them was familiar.

Voyages were divided into distinct segments called *etaks*; depending on the voyage, there could be from a few to more than ten *etaks*. An *etak* was never an absolute measurement of length, but varied according to the reference points on the way. As a rule, it was reckoned that when an island appeared on the horizon, the distance to it was one *etak*. Because an island with mountains was visible from much farther away than a low atoll, which could only be seen from a short distance, the absolute distance of an *etak* was variable.

9. Polynesian Migration

In their maritime migrations, the inhabitants of New Guinea extended their voyages until eventually all the island groups of the Pacific Ocean were populated. This is a remarkable feat considering that the Pacific Ocean covers nearly one half of the Earth's surface, and that it was accomplished in vessels absurdly small by European standards.

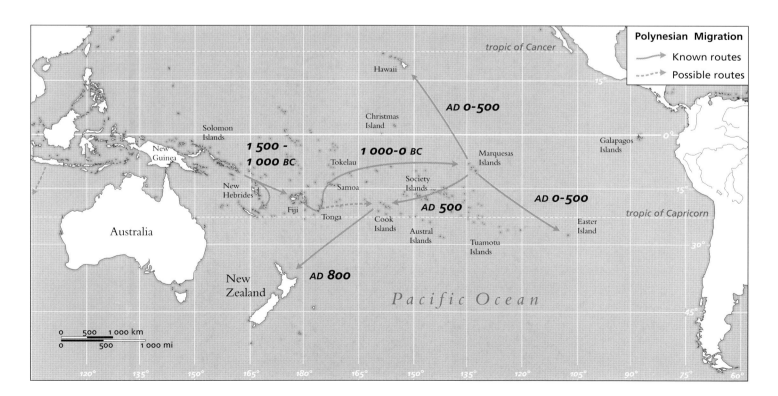

Navigators constantly estimated the speed of the boat and the distance it had travelled, maintaining their heading mainly with the stars at night and the waves during the day. They observed the progress of the boat along its heading, *etak* by *etak*, using the islands passed by the boat as points of reference. Very often they did not see the islands at all, but could imagine them bypassing their boat on either side. Stars rising from the horizon at known directions guided the navigators in estimating their bearings. In their voyages, they followed the path of the star, and experienced navigators could understand their

10. Islands of the Lateen Sails by Antonio Pigafetta, 16th century

In this illustration from the account of Magellan's expedition to circumnavigate the globe, a vessel of the Marianas or Ladrones is shown. The sails are made of palm leaves sewn together like a lateen sail, causing Magellan to name the islands *Islas de las Velas Latinas* (Islands of the Lateen Sails). There is no difference between the stern and the bow of these boats, which are 'like dolphins jumping from wave to wave.'

BIBLIOTHÈQUE NATIONALE DE FRANCE, PARIS

11. Native Watercraft of the Island of Anamocka by Abel Tasman, 1642

Abel Tasman encountered the native watercraft of the Solomon Islands during his voyage of 1642–43. He was impressed with how speedily they could move. The distinctive inverted triangular – shaped sail, shown here, is common to many traditional Pacific Ocean cultures. There were regional differences, such as the crab claw sail, so named on account of its appearance.

JUHA NURMINEN COLLECTION

position in relation to other, even far away islands, just like Tupaia did on Cook's voyage from Tahiti to Java.

In their long voyages the Pacific seafarers sailed hundreds of miles on passages lasting many days and sometimes weeks. The knowledge and navigational skills of Pacific seafarers were based on thousands of years of accumulated experience, passed down through generations from father to son. Early instruction took place on land and continued for years. Only selected and specially initiated youths were trained as navigators. The knowledge was often kept secret and women were also known to participate in the training and practice of navigation. The heavens and the movements in it were studied night after night until the student had learned to identify every crucial star in the sky and knew its position. Exercises were then continued at sea in realistic conditions and on voyages between islands. Students learned to use visualization and cognitive or mental maps to stay on course and estimate the distance travelled. When sufficiently experienced at sea, they could also absorb the skills of wave navigation and learn to read ocean swells. It could take a decade to become a proficient navigator on the South Seas.

Navigation on the Open Seas

In contrast to the Viking sailors of Scandinavia, whose destinations were located on long coasts, thereby reducing the risk of sailing past them by accident, the mariners of the Pacific sailed to small groups of islands, sometimes even minuscule atolls, which were hundreds of miles away. They could not afford the risk of sailing past their destination, for the consequences could have made their life difficult, and in the worst case been fatal.

To hold their course without the help of a magnetic compass, the Pacific navigators used the stars on the horizon at night and the position of the Sun during the day, and when the sky was overcast and stars or the Sun could not be seen, they observed the waves, ocean swells, and the appearance of the sky. They knew where on the horizon individual stars rose or set. These seafarers also understood that at any given latitude, the position remained the same, but that the time of their rising and setting varied according to the season.

To assist them, the Pacific navigators devised a star-compass based on known stars as they rose and set on the horizon. It was similar to the European compass rose except that instead of north, south, east and west, it indicated directions based on easily recognizable stars. This same system was used by Arab navigators in the Indian Ocean before the arrival there of the Portuguese. Skilled navigators from Oceania could name stars rising from the horizon in a particular direction and time. For example, when Sirius had risen well above the horizon, they could recognize the stars that rose in the same direction as the night progressed. Usually, they chose a horizon star that was in the direction of their

destination. But if the sky in that direction happened to be overcast, they chose another star, perhaps one on the traveller's reciprocal course. Because they were so knowledgeable about the sky and its stars, Oceania seafarers could also use a star that was off the vessel's course, taking care that the angle between the vessel's direction of travel and the bearing of the star remained constant. This knowledge provided them with a dependable and accurate gauge for holding course as they sailed towards their destination. Sailors were taught the bearings of neighbouring islands with the star compass. For longer voyages, which progressed from island to island, they also had to know the bearing of their destination from islands other than their own.

During daylight hours, the progress of the Sun helped the navigators hold their course. Observations of the directions of sunrise and sunset and its position at noon were essential to navigation. The information provided by the Sun, however, was not nearly as accurate as that available from the stars.

When neither the Sun nor the stars could be seen, observation of waves and swells enabled Oceanic navigators to estimate their heading. In the Pacific, there are different prevailing wind systems that vary according to season and region. The best known of these are the trade winds, which occur close to the equator, and the westerlies, which occur in the southern latitudes. The maritime people of Oceania were naturally very familiar with the seasonal changes to the winds, and planned their trips to take advantage of the best seasonal wind pattern. Pacific navigators also used the large, regular ocean swells, caused by the winds blowing hundreds if not thousands of miles away, to provide navigational data. These swells are quite different, and easily distinguished, from the short, steep waves caused by local winds. Navigators of the South Seas could recognize those arriving simultaneously from as many as four or five different directions, caused by distant wind conditions. They could distinguish them by the movement of the boat and with their own bodies, and assess their boats' courses accordingly. A skilled navigator could also estimate the strength of a current by observing the shape of the waves. For European seafarers accustomed to navigation by instruments, the accuracy of this natural method was difficult to comprehend.

In some regions of the Pacific navigators used a wind rose, based on the direction of the prevailing winds, as a kind of compass to determine direction. In early antiquity, sailors of the Mediterranean Sea used the identical method of prevailing winds to indicate direction. The Oceanic navigators, however, never used the star compass or the wind rose at sea, but only for training purposes on land. In the Caroline Islands it was common to make a star compass on sand, using sticks, shells and other available materials. They made a circle with sticks and divided it into eight sections, assigning pieces of coral to stand for the stars used. Their traditional twin-hulled canoe was always depicted at the centre of the compass.

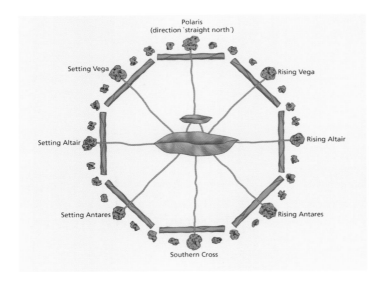

12. Carolinian Star Compass

By diagrams such as this, Polynesian seamen were taught how to navigate by the stars. Lacking the magnetic compass, they used the rising and setting of certain selected stars as their direction guide. With the materials at hand, a kind of 'star compass' was created: the lumps of coral represented the stars (what we would think of as the compass points), while bundles of coconut leaves designated the direction of ocean swells. This same system of sailing by the stars was used by Arab navigators in the Indian Ocean before the arrival of the magnetic compass.

13. Sailing toward a Star

In order for the navigator to arrive at his desired destination, beneath the appropriate selected star, he has to take into account the effect of wind and current upon his ship. As seen here, the heading of the ship is to the left of the goal, but the course to the destination is eventually made good.

In some areas of the Pacific the navigators also used so-called 'zenith stars' to guide their way to the destination. According to known zenith stars they could estimate the correct latitude to their target island. This was a form of latitude sailing commonly used by Arabs and Europeans in other oceans and is handled later in this book.

Voyages were usually timed so that most of the sailing could be downwind or across the wind. When they were forced to sail upwind, the navigators of the Pacific commonly applied a method of tacking in a tapering zigzag pattern that made certain of finding their destination, even if they were bound for a small atoll. The points where tacks were made were estimated using directional stars behind their destination, even when the island itself was not visible. Its bearing was estimated on the basis of the distance travelled from the previous tacking point. And that distance was estimated, based on experience, on the speed of the boat. No instruments were used. To find the proper place to tack, a navigator would position two targets along a single lane, one of which he could not see. Skilled navigators were good at imagining these unseen targets. The system proved itself even on long upwind passages when numerous tacks had to be made to reach the destination. This approach, based on visioning and directions, was foreign to European navigation, which was based on true observations and measurements. Even on long voyages, experienced Pacific navigators were able to keep their course within an error less than three to five degrees. This was possible during their voyage even if they encountered different weather types and side-

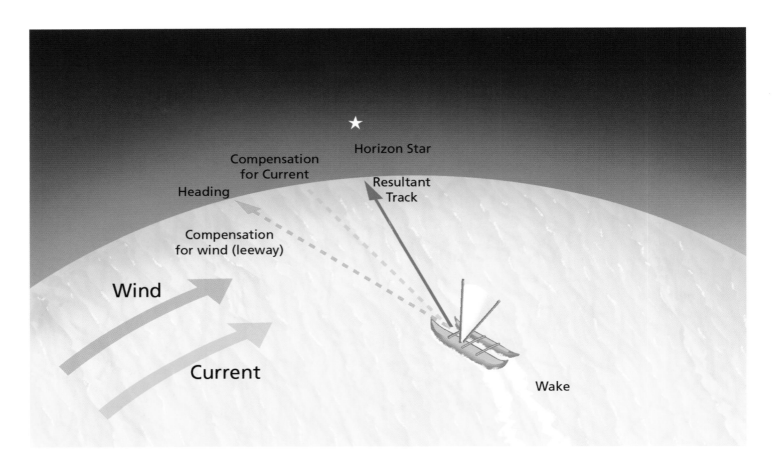

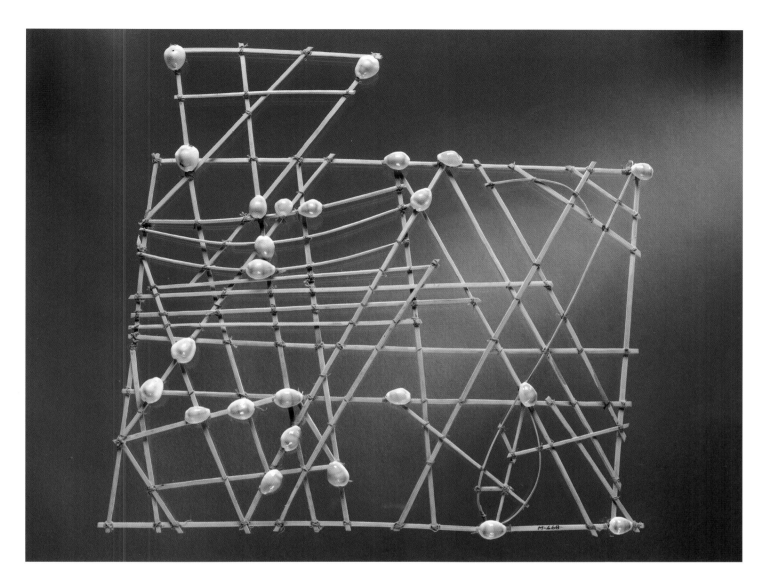

pushing currents. But if the voyage to a small destination was very long, an error of five degrees could be enough to bring the navigator past his destination without his seeing it. Therefore, these remarkable navigators had developed special means of coastal navigation to lead them finally to their target.

Coastal Navigation

When their island destination was two *etaks* away, but not yet in sight, Oceanic navigators began to look for natural signs. At this distance the first indication of an island was the appearance of birds, which widened the target area. Navigators did not have to find a small island; they could seek out a much wider circle defined by the extent to which birds flew from land. With a chain or cluster of islands, the risk of accidentally sailing past a target was obviously even smaller. Terns, boobies and frigate birds flew a distance of about 25 miles over the sea to catch fish, while other species ventured twice as far in search of food. Consequently, a frigate bird sighting would be a sure sign that an island was fairly close, and its bearing could be estimated from the direction of the bird returning to its island.

14. Navigation Chart from the Marshall Islands

Stick charts, constructed of palm ribs bound by coconut fibre, with shells embedded to represent islands, were not navigational charts as used in the Western World; instead, they often served to act as a memory device for patterns of wave swell and ocean currents. The particular stick chart shown here covers a wide area and is more concerned with the relative position of islands to one another than to swells and currents.

DEPARTMENT OF ANTHROPOLOGY, SMITHSONIAN INSTITUTION, MARYLAND

Clouds also assisted mariners in determining the location of land. They revealed the presence of an island long before the island itself came into view. As the Sun heats the land, the warm air rises until it reaches the colder air of the upper atmosphere, and there it condenses to form a cloud. A solitary cumulus cloud, in an otherwise cloudless sky, is a sure indicator of land below it. This is true even in a cloud-filled sky, for this cloud will not be moving, as are all the other clouds. However, the presence of clouds is not as reliable a sign as the birds are, and both were useful for navigation only during the daytime.

In certain areas during night-time seafarers used another visual guide, the presence of phosphorescence from the ocean floor. This glow emitted from phosphate-bearing rock, which sometimes appears in proximity to tropical islands, has not been explained. Nevertheless light glowing from deep under the surface guided nocturnal sailors as they approached the shallow waters of an island or group of islands. This phenomenon is different from that of bioluminescence, which is the emission of light by plankton when the water is disturbed. The best known forms on land of this type of light are fireflies and glow worms. The glittering splashes of light emitted from plankton did not guide the navigator, but gave delight to nocturnal tropical seafarers when they saw the shimmering wake extending far behind their boat.

Seafarers from the Marshall and Gilbert Islands (Micronesia) learned to locate islands that were not visible by observing the wave patterns around them. The pattern of large ocean swells, originating from distant locations, is altered when they approach and pass an island. An 'echo' occurs as the waves reflect back off the island, while on the opposite side of the island a calmer area is formed – like a wave-shadow. These altered swells advance far from the island, covering an expanding sector. When swells from two different directions pass an island, there is a heaping up of the water at their point, or node, of intersection. The presence of these nodes alerts the navigator that an island is nearby, and a series of nodes in alignment can direct him to that island. Navigators were taught to recognize the sequences formed by these nodes from wave charts, locally called *mattang*, made with sticks, twine and shells.

Two types of wave charts have been found in Micronesia. They were generally cruciform and showed wave formation in average conditions for a simple, circular island. There were also more complex charts for a particular island or group of islands. Neither type of chart was used at sea, but remained on land for training purposes. Their main use was to show

typical wave patterns and their intersections. The intersecting points, or nodes, of the waves were often marked on the charts with shells. It is difficult to grasp how seafarers could have recognized such shapes or aberrations in the normal motion of the sea. Nevertheless, in numerous tests the seafarers of the Marshall Islands have shown that they are indeed capable of finding their destination on the basis of wave patterns.

ARCTIC SEAFARERS

During Cook's voyage to the northernmost parts of the Pacific Ocean in 1778, he encountered indigenous people in Asia and North America and learned about their skills in seafaring. He admired the speed and seaworthiness of the skin-covered boats of the Aleuts (indigenous people of the Aleutian Islands) and of the Alaskan Inuit. Their kayaks, baidarkas (an ocean-going kayak of the Aleutian Eskimo), and umiaks were made of seal or walrus skin pulled over a frame of arches made of available materials such as whalebone or wood. The umiak, a significantly larger vessel than the kayak, was designed for the principal purpose of transporting people and goods, while the slender kayak was used only to hunt sea mammals. It was fast, silent and light. When the hunter pulled his waterproof anorak around the sides of the cockpit, his wrists and head, he and the kayak were inseparable. Despite being unsteady, the kayak was seaworthy even in heavy seas, and a skilled kayaker could easily right his upturned craft. The kayak sometimes weighed less than twenty kilos; hence it was easy to carry across land or ice.

Their superior boatbuilding skills and seamanship enabled the Arctic hunting culture to encompass a region extending from Asia to North America and Greenland, where they had first been encountered by European Vikings in the late tenth century.

While hunters in Arctic waters made very long hunting trips, unlike the peoples of Oceania they rarely had to navigate in open sea, away from the coast. Their passages were generally confined to coastal sailing where deep fjords, inlets and islands provided sheltered waters. Navigation was no less difficult, however, since the seascape of the Inuit was ever changing. In spring, the frozen winter sea breaks up into drifting ice floes, constantly moving with every shift of wind and current. Masses of ice may at times coalesce into a solid sheet, and then split apart to provide leads of open water. The Eskimo, like the Polynesian, found his way about the sea by carefully noting the signs and rhythms of sea and sky, and minute changes in the direction and the sounds of waves. To them it was more important to know the effect that wind would have on the movement of the ice, than which direction the wind came from. They had many expressions for different winds that took into account its temperature, strength and effect, as well as the direction.

When they did have to navigate to distant islands, such as the Aleutians, or in crossing the Bering Strait on trading voyages, they relied on the natural signs with which they were familiar: the path of the Sun across the sky, and the North Star. The latter was familiar to northern people and important in that it indicated north. It was the only immovable star, and the entire vault of heaven rotated around it.

The navigating skills and techniques of indigenous peoples of Oceania and the Arctic seas evolved differently from that of European navigators because their relationships with the sea and their motivation to take to the sea were so different. The

16. Inuit Kayak, 1675

From his expedition to the Canadian Arctic in 1576, Martin Frobisher (1535–1594) brought back to London an Inuit kayak, along with its Inuk occupant. There, the Inuk impressed everyone with his remarkable skill with a bow and arrow. Queen Elizabeth, however, was not so pleased when he shot her swans on the lawn of Hampton Court.

JUHA NURMINEN COLLECTION

15. Singalesian Outrigger by Björn Landström, 1964

COURTESY OF OLOF LANDSTRÖM

basis of European livelihood was mostly land and agriculture, whereas the indigenous peoples lived from the sea. They were born with a sense of the sea; for them it was not an adversary to conquer but a friend that provided their sustenance, clothing, shelter and vessels. Their navigators learned to read the sea and other natural phenomena with all the senses. They observed the starry sky and the path of the Sun, the movement of waves and the colour of the sea, smelled the wind, listened to the sounds of birds and watched their flight, and felt the changes in the motion of the sea with their entire bodies. The sea was their home. To the Europeans, the sea was often a great unknown that raised fear and inspired awe, but also represented a fascinating opportunity.

Pag. 229.

A

Scheeps Timmeren inde Virgines

XCI

17. Ship Carving in the Virgin Islands by Nicolaes Witsen, 1671

The first boats were logs, hollowed out with stone tools and fire. They were used all over the world. Some indigenous people still possess the skills to make dugouts. A boat built from a single tree trunk was strong, and the seamless construction made it watertight.

JUHA NURMINEN COLLECTION

The First Boats and Ships

Historians estimate that the first attempts to cross bodies of water were made from 25,000 to 30,000 years ago. Although no boats are known to be preserved from the prehistoric period, we know that man caught seals and whales, which suggests that he had the means of travelling by sea. In the beginning everything that could float was used on calm waters: logs, rafts or reed bundles. The first true boats were probably dugouts, made by hollowing out logs with fire and with stone tools. Boats made of animal skins, which were sewn together and stretched over frames of wood or whalebone, also date back to this period. Although they required more sophisticated skills, they were relatively easy to build, because no cutting and working of large timber was needed.

These primitive ship-types may still be found in use around the world, some in their original form, and others with more recent modifications. Hulls made out of tree trunks are still in use in Africa, South America and Australia. Reed rafts are used in South America, on the Nile and in Africa and Iraq. Skin boats are found on Greenland (the umiak), in Tibet and Great Britain (coracle). The kayak represents the very best in Inuit boatbuilding; optimized for their resources and way of life, there was no need to develop it further, hence its widespread continued use.

The description in the Bible of Noah's Ark was of a large, box-shaped hulk, with no sails or oars. But as there is no archaeological evidence to support that description, the first ships for which evidence does ex-

18. Kayak by W.A. Graah, 1832

The kayak developed throughout centuries to correspond to local conditions and demands. The framework was usually built of driftwood or whale bones, over which whale hide was stretched, then sealed with whale fat. The kayaks of the Inuit people were narrow and shallow, and they were used both for transport and for hunting.

JUHA NURMINEN COLLECTION

ist are the ancient Egyptian and Mesopotamian reed boats, depicted on pottery more than 5000 years old. The hulls were made of lashed papyrus reed, because there was virtually no suitable wood available. The life span of such boats was short, because papyrus is weak and gets waterlogged easily. On the other hand it was a cheap, readily available raw material. The papyrus boat had a flat bottom and was shaped like a sickle. The bow was a little raked, and the stern was drawn inwards by a cable which stressed the hull into a curve that gave the vessel better manoeuvrability and carrying capacity, and facilitated landing on shallow shores. This was to become the main characteristic of the Mediterranean vessel for millennia.

The invention of the sail was revolutionary. It is possible that the Egyptians were the first to use sails as the first depiction of them is to be found on an Egyptian amphora from about 3500 BC. Only square sails were used in such Egyptian sailing vessels. The mast was situated in the fore part of the ship, which indicates that the sail was only used in following winds. On the Nile the wind usually blows from north, which means that southward bound up river the sail was raised, while it was lowered when travelling north down stream. There were steering oars aft. At first, these vessels were paddled, but later they were rowed, which enabled the building of considerably larger vessels. In 1969 and 1970 Norwegian explorer Thor Heyerdahl built the reed boats *Ra* and *Ra II* according to ancient prototypes and proved the seaworthiness of the papyrus boat by sailing them on the Atlantic.

19. Queen Hatshepsut's Ship by Björn Landström, 1961

Queen Hatshepsut sent five merchant ships to the mysterious land of Punt about 1500 BC to bring back incense, ivory and other valuable goods. These ships represented the ultimate shipbuilding skill of Egypt. When powered by sail they used a wide, square sail; at other time they were propelled by thirty oarsmen.

COURTESY OF OLOF LANDSTRÖM

THE SEAFARER'S NATURAL WORLD

Of a sudden they fell into that numbing ocean's dark mist which could hardly be penetrated with the eyes. And behold, the current of the fluctuating ocean whirled back to its mysterious fountainhead and with most furious impetuosity drew the unhappy sailors, who in their despair thought only of death, on to chaos.

ADAM OF BREMEN, *c.* 1080

Sailing in primitive vessels thousands of years ago, people first navigated inland waters successfully, then extended their journeys to astonishing distances from their homes across the open sea. When making a passage in coastal waters, familiar landmarks led sailors onward from headland to headland. On the open ocean, careful observation of waves, direction of wind, bird life and marine species all provided 'seamarks' to indicate direction to their destination. Gradually, seafarers developed an understanding of the winds and currents of the sea. They also learned to use the stars, Sun, Moon, and the Earth's magnetic field to guide them. For millennia, nature has posed these challenges to navigation.

UNDERSTANDING THE WINDS

Understanding the winds is of fundamental importance to seamen, but the science of meteorology lagged behind the practical observations of seafaring men. The fourth century BC Greek philosopher, Aristotle, believed that winds were caused by exhalations from the Earth, in which air rises and is swept away by 'the revolution of the heaven'. That notion remained dominant until the seventeenth century when the great Italian astronomer, Galileo Galilei (1564-1642), suggested that winds were the result of the rotation of the Earth, with the air trailing behind.

We now know that winds are created when solar radiation causes local changes in the temperature of air and water masses. As the air heats it loses density and rises, causing atmospheric pressure to decrease in the area. Air begins to flow from cooler areas of high pressure towards the low-pressure area, causing winds. This flow is affected by the topography of the Earth, and by friction between land and air, and within the air itself. The motion of wind and water is influenced by the rotation of the Earth, causing them to be deflected in a circular motion, known as the Coriolis effect. Because the flow systems of the atmosphere and the oceans and seas are in constant interaction, and air moving with the wind receives and releases energy in a constantly changing environment, the currents of air and sea are complicated.

When seafarers extended their voyages across the oceans in the sixteenth century, they began to pay more attention to the pattern of winds, especially to the trade winds, and to speculate on their causes. But they continued to describe their discoveries in Aristotelian terms.

Seafarers were less interested in what caused the winds than in using them to get to their destination quickly and safely.

20. Sea Painting by Johannes Holst, 1913

PETER TAMM COLLECTION, HAMBURG

The Earth in its Orbit

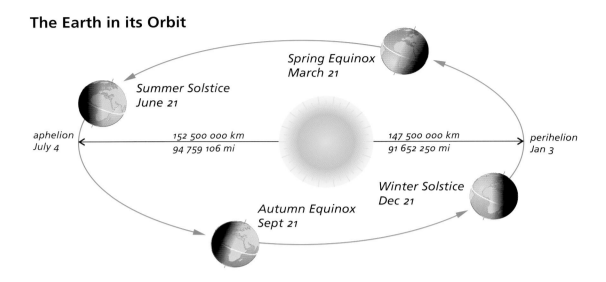

Spring Equinox
March 21

Summer Solstice
June 21

aphelion
July 4

152 500 000 km
94 759 106 mi

147 500 000 km
91 652 250 mi

perihelion
Jan 3

Winter Solstice
Dec 21

Autumn Equinox
Sept 21

Equinoxes and Solstices

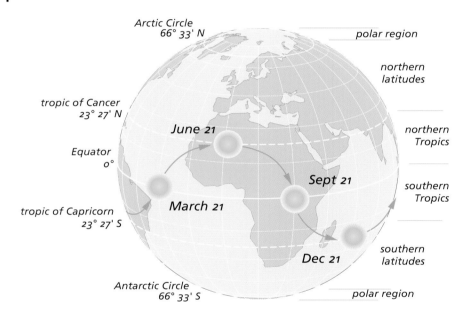

Arctic Circle
66° 33' N

polar region

northern
latitudes

tropic of Cancer
23° 27' N

June 21

northern
Tropics

Equator
0°

Sept 21

March 21

southern
Tropics

tropic of Capricorn
23° 27' S

Dec 21

southern
latitudes

Antarctic Circle
66° 33' S

polar region

21. The Earth in its Orbit, Equinoxes and Solstices

Although the Earth's axis is at a fixed angle of 23° 27', in its annular orbit around the Sun it changes relative to the Sun. During the period from 21 March (Vernal Equinox) to 23 September (Autumnal Equinox) the northern point of the Earth's axis is inclined towards the Sun. At this time, the Sun is relatively high in the sky in the northern hemisphere and summer weather is experienced there. From 23 September to 21 March, the situation is reversed, with the southern hemisphere tilted toward the Sun and having its summer weather. This shift in the declination of the Sun creates a likewise shift in the equatorial belt of heating and causes a corresponding move in the belts of pressure with their associated winds.

Gradually, with experience, they learned to make use of wind systems. The Vikings used their knowledge of prevalent winds of the North Atlantic to plan their annual voyages to colonies in Iceland and Greenland.

In the fifteenth century, when the Portuguese first sailed south along the western coast of Africa, they proceeded cautiously, for they knew that the prevailing northeast trade wind and the Canary Current (which flows southward) would be against them on the return passage. They soon discovered that on the homeward voyage, if they sailed in a wide arc west and then north into the Atlantic, they would reach an area where prevailing westerlies would take them to their home-ports of Lagos and Lisbon. On these voyages, they rediscovered the Atlantic archipelagos of the Canaries, Azores, Cape Verde and Madeira. On their voyages to the New World the Spaniards used the trade winds to take them westward. Returning to Spain, they learned to choose a northerly route

22. Ocean Winds

No wind was of greater importance to sailors than the trade winds; their near constancy in strength, position and direction might well earn for them the title of 'Queen of the Winds'. To the mariner, it mattered little what caused these winds, as long as they propelled his vessel with surety and swiftness to his destination.

23. Ocean Surface Currents

The course of ocean currents remained virtually unknown until a sufficient number of voyages had been made. It was not until the sixteenth and seventeenth centuries that seafarers began to understand how to use currents and to chart them. Conventionally, these currents are shown on maps or charts as simple straight or curved lines, but they are much more complex. Currents are subject to local, transitory and seasonal influences, such as surface temperature of the sea, which cause them to migrate or meander.

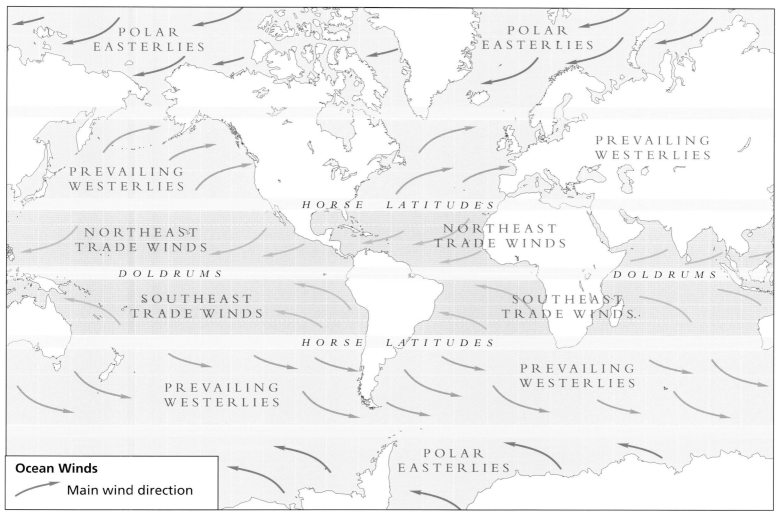

POLAR
EASTERLIES

POLAR
EASTERLIES

PREVAILING
WESTERLIES

PREVAILING
WESTERLIES

HORSE   LATITUDES

NORTHEAST
TRADE WINDS

NORTHEAST
TRADE WINDS

DOLDRUMS

DOLDRUMS

SOUTHEAST
TRADE WINDS

SOUTHEAST
TRADE WINDS

HORSE   LATITUDES

PREVAILING
WESTERLIES

PREVAILING
WESTERLIES

POLAR
EASTERLIES

Ocean Winds

Main wind direction

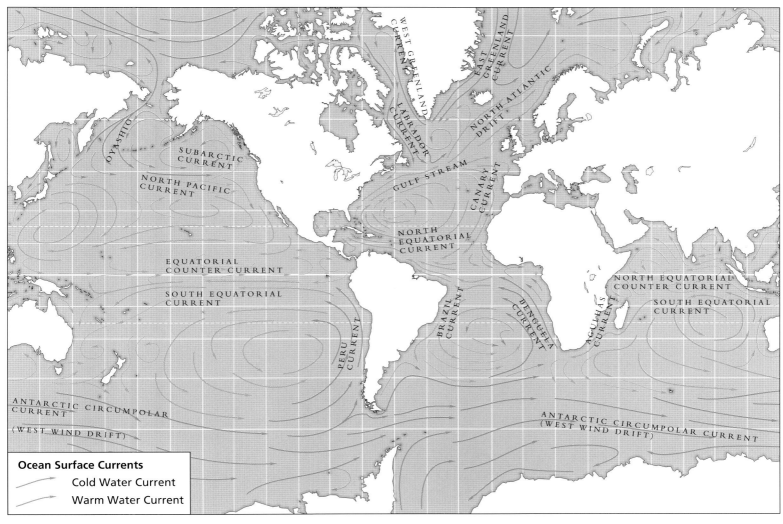

WEST GREENLAND CURRENT

EAST GREENLAND CURRENT

LABRADOR CURRENT

NORTH ATLANTIC DRIFT

OYASHIO

SUBARCTIC
CURRENT

NORTH PACIFIC
CURRENT

GULF STREAM

CANARY CURRENT

NORTH
EQUATORIAL
CURRENT

EQUATORIAL
COUNTER CURRENT

NORTH EQUATORIAL
COUNTER CURRENT

SOUTH EQUATORIAL
CURRENT

SOUTH EQUATORIAL
CURRENT

BRAZIL CURRENT

BENGUELA CURRENT

AGULHAS CURRENT

PERU CURRENT

ANTARCTIC CIRCUMPOLAR
CURRENT

(WEST WIND DRIFT)

ANTARCTIC CIRCUMPOLAR CURRENT
(WEST WIND DRIFT)

Ocean Surface Currents

Cold Water Current

Warm Water Current

that would bring them to the westerly winds of the northern hemisphere.

The first practical sea route from Europe to India was discovered by Vasco da Gama (c. 1469–1524) when he decided to bypass contrary currents and winds along the southwestern African coast by sailing far west, close to the coast of Brazil, and into prevailing westerlies which carried him on a southeasterly course towards the Cape of Good Hope. Rounding it, he then headed for India. For the next 300 years, seafarers continued to use this same route.

When Europeans sailed in the Indian Ocean, they encountered the monsoon winds, a system that Arab seafarers had known for a long time. Unlike the trade winds, they change direction according to the seasons. When explorers reached the Pacific and the waters of Southeast Asia, they discovered that these waters had similar systems of trade winds and monsoon winds as in the Atlantic and Indian Oceans. The Dutch spice trade, which began in the sixteenth century, used routes in the Indian Ocean that were largely based on their knowledge of the monsoon system. The Spaniards also made use of trade winds to carry silver from Mexico to the Philippines, and across the Pacific. By the eighteenth century, sufficient knowledge of oceanic winds had been accumulated to make possible the publication of charts indicating the average direction and force of the winds at different times of the year.

COMPREHENDING THE CURRENTS

Ocean currents are mostly caused by wind and differences in temperature. Seafarers came to know the force and direction of coastal currents, such as the inflow into the Mediterranean from the Black Sea at the Dardanelles and from the Atlantic at the Straits of Gibraltar, at an early time, but oceanic currents long remained a mystery. Like the winds, explanation of the general circulation of the oceans was first described in Aristotelian terms; the rotating heaven was believed to drag the air and the oceans with it. According to his theory, everything moved from east to west. However, doubts were cast on the Aristotelian model when seafarers sailing in the Atlantic discovered currents that flowed north and south. Discovery of the west-flowing North Equatorial Current renewed confidence in Aristotle's premise. But that confidence was dispelled when it was also discovered there was no channel west from the Gulf of Mexico or anywhere in the Americas through which the current could continue its westward flow. The ancient theories of oceanic circulation were finally abandoned.

During the three centuries following the great discovery voyages of the fifteenth and sixteenth centuries, a general idea of ocean currents was slowly developed, and seafarers learned to use them to hasten their voyages. They also learned to avoid contrary currents and areas of dangerous winds and currents. If the direction and speed of a current was not taken into account, a ship could be set off course by many nautical miles in a single day.

ACCOUNTING FOR THE TIDES

Knowledge of local tides was also important to seafarers when sailing in shallow coastal waters, and when entering and leaving harbours. Since there is almost no tide in the near land-locked Mediterranean, seafaring communities of that area developed an understanding of the tides only when they ventured out past the Straits of Gibraltar. The ancient Greek mariner Pytheas (c. 350 BC) discovered the relationship between the Moon and tides on his voyage from Massalia (Marseille) into the Atlantic and to northern Europe. Scientists of antiquity later more fully described the tides based on the lunar cycle. Through his writings, the Roman scholar and scientific authority, Pliny the Elder (c. AD 23-79), made the phenomenon more widely known.

The Venerable Bede (673–735), an English Benedictine scholar, gave an accurate description of the relationship between the cycle of the Moon and tides in a commentary on the calendar, entitled *De temporum ratione* (On the reckoning of time, 725). According to Bede, the time between the tides was 24 hours and 50 minutes, which is close to the actual value of 24 hours and 52.5 minutes. The interval is longer than 24 hours because the tides are influenced by the movement of the Moon. That the Moon revolved around the Earth was well known; early observers also knew that it moved with the stars from east to west, but at a slower rate by 12 degrees east every day, corresponding to roughly 50 minutes. Bede also knew that high tides did not occur at the same time everywhere and that while the tide is rising in one location, it is falling in another. Apparently he understood that the tide was water moving from one location to another. He also knew that high winds could alter the height and timing of tides.

Later medieval scholars had difficulty explaining exactly *how* the Moon caused the tides. They believed that the 'heat' of the Moon warmed the bottom of the oceans, causing water to expand and the surface of the sea to rise. Another explanation was that in a continuous cycle the Sun caused evaporation of water at the equator and the Moon condensed the water at the poles. The most common explanation, though, was astrological, and the real cause was not discovered until the turn of the seventeenth and eighteenth centuries. Isaac Newton (1642-1727) first proposed how general gravitation caused the tides in his 1687 work *Principia*. Later in his *Hydrodynamica*

25. Low Tide, Sunset by Eugène Boudin, 1880–1885

The French Impressionist painter Eugène Boudin (1824–1898) is known for his expert rendering of all features of the sea and its shores. Sailors would not, however, be fooled by this placid scene. Three hundred and fifty years ago, Jonathan Swift, the British satirist and clergyman, wrote, 'How is it possible to expect mankind to take advice when they will not so much as heed warnings'. Throughout the centuries, however, seamen have heeded the signs and portents of weather changes, codified them, and as a memory device frequently set them to rhyme, such as the familiar 'Red Sky at Night'.

ASSOCIATION PEINDRE EN NORMANDIE, CONSEIL RÉGIONAL DE BASSE-NORMANDIE

24. Savannah, Moonlight over the Savannah River in 1850 by John Stobart, 1987

Unable to manoeuvre within a limited space, large sailing ships remained at dock or at anchor until the tide turned in their favour. Then they could be towed downstream by a small boat to where sail could be hoisted.

USED BY PERMISSION OF DUTTON, A DIVISION OF PENGUIN GROUP (USA) INC.

26. Coordinates in Celestial and Terrestrial Spheres
Although the terminology differs slightly, the grid pattern for locating stars and planets in the celestial sphere is but an extension into space of the same system used to situate position on the Earth.

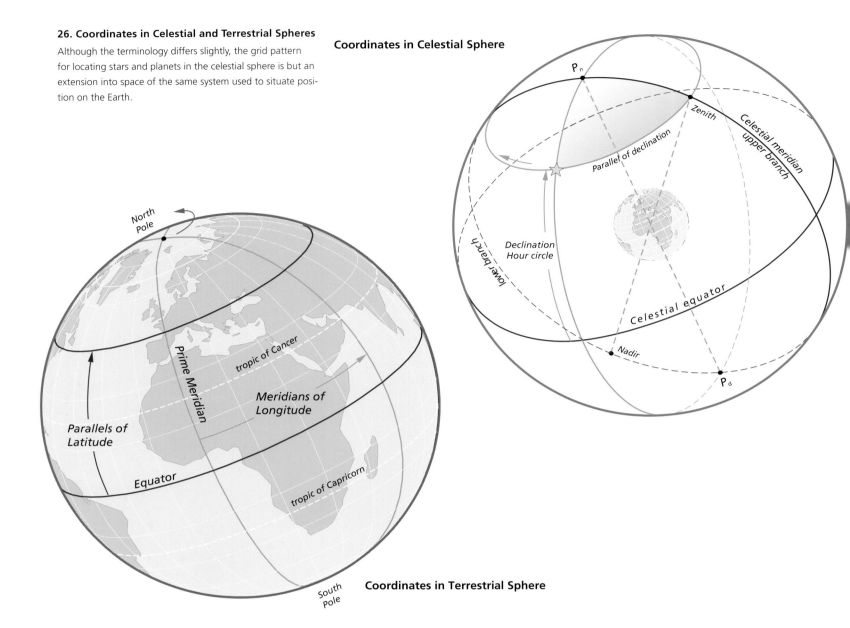

Coordinates in Celestial Sphere

Coordinates in Terrestrial Sphere

published in 1734, the Dutch Mathematician Daniel Bernoulli (1700-1782) explained the mechanics of fluids.

DEALING WITH THE WEATHER

Of all natural conditions, the weather has been the most tangible to seafarers, and probably the most decisive factor in their daily activities. Weather determined the movement and speed of their ship, the safety of the crew and cargo and the success of the voyage itself. Sailors were at the mercy of the weather, but skilled navigators knew how to use it to their advantage and to avoid dangers and impediments. It was vital to understand the complex inter-relationship of winds, currents, temperature and atmospheric pressure that caused weather. It was also important to be aware of the special and unexpected characteristics of local weather conditions, which could take even the most experienced sailor by surprise.

Seafarers have always tried to forecast weather. From various natural phenomena and signs, they have attempted to predict the wind, its strength and direction and their effect on the oceans. They had to know whether to expect rain or fog, which would reduce visibility. Often the weather signs were expressed in rhymes to make them easier to remember. These rhymes were frequently accurate and had a sound meteorological basis. For example:

A red sky in the morning is a sailor's warning;
But a red sky at night is a sailor's delight.

When rain comes before wind,
Halyards, sheets and braces mind!
But when wind comes before rain
Soon you may sail again.

The barometer, which measures atmospheric pressure, was invented in 1643 by a student of Galileo, the Italian Evangelista Torricelli (1608–1647). Soon after, the connection between atmospheric pressure and changes in weather was discovered. The barometer later became standard equipment for seafarers. Systematic weather forecasts, based on observation and atmospheric pressure, were begun by Admiral Robert FitzRoy in the second half of the nineteenth century in Great Britain, the forerunner of the Meteorological Office.

WATCHING THE HEAVENS

Early seafarers were helped to their destinations by simple observations of the Sun and sky. The path of the Sun as it rose and set provided the two cardinal points of east and west, and from midday Sun, bearings to the south could be estimated; stars close to the celestial pole indicated north. All other intermediate points could be derived from these simple bearings.

Ancient Greek and Hellenistic cultures developed the concepts of the equator, the celestial poles and the two equinoxes of spring and autumn, that point at the equator through which the Sun moves from the southern to the northern hemisphere during its annual cycle. They used these reference points to describe and calculate the apparent movements of celestial bodies in relation to the dome of the sky and to the horizon, the times of the rising and setting of the stars, and the duration of the night and the day.

Everywhere on the Earth, the sky and the stars appear to move westward, rotating around a fixed pole, and making a full circle once a day. Seafarers also discovered that the height of the north celestial pole increases as the traveller moves north from the equator, and the south celestial pole increases in height as one sails south from the equator. At the Earth's poles the celestial poles are at their zenith, and the movement of the stars circles the sky parallel to the horizon. At the equator, the celestial poles are opposite each other on the horizon and the stars rise and set perpendicular to the horizon. Of great importance to navigation, it was observed very early that a particular fixed star always rises from the same place on the horizon, and follows the same path across the sky when observed from the same location.

The Sun, Moon and the five planets known to the ancients also follow the same daily pattern, but their tracks and speeds are all different and more complicated. The Moon moves rapidly, while Saturn, the most remote planet, takes almost thirty years to traverse the sky. To an observer on the Earth, the motion of planets is eastward on the celestial sphere, against the stars. Their rate of movement and their brightness, however, does not appear to be consistent; their speed varies and sometimes their direction appears to reverse to the westward. For centuries, the movement of planets continued to pose a problem to astronomers, until it was understood that they revolved around the Sun instead of the Earth.

Towards midsummer, the elevation of the Sun at noon increases day by day, until it reaches a point known as the tropic of Cancer at the time of the summer solstice. Then it begins its descent to the winter solstice at the tropic of Capricorn from where it returns to climb north. During its journeys between the two solstices, the Sun crosses the equator twice each year at the spring and autumn equinox. The apparent annual path of the Sun against the fixed stars is known as the zodiac, or the ecliptic. Seafarers observed the yearly path of the Sun at their homeport, and noted the direction from which it rose or set as the seasons changed. This enabled the Vikings, for example, to know the right time of the year to set sail for the long voyages to their western colonies in Iceland and Greenland. They inherited this knowledge from their farming ancestors who had watched the progression of the Sun and other celestial events in order to determine when best to sow their fields.

Once the geometry of the celestial sphere had been established, with a spherical Earth forming the centre, it was easy to apply the same system of coordinates to the Earth's surface. The equator, with lines of latitude running parallel to it, and lines of longitude perpendicular to the equator, were simply transferred to the surface of the Earth. The key unit of distance in navigation, the nautical mile, is one minute of arc along a great circle, and is derived from spherical geometry. In modern sea charts nautical miles are indicated on the vertical, meridian line, which normally is on the side of the chart. To determine the distance of a planned voyage, the navigator uses a pair of dividers to take an appropriate number of units (nautical miles) from the scale, and measures them off on his chart from the point of origin to the destination of his voyage.

In antiquity, geographic coordinates had little importance to navigation, because of the enormous difficulty in providing accurate longitudes. And those astronomical measurements of longitude that could be attempted ashore were impossible on a ship at sea. More sophisticated navigation, using the stars, did not develop until sailors began to make long north–south voyages. In the Mediterranean region the night sky at Carthage, Athens, or Alexandria looks much the same, continuing its rotation across the heavens night after night. But in the course of a journey of several weeks southward, on the Red Sea or the Indian Ocean, a change in the star paths becomes apparent. The north celestial pole slowly descends towards the horizon and new constellations appear from the south. When mariners discovered this they soon learned to estimate their geographic latitude by measuring the approximate elevation of the celestial pole from the horizon using the stars closest to the pole. Today that star is *Polaris* (also known as the North Star or Lode Star); in antiquity other stars occupied that place. The starry sky helped seafarers to know when they had arrived at a desired latitude, and enabled them to remain on course after days or weeks of sailing. At the desired latitude, a ship needed only to continue sailing due east or west by keeping the star at the same elevation until it reached its destination. They arrived at this practi-

Latitude Sailing

For simplicity and ease of use, no celestial navigation practice has served mariners throughout the world as well as that of Latitude Sailing. 'Running down ones easting (or westing)', or following one line of latitude, was the preferred method of European mariners, as well as Arab navigators in the Indian Ocean, and the early seafarers of Oceania.

The navigator planned his departure from a port known to be at the same latitude as his destination. Alternatively, he sailed north or south until he reached the latitude of his destination, then maintained a course on that latitude. This method required no time-consuming, complex calculations; all that was needed when travelling in an east/west direction was to keep a celestial body at the same meridian altitude – its angular height above the horizon at meridian. At night, the North Star, *Polaris*, with a correction for time, served this purpose, and during daytime a sighting of the Sun at its meridian passage at noon – when it reaches its highest point in the sky – was sufficient. There was no need to know longitude, for as long as the latitude was maintained, the navigator could be assured of reaching the desired destination.

The use of instruments, such as the cross-staff or quadrant, enabled the mariner to determine his latitude, but upon reaching the latitude of choice, it could be maintained without any instruments. During the daytime, it was only necessary to keep the shadow of any upright post on the boat the same length at noon each day.

In ancient times, Greek sailors used the latitude sailing method when voyaging between Alexandria and Crete. Latitude sailing enabled the Northmen, or Scandinavian Vikings to reach their desired landfall when sailing even greater distances across the Atlantic Ocean, between Norway and Greenland. And Vasco da Gama practised latitude sailing when he set out in 1498 to round the Cape of Good Hope to reach Calicut, India. Until then, the practice had been to follow the west coast of Africa to the cape, but the combined forces of adverse winds and dangerous currents made this a difficult passage. Instead, da Gama chose to hold a southerly course far to the west of Africa, and thereby avoid these hazards. The

Southeast Trade Winds propelled his ship in a region totally unfamiliar to European mariners, but he knew he need not be concerned until he reached the latitude of the Cape of Good Hope. Then he ran down his easting to double the cape and resumed the planned course to India.

A favourite landfall on the western side of the Atlantic for French navigators, such as Jacques Cartier (1491–1557), was Cape Bonavista, Newfoundland. Leaving Saint-Malo, France, at 48° 39' N, after clearing the coast of France, by continually sailing west they would certainly stand a very good chance of arriving at Cape Bonavista at 48° 42'N, a difference of only three nautical miles from his home port.

In order to protect British trade interests in the Pacific from Spanish attacks, the British Admiralty sent Captain George Anson (1697–1762) to raid and destroy Spanish settlements along the South American coast. At the same time, Anson set about to correct and improve charting of the Pacific for future English mariners. After Anson's squadron passed through Le Maire Straits and beat its way around Cape Horn into the Pacific, it turned out to be even less hospitable than the turbulent neighbourhood of Tierra del Fuego and Cape Horn. Furthermore the expedition was seriously hampered by the loss to scurvy of over 200 men. It was necessary to get to land as quickly as possible in order to give the enfeebled crew a chance to recover, and to refit Anson's badly damaged vessel, which had become separated from the rest of the squadron. Since he was coming close to Juan Fernandez Island (discovered by Fernandez in 1574), Anson set direct course in search of the island. When the island failed to appear, Anson headed over to the coast of Chile to make a new departure to westward following the principles of latitude sailing. Running down the known latitude of Juan Fernandez, on 9 June 1741, he at last discovered the long-wished-for island. His decision to cast back eastward to the Chilean coast cost him many more days in which additional men died of scurvy. But by chance, the delay saved him from even greater misfortune, for a strong Spanish naval force was awaiting him at Juan Fernandez Island, and had departed just before his arrival.

Long before Anson's arrival in the Pacific, Polynesian navigators had their own form of latitude sailing using

'zenith stars' as an aid to locate islands. They knew which star or group of stars when at their zenith, that is at their highest point in the sky, was directly above a specific island or island group. The skilled Oceanic seafarers could recognize and name 'zenith stars' for numerous islands or island groups and used them as a guide to their destination. If the zenith of that same star was directly above the navigator's canoe, he knew that he was in the same latitude as his destination. The position of the star could be determined by sighting up the mast, provided the sea was reasonably calm. By remaining in that latitude (sailing east or west) through observing the path of the sun during the day and the stars at night, especially the zenith star or stars of the required destination, the mariner would reach his goal. This method of using zenith stars for navigation was especially practised on longer voyages, and helped seafarers avoid accidentally sailing past their destination.

Very good navigators have an instinctive sixth sense when to trust their observations; it is as much an art as it is a science. Some navigators have a definite feel for their work and consistently achieve good results, while others never quite manage. One navigator who could not 'get the hang of it' was Captain Bartholomew Gilbert. In 1603 he made a voyage to Virginia in the Bark *Elizabeth*. The ship left Plymouth, England, on 10 May and sailed south toward Madeira to pick up the trade winds. Sixteen days later Gilbert was at the latitude of 32° N, but failed to sight Madeira. Missing the island, he turned the *Elizabeth* westward, following the latitude, and expecting to raise the island of Bermuda. On 1 June he sighted land, but upon landing he found that the island was St. Lucia, one of the most southerly Windward Islands of the West Indies. The error was extraordinary, since St. Lucia is 1100 miles south of Bermuda. Describing this remarkable event, Samuel Purchas (the English historian and a contemporary of Gilbert) said: 'That does scant credit to their navigational skill, and speaks volumes for their courageous ignorance'.

27. A Detail from Louis Renard´s map, 1715

JUHA NURMINEN COLLECTION

28. Celestial map published by Johannes Covens – Cornelis Mortier, c. 1759

For millennia, the stars, planets and celestial events have been used to predict human affairs and earthly events. They have also served mariners as an aid to navigate across the open sea. Although the constellation figures filling these dual celestial hemispheres are mythological in origin, and thought to have astrological significance, they still serve a practical purpose in defining regions of the sky. In this map, the spaces between the constellation figures contains a summation of eighteenth-century astronomical knowledge.

JUHA NURMINEN COLLECTION

cal knowledge through experience, without needing to think about the shape of the Earth or the structure of the Universe.

There is no visible star at the exact celestial pole, and the location of the pole changes slowly under the influence of the gravitation of the Moon and the Sun, which affect the tilt of the axis of the Earth. As a result, the Earth's geographic pole slowly makes a full circle around the pole of the ecliptic every 26,000 years. Navigators in antiquity were forced to select a different star for their observations than the one currently used. As long ago as 800 BC, mariners from Crete sailed from their island to Egypt, a distance of some 300 miles. At that time, *Polaris*, the present-day North Star, was fourteen degrees from the pole. For their measurements they used instead the second brightest star of the Little Bear (Little Dipper), called *Kochab*, which was about seven degrees from the north celestial pole. Now *Polaris* is much closer to the celestial North Pole, and will reach its closest point in the year 2115.

If weather conditions prevent seeing the Pole Star, if the ship is in the southern hemisphere, or if the star's elevation is difficult to establish for any other reason, then geographic latitude can be determined using another star of known declination (its angular distance) from the equator. This can be arrived at by measuring the zenith angle of the star when it is at its highest point (its meridian) in the sky. When the coordinates of a star are known, latitude can be calculated. Unfortunately, throughout the history of navigation, there has never been a suitable star close to the southern celestial pole. The Sun can also be used to determine geographic latitude in both hemispheres. This method is somewhat more complicated than using a star, because the declination of the Sun, varies throughout the year. The technique for finding latitude by measuring the Sun's altitude at the time of its meridional passage was known in antiquity, and when instructions and tables showing the path of the Sun were drawn up it became useful in navigation.

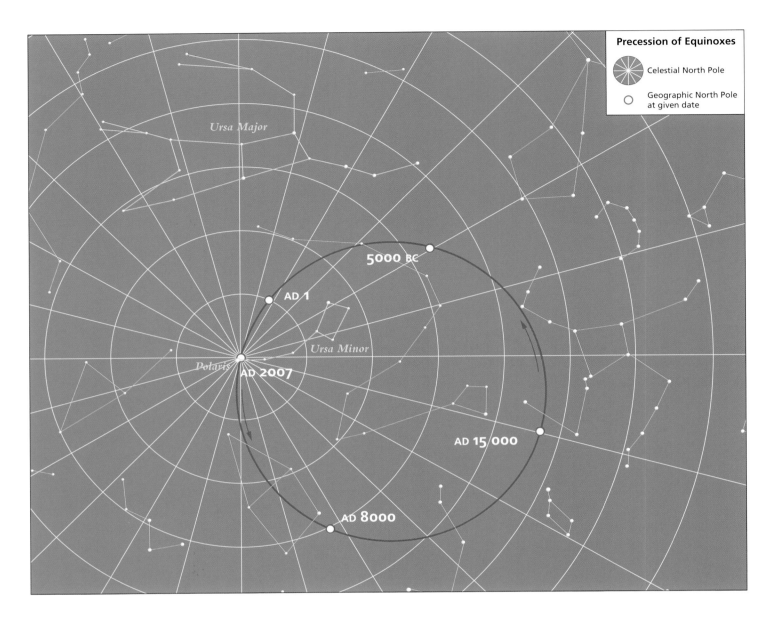

Precession of Equinoxes

Celestial North Pole

Geographic North Pole
at given date

Ursa Major

5000 BC

AD 1

Ursa Minor

Polaris

AD 2007

AD 15,000

AD 8000

29. Precession of Equinoxes

Polaris, the North Star, so useful to sailors in the northern hemisphere for determining geographic north, has not always been so favourably located. Presently,
Polaris circles within one degree the Celestial North Pole. At the time of Christopher Columbus (1451-1506), however, it circumscribed the pole at 3.5 degrees.
As the result of precession of the equinoxes, over the centuries other stars have
approximated that position.

Determining longitude was extremely difficult on land,
and nearly impossible at sea, until the mid-eighteenth century. In theory it is a simple matter. The difference in longitude between two locations is the difference between their
local times. The Earth rotates 360 degrees every 24 hours;
thus, each hour is equal to 15 degrees of longitude. A difference of two hours, time between two locations equates to a
difference of 30 degrees of longitude. Local time at a place
of observation can be determined using the Sun or the stars.
The problem lies in knowing the local time at the other location. Navigators struggled for centuries to find longitude

using lunar eclipses. The difficulty with this method was the
infrequency of lunar eclipses, and the inability to simultaneously compare the local times between two places in distant locations. Finding longitude at sea was finally solved
with the invention of a timepiece – the marine chronometer
– that could keep accurate time while at sea. When the time
at the port of departure, the reference meridian, was known
during a journey, and local time was determined from the
sky, longitude of the present position could then be calculated. With the industrial manufacturing of adequately precise chronometers, they became the most commonly used
instrument to determine longitude and changed seafaring
forever.

Another approach to finding longitude while at sea was
measurement of the distance of the Moon from a number
of important stars. This method, called Lunar Distance, did
not become practical until instruments capable of accurate
angular measurement, such as the octant, were developed,
and accurate tables of the Moon's motion produced. Master
navigator James Cook used the lunar distance method, as

well as his newly acquired chronometer, to determine his location when he was charting unknown regions of the Pacific between 1768 and 1780.

ESTABLISHING LOCATION

As long as sailors were limited to line-of-sight pilotage, assisted by sounding for depth, there was no need for charts. But when advances were made in navigational technology, charts were soon produced, and permitted voyaging beyond sight of land. When the magnetic compass was introduced in Europe in the late Middle Ages, portolan maps soon appeared. They did not use the coordinates of latitude or longitude, but were based on compass directions between coastal ports and rough estimates of distances given in the number of days at sea from port to port. Portolan maps of the Mediterranean represented coastlines fairly accurately. When instruments and tables were developed to measure stellar or solar altitudes, charts began to be published with latitude and longitude scales.

The equator, first developed for astronomical description, was a natural starting point for the measurement of latitude. Latitude coordinates, as arcs or angles, were measured from the equator towards the poles. Longitude, however, has no natural starting point for measurement. Accordingly, some point had to be arbitrarily chosen. Mapmakers sometimes based their selection of a zero meridian, or Prime Meridian, on political motives, and sometimes on practical needs. In the early Hellenistic period (fourth to first century BC) geographers calculated geographic longitudes from several places, including the meridian of Alexandria, Rhodes or the Straits of Gibraltar. In late antiquity, longitude was commonly counted eastward from the edge of the known world, which at the time was the Canary Islands or the Azores. Since 1884, based on an international agreement, the Prime Meridian has passed through an observatory at Greenwich on the outskirts of London, England.

FINDING DIRECTION

The magnetic compass, invented in China by the first century AD, began to be used by seafarers in the Mediterranean and Northern Europe by the end of the twelfth century AD. This device surpasses all other navigational aids in its importance to marine navigation. More than a thousand years ago Arab seafarers in the Indian Ocean, Polynesian navigators in the Pacific, and the Vikings in the North Atlantic had all found their way to remote destinations over the open sea without the aid of the magnetic compass, but it is impossible to imagine the great voyages in the Age of Discovery without it. The further from its homeport a ship sailed, the more important the compass became.

The magnetic compass aligns itself with the magnetic field of the Earth, which is not the same as the geographic axis of the Earth. As long as ships maintained a course along the west coast of Africa or Europe, the compass served to guide them well, because the magnetic north indicated by the compass was roughly equal to the true north of the geographic North Pole. But when seafarers ventured west across the ocean, they discovered that these two norths no longer coincided. The difference between them increased the further west and north a ship sailed. If a ship sailed west from Great Britain towards Newfoundland and followed the compass without taking into account the westerly magnetic variation, its course would slowly be directed south and the ship would end up somewhere halfway down the eastern coast of the United States.

This discrepancy between true, or geographic north, and magnetic north is known as 'variation' or 'declination'. When the needle of a compass is deflected east of true north, the variation is said to be easterly, and when it is deflected west of true north it is westerly. The amount of magnetic variation, as well as its easterly or westerly direction, varies in different regions of the globe. It also varies over a period of time, because the magnetic poles are not stationary. When magnetic variation was discovered, instrument makers in northern Europe began manufacturing different compasses to solve the problem; either the compass was made to be adjustable for variation, or permanently fitted to local variation. The problem was eventually solved by taking comprehensive measurements of variation and publishing them, as Edmond Halley (1656–1742) did in the chart of the Atlantic he published in the early eighteenth century. This information allowed mariners to make the necessary adjustments to the course of their ships. Attempts to determine longitude using magnetic variation, or by vertical dip of the compass needle, called 'inclination', failed.

Another cause of compass error is the influence of the immediate environment, such as cannons or any ferrous metal, on the ships' compass. This is known as 'deviation'. Although seafarers undoubtedly noticed deviation when they first started using the compass, the term was first used by João de Castro (1500–1548), a marine officer with the Portuguese fleet in India, when he was investigating compass variation in 1538–1541. The need to take this type of compass error into account became critical to navigation when in the early nineteenth century wooden warships began to be plated with iron, and especially when shipbuilders started to make ships entirely out of steel. Gradually, as detailed later, the means was found to minimize magnetic deviation of the compass caused by the ships themselves.

30. Parhelion by Joan Blaeu, 1665

Sometimes, two very bright spots (parhelion) are seen on each side of a halo around the Sun. Called sun dogs, they are created when light refracts through flat, hexagonal ice crystals in the atmosphere, producing auxiliary images of the Sun.

THE NATIONAL LIBRARY OF FINLAND, HELSINKI

tion for work outdoors. The civil twilight ends when the Sun is 6° below the horizon. Fainter stars can then be seen, but it is still possible to see the horizon. From that time until the centre of the Sun is 12 degrees below the horizon is called 'nautical twilight', and after that, until the Sun is 18° below the horizon is 'astronomical twilight'. During astronomical twilight, and the following period of complete solar darkness, observation of stellar altitudes is only possible if the horizon is revealed by moonlight. Between the tropics of Cancer and Capricorn the twilight periods last a little more than 20 minutes. Complete darkness sets in about one hour after the sunset. At 50° latitude each twilight period lasts about 40 minutes. Closer to the poles the twilights last even longer and vary considerably with the seasons. The period of time available for measuring the altitudes of stars is thus short. However, the method of finding time by measuring lunar distances is not similarly limited.

Mirages

It often happens that the layers of air above the sea are at different temperatures, when they may act like lenses or mirrors, refracting or reflecting light. If the air above the sea is warmer and thus less dense than the air above it, a distant object at the horizon is seen as an inferior mirage, often simply called mirage. The mirage of the object may be seen beneath the object, either the right way up or upside down depending on refraction of the light rays. On both sides of the mirage the sky can often be seen in reflection. So a distant island might appear in duplicate, upside down or even as if hovering in the air. The true horizon is where the island and its mirage are united.

When there is a warm and less dense layer of air above a cooler and denser layer over the sea a superior mirage or looming is seen, where an image appears above a distant object. Again, it might appear upside down or the right way up. A looming can make objects visible even a 100 kilometres away beyond the horizon. An archipelago far away vibrating over the horizon can create an impression of a fairytale city. The phenomenon is called air castle or 'fata morgana' after Queen Morgan Le Fay of the tale of King Arthur. Mirages are normally caused by refractions and reflections in horizontal layers of air, but vertical ones can be seen, for instance, close to steamer funnels.

When taking altitude measurements with a sextant, mirages make it difficult to see the horizon clearly.

Temperature differences that cause mirages can also give rise to a phenomenon in which the surface of the sea looks either convex or concave, making the horizon look exceptionally close or far away.

The setting Sun can look horizontally sliced like a Chinese paper lantern because of air layers at different temperatures. The shortest wavelengths, violet, blue and green are refracted more than yellow and red

Natural Phenomena

LIGHT PHENOMENA IN THE ATMOSPHERE

The interaction of the air and the light passing through it gives rise to many phenomena. The air is a mixture of gases. Its main components are nitrogen and oxygen, and in addition small amounts of argon and other noble gases, carbon dioxide, and variable amounts of water vapour. The air usually also contains water drops, crystals and dust.

The colours of the sky

When passing through the air, light is scattered by molecules and other particles, it is refracted, reflected and diffracted. The blue colour of the sky is a consequence of scattering. Sunlight contains all colours of the spectrum from violet to red. The short-wave violet and blue lights are scattered most widely, and that scattered light is reflected from all parts of sky which is seen as blue. Distant objects are seen in a bluish hue and in lighter colours because of the scattered blue light. The phenomenon is called atmospheric perspective. Light scatter also causes reddening of the Sun

and the Moon close to horizon, and the red colour of sunset and dawn.

Refraction

The path taken by light is bent by refraction in the atmosphere, so that the light from a star, the Sun or the Moon, is refracted down when it penetrates into denser layers of air. Refraction is strongest at the horizon, at about 35 minutes of arc. This means that when the Sun is seen at the horizon, in reality it is below the horizon. It will also appear to be flattened because refraction is strongest near the horizon, with the result that the Sun's lower limb is lifted more than the upper limb. When taking altitude measurements with a sextant, refraction must be taken into account, and stars should not be used for navigation if they are less than 10° to 20° above the horizon.

Twilight and darkness

When using a sextant for astro-navigation, the sky must be dark enough for the stars to be seen, but it must not be too dark to see the line of the horizon. Twilight according to civilian uses commences at sunset. Scattered sunlight still provides enough illumina-

Fig.1.-July 18ᵗʰ

31. Aurora Borealis after Fridtjof Nansen, 1897

The aurora is often seen as many parallel rays, stretching across the sky, such as seen here in a colour woodcut based on a sketch from 1883 by the great polar explorer, Fridtjof Nansen.

JOHN NURMINEN FOUNDATION

32. Optical Phenomena of Unequal Refraction by William Scoresby Junior, 1823

At times, mirages have assisted mariners by allowing them to see land or ice lying beyond the horizon.

JUHA NURMINEN COLLECTION

in the air. When the horizon is very clear, this brings about the phenomenon of the 'green flash' at the last moment of sunset, when the green part of the spectrum from the setting uppermost segment of the solar disk is all that can be.

HALO PHENOMENA

Rainbows

Water drops suspended in the air scatter the light of the Sun and the Moon. The best known of these phenomena is the rainbow. A rainbow is created by water droplets in the air when the Sun is lower than 42° in the sky, and with the Sun behind the back of the observer. Sunlight is scattered and refracted by the droplets, and a colourful arch is created in the sky with an apparent radius of 42°. All colours of the spectrum are seen on the rainbow with a red outer and a violet inner rim. Due to scatter the sky looks brighter within the arch than outside it. Often a secondary rainbow with a radius of 51° is visible outside the primary one but with the colours in the opposite order.

Colour clouds

An occurrence known as 'colour clouds' belongs to the same family of phenomena as the rainbow, and are caused by sunlight or moonlight being scattered by very small droplets of water or ice crystals.

Halos

Many kinds of bright arches, rings and spots can be created when sunlight or moonlight are scattered by ice crystals of different shapes and positions in the air. Tens of halo formations are known. The visibility of halos is controlled by the altitude in the sky of the Sun or the Moon. Maybe the most common phenomena of this kind are the 22° circle around the Sun or the Moon, the sun pillar, and the parhelion, also called 'sundog' or 'mock sun' (in German *Nebensonne*) seen at 22° from the Sun on one or both of its sides. An unbroken 22° circle is usually caused by a smooth cirrostratus or gauze cloud. It moves at high altitude and precedes a low pressure. On average rain will come within 36 hours.

Thunder and flashing

The vertical motions of air masses at different temperatures and of the particles carried by them move large electric charges between the lower and the upper parts of tall clouds. Big electric tensions are created and they discharge in different ways between the clouds, or between a cloud and the Earth. The energy of the discharge heats the air until it glows, and that is seen as lightning and heard as thunder.

Another electrostatic phenomenon is called St. Elmo's fire. On nights of thunder it is seen as flame-like discharges, usually from the tops of ship masts and the ends of yards. This is a coronal discharge from a sharp tip and is caused by the electric tension between the ship and the air. It was given its name from the patron saint of sailors, St. Elmo or St. Ulmo (d. AD 303).

Noctilucent clouds

At high geographic latitudes, thin clouds of ice crystals, illuminated by the Sun from behind the horizon at heights of about 80 kilometres, are often seen, especially at summer nights. They appear thin and wispy, glowing electric blue.

Aurora or Northern lights

An aurora is created when particles of solar wind are trapped by the Earth's magnetic field, making them plunge into the atmosphere in the vicinity of magnetic poles. The particles collide with molecules of atmospheric nitrogen and oxygen at the height of about 100 to 1000 kilometres, gaining energy that will be released as light. The light is seen as an aurora against the dark night sky and appears as an oval with a distance from the magnetic pole varying between 16° and 24°. These are visible at great distances since they are created at such high altitudes. The colours of an aurora – violet, blue, green and orange – are determined by the gases participating in the collisions.

Zodiacal light

The light radiated by the Sun is scattered by interplanetary dust consisting of microscopic solid particles. This may appear on Earth in the night sky, after sunset and before sunrise, as a patch of dim light in the ecliptic (path of the Sun), and is known as zodiacal light. At dusk the zodiacal light disappears with the lowering Sun and it reappears just before sunrise in the morning sky. The phenomenon is most prominently seen in the tropics. At high latitudes the sky darkens so slowly after the sunset and brightens so early before sunrise that no zodiacal light can be seen.

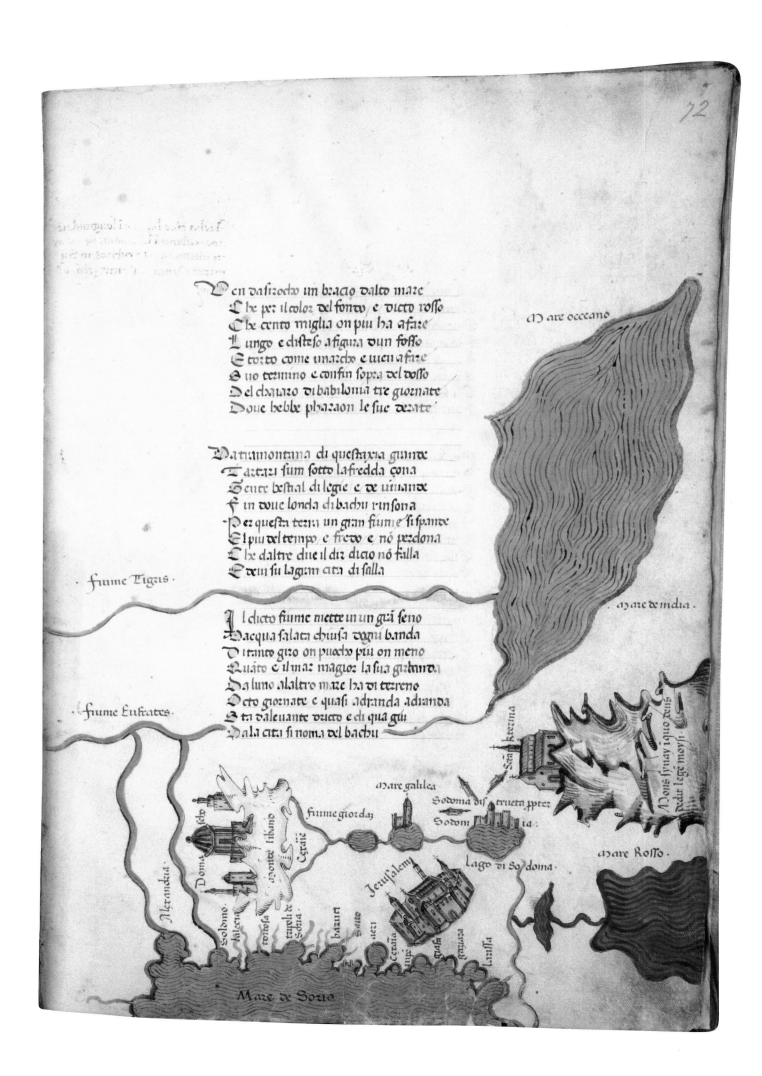

Ven dasirocho un bracio dalto mare
Che per il color del fonto e dicto rosso
Che cento miglia on piu ha afare
Lungo e disteso afigura dun fosso
Storto come unarcho e wen afare
Suo termino e confin sopra del dosso
Del chauazo di babilonia tre giornate
Doue hebbe pharaon le sue derate

Da tramontana di questa xia giunte
Tartari sum sotto lafredda zona
Sente bestial di legie e de uiuande
Fin doue loncla di bachu rinsona
Per questa terra un gran fiume si spante
El piu del tempo e fiero e no perdona
Che daltre due il diz dicto no falla
E deni su lagem cita di salla

Il dicto fiume mette in un gra seno
Dacqua salata chiusa dogni banda
Di tanto giro on puocho piu on meno
Quato e ilmar magior la sua girdura
Da luno alaltro mare ha di terreno
Octo giornate e quasi adranda adranda
Sta daleuante ureto e di qua giu
Dala cita si noma del bachu

Mare occeano

ayare de india

fiume Tigris

fiume Eufrates

Mare galilea

Scta kcrina

Mons synay iquo xius redit legi moysi

Sodoma distructa ppter

Sodomia

Lago di Sodoma

Mare Rosso

fiume giordan

Montes libano

Ceralc

Alexandria

Domas cho

Jerusalem

Mare de Soro

ANCIENT SAILING ROUTES
AND PERIPLI

Wonders are many on earth, and the greatest of these
Is man, who rides the ocean and takes his way
Through the deeps, through wind-swept valleys of perilous seas
That surge and sway.

SOPHOCLES, *ANTIGONE*

With the Mediterranean to the north of Egypt, and the Red Sea to the east, it is only natural that at a very early time Egyptians should venture into these waters to acquire the necessary goods and luxury items they desired. The first written account of Egypt's sea-trade is of a voyage made in 3200 BC by the Pharaoh Snefru when he sent forty ships east to Byblos, a wealthy city in Phoenicia, present-day Lebanon. By 3000 BC a flourishing trade between Egypt and Phoenicia was already established, with cedar wood for ship building one of the principal cargoes. In 2750 BC, Hannu (not to be confused with Hanno) led an expedition down the Red Sea, from where he brought back precious metals, and myrrh, a gum resin used in perfumes, medications and incense.

EGYPTIAN VOYAGES TO EAST AFRICA

During the reign of Sahure, in 2500 BC, Egypt began regular trade with a country called Punt, or Pwanet, more accessible by sailing the Red Sea than by overland caravans. Conventionally, the land of Punt is identified as Somalia, but recent evidence suggests that Punt may not have been quite that far south, and was instead the Sudan or east-northeast Ethiopia.

Of the many expeditions to the land of Punt that followed, none is better known than that undertaken in the reign of Queen Hatshepsut, (1473–1458 BC). Lengthy hieroglyph in-

33. A Page from *La Sfera* by Gregorio Dati, 15th century

Gregorio Dati's *La Sfera* (The Spheres), written in the fifteenth century, may well be the first primer of astronomy, cosmography and geography in the western world. Intended as a teaching tool for students and educated merchants, it is written in rhyming stanzas.

THE NATIONAL LIBRARY OF FINLAND, HELSINKI

scriptions and murals on the walls of her mortuary temple at Deir-el-Bahri, Egypt, tell how in 1493 BC Queen Hatshepsut sent a fleet of five ships, each with thirty rowers, to the land of Punt. There they obtained valuable woods (ebony and cinnamon), ivory, gold, frankincense, myrrh and saplings of the tree that produced that resin. In addition to these trade goods, exotic animals – giraffe, elephant, apes and a horse – were brought back to Thebes 'for the gratification of Hatshepsut'.

In the thousand years since the voyages under Sahure, much had been learned about sailing conditions in the Red Sea. Expeditions headed south during the months of June to December, with the prevailing northerly winds, even though they brought rough weather, and returned north with the mild southerlies that blew from December to June. Advances in shipbuilding had made the grand scale of Hatshepsut's expedition possible. Ships were larger, structurally more complex, and more sturdily built to accommodate cargoes.

Nine hundred years after Queen Hatshepsut's expedition in about 600 BC, there was an equally significant voyage. Pharaoh Necho first attempted to strengthen Egypt's control over trade in African and Arabian commodities by finishing a canal from the Nile River to the Red Sea – a project begun centuries before, and abandoned. There was a strong economic incentive for doing so. The Greeks controlled the northern shores of the Mediterranean, and the Phoenician sphere of influence extended to the western Mediterranean and beyond the Straits of Gibraltar, or Pillars of Hercules, into the Atlantic. With limited access to trade in the Mediterranean, a Red Sea canal could give Egypt direct access to East Africa and the Arabian Peninsula. When the canal project proved to be beyond Egypt's means, it appears that Necho was prompted to measures even more drastic to gain the wealth of trade with East Africa and beyond, and mounted an expedition to find new profitable markets on Africa's western coast.

Herodotus (c. 485–425 BC) credits Necho with being the first to demonstrate what some cosmographers believed – but had never been able to prove – that all Africa, then known as Libya, was surrounded by water and thus circumnavigable. According to Herodotus, Necho 'sent out a fleet manned by Phoenician crew with orders to sail west about and return to Egypt and the Mediterranean by way of the Pillar of Hercules', the Straits of Gibraltar. In two years, he says, they rounded the Pillars of Hercules and in the course of the third year returned to Egypt.

That such a voyage was completed is certainly *possible*. Their ships were seaworthy, and a clockwise circumnavigation of Africa would have given mariners favourable winds and currents until they reached the western coast of Africa north of the equator. As long as they kept within sight of the coast, no navigation was necessary. Whether the voyage was *probable* is a different matter. The source for Herodotus's narrative is unknown. Although he had faith in the truth of what he related, Posidonius (c. 135–51 BC) and Strabo (c. 63 BC–AD 21) doubted its authenticity, citing 'insufficient evidence'. Those present-day authors who believe the voyage actually took place point to one part in the story: 'as they sailed on a westerly course round the southern end of Libya, they had the Sun on their right – to the northward of them.' This certainly would be the case in southern latitudes. Unfortunately, no other navigation information or geographical details are present to allow us to test the truth of Herodotus's narrative.

34. Queen Hatshepsut

Among her many accomplishments, Queen-pharaoh Hatshepsut, fifth pharaoh of the eighteenth dynasty of ancient Egypt, re-established previously disrupted trade networks. EGYPTIAN MUSEUM, CAIRO

35. Queen Hatshepsut's Ship leaving from Punt, redrawn by Björn Landström 1961 from the original mural carving from Deir-el-Bahri

Ships constructed for the Queen's expedition down the Red Sea were roughly 22 metres (72 feet) long and 5 metres (16½ ft) wide. There was no keel to provide longitudinal stiffness; instead, this was provided by a long rope attached at the stem and stern, with intermediate vertical supports, tightened with a tourniquet. A square sail, 15 metres wide (49 ft), set on a single mast was used when winds were favourable, otherwise, fifteen rowers on each side provided the propulsion. The carved lotus flower decorating the sterns (seen on the far left of the carving), instead of a plow-like protuberance used as a ram, indicates these are trading vessels and not warships. These vessels were of shallow draft, enabling them to sail in the weed-chocked coastal waters of the Red Sea. At port there was no need for a quay or dock, for they could simply be pulled up on the beach and loaded from a gangplank. COURTESY OF OLOF LANDSTRÖM

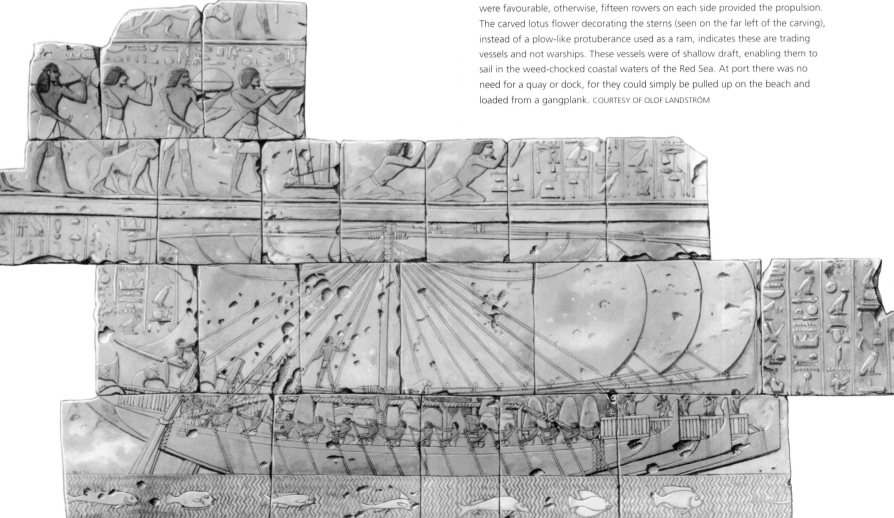

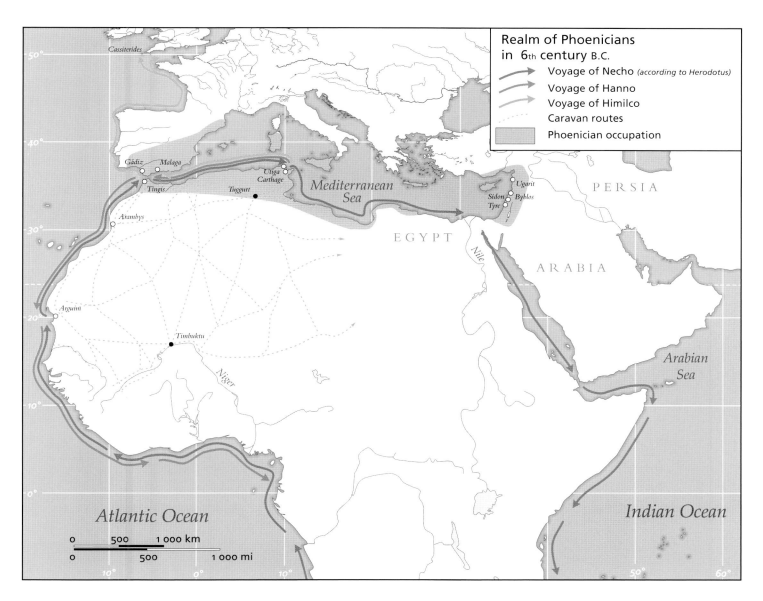

Realm of Phoenicians
in 6th century B.C.
Voyage of Necho (according to Herodotus)
Voyage of Hanno
Voyage of Himilco
Caravan routes
Phoenician occupation

36. Realm of the Phoenicians

In their desire to find new markets Phoenician and Egyptian mariners extended the range of their voyages beyond their familiar Mediterranean. Phoenicians were the first to pass through the Straits of Gibraltar out into the Atlantic Ocean. Far from their native shores they set up trade stations and established colonies.

PHOENICIANS: THE FIRST
OPEN SEA NAVIGATION

In the history of seafaring, no other Mediterranean culture has exceeded the Phoenicians in the range of their voyaging and the establishment of far-flung colonies. From its coastal cities of Byblos, which gave its name to the Bible, Tripoli, Beirut, Sedon and Tyre, their mariners spread out across the Mediterranean to establish colonies and trading stations. By the thirteenth century BC their settlements extended to include Cyprus for its copper mines and timber, Sardinia for its metals, and Rhodes, Crete, Malta, Sicily, Marseilles, Cádiz and Carthago (Carthage), each supplying commodities lacked in Phoenicia. Through Byblos papyrus was delivered to Greece. The name of the city originates from a Greek word *bublos*

meaning papyrus. Many papyruses are *biblio*, which translates as the word 'book'.

Perhaps as early as the eleventh century BC, but certainly by the seventh century BC, Phoenician ships passed through the Straits of Gibraltar to become the first Mediterranean nation to enter the Atlantic. They sailed north to the Scilly Islands off the southwest coast of England, the Cassiterides as they called them, to obtain tin, a necessary ingredient in the manufacture of bronze which was needed for tools, arms and all manner of utensils. Tin trade with the Cassiterides was constant, not only to supply the needs of Phoenicia's own people, but as a useful trade item with other nations.

In the other direction, sixty miles south from the Straits of Gibraltar, Phoenicians founded the cities of Lixus off the coast of Morocco, and Mogador (Essaouira) an additional 250 miles farther down the coast. By the fourth century BC Phoenicians continued a regular trade on the west coast of Africa for its ivory and gold, and leopard and lion skins. There is every likelihood Phoenicians also visited the Canary Islands, although there are no written records of such ventures by any ancient authors. Phoenicia's trade also took her east, into the Black

Sea, where she made a profit by selling her own goods, as well as those obtained from other countries. Whether Phoenician mariners reached the Azores, North America or Brazil, as has been suggested, is problematic.

When Phoenicia was conquered by Persia in the mid-sixth century BC, one of its famous colonies, Carthage, became the chief Phoenician city. Two contemporaneous Carthagenian mariners – Himilco and Hanno – made notable voyages at the end of the sixth century BC.

Himilco's original account is lost, but the narrative of his voyage is recounted by Pliny the Elder (AD 23–79) in his *Natural History*. Himilco's aim, Pliny states, was 'to explore the outer coasts of Europe'. After passing through the Straits of Gibraltar, Himilco sailed north until he reached the south-west corner of England, where he 'discovered' the Cassiterides – the Tin Islands. He described the difficulties in navigation he encountered along the way that slowed his progress: lack of wind, heavy and sluggish nature of the sea, quantities of seaweed that impeded his ships, and whales, 'monsters of the deep [which] swam to and fro among their ships as they were creeping on their languid course'. Himilco's voyage was not for 'discovery' in the sense of finding new lands; he knew where he was going and what he was looking for. The principle object of Himilco's exploration was to establish a direct sea route to the Cassiterides to avoid obtaining tin through intermediate traders, and thus give Phoenicia a monopoly on tin, adding greatly to her wealth.

Hanno's instructions were to sail south along the west coast of Africa and create Carthagenian colonies there. He founded four colonies, and continued to explore the coast of Africa almost to the equator, before turning back. His is the only known first-hand account of exploration along that coast until Portuguese explorations at the end of the fifteenth century.

Phoenicia's wide-ranging voyages could not have been possible without development in the fields of ship design and navigation. They strengthened the hull of their vessels by the addition of a keel which gave the boats greater longitudinal stiffness and prevented them from 'hogging', that is, sagging at the ends. Egyptian vessels achieved the same thing by using a long rope attached at the stem and stern and tightened with a tourniquet. The keel had one major advantage over the rope in that it not only provided stiffness, but it also gave the boat directional stability, preventing it from slewing about through the action of wind and wave. Phoenicia's more seaworthy vessels enabled them to travel the Mediterranean widely, and beyond into the open Atlantic Ocean.

The Phoenician's other significant contribution to navigation was the addition of sail to oared vessels. By using the

37. Amphora, c. 350 BC

Amphorae, such as this one from 350 BC, were in use in the Mediterranean from the fifteenth century BC until about the seventh century AD. They were the principle means of storing and transporting a wide range of goods, such as olive oil, wine, grain and fish. Most were around 45 cm (18 inches) high, but they ranged in size up to 1.5 m (5 feet).

JUHA NURMINEN COLLECTION

38. Kyrenian Ship by Kari Jaakkola, 2000

Greek commercial trade ships of the fourth century BC, such as this painting of a vessel from Kyrenia, on the north shore of Cyprus, plied the Aegean Sea near the coast of Turkey. These ships transported more than 150,000 tons of grain a year, and carried more than 300 amphoras.

JOHN NURMINEN FOUNDATION

39. Map of The Nordic Countries by Sebastian Münster, 1540

The island of Thule was first written about by the Greek explorer, Pytheas of Massalia (c. 380–310 BC), between 330 and 320 BC. Reportedly located six days' journey north of Britain, the island is most commonly associated with Iceland; yet perhaps it may be taken to represent the farthest reaches of the known world. Cartographers like Münster added the island of Thule to their maps.

JOHN NURMINEN FOUNDATION

wind for propulsion, it gave them a far greater range of travel. Fewer men were needed as rowers, and fewer provisions were required, allowing more space for profitable cargo. Rowers were still essential when there was no wind, or it was from an unfavourable direction, and when greater manoeuverability was required, as in harbour. Knowledge of the winds, the direction from which they blew, their local as well as seasonal variation, was important in determining when and where they would embark on their trading voyages. Generally, they sailed between the months of March and October when the weather was most settled and favourable.

Within the Mediterranean, sailing was primarily coastal, going from point to point using recognizable landmarks to determine positions. This was sufficient when sailing on an east-west axis, for land would always be within sight. Even when their route took them away from any visual reference, such as sailing from the African coast to the Balearic Islands, or across the Channel of Sardinia, voyages were sufficiently short that they could reliably arrive at their destination.

The most important navigation tool at their disposal was the lead line, used to determine depth. This was particularly sig-

nificant when approaching Alexandria on the Egyptian coast, with its reefs and shallow waters extending as far as sixty miles off shore. Placing a lump of tallow or other sticky substance on the bottom of the lead in order to bring up a sample of the sea floor was already a common practice to help identify their position.

Voyages within the Mediterranean usually followed either the north or south coast; making it unnecessary for navigators to have a knowledge of latitude. It was a very different matter once out into the Atlantic, sailing either to the north or south. The ability of Phoenician navigators to determine their latitude from the star *Kochab*, enabled them to sail with confidence when out of sight of land. There is no evidence they had an instrument to measure its angular height, but most likely they used the same method Arab navigators first used in the Indian Ocean: holding their hand up to the night sky and measuring the number of star's fingers the star stood above the horizon. Alternatively the stars altitude may have been measured by its apparent position along the height of the ship's mast.

Phoenicia's sovereignty of the seas in commerce and military action brought with it the necessity for a code of maritime law. One of her greatest legal, and maritime, achievements was the drafting of a sea law defining the rights and responsibilities of ship owners, captains, passengers, merchants, and local port authorities of the many nations with which it traded.

This law, known as *Lex Rhodia*, served Phoenicia and later formed the basis of Roman maritime law, which continued almost unchanged in practice into the Middle Ages. Much of this code of law was also copied with little alteration by the nations of Western Europe, as well as by Muslim traders. In 1010, Italy used the *Lex Rhodia* to form her maritime law of *Tabula Amalfitana*. From the Mediterranean it extended to France as the *Rolls of Oléron* under King Louis IX (r. 1226–1270). By the fourteenth century, the *Lex Rhodia* had been adopted with local variation by England, Flanders, and towns of the Hanseatic League. With Spanish expansion it spread to the New World and Asia.

It is testimony to Phoenicia's careful construction and clarity of expression in her seafaring code that much of today's international maritime law can be traced directly to the *Lex Rhodia*.

PYTHEAS OF MASSALIA:
THE FIRST SCIENTIFIC NAVIGATOR

The voyage made by Pytheas of Massalia around 350 BC, or perhaps even earlier, was unlike any that preceded him. His concerns were more of an intellectual nature, rather than about profitable trade routes. The object of his expedition was a quest for knowledge regarding the ocean beyond the confines of the Mediterranean Sea, and about the lands of northern Europe, which at that time were only vaguely perceived. The account by Pytheas, *On the Ocean,* survives only as fragments, starting to appear around 320 BC in the writings of later historians. That his journey was considered of great importance is evidenced by his name being referred to by no less than eighteen writers in antiquity.

Since Pytheas came from the Greek colony of Massalia, the present-day Marseilles which was an important trade centre in the Mediterranean at the time, it is only natural he would not neglect to report information that might be of use to his countrymen, such as the products of the area he visited, as well as its social and political structure. But there is no evidence of any direct commercial contacts as the result of his voyage.

Partly by sea and partially by land, Pytheas journeyed to the British Isles, travelled over the greater part of them, and was the first Greek writer to give an account. He visited Cornwall, the source of tin for Greek colonies. He related the varying methods of threshing grain, and how mead was fermented from honey. The information gained from his expedition about the British Isles, and the coasts of outer Europe, became the foundation for the knowledge of western geography of all the writers of later antiquity.

To the north, beyond Britain and Ireland, lay a land he named Thule, where, according to Pytheas, there was no earth, air, or sea, but a mixture of all these things. The area had a thick and sluggish nature, with the consistency of jellyfish, and made navigation impossible.

The information about Pytheas's journey is very often vague, and sometimes conflicting, which has led to much conjecture about the route he took and the identification of Thule. Some present-day historians believe that Pytheas travelled to Iceland before returning home, while others are of the opinion he voyaged north along the coast of Norway to the latitude of Iceland. It is even possible, considers one historian, that Pytheas entered the Baltic Sea where his journey took him east to the island of Saaremaa off the coast of Estonia, and farther, to the mouth of the Neva River. Part of the difficulty in trying to reconstruct the route of Pytheas lies in the fact that he recorded distances travelled by the number of days it took to sail from point to point. These temporal measurements were later converted by another author into distance measurements, accounted in numbers of stadia. Nevertheless this conversion produced wholly inconsistent and unreliable results.

However, it is not the route taken by Pytheas, nor the length of the journey, that was his most notable achievement; it was indeed the observations and descriptions he provided that make his expedition so important. The account he made of the tides he encountered in the Atlantic, a phenomenon practically nonexistent in the Mediterranean, and his observation that they were produced and regulated by the Moon, according to its phases, was an important milestone in navigational science. Though his reasoning on how the Moon influenced the tides was faulty, nonetheless, he was the first to recognize there was a relationship between the two.

His interest and ability in astronomy is clearly evident from the number of observations of the Sun's height above the horizon, his description of the changes in constellations, and the variation of length of daylight, as he travelled north. To determine his latitude, Pytheas used the rising and setting pattern of the stars. He also used Sun heights as measured from the length of the shadow cast from a gnomon, a vertical post where the shadow is used for measurement. Because he gave the Sun's height above the horizon at the winter solstice, it would be safe to assume his voyage extended over at least a two-year period. He could not use *Polaris*, the North Star, to determine latitude, for in the fourth century BC *Polaris* was not at the celestial North Pole. Nor, apparently, did he use *Kochab*. His skills in astronomical observation, however, allowed him to make use of asterisms, a cluster of stars smaller than a constellation, near the celestial pole. As the stars he selected rotated during the course of the night, they indicated the position of the celestial pole.

Identifying Thule, and determining whether Pytheas got that far, is as thorny a problem as trying to determine his route. Pytheas does not explicitly state that he visited Thule; he only reports its existence and says that it was a six-day voyage north of Britain. Beyond Thule lay the 'sluggish' sea. It appears Pytheas knew about Thule only by hearsay, having vaguely heard of it sometime during his voyage. He does not even mention that Thule was a large island. That idea comes from the third century Roman emperor and author, Julius Solinus (fl. AD 250), who for the most part recast the work of Pliny without acknowledgment. In it, Solinus repeated Pliny's statement that at Thule daylight lasted for six months while the Sun passed through the tropic of Cancer during the summer solstice; which if true would have moved Thule from the Arctic Circle to the North Pole. The Greek astronomer Cleomedes, who may have written his *On the Circular Motions of the Celestial Bodies* at any date between the first century BC and the fourth century AD, had been nearer the mark when, also writing about Pytheas, he stated the period of perpetual light at Thule to be thirty days. Indicative of the persistence of erroneous statements is the fact that in the sixth century, Bishop Isidore of Seville could still write 'Thule is the farthest island of the ocean, lying between north and west beyond Britain, getting its name from the Sun, since at it the Sun reaches its summer solstice'.

Not until thirteen centuries after Pytheas's voyage do we have the first reliable connection of Thule with Iceland. In 825, Dicuil, the Irish monk and scholar who taught in

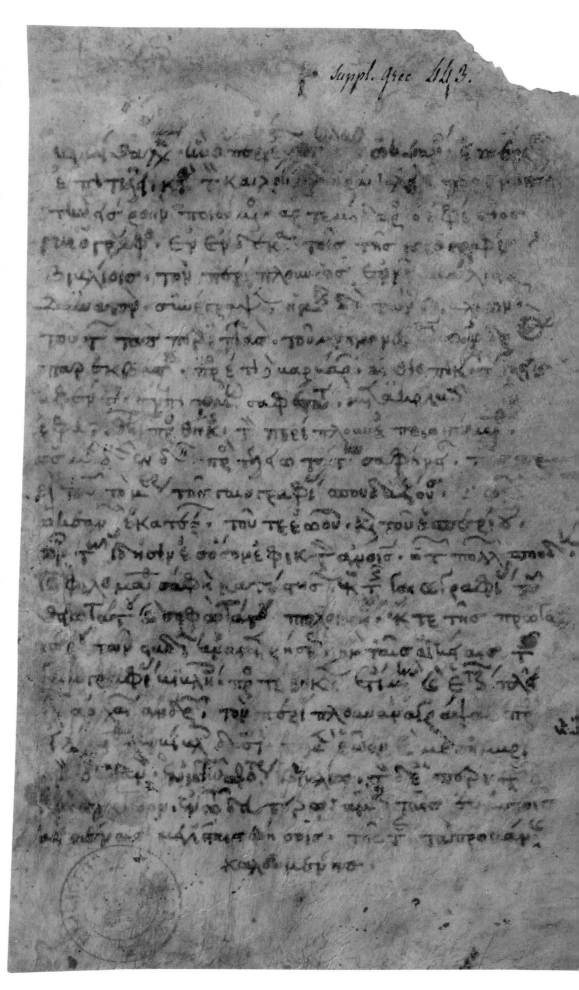

40. Periplus of Scylax c. 1200 attributed to Scylax of Caryanda

Written as a sequential description of a voyage, the *Periplus of Scylax* served as a guide to mariners in the Mediterranean Sea and Black Sea. It is the earliest 'way-finding', or navigation guide, known to exist.

BIBLIOTHÈQUE NATIONALE DE FRANCE, PARIS

the court of Charlemagne, wrote his compendium of history entitled *De mensura orbis terrae* (The Measure of the Whole World). In it he tells how Irish monks, in their need to flee from the Vikings and seek a land where they could pray in solitude, arrived in Iceland in AD 795. He states that this is the land called Thule, and gives a detailed description of the midnight sun.

Acceptance of Iceland as the Thule of Pytheas has since grown in strength, mainly through persistent repetition. Various islands, including the Faeroes, the Shetlands, the Orkneys and those off Norway, have also been suggested as the possible Thule, as has been the coast of Greenland.

Perhaps Pytheas never conceived of Thule as an actual territory, but as a realm beyond human knowledge – a goal beyond reach. In the traditional Greek concept of *oikoumene*, Thule was that place that lay *beyond* the farthest extreme of geography. The Greek writer Strabo called Thule 'an island being not only remote beyond Britain, but just barely habitable because of the cold, so that parts even more remote are considered uninhabitable'. As far as Strabo was concerned, the parallel through Thule was the north boundary of the inhabited world. The counterpart of Thule in the north would be the land of paradise, the abode of Adam and Eve, in the east; the land of Gog and Magog, the mythical enemies of civilization who dwelt in the far northeast; and the 'promised land' sought by Saint Brendan and his fellow monks that lay somewhere in the west. All these 'realms' are just beyond the known world, created at this time in order to comprehend the cosmos and man's place with in it.

Casting aside all conjecture about the route taken by Pytheas, and the location of Thule, the corpus of works on Pytheas demonstrates his considerable achievements. He is regarded as 'an investigator with a curiosity and breadth of interest like that displayed by Herodotus a century earlier, and a drive for scientific precision like that of Hipparchus two centuries later'. The observations of Pytheas are a significant advance in the history of navigation, rightfully according to him the title of the first scientific navigator.

FROM PERIPLI TO RUTTERS AND SAILING DIRECTIONS

As commerce by sea expanded its geographic range, mariners could no longer rely solely on memory to guide them safely to their destination and back to their home. Accumulated knowledge of route finding from the increasing number of voyages was set down in manuscript form. These first sailing directions were called *peripli* (*periplus*, singular), from the Greek word meaning 'voyaging around' or 'circumnavigation'. They listed in sequential order ports around a coast, along with distances and the amount of time required to travel between each port. They also described coastal landmarks, and related pertinent navigational information.

It would be reasonable to assume the Phoenicians had some form of sailing directions manual, but none have survived. The first extant sea manual is the *Periplus of Scylax*. According to Herodotus, the Persian Emperor, Darius I (550–485 BC), wished to know where the River Indus in India flowed into the Arabian Sea, and the extent of the shores beyond in the Indian Ocean. In 510 BC, Darius sent the Greek navigator, Scylax, in command of ships to sail down the Indus. Upon reaching the sea, the expedition turned west, and followed the coast until in its thirtieth month it arrived at 'the place from whence the king of the Egyptians, [Necho] had sent out the Phoenicians.

Some scholars question whether the voyage of Scylax actually occurred. The original manuscript by Scylax no longer exists; all that is left is the meager account given by Herodotus, quotations from the work of Scylax by Hecataeus, and excerpts by later authors such Aristotle and Strabo. Of the mariner Scylax, little is known other than that he was a native of Caryanda, a Greek colony in Asia Minor, corresponding to present-day southwest Turkey.

The periplus that has come down to us bearing the name of Scylax was written at a later time. From the place-names used, the closest one can come to dating this periplus is sometime between 360 and 348 BC. Early editions erroneously attributed authorship to Scylax of Caryanda; even when his credit was later corrected, the name was retained in honour of Scylax. There are also indications that this more recent periplus is a compendium of texts from a number of different authorities – of varying degrees of value – further corrupted by interpolations and errors from later copyists. Nonetheless, the *Periplus of Scylax* is still the earliest extant geographical treatise to give us a picture of the Greek world bordering the Mediterranean Sea, and the first written truly as a guide for mariners.

The periplus begins at the Straits of Gibraltar and follows the northern coast of the Mediterranean eastward to the Adriatic, and beyond into the Black Sea. It then turns west and follows the north coast of Africa until it arrives back at the starting point. The account of the shores of the Aegean Sea, and of the Greek colonies on the Black Sea which were best known, are given in full and clear detail. Outside the Pillars of Hercules, in the Atlantic Ocean, the author has only this to say: 'There are many trading stations of the Carthaginians, much mud, and high tides, and open seas'. But he does vaguely suggest that Africa was in fact a great peninsula. It makes no mention at all of the Indian Ocean or the Red Sea.

Nearly contemporary with Pliny the Elder, a Greek merchant residing in Alexandria wrote the *Periplus of the Erythræan Sea* (c. AD 89). In a narrow sense of the word, the Erythræan was the Red Sea, but in the Greco-Roman world it was taken to mean that entire northern portion of the Indian Ocean, now called the Arabian Sea, between the coasts of India and Africa and bounded on the north by the Arabian Peninsula. The name of the author of this periplus is not known, but it

41. The Sea Battle of Salamis by Wilhelm von Kaulbach, 1858

From 499–492 BC, the armies and vast armada of the Persians, under King Xerxes, swept westward across Asia, burning and sacking Greek city-states. At the battle of Salamis, fought in 480 BC, the Greek fleet gained a decisive victory over the invading forces. Although vastly outnumbered by the Persian fleet, the Greek vessels feigning retreat lured attacking vessels into a narrow strait near Athens. There, unable to manoeuvre in the restricted waters, the Persian vessels were rammed and driven upon the Attic shore. This was a turning point in the war. As a consequence of the victory, Hellenistic culture began to flourish and ultimately become the cornerstone of a distinctive Western culture.

BAYER.STAATSGEMÄLDESAMMLUNGEN

is evident from the information he presents that for the most part it is a first-hand account of a voyage in which the primary purpose was commerce.

The *Periplus of the Erythræan Sea* is divided into two parts. The first begins at Myos Hormos on the western side of the Red Sea, near its northern end, which the author says is 'the first of the regular trading ports on the Egyptian coast'. From there the author proceeds south along that coast, through the Gulf of Aden to the port of Rhapta on the east coast of Africa. This was the last market town on the continent and a place of considerable trade in ivory and tortoise-shell. Beyond Rhapta, says the author, 'nothing is known'. However, he conjectures that 'the unexplored ocean curves around toward the west, and running along by the regions to the south of Ethiopia and Libya and Africa it mingles with the Western Sea'. Thus he believed the Indian Ocean was not an enclosed sea, as the geography of Ptolemy would have it, and that Africa could be circumnavigated into the Atlantic.

The author is diligent throughout his periplus to provide information on the various kingdoms and tribes along the way, and of its rulers – if they were friendly or not, and whether they were predisposed to trade. He lists the various items available for export at these ports, as well as trade goods desired there for import. His navigational observations are detailed and useful. He reports, for example, that the port of Barygaza (roughly 22° N lat.), beyond the Indus River, was one of the large centres of trade in India, but that the small gulf leading to it was very dangerous to navigation. He warns: 'The water is shallow, with shifting sandbanks occurring continually and a great way from

shore; so that very often, when the shore is not even in sight, ships run aground, and if they attempt to hold their course they are wrecked.' He gives directions on how to enter the gulf safely, but even then navigation is troublesome, for 'the waves are high and very violent, and the sea is tumultuous and foul, and has eddies and rushing whirlpools. The bottom in some places abrupt, and in others rocky and sharp, so that the anchors lying there are parted, some being quickly cut off, and others chafing on the bottom.' The appearance of large, black water snakes, 'serpents', is an indication, he says, that one is approaching this gulf, for in other parts of this coast the serpents are much smaller, and bright green to gold in colour.

Before the author of the *Periplus of the Erythræan Sea* turns the navigator homeward he mentions that it was now possible to avoid taking the route close off the long coastline. Instead they could take a departure from the Arabian Peninsula or African coast and sail directly across the open Erythræan Sea, thus saving considerable time and distance. It was the Greek

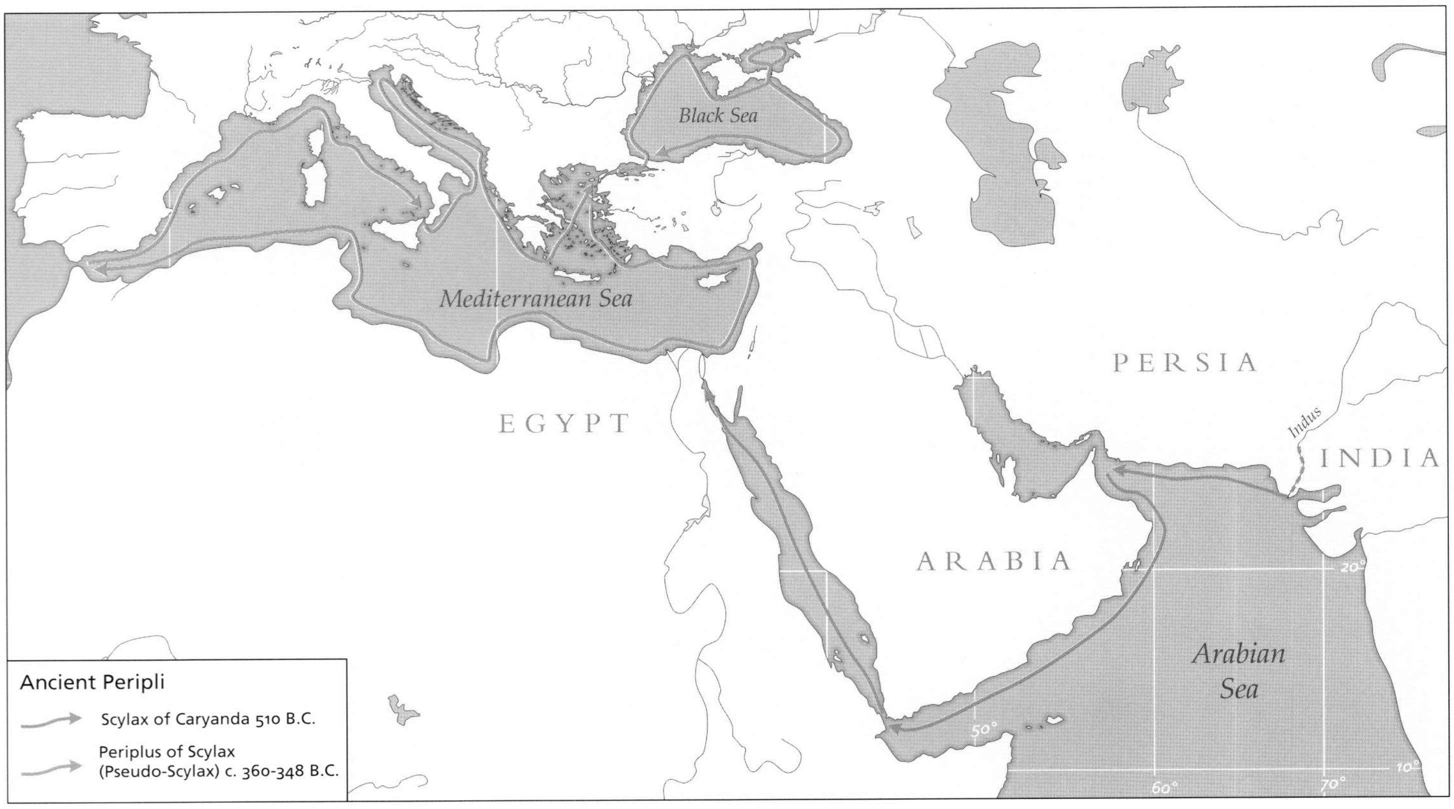

Ancient Peripli

Scylax of Caryanda 510 B.C.

Periplus of Scylax
(Pseudo-Scylax) c. 360-348 B.C.

42. Ancient Peripli

Shown here, as described in the writings of Herodotus and other Greek historians, is the route taken by Scylax of Caryanda in 510 BC, and the 'Pseudo-Scylax' periplus of the fourth century BC. With the *Periplus of the Erythraean Sea*, written almost six centuries after Scylax of Caryanda, the geographic range was much extended and a considerable amount of information relevant to navigation along these coasts included.

mariner Hippalus, he tells us, who first became aware of the pattern of monsoon winds in the Indian Ocean while engaged with trade in India, and learned how to take advantage of them. By the time the Erythræan periplus was written, this was already an established practice.

Later, during the second half of the third century AD, when the Roman Empire was still great and flourishing, it produced a manual of sailing directions called *Stadiasmus maris magni*. Starting at Alexandria, it covered the Mediterranean coasts from the Straits of Gibraltar in the west, to the entrance of the Black Sea in the east. Unfortunately, portions of this periplus are missing, and those that have survived are of unequal value in its geography and in the navigational information provided. The section on the North African coast from Alexandria to Utica, however, is presented in precise detail and with unquestionable accuracy – good evidence that it is a first-hand account and one intended as a practical guide for navigators. For each station along the way, the unknown author gives a brief note on the nature of the port – whether it is a good, protected harbour, or merely an open roadstead for anchoring – any landmarks, and other information the navigator should know about.

At the time of the fall of the Roman Empire in the third quarter of the fifth century, trade routes in the Mediterranean Sea and Indian Ocean were thoroughly established. When the Roman world became Christian, these same routes continued to be used through the early Middle Ages; but instead of being under control of Persian, Greek or Roman empires, they were now under the control of the Christian nations of western Europe: Italy, Spain and southern France.

When the introduction of the magnetic compass in the twelfth century provided mariners with a reliable means to set their course, and an astrolabe to fix their latitude, the older route-finding directions of the periplus, rather than being discontinued, were supplemented with new navigation information. Advances in astronomy, improved tables of ephemerides (positions) of the planets, with tables and rules for fixing position, were all incorporated into greatly expanded navigation manuals. By the end of the thirteenth century (1296) Italy had its *Compasso da Navigare*, Portugal in the fifteenth century, its *roterio*, immediately followed by Spanish manuals, which when adopted in England were called rutters. From the thirteenth century onward, navigation manuals began to be supplemented with the introduction of the portolan chart, which presented navigational information in purely graphic form. The wind-rose and rhumb lines of the portolan were eventually replaced on charts by a grid of longitude and latitude, and a compass rose divided into degrees of a circle. Navigation manuals have continued to the present day in Admiralty Pilot Books and United States Sailing Directions.

43. Alexandria Harbour

Founded by Alexander the Great in or around 334 BC, Alexandria became one of the greatest cities in the Hellenistic world. From its port, Egyptian grain was shipped to feed the Greek peninsula and islands. Under subsequent Roman rule, Alexandria was the chief harbour in the eastern Mediterranean for transport of goods to and from Rome's harbour of Ostia.

44. Lighthouse of Pharos

Many classical authors, as well as Arab traders visiting Alexandria, have described the Pharos lighthouse. Pliny the Elder (d. AD 79) wrote of the Pharos: *Over and above the Pyramides . . . a great name there is of a tower built by one of the kings of Aegypt within the Island Pharos, and it keepeth and commaundeth the haven of Alexandria. The use of this watch tower is to shew light as a lanthorne* [lantern] *and give direction in the night season for to enter the haven and where they shall avoid barrs and shelves.* Light from a fire was focused by mirrors, perhaps made of polished bronze, to reflect the light far out to sea. Some accounts also spoke of a huge lens to increase the range and visibility of the light. To strengthen the base of the lighthouse against heavy pounding by the sea, the blocks of granite were joined by lead, rather than mortar.

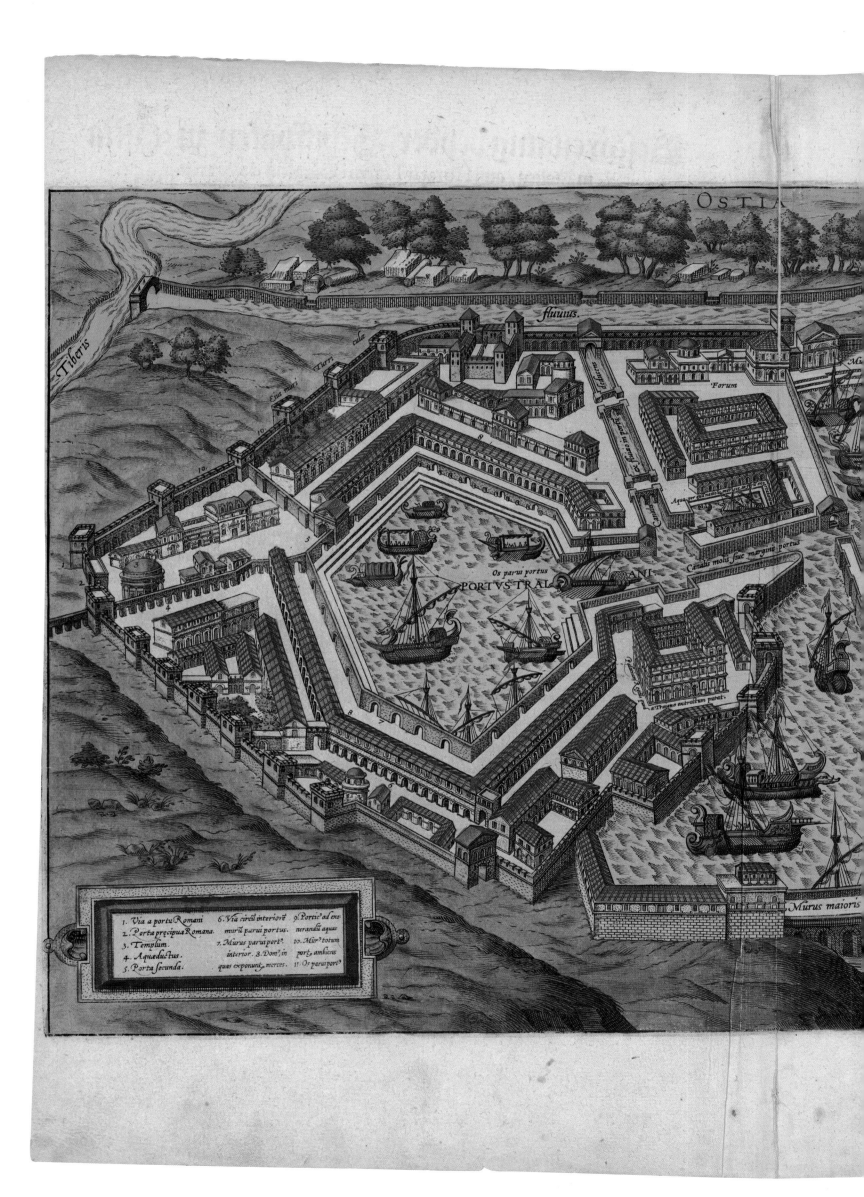

OSTIA

Tiberis

fluuius.

Turricula.

Eius Turricula.

Forum

Os parui portus
PORTVS TRAIANI

Ex fluuio in portu

Canalis

Aquæ

Canalis molis siue margine portus

a Traiano extructum portu.

Murus maioris

1. Via a portu Romani
2. Porta præcipua Romana.
3. Templum.
4. Aquæductus.
5. Porta secunda.
6. Via circũ interiorẽ murũ parui portus.
7. Murus parui portꝰ interior. 8. Domꝰ in quas exponunt merces.
9. Porticꝰ ad exenerandũ aquas
10. Mũrꝰ totiũ portꝰ ambiens
11. Os parui portꝰ

Os fluuij.

SEPT.

OCCID. ORIE.

MERI.

Os portus Orientem uerfus.

PORTVS CLAVDII.

fiue margo parui portus.

loci multa uacant aedificia

Bafis Colofsi Imperatoris

uerfus, in arcus, quo mare fluxu arenas expelleret, coftructus

Os portus, orientem uerfus, largum cannas quinquaginta.

45. Ostia published by Georg Braun – Frans Hogenberg, 1590

To serve the need of a port for Imperial Rome, the Emperor Claudius had a harbour excavated at the mouth of the River Tiber. Construction was completed in AD 64 during the reign of Nero. A large lighthouse, in appearance much like that of Pharos, guided sailors to its entrance. Although this map shows only a few vessels protected within its breakwaters, the harbour had sufficient capacity to hold 200 ships in the basin.

JOHN NURMINEN FOUNDATION

Overleaf
46. The North coast of Africa by Gregorio Dati, 15th century

In Dati's *La Sfera,* beautiful maps of the coastline of the Mediterranean are interwoven with the text, and distances are given between ports. However, with their lack of rhumb lines and a direction-bearing system, the maps cannot be used for navigational purposes other than to aid a seafarer's progression along the coast.

THE NATIONAL LIBRARY OF FINLAND, HELSINKI

da affricha achapulia zas facesse
son molte fratte dallito remote
echi uuol nauichar ich achapesse
tea esse z lito priol sipuote
et seguir poi fin araffamre besse
ma qui bisogna chi fuoe si rote
da fimasi insingui pmaesticale
tecento miglia son pdritto sicale

poi trepoli citta dala becria
cen venthanque miglia infr levante
itisuicata fu pquella via
dugento miglia idue bolte altretante
son fitto oreaufeu pheaufesia
doue fa bnchapo elgron monte athalonte
lassando bn gholfo oue ama diuiota
zgmonca epos bernicho itholometta

echi graffi elgholfo zhostra
farebbon piu selle miglia dugento
dalchapo breaufen a bonombeca
soncento miglia pur pfretto bento
luncho piu fu dugento par chsen
eomb abalt zondera aquatreo cento
aquasi fmezo desse sta laraffa
zin questo paese secra bassa

Olusho

boñadca

chapo dicaufeis

roloncerta

bernico

mm

misuerua

Raftaurabesse

cape

facessa

capilia

afetta

Zumih

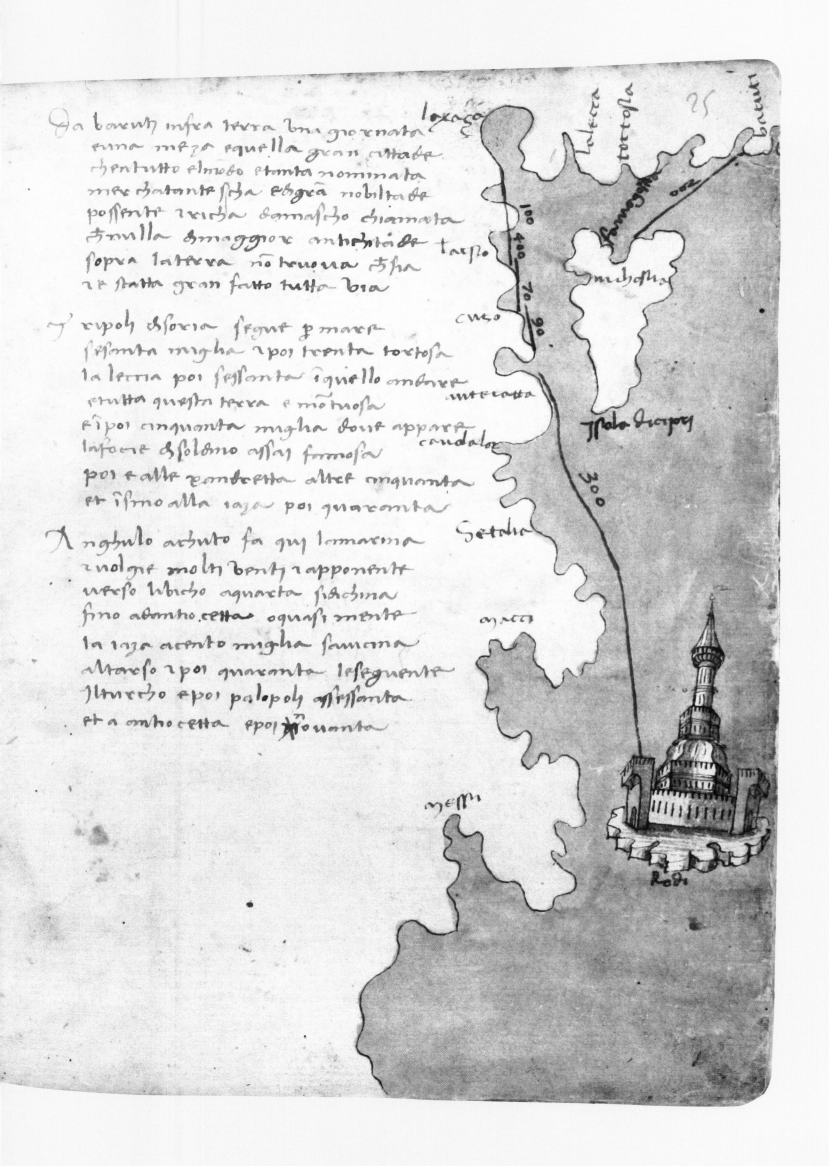

Da bayruth infra terra una giornata
e una mezo e quella gran cittade
chentutto elmodo e tanta nominata
infra chatante sta e dgrea nobilitade
posente richa damascho chiamata
e nulla dmaggiore abitade
sopra latterra no teuoua cho ha
re statta gran fatto tutta via

J rypoli dsoria segue p mare
sesanta migla e poi trenta tortosa
la terra poi sesanta iquello amore
e ruta questa terra e motuosa
e poi cinquanta migla doue appare
lasoce chsolduno assas formosa
poi e alle tondretta altre cinquanta
et istmo alla raza poi quaranta

A nghulo achuto fa qui lamarena
e nolge molti benty e apponente
uteso lbricho aquarta fidchina
fino abontho cetta oquasi mente
la raza acento migla samcina
altaeso e poi quaranta leseguente
Ituecho e poi palopoli assessanta
et a ontho cetta e poi nouanta

loxaza
talecca
tortosa
baruel
oba
sarmegatto
michossa
tarso
cuso
antecatta
Jsola dcapes
caudalo
300
Setalia
ayeci
messi
Rodi
100
400
70
90

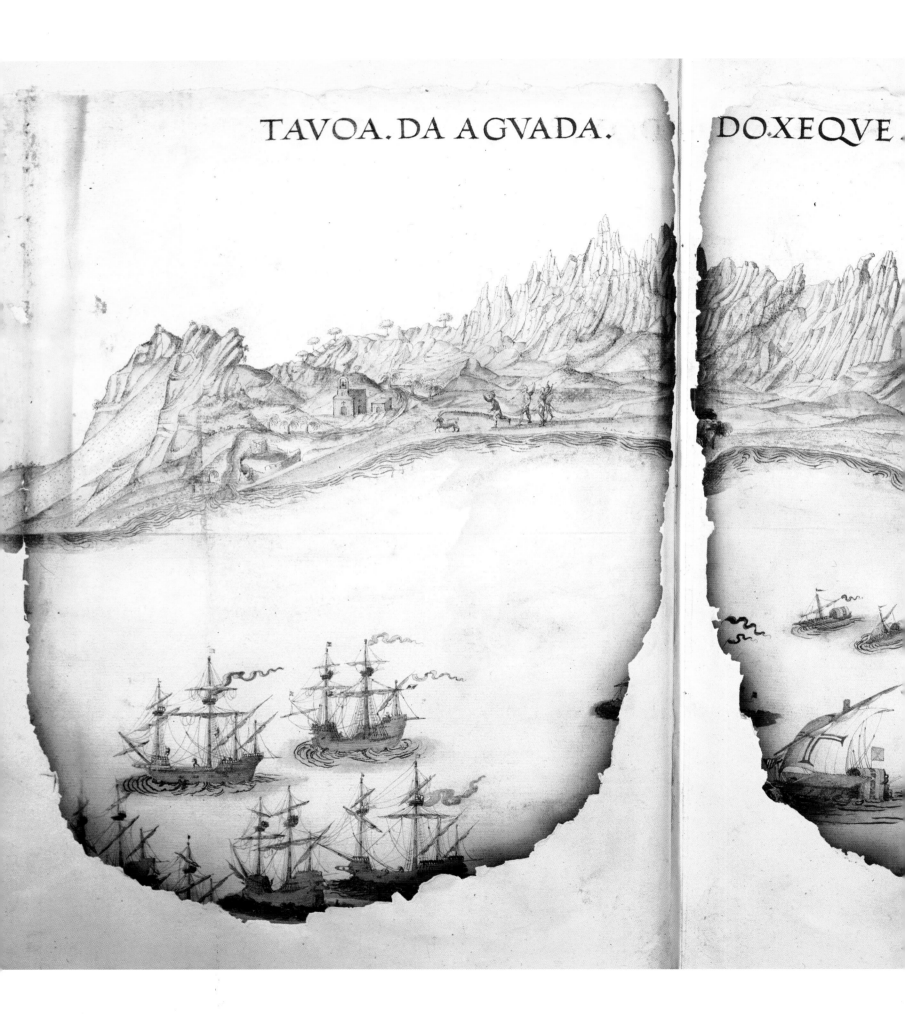

TAVOA. DA AGVADA.

DO.XEQVE

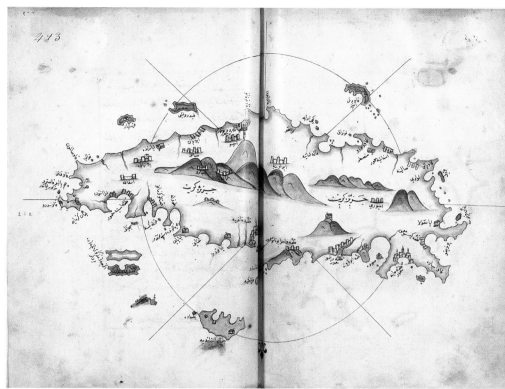

48. Crete by Piri Re'is, 16th century

The Turkish Admiral (Re'is), Piri Ibn Haji Mehmed (c. 1465–1554) accumulated extensive first-hand hydrographic information during his many years of fighting against the Spanish, Genoese and Venetian navies. Of the many maps and charts he produced, Piri Re'is is best known for his world map of 1513. This page from his *Kitâb-i-Bahriye* (Book of Maritime Matters), depicts the island of Crete. His book was the Islamic counterpart to the Italian produced *isolarii* (Island Books).

BIBLIOTHÈQUE NATIONALE DE FRANCE, PARIS

47. View of Aquada by João de Castro, 1542

Over time, sailing directions increased in pictorial content as an adjunct to the verbal information. Part journal and part sailing directions, the *Roteiro of the Red Sea* is from a Portuguese expedition in 1540–1541 to Goa, India, and into the Red Sea. Its author, João de Castro, sailing on this voyage, carefully set down the hydrographic and magnetic variations he observed along the way with an instrument designed by Pedro Nuñes (1502–1578). The *tavoas* (harbour charts), with coasts depicted either in a birds-eye view, or in horizon profile, provided additional and detailed information on navigation into the harbours. These graphic sea-views were an important innovation.

THE BRITISH LIBRARY, LONDON

The Ancient Mediterranean

PHOENICIAN MERCHANT SHIPS

The Phoenicians are regarded as the most successful seafarers and traders of the ancient world. Setting out from the Levant, which is present day Lebanon, they sailed the Mediterranean long before the Greeks. They built the largest and the best merchant ships and warships of their time, apparently capable of undertaking voyages lasting up to several years.

The most remarkable achievement of Phoenician shipbuilding was the 'round ship', propelled mainly by sails, but also by oars. The name is derived from the wide hull, which was close to a third of the ship's length, and which allowed for a large cargo capacity and a strong hull. It was built of cedar planks forming a length of approximately 30 m, with a partially covered deck to provide shelter from weather and wind for the crew and the cargo. The bow and stern were rounded and it is probable that the Phoenician ships had a keel, making them more stable on course and thus enabling sail on open seas. Such vessels were difficult to manoeuvre due to their heavy construction and weight. They had one mast and a square sail, which was effective only in a following wind and rowing was an option only if there was no wind. Navigation, in consequence, depended upon careful timing to take advantage of winds blowing in the intended direction. When these round ships were further developed they were able to sail all over the Mediterranean, to Britain, and to the west of Africa.

The Greeks called these vessels either 'bathtubs', because of their shape, or 'horses' because of the Phoenician preference for a figurehead in the shape of a horse head. They were so well adapted to their purpose as freighters that the Phoenicians built vessels of this type for a thousand years. Often they had small boats attached to them, used for discharging cargo onto shallow shores and as lifeboats.

The credit for developing the multibanked galley is also often given to the Phoenicians. These vessels were named after the number of banks for oarsmen: *bireme* (two rows) and *trireme* (three rows). By placing the oarsmen in different levels above each other, the number could be increased which meant a greater speed without lengthening the ship.

The trireme was the most common and best-known type of ship on the ancient Mediterranean. It was in operational use from the fifth century BC to the fourth century AD. In a galley speed and manoeuverability were essential qualities, therefore these vessels were built light and slim. As many as 170 oarsmen were seated in three levels, on each side of the ship, using oars of equal length. In favourable conditions the speed of a trireme could reach 7 to 9 knots. On long journeys sails were set, but the masts were left ashore before a battle. The main armament was a sharp bronze-clad ram on the bow below the waterline, used to pierce the hull of an enemy vessel.

GREEK MERCHANT SHIPS

Gradually other peoples began to follow the Phoenicians to sea. During the Trojan War of c. 1200 BC, Greek vessels were light, long and uncovered; they had tens of oarsmen and were beached for the night. Cargo was carried in clumsy sailing ships to avoid the expense of hiring oarsmen. Sea transportation saved a lot of time and was the only way to trade as Greece has a mountainous and difficult terrain. Initially, the Greeks traded in sheltered waters between the islands, enabling navigation by landmarks. Their harbours and trade centres were situated on shallow, sandy beaches, where it was possible to pull the ships ashore.

In the eight century BC the Greeks started to challenge the Phoenicians, colonizing Southern Italy, North Africa and the shores of the Black Sea. Greek merchant vessels shipped both import and export goods including wine, wheat, olive oil, vases, jewellery, clothing and metal tools. The general unit for carrying cargo was the amphora, which as early as the fifth century BC had standardized dimensions. This trade made Greece prosperous.

The Greek and Phoenician shipbuilders constantly adapted to meet the growing demands. Many types of merchant vessels sailed on the Mediterranean, but very few graphic depictions have survived. With their rounded stem and stern it is unlikely that such vessels could reach speeds of more than 5 knots. They had low draft because there were only a few suitable ports with quays and cargo was most frequently discharged directly on the beach. In the stern two steering oars were permanently fixed on both sides.

Valuable information has been acquired from a Greek shipwreck at *Kyrenia* off Cyprus. The ship sank about 300 BC and was then some 80 years old. It has been named Kyrenia after its place of discovery. This open, single-masted, sailing vessel was 14.7 m long and 3.4 m wide. It had small decks in the bow and stern and it's estimated that square sail measured 10.7 m x 6 m. When she sank, she was loaded with almonds and 404 amphorae, which were been used to ship wine from Rhodes. From the dishes found onboard it is likely that the ship had a crew of four.

During the Hellenistic era the freighters grew larger

49. Phoenician ship

The Phoenicians were regarded as the ancient world's best shipbuilders and seafarers. Their ships were bulky, which was important in trading. These wide, single-mast ships were sturdily built, but still they had good sailing qualities in open sea.

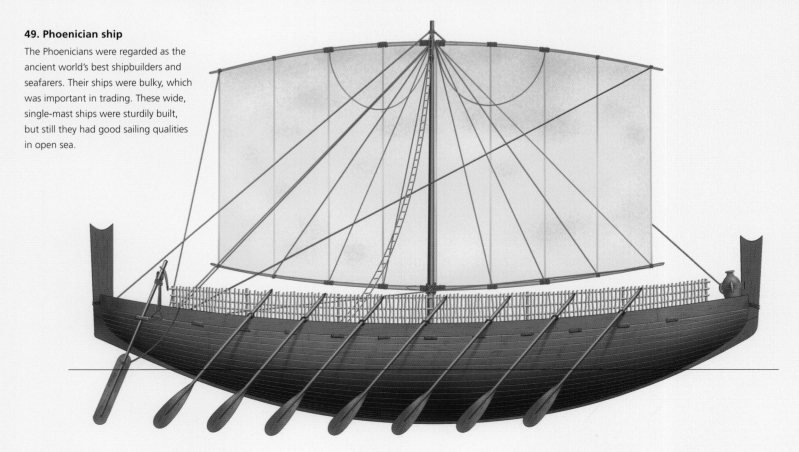

50. Mediterranean ship by Björn Landström, 1969

The ancient freighters were round, broad beamed, and high. They were equipped with a wide square sail, but they were not good for sailing to windward. During the Hellenistic age two or even three-masted vessels were built. The Romans constructed the largest ancient vessels, but they still had the same hull shape as Greek ships. The picture shows Björn Landström's impression of a Roman merchant ship, trading on the Mediterranean about 200 BC.

COURTESY OF OLOF LANDSTRÖM

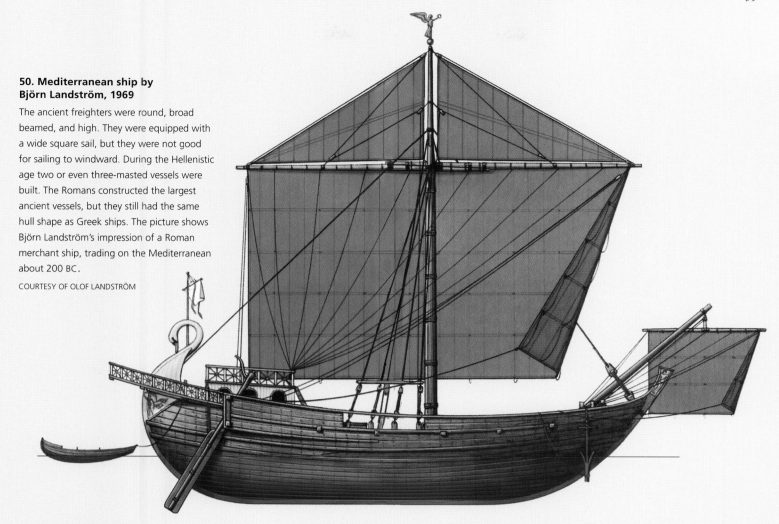

and deep-water harbours with stone piers were built. The largest ships had two or even three masts and more sails were added. The wide square sail evolved into a large bulging sail with a complicated system of brails.

The largest ancient vessel we know of was the three-masted *Syracusia*, which was ordered by the king of Syracuse in 230 BC. It was 180 m long and 31 m wide and had three decks. Freight was carried on the lowest deck. On the 'tween deck there were thirty cabins, a chapel, lounges, a library, a bath and other passenger spaces. The soldiers and the armament were carried on the weather deck. The ship was decorated with expensive materials and was built for shipping grain and also carrying the royal family and other important passengers. It may be regarded as an ancestor to the cruise vessels of today. Somewhat unsurprisingly it turned out to be too large for most of the ports and the king decided to rename it *Alexandria* and hand it over as a gift to his ally the king of Egypt.

In addition to the main sail, Mediterranean sailors started to use a square sail on the bowsprit, mainly for improving manoeuvrability. In many vessels there were also triangular topsails and the largest merchant vessels even had a mizzen sail at the stern.

ROMAN MERCHANT SHIPS

Seafaring never played as central a place in Roman life as it had for the Greeks, but the galleys and freighters of Rome came to dominate the Mediterranean – the *Mare Nostrum*, our sea, as the Romans self-importantly named it – until the Roman Empire disintegrated in the fifth century AD. While the Roman Empire flourished, the Mediterranean trade was richer and more varied

than ever before, and the cargoes were enormous.

To satisfy the requirements of commerce, the Roman Empire needed vessels of varying sizes. Parallel to slow sailing merchantmen there were light and fast merchant galleys propelled by oars for carrying goods which needed to reach their destination in a short time, such as wild animals from Africa and Asia for the gladiator games. When necessary, merchant galleys could be used for military purposes.

The cargo capacity of an average merchant vessel was 200–300 tons, but the largest grain carriers trading between Rome and Egypt could load up to 1200–1300 tons. Grain was the basic foodstuff for the Romans. Each year some 135,000 tons was imported from Egypt, which corresponded to a third of the Roman consumption and in the summer arrival of the grain ships from Alexandria was an important event. Warships escorted the freighters and smaller vessels arrived in advance to report the arrival to the waiting merchants. Large volumes of oil were also imported, which was used both in cooking and in the Roman baths.

About 40 AD Emperor Caligula (AD12–41) ordered the construction of a vessel even larger than the grain carriers, to transport an obelisk from Alexandria to Rome. This 40 m high obelisk had a weight of almost 500 tons and still stands today in the piazza in front of St Peter's Basilica. It was not until the 16th century that vessels as large were on the Mediterranean.

Different types of cargo vessels had their own names (*corbita*, *gaulus*, *ponto* and so on), which were derived from their hull shape or geographical origin. Nevertheless, all Roman merchant vessels were of about the same basic type, and from their Phoenician and Greek predecessors they differed only in their size. They were still roomy, round and broad

-beamed ships, with a curved bow, which often was lower than the stern. Usually the sternpost ended in a swan's neck, which faced amidships. The steering gear consisted of two long paddle-like side rudders, which could be lifted up from the water with tackles. The largest Roman vessels had several anchors made of lead or iron, examples of which, weighing up to one ton, have been found.

A deckhouse was usually situated aft and the helmsman stood upon it. In the aft section there were also a latrine overhanging the sea and an altar with an image of the ship's patron god. The ships were often named after the gods and the name was carved or painted on both sides of the bow. A small cabin aft housed the master and important passengers. The crew and less important passengers had to sleep on deck or in the cargo hold if it was raining. Most of the hold was reserved for cargo, fresh water and stores. In small ships, buckets were used to empty the bilge water in the bottom of the ship, but in larger vessels there were pumps for this purpose.

The freighters mostly had two masts but the largest had three masts. The main mast with its large square sail was situated amidships. In the top a triangular topsail could be set. It was not until a thousand years after the fall of the Roman Empire that this sail was to be used again. Another mast was situated forward and had a smaller square sail to improve manoeuvrability. In a following wind a speed of 4 to 5 knots could be reached, but in a headwind the vessels were very slow. Indeed, details have been found of one journey from Spain to Italy taking an incredible three months.

COSMOGRAPHY OF THE ANCIENTS

*Our universe is a sorry little affair unless it has
something for every age to investigate . . . .
Nature does not reveal her mysteries once and for all.*

SENECA, *NATURALES QUESTIONES*, BOOK VII

Many of the primitive methods of navigation continue to be used to the present, mostly by seamen in small craft. The great oceanic voyages of the early modern era, however, could only have been undertaken by seamen equipped with scientific means of navigation, based on a sound knowledge of geography and cosmography. Since the early sixth century BC, philosophers on the Ionian coast of Asia Minor have speculated on the physical, mathematical and astronomical aspects of the Earth. Two millennia later, it was to be the worldview they and their successors developed that guided Christopher Columbus on his voyage across the Atlantic in 1492.

Although the geographies postulated by Thales of Miletus (c. 624–c. 546 BC), founder of the Ionian school of philosophy in 580 BC, and by his followers, were to prove entirely wrong, their work was important because it made major advances from the Homeric tradition of explaining natural phenomena in mythological terms.

PYTHAGOREAN SCHOOL

With the Pythagorean School, founded by Pythagoras (566–470 BC) in 530 BC, the study of geography and cosmography assumed a regular and systematic approach. Pythagoras identified science with mathematics and was the first to understand that the Earth was a sphere and not a flat plane,

51. A Roman Mosaic depicting a scene from Homer's *Odyssey*, c. 300

From the shores of the Mediterranean where Western civilization had its nascence, epic tales are told of the voyages of Odysseus and Aeneas. These mythical heroes travelled in splendid galleys over the seas to fulfill their destiny as prophesied by the gods and goddesses. Their voyages are made to seem real by the inclusion of an intimate knowledge of the Mediterranean Sea and of navigation practices. In this mosaic of a scene from Homer's *Odyssey*, Odysseus is tied to the mast to avoid the temptations of the sirens when his ship is forced to come close to land due to a storm.

LE MUSÉE NATIONAL DU BARDO, TUNISIE

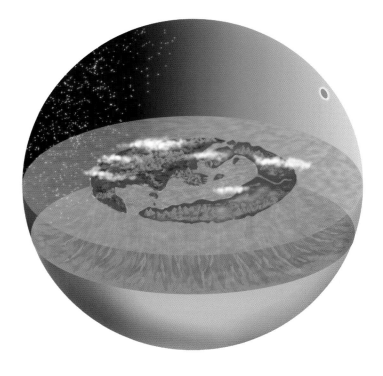

be nearly two millennia before the Polish astronomer Nicolaus Copernicus (1473–1543) postulated a heliocentric solar system, one in which the Sun instead of the Earth was in the centre of the universe, which he published in 1543 as *De revolutionibus orbium coelestium*.

Around 500 BC, Hecataeus of Miletus (c. 550–480 BC) wrote the first regular treatise on geography and history. Hecataeus

52. World view according to Homer

Homer's poems, the *Iliad* and the *Odyssey*, written in the eighth century BC provide the earliest comprehensive view of geographical knowledge at the time. In this modern reconstruction, the inhabited world is represented as a flat, circular disc of land, embraced by a circumfluent world-river, the *Oceanus*. From its periphery rises the dome of the sky. The Greek historian Strabo, who surpassed all other writers of antiquity on geography, termed Homer '. . . the founder of all geographical knowledge, and no less eminent in this respect than for his poetical excellence, and his political wisdom.'

53. Sailing Routes of Aeneas and Odysseus

Based on the description of geographical locations, and the navigability of certain routes, the peregrinations of Odysseus have been reconstructed. This traditional view, which limits their travels to the eastern and central Mediterranean, is not upheld by all scholars. Some believe the wanderings extended into the western Mediterranean, while others doubt that many, if not all, of the places described were even real. In Virgil's *Aeneid* (written in the first century BC) the journey of Aeneas roughly parallels that of Odysseus.

but he probably arrived at this conclusion from theoretical speculation and on the basis of aesthetic values, rather than by mathematical calculations. Pythagoras left no writings, but Aristotle reported that Pythagoras believed the Earth to be a sphere 'because the sphere was the most perfect form'. He conceived the cosmos as one in which the Earth was not in the centre of the universe, nor was it fixed, but moved in the heavens around a 'central fire'. The Sun, Moon and planets all moved with the Earth in the same direction. The nature and purpose of this central fire he left unexplained. It was to

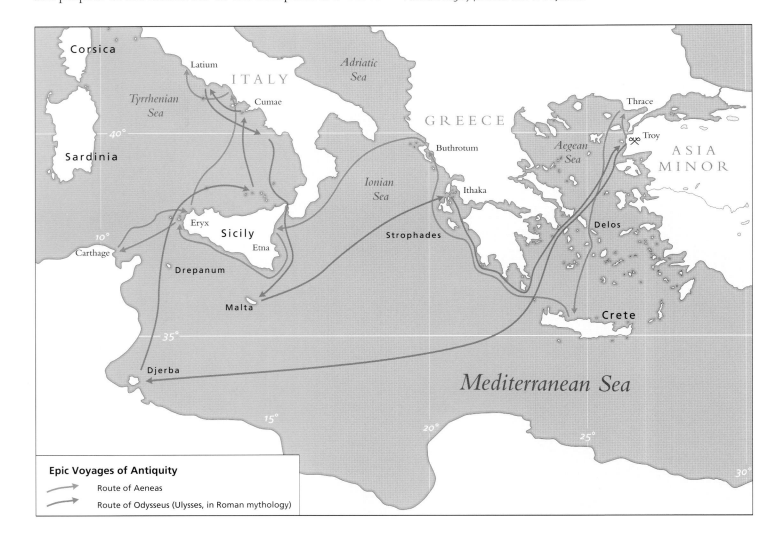

Epic Voyages of Antiquity

→ Route of Aeneas

→ Route of Odysseus (Ulysses, in Roman mythology)

travelled widely, and much of the geographic information in his *Periegesis* (Guide Around) was acquired this way. For the most part, the world of Hecataeus was bounded by the extent and distribution of Greek colonies and settlements. The rest of his information he collected from other sources, which he combined with Greek fable and myth. Though his geographic information was scant, it was a major step from the contemporary speculation on the form of the Earth, and its position in the cosmos, towards an orderly description of the inhabited world. This earned for him the title 'Father of Geography.'

Herodotus, successor to Hecataeus, furthered progress in the study of geography. Like Hecataeus, Herodotus was an adventurous traveller who gathered information from personal ob-

54. World view according to Hecataeus

In keeping with the Homeric tradition, Hecataeus displays the earth as exactly round, with Greece in the centre of the world, all being surrounded by a river-ocean. With a desire for order and symmetry, Hecataeus divides the earth into two continents of equal size.

55. World view according to Herodotus

Herodotus rejects the portrayal of the Earth as a round disc. Whereas Hecataeus assumed an ocean to surround the earth on all sides, Herodotus did not give credence to this, saying that '. . .though he had taken much pains to enquire, he found none who by personal observation could confirm the presence of a sea north of Europe.'

servation, and combined it with material from other sources. His book, *History*, written in the mid-fifth century BC, was primarily intended as a history of the Greek struggle with the Persian Empire. But it is filled with so much descriptive detail of the lands involved in this history that it gives the most complete picture of the world as was known to the Greeks at that time.

Of all the philosophers of greater Greece, none exerted more influence than Aristotle (384–322 BC), who defined the basic concepts and principles of many of the sciences. Two of

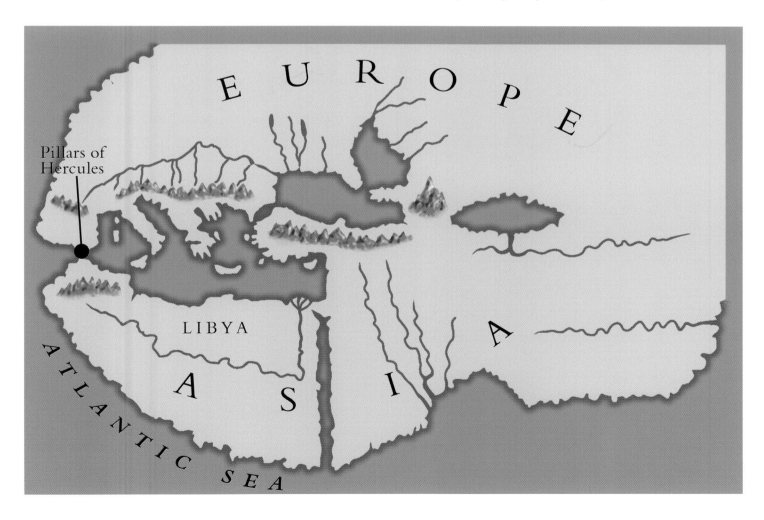

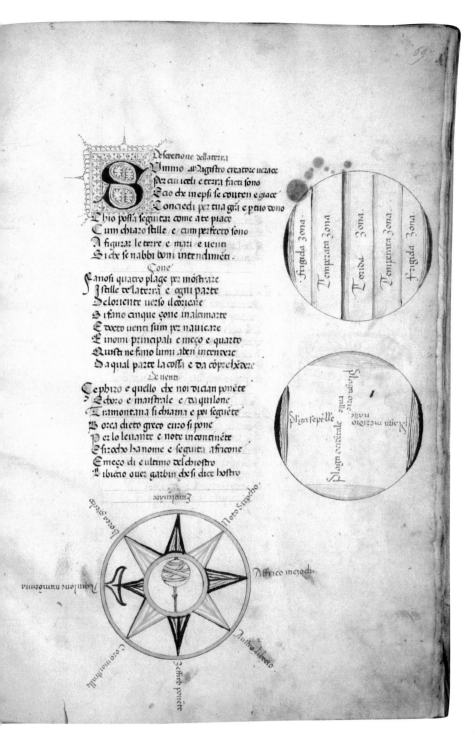

56. Habitable Bands of the World by Gregorio Dati, 15th century

According to Aristotle, there were only two habitable bands in world, located in the temperate climate zones. In the polar regions it was too cold to sustain life, and in the equatorial region it was too hot.

THE NATIONAL LIBRARY OF FINLAND, HELSINKI

concerned with the general distribution of land and water over the Earth's surface. He described the geography of the known world – its lands, seas, mountains and rivers. It was a world of ordered architecture in which masses of land were distributed over the surface of the Earth in a balanced fashion, and all the waters were interconnected and in constant flow. This symmetry necessitated the principle that whatever was in the north – land, water, winds – would also be found in the south.

In Aristotle's formulation of the world there were only two zones where habitation was possible. 'Habitation,' Aristotle said, 'ceases on one side' of the habitable zone band 'because of the cold, and on the other because of the heat.' The band in the temperate zone of the northern hemisphere contained the familiar countries of the Mediterranean. But the existence of a southern hemisphere band was by speculation only, needed to fulfill a sense of order, balance and symmetry. These zones geographers later extended, and further subdivided.

The concept of climate zones so strongly affected the thinking about the habitable regions of the Earth that, fully eighteen centuries later, Columbus's crew were afraid to enter the region of the equator between these two habitable bands. They believed their blood would boil on account of the intense heat, or failing that, their skin would turn black and remain so permanently, like the skin of the natives of the region.

Like Pythagoras, Aristotle believed that the Earth was a sphere. Aristotle, however, looked for physical proof, and put forward four arguments for the Earth being spherical: 1. At an open place, the horizon always seems to be equi-distant in all directions; 2. When viewed from land, as a ship sails over the horizon it slowly disappears from sight, starting with the hull and ending with only the top of the masts being visible; 3. The altitudes of stars change proportionally with changes in the observer's latitude; 4. The Earth's shadow at eclipses of the Moon is unvaryingly circular. Aristotle is usually credited as being the first to find this proof.

Aristotle's philosophical construct of the Earth, with its balanced masses of land and sea, became the unshakeable basis of the search nearly two millennia later for the Northwest and Northeast Passages to Cathay. After the Southeast Passage around the Cape of Good Hope and the Southwest Passage around Cape Horn had been accomplished, the other two passages in the north *had* to be present, for they were believed to be necessary to balance those in the south.

his major works, *De Caelo* (The Heavens) and *Meteorologica,* dealt with the properties of heavenly bodies, the phenomena of the atmosphere and physical geography. His ideas were accepted by later writers of antiquity, and through translations directly from the original Greek texts and from Syriac translations, were again taken up and developed by Moslem scholars in the Middle Ages.

Aristotle's notion of the world was based on philosophy and logic, rather than on knowledge of distant regions gained from travel and discovery. Like other Greek writers, Aristotle was

ALEXANDRIAN SCHOOL

Knowledge of the Earth's dimensions was to be greatly advanced by the school that grew up in Alexandria, Egypt. Under Alexander the Great (356–323 BC), king of Macedonia, the Macedonian Empire stretched between Europe, Egypt and India. When Alexander reached Egypt he ordered a city to be founded there at a prehistoric harbour by the island of Pharos.

As a regional capital for his vast empire it was ideally located in the Mediterranean halfway between Greece and the rest of Egypt. A passage connecting the Nile River with the Red Sea had finally been excavated by the Persian King Darius in the fifth century BC after his conquest of Egypt. Although of limited use due to sandstorms, it gave Alexandria ready access to the Indian Ocean. In consequence, the city prospered as a centre where goods from the Far East were brought, bartered and further transported to Europe.

After Alexander's death one of his generals, Ptolemy Soter (Ptolemy I, 367–283 BC), secured the kingship of Egypt. Alexandria grew under the Ptolemaic dynasty to become one of the largest and richest cities of the world, and the maritime centre of the entire Hellenistic Mediterranean. The city was distinguished not only for its trade, but also for its culture; many races and religions peacefully co-existed, their languages and ideas richly mingling. To guide sailors safely to its harbour, a lighthouse, crowned with a statue of Poseidon, was built on Pharos of Alexandria. Completed around 283 BC during the rule of Ptolemy II (309–246 BC), it rose 400 feet into the air, making it one of the highest structures on Earth.

Ptolemy I founded an academy of philosophers, a museum and three co-existing libraries in Alexandria. In them half a million books and scrolls, covering the entire range of knowledge, were collected from all over the world. Demetrius of Phaleron, a student of Aristotle, created a school of learning at Alexandria devoted to research and instruction in philosophy and the sciences, modelled on Plato's Academy in Athens founded 385 BC. The most gifted scholars were to be found here, and by the beginning of the third century BC the intellectual centre of the world shifted from Athens to Alexandria. The study of geography now changed from the earlier theoretical concepts of the universe to one that that was centred on mathematical calculations of the shape and size of the Earth.

Once the globular form of the Earth had become unassailable doctrine, successors to Aristotle set about to determine the Earth's circumference. Eratosthenes, who flourished in the middle of the third century BC, was an astronomer and mathematician at the library of Alexandria. He calculated a circumference of 250,000 stadia, which he later changed to 252,000 stadia. The initial figure of 250,000 stadia, which corresponds to 24,662 miles or 39,690 kilometres, was the more accurate of the two. It is likely that Eratosthenes later added the additional 2,000 stadia in order to arrive at a figure easily divisible into 60 parts, or into the 360 degrees of a circle. Either calculation was certainly much more accurate than the figure of 400,000 stadia claimed by Aristotle, or the 300,000 stadia calculated by Aristarchus of Samos (fl. 281 BC), one of the earliest astronomers of the Alexandrian school. The calculations of Eratosthenes were remarkably close to the Earth's true circumference of 24,902 miles at the equator, slightly less at the poles.

57. Madagascar by Lopo Homem, 1519

Climate zones continued to be shown on maps well into the sixteenth century as vestigial remains of the Aristotelian classification. In this Indian Ocean segment of a map made in 1519, Lopo Homem, cosmographer to the royal family of Portugal, aided by Pedro Reinel (fl. 1485–1535), placed four equally spaced and numbered climates beneath the equator. By now, this system had outlived its relevance, for the climate of lands in the New World could not be correlated with European climate simply on the basis of latitude.

BIBLIOTHÈQUE NATIONALE DE FRANCE, PARIS

Hipparchus of Rhodes (190–120 BC), one of the greatest of Greek astronomers and the founder of trigonometry, accepted the calculations of Eratosthenes, as did Pliny the Elder, and other philosophers. But these calculations did not go unchallenged. Posidonius of Rhodes made his own estimate of the circumference of the Earth by using the difference in altitude of the star *Canopus* between Rhodes and Alexandria. He arrived at a figure of 240,000 stadia – a result not far from the

250,000 stadia of Eratosthenes. Deciding his calculations were based on several erroneous assumptions, however, Posidonius made new calculations and came up with a circumference of the Earth at 180,000 stadia – 28% smaller than that calculated by Eratosthenes! This markedly reduced figure was accepted by later Greek geographers, most notably by the Greek astronomer and geographer Claudius Ptolemaeus, known as Ptolemy (AD 85–165).

Far from being of merely academic interest to mathematicians, this miscalculation of the circumference of the Earth had very great and direct consequences in the exploration of the Atlantic 1600 years later. Christopher Columbus and many other intellectuals of his time accepted the smaller number. Coupled with other information about the geography of the Earth, Columbus was led by this error to believe the distance between the shores of Europe and Japan was much less, making it appear that the passage between the two would be shorter and safer.

From the calculations made by Eratosthenes, Crates of Mallos (180–150 BC) concluded that the portion of the Earth known to be habitable was much smaller in relation to the entire globe than had previously been thought. To correct this, and in keeping with the need for symmetry and order, Crates added three other unknown continents, similar to the known one. These four habitable landmasses were divided by a meridional and a latitudinal (equatorial) ocean. This speculative formation created an antipodes, and antipodal peoples, a problem much debated by ecclesiastical scholars in the Middle Ages.

58. Eratosthenes

The Greek geographer, Eratosthenes (c. 276–194 BC), was the first to calculate the circumference of the Earth.

THE BRIDGEMAN ART LIBRARY

ROMAN CONTRIBUTIONS

After Rome became the leading power in the Mediterranean, the Alexandrian school of science declined. Roman writers were less concerned with astronomy and the mathematics of science, and turned their attention to a description of physical geography. For the most part their works were compendia of the scientific accomplishments of the Greeks, and added relatively little of their own.

Strabo wrote his treatise, *Geographia*, in the first decades of the Christian era. It comprised an historical review of all the Greek writers who preceded him. Although he generally agreed with the earlier writers on the geography of the world, his description of physical geography covered a wider range. But the map of the world he constructed was adopted almost entirely from Eratosthenes.

The earliest Roman geographer Pomponius Mela's compendium on geography, *de Chorographia*, written after AD 43, also followed the views of Eratosthenes. However, his depiction of the habitable world differed by the introduction of a continent in the southern hemisphere to mirror the northern hemisphere counterpart of Europe, Africa and Asia. This

symmetrical construction was purely hypothetical on his part. Nonetheless Mela asserted that the southern continent was inhabited.

SECOND ALEXANDRIAN SCHOOL

In the second century AD, mathematical sciences at the Alexandrian school once again flourished. The leading figure was Ptolemy. We know little about his life, other than that he was of Greek descent, living in or near Alexandria; everyhting else must be discerned from his writings.

Ptolemy created a body of knowledge of unrivalled extent, covering a wide range of subjects, including optics, music, geography, trigonometry, astrology, astronomy and astronomical instruments. His two best-known writings are the thirteen-volume *Mathematike syntaxis* (*Almagest*), and an eight volume work on geography, *Geografike Hyfegesis* (*Geographia*), accompanied by an atlas. The *Syntaxis* was a compilation and synthesis into a coherent whole of all astronomical writings preceding Ptolemy,

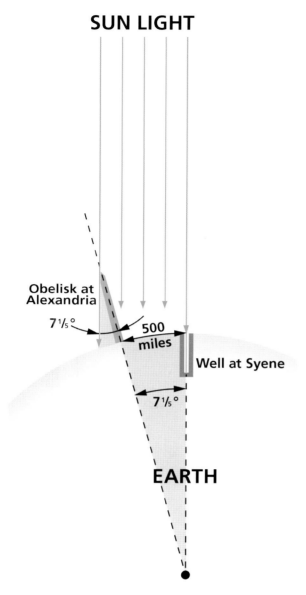

SUN LIGHT

Obelisk at Alexandria

7 1/5°

500 miles

Well at Syene

7 1/5°

EARTH

plus all his own observations and original mathematical theory of planetary motion. Ptolemy's original astronomical work is one of the greatest achievements in the history of science. His chief authority for the initial mathematical theory was Hipparchus of Rhodes, to whom he gave full credit.

The introductory chapter of Ptolemy's *Syntaxis* presented his concept of the cosmos – a belief in a stationary, spherical Earth situated in the centre of the universe, and the order of celestial spheres of the planets in relation to the Earth.

59. Measurement of Circumference of the Earth

To determine the circumference of the Earth, Eratosthenes measured the meridian altitude of the Sun from two different geographic points of latitude, but at roughly the same meridian of longitude: a deep well at Syene (Aswan) and an obelisk at Alexandria. He made observations on the same day at noon, as determined when the Sun was reflected in the water at the bottom of the well. He knew the distance between these two points of latitude, the height of the obelisk, and the length of its shadow; from these three figures Eratosthenes calculated the angle subtended at the centre of the Earth (the same as the angle of the shadow cast from the obelisk) to be roughly 7 1/5 degrees. This enabled him to arrive at a figure of the Earth's circumference that was accurate to within 2–5% of its true circumference of roughly 25,000 miles (40,000 kilometres).

60. World view according to Eratosthenes

Eratosthenes established the presence of a Northern Ocean, doubted by Herodotus, and placed in it the island of Thule, described by Pytheas of Massalia. He showed the Atlantic Ocean continuous with the Erythræan Sea (Indian Ocean), thus making it possible to circumnavigate Africa. Eratosthenes conceived '. . .if it were not that the vast extent of the Atlantic Sea rendered it impossible, one might even sail from the coast of Spain to India along the same parallel.'

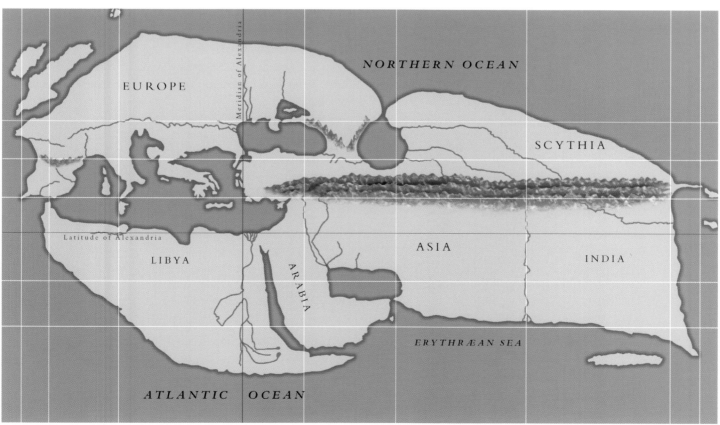

EUROPE

NORTHERN OCEAN

SCYTHIA

Meridian of Alexandria

Latitude of Alexandria

LIBYA

ARABIA

ASIA

INDIA

ERYTHRÆAN SEA

ATLANTIC OCEAN

61. Spread of *Almagest* by Claudius Ptolemaeus, translated by George Trebizond, c. 1451

Ptolemy's *Mathematike Syntaxis*, better known by the name of *Almagest*, contained a star catalogue and a model of the complex motions of the planets. Completed sometime before AD 150, the system of Ptolemy's astronomy, inherited from his Greek predecessors, was kept alive through the commentaries written by Hypatia (AD 355–415), the first great woman of science, and her father Theon. Translated into Arabic in the ninth century and into Latin in the twelfth century, the *Almagest*, with its geocentric model of the universe, remained the authoritative work on astronomy for many centuries.

BIBLIOTECA APOSTOLICA VATICANA

Through a complex system of small circles, called epicycles, revolving in larger circles, which in turn revolved around the Earth, Ptolemy explained the motions of the Sun, Moon and planets. The remaining chapters contained specific astronomical problems, his observation of eclipses, and his study of stars, which included a catalogue of 1020 stars with their magnitudes (brightness), latitudes and longitudes.

So thorough and complete was Ptolemy's work on astronomy that for the next 1500 years it dominated all subsequent studies. From the original Greek texts and Syriac translations, the *Syntaxis* was translated into Arabic at the end of the eighth century, when it was renamed *Kitāb al-Majistī*, or *Almagest* (The Greatest). This served as the basis for ninth- and tenth-century Arabic treatises, such as Al-Farghānī's (known in the west as Alfraganus) *On the Elements of Astronomy*, and Al-Battānī's *Astronomy*. Through Moorish centres in Spain, Arabic texts were translated into Latin, and Ptolemy's astronomical work made its way into Christian Europe.

Ptolemy's *Geographia* formed a sequel to his books on astronomy. The first volume discussed the basic principles of cartography, and the problem of how to represent the curved surface of a sphere onto a flat plane. In it he gave examples of different projection plans. In the remaining volumes (two through seven) Ptolemy gave the coordinates in latitude and longitude for 8000 places. By establishing the exact determination of places he hoped to be able to provide a scientific basis for cartography. He said: 'one must contemplate the extent of the entire Earth, as well as its shape, and its position under the heavens, in order that one may rightly state what are the peculiarities and proportions of the part which one is dealing, and under what parallel [latitude] of the celestial sphere it is located. *It is the great and exquisite accomplishment of mathematics to show all these things to the human intelligence.*'

To create the table of coordinates for his maps, Ptolemy used direct astronomical observation to establish the latitudes of

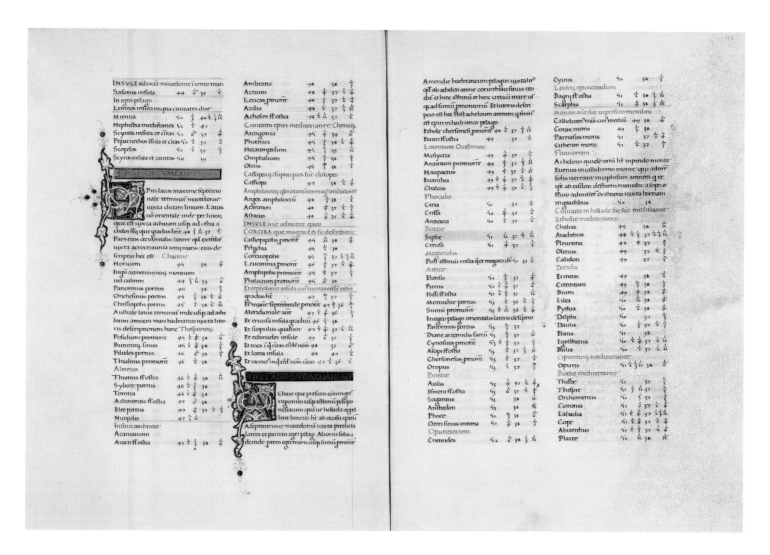

places. But for their longitudes, he had to rely on information gathered from the diaries of travellers whose statements of the distances they travelled were only estimates. These estimated longitudes were further influenced by Posidonius's incorrect computation of the circumference of the Earth, thereby changing the global relationship of land to water. As a result, Ptolemy's maps showed an elongated Mediterranean Sea covering 62° of longitude, instead of the actual 42 degrees.

An atlas accompanied Ptolemy's books showing all that was known of the inhabited world. There were different versions of the atlas manuscript. The so called version A consisted of one 'master map' of the entire world, plus twenty-six detailed, regional maps. Printed atlases were based on this version. For the master map, Ptolemy used a conical projection plan, or a modification thereof, in which the parallels of latitude are seen as curved lines maintained equidistant from north to south, while meridian lines of longitude converge toward the pole. Curiously enough, he did not use this system for the remaining twenty-six maps, but reverted to a grid system of earlier mapmakers where lines of latitude and longitude were all at right angles to each other and all equidistant. This reversion to a grid projection is all the more surprising, since Ptolemy himself criticized the inherent problems of deformation in the size and shape of land and sea in a right-angle grid system.

62. Spread of *Geographia* by Claudius Ptolemaeus, translated by Jacopo d'Angelos, 1406–1410

These pages, from the oldest Latin translation of Ptolemy's *Geographia* by Jacopo d'Angelos of Scarperia, show the coordinates of latitude and longitude for locations in Greece. Maps based on this translation followed within twenty years. Together, they re-awakened interest in geography.

BIBLIOTECA APOSTOLICA VATICANA

Overleaf
63. Ptolemy World Map, 1466

In Ptolemy's time there was no knowledge of the geography along the northern edge of Asia, thus the boundary of his master map ended at 63° North latitude. There was, however, some slight inkling about the existence of Scandinavian lands, represented as the islands of Scandia and Thule. In the west, the known limits of the habitable world were the Fortunate Islands (Canary Islands). In spite of an earlier awareness by Herodotus and Eratosthenes that Africa could be circumnavigated, Ptolemy enclosed the Indian Ocean, making it an inland sea.

BIBLIOTECA ESTENSE UNIVERSITARIA, MODENA

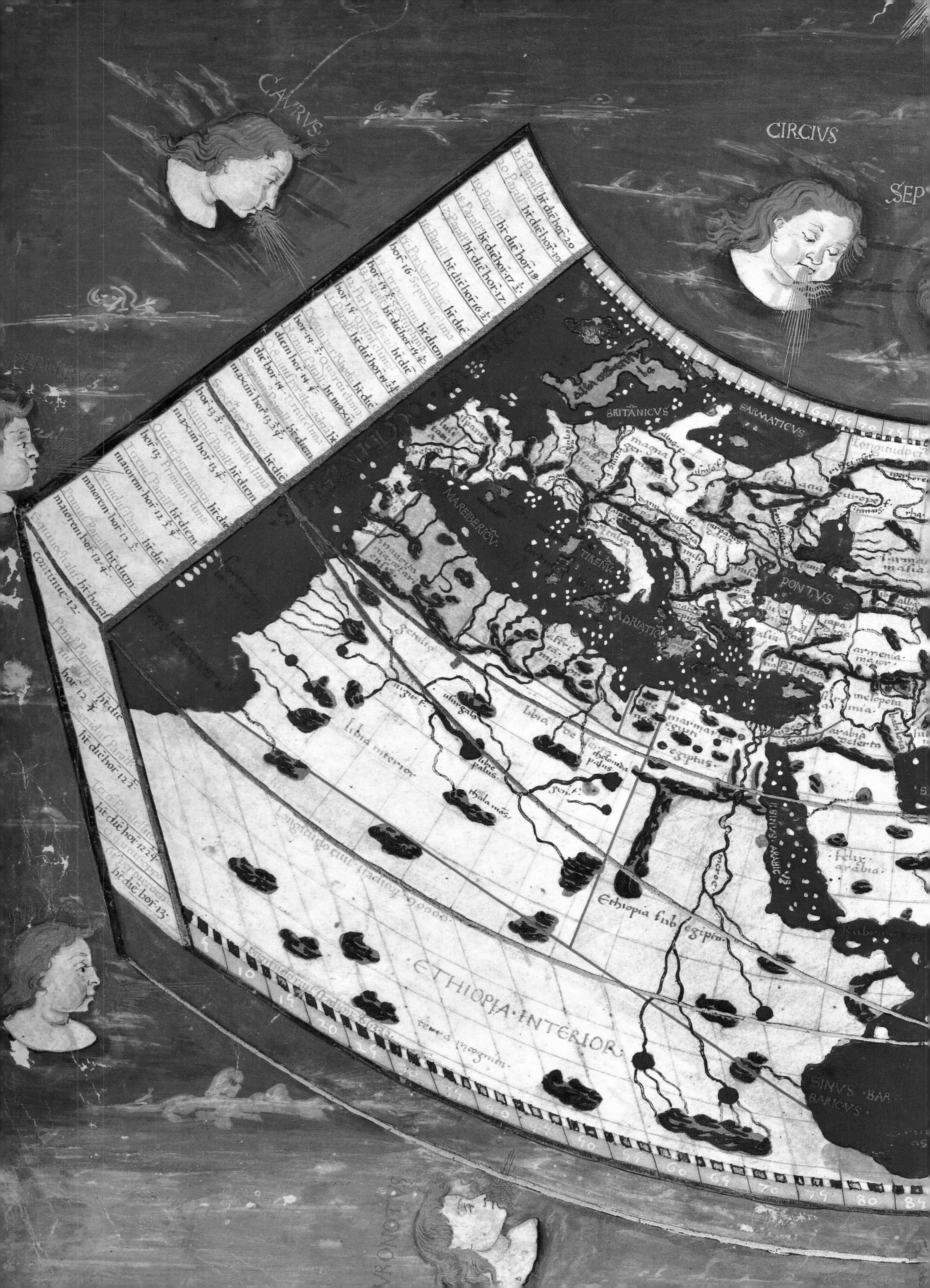
CAVRVS
CIRCIVS
SEP
BRITANICVS
SARMATICVS
MAREIBERICV
TIRENV
ADRIATIC
PONTVS
libia interior
egiptus
felix arabia
armenia maior
arabia deserta
Ethiopia sub egipto
ETHIOPIA·INTERIOR
SINVS BARBARICVS
VRONOTVS

AQVILO
VVLTVRNVS
Serica Rego
Sathia intra imaum montem
Sathia extra imaum montem
Sacha regio
Sogdiana
INDIA EX TRA GAN GEM
INTRA GANGEM
INDIA
ARIA
MARE
INDICVM
taprobana insula

Tabula noua totius orbis.

We might conjecture he did this as a matter of convenience in adopting much of the data from Marinus of Tyre (c. AD 70–130), a geographer and mathematician who used a similar grid system of equally spaced lines of latitude and longitude.

Ptolemy brought to his mapmaking not only a scientific approach, but a very pragmatic one as well. In chapter five of the first book he says: 'Anyone who wishes to draw a geographical map should found his work on trustworthy observations

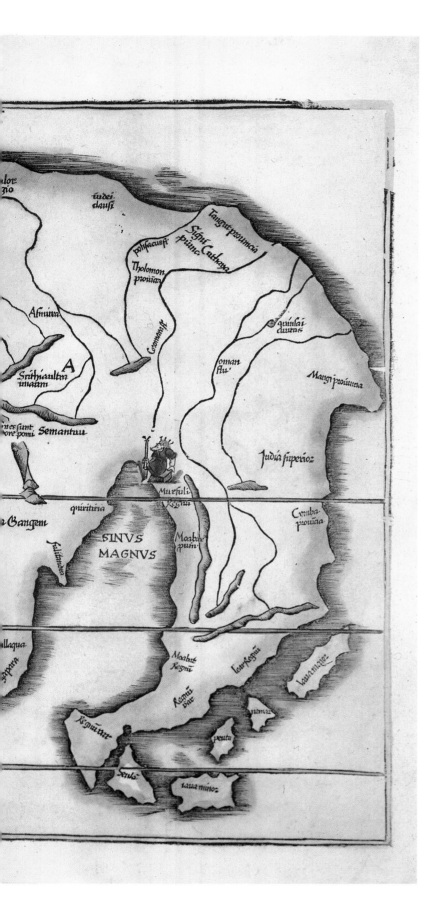

64. A modern world map by Martin Waldseemüller, 1541

In this 1541 map by Martin Waldseemüller, we see a greatly expanded view of the world since the time of Ptolemy: it is one of the first maps in which the Americas are shown. The Cape of Good Hope, at the southernmost tip of Africa had been doubled, and the Indian Ocean is no longer a completely enclosed sea; India and the Far East could be reached by sailing eastward from the Atlantic Ocean. Although the southern coast of Greenland had been visited and inhabited by the Norse five and a half centuries earlier, it was still not determined where that continent fitted into a world cosmographical view. During the time of Christopher Columbus, many geographers believed it to be a part of Asia. Here, it is shown as a long peninsular extension from a region of northern Russia.

JUHA NURMINEN COLLECTION

and then insert the remaining less reliable materials with as much accuracy as possible. As changes and variations often occur, the latest itineraries should principally be relied upon, but with due criticism and selection.' Certainly there were er-

rors and distortions in his maps, but his methodology cannot be faulted.

For more than a thousand years, the whole of Ptolemaic knowledge disappeared from the Western world. During the Middle Ages, mariners plying the Mediterranean developed a different cartographic tradition – the portolan chart – for navigation purposes. However, the Byzantine and Arab world kept the knowledge of Ptolemaic geography alive, and it re-emerged in Latin Europe in the fifteenth century when the Byzantine scholar, Manuel Chrysoloras (AD 1355–1414), a teacher of Greek living in Constantinople, began the work of translating Ptolemy's works from the original Greek into Latin. Chrysoloras died before finishing the translation, but it was completed by one of his pupils, Jacopo d'Angelos of Scarperia. From the time of the first printed edition of Ptolemy's atlas in 1477, it was the standard authority on geography for the next hundred and fifty years, with the maps being reproduced in many editions.

Ptolemy's atlas also formed the basis for all future advances in cartography. As new information became available, additions, corrections and modifications were made in successive editions by many famous cartographers, from Johannes Müller of Königsberg (called Regiomontanus, 1436–1476) in the fifteenth century, to the sixteenth century Gerard Mercator (1512–1594). Even today, Ptolemy's dominance is still felt and many of his practices adhered to. Differentiating the boundaries of land from sea by the use of shading is unchanged, as well as his practice of orienting north at the top of the map. He recognized the importance of determining as closely as possible the longitude and latitude of geographic locations, and his conical projection plan for maps, developed in Hellenistic Alexandria in the second century, is still in use. His pragmatic use of Marinus of Tyre's rectangular grid projection of latitude and longitude lines in most of his maps was later to make possible scientific navigation.

Cylindrical Projections

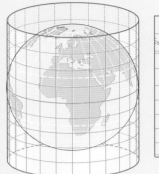
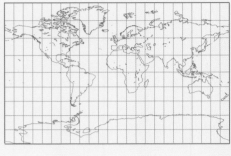

Conical Projections

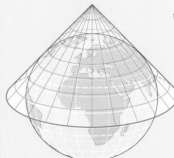
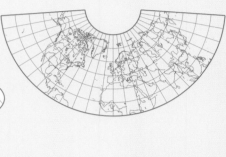

Stereographic Projections

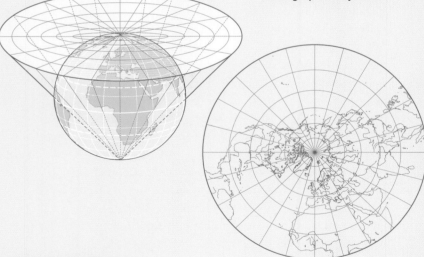

65. Map projections

66. Generale Ptholemei by Martin Waldseemüller, 1513

This Waldseemüller map is based on the tradition of Claudius Ptolemaeus – the father of cartography, and it is in conical-projection.

JUHA NURMINEN COLLECTION

67. Universalis Cosmographica by Johannes Honter, 1595

Another projection plan, technically named pseudo-conical equal-area, but more commonly known as a cordiform projection on account of its heart shape, was sometimes used to represent the three-dimensional globe on a flat plane. It had the advantage of suggesting the Earth's roundness.

JUHA NURMINEN COLLECTION

Map Projections

Before it was possible to begin mapping the Earth with any degree of accuracy, its cosmography had to be determined. In the fourth century BC, observations convinced philosophers that the shape of the Earth was spherical. In the next century, the circumference of the Earth was measured and its correct magnitude determined. These were the prerequisites for a geographical coordinate system and a scale of mapping.

From the very start, it was recognized that geographical positions could be recorded only if there was a grid system in which to place them. Mapmakers struggled with how to represent, with a minimal amount of distortion, the spherical form of the Earth on a flat plane – a parchment or piece of paper.

Claudius Ptolemaeus (Ptolemy) of Alexandria, the greatest of all cartographers of classical antiquity, created a body of knowledge of unrivalled extent. In about AD 150, Ptolemy wrote a synthesis of geography, and a world atlas, called *Geografike hyfegesis* (Introduction to Descriptive Geography). It contained three different proposals for projecting the spherical surface of the Earth onto a flat plane. In the first of Ptolemy's projections, he projected the globe onto a cone placed over it. When unrolled into a flat plane the parallels of latitude are seen as concentric, curved lines, parallel with the equator, and maintained equidistant from north to south, while meridian lines of longitude are broadest at the base and converge to a point at the pole. This projection plan, called conical projection, is a basic form, and is one of the three main families of map projections. In order to avoid excessive distortion of the southern regions, Ptolemy folded his map along the equator, making the meridians converge towards the south.

In Ptolemy's second projection, only the central meridian was a straight line, with all the parallels of latitude and meridians of longitude being curved. That rendered the map in the shape of a cape. The third projection, presented the Earth as seen in the middle of the celestial circles. For each projection, Ptolemy showed how the scale systematically varies in different parts of the map.

Even though the sound basics had been established for an exact representation of the surface of the globe, on Ptolemaic maps geographical positions of most places of the world were not determined with any accuracy. Once mariners extended their voyages beyond the confines of the Mediterranean, in order to safely navigate they needed charts drawn to proper scale, with true bearings and coordinates.

Representing the curved surface of the Earth on a flat plane continued to remain a problem for mapmakers. At the beginning of the sixteenth century, solutions based on geometry or trigonometry of the sphere went through many forms. Conical, azimuthal, cylindrical and cordiform projections were all experimented with. There was no perfect answer to the problem; all in some way caused distortion and skewed relationships and distances.

In the azimuthal projection, another of the three main families of map projections, the globe is projected onto a plane. In polar aspect, it maps a plane tangent to the earth at either of the poles; parallels of latitude are complete circles centred at the pole, while meridians of longitude radiate outward from the pole. This type of projection may be used in an equatorial or oblique aspect. Although the azimuthal projection cannot display the entire Earth, at least it gives a general sense of a globe.

The third main family of map projections is the cylindrical projection, where a flat sheet is wrapped in the form of a cylinder around the globe. When unrolled, the scale for the meridians remains the same, while the scale for the parallels increases as they approach the pole. Each of these three main families of map projections has many variations. The cordiform (heart-shape) projection, another geometrically constructed plan, has a set of complex meridian lines.

None of these projection plans were of any use for navigation. In principle, a vessel leaving a port and crossing the ocean on a constant bearing, a rhumb line, would reach its destination. In practice, how-

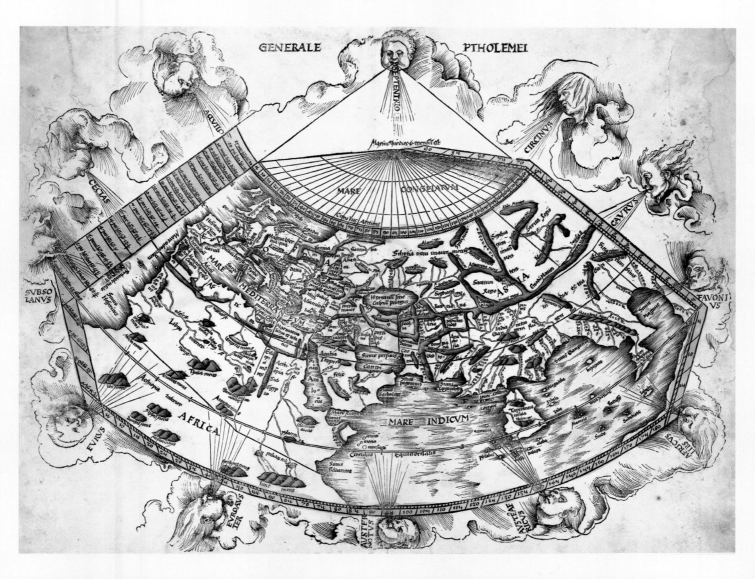

GENERALE PTHOLEMEI

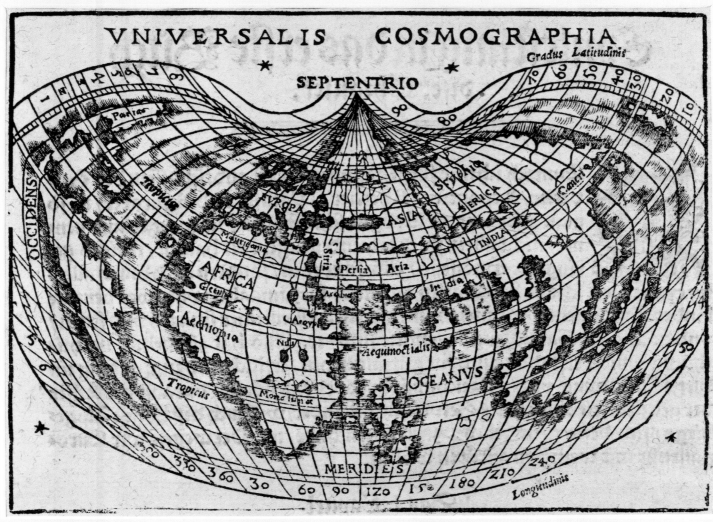

UNIVERSALIS COSMOGRAPHIA

ever, it is a different matter. Since all the meridians converge to a point at the poles, all rhumb lines curve turning continuously towards them. The only exception is if the rhumb line follows one of the cardinal points of the compass, and therefore follows along a parallel of latitude or a meridian of longitude. One of the first to study the geometry of these curved lines, later called loxodromes, was Pedro Nuñes, who wrote his *Navigandi libri duo* in 1546. Gerard Mercator, the Flemish born mathematician and cartographer, corrected the curve established by Nuñes, and showed that it was actually a helical line, which he depicted superimposed on a globe. Mercator used the projection plan, now bearing his name, on his great wall map of the world in 1569.

By all appearances, the projection plan devised by Mercator is much the same as a cylindrical projection, but it differs in that the parallels of latitude and meridians of longitude are the same scale on each point on the chart. With the scale proportionately increased with the increase in latitude. In his projection Greenland appears to be the same size as South America, although in fact it is only one-ninth the size, but at any point on the chart or map, the shape of the land features remains correct and undistorted. The perceived distortion is created only when one compares the larger scale of lands toward the poles with lands in lower latitudes.

Technically called a conformal, or isogonic cylindrical projection, Mercator's projection preserves equal angles, and the rhumb lines and bearings are straight lines, which are necessary for navigation. He was unaware of the mathematical formulation of his projection, and had empirically arrived at the solution to the problem of spiral rhumb lines on a plain chart. Three decades later, Edward Wright (1561–1615), professor of mathematics and a geographer, worked out the trigonometric tables for Mercator's projection.

With a chart based on the Mercator projection, the mariner could now plot a proper course to his destination, and upon his return, report to his sovereign the location of his discoveries that they might be incorporated by cartographers and into a new view of an expanding world.

68. A Plat of All the World by Edward Wright, 1600

The map shown here, drawn by the great mathematician and astronomer, Edward Wright, was published in Richard Hakluyt's *Principle Navigations, Voyages, Trafiques and Discoveries of the English Nation* (1588–1600). It is one of the very first to present Mercator's new plan for projecting the surface of the globe on a flat plane. In spite of inevitable distortions inherent in any plan, its great advantage over all others was the ability to use it for navigational purposes. It allowed the navigator to plot a ship's course as a straight line and a constant angle, no matter how it cut across the meridians.

COURTESY OF THE JOHN CARTER BROWN LIBRARY AT BROWN UNIVERSITY, RHODE ISLAND

Cy comence le xiij.liure
q̃ parle de leaue et de ses pietes.

Le premier chapitre
parle de leaue en general

R escriptes les ꝓpietes
du feu et de lair. il est
temps que nous disõs
maintenant de leaue
et de ses œuures entant cõme il en apptient
a ceste petite œuure. Leaue est ainsi appellee

ꝑ ꝑuir quelle est egalle et vnie. car elle
ne cesse onques de soy mouuoir tant qͤlle
est toute esgalle par dessus si cõme dit
ysidoie. ou xiije liure des ethimologies.
Leaue selon cõstantin est vng element
froit et moiste subtil et delie et cler au re

NAVIGATION IN THE MIDDLE AGES

As geography without history
Seems as a carcass without motion,
So history without geography
Wanders as a vagrant without habitation.

CAPT. JOHN SMITH, *A DESCRIPTION OF NEW ENGLAND*, 1616

Mathematicians and astronomers of classical antiquity had made great progress toward a secular understanding of the cosmology of the universe and the geography of the world. But following the adoption of Christianity throughout the Roman Empire, the same questions asked by Greek philosophers regarding the shape of the Earth, its position in the universe, and whether space was finite or infinite, were asked anew. With the political and military decline of the Western Roman Empire Christianity filled the political vacuum and became a dominant force in the minds of men. The next seven centuries were to witness attempts to reconcile the past science of the Ancients with the theological dogma of a new religion.

69. The Earth, its Rivers and their Tributaries by Jean Corbichon and Evrard d'Espinques, 1480, from the original work by Bartholomeus Anglicus of the 14th century

The detailed appearance of this elaborate late fifteenth-century T-O map, would suggest that its creator Bartholomeus Anglicus intended some semblance of geographical reality. This can be seen most clearly in the verdant natural landscape and carefully executed drawing of contemporary ships. But it is yet another rendering of a Biblical landscape. East, with Paradise, is oriented at the top of the map; it is not by accident that there are four rivers pouring forth from Eden. In the second book of Genesis, after watering the Garden of Eden, the river divided into four major rivers that nourished the rest of the world.

BIBLIOTHÈQUE NATIONALE DE FRANCE, PARIS

70. T-O Map by Isidore of Seville, 1472

In Isidore of Seville's T-O map, a tripartite world with a circumfluent ocean is retained from Ancient Greece. He identifies the three known continents of Europe, Africa and Asia, with the three sons of Noah - Shem, Japhet, and Ham – who were apportioned divisions of the Earth. These maps functioned more as a diagrammatic representation of the Earth than any attempt to depict its geography. The *Etymologies*, in which this map first appeared (around AD 620), was in manuscript form. The illustration here is a copy made seven centuries later (1472), and is the first printed map in Europe.

THE LIBRARY OF CONGRESS, WASHINGTON D.C..

NEW VIEWS IN THE MEDIEVAL WORLD

Medieval Cosmography

Although the doctrine of a spherical Earth was well established centuries earlier, the Catholic hierarchy did not readily accept it, and replaced a Greek universe based upon science, with a 'new' universe re-ordered according to Christian faith. Many distinguished leaders of the Church condemned the doctrine of a spherical Earth, and especially its corollary – the existence of an Antipodes – a region on the opposite side of the globe inhabited by people with 'opposite facing feet.'

The best-known, and most influential, ecclesiastic to denounce the Antipodes was Saint Augustine (AD 354–430), one of humanities most prolific geniuses. He cautiously agreed with Aristotle on the spherical nature of the Earth, but was against an inhabited Antipodes. Biblical tradition, with a strict, literal interpretation of Scripture, was incompatible with the concept of an inhabited southern continent. Nowhere in the Bible, he said, is there anywhere to be found an account of a race descended from Adam living in the Antipodes. More pragmatically, he believed the immensity of the ocean would make it impossible for descendents of Adam and Eve to sail to and populate the Antipodes. There were, however, those who kept the learning of antiquity alive. Chief amongst them was Bishop Isidore of Seville (Isidorus Hispalensis c. AD 560–634) who was a powerful ecclesiastic and one of the greatest encyclopedists and excerptors of late antiquity. Known for his many books on history, natural science and theology, his greatest work, called *Etymologies*, was drawn from both Classical and Biblical sources, as a compilation of the entire range of human knowledge.

The Spanish bishop considered the geography of the world, portrayed the ocean, the tides, inlets of the sea, and lakes and rivers of the Earth, and was the first person to define the Mediterranean Sea clearly by the use of that name. Although he quoted from many of the classical writers who believed in a spherical Earth, it appears that he still favoured the idea of a flat Earth, covered with a spherical heaven.

Isidore of Seville's work was immensely popular and was copied in the eighth and ninth centuries by monastic encyclopedists. In the Middle Ages, geographic knowledge was considered an important subject for a well-rounded education. All the manuscript compendia of knowledge had specific sections describing the physical geography of the known world, and were illustrated with maps. They were, however, limited by the paucity of information available about distant places, while dissemination of the texts was restricted by the need for scribal copying.

Medieval Cartography

…if one does not understand the physical form of the world, history is apt to become a stale and tasteless crust…

ROGER BACON, *OPUS MAIUS*, C. 1268

The primary purpose of the maps in the manuscript compendia was neither geographical nor navigational; they were schematic representations of the world as it was then understood, and combined historical and theological knowledge with geographical information. The Ptolemaic system of mathematical geography using latitude and longitude had been lost to western scholarship. And, had it been known, it would not have been accommodated easily into the several types of maps produced from the seventh century onwards by ecclesiastic cartographers, for whose purpose it was as important to show the significance of places, as it was to show their location. Thus, Jerusalem, although not in the geographical centre of the inhabited Earth, was put in the centre of the map as a statement of its spiritual centrality.

Circular maps, popularly called T-O maps, may have been conceived as early as the fifth or sixth century BC by philosophers of the Ionian School, but it was through Isidore of Seville that the western world came to know them. These maps adopted from classical writers the concept of a world disc divided into three continents – Europe, Asia and Africa – all surrounded by an Ocean River. Three major waterways separated the continents to form the 'T' within the 'O' of the map: the river Don (*Tanais*) divided Europe from Asia; the river Nile divided Africa from Asia; and the Mediterranean Sea lay between Europe and Africa. The Ancients considered Europe to be equal in size to the other two continents combined, but from the time of St. Augustine onward the proportions changed and Asia was shown as the largest of the three continents.

On this simple plan, medieval minds overlaid their own view of the world, one dominated by a Christian theology. The maps were oriented with East at the top, for that is the place from where warmth and light came. Here too, was found the Garden of Eden. Occupying the central position, the place of greatest importance, was the holy city of Jerusalem. This became the prototype for all other T-O maps illustrating the habitable world of the Earth, and it was replicated with many variations as a cartographic tradition until late in the seventeenth century.

Yet another form of circular map divided the Earth into the horizontal bands established by the classic philosophers. These were zonal maps, or a variant called *climata* maps. Aristotle became the accepted authority for there being at each pole a frigid zone, uninhabitable on account of the extreme cold; a torrid zone in the middle, at the equator, that also was uninhabitable on account of the intense heat; and only two habitable temperate zones, one in the northern hemisphere and the other in the southern hemisphere. Aristotle, however, was not the only classical authority used by medieval mapmakers. In

71. Arabic Circular World Map
by 'Ali ibn Musa ibn Sa'id al-Maghribi, 1570

This world map from an anonymous Arab treatise titled *Kit b al-Bad' wa-al-ta'rikh* (Book of Creation and History), is in the Islamic tradition, yet the seven concentric arcs are the astronomically defined 'clime' zones of Greek predecessors. Oriented with East, rather than the traditional South, at the top, Baghdad occupies a position a little below the centre of the map.

THE BODLEIAN LIBRARY, UNIVERSITY OF OXFORD

Overleaf
72. Map of the World by Pietro Vesconte, c. 1320–1325

Pietro Vesconte's map, drawn in 1321, introduces a new geographic realism. No longer a simple T-O map, and devoid of religious content, it combines a map of the world with a sea-chart. As a nautical chart-maker in Genoa, Vesconte's maritime experience is clearly evidenced by the realistic representation of the geography of the Mediterranean Sea, Black Sea and the Atlantic Ocean. The map is oriented with East at the top.

THE BRITISH LIBRARY, LONDON

the second century BC, Hipparchus of Rhodes (190–125 BC), had enumerated the climate zones in a different manner and increased their number from three to seven *climata*. The seven *climata* of Hipparchus were portions or segments of the habitable world included between two parallels of latitude, which he defined according to the length of the longest day – a rough means of determining latitude. In the second century AD, Ptolemy took the seven climate bands and extended the number to thirty-three parallels at regular intervals, extending from the equator to Thule. Islamic mapmakers continued with Ptolemy's use of climata division in their own maps. In the western world, following the publication in 1409 of the Latin translation by Jacobus Angelus (Jacopo d'Angelos) of Ptolemy's *Geographia*, climate bands were shown on maps well into the sixteenth century – the last vestigial remains of this cartographic system. The first printed version was published in 1475 without maps, followed two years later with a version containing maps.

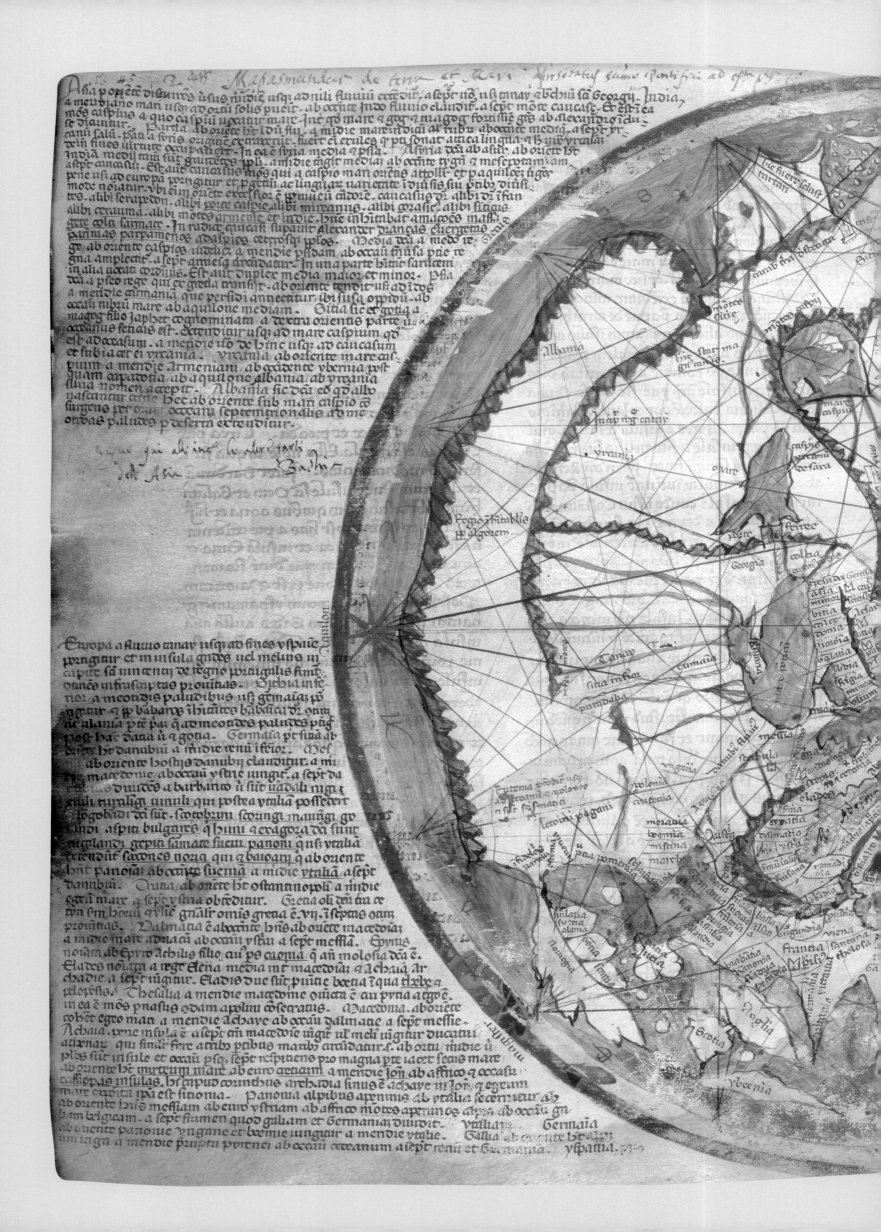

Asia porrecta dicit u. us usus uidie usqs ad nili fluuiu ectedit. a septrnõ ust tanay abchnu sã Georgij. India
a meridiano mari usqs ad ortu solis pueit. ab octte jndo fluuio claudit. a sept mote caucase. Et est ea
mõs caspius a quo caspiu uocatur mare. Int qd mare q gog q magog fortisse gtes ab alexandro uclu-
se dicuntur. Partia. ab ouete bt idu flu. a midie mare idiai at rubu abocute medtã. a sept yr-
canu salu. phã a suris origine ertraxerit. fuerit ei erules q ptisonat attica lingua. q h uir uirali-
dein fines uirtute occupauerit. In ea e syria media q psla. Assiria dã ab asiur. ab ouete bt
india medij tui sui gaudetes. psli. a midie tingit mediã. ab octte tygri q mesopotamiam
asept caucasu. Est aut cancasius mõs qui a caspio mari oriens attolli. et paquilorz sugru
pene ust ad europa pringitur. et p gtiu ac linguarz uarietate iduisis siu ptibz diuisis
mote noiatur. ubi ei in ouete ercelsior e pymueu caidoie. caucasi g alibi di isun-
tres. alibi serapedon. alibi porte caspie. alibi mirannus. alibi corasie. alibi sitiais
alibi cerauna. alibi motes armenie. et indie. huic inhibitar amazoes massa-
gere cola saimare. In radice caucasi supauit Alexander priancas euergetus
primas parpamenos adaspico cerosq iplos. Media tra a medo rege. ab ouente caspios intelie. a mendie ysidam. ab occau thiusa pnte re-
gna amplectit. a sept armeia deiaidatur. In una parte hitie saricem
in alia uocat cordiune. Est aut duplex media maior et minor. Psia
tra a pseo rege qui ex gecia transit. ab ouente tendit ust ad idos
a mendie carmania que persidi annectitur. ibi sua oppidu. ab
occau rubru mare ab aquilone mediam. Sitia sic et motia a
magog filio iapher cognominata. a detra orientis parte ua
occauus senais est. extenditur usqs ad mare caspium qd
est ad ocrasum. a mendie usd de hinc usqs ad caucasum
et subia ct ei yrtania. yrtania ab ortente mare caspium a mendie Armeniam. ab occidente ybernia post
quam cxpardia. ab aquilone albania. ab yrtania
fluuia nomen acepit. Albania sic dca eo qd albo
nascantur crine. hec ab ouente sub mari caspio co-
surgens per ora occeana septemtrionalis ad me-
otidas paludes p deserta extenditur.

Sequer qui alii ine bedure parti
dell Asia

Europa a fluuio tanay usqs ad fines yspaie
pringitur. et in insula gndes uel melius in
capite sã uin cenij de regno pringilis finit.
oance infrascriptas prouitias. Sithia inferior. a meotidis paludibus ust gemaiarz tõ
uigitur q p babaros iliuctures babaica di onu
ac alauia prê par q ad meontdes paludes pag
post hac baua u a gotia. Germaia pr sinu ab-
oziete bt danubii a midie renu istior. Mel-
ab ouente bostis danuby claudit. a midie macedonie. abocau ystrie uingit. a sept da-
euluis diuides a barbario u sut uadali rugi q
euli turaligi. tiuuli qui postea utalia possederit
sogobadi di sut. scouobzim secungi mauigi go-
hindi aspit bulgaris q huni q euagora di sunt
nugelandi gepit samare sueu panoni q ust ytalia
extendit saxones nona qui q baioary q ab ouente
hut panoia. ab ocrte sueuia a midie ytaliã. a sept
danubiu. Oruia. ab ouete bt ostantinopli a midie
egeu mari q sept ystaia obtedijr. Grecia oli tã tã ce-
tyn bin bonu q ulie gualit omis grecia e. uij. i septis oam
prouitas. Dalmatia e abocente hris ab ouete macedoiarz
a raidie mari adriaiu ab ocrau ystau a sept messiã. Epyrus
noiã ab Epyro Achilis filio. au ps caonia q au molosia dca e.
Clades noiata a rege Elcia media int macedoiarz q achaiã ar-
cadie a sept iugitur. Eladis due ste puntc boena q qua tlrbe q
pelopris. Thesalia a mendie macedonie ouieta e au pua atype
in ea e mõs pnasus odam apliui coseratus. Macedonia. abocrete
cobet egeo mari a mendie achaye ab ocrau dalmaie a sept messie.
Achaia. pene insula e a sept cm macedoie uigi ul meli uigitur ducatui
atirnar qui simar fire atibz pribus maribz arciuditur. c. ab ortu midie u
ples sur insule et ocrau psq sept respiciens pro magua pte iacet seuis mare
ab ouente murteum mare ab euro artaiu a mendie ion ab affrico q occasu
cassiopas insulas. ht caput corinthus archadia sinus e achaye in ior q egeam
mare expoita ipa est sitiouia. Panonia alpibus aperninis ab ytalia secernatur ab
ab ortente hris messiam ab euro ystiam ab affrico motes aperinos absq ab occau ga-
ham belgicam. a sept flamen quod galiam et germaniã diuidit. Ytaliarz. Germaia.
ab ouente panonie yngane et bcemie iungitur a mendie ytalie. Galla. ab ouente bt alpi-
um inga a mendie pripta pyrenei ab occau occeanum a sept renu et germania. yspania.

73. Astrolabium nocturnam, 12th century

Eighth- and ninth-century Muslim centres of learning kept alive the scientific knowledge of Aristotle, Ptolemy and other great philosophers in antiquity. Through Muslim conquests in Spain, this information was transferred to Christian Europe. In the Middle Ages, in addition to liturgical texts, scribes in Monastic centres of learning reproduced treatises comprising the disciplines of mathematics, and the practice of geometry and astronomy. In this twelfth-century manuscript an astronomer is taking a sighting of the Pole Star with a nocturlabe, a night astrolabe, to determine time at night. Through the seventeenth and eighteenth centuries, the instrument was also used by sailors to calculate the time of tides and to measure latitude.

MUSÉE DES MANUSCRITS DU MONT SAINT-MICHEL

Medieval Trade Routes in the Mediterranean

In addition to Islam being the heir and transmitter of the Hellenic civilization, its rise in the Mediterranean created a major political force during the early Middle Ages. By the eighth century, the Arab world ringed the Mediterranean from the Anatolian border of Byzantium, westward around the shores of North Africa, and eastward to include much of Spain, Sicily and the boot of Italy. By the tenth century the Muslim world had virtually made the Mediterranean a 'Muslim lake'. But in the middle of the tenth century Arab unity was weakened by internal dissention amongst the local Islamic dynasties, and Christendom found the degree of unity needed to bring Islamic expansion to a halt.

At the end of the tenth century, fleets from Genoa and Pisa attacked Muslim pirate bases in the western Mediterranean and regained control of Islamic shores of North Africa, while Venetian warships cleared the Adriatic and Aegean Seas. By 1123, with the Venetian naval victory over the Egyptian fleet at

Ascalon, a Muslim port near Jerusalem, the two city-states of Genoa and Venice came to dominate the Mediterranean.

By the beginning of the thirteenth century, Venice was a world power, with possessions stretching from the Adriatic throughout all the Aegean. Her routes to Alexandria and Constantinople enabled her to trade in precious silks, perfumes, rare woods and porcelain from China; cloves, cinnamon and other spices from Asia; carpets and tapestries from Persia – all of which were redistributed throughout Europe. The most lucrative of her trade items, 'the very milk and nourishment' of the city's being, was pepper from India and the Moluccas (island group of the Malay Archipelago), which came by sea across the Indian Ocean, Red Sea and Nile River to Alexandria. Alexandria was an important trading port for Genoa as well for Venice, and furnished Genoa with most of her oriental wares.

Venice, the eldest child of Liberty.
She was a Maiden City, bright and free;
No guile seduced, no force could violate;
And when she took unto herself a mate,
She must espouse the everlasting sea.

WILLIAM WORDSWORTH

To support her trade, Venice had an empire of bases at important positions along her sea-routes, as well as possession of Crete, Cyprus, Rhodes and Corfu. Additionally, there were many smaller islands and ports throughout the Adriatic and Aegean where her ships were welcome, linking her at the eastern end of the chain to her major colony in Constantinople. Fortified bases along the way protected Venetian commercial routes and served as places they could rest and re-provision. Constantinople, at the eastern terminus of Venetian trade, was strategically important; from there, all traffic to and from the Black Sea was controlled. In as early as 1082, Venetian merchants had their own quarter in Constantinople, and by 1177 ten thousand Venetian merchant-colonists lived there.

When Venice founded Tana, near the estuary of the Don River on the Sea of Azov, it extended her trade links to the Russian Arctic for its valuable furs and grain. Tana was strategically located, not only for obtaining products from the north, but also because it was the terminus of caravan trade routes from central Asia and China.

Genoa went one step further. From the Sea of Azov her ships sailed north on the River Don through southern Russia, and were carried overland to the Volga River, by which they sailed into the Caspian Sea. The colonies Genoa established there brought her closer to the source of goods arriving through central Asia from the Far East and provided a quicker and less expensive return route than that available to Venice.

Although not nearly as exotic as the luxury goods of silks, porcelain and spices from the Indian Ocean and western Pacific, and certainly more bulky to carry, salt was an extremely

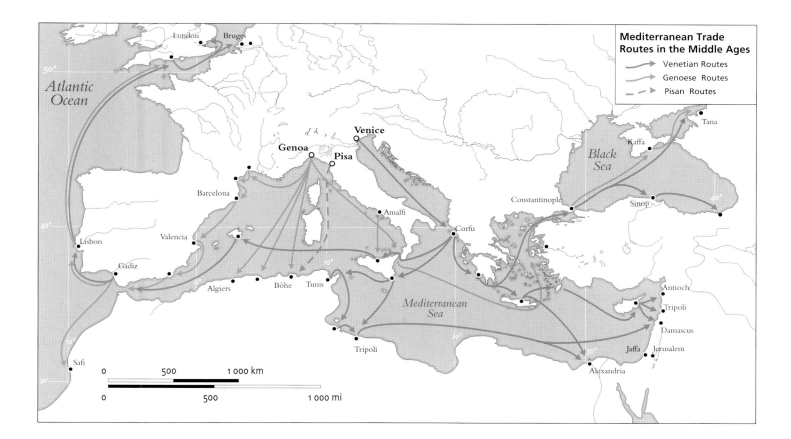

74. Mediterranean Trade Routes in the Middle Ages

Trade flows in the Mediterranean, as anywhere else, depended upon distribution of goods and market forces. Foreign and domestic conflicts, shifting ideologies, changes in population levels and political structure, all affected trade.

important commodity of trade in the Mediterranean. It was a necessary item in the daily life of all people to preserve meat and fish and ensure their edible state over a long, lean winter. Venice supplied the inhabitants of the countris immediately to her north with salt from her own salt marshes in the northern Adriatic, and from marshes and salt lakes of Cyprus.

From the quarries at Phocaea, northernmost of the Greek Ionian cities in the Aegean, Genoese vessels carried alum, another equally common but important commodity. Alum was an essential ingredient, for dying the woollen cloth manufactured in England and at Bruges in Flanders. The transport and sale of alum significantly contributed to Genoa's economic prosperity.

Most profitable of all was the shipping of people. Slave owning was a widespread and common practice in the Mediterranean, and a considerable volume of slaves were transported to be sold as domestic servants, concubines, field workers and foot soldiers for armies. From North Africa, Venice transported Muslim-owned black slaves eastward, and shipped white slaves from Tana and Crete westward to Italy, Spain and France. Genoa, too, profited in the slave trade, shipping human cargoes from North Africa and Genoese colonies in Kaffa and Tana on the Black Sea and Sea of Azov.

For pilgrims desiring passage to the Holy Land, as well as for the waves of crusaders travelling to the Levant to fight the infidels, Venice was the major departure point. Jaffa, the port for Jerusalem, was the destination of some pilgrims, while others went to Tripoli or Alexandria. In the first crusade from 1095 to 1099, to recover Jerusalem and free the Holy Land, Genoan,

Pisan and Venetian ships all ferried crusaders to Palestine. In the fourth crusade from 1202 to 1204, Venice constructed a fleet of 200 transports and 50 fighting ships. Initially they were destined for Egypt, but instead they swept on to conquer Constantinople. From the captured city Venice gained a great deal of wealth directly by looting, and also obtained possession of three-eighths of the city itself, and acquisition of other lands. This gave her a strategic position to control her commercial trade routes in the Adriatic, the Aegean and the Black Sea.

Best known of all Venetian merchants are the Polo brothers, Maffeo and Niccolò, and Niccolò's youngest son Marco (1254–1324), who left Constantinople in 1271 to trade with Russia and Mongolia. They arrived in Beijing in 1275, where Marco Polo won favour with Kublai Khan (1215–1294) and made in his service several voyages to various parts of China as well as to

Overleaf
75. A Braun and Hogenberg map of Venice, 1572

Venice embraced the sea, making it the very core of her being, as much as the meagre islands of the lagoon on which she built her *palazzi*. In return, from the Barbary Coast, from Constantinople, Russia, the Crimea, Bruges, Damascus and Alexandria, the sea brought to Venice all the trade goods and riches of the world.

JUHA NURMINEN COLLECTION

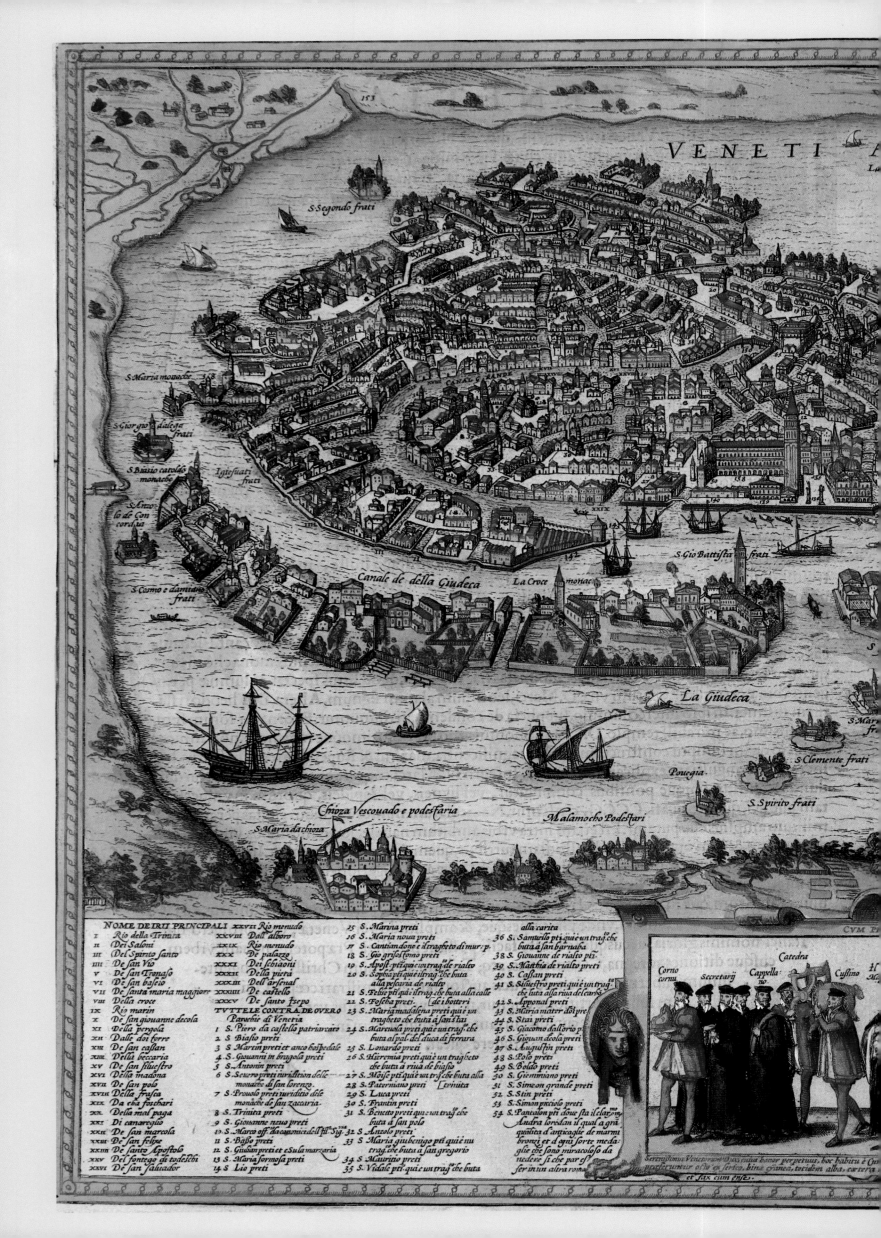

Torcelo Vescouado e.Podestaria

S.Bernardo monache   Matthia frati   S.Giac.mo de Paludo frati

man.ache   S.Nicolo de Lio frati   Mazorbo   Buran

o habe   S.Franc. del deserto

Miuran Podestaria

S.Christoforo frati

Lazaretto nouo

72

XXXI   XXXII   XXXIII   XXXIIII   XXXV

S.Andrea da lio frati certosini

frati et Badia

S.Lazaro

S.Helena frati

Lazare to.Vecchio.Hospedal della.sanita

S.Seruolo monache

erenissi: Ombrela   Oratores diuersor: Principum   Ambascia tori di varij Principi   La Spada ensis.

sed raro, cum annitoata splendido atq, magnifico, vexilla har sex, vlnarum triu, sella, puluinar, ombraculu aureu.

Merchant Ships of the Middle Ages

In the eleventh century the Vikings were losing their grip of Northern Europe. Many German trading towns joined forces to protect themselves and their ships as well as their commercial interests. The most important alliance was the Hanseatic League, which at the end of the Middle Ages ruled trade, shipping and politics in the Baltic Sea and North Sea areas.

The Hanseatic League employed a new ship type known as a *cog*, a large and seaworthy freighter. The design was influenced by the Vikings' *knarr*, but the cog's deep draft enabled it to carry five times as much cargo as the knarr, so was used especially for bulk and break-bulk cargoes such as salt, sulphur, fish, grain and wood. These shipments did not bring large profits, but the Hanseatic League had a monopoly on many categories of goods. The dominance of the cog in the ocean trades of northern medieval Europe is reflected by the fact that many ports were moved from positions on rivers far upstream, to new locations

78. Venetian Ship by Björn Landström, 1961

The lateen sail was used in Mediterranean ships for a 1000 years as it offered many advantages, especially in smaller vessels. Unlike European ships, the larger Mediterranean vessels had several masts. Because the handling of a large lateen sail was quite difficult, the square sail (inspired by the cog) was introduced in the Mediterranean.

COURTESY OF OLOF LANDSTRÖM

77. The Hansa Cog by Björn Landström, 1961

The cog evolved from the Viking ship. In the beginning it was an open ship with a single mast and a square sail, but it could also be rowed. Later, the cog was built with a shelter deck and castles (high structures at the bow and stern). It became very popular among merchantmen within the Hanseatic league as it was able to carry large amounts of cargo of various kinds.

COURTESY OF OLOF LANDSTRÖM

closer to the sea and in deeper water where the large cogs could serve them. In addition to cogs, which in some ports were referred to as hulks, knarrs continued to sail the northern waters.

In 1962 a remarkable shipwreck was found in the River Weser close to Bremen: a fourteenth-century cog. This has provided maritime historians with more technical detail of the cog than had previously been interpreted from depictions on seals and coins of the Hanseatic cities.

Cogs had clinker built outer planking, with planks partly overlapping and clenched together with nails, and one mast with a square sail. Their sterns and stems were straight, as opposed to the rounded forms of the Viking ships. They were flat bottomed, enabling loading in shallow waters with the tide, and the high freeboard offered good protection against pirates. The earliest cogs were open and could be rowed shorter distances. However, by the thirteenth century cogs were larger and decks and castles began to appear. The castles were superstructures in the fore and aft part of the ship which were used both for accommodation and in battle. A revolutionary feature in the design of the cog was the rudder, which from the 1240s replaced the steering oar. It was hinged on the sternpost and controlled by a tiller.

The earliest cogs could sail only in fair winds, but the rudder made sailing against the wind easier. In addition to the square sails, bonnets were often laced to the foot of the sail in light wind conditions. The sails were usually tanned red to protect them from rot, mould and mildew. In old manuscripts striped red/white and green/white sails, and even completely black sails, are also mentioned. The long and heavy yard was hosted by a windlass, which was also used to weigh the anchor.

If possible, the cogs sailed close to the coast within sight of land, as there were no charts and compasses to guide the navigators. In dangerous waters the depth was sounded regularly from the bow; in fog or storms the crew anchored and waited for better weather conditions. It was not until the introduction of the magnetic compass in the fourteenth century that these navigation techniques changed.

Cogs sailed to the Mediterranean in the twelfth century, participating in the fleets of the crusaders. They were also used by pirates. But as late as the thirteenth century the round hull form still dominated both large and small vessels in the Mediterranean, little changed since the Roman Empire. They were usually equipped with two masts and they had two or three decks.

The main difference between Mediterranean shipbuilding techniques and those of northern Europe was the way the hull was constructed. Northern Europeans used clinker construction, while Mediterranean ships were always carvel-built with flush, even planking, and their frames were erected before the planking was fastened. In the fourteenth century, however, there began to be a convergence between northern and southern European shipbuilding methods. The southern way of constructing a hull was gradually adapted in the north, enabling the building of larger and stronger ships due to the more compact hull with heavier planking. For example, the Bremen cog was partially carvel-built. At the same time southern shipbuilders began to adopt the simple square sail of the cog, which was easier to handle in large ships and required a smaller crew than did the lateen sails used throughout the Mediterranean since the fourth century. Lateen sails and square sails both have their advantages and disadvantages. Mediterranean sailors were used to lateen sails in vessels with several masts, and they found that a square-rigger was difficult to keep on the right course. They met that problem by adding a shorter mizzenmast aft of the main mast, on which they placed a lateen sail to improve the course stability. In the north, vessels with several masts were not seen until the fifteenth century, but from that date the transfer of sail-design technology was rapid.

At the time that the Hanseatic League sailed the northern seas, three Italian republics, Genoa, Pisa and Venice, with Marseilles and Barcelona, dominated Christian shipping on the Mediterranean during the Crusades. Their shipyards were busy and the large merchant fleet of the Mediterranean brought valuable cargoes from the Levant.

In the fourteenth century the development of the cog stagnated. Larger vessels were required to carry greater volumes of cargo and a bigger crew, but it was impossible to increase the tonnage of the cog. A new generation of ships would need to operate at sea for longer periods of time. Furthermore, there was a need for heavier armament both for offensive movements and defence. To meet these new requirements a new type of ship evolved, the carrack, which exploited the best qualities of both the cog and the Mediterranean ship.

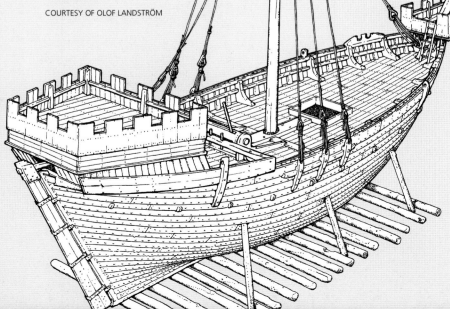

79. Carta del Mar della Tana (Mar d'Azov) by Leonardo Dati, 15th century

The Sea of Azov, a shallow branch of the Black Sea, was the farthest northeast-ern extension of the Greek cultural sphere. Trade goods came here from the Far East, the Russian north and the Mongol-Tartar tribes. In the thirteenth century, Genoa and Venice had mercantile colonies in the town of Tanais (Tana) on the Sea of Azov. This was an important transit point for these goods to be trans-ported to the Byzantine Empire and western Europe.

BIBLIOTECA RICCARDIANA, FLORENCE

80. Marco Polo leaving Venice, from *Li livres du graunt caam*, 1400

This image depicts Marco Polo, along with his father Niccolò Polo and uncle Maffeo Polo, leaving Venice in 1271 for China (then called Cathay). Most of their travel was overland by way of Silk Road. They returned home in 1295 after being employed in the court of Kublai Khan for seventeen years and engaging in trade. Their return route was almost entirely by sea.

THE BODLEIAN LIBRARY, UNIVERSITY OF OXFORD

Annam, Tonkin, India and Persia. On returning to Venice by sea, captured by the Genoese, Marco Polo recounted in his book *Il Milione* in 1298 all he had seen and heard on his venture. It provided the western world an abundance of information about Asia, which was until then almost totally unknown, and stimulated later European explorers to seek a sea-route to the land of riches he described.

Although the Venetian Republic dominated the eastern end of the Mediterranean it was by no means the sole power in trade there. Her rival, Genoa, also had a base in Constantino-ple and in Chios, threatening Venetian control of goods from the Black Sea.

Until the middle of the thirteenth century, an uneasy bal-ance of power existed between Venice and her rival city-states of Genoa and Pisa. Over the next century and a half, they challenged Venetian control of the eastern Mediterranean in four wars. In the end, Venice dominated the western Aegean,

while Genoa commanded the eastern Aegean, and both city-states shared the Black Sea and Tana on the Sea of Azov.

In 1238 the Algarve port of Tavira was captured from the Moors by Portuguese forces, and within ten years Cordoba, Valencia and Seville were re-conquered by Castile. With the Barbary Coast of North Africa already cleared of its Mus-lim pirate bases, and the Moorish occupation of Andalusia (with the exception of Granada) now ended, it was reasonably safe for Christian merchants from Genoa and Venice to sail through the Straits of Gibraltar out into the Atlantic to carry their seaborne trade to the ports of northern Europe and the west coast of Africa.

Genoese galleys led the way in oceanic discovery. Before the close of the thirteenth century they were already searching south for a sea-route around Africa to India. They established trade ports on the Atlantic coast of Morocco at Safi, and with the voyage of the Vivaldi brothers in 1291 sailed beyond Cape Nun at 32° 18' North latitude. In the other direction, as early as 1227 Genoese ships were in the Bay of Biscay, and by 1277 they were sailing directly from Italy into the English Channel, to Bruges. This great accomplishment established a new and major sea-route linking the Mediterranean with northern Europe.

In the Middle Ages Bruges was the most important trad-ing centre of northwest Europe, with a long tradition as an international port. Scandinavian Vikings traded here in the eighth and ninth centuries. And by the eleventh century it was the commercial centre of Europe. By the first quarter of the fourteenth century, Genoese vessels were voyaging yearly to Bruges, bringing the much-needed alum to her wool-len cloth manufactures. Venetian vessels also sailed to Bruges, and to London and Southampton in England, bringing ori-ental commodities from its trade in the Levant, and return-ing homeward with wool and woollen textiles. From Bruges, sea trade extended eastward into the ports of the Hanseatic League of the Baltic.

Navigational Innovations

Throughout the first millennium of the modern era, when mar-iners lost sight of shore due to the dark of night, were blown off course by winds from an unfavourable direction, or lost all sense of direction by storms, they had no way of knowing which way to turn to resume their proper course. On long passages made out of sight of land in the Mediterranean, navigators depended upon dead reckoning based on estimates of time, direction and speed. Once they reached the distant shore, they depended on recognition of headlands, capes and other landmarks to set them to their destination. This, however, was of little help if the shore they approached was a dull, featureless stretch of land.

In the twelfth century two principal navigational tools – the sea chart and the magnetic compass – simultaneously made their appearance in Latin Europe. They expanded the capabilities of

Ci commence li liures du grant Caam qui parole de la grant Ermenie. de perse.
et des tartars et dynde. Et des grans merueilles qui p le monde sont.

Pour savoir la pure verite des
diuerses regions du monde. si
preneꝪ cest liure si trouuereꝪ les
grandismes merueilles qui sōt
escriptes en la grant hermenie.
et de persse. et destartas. ꝫ dynde
et de maintes autres prouinces. si conune nre liures
nous contera tout par ordre des que nre sire mare. pol
saiges et nobles si toies de neuue raconte pource que il
les uit. mais auques il y a choses,

Quil ne uit pas. mais il entendi dou
nies certains par uerite. Et pource
metrons nous les choses ueues pour
ueues. Et lentendue pour entendue
a ce que nre liure soit uraus et uerita

bles sanꝪ nule mēcōge. Et chascais qui ce liure ora
ou lira le doit croire. pource que toutes sont choses ue
ritables. Car ie uous fais a sauoir que puis que nre
sire diex fist adam le premier pre ne fu onques de
nul homme generacion qui tant seust ne cerchast
des diuerses parties du monde cōme cest nne sire mare
pol en soc. et pource pensa que ce seroit granꝪ maus se
ce ne fist metre en escrit ce que il auoit ueu oz aꝑ te
rette. A ce que lautre gent que ne sont uenue oz le sa
chent par cest liure. Et si uous di quil de noura a ce
sauoir. en ce druises parties bien. xxuj. ans le quel
liure puis que demourant fu en la carcere de genes fist
retraire par ordre par mesire Rasta pysā. Qui en ale
meismes prison estoit au temps que il couroit de
crist. mjl. C. C. xxiij. et xxiiij. ans a lincarnacion.

Dividing the Horizon:
From Wind Rose to Compass Card

The winds, as at their hour of birth,
Leaning upon the ridged sea,
Breathed low around the rolling earth
With mellow preludes, we are free.

ALFRED LORD TENNYSON

Winds were the earliest markers used to divide the horizon into named parts in order to express direction. A twelve-wind classification appears to have originated in Babylonia as early as 1750 BC. The first mention of them in literature is in Hesiod's *Theogony* (c. 700 BC), where he named the winds, described their genealogy, character, their origin in the heavens and placement therein. In his epic poem, the *Odyssey*, Homer recognized only four winds, consisting of the four cardinal points we now call north, east, south and west. Later, in his *Meteorologica*, Aristotle continued with Hesiod's personified winds by enumerating twelve winds and the places from which they blew. Four of Aristotle's winds had directly opposite counterparts. *Boreas* (*Apartica*), the north wind, blew from the region of the Great Bear (*Ursa Major*). Opposite *Boreas* was *Notus*, the south wind. *Apeliotes*, and

81. Tower of the Winds frieze

The eight winds on the frieze of the entablature are: *Boreas*, blowing a cold wind from the north; *Kaikas*, the northeast wind; *Apeliotes*, the east wind; *Euros*, southeast wind; *Notos*, south wind; *Lips*, southwest wind; *Zephros*, west wind; and *Skiron*, from the northwest.

82. Tower of Winds in Athens

Still standing in the Roman agora of Athens is the monumental construction built around 100 BC by the astronomer, Andronicus, from Kyrrhos in Macedonia. Commonly referred to as Tower of the Winds, its most prominent feature is the carved personification of the eight winds used to indicate direction. The figures on the tower are sculpted to give an idea of the weather conditions one would expect when wind blew from a particular direction. In conjunction with a wind-vane surmounting the tower, the sculpture functioned as a simple weather-forecasting station.

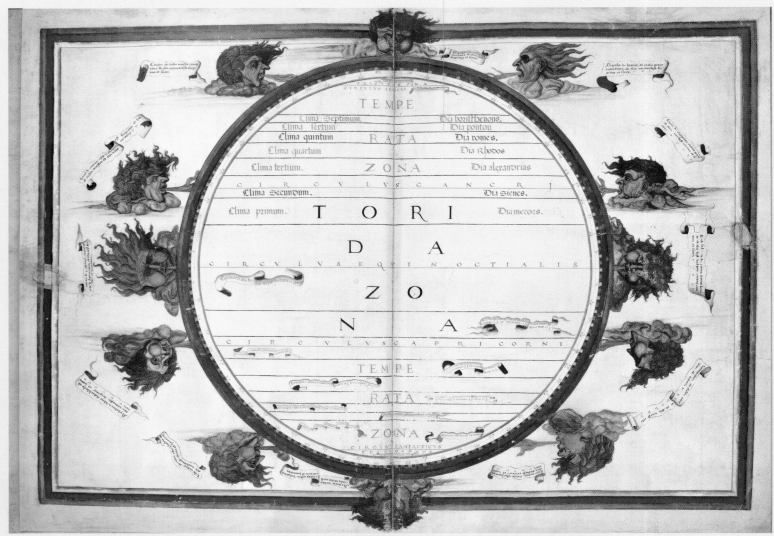

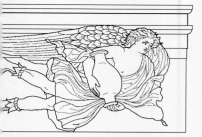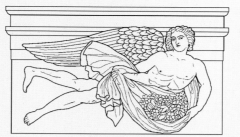

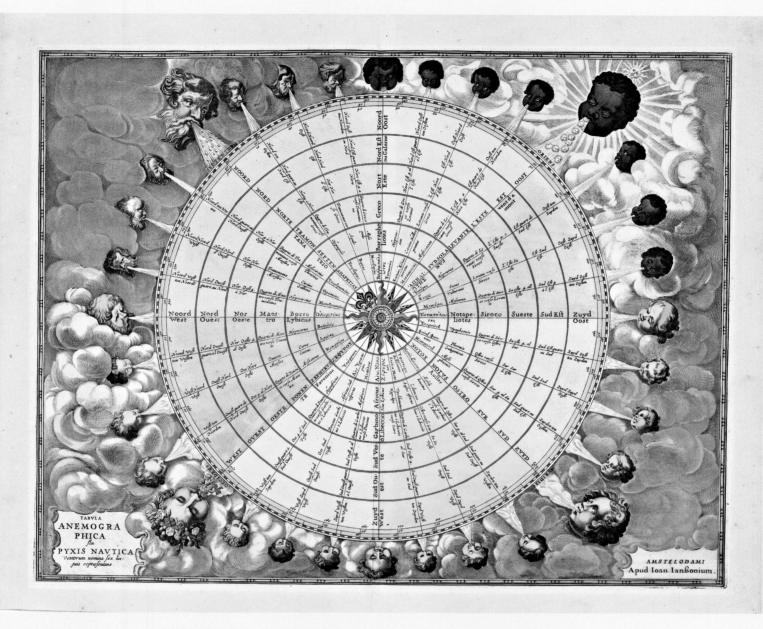

84. Wind-rose by Johannes Janssonius, c. 1650

Over the centuries an increased diversity of names for the winds, and ambiguity about the direction they came from, produced a multitude of different wind names. To create a sense of order from this tangled confusion of names and directions, cartographers produced wind roses such as this one with thirty-two rays by Johannes Janssonius.

JUHA NURMINEN COLLECTION

83. Temperature zones and winds by Diego Homem, 1558

Aristotle enumerated twelve winds and the quarter from which they blew. This twelve-wind division can be seen on many maps, such as the map manuscripts based on Ptolemy's *Geographia*, and were used by astronomers until the sixteenth century.

THE BRITISH LIBRARY

its counterpart *Zephyrus*, respectively blew from the east and west where the Sun rose and set during the spring and autumn equinoxes. Sunset and sunrise at the summer and winter solstices were used as intermediate points between the four cardinal directions. Personified as deities, these winds were depicted by heads with the wind issuing forth from their mouths. In keeping with the mythological origin of winds in the heavens, to indicate direction on maps they were by necessity placed around the border, beyond the confines of the known world. Aristotle's twelve-wind system can be seen on many maps, such as those in fifteenth- and sixteenth-century editions of Ptolemy's *Geographia*.

Although the twelve-wind division of Aristotle found acceptance throughout the Roman Empire from Egypt to Spain, and continued to be used by later writers into the sixteenth century, it was eventually replaced by an eight-wind system. This arrangement was derived from Eratosthenes, and accepted by the

Roman authority, Pliny, as better than the 'too subtle and meticulous' twelve division of Aristotle. The eight-wind system could be continuously halved from four to eight, to sixteen and thirty-two divisions, whereas the twelve-wind system required a cumbersome division of thirds. The eight-winds comprised the four full-winds of *Boreas, Notus, Apeliotes* and *Zephyrus*, and four half-winds, *Caecias, Eurus, Lips* and *Argestes* – all equally spaced around the horizon. Instead of astronomical positions of solstices and equinoxes to designate direction of the winds, they were identified and personified according to the weather they brought with them, or named after the deities who reigned in each region.

During the Middle Ages, a new set of named wind directions emerged, taking their reference not from astronomical solar positions, or mythological personifications, but from general geographic regions. Though still an eight-wind system, Mediterranean sailors named winds after the lands from which they

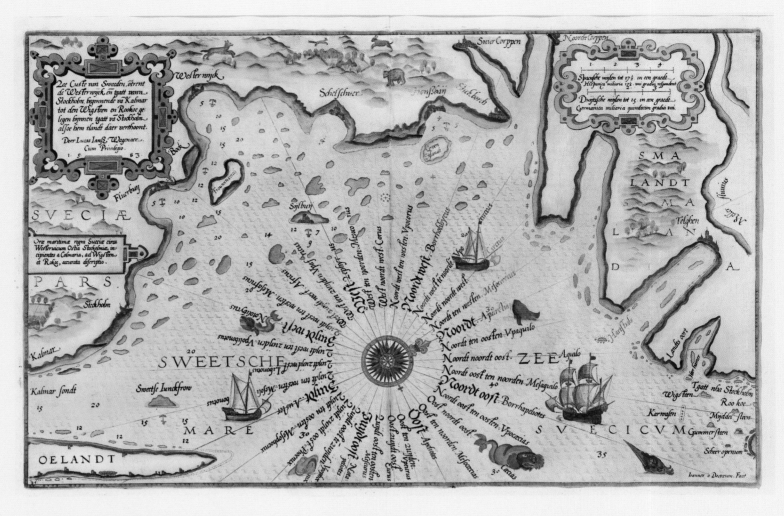

85. Coast of Sweden by Lucas Janszoon Waghenaer, 1584–86

The thirty-two points dividing the horizon are less decorative here on this map and designated by the teutonic words for direction that we are familiar with today. Any good mariner could 'box the compass', that is, give the proper names of each of the thirty two points in sequence.

JOHN NURMINEN FOUNDATION

86. Compass rose by Peter Plancius and Nicolas Cornelis Claesz, 1594

JUHA NURMINEN COLLECTION

originated. Thus, the southwest wind, *Libeccio*, came from Libya, at the time a general term referring to all of Africa. *Greco*, from Greece, designated the northeast wind, and *Tramontana*, which came from 'across the mountains', a north wind.

However, to sailors plying the waters of the open ocean, a wind blowing from Thrace (*Thracias*) lost all relevance in defining direction and so personified winds came to be replaced by the more abstract arrangement of a wind-rose. The wind-rose appeared late in the thirteenth century on sea charts of the Mediterranean (portolans), with the introduction of the magnetic compass. Enclosed within a circle were the four cardinal points of north, east, south and west, each cardinal point representing one of the 'full winds'. This was bisected with intermediate points of 'half-winds', and further bisected into 'quarter-winds',

and 'eighth-winds'. A network of fine lines - vestigial remains of the wind issuing forth from the mouths of gods – converge from the edge of the chart inward toward the centre of the wind-rose, in which all the lines intersect. Variously called wind lines, rhumb lines or loxodromic lines, they indicate the direction from which the wind is blowing.

The points, with their extended lines, also functioned to help navigators determine their direction steer their ship along the recognized direction of the winds to the desired goal. Although the division of the four cardinal points of north, east, south and west, into thirty-two equally spaced segments, or points, made the angular distance between points 11.25° (360 ÷ 32 = 11.25), it better filled the mariner's need for more precision in navigation, and became the basic directional schema, persisting in use through the nineteenth century.

Eventually, the wind-rose became overburdened by a multiplicity of names and obtuse symbolism.

Although it was a conveniently simple arrangement, the problem nonetheless remained of what name to give to all the directions. In the time of Charlemagne (AD 768–814), Frankish and Flemish mariners used a different system of direction naming: the Teutonic monosyllabic words of *Nord, Est, Sund* and *Oëst* (North, East, South and West) for the four cardinal points. The etymological significance of these four words has long been lost, although West and East were apparently originally 'evening' and 'morning', while south may have been 'noon'. Remaining intermediate directions were designated by simple compounds of these four words. Portuguese mariners in the early sixteenth century were the first to adopt the Flemish wind names over the Italian. João de Lisboa used them exclusively in his *Trattado de navegar* (Navigational Treatise) published in 1514 and this system of named winds continues to be in use throughout the world.

The distinction between a wind-rose and a compass rose is blurred; both carry certain features in common, like the points, dividing the horizon into thirty-two equal segments. Some define the change-over from one to the other to have occured when Teutonic names for directions replaced wind names for direction, and link it with the use of the magnetic compass. Often, however, these roses did not display any names. The one thing evidence does suggest is that the difference appears to be more time related - that is, when used in conjunction with the magnetic compass – than a stylistic distinction.

As early as 1269, Pierre de Maricourt (Petrus Peregrinus) proposed dividing the wind-rose into increments of 360 degrees, but it was not until the nineteenth century that the system of wind points to mark direction was supplanted by a circle marked in degrees, to become the present-day compass card.

commercial fleets in the Mediterranean, and became the dominant force in the furtherance of all oceanic voyaging and exploration. At what precise date, and by what pathway, the magnetic compass as a navigation instrument was introduced to Christian Europe is unknown. By the second century AD the Han dynasty (200 BC–AD 220) of China was as mighty an empire in the east as that of the Roman Empire in the west. Engaging in trade, their sea-going junks sailed to India and could be seen on the Euphrates River. By the Sung (Song) Dynasty (960–1279), maritime trade expanded, and guided by the magnetic compass (with a south-pointing needle) Chinese junks were making regular voyages to all parts of the Arab world in the Indian Ocean. These links between the Arab world and China were reciprocal, and by the early part of the tenth century, Arab seafaring routes extended to Indonesia, China and Japan. There is no verification that this is how Arab mariners acquired the use of the magnetic compass, and one cannot entirely discount the possibility of it being an independent Muslim or Byzantine discovery.

From the Arab navigators it was transmitted to Christian mariners at their mutual trading ports. According to tradition, it was Flavio Gioia (fl. 1302), a citizen of Amalfi in Italy, who in 1302 invented the compass, that instrument 'without deceit or failure'. It is possible that the magnetic compass was introduced into Italy at Amalfi, or somewhere along the section of coast around the Bay of Naples, for these ports were a centre for trade with the Arab world. Its mariners were in direct contact with Arab knowledge and their use of the magnetic compass, and adopted it for their own use. However, introduction of the compass must have occured at a much earlier date than during the lifetime of Flavio Gioia. Over a period of time, improvements were most likely made on the overall design of the instrument by a number of people, until Gioia brought it to completion by attaching a compass card with a wind rose to a magnet and placing it in a box.

The English monk and scholar, Alexander Neckham (1157–1217), provides the first written record of the magnetic compass used as a guide to European seamen. In his *De Utensilibus*, written around 1180 and again in his *De naturis rerum*, Neckham relates that one of the essential items one must have aboard a ship is 'a needle placed upon a magnet, which would revolve until its point looked north, and thus guide sailors in murky weather or on a starless night'. Neither Neckham, nor any other twelfth- or thirteenth-century author who describe the magnetic compass, present it as a remarkable new discovery. This casual acceptance of the magnetic compass leads most historians to believe that it was already commonly in use from the middle of the twelfth century. Whether the compass

87. The City and Harbour of Genoa by Charles Wylde, 1673

Venice's only rival for trade in the Mediterranean was Genoa. While Venetian ships monopolized the spice trade, Genoese ships handled the silk trade through their merchant colonies in Constantinople and Kaffa. When Constantinople fell to the Turks in 1453, Genoa lost her access to the eastern markets. Rather than see that trade fall into the hands of Venice, Genoa financially backed the Portuguese in their search for an alternative sea route.

THE BRITISH LIBRARY, LONDON

88. Carte Pisane, 1291

The *Carte Pisane*, drawn sometime between AD 1275 and 1291, is the oldest extant portolan chart.

BIBLIOTHÈQUE NATIONALE DE FRANCE, PARIS

89. Mare Mediterranea by Domingo Olives, 1568

In this beautifully embellished navigation chart of the Mediterranean Sea, ownership of territories is indicated by the relevant flags. Major ports and important brading cities are shown, with Venice and Genoa given prominence. Wind roses and rhumb lines necessary for navigation are present, yet the ancient eight-wind system for direction-bearing is still retained with its personified wind gods.

THE NATIONAL LIBRARY OF FINLAND, HELSINKI

needle was given to Western sailors by an Amalfitan or any other, there is clear evidence it was in regular use during the time of the third Crusade in 1189 to recapture Jerusalem.

With the magnetic compass aboard Genoese and Venetian ships, the passage to the Levant and North Africa was markedly shortened. Seafarers no longer need follow a coastline from point to point, or wait out a winter at their destination or at some intermediate point before returning home, but could set their course directly to their destination. The saving in time allowed two round-trips a year, thus increasing the profit and the prosperity of these two city-states. By the end of the thirteenth century, their trading ships were sailing the Mediterranean safely and efficiently at all times of the year.

Genoese and Venetian voyages across the Atlantic to distant ports of northern Europe, owed their commercial success to the compass. With this instrument to guide them, upon arriving at Cape Finisterre, the rocky promontory at the northwest corner of Spain, they could safely sail directly across the Bay of Biscay to the Brittany coast of France to enter the English Channel, and thus save many miles.

That the magnetic compass pointed north was based solely on empirical evidence, which at the time was sufficient for mariners. It took another hundred years before the French mathematician and physicist, Petrus Peregrinus (Pierre de Maricourt, b. c. 1220), was able to provide a general explanation of how the compass worked. In 1600, English scientist William Gilbert (1540–1603) published his *De magnete*, which provided a basic understanding of the mechanisms of magnetism. He established that the Earth was itself a giant magnet that influenced the magnetic needle of a compass, or any other magnetic object.

As with the compass, it is difficult to determine an exact date for the emergence of a true sea chart, but it appears to be directly linked with the use of the magnetic compass. The direction-bearing arrangement displayed on the compass card was the Aristotelian eight-wind system, further divided into sixteen half-winds. This same display, as a compass-rose with the addition of radiating lines, was also drawn on charts for navigational purposes.

By the end of the thirteenth century, mariners plying the Mediterranean and eastern shore of the Atlantic had available to them written sailing instructions called *portolani* (or portolans in English). Like the periploi of ancient Greece, they contained distances and directions and gave detailed descriptions of principle harbours, coastal landmarks, depths and hazards to navigation. In these portolans directions were now given in magnetic compass bearings. There is no evidence of a continuous tradition between the periploi and the portolans of the Middle Ages, but it is hardly credible that this information which was so painstakingly accumulated and recorded over centuries of experience, should have been forgotten altogether, only to be relearned.

The earliest set of portolan sailing directions is *Lo compasso da navigare*, written about AD 1230. The word *compasso* is used here in the sense of 'circuit', going from port to port in a clockwise fashion around the Mediterranean Sea. Since *Lo compasso* was a compilation of sources, named compass bearings were given in a variety of ways: the Teutonic monosyllabic words of *Nord, Est, Sund* and *Oëst* (north, east, south and

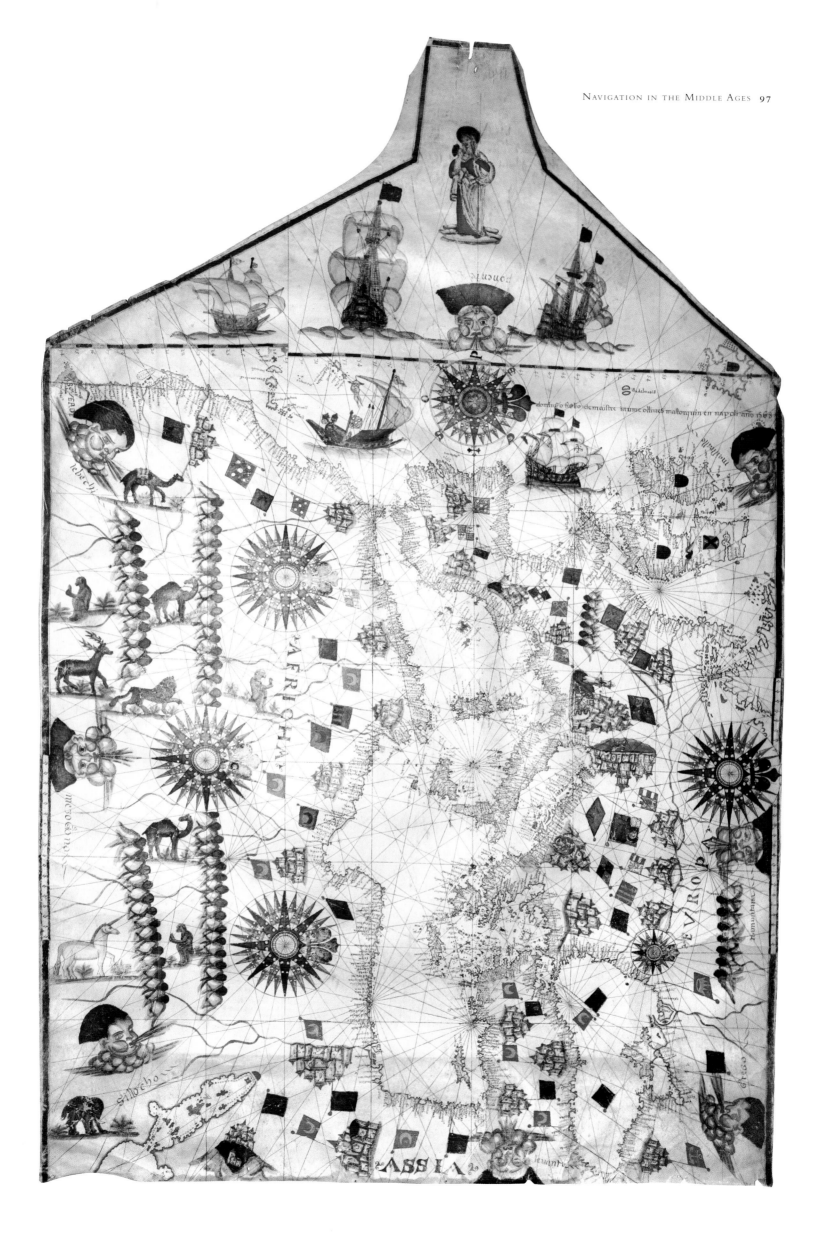

Michael of Rhodes

Michael of Rhodes, served on Venetian Trade vessels and on war galleys from 1401 to 1445. He rose from being a simple oarsman on galleys to that of *armiraio*, assistant to captain of the entire fleet, and the highest possible rank a non-noble could hold in Venetian maritime service. His voyages took him to all the major ports of the Mediterranean, eastward to Tana on the Black Sea, and westward into the Atlantic where he sailed to London and Bruges. Altogether, he made forty voyages and participated in five major sea battles, including the defense of Salonika. His name and achievements, like countless others of the time, would have been long forgotten if it were not for the manuscript he wrote in which he transcribed all the information on navigation he had accumulated throughout his career.

His 440-page document is a compendium of mariner's knowledge in the first half of the fifteenth century, composed in four major sections: mathematics, ships and shipbuilding, navigation and time reckoning. The section on navigation practices is understandably large, and invaluable for our understanding of navigation practices in late-medieval Northern Europe. Michael presents methods for recovering one's course to an intended destination when unfavourable winds blew the ship off course, working with multiple course changes, and plotting a course in advance. The mathematical technique for this, based on the trigonometry of right-angle triangles, was called marteloio, but no mathematics were required of the mariner, nor was any sea chart needed. It was necessary only to memorize a set of rules; he called this navigating 'mentally'. The direction-bearing dial Michael used was that of the eight quarter winds of the Mediterranean. In effect, his system was the same used by Polynesian navigators, with the difference being that they used the rising and setting of certain stars as their direction-bearing dial.

Included in Michael's manuscript are some of the earliest surviving portolans. These instructions written as an aid to navigation gave the distances and directions between ports, and all the local information – tides, currents, winds and landmarks – needed to safely enter them. In addition to portolans for the Mediterranean, he also included portolans for the major ports in the Atlantic between Spain and Bruges in Flanders (now Belgium).

90. Galley of Flanders at sea, 15th century

Galleys such as this, were not only used to ply the Mediterranean, but also made extended voyages out into the Atlantic to such far off ports as London and Bruges, the dominant centre of trade in Northern Europe during Michael's time. Whenever possible, sails were employed in order to lessen the workload of the oarsmen. Although the lateen sail was well suited to sailing close to the wind, it was difficult to handle in stormy weather, and unwieldy in coming about on another tack.

THE MICHAEL OF RHODES MANUSCRIPT, REPRODUCED WITH PERMISSION OF THE MICHAEL OF RHODES PROJECT

91. Square-rigged Ship

The galley, with its lateen sail, was eventually replaced by the square-rigged vessel for use in commerce. It did not require a large crew to handle it, was more manoeuvrable, and it was better suited for carrying a large cargo.

92. Lateen Sails

The triangular lateen sail has a 2000-year history of use in Europe. Adapted in the third century by the Romans from Arab mariners, it was the preferred choice of sail type in the Mediterranean Sea and parts of the Indian Ocean. The lateen sail was developed independently in Polynesia. Michael paid a great deal of attention to detail in the construction of these sails.

93. Frame Diagram

One of the earliest treatises on the methods of ship construction is provided by Michael of Rhodes in his manuscript. He covered the construction and equipping of five different kinds of vessels. The diagram here shows a stick frame, around which battens were bent to arrive at the proper curvature of the hull.

THE MICHAEL OF RHODES MANUSCRIPT, REPRODUCED WITH PERMISSION OF THE MICHAEL OF RHODES PROJECT

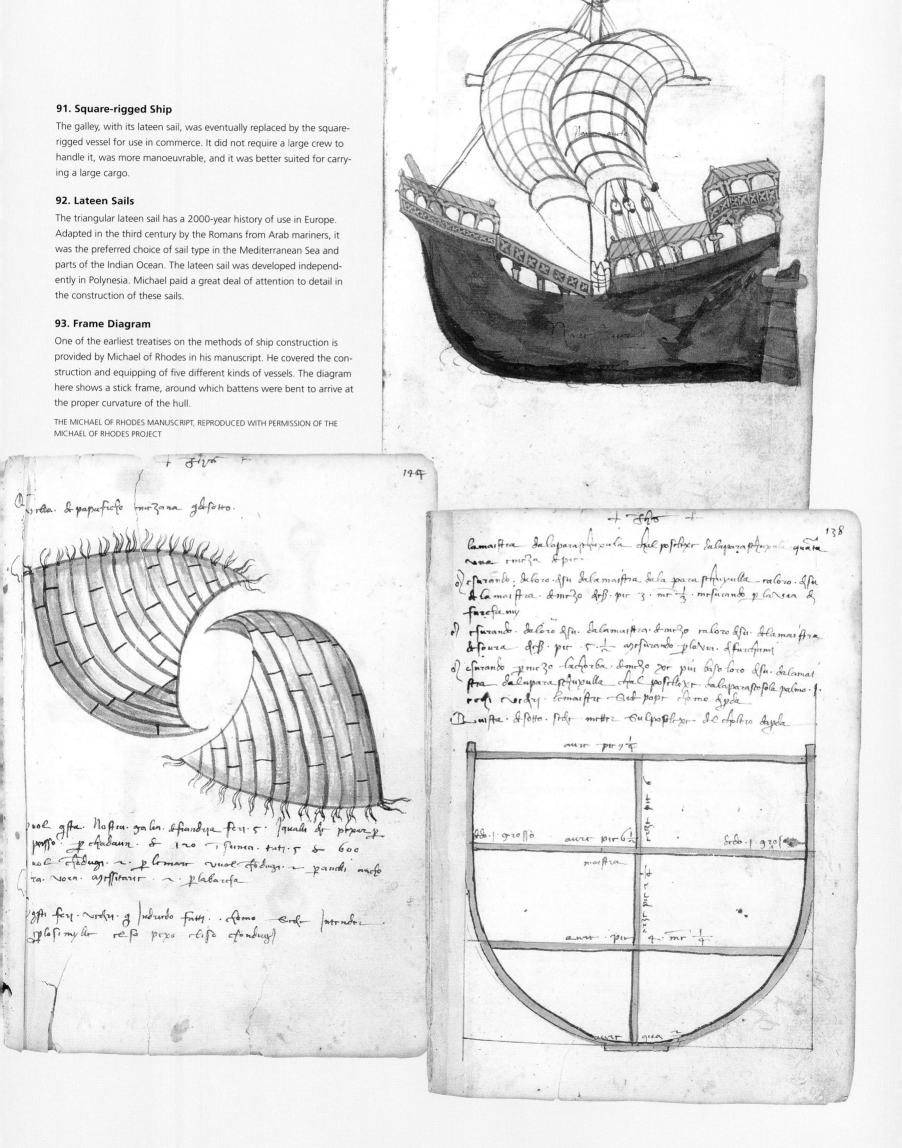

west); the older wind system names, such as Greco and Levant; and compass bearings occasionally given in divisions of quarter-winds, eighth-winds, and so forth.

A portolan chart, or a major portion thereof, existed in 1270, when King Louis IX of France, known as Saint Louis, participated in the eighth Crusade against Tunis. Twenty-five years later, in his *Arbor Scientiae* (the *Tree of Science*), the Catalan philosopher, Ramón Lull (1232–1315), stated that a *charta* is as necessary for sailors as the compass, needle and Polaris, the 'star of the sea'. The term, portolan, used for written sailing instructions, is also used for the sea chart; the two were intended as complementary documents. The earliest extant portolan chart, the *Carte Pisane*, was drawn sometime between AD 1275 and 1291, and served as the visual companion to the text in the *Compasso*.

The absence of any examples of a chart portolan earlier than the *Carte Pisane* may be attributed to their destruction through constant use, or to their being discarded when new charts with corrected and more complete information were available. Venice and Genoa were the first known centres of portolan production. The maker and place of origin of the *Carte Pisane* is unknown, but most scholars believe it originated in Genoa, although its name derives from the fact that is was found in Pisa, where it was owned by a Pisan family. That it was the result of a piecing together of earlier charts

from different authors is evident from the different degrees of geographical accuracy found in different regions, the different languages used and a variation in toponymic vocabularies.

The look of portolan charts is in startling contrast to the theoretical and schematic maps of classical antiquity, and to the theological maps of the early Middle Ages. Here is an easily recognizable physical geography we can relate to, with coastlines of countries scarcely different from that on present-day maps.

The portolan chart differed from all previous charts in that it was based on knowledge gained by sailing experience, and displayed a continuous improvement in cartographic technique. Ptolemy's overestimation of the linear extension of the Mediterranean basin in an east-west direction, by one-third, is corrected in the *Carte Pisane* to within one-percent of its true length.

Since the portolan was created for navigation purposes, intended for the very practical purpose of getting from one port to another, depiction of land is confined to that thin strip at the edge of the sea, containing harbours, important ports and seaside towns with an established trade. The interior is left blank; only those features of land visible from the sea, such as headlands and prominent features necessary to correctly identify a landfall, are depicted. The shoreline fairly bristles with names of all the harbours, towns and practical features; those of greater importance are written in red instead of the cus-

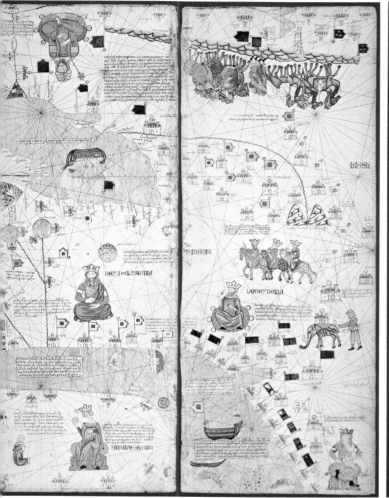

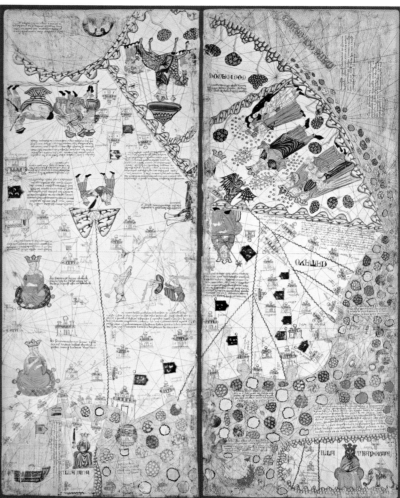

94. Mappemundi by Abraham Cresques, 1375

On Abraham Cresques' map of the world, nine monarchs are depicted who reign in countries outside of Europe – each crowned, enthroned and holding a sceptre. In the centre of the Sahara desert of Africa a black king, the 'The Lord of Guinea', is seated, holding a large nugget of gold in his hand. Prince Henry the Navigator promoted Portuguese voyages to reach the source of this gold directly by sea, down the west coast of Africa.

JUHA NURMINEN COLLECTION

95. Khios and adjacent mainland by Bartolomeo dalli Sonetti, 1485

The first printed sea chart was an Isolario – Island-book – compiled by a fifteenth century Venetian sailor, Bartolommeo Zamberti. Having written the navigational text in the form of sonnets, he took on the name of Bartolomeo dalli Sonetti. Shown in the colour woodcut here is the island of Khios, with part of the mainland of Greece. Direction-bearing is provided by an eight-wind system, named after the lands from which the winds blew.

NATIONAL MARITIME MUSEUM, LONDON

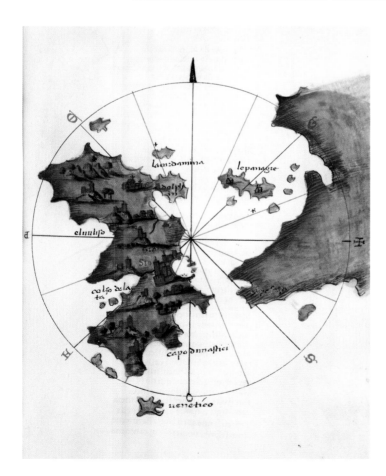

tomary black. Many portolan charts also showed the eastern Viking routes through the river system of present-day Russia. Ownership of territories and ports is indicated by painted flags, or by the particular emblem or symbol of the sovereign.

The portolan chart is oriented with north at the top, indicating its intended usage and inter-relationship with the magnetic compass. Lacking is any rectilinear grid of longitude or latitude lines, or *climata* divisions. In their stead, the chart is covered

**96. 16th-century manuscript showing
the teaching of astronomy using an astrolabe**

From the ninth to the eleventh centuries, Muslim scientists and mathematicians
dominated the field of astronomy. They corrected the measurements of coordinates for stars made by Ptolemy, and refined the complex motions of the stars and
planets he proposed in his *Almagest*. Their calculations, transmitted through Latin
translations, started a scientific reawakening in Europe. Among those influenced
by their Islamic predecessors were Alfonso X, Regiomontanus, Copernicus and
Tycho Brahe. As the most important instrument for these astronomical studies,
the astrolabe occupies a prominent position in this image.

© COURTESY OF UNIVERSITY LIBRARY ISTANBUL / MUSLIM HERITAGE.COM

**97. Astrolabe with Geared Calendar by
Muhammad b. Abi Bakr, 1222**

In the twelfth century, interest was shown in devising more accurate methods for
using the planispheric astrolabe to determine latitude, and some intriguing possibilities were presented for using it to establish longitude.

MUSEUM OF THE HISTORY OF SCIENCE, UNIVERSITY OF OXFORD

Opposite
98. Astrolabe by Jacques de Vaulx, 1583

The planispheric astrolabe, stripped of all but the essential parts needed for
determining the altitude of a celestial body, was transformed into the mariner's,
or sea astrolabe. No longer tied to astrological and surveying purposes, it became
the navigator's chief instrument for determining latitude.

BIBLIOTHÈQUE NATIONALE DE FRANCE, PARIS

with an inter-lacing pattern of lines radiating from one or more
nodal points of 'compass roses'. These compass roses did not
divide the horizon into degrees of arc, as on today's compass,
but represented the Aristotelian eight-wind system, further divided into sixteen half-winds. The mariner used the lines, called
rhumb lines or loxodromes, radiating from the compass rose, to
help project their ship's course. No grid system was required, for
with only a ruler, a pair of dividers and a compass the navigator
could plot a course and arrive at his intended destination.

As the number of voyages increased, aided by portolans, new
information was provided that improved their accuracy and
detail, and stimulated further voyaging, all of which created
a marked demand for charts. Soon there were major cartographic workshops in the Catalan towns of Palma de Majorca,
Barcelona and later, Valencia. All the defining characteristics of
the *Carte Pisane* were continued as the basic plan for the many
portolan charts that followed.

With the shift of chart making from Genoa and Venice to
Catalonia, portolan charts correspondingly changed in appearance. They became more elaborate in design and more
lavish in the use of colour and decorative embellishment.
Although still primarily intended for navigational purposes,
the interior land space, once empty, came to be filled with
illustrations of cities, geographic features, extensive legends
and portraits of rulers. As a wealth of new information about
the world poured forth from extensive trade voyages and
from the journals of world travellers and missionaries to
China, Catalonian cartographers portrayed an increasingly

aniere·de·treũer·Combien·

lon sera eslongé De la ligne Equinoctialle en chacun lieu Par lastralabe ordinaire
Sellon la declinaison que le solleil faict chacun jour de lan entre ses deux Tropicques

Le solleil decline entre les tropicques chacun ay passant par les 12 signes 47 degrez & minuttes
ET en faisant ceste declinaison Il passe deux fois par la ligne equinoctialle Donc est a entendre
que depuis le 21e Jour de mars Jusqua au 24 Jour de septembre le solleil est deuers le nord
de ladicte ligne equinoctialle ET depuis le 24e Jour de septembre Jusqua aus 22 Jour de mars les Solleil est de la part du su dicette ligne
Dont sellon la partie australle ou septentrionalle ou le solleil est de lad ligne equinoctialle lon y puist prendre son esleuation et treuer la
haulteur que chacun lieu est long de lad ligne equinoctialle en la maniere qui ensuict par lastralabe ordinaire aux pillottes Dont sensuict la figure

·1583·

Pour bien sçauoir treuer Par la presente figure de lastralabe ordinaire la haulteur ou eslongnement que chacun lieu
est long de la ligne equinoctialle Premierement Il conuient sçauoir en quelle part le solleil faict sa declinaison
de la ligne equinoctialle sçauoir sil est en la partye du su ou en la partye du nord dicelle ligne / pour lors / cest...

Quand le solleil est deuers le nord de la ligne equinoctialle ET Il vous faict ombre au nort voyez a lesleuation
que vous trouuez a vostre astralabe combien Il sen fault quil ny aye 90 ET auec ce qui se en faultra vous adiousterez les degrez que le solleil
tient de declinaison en ce jour ET letout mis ensemble autant estes long de la ligne equinoctialle de la bande du nort

Et sy au mesme temps que le solleil est deuers le nort audict equinoctial cest vous faict ombre deuers le su vous adiousterez la declinaison du so
aues lesleuation que vous trouuerez au solleil ET sy letout mis ensemble passent 90 Ce qui passera autant estes long de la ligne verale
nord ET sy lesleuation et la declinaison ne font 90 autant estes long de la ligne en la bande du su ET sy la haulteur et la declinaison
font Justement 90 Vous serez en la ligne Æquinoctialle

Touttes les fois que vous trouuerez a vostre astralabe que le solleil sera esleue 90 que vous naurez ombre de costé ny daultre cest a
dire que le solleil sera droit a vostre zemis sus vostre teste Regardez de quelle part cest que le solleil faict sa declinaison de lequinoctial ET autant
serez long dudit equinoctial au costé ou sera le solleil come Il y aura en ce jo de declinaison Soit de la part du nort ou de la part du su

Arab Dhow

During the Middle Ages the Arabs ruled the sealanes of the Indian Ocean until the European arrival in the fifteenth century. Their trade reached as far as China, India and the spice islands of Indonesia. In the wintertime the monsoon winds blew from the northeast, taking the ships towards the East African coast and in the summer the wind came from the southwest taking the ships to Arabia and India. On the Indian Malabar Coast the vessels loaded wood, in Africa they loaded wood, ivory and slaves. In the tales of a *Thousand and One Nights*, stories about Sinbad the Seafarer are thought to be based upon the Arabs' voyages from the Persian Gulf to China. A roundtrip to China took some one and a half years and the vessels brought back, among other things, silk and spices. By the eight-century the Arabian language and science, and the Islamic faith, were very widely spread.

The Arabs were the masters of the seas, experienced navigators, meteorologists and geographers. They believed that the Earth was round and that there were three continents: Asia, Africa and Europe. They adapted Ptolemy's system to include the latitudes and longitudes on the charts. These maps were often kept secret from other captains because the competition was fierce on the trade routes. No later than the thirteenth century they started to use the magnetic compass and they had much more experience than the contemporary Europeans. The Arabs did not apply their skills on voyages of discovery because in their opinion they could not gain any real economic benefits from them – there were riches much closer. They were also superstitious about the southern oceans and regarded the South Atlantic as a scary 'green sea of darkness', where monsters lurked in the depth.

The shipbuilding skills of the people in the Middle East and North Africa have their roots in the wooden and reed rafts in the ancient civilizations of Egypt and Mesopotamia. We don't know much about ancient and medieval Arabic boats as no wrecks have been found. It was European seafarers who gave the name *dhow* to the vessels they later found in the Indian Ocean, the Arabs themselves called them just 'sailing ships'. The traditional Arabic dhow is still used in the Indian Ocean.

There are more than 200 names for different types of dhows, including boom, sanbuq, zaruq and baghlah. Rather than following the European practice of designating vessels by the number of masts and the layout of rigging and sails, dhow names derive mainly from differences in hull shapes and sizes, but also from the intended usage. The hulls were always carvel built. In the Middle Ages teak and coconut-palm wood were used for the hull and the masts. Unlike the Europeans, the Arabs did not use wooden treenails or iron nails. They assembled the side planks by sewing with greased or waxed coconut fibres. The chinks between the planks were then tightly caulked. Towards the end of the fifteenth century they also started to use nails. These vessels were built to sail in the Indian Ocean and the Arabic Sea, where light and manoeuvrable ships were needed.

In the Middle Ages large Arabic freighters, sailing in convoys, traded alongside smaller and more traditional vessels on the Mediterranean. Most of the bulk cargoes were loaded into barges and towed after the ships. For trading on the oceans the Arabs used two main vessel types.

The boom was apparently the older and more traditional vessel. It was single decked with a large cargo hold, the bow and the stern were pointed, it was equipped with a rudder and had two lateen sails.

In the seventeenth and eighteenth centuries the majestic two-masted *baghlah* started appearing on the seas. This 40 m-long ship with a transom stern had a superstructure aft with windows and a decorated gallery. It is probable that European merchant vessels affected the design and the decorations. A crew of more than 20 men operated it, and it could be armed with guns.

The triangular lateen sail was common on all Arabic ships, as it was better for windward sailing than the square sail. It was carried on an oblique yard, running parallel to the keel of the ship, and was called a lateen sail by northern Europeans who only encoun-

tered them in the latin Mediterranean, but it is possible the name comes from the Arabic words '*alla trina*', meaning triangular. It is not known when the lateen sail was developed or if its origin is even Arabic. However, the Arabs brought it to the Mediterranean, where it was the only design from the ninth until the thirteenth century, when the Northern Europeans re-introduced the square sail. Most likely it has its origin in the Red Sea, where passages often had to be made against headwinds. It was also a good sail in the monsoon winds on the long trading routes of the Indian Ocean.

100. Arab Dhow

The dhow is a traditional Arab sailing ship, which still is in use on the Indian Ocean. The designation is used for several types of one- or two-mast sailing ships. They differ from European ships in the hull construction method and use of the lateen sail. All Arab ships have the triangular sail in common, it enabled better sailing capability than a square sail in following wind. All Arab ships have in common the triangular sail, which enabled them to sail better to windward.

99. Arab dhows in the harbour of Aden by Björn Landström, 1961

COURTESY OF OLOF LANDSTRÖM

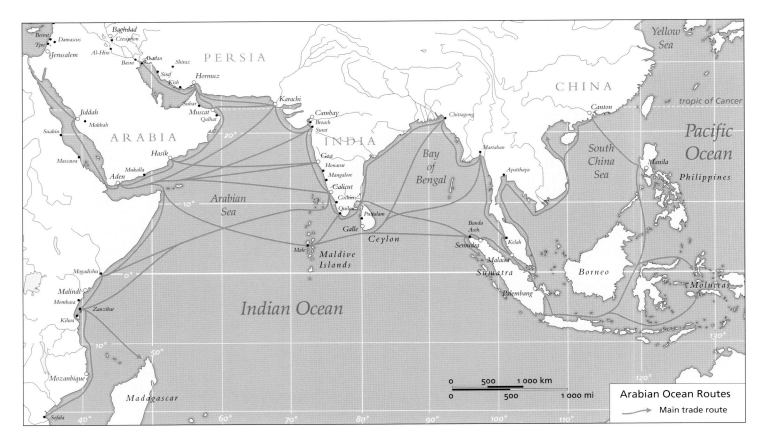

101. Arab Ocean Trade Routes

Maritime traffic in the Indian Ocean, principally in the trade of spices and aromatic products, tied together a vast geographic region ranging from China and Southeast Asia to the east coast of Africa. Arab control of trade was taken over by the Portuguese upon their arrival in the Indian Ocean at the beginning of the sixteenth century. By the mid-sixteenth century, Portuguese control of the sealanes and trade weakened, to be replaced by French and English domination.

realistic depiction of the world into the traditional framework of the portolan.

The most famous Catalonian cartographer was Abraham Cresques (d. 1387), from a Jewish family of cartographers and instrument makers who had been established for generations in Majorca. Charles V of France commissioned Cresques to produce an 'atlas' of the world containing the latest information. This atlas, called the Catalan Atlas and dated 1375, was given the title *Mappamundi, that is to say, Image of the World and of the Regions which are of the Earth and of the Various kinds of Peoples which Inhabit it* – which clearly expresses its all-encompassing content. Its basic form is that of the portolan chart, with compass roses, loxodromes, and named port and coastal cities. But it also incorporated the latest geographic information in Marco Polo's *Description of the World*, and in the written account, *Description of Eastern Regions*, by Oderic of Pordenone, an Italian monk who journeyed throughout the greater part of Asia between 1316 and 1330. For the first time, the continent of Asia assumes a recognizable form, filled with explanatory texts on the customs of the people and its economic resources.

Although the Catalan Atlas was intended as a lavish showpiece and not for practical use by navigators, it had a profound effect on the history of navigation for it would stimulate later Portuguese monarchs to search for a sea-route around Africa, and eastward to the coasts of India and *Catayo* (China) seek-

ing the treasures of the fabulous empire of the great Kublai Khan. It also prompted Christopher Columbus to seek the same lands by sailing westward.

Portolan charts were sufficiently accurate for navigation within the limited region of the Mediterranean and Atlantic shores of northwestern Europe and Africa, and continued to be used for three centuries. They did not have to deal with the problem of transformation of a curved surface onto a flat plane since the area represented was small enough to be relatively free of distortion. But as mariners extended their voyages farther out into the Atlantic, and cartographers attempted to make the portolan cover a larger area, their usefulness diminished. Without a consistent and mathematically based projection, the topography became distorted.

The shortcomings of the portolan chart are insignificant considering their importance as the first true sea chart, designed expressly for the navigator. From these beginnings evolved our present-day nautical chart. And the written portolan, with its possible origin in some Byzantine peripli, such as the *Stadiasmus maris magni* (Measurement in stades of the Great Sea) originally drawn up perhaps as early as the third or fourth century, is the ancestor of today's pilot books.

Movable-type printing transformed chart making from the earlier manuscript charts and introduced a variation on the portolan chart called an *Isolario* (Island book). Colour woodcuts in these printed books accompanied the written text of navigation instructions. As its name, island book, implies, the woodcut charts generally covered islands in the Mediterranean, and were produced mainly by Italian map-makers.

Before engraving became the predominant technique for printed maps, woodcuts were the popular medium. They lacked the ability to show the subject in any great detail, but had the great advantage over manuscript maps in the ease with which they could be faithfully reproduced, and widely disseminated. Within its restricted geographical area, *Isolarii* depicted all relevant detail for the navigator, including harbors, habitations and some topographical detail, upon which a direction-bearing dial was overlaid.

…with compass to the wind I have stepped repeatedly
upon each isle its ports and bays, its rocks both bare and filled with
growth, and with a stylus marked their true position on a chart.
BARTOLOMEO DALLI SONETTI

During the last half of the sixteenth century, Italy's lead in chart-making, for a variety of historical and commercial reasons, waned, to be replaced by States in the Low Countries.

ARAB SCIENCE SPREADS NORTHWARD

By the end of the sixth century the Byzantine Empire included Syria, present-day Turkey/Anatolia, Egypt, and all other lands bordering the eastern Mediterranean. Its ports controlled the Mediterranean trade routes, where goods from the Far East were brought, bartered, and further transported to Europe. In the years following Alexander the Great's founding of the city of Alexandria in Egypt in 331 BC, Greek colonization made it the cultural and scientific pole of the Greek World. Its most gifted scholars were to be found in its institutions, and its library contained the wisdom of the ages. Greek colonies in Greater Syria, with its major trading centres at Damascus, Antioch and Palmyra, made Syria virtually a Near Eastern Hellenism.

Arab traders reached Alexandria by way of the Red Sea, where in its institutions they gained knowledge of Greek astronomy and nautical science. When Syria was conquered by the Arabs in AD 636, it gave them direct access not only to the works of its Greek heritage, but also to those of the Persian Empire to the east of Syria. From these Greek colonies scientific knowledge was transferred to the Arabic world, either through direct translation from the original Greek works, or through intermediate Syrian and Hebrew translations.

Drawing upon prior Greek, Indian and Persian knowledge, mathematical science and astronomy emerged in the Arab world. A library of Greek works, including Ptolemy's *Geographia*, Euclid and Archimedes, were collected and translated into Arabic. When al-Ma'mun became Caliph (AD 813–833) of an Islamic empire that stretched from Mesopotamia to India, he founded an academy in Baghdad called the House of Wisdom. There, Greek philosophical and scientific works were translated, and an observatory set up for Muslim astronomers. Amongst its notable scholars was al-Khwārizmī, who wrote works on the astrolabe, sundial and the calendar. Through his work, and that of others, a greater number of observations were made of latitude and estimated longitude for principle cities, mountains, rivers, and other important geographic sites. This led to cartographic improvements, particularly in Islamic Africa and the Near East.

For taking astronomical observations, the astrolabe has a history of over two thousand years, making it perhaps the oldest scientific instrument in the world. This record is all the more remarkable in that the astrolabe is a complicated and sophisticated device capable of solving a multitude of problems in positional astronomy. Its name comes from a Greek word, meaning literally 'taking of the stars'. In effect, the astrolabe projects the three-dimensional celestial sphere onto a two-dimensional plane or flat surface. With the proper combination of its moveable plates and alignment of a superficial fretwork called the *rete*, all problems in spherical geometry can be solved, making the astrolabe invaluable for determining the position of celestial bodies, the Sun, Moon, stars, and planets. It could also be used to find the time during the day or night, and to calculate the time of celestial events such as sunrise and sunset.

Some credit Hipparchus with inventing the astrolabe, but since no instrument from this period exists, it would perhaps be better to credit him with devising the theory and principle of the astrolabe. Nearly four centuries later, Ptolemy, the greatest of all astronomers and geographers of classical antiquity, built on the work of Hipparchus. In his *Planisphaerium*, Ptolemy provided the mathematical basis for the stereographic projection used in the planispheric astrolabe. And early in the fifth century, Synesius of Cyrene constructed an astrolabe.

Arabic treatises on the astrolabe found their way through North Africa into Spain with the Islamic conquests of the eighth and ninth centuries. From there it spread to Latin European culture through Christian monasteries in northern Spain.

While the date of the oldest European astrolabe is controversial, its origin in Catalonia about AD 1000 appears plausible to many scholars. Through numerous treatises, knowledge of the astrolabe grew quickly in the Latin West during the eleventh century. Walcher of Malvern in England is known to have constructed an astrolabe in 1092. Ascelin of Augsburg and Hermanus Contractus, the polymath monk of Reichenau, wrote treatises on the astrolabe (*Mensura Astrolabi*). Initially, these treatises were merely direct translations from the Arabic into Latin, and dealt with the simple issues of construction and use of the astrolabe. By the mid-twelfth century a thorough knowledge of the astrolabe prevailed in Christian Europe, and by the end of the century virtually all of the Arabic science of astronomy and mathematics had been assimilated.

In the late Middle Ages the astrolabe also served as an educational tool to promote the study of science. Geoffrey Chaucer, best known for his *Canterbury Tales*, wrote a treatise in 1391 on the astrolabe for Lewis Clifford, the eleven-year-old son of a friend. Chaucer considered the astrolabe to be the most admirable tool for teaching science and mathematics; in consideration of the youth of his audience, he kept the text 'full light reules and naked wordes in English'.

The planispheric astrolabe, requiring as it did a different plate for each latitude, was too complicated for navigational purposes. This system was improved with the development of the Uni-

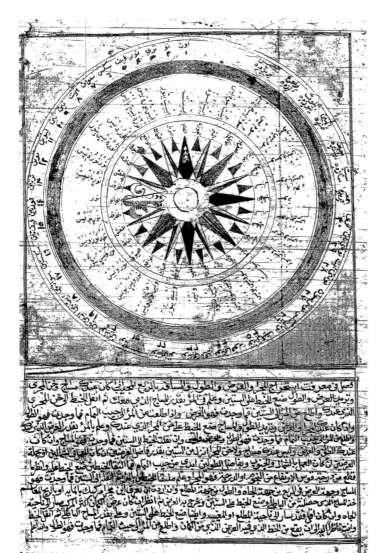

102. Arab compass

An Arab compass card with its thirty-two rhumbs, designated by the rising or setting of selected stars on the horizon, is shown in this late Ottoman manuscript. Arab navigators did not use the fleur-de-lis to designate north. Instead, the North Star (*Jaʿh*) and the South Pole (*Qutb*) divided the compass card into an eastern and western half. The stars or constellations used for the remaining thirty rhumbs were: *Ursa Minor, Ursa Major, Cassiopeia, Capella, Vega, Arcturus, Pleiades, Altair, Orion, Sirius, Scorpius, Antares, Centaur, Canopus and Archernar.*

ILLUSTRATION COURTESY OF THE AMERICAN RESEACH CENTER IN EGYPT, INC.

103. Kamal (latitude hook)

Each knot tied in the string of the *kamāl* when used in conjunction with the moveable board, was the measure of an angle between the horizon and a celestial body. The target star most often used was *Polaris*, for its height above the horizon was independent of time.

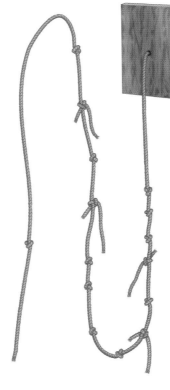

versal astrolabe equipped with a single plate that could be used at any location. This extended its use in marine navigation, but with limited success; to accommodate the increased amount of information, and still retain accuracy, the instrument had to be made larger, and thus became heavier. All that mariners needed in order to determine latitude at sea was the ability to measure the altitude of a celestial body – the Sun, or stars.

To facilitate this task the planispheric astrolabe was simplified by removing all its plates with astronomical information engraved on them, leaving only the circular main body and a rotating bar, called the alidade, with two pinhole sighting vanes. The celestial body was viewed through these openings and the altitude read off a scale on the circumference of the instrument. To keep this modified astrolabe level and steady while taking measurements on the ever-shifting deck of a ship, it was made heavier, weighted at the bottom, and had an articulated ring added at the top by which it could be held. These improvements made it more functional at sea, and thus it was called a sea astrolabe or mariner's astrolabe. The names of those places and ports for which latitude had already been ascertained, were written directly on the scale of the sea astrolabe, thus eliminating the need to read degrees of altitude and to correlate them with latitude.

The earliest known use of this new type of astrolabe was by Diogo d'Azambuja during a voyage down the west coast of Africa in 1481. Bartolomeu Dias (c. 1450–1500) used astrolabes on his voyage of 1487–88, as did Vasco da Gama on his voyage in 1497 when he sailed all the way to Calicut, India. Columbus attempted to use the astrolabe on the return leg of his first voyage started in 1492. William Barentsz (1550–1597), in his epic voyages in far northern latitudes at the very end of the sixteenth century, used the sea astrolabe, as well as the cross-staff, to determine his latitude.

Through the introduction of scientific learning from the Arabic world, where the cosmography of the ancients had been assimilated, and practical applications of its science had developed, navigational techniques in Western Europe were dramatically accelerated.

INDIAN OCEAN - THE SILK ROAD'S WATERY PATH

And He it is who appointed the stars to you,
that you might guide yourselves by them
through the darkness of land and sea

THE QUR'AN, SURA VI, VERSE 97

The communications established between Islamic and Christian scholars had little parallel amongst practical seamen of the two communities, who were in effect still at war. The common fate of Christians who fell into the hands of Islamic seamen was slavery, often reduced to pulling an oar in a galley, and the fate of Muslim seamen who strayed into Christian territory was little different. Thus it happened that Muslim navigators made use of the techniques of astronavigation for centuries before they were established in Christendom. An extensive literature on Arab navigation practices already existed in the tenth century, but it is from the writings of a fifteenth-century Red Sea and Arabian Sea pilot, Ahmad Ibn Mājid (c. 1432–1535) that most of our information comes. Ibn Mājid wrote nearly forty treatises on navigation, the *Fawā'id,* a treatise in verse, and a prose work, the *Hāwīa,* dealing with the Indian Ocean.

As early as 2000 BC, ships from Arabia departed from the Red Sea and traversed the Indian Ocean to the Malabar Coast of India, sprinkling its shores with their trading colonies. By AD 700 Arab traders extended their markets to Ceylon, Canton, Cochin China, and as far east as Korea.

Some of the Arab sailing routes were coastal, and the shore could be followed until the desired port was reached; these routes called for the least technical navigational skills, but required local knowledge of landmarks and other visible signs. If a direct route were chosen from port to port across open water, navigators in the Indian Ocean had to possess a thorough knowledge of the monsoon winds. They determined the route to be taken, the seasonal timings of the voyages and the duration of the voyage. All navigational theory was useless without practical information about the winds that propelled the ship. Every Arab navigator knew the dates of the monsoons, with their change in wind direction and currents, and which were the most favourable for his intended voyage.

Offshore sailing out of sight of landmarks was more difficult, requiring knowledge of celestial navigation and the use of the compass. When a course change was necessary part way across open water, the navigator would follow the appropriate rhumb line from his starting point until he reached the latitude of his destination, then he maintained his course on that latitude. This is the same technique later used by mariners in northern waters, where it is called latitude sailing, or running your easting (or westing) down.

The magnetic compass is not mentioned in Muslim literature until AD 1232, but its use by Arabs goes back to the tenth century, as mentioned by the French theologian and orientalist, Eusèbus Renaudot, and possibly even earlier. That it was the same magnetic compass introduced later into Europe is evident from its name *ibra,* which literally means needle. Arab navigators were aware that the needle did not point to true or geographic north due to the effect of magnetic variation, but attributed this to defects in the needle, its mounting in the compass box, or to a faulty reading by the helmsman.

As with its northern counterpart, the Arab Indian Ocean compass card (*dīra*) was divided into thirty-two points, from which a rhumb line (*khan*) could be projected outward. Where the two cards differed was the reference used for direction. In Mediterranean and northern waters, winds, and the direction from which they blew, pointed the way on compass cards and charts.

The Arab compass card instead used the points on the horizon where selected stars set or rose. Navigational treatises, however, emphasized the need for navigators not to rely uncritically on the position of the stars as marked on the compass card, for they were only set on the rhumbs in approximate positions.

In their navigation of the Red Sea and Indian Ocean, Arab navigators took observations of the stars to determine their latitude, and as a guide to setting their course. *Polaris* was the star most frequently used to determine latitude, but when it was not available, the altitude of other stars was taken. Arab navigators had as many as six or seven basic methods to determine latitude from the stars, and were able to determine latitude from the relative position of stars or constellations, such as the Southern Cross, to one another. Ahmad Ibn Mājid claimed 'he knew seventy different ways of measuring, using nearly every bright star in the sky.' Until the arrival of the Portuguese in the Indian Ocean, Arab navigators did not use the Sun's meridian passage to determine latitude; in the Indian Ocean the Sun is almost directly overhead, making it difficult to determine the moment of meridian passage, and to measure its height.

The system of dividing the circle into 360° that the Greeks and Romans had adopted from Mesopotamia, was certainly known by Arab astronomers and authors of navigation treatises. But until Arab navigators adopted the western system, brought to them by the Portuguese, the unit they used instead of the degree was the *issabah,* literally meaning 'finger'. When the hand was held at arm's length, the finger subtended an angle of roughly 1.6°. Thus there were 224 *isba* in a circle. The *isba* was further divided into eight parts, each called a *zām.*

It is commonly believed the navigational instrument used by Arab sailors was the *kamāl,* which gauged the altitude of *Polaris,* or any other useful reference star, above the horizon. It consisted of a rectangular piece of horn or wood with a length of string extending from its centre. Knots tied along the length of the string provided the altitude scale, and corresponded to the appropriate latitude. With one end of the string held in the teeth (or brought up to the eye) at the appropriate knot, and by keeping the lower edge of the board on the horizon while its upper edge touched the desired star, the navigator knew he was at the proper latitude. In an alternate version of the *kamāl* the board was moved along the length of string to the appropriate knot. The knots on the string were at irregular intervals, dependent on the home and destination ports frequently visited. Later, Arab navigators created a measured scale, with each knot placed at an interval of one *issabah.*

Rather than finding location at sea, the *kamāl* was used to know when the appropriate latitude was reached; thereafter, by maintaining an east-west course, the desired destination would be reached. In short, it was a method for latitude sailing.

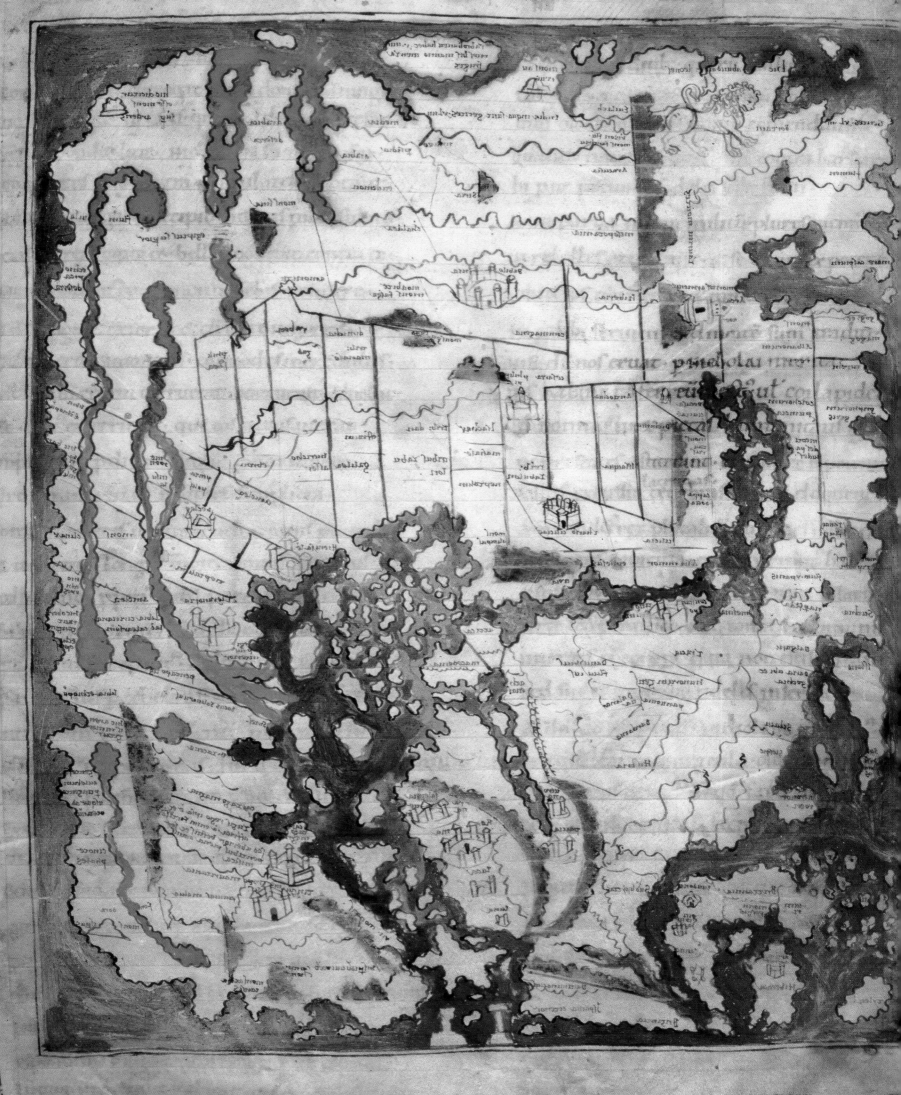

EARLY NAVIGATION
IN NORTHERN WATERS

Parallel to the story of navigation in the Mediterranean and Indian Oceans was the navigational experience of the far north of Europe. From the sixth century onward, seamen from England and Scandinavia sailed the eastern shores of the Atlantic seeking new lands to conquer or those that were better suited to habitation. Irish monks left their homeland and sailed north to the western shores of Scotland to establish monasteries of solitude and learning, and to promulgate the Christian faith. They extended their voyages to the archipelago groups still farther north, and by the eighth century reached Iceland. Norsemen in their larger and more seaworthy craft sailed still farther west to Greenland and the New World.

KING ARTHUR OF ENGLAND

It is difficult to separate fact from fiction in the accounts of the earliest voyages in northern waters. One of the first, which may be no more than fable but still contains a degree of historical value, is that of King Arthur's naval conquests. The record of Arthur's naval expedition comes almost exclusively from *Historia regum Britanniae* (The History of the Kings of Britain) completed in 1138 by Galfridus Monumetensis, commonly known as Geoffrey of Monmouth (d. 1155). According to this account, Arthur was

104. Mappa Cottoniana, 11th century

The Anglo-Saxon, or Cottoniana, World Map of the eleventh century is the first to depict the island of Iceland. The author of this map has utilized early sources of geography to which he has added information brought back from Norse discoveries and migrations. The map is oriented with east at the top, and Iceland can be seen in the lower left-hand corner. Island archipelagos north of Britain are shown east of Iceland.

THE BRITISH LIBRARY, LONDON

not contented with his kingdom, which he felt was too little for him, and proceeded to subdue 'all Scantia, which is now called Norway, and all those islands appertaining to Norway,' namely Iceland, Greenland, Sweveland, Gotland, Denmark, and 'many other islands beyond Norway, even under the North Pole.' The Kingdom of Britain supposedly extended from Greenland in the west to Lapland at the border of Russia in the east, south to Gaul, and north to the islands under the pole.

One who did not believe in King Arthur's voyages, and his population of Greenland with Britons, was Thomas Blundeville in his very popular *Eight Treatises on Navigation* (1561). 'In my opinion,' he says, 'these are mere fables.' Blundeville declared that those places were more suitable as dwelling places for whales and monstrous fishes than for men – especially English men little used to severe winters. 'If anyone should best do it,' he continues, 'me thinketh that the people of Finmarke [north-easternmost corner of present-day Norway] and Wardhouse [modern town of Vardö], or such like people bordering on the North Seas, should best doe it.'

Though their authenticity may be disputed, the voyages of King Arthur nonetheless influenced England's maritime future. Dr John Dee (1527–1608), mathematician, scientist and advisor to Queen Elizabeth I of England, made Arthur's conquest and annexation of lands beyond the British Isles the basis of England's challenge to Spain's claim to the Atlantic. He felt that Britain should not be faint-hearted, afraid, or shrink from enjoying 'so manifest right and possession of our sea-limits.' The voyages of King Arthur became firmly fixed as Britain's patrimony. Texts from Monumetensis's *History of the British Kings* are recorded in Richard Hakluyt's *The Principal Navigations Voyages Traffiques & Discoveries of the English Nation* (1589), and the great cartographer, Gerard Mercator, mentions the voyages of King Arthur four times in his 1577 letter to Dr John Dee.

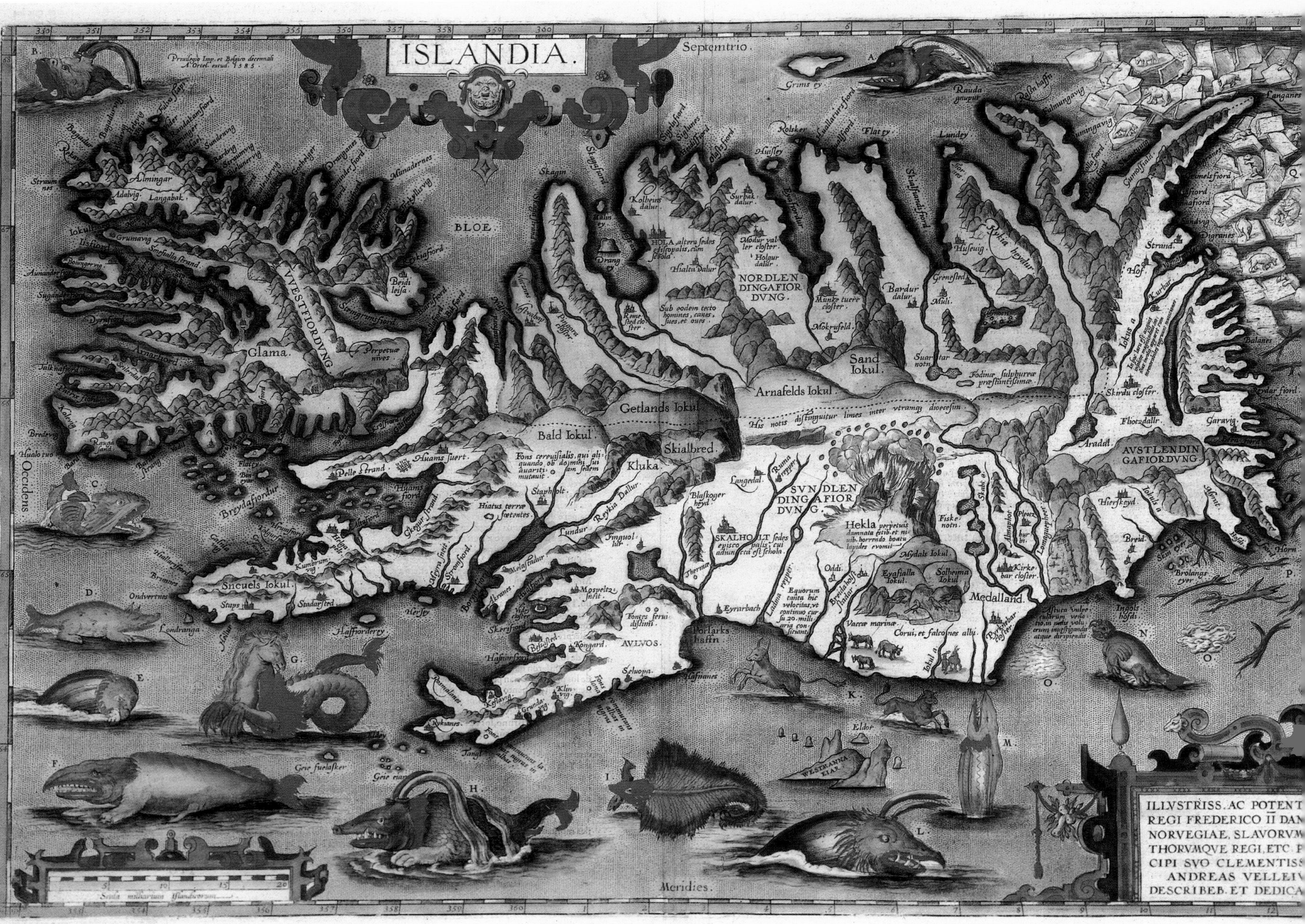

105. Islandia by Abraham Ortelius and Andreas Velleius, 1590

The numerous fantastic denizens of the deep that surround Iceland in this late sixteenth-century map give a false notion about its geographic realism, for the island's topography is well depicted. Its most famous volcano, Mount Hekla, with a centuries-long history of volcanic activity, is prominently shown. Saint Brendan pronounced Mount Hekla to be 'the gates of Hell.' When the island of Surtsey first erupted off the south coast of Iceland in 1963, the name first proposed for it was that of Brendan. Instead, it was named after the fire giant, *Surtur*, of Norse mythology. Visible in the sea east of the island, is timber that has floated all the way from Siberian rivers.

JUHA NURMINEN COLLECTION

AGE OF THE SAINTS

[We] the Uí Chorra of Connaught
Without fear against banks of billows,
Over the gravel of the mightily-roaring sea
For knowledge of the wonderful folk,
In a boat lasting, blessed, on a course satisfying, firm
We went on our pilgrimage
At the blast of the whistling wind.

IMMRAM CURAIG UÍ CHORRA

Saint Brendan

Ireland's sea-voyage stories called *Immrama* are northern counterparts to Homer's epic story of the adventures of Odysseus, and of Virgil's account of the escape of Aeneas from Troy to become the mythic founder of Rome. In Ireland's ancient Celtic past, legendary chieftains and clerics left their land to sail the foam-flecked sea in quest of some distant island that lay just beyond the edge of human experience. Their voyages are a combination of allegory and mysticism, upon which is overlaid a strong atmosphere of Christianity.

These wanderers stray among magic islands of the Otherworld with strange and wondrous attributes. There is always an island where birds speak to them, an island containing a very ancient and wise man, an island of fire and torment, an island of bounteous trees, fruit and berries, an island of sheep, and so on. Overwhelming as these tales are, with their fantastic visions and prophesies, they contain sufficient navigational detail to show that the authors had an intimate familiarity with the sea beyond the immediate shores of their land.

All these accounts are remarkably similar, differing only in the details to suit the reason for and nature of the search. These tales appear in written form at the end of the eighth and very beginning of the ninth century. But most likely they were formed in a much earlier time, and kept alive in oral tradition, until put into writing. Of all the *Immrama*, the best known and most widely read in its own time, and even today, is the voyage of the Irish monk, St. Brendan, as told in the *Navigatio Sancti Brendani*, and in the *Vita Sancti Brandani*.

In an early version of the *Navigatio*, written around AD 800, Saint Brendan, famous for his mighty works and spiritual father of nearly 3000 monks, receives a visit from another holy man, Saint Barrind, who describes a journey taken with his disciple, Mernóc, to a nearby island called the Promised Land of the Saints. Brendan resolves to go in search of this island himself. It takes him seven years to arrive at the heavenly paradise on Earth, after which he returned home to recount to all the other brothers of his monastery 'the marvelous wonders God deigned to show him.'

Into this highly stylized, abstract, narrative with its symbolic language, are skillfully blended elements of reality. Historical characters, places and events are so effectively introduced into the tale to increase its credibility and reinforce the power of its message that present-day historians have attempted to identify the true extent of the travels and actual lands visited by St. Brendan. Interpreting literally the navigational clues and descriptions of the islands found in the *Navigatio*, some authors claim Brendan's travels ranged all the way from Spitzbergen and Jan Mayen Island in the Arctic north to the Bahama Islands in the south, where flamingos dropped grapefruit into his curragh. It teases the imagination to believe this holy man reached the shores of North America almost a thousand years before Christopher Columbus.

Tim Severin, present-day author, historian and sailor, has taken a different approach to the problem of authenticating Brendan's voyage. He built a curragh as much like Brendan's as physically possible to see if it could be sailed to North America. Using the prevailing wind and current patterns of northern latitudes, Severin found a 'logical progression' of landfalls, one conceivably

106. Saint Brendan and the Whale from *Navigatio*, c. 1460

In the *Navigatio* of St. Brendan, elements of Celtic tradition, Greco-Roman mythology, and Christian teaching are all combined into a carefully structured tale to propagate the Christian religion. Among the varied and fantastic encounters of St. Brendan and his brethren is their arrival upon an island to celebrate Easter Sunday. To their surprise, they find they have landed not upon an island, but the back of a great whale. A remarkably similar event, but without any religious significance, occurs in the tales of Sindbad the Sailor.

UNIVERSITÄTSBIBLIOTHEK, HEIDELBERG

the same as Brendan's; the islands he visited and the events he encountered closely paralleled those of the ancient legend. On 26 June 1977 Severin and his crew landed in Newfoundland. But proof that a voyage by Brendan to the New World could be done is not the same as proof that it was done.

The life of Brendan and the legend of Brendan are two separate entities. Brendan was not a mythical figure but an esteemed monk, born in southwest Ireland in the last decades of the fifth century. After his ordination in 512, Brendan attracted a group of disciples and founded a monastery in Ardfert, north of Tralee. As his reputation and capabilities grew, so did the range of his travels: to the Hebrides Islands and to Wales; allegedly also to Brittany, the Orkney Islands, and even the Faeroes. He founded monasteries on all these island outposts, as far as 520 miles from his native shore of Galway,

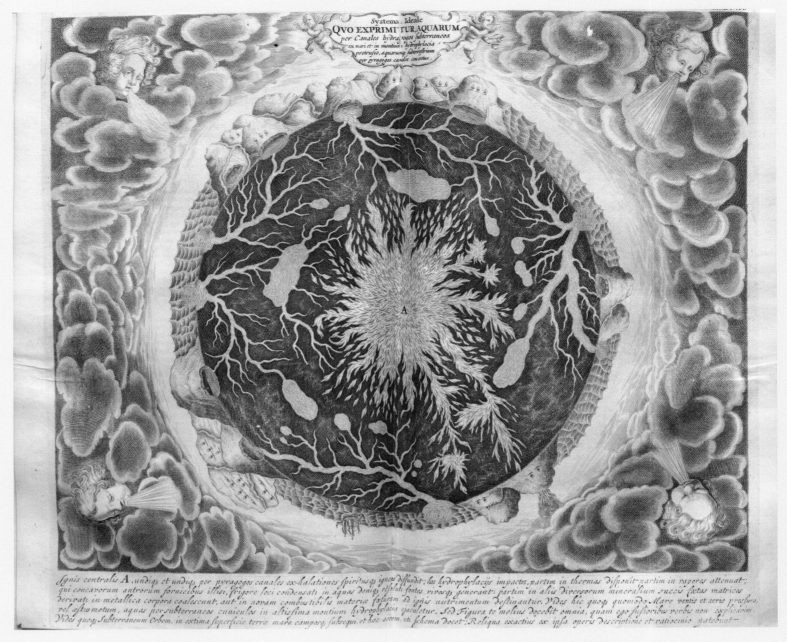

Systema Ideale
QVO EXPRIMI TVR AQVARVM
per Canales hydragogos subterraneos
ex mari et in montium hydrophylacia
protrufio, aquarumq; fubterrfirum
per pyragogos canales concetus.

Ignis centralis A .undiq; et undiq; per pyragogos canales ex-halationes fpiritusq; igneos diffundit; los hydrophylaciis impactos, partim in thermas difponit partim in vapores attenuat;
qui concaporum antrorum fornicibus illisi, frigore loci condensati in aquas deniq; effolut fontes rivosq; generant: partim in aliis Diverforum mineralium fuccis foetus matrices
derivati in metallica corpora coalescunt, aut in novam combustibilis materiae faturam ad ignis nutrimentum destinantur. Vides hic quoq; quomodo Mare ventis et aeris preffura,
vel aestu motum, aquas per subterraneos cuniculos in altissima montium hydrophylacia ejaculetur. Sed Figura te melius Docebit omnia, quam ego fufioribus verbis non explicarim.
Vides quoq; Subterraneum Orbem, in extima fuperficie terrae maria, camposq; fubresq; et hac aetem, uti schema Docet. Reliqua exactius ex ipsa operis descriptione et ratiocinio patebunt.

The Enigma of Currents

As European ships left the familiar shores of continental Europe to venture out onto the open Atlantic Ocean, they encountered great rivers within the sea: the ocean surface currents. In the sixteenth and well into the seventeenth century, the course of ocean currents was virtually unknown; there simply were not enough voyages made or a sufficient number of observations taken to construct a general pattern of the ocean's circulation.

With an ever-increasing number of expeditions to discover new lands and a sea route to the East Indies, mariners slowly accumulated knowledge about these currents. Gradually, general patterns began to emerge. In sailing toward India, Portuguese ships kept away from the westward-setting Agulhas Current off *Cabo de Buena Esperanza* (Cape of Good Hope) by sailing 100 or 150 leagues south of the cape. On the return voyage, they made use of this self-same current to speed their passage by sailing close to the cape. When they entered the northern Atlantic they steered clear of the contrary, south-setting Canary Current by making a wide sweep to the northwest before setting a final course homeward. The ships of Christopher Columbus and other Spanish explorers were propelled westward in the North Atlantic Ocean by the North Equatorial current. From the very start

they recognized its presence and made use of it. On their return from the West Indies, Spanish ships sailed north with the Florida Current (between the Bahamas and Florida) to higher latitudes before heading homeward, thus avoiding the problem of sailing against wind and current.

What happened to that westward-flowing water when it reached the other side of the ocean remained unanswered for almost three centuries. Since it was neither depleted at its source in the east, nor piled up in the west, philosophers of natural history concluded that there must be some means of egress, some strait or river in the Americas, through which the water could escape, to flow continuously around the world. The Gulf of Mexico, a plausible location for such an opening, was found to be totally enclosed at its western end. And exploration of North and South America showed it to be one long, continuous coastline, unbroken by any strait or passage leading to the Pacific Ocean.

Early explorers of the North American coast were quick to note the Gulf Stream, with its swiftness of current, distinctive colour and temperature. But it remained until nearly the end of the eighteenth century before the general path of the Gulf Stream was discovered and it was realized that it was one segment of a large clockwise gyre in the North Atlantic Ocean

– each portion of that gyre carrying a different name and set of characteristics.

Surface currents of the ocean are driven by the general pattern of prevailing winds produced by high- and low-pressure systems over the Earth; if there were no continental boundaries to the flow of surface currents they would continue in an uninterrupted belt around the globe. With the exception of the Antarctic Circumpolar Current (lying between latitudes 40° S and 60° S), all surface currents are confined to the three major ocean basins of the world, each flowing continually in a generalized closed loop. Due to the Earth's rotation the current is deflected from moving in a straight line; named the Coriolis effect, this results in the currents (and winds) in the northern hemisphere being deflected from the direction of the wind, toward the right, to rotate in a clockwise direction, while those in the southern hemisphere are deflected toward the left with a counterclockwise rotation. By moving the warm surface waters near the equator toward the pole, and cold water from the poles toward the equator, these closed loops, or gyres, in the ocean basins help equalize the distribution of global heat.

Wind is not the sole progenitor of the unceasing flow of the Earth's water. Differences in the density of ocean water, created by variations in temperature and

108. Map of the Gulf Stream by Benjamin Franklin, 1785

Isolated segments of the Gulf Stream were quickly discerned by the earliest explorers to North America. But it took another 160 years before two men, William De Brahm and Benjamin Franklin, almost simultaneously recognized that these seemingly disparate segments and qualities were all part of one continuous current – the Gulf Stream. Franklin, in this French engraving of his Gulf Stream chart, added annotations advising French mariners on how they would know they were in the stream 'by the warmth of water, which is much greater than the water on each side of it.'

LIBRARY OF CONGRESS, WASHINGTON D.C.

Opposite
107. Ocean currents and volcanoes by Athanasius Kircher, c. 1650

Athanasius Kircher's (c. 1601-1680) *Mundus subterraneus* contained a number of thematic maps, including one showing ocean currents. With this map he was trying to explain that volcanoes, tides and ocean currents existed because of the burning core of the Earth and underground water canals.

THE NATIONAL LIBRARY OF FINLAND, HELSINKI

109. Globe Terrestre by J. Forest, c. 1880

The chief advantage of a spherical globe over the plane, or flat, chart, is that it represents geographical information with relatively minimal distortion. Sometimes additional information is displayed. In the French globe seen here, currents are shown with different colours.

JUHA NURMINEN COLLECTION

salinity, produce currents that run deep beneath the surface. Water transported to polar latitudes by the surface currents is cooled by the atmosphere there and is increased in density by high levels of evaporation. Since the resultant denser water is heavier than the warm and less saline water, it sinks (downwelling) and moves towards the tropics, setting in motion a global 'conveyor belt' of current known as thermohaline circulation. In the middle of the North Pacific and the Indian Ocean this belt of deep, cold water rises toward the surface (upwelling) where it is replaced by warmer surface water and becomes a shallow near-surface current. Eventually it returns back to the surface and the starting point of the circuit.

This unceasing shift of warm and cold water currents brings the nutrient-rich phytoplankton and zooplankton in the cold, deep water toward the surface where these microscopic plants and animals form the bottom link of a long food chain for all of life in the seas.

Tides, generated by the Moon and Sun also create currents. Though they are negligible in view of the complete pattern of ocean circulation, to mariners they are important when navigating in coastal areas, particularly narrow channels and when entering and leaving harbours.

and none of them could be reached except by boat through treacherous, tide-ripped waters. His appellation 'Brendan the Voyager' was well earned.

Brendan was not the only Irish monk to make long ocean voyages. From the sixth century onwards, Irish abbots and their disciples ventured forth in their curraghs from island to island in search of remote, isolated places where, like Eastern anchorites (such as the third-century Saint Anthony) they could withdraw into a private 'desert island' in the ocean. Separated from home and friends, these hermits renounced their worldly goods to serve God in lonely solitude and prayer.

Saint Columba (521-597) of Donegal, after founding several monasteries in Ireland, took his disciples to the Island of Iona in the Scottish Hebrides where he founded a monastery. St. Brendan made several trips to Iona to visit Columba, and may even have founded a monastery of his own there. For hundreds of years, the 'Sacred Isle of Iona' was the spiritual capital of Scotland. Saint Columbanus (543-615) sailed from Ireland with twelve companions to Britain and from there crossed over to France, probably in 585, to begin his apostolic mission. Saint Adomnán, ninth abbot of Iona (c.

679) recorded four voyages made by Cormac ua Liatháin, a disciple of St. Columba, of which one took him as far north as Orkney. Adomnán's narrative contains specific details of the sails, rigging and construction of Cormac's sailing curragh.

Irish monks went far beyond the shores of Scotland, Wales and Brittany to preach the gospel or live as anchorites. They reached the Orkneys by 579, the Shetlands before 620, and later, the Faeroes. Eventually they reached Iceland in the year 795. It does not follow necessarily that these voyages were all made in a frail curragh. As far back as the time of St. Columba, Irish monks had 'long ships' made of 'hewn oak and fir.' In his *Vita S. Columbae* (Life of St. Columba), Saint Adomnán refers to many types of vessels: the *alnus, caupellus, cymba, cymbula, naves longae dolatae, navicula, navis oneraria, Scaphae.*

There is no literary evidence, or extant artifacts, to suggest these wandering clerics had charts and navigation instruments for their voyages. Undoubtedly, they used the time-honoured system of dead reckoning, combined with an accumulated knowledge from their experience with the sea: prevailing winds, currents, the colour of water, the presence of birds, and the sound of the sea breaking upon a shore (*tuindi fria tracht*).

In *Immrama* narratives, the wandering monks trust to 'the will of God' to determine the direction their frail vessel will

110. Early Maritime Ventures in Northern Waters

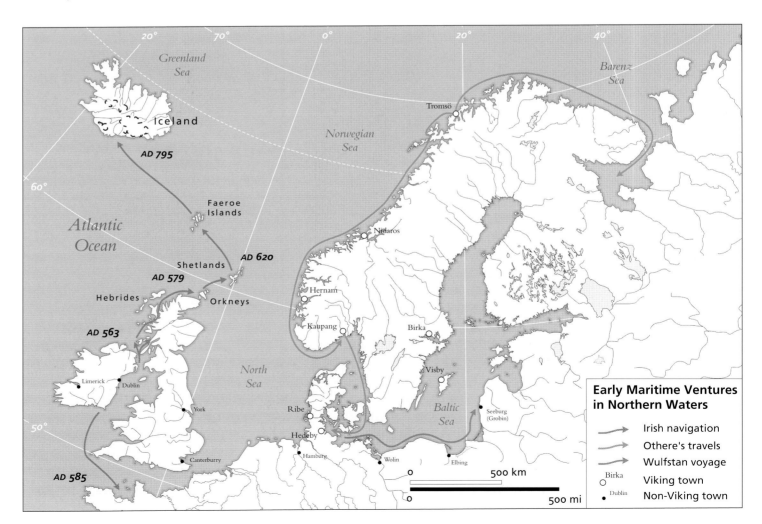

take them; a literary device to emphasize their saintliness. But in the better-documented voyages made by the Irish monks, when they stepped aboard their sea-going curraghs to journey to distant lands they were accompanied by professional seamen and pilots called *nautae* and *gubernata*. Since their voyages took them far from sight of land, to the extent of sailing directly to Iceland from Ireland without using the intermediate 'stepping stones' of the Shetlands and Faeroes, they must have used some form of celestial navigation. This is supported by the tradition of leaving for Iceland early in the year, probably before May. Thereby, they avoided summer fogs which hide the Sun, and the 'luminous nights' when the sky is so light as to obliterate the other stars, especially *Polaris*; both heavenly bodies were essential for latitude determination.

Dicuil

The Irish cleric Dicuil (b. 770) was an important figure amongst the early geographers, because he was both a traveller who voyaged across northern waters, and a scholar who made effective use of the earlier accounts. In his later years he went to the Frankish court of Charles the Great (768–814), popularly called Charlemagne, where he wrote two known and dated works, *Liber de Astronomia* (Book of Astronomy), and *De mensura orbis terræ* (Concerning the Measurement of the World), completed in 825. His astronomical work was a study of the heavenly bodies, primarily for the purpose of calculating the date of Easter and other religious holidays, but it also included his speculations on the distance between planets, and the possibility of a Pole Star at the Southern Celestial Pole, like that found in the north. The principle object of *De mensura*, as its name implies, was measurement of the world. He drew from as many as thirty Greco-Roman sources, some of them twenty to thirty volumes long, and compared Pliny's figures of latitudes and longitudes with the surveys of the Roman Empire, *Mensuratio orbis*, which had been ordered by the Emperor Theodosius II in AD 435.

Dicuil corrected Pliny's mistaken statement, which Solinus had publicized, that at Thule the Sun remains above the horizon for six months at a time. If that had been the case, Thule would have been at the North Pole. It was in support of his assertion that Thule was at the Arctic Circle that Dicuil recorded Pliny the Younger's quotation from Pytheas of Massalia, that Thule lies six days' sail north of Britain. Not content with an appeal to authority, Dicuil also relates the story of Irish anchorites fleeing the Faeroes. When the anchorites were invaded by the Norsemen they went to Thule, where they arrived on 1 February 795 and stayed until 1 August before returning to Ireland. They told Dicuil that at the summer solstice 'the setting Sun in the evening hides itself as though behind a small hill in such a way there was

111. The North Cape by Peder Balke, 1840

North Cape, Norway's most northerly point, is given its due prominence and grandeur in this romantic painting by Peder Balke. At the time that Othere visited it in AD 890, during his voyage to the White Sea, no one preceded him in sailing any farther north.

NATIONAL GALLERY, OSLO

no darkness in that very small space of time, and a man could do whatever he wished as though the Sun were there.' They thought, 'If they had been on a mountain top, perhaps the Sun would never have been hidden from them.' Dicuil correctly perceived that the same thing, only in reverse, must occur during the winter solstice, when for a few days it would be dark most of the time, with only a brief period of dusk. These observations correspond so completely to the conditions of Iceland, the northern coast of which lies at 66.5°, just upon the Arctic Circle, as to leave no doubt that was the land the Irish occupied and named Thule.

That Thule was completely surrounded by solid ice was another misconception Dicuil corrected. These same men had voyaged there 'at the natural time of great cold [February]' entered the island and remained on it day and night except for the period of the solstice. They did find, however, that the sea was frozen over a single days' sail north of Thule.

Not all Dicuil's depiction of the northern Atlantic was second-hand. He personally travelled to the islands around Ireland and Britain. 'Among these I have lived in some, and have visited others; some I have only glimpsed, while others I have read about.' He describes the Faeroe Islands, which lay beyond the farthest limit attained by the Romans. Talking of the sea that lies between Ireland and Britain, Dicuil says it is 'rough and stormy all the year round, and is only navigable for a few days.'

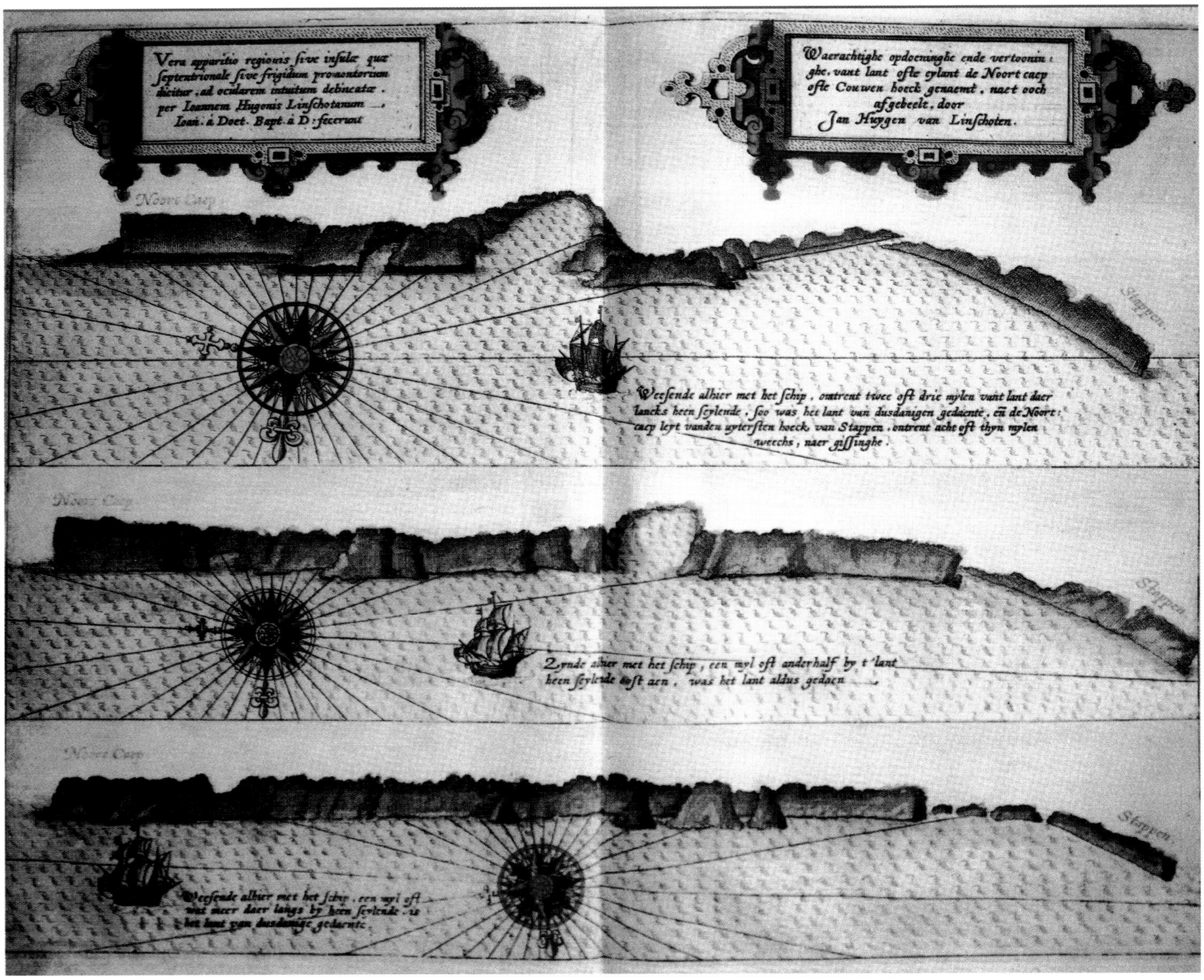

112. North Cape, Norway by Jan Huygen van Linschoten, 1601

North Cape received its name when Richard Chancellor (d. c. 1555) visited it in 1553 on his search for the Northeast Passage. For future navigators it was an important landmark in fixing their position. In his atlas of sea charts, Linschoten shows it in profile plan, just as the mariner would see it. In the three stages of approach to North Cape note the progress of the ship and the accompanying shift in direction of north in the compass rose.

UNIVERSITY LIBRARY OF TROMSÖ

THE VOYAGES OF OTHERE AND WULFSTAN

He sæd þæt he

Æt suum cirre wolde fandian hu longe þæt land

Norþryhte

Læge, oþþe hwæþer ænig mon be norþan þæm

Westenne bude,

Þa for he norþryhte be þæm lande:

'He said that he at some time wanted to find out how long the land
extends to the north, or whether any man lived north of the waste.'

OTHERE C. 890

With these words begin the oldest recorded eyewitness account of a voyage from northern Norway to the White Sea. Here, the task of separating legend from reality no longer exists as it did for the voyages of King Arthur or the Irish *Immrama*. King Alfred the Great of Wessex, England, who ruled during the end of the ninth century, wrote a universal history for the people of Britain. He used two main sources for his compendium: the *Historia adversus Paganos* (History against the Pagans) by Paulus Orosius's, a fifth-century Spanish ecclesiastic, and the *Historia Ecclesiastica* (History of the Anglo-Saxon Nations) by one of his own countrymen, the Venerable Bede. To augment this history, particularly regarding the geography and ethnography of far northern lands, King Alfred inserted in his work the accounts of Othere and Wulfstan (both fl. 880–890) as they were related to him.

Little is known of Othere's background, other than that he was a Northman, living at the northernmost border of Norwegian settlements in the region of Tromsö. Although England in the ninth century suffered many raids by Vikings, who eventually occupied and ruled much of the eastern half of that country, it is likely that Othere's contact with King Alfred was of a peaceful nature, as a Norse merchant or trader. In addition to giving Alfred much detailed information on his voyage, and descriptions of the peoples he met there, he also presented the king gifts of walrus ivory.

In the Middle Ages, whaling was one of the mainstays of the Scandinavian economy, providing meat and blubber for food, bones for building materials and tools, and valuable ambergris for medicinal purposes. Othere was actively engaged in whaling. The principle purpose for his travel, he states, 'was to increase the knowledge and discovery of these [northern] coasts and countries, and for the more commodities of fishing of horsewhales.' The horsewhales, as he calls them, were the walrus, or morse, and thought by Othere to be a kind of whale, much smaller than the common whale he knew off the coast of Norway.

In 890, Othere left his native land Hålogaland (Helgeland), to sail north toward the pole. Only a single settlement lay ahead; past that stretched an uninhabited, barren moor, visited only on occasion by a few Finns who came to hunt and fish. For three days he held his course northward until the coast trended toward the east. Here, at the North Cape of Norway (71° 15' N), he reached the limit of travels of the whale hunters. Beyond that point no man had ever sailed. Continuing east from the cape, he followed the coast as it gradually turned toward the south, rounded the Kola Peninsula, and entered the White Sea. After five days of sailing south, he came to a 'mighty river'; in all likelihood this was the Northern Dvina River. Now, for the first time since the departure from his own dwelling, he encountered an inhabited land.

The people here were called the Biarmes, he says; they tilled the land, in contrast to the Finns who were hunters and fishermen, and hunted walrus. Othere was particularly interested in the various uses to which the Biarmes put the walrus. Not only was the ivory of their 'teethbones' a valuable commodity, but their skins were also made into excellent cables for ships. Fearing attack, Othere did not enter the river to explore it further, but decided to conclude his voyage and return home. Not until 663 years later, with the expedition of Hugh Willoughby (d. 1554) for the Muscovy Company of England, would such a feat of voyaging again be accomplished.

Othere's account of his second voyage, south along the coast of Norway to the Viking port of Haithabu (Hedeby) at the base of the Jutland peninsula, is considerably briefer. He gives no detailed description of the geography of the land, as he did on his first voyage, or the names and manners of the people, only the courses held and the sailing times to his destination.

Leaving Hålogaland, Othere sailed south to a port or strait called Sciringes-heale, which seems to be Kaupang, an important Viking trading post at that time. He sailed through the narrow strait between Denmark and Sweden to the Baltic Sea. Keeping Jutland and Sjaelland to starboard, and the Baltic Sea

113. Adult walrus with her pup by Joan Blaeu, 1662
The European's reaction to first encounters with these creatures bordered on incredulity. Jacques Cartier (1573–1649) described the walrus as 'a beast big as an oxen, with two teeth in its mouth like an elephant, who lives in the sea.' Killed for their valuable ivory tusks, their hides which could be made into leather, and their blubber which could be used for lamp oil, a lucrative industry was set in motion, and the walrus population quickly became nearly decimated.
JOHN NURMINEN FOUNDATION

to port, Othere arrived at Hedeby (53° 45' N, 10° 00' E) in five days. At this other important Viking trading town founded by the Danish King, Godfred, in c. 800, Othere ended his second voyage.

Coincidently, from this very same port, and in the same year, another voyage commenced, eastward into the Baltic Sea. This voyage was by a Dane called Wulfstan, who related the events to King Alfred. Much like Othere's second voyage, we have here a periplus of the sailing route, with many geographic names, but unfortunately scant in narrative description.

Wulfstan left the Viking settlement of Hedeby and sailed eastward, all the while keeping the mainland of Europe to starboard, and all the islands belonging to Denmark to port. He also kept Bornholm Island to port, which at that time did not belong to Denmark, but had its own king. Maintaining his easterly course, he kept south of the mainland of Sweden and the two large islands of Öland and Gotland east of it, until he reached Trusco on or near the river Elbing. He describes the nearby Vistula River (Wixel, as he calls it) that empties into the Baltic Sea at present-day Gdańsk in Poland, and a land he calls Eastland, which he reported to be 'a very large land with many cities and towns, each having their own king; whereby there is continual strife and contention among them.'

From this point onward, antiquated toponymy and ambiguous, undefined borders of the countries make it difficult to determine the farthest extent of this voyage. Eastland, in his narrative, may have been Lithuania, but perhaps he sailed still farther east to Estonia.

Soundings

*'til ye come in to xxiiij fadome deep and if it be
stremy grounde it is between huschant and cille
in the entre of the chanel of fflandes and soo goo
yowre cours til ye haue sixti faduu deep. Than goo
est northe est a long the see. &c.'*

SAILING DIRECTIONS C. 1460–80

Knowing the depth of water is important to the mariner for the safety of his vessel lest unawares he should run his ship upon a shore or rocks, and also to give a general idea of his position. The lead-line, or sounding-lead, used to measure depth and determine general position at sea, is unequalled in simplicity of construction, ease of use, and reliability of results. As the oldest navigational tool, it has been virtually unchanged in structure from the time man first put to sea in his frail craft. When charts were crudely drawn or unavailable, and the compass not yet introduced to the western world, the only means by which a navigator could determine his position was local knowledge of the region's geography, and the sounding-lead. As its name implies, the sounding-lead was a lead weight attached to a length of line knotted at regular intervals. The unit of measurement between knots was a fathom. Originally, a fathom was defined as the distance between the tips of hands of outstretched arms; later, it was standardized to six feet, and used as a common unit among all nations.

Upon nearing a coast, 'soundings' were taken by heaving the line overboard and letting it run out until the lead reached bottom. Noting the depth enabled the navigator to know whether or not it was safe to proceed on the present course. Tomb paintings from ancient Egypt early as 1800 BC depict mariners measuring depths by this method. Bas-relief carvings from the tomb of Queen Hatshepsut, commemorating a voyage to the land of Punt around 1500 BC, show a lead-line being used to measure the depth of water.

The sounding-lead was used by Greek and Roman navigators since the sixth century BC as evidenced from excavations of shipwrecks in the Mediterranean. Writing in the fourth century BC, the Greek historian, Herodotus, warned navigators in their approach to Alexandria to take careful soundings with a lead-line: 'When you get eleven fathoms and ooze [yellow mud, deposited by the outflow of the Nile River] on the lead, you are a day's journey from Alexandria.'

From its very inception, the lead cone of the sounding-line had a small hollow at its base which was filled with tallow or some other sticky substance. When the lead was lowered, samples of the seabed adhered to the tallow. Brought to the surface, the character of the ocean floor was assessed and small differences in the composition of the aggregate – sand, pebble, shell, or mud – provided confirmation, in addition to depth, of the ship's position.

Throughout centuries of voyaging, these findings were carefully recorded in the logbook, to be marked on charts as an aid to future navigators. Sailing directions, or rutters, such as the 1574 *A Regiment for the Sea* by William Bourne (c. 1535–1582) gave detailed information on depths and the type of sea floor found. But it

was not until 1584, when Lucas Janszoon Waghenaer (c. 1533–1606) of Holland produced the first sea atlas, *Der Spieghel der Zeevaerdt* (Mirror of the Sea), that the earliest charts showing actual sea depths, along with the character of the bottom, were produced. In the New World, the first charts with printed depths, as well as the first to use the Mercator projection, were those in Robert Dudley's (1573–1649) atlas, *Dell' Arcano del Mare* (Secrets of the Sea), printed in 1647.

114. Guthlac Roll, c. 1210

In shallow coastal waters and rivers, a long pole rather than a lead-line suffices to measure the depth. St. Guthlac (c. 674–714) is shown here sailing up the river to Crowland, on an island at the western edge of Peterborough Fen, England, where he would become an anchorite. At the bow of the vessel, a figure is taking depth soundings with a long pole.

THE BRITISH LIBRARY, LONDON

115. The Rutter of the Sea by Pierre Garcie, 1521

The taking of soundings to safely enter the English Channel is given in this late fifteenth-century set of sailing instructions. The caption reads: '...until you come to twenty-four fathoms deep, and if there are strong tidal currents it is between Ushant, France and the Scilly Islands of England at the entrance to the Flanders [English] Channel, and so hold your course until you have sixty fathoms deep. Then go East Northeast along the sea, and so forth.'

THE BRITISH LIBRARY, LONDON

In proximity to the coast, the average weight of the lead was about ten pounds. For deep water heavier weights were used, otherwise the ship would outrun the line before the weight touched bottom, and give a false reading. According to the Greek historian and geographer, Strabo (63 BC–AD 24), Posidonius (in about 100 BC) took soundings of the depth of the Mediterranean somewhere between Rome and present-day Sardinia, and found it to be 1000 fathoms deep. This, however, was an isolated early example of deep-sea soundings.

Before the advent of the chronometer to keep accurate time at sea, thus allowing the navigator to determine longitude, the lead line provided a reliable check on the ship's position. As shore was approached from the open sea the lead-line revealed a change from 'bottomless depths' to a measurable number – 'coming into soundings', as it was known – and the navigator knew he had reached the continental shelf. With the accumulated knowledge from earlier voyages, recorded and marked on charts, the ship's longitude could thus be determined.

Charting and surveying of the ocean depths did not begin systematically until the last quarter of the eighteenth century. In 1773, Captain Constantine John Phipps measured the depth of the Norwegian Sea using a 150 lb weight. He found seafloor at 683 fathoms, and brought up fine blue soft clay. At such depths, the length of rope line required was bulky, and subject to stretch or shrinkage, giving false 'readings'. During an expedition of 1838–1842, Charles Wilkes

(1798–1877) overcame this by using a wire line. Ocean deep-water soundings now reached as far as 2425 fathoms. By the mid-1850s, recorded depths of the Atlantic Ocean Basin were numerous, in part due to the desire to lay the Trans-Atlantic cable. And in 1855, Lieutenant Matthew Fontaine Maury (1806–1873), one of America's greatest oceanographers, published his *Physical Geography of the Sea and its Meteorology,* which contained in addition to worldwide patterns of the ocean's winds and currents, a bathymetric map of the Atlantic with contours at depths exceeding 4.5 miles.

Today, depth sounders and sonar have taken over the task of determining depth; even so, we still use the phrase 'plumbing the depths', which takes its origin from the Latin word *plumbum* for the lead used in the lead-line.

116. Sounding Weights

Present-day sounding weights have barely changed over the centuries in appearance and structure from these ancient Roman leads retrieved from sunken vessels.

COURTESY OF JOHN PETER OLESON

117. The Coast of England by Lucas Janszoon Waghenaer, 1584

Information about depths in coastal waters and river channels, gathered by direct experience, was collected and placed on charts to aid future navigators. Waghenaer's atlas of sea-charts, which here shows a detail of part of the coast of England, was the first to add tidal data and give soundings.

THE NATIONAL LIBRARY OF FINLAND, HELSINKI

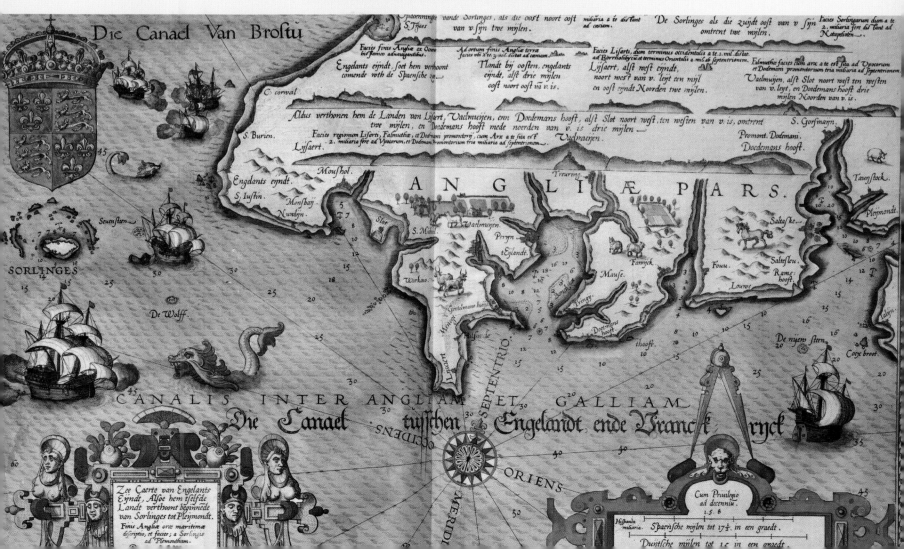

VIKING ROUTES
AND LONG DISTANCE NAVIGATION

SEA KINGS OF THE NORTH

Within a span of three hundred years, Viking raiders from Scandinavia extended their sphere of activity, penetrating many parts of the Baltic and taking part in trade on routes through the river system of vast inland Russia. By the middle of the ninth century they reached the Mediterranean by sailing around the edge of continental Europe. The Vikings quickly assimilated themselves into the local population and established permanent settlements in Russia, England, Normandy and Sicily. Crossing the Atlantic, they left outposts in Greenland and Newfoundland.

Traditionally, the start of the Viking age is marked when Vikings from Denmark crossed the North Sea to the northeast coast of Anglo-Saxon England in AD 793 to attack the Lindisfarne monastery. Archaeological evidence, however, shows that there was already contact between Norway and the British Isles as early as the end of the sixth century. From the first

decades of the ninth century until the beginning of the eleventh century, the entire coast of Ireland was ravaged. Danish voyages of exploration and raiding, and eventually colonization, were mainly southward to the British Isles and France. They continued south to Cádiz, Spain, sailed up the Guadalquivir River to conquer Seville, and entered the Mediterranean, reaching Pisa, Italy, in 860. Swedish Viking routes were predominantly eastward through the Baltic Sea and Gulf of Finland to Russia, where they founded the city of Novgorod in 862. Sailing south on the Volga River they reached the Caspian Sea. On the Dnieper River they founded the city of Kiev about 900, and journeyed onward to the Black Sea to reach the city of Constantinople. These Viking travels, thousands of miles from their homelands, connected them with trade goods from Southern Europe, North Africa, the Ural Mountains and Central Asia.

This division of Danish and Swedish Viking routes is a generalization, for along with their Norse brethren they un-

119. Gronlandia Iona Gudmundi Islandi by Jón Gudmonson, c. 1640

On this map, Greenland, with its Norse Eastern Settlements and Western Settlements, is separated from Norway by an incredibly narrow Atlantic Ocean. Greenland's eastern extremity is severed from Norway, and its southern extremity from the North American continent. Whether its western edge is attached to Asia is indeterminate. Jón Gudmonson, an Icelander, drew this map in about 1640, relying on earlier sources from sometime before the twelfth century. Although not identified, the strait between Greenland and North America is most likely Hudson Strait, indicated by the spiral symbol representing the 'furious overfalls' John Davis described during his 1587 voyage.

DET KONGELIGE BIBLIOTEK, COPENHAGEN

118. A detail from the Bayeux Tapestry

The Bayeux tapestry, dating between 1066 and 1077, tells the story of events leading up to and including the Battle of Hastings, England, in 1066. From Bayeux, an ancient Viking settlement in Normandy, William 'the Conquerer', Duke of Normandy, and descendent of Rollo the Viking, is seen here leaving to invade and conquer England.

MUSÉE DE LA TAPISSERIE DE BAYEUX

doubtedly shared to some extent travels in all directions. But voyages westward across the Atlantic, belonged to the Norsemen alone. Norway's land was unable to sustain its growing population and forced its inhabitants to emigrate, who established settlements in the Orkneys and the Hebrides of Scotland, where they could find arable land and pastures for grazing their stock.

As population pressures increased it was only natural to continue moving *vestan um haf,* westward over the sea, from initial outposts to the Shetlands, Faeroes, Iceland, Greenland and eventually the shores of North America. The general pattern was one of initial discovery by accidental landfall when driven by a storm or unfavourable wind, followed by voyages of exploration, and finally actual settlement. The accomplishment of these extended navigations required honing skills in latitude sailing and dead reckoning, and through careful observation, gaining familiarity with new landmarks. New courses and bearings had to be memorized; they had no maps, for there was no Norse tradition of cartography.

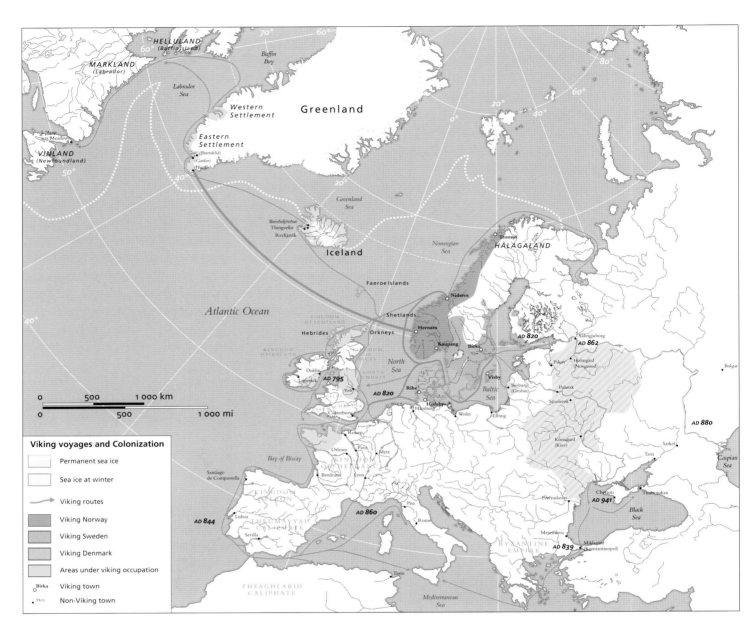

120. Viking Routes and Colonization

What cannot be shown on this map is the regularity of ocean traffic by settlers and merchant ships between the Norwegian homeland and its overseas dependencies in the twelfth, thirteenth and early part of the fourteenth centuries. By the twelfth century there were over 300 settlements in the Greenland colony. At its most flourishing time the population was over 3500. The Eastern Settlement had twelve parish churches, a cathedral, Augustinian monastery and a Benedictine nunnery.

Our knowledge about Norse exploration and colonization of lands in the western Atlantic comes from sagas passed on as oral records through generations and eventually written down during the thirteenth and fourteenth centuries. It was an age when the accuracy of oral memory was carefully protected, but nevertheless the sagas should not be accepted as historical fact even though they recount actual events, persons and dates, but rather as a 'historical source for the conceptual world of the Old Norse and Icelandic peoples', incorporating details of events.

To navigate across the Atlantic, Norsemen relied on the cumulative experiences of previous voyagers, disseminating by oral tradition knowledge of the routes. Long before they immigrated to the Shetlands in c. AD 700 and to the Faeroes in the early ninth century, Norse fishermen had gained a significant background in seamanship and navigation in the North Sea. They used the shallow quickly deepening water off the coast, recognized by the change in colour of the water, to give them their approximate position. The direction and strength of ocean currents and local tidal streams provided additional bearings. Landmarks were an important part of Viking navigation; they steered for well-known promontories, such as the steep headland of Reykjanes in Iceland, West Cape at Stad, Norway's westernmost point facing the North Sea, and the high land of Hvarf (Cape Farvel) in Greenland. At the approach of land they were alerted by rocks, skerries, ground swells, overfalls, and other manifestations of the sea to help shape their course.

The appearance of local seabirds also served to give the mariners an inkling of their position. In the vicinity of the island groups, puffins and common guillemots gave assurance land was close by. Further offshore, in the northern area, the gannet, Brunnich guillemot and a dark variety of the fulmar predominate, while in the southern area the birds observed more frequently were the common guillemot, gulls and the razorbill auk. While halfway between Scotland and Iceland the Vikings would encounter the Icelandic great skua. When they were about 150 miles south of Iceland, an abundance of birds and whales appeared as the result of surface currents providing a rich mixture of nutrients. With the high frequency of fog in these northern waters, any aid to locate their position, no matter how imprecise or subtle, was of value.

Not until the introduction of the sagas in the thirteenth and fourteenth centuries did written sailing directions appear in a northern equivalent of the *peripli* of ancient cultures of the Mediterranean. In the *Óláfs saga helga* (Saga of Saint Olaf), the course advised for sailing down the coast of Norway is to 'have the sea half-way up the mountain'. And in a passage from the *Landnámabók* (Book of Settlements), the course laid down for sailing from Norway to Hvarf, at the southern tip of Greenland, is: 'From Hernan in Norway [approximately 61° N latitude] steer due west for Hvarf in Greenland. You will then pass the Shetland Islands so close that you may see them in clear weather, and so close to the Faeroe Islands that half of the mountain is underwater, and so close to Iceland that you may have birds and whale from there'. The distances between landmarks in the first 360 miles were sufficient that any errors in dead reckoning could be compensated. Beyond the Faeroes, however, lay 1440 nautical miles of open ocean that required the ability to maintain a course due west without the aid of a magnetic compass, which had not yet reached northern Europe.

To make the transatlantic passage, Norse seamen would take advantage of the easterly winds prevalent in the spring and sail south until they reached the proper latitude that would enable them to hold a course due west to their destination. Neither the sagas, nor the *Konungs skuggsjá* (King's Mirror) of the early thirteenth century, make any mention of instruments the Norsemen might have used to maintain a course of constant latitude while sailing out of sight of land. This may either mean they had no instruments, or that they were so commonly used it did not seem necessary to mention them.

For the Norsemen to practise latitude sailing, two tools were necessary: one, a means to ascertain latitude so as to know where to turn west, or east on the return passage, and then to keep their course along that latitude; the other, a form of 'compass' providing a reference point in the circle of the horizon in order to maintain a proper course.

The *Solskuggerfjól*, or Sun shadow board, answers for the first tool. Mariners in the Faeroes used it during the seventeenth and eighteenth centuries, and it is conjectured that it is the same tool as that used by the Norsemen. It was a wooden disc with an adjustable gnomon at its centre that could be raised or lowered according to the time of the year. Concentric cir-

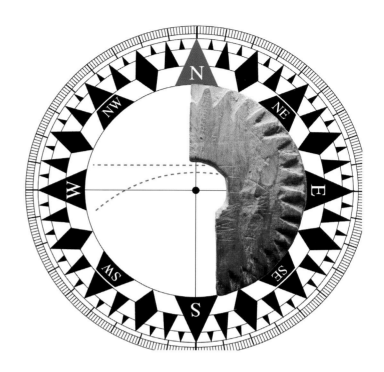

121. Viking 'Sun Compass' (placed in present-day compass card)

When used in conjunction with all the other navigational clues - wave patterns, prevailing winds, colour of water, and migration patterns of birds and whales - this seemingly crude direction-bearing dial from Unartoq Fjord, Greenland, enabled the Norsemen to effectively make repeated voyages across the Atlantic. When used simultaneously with a modern magnetic compass, it has been shown to be accurate within several degrees of arc, even on a small boat in heavy seas.

SUN COMPASS USED BY COURTESY OF SØREN THIRSLUND

cles of increasing diameter inscribed on the surface indicated the altitude of the Sun at a particular latitude. The mariner would know whether he was north or south of his anticipated latitude from the position of the tip of the shadow of the gnomon at midday. In order to keep the disc level and not give a false reading, it was floated in a container of water.

A wooden disc recovered from an archaeological site of known Norse occupation in Unartoq Fjord, Greenland, may well be the remains of a navigating instrument used as a direction-bearing dial. The periphery of this disc is divided by points into thirty-two equal spaces, and at its centre is a hole which is presumed to have contained a gnomon. Across the surface of the disc a straight line and hyperbolic curve are incised. The straight line is the path of the Sun at the vernal and autumnal equinoxes, as shown by the shadow cast by the gnomon, while the curved line is the Sun's path over the course of a day, shown by the shadow of the gnomon at the summer solstice. By rotating the disc to make the tip of the gnomon's shadow touch the curve, one has, in effect, a 'solar compass'. Instead of the north orientation of a magnetic compass, the solar compass provides an east/west orientation – one that is equally useful and effective.

Norse mariners were familiar with *Polaris*, calling it *Lei-darstjerne*, the leading or guide star, but unless voyages were

123. A Map of the Northern Regions by Abraham Ortelius, 1598

As voyages of exploration across the Atlantic Ocean increased in number, cartographers incorporated into their maps the new information and empty spaces began to be filled in with new geographic information. But geographic fallacies, as well as non-existent islands with names such as Heather-Bleather, Drogeo, Podanda and Neome, also appeared on some maps. One of the most unusual and controversial islands in the chronicles of cartography was that of Frisland, resulting from a voyage made in 1380 by a Venetian nobleman, Niccolò Zeno. If one were to believe his narrative and its accompanying map, Niccolò Zeno was the first to discover America. Cartographers and historians were reluctant to give up on the existence of Frisland, but eventually it was removed from the face of the map.

JOHN NURMINEN FOUNDATION

122. A page of the *Flateyjarbók*

The *Flateyjarbók* (Flat Island Book), written sometime between 1380 and 1400, takes its name from the place of the owner who resided on Flat Island in Breijdafjord, Iceland. The artistic excellence of this book is matched by the wealth of information it contains on early Norse voyages to Greenland and lands to the west. It records the first sighting of North America by Bjarni Herjólfsson, and Erik the Red's discovery and settlement of Greenland, as well as the voyages of Leif Eriksson and his brothers, Thorvald and Thorstein.

STOFNUN ÁRNA MAGNÚSSONAR Í ÍSLENSKUM FRð, REYKJAVIK

made in early spring or autumn, it could not serve as a guide. During the middle of the summer, persistent twilight in high latitudes obliterates this useful but faint star.

By all appearances, the most important tool in guiding the Norsemen on their open-sea voyages was an innate sensitivity to the subtle variations in seasonal winds, and nature of the water, rather than reliance on astronomy and instruments.

Westward Over the Sea

According to the saga *Landnámabók*, a catalogue of the first Norse settlers, one of the early voyagers to Iceland was a Viking named Naddod (c. AD 860). Upon arrival, he named the land *Snaeland*, or Snowland. Naddod was followed by Flóki Vilgerdarson (c. AD 865) who tried to settle there. But the first winter was so severe it killed all his cattle, and he departed, renaming the place Iceland. By the end of the ninth century a steady stream of immigrants seeking land arrived from coastal Norway and its satellite colonies in Ireland and the Scottish Isles, quickly displacing the few Irish monks remaining on the southeast coast.

Winds of the World

The Earth's atmosphere is composed of several layers, all constantly in motion. It is this planetary circulation of air that controls our weather, produces the major high- and low-pressure systems of the Earth, and is responsible for belts of calms, variables, and the persistent flow of Trade Winds.

PERMANENT SYSTEMS

The basic pattern of circulation is the result of air being heated in the tropical zone and rising to higher altitudes. These winds aloft flow toward the Polar regions. The rising currents near the equator produce a permanent belt of low pressure in the lower latitudes, while the descending currents produce high pressure in the Polar zones. Cooler and accordingly heavier air from the Polar zones flows down over the surface of the Earth to replace that which has risen, thus, a constant balance of heat is maintained. But this simplified pattern is rendered more complex by two major factors: the rotation of the Earth, spinning on its axis, and the angle of that axis relative to the Sun.

In 1835, Gaspard-Gustave Coriolis (1792–1843), a French engineer, introduced the concept that takes his name – the Coriolis Effect. He stated that a moving body on the Earth's surface is deflected by the rotation of the Earth. In the northern hemisphere the deflection is to the right from the direction of its motion, and to the left in the southern hemisphere. This accounts for direction of circulation in major water and air currents. As a result, air aloft, in its trajectory toward the poles, flows almost due east by the time it reaches a latitude of 30° in the northern hemisphere, and almost due west in the southern hemisphere. Due to the conservation of angular momentum, the sheer weight of this mass of air is overcome by gravity causing the air to descend to the Earth's surface where it then spreads both north and south. Where this occurs (in a region called the 'Horse Latitudes') a belt of high pressure, with its calms or light and variable winds, is created. Thus, the major flow of air from the poles toward the equator is broken up into several important sub-groups: Polar Easterlies, Westerlies and Northeast Trade Winds. Flow of returned air toward the equator is deflected westward by the Coriolis Effect, producing the Trade Winds in both the northern and southern hemispheres. At lower levels, the air that flows toward the pole is deflected eastward, producing the predominating Westerlies in both hemispheres. Occasionally, masses of cold air pour down from the polar region into lower latitudes where the Coriolis Effect sets them spinning, creating high pressure cells.

Another major variable in creating surface winds of the Earth is the angle of the Earth's axis. Although it is a fixed angle of 23.5° in its annular orbit around the Sun, it changes relative to the Sun. This shift in the declination of the Sun creates a likewise shift in the equatorial belt of heating and causes a corresponding move in the belts of pressure with their associated winds. It also causes the broad band of Northeast Trade Winds to shift north and south, with corresponding shift in the declination of the Sun.

This planetary circulation explains the general system of surface winds as they flow over the open ocean. Superimposed upon this are wind patterns caused by islands and continental landmasses. Navigators learned to use these systems, which are the same in the Pacific Ocean Basin as they are in the Atlantic Ocean Basin, to their advantage in determining the course of their voyages. In the Atlantic Ocean, Columbus and his successors learned to use the prevailing Northeast Trade Wind to their advantage in sailing westward. On their return voyages they sailed north until reaching the prevailing Westerlies, which propelled their ships homeward. In the Pacific Ocean, the same course of action was learned by the Spanish treasure fleets sailing between Mexico and the Philippines.

SEASONAL PATTERNS

In a narrow band of water along the coastline a daily pattern of 'sea breeze' alternates with a 'land breeze'. During the day, land is heated by the Sun and the

124. Monsoon Winds

Monsoon winds, with their accompanying rainfall and seasonal shift, are common to many parts of the world, such as Australia and the southwestern United States. The best known monsoons are those of the Indian subcontinent and southeast Asia. Determined by land and sea temperature differences, the Indian summer monsoon takes place from June to September and brings winds from the southwest and heavy rainfall. From September to March the pattern is reversed, with a dry winter and northeast winds. These changes in wind direction were used by navigators in the Indian Ocean for their passage planning.

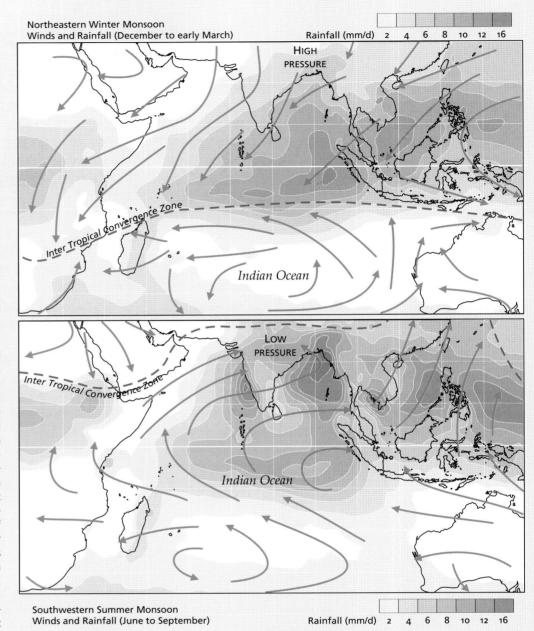

Northeastern Winter Monsoon
Winds and Rainfall (December to early March)　Rainfall (mm/d)　2　4　6　8　10　12　16

HIGH PRESSURE

Inter Tropical Convergence Zone

Indian Ocean

LOW PRESSURE

Inter Tropical Convergence Zone

Indian Ocean

Southwestern Summer Monsoon
Winds and Rainfall (June to September)　Rainfall (mm/d)　2　4　6　8　10　12　16

125. Global Wind Patterns

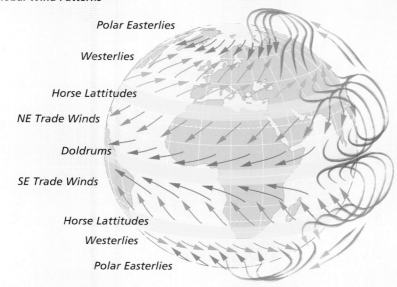

Polar Easterlies

Westerlies

Horse Lattitudes

NE Trade Winds

Doldrums

SE Trade Winds

Horse Lattitudes

Westerlies

Polar Easterlies

warm air rises creating a localized area of low pressure. Cooler, moister air from the ocean blows toward the land as a sea breeze, replacing the air that has risen. Water absorbs heat from the Sun more slowly than land does, but it retains the heat longer. As a result, when land quickly cools during the night, the pattern is reversed, and the wind now flows toward the ocean as a land breeze.

This same alternating pattern of winds caused by differences in temperature between land and the ocean occurs on a global scale, where they are much stronger and constant. Seasonal changes in temperature, shifting of dominant high- and low-pressure systems, and a change in the jet-stream, that narrow band of relatively strong winds in the atmos-

phere, creates the climatic system of monsoons. Its name comes from the Arabic *mausim*, meaning a 'season', referring to the seasonal shifting in winds and rain. Although monsoon winds and rain occur in other parts of the world, such as Australia, Africa, and Central America, best known are those in the Indian Ocean affecting the Indian subcontinent and southeast Asia. Here, during the winter monsoon season, the winds are from the north, northeast, and carry little moisture. During the summer monsoon season, winds are from the south, southwest, bringing with them abundant rain. Arab navigators, and later the Portuguese, used this seasonal change in direction of winds to set the time and direction of their voyages.

Without wind, a ship cannot sail – a cause of great-

er anxiety to seamen than that of gales and storms. Near the equator, where the northeast and southwest Trade Winds converge, is a region without any steady surface winds. Sailors call it the doldrums, while meteorologists call this area of calms the Intertropical Convergence Zone, or ITCZ for short. The doldrums, as well as the Trade Winds, shift with the seasons brought about by the shift in declination of the Sun. For European mariners to reach the southern oceans it was necessary to pass through this difficult zone with its prolonged calms, trapping a ship for days or even weeks, interrupted sporadically by severe thunderstorms and squalls.

This is the region where hurricanes and typhoons - the most violent of oceanic winds – originate. The generic term for them is 'Cyclone' which refers to any circular windstorm generated by a surface low-pressure system. In the Atlantic Ocean and the eastern Pacific Ocean they are called hurricanes, while in the western Pacific they are termed typhoons. The name typhoon is derived from the Cantonese *t'ai fung*, meaning a 'great wind'. Surface winds blowing in a tightening spiral toward the centre of these deep pressure systems can reach a velocity in excess of 155 miles per hour. This is a category 5 in the Saffir-Simpson numeric scale of cyclones according to their intensity.

126. Rainbow by Ivan Aivazovsky, 1873
Ivan Aivazovsky's evocative painting captures all the drama of a sinking ship in a windstorm, and the rescue of its crew with lifeboats.

THE TRETYAKOV GALLERY, MOSKOW

127. Picture Stone from Gotland

Remnants of Gotland's Viking past are present in the many *bildstens*, or 'picture stones' found there. On this small island off the east coast of Sweden, as wherever the Vikings lived, their expeditions, battles, and important personal events were commemorated on carved limestone plaqiues. The most frequent thing represented in these stones was that of their ships; an indication of the great importance in their life that they attached to it.

A MUSEUM OF NATIONAL ANTIQUITIES, STOCKHOLM

To Gunnbjörn Ulfsson of Saxahvoll (c. 900) is accorded the honor of being the first Icelander to sight Greenland. Early in the tenth century, while he was hunting walrus, his ship was blown far westward until he saw on the horizon an unknown shore, with offshore rocky skerries which were given the name of *Gunnbjarnarsker*, or Gunnbjörn's Skerries. He made no attempt to land, and when a favourable wind came up he returned home. His discovery, perhaps reinforced by seeing the migratory flight of geese toward that direction, or by an early sighting of land through the phenomenon of Arctic mirage, was sufficient to establish in the minds of Icelanders that land lay to the west.

Years later in c. 950, when Gunnbjörn's sons were living in Iceland, two newcomers arrived from Norway: Thorvald Asvaldsson, and his sixteen-year-old son Erik the Red (Eiríkr Rauði or Eirik Torvaldsson). Forced to move on account of blood feuds and slayings, and unable to return to Norway, Erik sailed still farther west. On the coast of Greenland he found two sites suitable for settlement. These two places were to become the Eastern Settlements (*Eystribygd*) and the Western Settlement (*Vestribygd*) of Norse Greenland. Erik returned to Iceland and convinced 400 to 500 people to accompany him in settling a land that he called a 'Green Land'. Since Greenland at that time had sufficient pasturage along its coastal margin to support cattle, Erik's appellation is not entirely without merit.

The navigation was not difficult. The colonists needed only to sail due west until reaching the Greenland coast. Along the west coast of Iceland the Irminger Current, with its relatively warm and saline water, flows northward, while the East Greenland Current flowing southward contains very cold water with a low salinity. About halfway between the two lands, this well-defined change in the colour and temperature of the water helped fix their position. Upon reaching the Greenland shore, it was a matter of coastal sailing. The current set in their favour. But seamanship of a high order was required, because the sea in that region is often violent and fog-shrouded. Of the twenty-five ships that started out in Erik the Red's expedition, only fourteen made it to their destination.

The voyage of Bjarni Herjólfsson in 986 advanced westward expansion of the Norsemen one step farther. According to the *Grœnlendinga saga*, one of the oldest of the Icelandic sagas, Bjarni was in Norway picking up cargo, when his parents decided to move from Iceland and re-settle in Erik's new colony in Greenland. When Bjarni returned home to find his parents gone, he continued his voyage directly to Greenland without even stopping to unload the cargo.

Contrary winds and dense fog caused him to lose his way, and when he finally sighted land, it was not the rocky, mountainous terrain of Greenland that had been described to him, but low, thickly wooded hills. He shaped his course north, and when another land came into view he determined this too could not be what he sought, for it was low-lying and lacked glaciers. Without lowering sail, Bjarni continued north until he sighted a land containing some of the topographic features of Greenland, but this he ignored as well. Then he changed his course to the east and finally reached the coast of Greenland, and his parents', dwelling.

The journey of Bjarni Herjólfsson is remarkable in two ways. It makes him the first documented European discoverer of America, although he did not set foot on land. And it shows in a good light the navigational skills that enabled him to sail 800–1200 nautical miles in totally unknown waters, come upon unfamiliar lands, and yet still maintain sufficient conviction in his navigation to reach his destination. The narrative relates that after being in a state of *hafvilla*, a loss of all sense of direction, for several days, 'at last they saw the Sun and were able to get their bearings'. With the fog dispersed, Bjarni was able to view the horizon, recover his sense of direction, and reset his course. Several times in the saga reference is made to his knowing he was 'too far south'. It is apparent that he was able to make some kind of latitude calculations from observation of the Sun, which showed him he must continue sailing farther north before he could change course to the east and reach Greenland.

The danger in relying too heavily on any one saga to determine the exact nature of events is exemplified by the voyage of Leif Eriksson (Eiríksson), the son of Erik the Red. In *Eiríks saga rauða*, Bjarni Herjolfsson has little to do with Leif's voyage. Leif's Vinland voyage began in Norway at the court of King Olafr Tryggvason, who charged Leif with the task of preaching Christianity in Greenland. On the way 'he ran into prolonged difficulties at sea and finally came upon lands whose existence he had never expected.' In the *Grœnlendinga saga*, however, Leif made a conscious decision when he was in Greenland to organize an expedition to explore the lands Bjarni had sighted.

According to that version, having learned what he could from Bjarni about the navigation, Leif started out in around the year 1000 to retrace Bjarni's travels, but in the reverse order. The first landfall made was in the country Bjarni sighted last, and was low and flat. Leif named it *Helluland*, or Flat-stone Land. He anchored there and went ashore in the ship's boat. By this act, he became the first European to actually set foot on North American soil. His landing is believed to have been on present-day Baffin Island. The second land, which was heavily forested, he called Markland, or Forest Land, now generally regarded as the Labrador coast. Leif continued to sail south for some time until he came to a third land, named in the saga as Vinland. Traditionally it was believed that the name referred to wine and grapes, and Leif's choice of it was interpreted as rude propaganda for settlers. But this is probably wrong. The word 'vin' with a short 'i' in ancient Norwegian had a meaning of grass or meadow. Leif and his crew over-wintered here, built houses, and explored the surrounding country. In the spring of 1002 they loaded their ships with timber, left the settlement and returned to Greenland.

In the following years Leif's two brothers, Thorvald and Thorstein, made separate trips to his settlement at 'Vinland the Good', as did Freydis Eiríksdottir, the illegitimate daughter of Erik the Red. In about 1010, Thorfinn Karlsefni, an Icelandic sea captain and merchant, organized an expedition to colonize Vinland. A party of 150 men, five women and a quantity of livestock, went there in three ships for the new settlement. But after several years, increasing conflicts with the native North Americans, who the Norse named Skraelings, made it advisable to leave. A single ship of Thorfinn's fleet, loaded with a cargo of timber and hides, returned to Greenland. So completely was the settlement on Vinland lost that when in 1121 Bishop Eirík Gnupsson of Greenland tried to go there, the course to reach it and its exact location had already been forgotten. With that last step of westward expansion from Greenland to Vinland, the Norse had reached their limits of nautical and navigational abilities.

To this day, the exact location of Vinland is still being debated; it could be anywhere between the Labrador coast and the southern coast of New England. The difficulty in fixing the landing place of Leif Eriksson and those who followed lies in the paucity of clues in the extremely terse wording of the sagas, and in the differing accounts between sagas. But

128. King's Mirror, the Viking View of the World

The Viking view of the world, as described in the *King's Mirror*, was one in which all the landmasses of the Earth were contiguous; this single continent was called the *Heimskringla* (Home-circle). Greenland was not an island, but attached to the mainland on the extreme side of the world to the north. The Atlantic Ocean was conceived as a 'channel gap' between Norway and Greenland. No land lay beyond Greenland in the Home-circle, only the 'great ocean that runs around the Earth.' The Viking concept is an echo of Homer's construct of the world, in which the Earth was thought to be a flat disc surrounded by a circumfluent world-river, the *Oceanus*.

the most likely candidate for Leifsbudir, the settlement of Leif, is the site of L'Anse aux Meadows at the northern tip of Newfoundland. Here, undisputed archaeological evidence is present for Norse occupation at the time of their exploration and nascent colonization in North America. The remains of this Norse settlement in L'Anse aux Meadows was discovered in 1960 by Norwegians Helge Ingstad and Anne Stine on the evidence gathered by the Finnish geologist Väinö Tanner during his studies in Labrador in late 1930s and 1940s.

The *Landnámabók* and the *Saga of St. Olaf* both mention a land, Hvitramannaland, or White man's land, 'west in the ocean from Ireland … near Vinland the Good, and a little beyond'. According to these sagas, this land, sometimes called Albania or Greater Ireland, should be located six days, sail from Ireland. It has been suggested that the six days does not refer to the passage from the north of Ireland to Newfoundland – a course due west by latitude sailing – but to the next course beyond Newfoundland. If so, from L'Anse aux Meadows at Belle Isle Strait, this would place landfall at Hvitramannaland somewhere on the western shores of the Gulf of St. Lawrence.

Ari Marsson, who was a relative of Erik the Red's wife, purportedly visited the land. It has been supposed that the inhabitants of Hvitramannaland were Irish monks who migrated westward in the wake of Viking invasions, but they could have been Danish Vikings who had settled in the Shannon estuary of Ireland in the second half of the ninth century, and later sailed across the Atlantic.

THE KING'S MIRROR

The Middle Ages produced a number of books on the history of the world; written by monks or ecclesiastics, they were a compendia of the works of the best writers from the Classical world, to which were added history and geography of northern Europe. These were usually written with the purpose of passing on to the general public the wisdom of the ages. A more specific readership was intended for the encyclopedic work *Konungs Skuggsjá*, or the *King's Mirror*, which was written by a now forgotten author as a teaching text to a very limited and specific audience, the sons of King Hákon Hákonarson (1217–1263) of Norway. Nonetheless, it contains information of interest to a wider audience. Rather than taking the form of a treatise, the *King's Mirror* is written as a dialogue between a learned father and an eager, responsive son – a Norwegian adaptation of Plato's dialogues. Through their conversations, the future king learns about the four areas of work in the world: royal courtiers, the clergy, merchants and peasants. Only two of these four sections have survived to the present day, but fortunately the remaining parts provide us with much information on the Norse Greenland settlements in particular, and generally on five centuries of seafaring to the distant Norwegian colonies.

The author of the *King's Mirror* supports the concept of a spherical Earth, using as his guide the work of Bishop Isidore of Seville. He divides the world into the usual five zones or climates completely encircling the globe: a Torrid Zone, in which men cannot live on account of the extreme heat; a temperate, habitable zone on either side of the Torrid Zone; and to the north and south of these, frigid belts which cannot support habitation any more than the Torrid Zone, for there 'water casts aside its nature' and turns both the land and water into ice-masses.

Norway, he asserts, lies on the northern boundary of the habitable zone, close to the frigid belt, while Greenland lies totally within the Frigid Zone. That there are settlements in Greenland and the climate is good, even though the land is full of ice and glaciers, is in conflict with the theory that lands in the Frigid Zone are totally uninhabitable. The author reconciled the problem with the observation that during the summer, when the Sun is at its highest, the almost continuous daylight manages, though just barely, to melt the ice and warm the soil, thus making a narrow strip of land on Greenland's coast capable of supporting vegetation and sustaining habitation.

The proper season for navigation to the Greenland settlements is addressed in the *King's Mirror*. Over the course of many voyages, the most opportune times to set out across the Atlantic had been learned. By 16 March, at the Vernal Equinox according to the Julian calendar, when the days lengthen, the Sun rises higher and the nights grow shorter, ships could begin to venture out. At that time 'the North wind gently clears up the face of heaven with a light and cool breeze, brushes away the restless and storm-laden clouds ... peace is renewed among the winds, for they all yearn for rest after the season [winter] of violent wrath and wearisome blasts. The showers cease, the waves sink to rest, the breakers flag, the swell of the noisy ocean dies away, all the storms weaken, and quiet follows upon restless turmoil'. By the beginning of October at the start of Equinoctial gales, prudent sailors should hardly venture over the seas, 'for at that time the sea begins to grow very restless, and the tempests always increase in violence as autumn passes and winter approaches'.

Although the mechanics of wind systems of the Earth was not yet known, the Norse knew from practical experience what every wind, and its shift in direction, would portend. They knew from the winds how to anticipate the weather, and used them in their navigation to steer their ships over the perils of the ocean. Ptolemaic maps personified the winds as Gods, depicting them as heads with wind issuing forth from their mouth. The *King's Mirror* goes beyond this in giving winds the power of thought, emotion, and the soul of a poet. 'When the southwest wind observes how friendship [with the south wind] has cooled, now that the truce [among winds] is broken, he sobs forth his soul's grief in heavy showers, rolls his eyes above his tear-moistened beard, puffs his cheeks under the cloudy helmet [of the sky], blows the chilling scud violently forward, leads forth huge billows, wide-breasted waves, and breakers that yearn for ships, and orders all the tempests to dash forward in angry contest.'

The author of the *King's Mirror* shows an understanding of the workings of tides. He describes the diurnal periodicity of the flooding and ebbing of tides, and explains how they are related to the waxing and waning of the Moon. There is a full discourse on the Sun's path over the course of a year, from winter solstice through to summer solstice, and back again, with attention paid to the differences in climate between southerly latitudes and those of Greenland and Norway, and to the reasons for it.

129. The Gokstad Ship

The Viking ship found at the Gokstad farm near Sandefjord Norway, in 1880 was built around AD 890. This 24 metre-long and 5 metre-wide ship carried 32 oarsmen. It ended up as a burial ship for an important chieftain some ten years later. Its seaworthiness was proved when a replica of the ship in 1893 crossed the Atlantic in 28 days.

MUSEUM OF CULTURAL HISTORY, UNIVERSITY OF OSLO

While the rest of Europe at this time attributed the aurora, the Northern Lights or *Nordurljos*, to dancing spirits in the sky, and wove around them fanciful mythology and superstition, the *King's Mirror* seeks to explain them in terms of natural phenomena. It postulates that the aurora may be an occasional gleam of light from the Sun, shot up into the sky when it is on the opposite side of the Earth, or may be reflections from frost or glaciers, radiating forth flames of light.

Safe passage for settlement and trade in the colonies of Greenland depended as much on the proper construction and maintenance of the vessels as it did on an understanding of the ways of the sea. The author's advice is to keep ships well tarred over the winter so as not to let the planks dry out. Reliable tackle and a good supply of materials to repair sails must be kept aboard at all time, as well as all the tools and materials needed by the carpenters. Nor does he overlook advice on the manners and ethics of the men in charge of the ships. 'Keep your ship attractive', he says, 'for then capable men will join you and it will be well manned'. And he gently reminds those involved in trade not to let the King's belongings fall into their purse, for 'it is easier to be cautious beforehand then to crave pardon afterward'.

This document is as relevant today as it was in its time for its wise advice and the sheer poetry of its language.

NICHOLAS OF LYNN

The account of a voyage to the North Pole undertaken in 1360 by Nicholas of Lynn, an English Friar, falls into a genre of travel literature popular in the Middle Ages. These works contained a certain amount of fable and other fantastic mate-

130. Prow of the Oseberg Ship

The stempost of the Oseberg ship, found in Vestfold, Norway, in 1904, is skillfully carved in a characteristic animal style. Built in the beginning of the ninth century for coastal waters, the Oseberg ship represents an early type of Viking ships and was probably used as a royal pleasure craft.

MUSEUM OF CULTURAL HISTORY, UNIVERSITY OF OSLO

131. Polar map drawn by Gerard Mercator, 1569

In a Polar insert to his 1569 World Map, Gerard Mercator depicts the four polar islands divided by four rivers or canals converging at the North Pole into the Maelstrom – the ind-welling seas. We may infer that since the islands, ringed by mountains, are placed at 78° N latitude, this was the farthest north reached by Nicholas of Lynn, as he had ascertained by observations taken with his Planispheric Astrolabe. In the very centre of the whirlpool where waters descend into the centre of the Earth, sits a large magnetic rock or mountain. Here, most likely, Mercator conflated Cnoyen's description with his own knowledge about the Maelstrom off the north coast of Norway at roughly 68° N.

MARITIEM MUSEUM ROTTERDAM

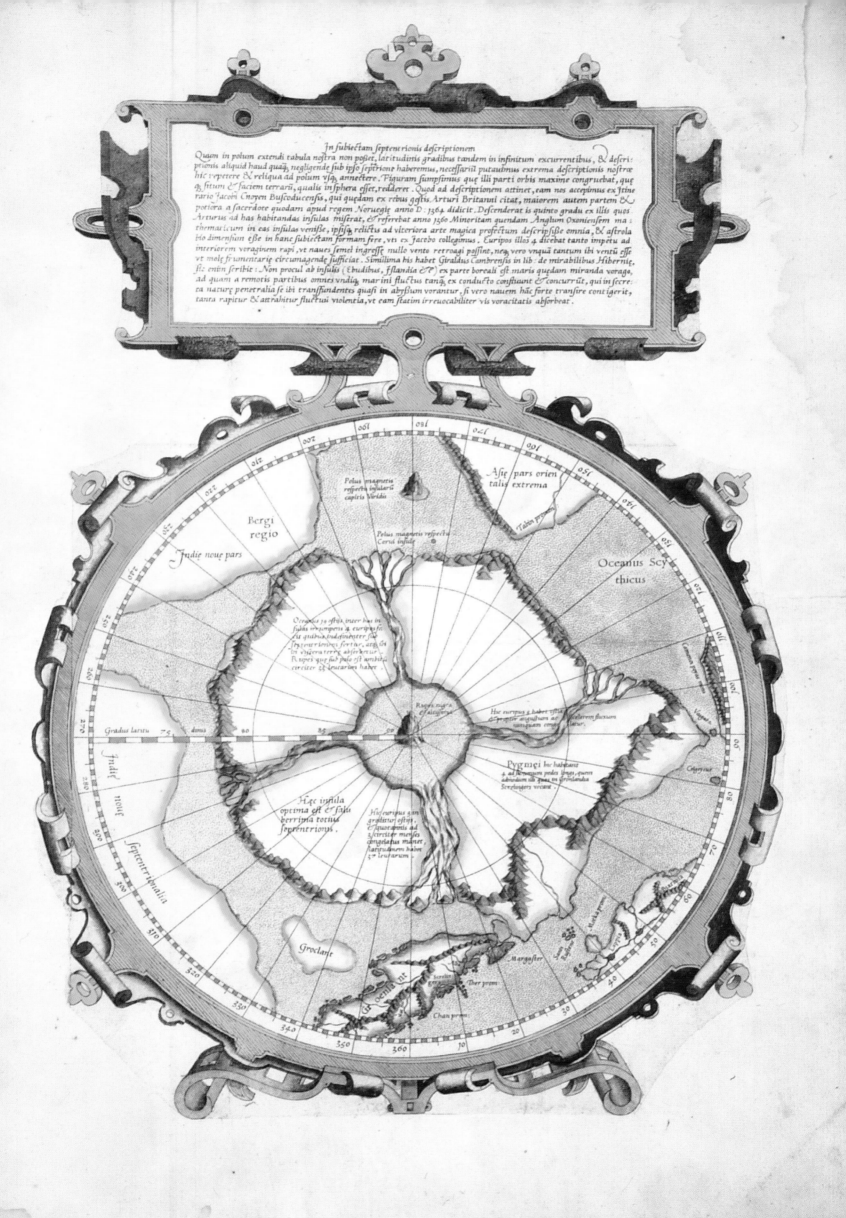

In subiectam septentrionis descriptionem

Quam in polum extendi tabula nostra non posset, latitudinis gradibus tandem in infinitum excurrentibus, & descriptionis aliquid haud quaq, negligende sub ipso septrione haberemus, necessariu putauimus extrema descriptionis nostrœ hic repetere & reliqua ad polum vsq, annectere. Figuram sumpsimus que illi parti orbis maxine congruebat, que q, situm & faciem terraru, qualis in sphera esset, redderet. Quod ad descriptionem attinet, eam nos accepimus ex Itinerario Iacobi Cnoyen Buscoducensis, qui quędam ex rebus gestis Arturi Britanni citat, maiorem autem partem & potiora a sacerdote quodam apud regem Noruegie anno D: 1364 didicit. Descenderat is quinto gradu ex illis quos Arturus ad has habitandas insulas miserat, & referebat anno 1360 Minoritam quendam Anglum Oxoniensem mathematicum in eas insulas venisse, ipsis, relictis ad viteriora arte magica profectum descripsisse omnia, & astrolabio dimensiu esse in hanc subiectam formam fere, vti ex Iacobo collegimus. Euripos illos 4 dicebat tanto impetu ad interiorem vereginem rapi, vt naues semel ingresse nullo vento retroagi possint, neq, vero vnquā tantum ibi ventū esse vt molę frumentarię circumagende sufficiat. Similima his habet Giraldus Cambrensis in lib: de mirabilibus Hibernię, sic enim scribit: Non procul ab insulis (Ebudibus, Islandia &c) ex parte boreali est maris quędam miranda vorago, ad quam a remotis partibus omnes vndiq, marini fluctus tanq, ex conducto confluunt & concurrūt, qui in secreta naturę penetralia se ibi transfundentes quasi in abyssum vorantur, si vero nauem hāc forte transire contigerit, tanta rapitur & attrahitur fluctui violentia, vt eam statim irreuocabiliter vis voracitatis absorbeat.

Viking Ships

Perhaps the most remarkable achievements of the Vikings were their voyages over the seas, made possible by first-class seamanship and excellent ship-building skills based upon centuries of traditions. The Viking ships – the extremely seaworthy *knarr* and the fast *drake* – represent the peak of this development. With these vessels the Vikings sailed over the North Sea and the North Atlantic.

The popular concept of Viking ships is an image of a sleek ship with a striped square sail and colourful shields. In the high bow there is a dragon figurehead. Such fast warships indeed existed, but the Scandinavians also sailed with broad-beamed freighters and different coastal vessels. It is not clear at what stage the hull form and construction of a warship started to differ from those of a merchant ship, but there is evidence from the eleventh century of such a development. Voyages on the Atlantic Ocean were mainly made by the inhabitants of the western part of Scandinavia. They developed the best ship types for use in the open sea, of which the knarr was the most seaworthy. With these they sailed to Iceland, Greenland and further to the northeast coast of the North American continent.

The oldest Scandinavian archaeological boat find is the 2300-year-old Hjortspring boat, which has a length of 19 m and a breadth of 1.9 m. The keel plank of limewood is slightly hollowed and the thin lime-wood hull planks are sewn together. The frames are made of bent hazel. As there are no signs of tholes, it is assumed that this slender canoe-like boat was paddled.

The next known Scandinavian find chronologically is the Nydam boat from the fourth century AD. It shows clearly the enormous technological advances achieved in the seven centuries that followed the contruction of the Hjortspring boat. The Nydam boat is of Western Scandinavian origin and was found in a swamp in Southern Jylland, Denmark. The shell-built hull of oak has a length of 24 m and a width of 3.8 m. The hull planks are nearly fulllength and fastened by iron rivets. The depth of the keel is 1.2 m and there was no mast. The boat was rowed and it is likely that this type of boat was used both for trading and plundering.

Vessels designed for both coastal trading and voyages on open sea sailed well and were slender, which also made them easy to row, and they were shallow drafted and easy to manoeuvre. The main building material was oak, but pine or lime were also used. The hull was shell-built in a traditional manner.

One of the features that provided the Scandinavian vessels with outstanding seagoing qualities was the keel. It made them stable, and it was even possible to a certain extent to sail against the wind, although maritime researchers offer differing opinions about that. It is likely that the knarr had better qualities for sailing to windward than had the drake. Some believe that the sails of Viking ships were so difficult to handle that the Vikings preferred to wait for fair wind.

Although the vessels were equipped with a steering oar on the starboard quarter, if they were well built and correctly loaded they kept their heading no matter how strong the wind. But it was of great importance how the crew was situated on board and how the sails were sheeted home and braced. The rudder was only required for fine adjustments of the course. The flexible construction of the hull helped to give the Viking ships good sea-keeping qualities in rough weather.

The ships were open and the cargo and crew were fully exposed to weather and wind, though canvas was stretched over them to provide shelter. Emptying the ship of water was a constant routine; the baler was an on-board necessity. Despite their sea-worthiness, the vessels were small and the freeboard low. When the design of the ocean-going vessels gradually improved, a couple of wash strakes were added to raise the freeboard; this 'upper' hull provided better shelter from splashing.

The conditions on board were extremely primitive. On the coastal routes it was usual to beach for the night and sleep in tents. On the open-sea routes the men slept on the bottom in sleeping bags of skin under bare skies. The ships were apparently equipped with a large pot for cooking, but as there was no fireplace on board it was probably used only on shore. There were no latrines on the ships; all needs were satisfied overboard. The men kept their personal things in lockers, which probably also served as benches when they were rowing the ship.

It is not known when the Scandinavians began using sails, but it was later than in other cultures. During the eight century Viking ships had one mast and a

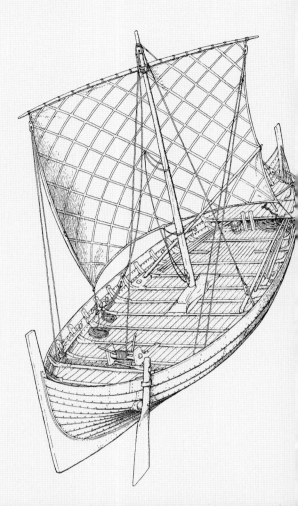

square sail, which was woven of wool and became stretchy when wet. Therefore the diagonal lines seen on pictures are probably reinforcements. The mast was fastened in the mast step above the keel and in the mast partner spanning several cross beams longitudinally, and was probably lowered and raised quite frequently.

The typical freighter of the Viking Age was the knarr. The merchantmen were designed to carry as much cargo as possible with a minimum of crew. They had a greater beam and were heavier than the warships and in practice they always set sail on open sea. They were equipped with a couple of pairs of oars,

132. A Knarr drawn by Björn Landström, 1961

A reconstruction of a knarr by the artist Björn Landström. This ship had no rudder, but only a steering oar on the starboard quarter.

COURTSESY OF OLOF LANDSTRÖM

133. Viking Ship by Björn Landström, 1961

The Viking's freight ship was called a knarr, and it was shorter and wider than their warships. It was ideal for carrying cattle, wool and grain. The knarr had no deck, so the cargo and crew were exposed to weather and wind, but the ship was extremely seaworthy.

COURTSESY OF OLOF LANDSTRÖM

intended mainly for manoeuvring when coming to shore or in narrow waters, although they could also be used for propulsion in a calm. The dimensions of the hull grew with the development of the trade. It is regarded as most likely that the Scandinavians had no purpose-built freighters before there became a need to ship larger amounts of cargo such as wood, dried and salted fish and grain.

A few well-conserved shipwrecks provide evidence of freighters of the Viking Age. Close to Roskilde five vessels were found in 1962 and a further one in 1997, all believed to date back to the eleventh century. Among these was a 16 m-long and 4.6 m-broad knarr with a displacement of about 6 tons. With a full cargo of 20 tons she had a draft of only a metre. A replica of this ship, named *Saga Siglar*, was built in Norway 1983 and has since sailed around the world. Between Greenland and Newfoundland she met a hurricane, but managed well as the crew used the same skills in seamanship as had their ancestors.

The Scandinavian attack on the Lindisfarne monastery in AD 793 is regarded as the beginning of the Viking Age, even if the Vikings undertook plundering expeditions before that. The era continued for nearly 300 years until the failed attempt to conquer Britain in 1066. The drakes (*drakskepp*) or long ships (*långskepp*) were long, slender and light, equipped with a large sail and easy to row. The larger warships were also named sessa. The Sagas describe ships with as many as 120 oarsmen, which mean that the hull length would have been around 70 m. If it were as-

sumed that such a ship would have been built by the same methods as were employed in the construction of the wrecks that have been found, it would have been weak. Most likely the author of the Sagas exaggerated, although very long ships have existed. The longest hull found on a Viking ship, the drake Roskilde 6, measures 36 m in length and 3.5 m in breadth.

In a storm the Vikings kept a course following the sea and along the direction of the wind, and there was a danger of capsizing should a strong wind strike them on the beam. Sometimes they lowered a rope from the stern, which assisted the helmsman steer the right course. The drakes and the knarrs managed well in storms due to their long keel and the large surface of the bow. Seafarers also used to set a smaller auxiliary sail, because the long ships behaved well in high speed with the waves, although it could not cope with excessive speeds. In experiments performed in replicas it was found that when they reached a speed of 17 knots, planing in strong wind, the ship becomes unmanoeuvrable.

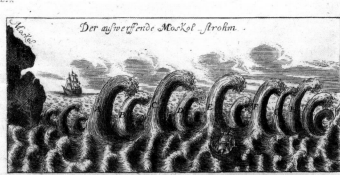

134. Maelstrom by Eberhard Werner Happel, 1708

Powerful tidal forces create swift currents in the dangerous whirlpool of Maelstrom, off the north coast of Norway. In the sixteenth century it was believed that ships were in peril of being snatched down in spiraling abysses to the very bowels of the Earth. Even today, for those who sail at the wrong time, navigation upon this sea can be dangerous.

JOHN NURMINEN FOUNDATION

rial, mixed in with factual elements. It is difficult to extricate fact from fiction, for the full written accounts of Nicholas's voyage are no longer available for study, and what remains relating to it in the form of letters is fragmentary. The principal source is *The History of the Voyage of Jacobus Cnoyen Buschoducensis, throughout all Asia, Africa and the North*, a compilation of three separate writings: Ívar Bárðarson's *Description of Greenland*; Nicholas of Lynn's own book *Inventio Fortunata*, and parts of the *Gesta Arthuri*, a source mentioned by Gerard Mercator for exploits of the sixth century King Arthur of England.

Cnoyen's narration begins with a description of northern Norway, and all the islands beyond, including Greenland and Iceland, which King Arthur had subdued and populated. The story then abruptly moves ahead another eight centuries to AD 1364, when we learn of a priest returning to Norway from Greenland, having in his possession an astrolabe which he used for the taking latitudes. Doubtless, that priest was Ívar Bárðarson, superintendent of the See of Greenland, who in that year had returned to Bergen, Norway, along with seven companions who presumably were also from Greenland, to assume

the position of canon at the Church of the Apostles in Bergen. We do not know whether Cnoyen received his information about the northern islands directly from Bárðarson while on a visit to Norway, or from Bárðarson's published *Description of Greenland*. But we learn that Bárðarson received this astrolabe from an English Franciscan from Oxford, England, who had visited Greenland and gave it in exchange for a New Testament. This had to have been a Planispheric astrolabe, which at this time was already in use in northern Europe.

It was Dr John Dee who identified the friar as Nicholas of Lynn, whom he believed to be knowledgeable in mathematics and astronomy. He says that in 1360 in the thirty-fourth year of the reign of King Edward III, 'a Friar from Oxford, being a good astronomer, went in companie with others to the most Northern Islands of the world, and there leaving his companie together, he transited alone, and purposely described all the Northern Islands, with the indrawing seas: and the record thereof, at his returne he delivered to the King of England. The name [of] which booke is *Inventio Fortunata, incipit a gradu 54. usque ad polum*', that is, begins at 54° and continues to the Pole.

In his description of the polar region, Nicholas of Lynn asserted there to be four large islands surrounded by a circle of mountains at 78°. Through these islands, currents flow into the centre of the world from the outer oceans, there to converge in a whirling maelstrom at the North Pole and plunge into the middle of the Earth. 'The currents here', he says, 'are so swift that sailing is dangerous'.

It is quite probable that the text as it is now known has been compromised to some degree by the number of hands through which it passed – Jacobus Cnoyen, John Dee, Gerard Mercator and Abraham Ortelius. Most likely, errors have unintentionally crept into the tale, and paraphrased information subtly shifted in meaning from the original text.

In this questionable text, Nicholas's voyage is given as starting at 54°. Even this simple statement lends itself to varying interpretation. Fifty-four degrees divides one climate parallel from another, with everything north of 54° being in the seventh climate. In this sense, we are given only the most general idea of where the voyage started. Dee, however, is explicit in stating that the Franciscan took leave 'from the haven in Norfolk [Lynn] from which he took his name', If so, the harbour of Lynn at 52° 47'N approximates the latitude for departure.

Lynn was one of the most prosperous harbours on the east coast of England, trading primarily with Scandinavia, but also with the Baltic, Low Countries, Rhineland, Flanders and north France. In 1200 its prominent merchants traded with Trondheim and Bergen. It is little wonder that Lynn was later to become an important port for the Hanse merchants who established their warehouses there in the fifteenth century for trade with the Baltic. Two other major seaports, lying on the north and south shore of the Humber River – Hull, at 53° 40'N, and Grimsby, at 53° 30'N – could also qualify as the departure point. From Lynn, with a favourable wind, it was only two weeks sail to Iceland where the English frequently engaged in trade.

From Iceland, Nicholas of Lynn sailed to Greenland's Eastern Settlement. Wishing to explore lands farther to the north, he left his English crew behind and 'journeyed further through the whole of the North, etc. and put into writing all the wonders of those Islands'. Needing a vessel better able to withstand the rigours of Arctic sailing, with its perverse weather and drift ice, Nicholas proceeded on the second portion of his exploration in a Norwegian ship. It is possible that it was this second departure, from Markland, that is Labrador at the latitude of Hamilton Inlet, which was 'begun' at 54°.

The Norwegian ship could well have belonged to Pál Knútsson, who was sent by the king of Norway for the purpose of trade in the Eastern Settlement of Greenland, or as a law-man there. In 1356–57, Knútsson made an auxiliary expedition to the Western Settlement. Although abandoned of inhabitants, the remains of tree-trunks and ship's timbers were there, evidence of the Greenlanders' travel to the Labrador for timber.

Sailing with Pál Knútsson and a crew experienced in Arctic sailing, in a ship better suited for the purpose than his English ship, it is well within the range of probability that Nicholas of Lynn crossed the Davis Strait from Greenland and ranged that strait's western shore from the coast of Labrador to far northern latitudes. If that summer happened to be warm and the seas ice-free, he perhaps made it as far north as Ellesmere Island. That he sailed all the way to the North Pole, as described by Cnoyen, is not possible, for solid pack ice would have prevented progress.

The polar geography supposedly visited by Nicholas of Lynn was a conflation of reality, somewhat displaced, and of classical mythology. Common to all the accounts of his voyage are whirlpools with the power to pull ships into the bottomless ocean, indwelling seas with swift currents pouring forth through deep channels, and wondrous magnetic effects. Some degree of authenticity can be found in these constituents. Nicholas of Lynn would have encountered some of the swiftest currents to be found in the northern ocean. The rivers and currents he described might have been Cumberland Sound and Frobisher Bay, both cleft deeply into Baffin Island, and Hudson's Strait. The first two might easily be confused with straits or rivers cut through mountainous islands, and the roaring and dangerous current that pours out of Hudson's Strait was described 225 years later by John Davis as 'loathsomely crying like the rage of waters under London Bridge'. It was no exaggeration on Nicholas of Lynn's part to call these channels a whirling maelstrom.

The Maelstrom vortex off the northern coast of Norway – named by some the Charybdis of the North – was known about from the time mariners first ventured along that coast. King Arthur, in conquering Norway and the northern islands, is said to have had nearly 4000 people swallowed up by the indwelling sea. Giraldus Cambrensis (Gerald of Wales),

the distinguished writer, historian and ecclesiastic of the early Middle Ages, described this whirling mass of water, the Maelstrom, as a place where 'all the waves of the sea from far have their course and recourse, as it were, without stop, which there conveying themselves into the secret receptacles of nature are swallowed up, as it were, into a bottomless pit, and that if by chance any ship passes this way it is pulled and drawn with such a violence of the waves that soon, without remedy, the force of the whirlpool devours the same.' Ívar Bàrðarson, in his *Description of Greenland*, places a maelstrom in the ocean north of the Western Settlement of Greenland.

Greek philosophers had described four indrafts of the Ocean Sea in the four opposite quarters of the world. In *Phaedo* (c. AD 36 0 BC), Plato explained that all the waters pierced the Earth to a sea called Tartarus at the centre, and that all the rivers, lakes and oceans were drawn into this primary and original mass of water. Writing in the eighth century, Paulus Warnefridi (c. 720–799) described the maelstrom as 'that very deep abyss of the waters which we call the ocean's navel'. And the seventeenth-century Jesuit priest, Athanasius Kircher, in an attempt perhaps to reconcile a geography of legend with a geography of reality said 'the celebrated whirlpool of Mosken Maelstrom on the north coast [of Norway] is about two miles wide and probably communicates with a subterranean passage through which the sea finds its way into the Gulf of Bothnia.'

Notwithstanding the sometimes confusing and conflicting information in Cnoyen's account, there is much in the story that can be corroborated. Even the magnetic island, and the region where the ship's compass does not hold, has a basis in fact. In approaching Labrador, the difference between the Earth's magnetic pole and true geographic north, is so great as to render the compass virtually useless. Here, magnetic variation exceeds 40 degrees.

Certainly the voyage of Nicholas of Lynn had a marked influence on the cartography of the sixteenth century, which showed geography in the polar region, complete with legends, taken directly from the voyage. The transition from word to line first appears on a globe made by the celebrated German scientist and cartographer, Martin Behaim (1459–1507), in 1492. Thereafter, the four polar islands from *Inventio Fortunata* become firmly fixed on maps of the most prominent and respected cartographers throughout the sixteenth century: Johannes Ruysch's *Universalior Cogniti Orbis Tabula* of 1507; the polar insert to Gerard Mercator's World Map of 1569; and in the 1584 Atlas, *Theatrum Orbis Terrarum,* by Abraham Ortelius.

Nicholas of Lynn's islands exerted such a strong influence on geographic concepts of the polar region that it took more than a century after Mercator displayed them before they finally disappeared from maps.

Chinese Junks and the Treasure Ships of Zheng He

Two of the world's largest rivers, the Huang – also called the Yellow River – and the Yangtze, have had a decisive influence on the development of Chinese history and culture over several thousand years. With their numerous tributaries, streams, lakes and canals, they formed a transportation network connecting towns and trading. Apart from the natural watercourses, China's Grand Canal is the longest and oldest canal in the world, the construction of which started in the fifth century BC. The development of a river fleet and inland trading remained the focus of Chinese shipbuilding and transport policy until the eighth century AD. Only then was Chinese interest in ocean trading aroused, and the building of larger sea-going vessels began.

The first plank-built riverboats evolved into junks, which became the classic Chinese sailing vessel. The earliest junks had one mast and probably a square sail. The first era of big sailing vessels appeared during the Qin and Han Dynasties (221 BC–AD 220).

The earliest Chinese ocean-trade routes were to Korea and Japan in the north. The Yellow Sea was comparatively shallow and to serve these routes Chinese shipwrights built flat-bottomed ships without keels, so as to prevent grounding on the constantly shifting sandbanks; in consequence they were called sand boats (shachuan). They had several masts and were also suitable for river traffic.

The Song Dynasty (960–1279) for the first time directed attention to the southern coast. This culminated in the twelth century with the establishment of the first naval fleet, and a large merchant fleet. The type

of junk developed for the southern oceans was called a fuchuan and had a deeply v-shaped hull with a keel. In the rough South China Sea the flat-bottomed sand ships would not have had adequate stability. Fuchuans were usually equipped with three or four masts, had a high bow and stern, and could have as many as four decks. The Chinese used to paint large dragon's eyes in the bow.

135. Faded Mural of Zheng He

The Song Dynasty, however, regarded foreign trade as of little importance, and strictly regulated it. Not until the Yuan Dynasty (1271–1368) did the Mongol emperors begin sending merchant ships to sea with any consistency, and to establish trading stations in Sumatra, Ceylon and southern India. The first west-

136. Sailing routes os Zheng He

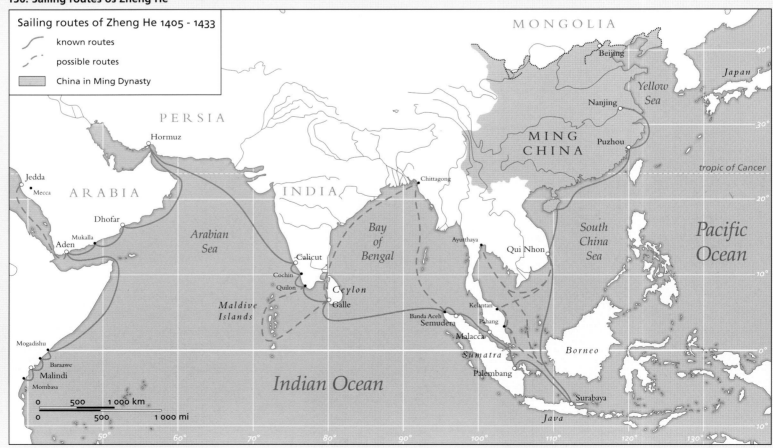

Sailing routes of Zheng He 1405 - 1433
- known routes
- possible routes
- China in Ming Dynasty

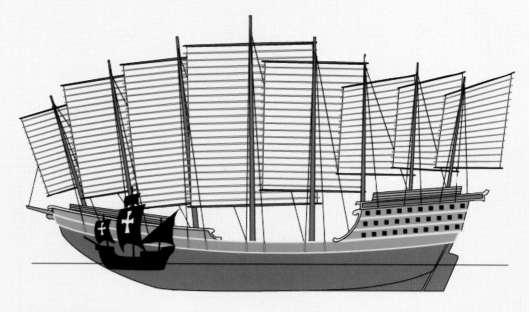

ern description of China originates from this era. On his journey to China, Marco Polo wrote about four-masted vessels sailing to India, equipped with private cabins for as many as 60 merchants and manned by up to 300 crew. Polo had travelled to China along the Silk Road through central Asia, but he did the first leg of his return voyage by sea, on board one of the fourteen junks carrying a Mongol princess to the court of the Khan of Persia, whom she was to marry. Polo continued by land from Persia to Venice.

According to Polo, the hull of the junk was double-planked, fastened with iron clamps and spikes. Additional layers of planking could later be added, up to a total of six layers. He also described the ship's bulkheads and rudder, which was hinged to the stern-post. The bulkhead and the rudder, together with the magnetic compass, are the most important maritime innovations of Chinese shipping, showing that they had developed their shipbuilding skills considerably earlier than did Europeans.

The watertight bulkheads, which made the hull stronger and improved safety, were usually transversal but sometimes also longitudinal. There could be up to thirteen transversal bulkheads. If a leak developed in one compartment of the ship, the bulkheads prevented flooding of the other compartments, and the vessel stayed afloat. In European ships, internal bulkheads were not to be introduced until the middle of the nineteenth century.

The hinged rudder appeared In China no later than the first century AD, 1200 years before European shipwrights adopted it in the thirteenth century. Chinese

138. Zheng He's name drawn by Jue Feng

137. The Ship of Zheng He

The famous Chinese explorer Zheng He carried out a total of seven expeditions to the Western world. Some of the vessels participating in the expeditions were so called 'treasure ships', huge wooden built sailing vessels. These junks could have nine masts and a length of 120 meters. They were able to carry up to 1000 passengers.

rudders were much larger in relation to the ships than were those later used in Europe. The large surfaces made them efficient, but they were also more difficult to control, although this was sometimes improved by making holes in them.

Junks had fore-and-aft lugsails, square sails in which the fore end is shorter than the aft end. Their heads were bent onto tilted yards carried parallel to the centerline of the ship. The sails were made of matting on bamboo battens, there was only one sail on each mast, and they could be hoisted or lowered like a venetian blind. Because bamboo is very strong, standing rigging could be simple, with few stays or shrouds, and the construction of the mast made it possible to turn the yard around the mast. Due to the structure of their rig, junks were fast, easy to handle and could be steered close to the wind.

By the Ming Dynasty (1368–1644), China controlled the sea from Korea and Japan in the north to Vietnam and Thailand in the south. The emperors of the Dynasty sent to sea seven exploration fleets, commanded by the Muslim eunuch Zheng He (1371–1433). Having arrived at court at the age of ten and been castrated, he had proved a successful soldier, and one faithful to the emperor during an attempted coup. He had gradually reached an important position in the court, and in 1403 Zheng He was appointed admiral of the fleet.

For his first voyage in 1405, 62 large and 255 smaller vessels were placed under his command. The largest were called treasure ships, with a displacement of 1500 tons. They were 120 m long and 50 m wide and could carry more than 1000 passengers. In addition to sailors and soldiers, their crews contained merchants, astrologers, craftsmen and priests – a total of 27,800 people. A single treasure ship was larger than the combined fleets of Columbus and da Gama.

In the construction of the treasure ships, the shipbuilding skills of north and south were combined. Their beam was wide in relation to their length, and they were exceptionally stable due to v-shaped hulls, long keels and heavy ballasting. They had nine masts with sails of red silk. Even though they carried guns, they were not classed as warships. These gigantic junks were appointed for luxury and were comparable to the cruise vessels of the presentday. The imperial envoys had huge cabins and the lounges were

equipped with windows and balconies. The hulls were brightly carved and painted in the bow were carved animal heads and dragon eyes, and aft were patterns symbolizing auspiciousness. Beneath the waterline, the hulls were whitewashed, and near the red waterline there was a sun-and-moon frieze. One may only imagine what Europeans would have thought if they had met these huge ships on the oceans, but an encounter never occured.

During the voyages the fleet sailed to India, the Red Sea and the east coast of Africa, visiting thirty-seven countries. They carried a cargo mainly of silk and porcelain that was to be traded for spices, tropical wood, wild animals and jewels. The principal purposes of the expeditions, however, were political. Despite the strength and heavy armour of the fleet, there was no intention of conquering new territories, or even of developing trade routes. China wanted to strengthen its empire's prestige in foreign countries.

It has even been suggested that Zheng He reached America, and that Columbus would have used his maps. However, there is no evidence of this in the history of discovery or in the history of cartography.

The powerful Confucian faction in the Chinese court was against the explorations of Zheng He and by 1450 they succeeded in bringing to an end all distant-water Chinese shipping. There may have been economic reasons behind this isolation policy, but the dominant consideration was the conviction that China was the centre of human civilization, and that Barbarian nations had little of value to offer with the prosperity already enjoyed in China, at least by the elite.

In the 1420s the Chinese navy had been the mightiest in the world, consisting of 400 large and 1350 smaller ships. There were 3000 freighters in the merchant navy, all of them convertible to warships. In addition to that, the merchant fleet included 400 huge bulk carriers for grain shipments and 250 large ocean-going vessels. But this development was brought to a rapid end by the close of the fifteenth century, when the emperor prohibited the construction of ocean-going vessels, or trading with vessels with several masts. Fearful of losing political control of Chinese mariners, he even forbade them to leave the country. The Chinese fleet collapsed: in 1474 it was only a third of the size during the early Ming Dynasty and in 1503 only a tenth of it.

Had the treasure ships of Zheng He been allowed to continue their voyages of discovery, and if the emperors of the Ming Dynasty had chosen to practise a strong colonial policy, the course of world history would have been fundamentally changed. As it was, however, the oceans were left open to the Europeans, who in the beginning of the sixteenth century were able to establish their control over the ocean trades.

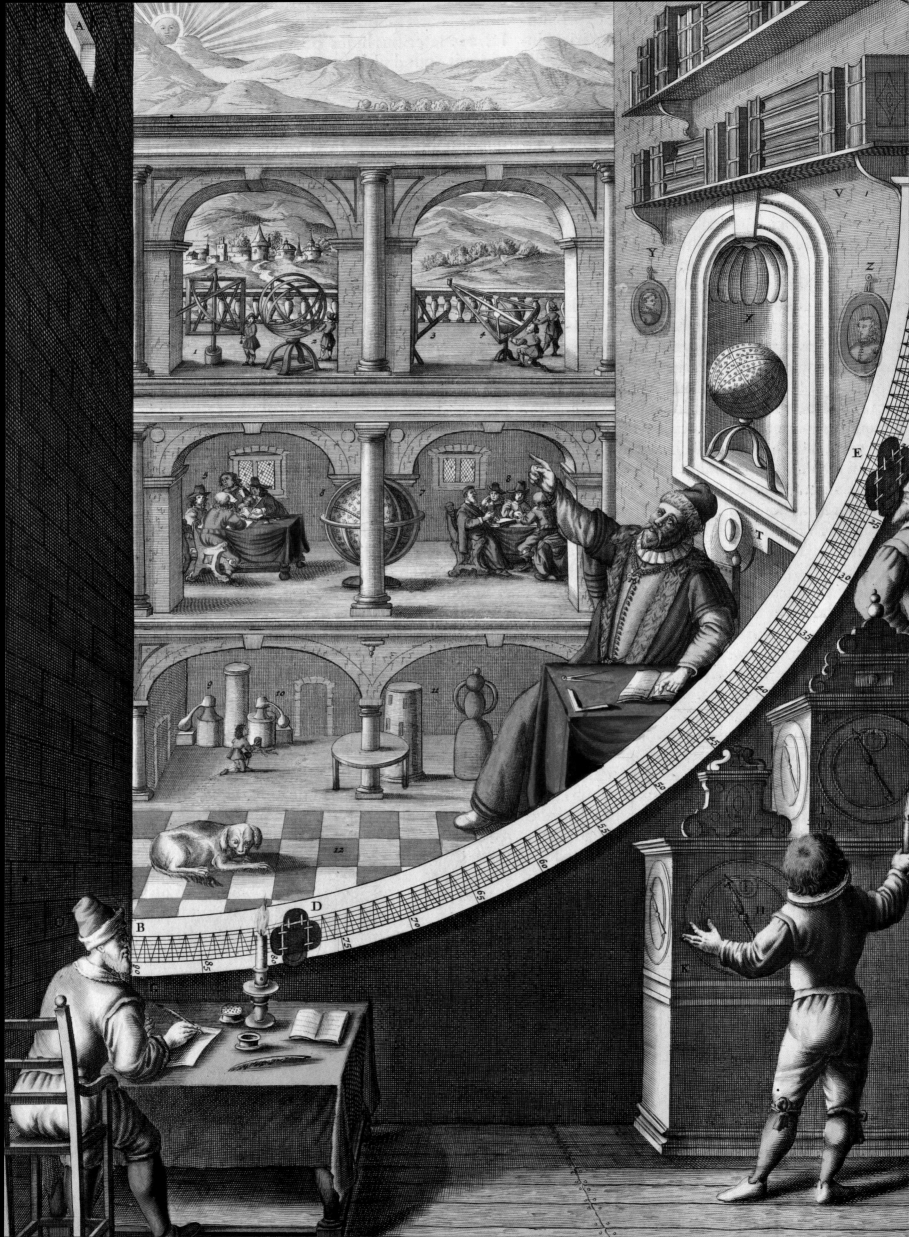

ADVANCES IN SCIENCE

The heavens themselves, the planets, and this centre.
Observe degree, priority, and place,
Insisture, course, proportion, season, form,
Office, and custom, in all line of order ....
Take but degree away, untune that string,
And hark! What discord follows ....

SHAKESPEARE, *TROILUS AND CRESSIDA*

SCIENTISTS OPEN THE SKIES

The New Astronomy: A Heliocentric Universe

Common to the Aristotelian and Ptolemaic cosmologies were three unshakable premises: a stationary Earth stood at the centre of the universe; all the planets moved in perfect circles and with uniform motion, or were composed of circular and uniform parts; objects in the heavens, being more perfect than Earth, could not change their character, such as brightness or direction of movement. In his *De Caelo* (The Heavens), Aristotle (382–336 BC) conceived the universe as a series of concentric spheres, each with a planet attached, rotating in a different plane to the others. He placed the Earth at the centre of the universe and surrounded it with spheres of the remaining elements – water, air and fire. Fixed stars lay in a sphere beyond the sphere of the planets. All these spheres were controlled by the outermost, called the *Primum mobile*, itself controlled by 'divine power'. This structure appealed to humanity's need to believe in a harmonious and ordered universe.

In the second century AD, Ptolemy noted that the Aristotelian structure of the cosmos did not fully explain the apparent movements of the planets, and devised a new system of planetary mechanics that could be used to predict and compute the

139. Tycho Brahe in his observatory by Joan Blaeu, 1662

The astronomical observatory Tycho Brahe built on the tiny Danish island of Hven became Europe's most famous observatory. It housed the instruments he devised himself, with which to measure the positions of stars and planets. To achieve greater accuracy, Brahe made his instruments extraordinarily large, such as the quadrant seen here, mounted on a wall. Brahe, seated, is pointing toward an aperture in the wall through which a star's altitude is being measured. Brahe's observations were the most accurate at the time, and helped resolve the conflict of the Copernican system of the universe over the Ptolemaic system.

THE NATIONAL LIBRARY OF FINLAND, HELSINKI

140. Epitome of Almagest by Regiomontanus, 1491

Seated beneath the armillary sphere are Ptolemy (on the left) and Regiomontanus (on the right), presumably in discussion on the ways in which current astronomical thought did not correspond with observed phenomena. Reforms proposed by Regiomontanus influenced astronomers of succeeding generations, including Copernicus, Tycho Brahe, Galileo and Kepler.

MASTER AND FELLOWS OF TRINITY COLLEGE, CAMBRIDGE

141. A Ptolemaic Depiction of the World's Structure by Andreas Cellarius, 1660

The Ptolemaic concept of the universe, inherited from his Greek predecessors, was one in which: the Earth is at the centre of the cosmos and immovable; the celestial realm is composed of the planets all moving in perfect circles; and in relation to the distance of fixed stars, the Earth is but a mathematical point.

JUHA NURMINEN COLLECTION

positions of celestial bodies at given times. Ptolemy's model consisted of circular planetary orbits, modified with epicycles, equants, eccentrics and deferents. The complexity of Ptolemy's arrangement was necessitated by the initial false premises of the nature of the cosmos. But his book on astronomy, the *Almagest* (The Greatest), became the basis of all mathematical astronomy for the next fourteen centuries.

As early as the fifth century BC, the Greek philosopher Philolaus (c. 470–385 BC) had proposed that the Earth was a planet, and that it did not occupy the centre of the cosmos. Heraclides Ponticus, who flourished in the fourth century BC, suggested

the Earth rotated on its axis. And Aristarchus of Samos (310–230 BC) placed the Sun, rather than the Earth at the centre of the universe. But their ideas were submerged under the weight of authority of Aristotle and Ptolemy. The impetus for the development of a new cosmological system was not to come until the first half of the fifteenth century AD when Nicholas Cryfts, called Nicholas of Cusa, joined the number of ecclesiastic scholars who were promoting the need for a reform of the calendar.

Nicholas of Cusa (1401–1464), Bishop of Brixen (Bressanone) in the southern Tirol of Italy, played an important role in Church reform, and travelled widely administering to its diplo-

142. A Depiction of the Copernican System by Andreas Cellarius, Pieter Schenk and Gerard Valk, 1708

In Copernicus's heliocentric universe the Sun, rather than the Earth, occupied its center. On the order of the heavenly spheres, he said: 'I feel no shame in asserting that the Moon and the Earth traverse a grand circle amid the rest of the planets in an annual revolution around the Sun. This should be admitted, I believe, in preference to perplexing the mind with an almost infinite multitude of spheres, as must be done by those astronomers who try to fix the Earth in the middle of the universe. On the contrary, we should rather heed the wisdom of nature, which especially avoids producing anything superfluous or useless, and frequently endows a single thing with many effects'.

JUHA NURMINEN COLLECTION

History of the Compass

As early as the second century AD, Chinese junks used iron rubbed with the lodestone for its polar direction ability. In the western world, one of the earliest forms of a compass to indicate North-South direction consisted of a thin magnetic needle attached to a piece of straw or wood and floated in a bowl where it could turn freely according to the Earth's magnetic field.

A mariner's compass was developed within a century by pivoting the magnetic needle on top of a vertical axis placed in a box made of wood or ivory and permanently fixed to the ship's navigation deck. A compass card attached to the needle turned with it, and on the rhumb scale on the card the heading of the ship could be read, using sights indicating the direction of the keel, now known as the lubber line.

In modern compasses the circle of the horizon is usually divided into a scale of degrees. The compass box is suspended on a Cardan frame, known as gimbals, in order to steady it when the ship was rolling. The magnetic needle, or rather a bunch of needles, used in early compasses did not retain their magnetism permanently, and a lodestone was carried on board or kept at ports to revive the magnetic power of the needle by 'stroking' the lodestone along the needle.

The lines of force of the Earth's magnetic field do not run parallel to the surface of the Earth; close to the magnetic poles they are almost perpendicular, which is why the magnetic needle tends to incline. When sailing in Polar regions, inclination must be taken into account, but in more temperate waters the effect is less important.

Magnetic compasses are also affected by the heavy iron guns carried on board wooden ships, an effect known as deviation from magnetic north, and this became even more serious when ships began to be built of iron. At the beginning of the nineteenth century Matthew Flinders (1774–1814) proposed a vertical iron bar to be placed close to the compass in order to neutralize the magnetic field created by all iron items aboard. At that time the electromagnetic theory of deviation was developed by Thomas Young (1773–1829). William Scoresby (1789–1857) observed that the magnetic field of the vessel and thus also the deviation are changed when the ship moves in the Earth's magnetic field.

The amount of deviation depends on the placement of iron masses on the ship, and it varies with the heading of the vessel. A deviation table had to be drawn up by testing the compass against shore

143. Compass as depicted by Gregorio Dati, 15th century

Picture of a simple dry box compass from *La Spera*.

THE NATIONAL LIBRARY OF FINLAND, HELSINKI

144. An Example of a British compass, 19th century

The compass case, made of brass, is suspended by gimbals in a wooden case in order to steady it when the ship is rolling. A sighting device on top of the box is used to determine bearings, and a dark filter eliminates glare.

JUHA NURMINEN COLLECTION

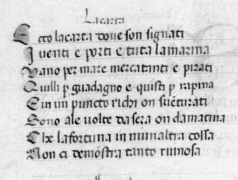

145. Lodestone made in St. Petersburg, c. 1790

Before compass needles were made to be permanently magnetized, the lodestone was carried aboard ship to periodically re-magnetize the needle.

JUHA NURMINEN COLLECTION

146. Deviation Graph

Deviation means the angle between the magnetic north and the north indicated by a magnetic compass, which varies according to the direction of a ship's travel. The deviation of the magnetic compasses of most ships are still measured. This graph shows the Finnish Navy cable ship *Putsaari's* sine-wave deviation.

THE FINNISH NAVY

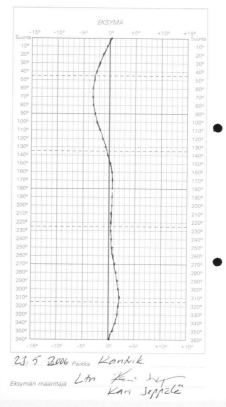

marks, or Polaris, on every point of sailing. Nowadays a deviation table is usually stored in the memory of the ship's navigation computer. Deviation must always be taken into account when navigating with a magnetic compass.

In 1838, George Airy, Astronomer Royal of England developed a method for compensating for deviation using magnets and pieces of iron. Soon John Gray's compass binnacle became a standard with its adjustable magnets and characteristic two iron cannon balls on both sides of the compass. And several technical improvements to the mariner's compass were developed by the physicist William Thomson, Lord Kelvin, of Scotland, between 1873 and 1878. He made the compass card lighter by devising a system of needles suspended on silk threads fixed on a card made of light rice paper, in order to reduce friction on the bearing of the pivot. He also devised a system to limit movement of the card due to the motion of the ship

by immersing the card in a fluid, using a float under the card to reduce fiction.

In order to make it possible for the captain to keep track on the bearing of the vessel even when laying on his bed an overhead compass hanging from the ceiling of the cabin was developed.

In the twentieth century new instruments on different principles have been developed which in part have replaced magnetic compasses. A gyrocompass depends on the principles that a spinning top maintains the orientation of its spinning axis in space, and that the spinning motion of the Earth will act on a spinning top left to turn freely so that its axis will settle parallel to the axis of the Earth. A gyrocompass senses any change of the ship's position as torsion, and gyros can be used to measure inertial forces acting on a ship in order to provide the navigator with a dead reckoning position. But the development of the inertial navigator has already been superseded by the Global Positioning System (GPS) based on man-made satellites.

147. The Compass Binnacle, 20th century

The compass binnacle, made of brass and wood, was placed on the navigation deck where the helmsman could see the compass to keep the course. The red and green balls compensate for magnetic deviation caused by iron parts of the vessel.

JOHN NURMINEN FOUNDATION

matic affairs, but he also maintained an active interest in mathematics and astronomy. From out of the jumble of dating systems, and the disparity between astronomical and ecclesiastical lunar computations, a new way had to be found to determine when Easter should be observed in the Christian world. This required an astronomical knowledge of the Sun and the Moon, and led him to publish improvements on the *Alfonsine Tables* of ephemerides which had been created in the thirteenth century by King Alfonse X to predict the movement of planets.

This work did not require Cusa to depart from Ptolemy's computations, but he was able to detach himself enough from Ptolemy's cosmography to propose, half a century before Copernicus, that the Earth revolved on its axis and that it circled the Sun. In contradiction to Aristotle and Ptolemy, and in advance of the thinking of Giordano Bruno (1548–1600) who was burned as a heretic by the Roman Inquisition for expounding views similar to those now put forward, Cusa expressed the belief that the stars were not confined within a fixed, celestial shell, but extended into infinite space. That Cusa's radical thinking did not result in derision or condemnation is most likely due to his having expressed it in a mystical and hypothetical way.

Johannes Müller of Königsberg (1436–1476), widely known as Regiomontanus, also re-examined the findings of Ptolemy, as well as the accuracy of the *Alfonsine Tables*. He set up an observatory in Nuremberg, Germany, where he could watch the planets, and built a workshop to construct better instruments for the task. He did not question the Ptolemaic geocentric construct of the cosmos, but he introduced a new approach to the study of astronomy – mathematical astronomy. Quantitative observation replaced the philosophical constructs of the Old Astronomy based on 'common sense'. Theories of the universe now had to be formulated in 'logical and mathematical terms'. Conversely, any mathematically derived explanation of the motion of planets had to be confirmed by observation. In his *Epitome of the Almagest* (completed in 1462) Regiomontanus showed that the position of the planet Mars was off by 2 degrees from Ptolemy's predicted position. From his observation of the motion of the Moon, he suggested that lunar distances could be used to determine longitude at sea.

Ptolemy's geocentric cosmology was finally replaced with a heliocentric model by the Polish astronomer Nicolaus Copernicus (1473–1543), when in 1543 he published *De revolutionibus orbium coelestium* (On the Revolutions of the Heavenly Spheres). The Coperinican system was based on the now familiar idea that a year represented one complete circuit by the Earth around the Sun, while the spinning of the Earth on its axis accounted for the alternating pattern of night and day. This rotation of the Earth also accounted for the appearance of the stars revolving around it in the opposite direction. He showed that the angle of the Earth's axis (23.5°) remains constant, but in its annual orbit around the Sun it presents a different 'face' to the Sun, which accounts for the variance of the length of days and nights in winter and summer.

With his placement of the Sun at the centre of the cosmos, Copernicus was able to simplify the complex and cumbersome Ptolemaic planetary mechanics. Although he retained the epicycles of Ptolemy, their arrangement was a simpler one and the number of epicycles reduced in number. His description of planetary motion also provided an explanation of why some planets appear to change direction and move backwards (retrograde motion) and why planets varied in brightness. Copernicus also calculated with great accuracy the radius of the orbit of planets around the Earth and Sun. But he was uncertain as to whether the Sun was at the exact centre of the cosmos, or whether it was slightly off to one side. If it was in the exact centre, then he had a truly heliocentric universe. But if the centre of the cosmos was the orbit of the Earth in respect to the fixed shell of the stars, which he retained from Aristotle's cosmological system, then the Sun was slightly off-centre, and this was a heliostatic system.

Acceptance of the heliocentric astronomy was slow in coming. It took almost one hundred years before his Sun-centred universe finally found confirmation and acceptance. The concept was readily understood, but Copernicus's detailed explanations were too complicated and difficult for most scholars to follow. His proposed construction of the universe was correct, and had been derived by theoretical analysis; what it lacked was quantitative observations, substantiated by precise data. A major step toward providing this was made by the Danish astronomer, Tycho Brahe (1546–1601). He devised improved instruments, which he used to determine with greater accuracy the motions of the planets. But Brahe lacked the use of a telescope which was not invented until decades later, and he was unable to measure any stellar parallax, the apparent angular change in position of stars when viewed from different perspectives. This led him to conclude that either the stars were too far away and therefore the amount of parallax was too small to be calculated, or that the stars were close beyond the planets, and that the Earth did indeed rest at the centre of the universe. Unfortunately, he decided the latter was true, and constructed a geocentric solar system, but one that included those heliocentric elements from Copernicus that seemed acceptable.

In this compromised structure, published in his *De Mundi aetherie recentioribus phaenomenis*, Brahe placed a solid, fixed Earth at the centre, orbited by the Sun, with all the remaining planets revolving around the Sun. Despite this significant mistake, the great number of careful measurements of planetary motions Brahe made, particularly those of the planet Mars, led to the next significant advance in astronomy.

In his latter years, Brahe had an assistant by the name of Johannes Kepler (1571–1630). Working with Brahe's extensive and precise data Kepler created a new model of the universe. Finding that his calculations would not fit with all the observed motions of the planets, he finally realized that the problem lay in the basic premise that planets moved in perfectly circular orbits. When, instead, he used an orbital motion in the form of an ellipse, the mathematics, calculations and obser-

vations all correlated. However, Kepler could not determine why the orbit of planets moved in an ellipse, rather than in a circle. In his *Harmony of the Worlds* (1619) he speculated it was caused either by magnetic forces or was due to angels flapping their wings to push the planets about.

Kepler's efforts reshaped seventeenth-century thinking on motions and orbits of the solar system, and in 1687, with the publication of *Principia*, Isaac Newton gave the foundations of mechanics on why celestial bodies move the way they do.

Following the invention of the telescope by Dutch spectacle makers, Galileo Galilei was able to view the heavens in greater detail than heretofore had been possible, and finally to prove Copernicus's theory of a heliocentric universe. His telescope was primitive, but through it Galileo saw the mountains and craters of the Moon, as well as sunspots on the surface of the Sun. These 'blemishes' disproved the Ptolemaic doctrine that the heavens were composed of an unchanging, perfect substance. The planet Saturn was revealed to have rings, which Galileo called 'ears', and the planet Jupiter had four moons. Galileo realized that the occultations and transits of these moons could be used to determine longitude at sea.

His most important observation, however, was that the planet Venus went through a complete set of phases, from crescent to full, in the same manner as the Earth's Moon. This could only occur if Venus orbited the Sun, and lay between the Sun and Earth. His discovery not only provided the observational evidence to support Copernicus's heliocentric universe, it also brought to a close the authority of Aristotle and Ptolemy in the nature of the universe.

CELESTIAL EPHEMERA FOR NAVIGATION

Important as these advances in comprehending the celestial harmonies of the universe were, to the navigator they were of little consequence. The only role in navigation provided by the progress in astronomy was the ability to predict the time

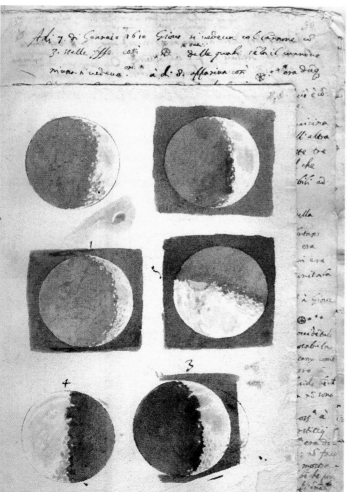

148. Galileo Galilei by Justus Sustermans, c. 1639

Through his systemic studies, quantitative experiments, and careful observations, Galileo changed Aristotle's abstract conceptual approach to astronomy to one of an understanding through scientific method. In 1608 the telescope had been invented, and within a year Galileo created an improved version capable of magnifying objects up to twenty times. It was now possible for astronomers to see beyond what the naked eye could perceive. Details of the surfaces of planets, and planetary motions, as revealed by the telescope, changed all previous concepts of the universe.
NATIONAL MARITIME MUSEUM, LONDON

149. The Phases of the Moon by Galileo Galilei, 1610

When Galileo turned his telescope to the heavens in 1609, the first celestial body he observed was the Moon, which he illustrated. This, along with his other discoveries, he published the following year in his book *Sidereus Nuncius* (Starry Messenger).
BIBLIOTECA NAZIONALE CENTRALE DI FIRENZE

150. Telescope, 19th century

Galileo designed an accessory to the telescope that enabled distances to be measured between Jupiter and its moons, thereby determining longitude at sea. In actual practice, however, the telescope was of little use for the purpose of navigation due to the rolling and pitching of the boat. Its most important function was to determine the nationality of a vessel – whether friend or foe – while the ship was still far enough away that evasive action could be taken, if necessary, while there was still time. In the approach to land, it was useful in identifying landmarks and potential harbours or dangers.

JUHA NURMINEN COLLECTION

of eclipses, which could be used to establish the longitude of important geographic locations. Solar eclipses, however, are so rare for any one place that it is impractical to depend on them for any navigational purpose. And while lunar eclipses may occur several times in each year, and were used in antiquity to determine the longitude of several locations, lunar motion is so complex that it was not until the nineteenth century that it was possible to use lunar eclipses for navigation. For mariners to calculate latitude and longitude to make their voyages across the oceans, they needed complete, accurate and reliable tables of the movement of the heavenly bodies. These astronomical tables, known as ephemerides, were published in almanacs.

Unfortunately the publication of Copernicus's *De revolutionibus* did little to increase the accuracy of declination tables for the movement of the Sun and planets. Although his calculations were based on the 'new' heliocentric hypothesis, their dependence on the old Aristotelian/Ptolemaic system, in which the orbits of planets all moved in perfect circles, made them no more than approximations of observed movements. The basic cosmological system remained unchanged from the time of Aristotle. The universe was still conceived as a finite whole, constructed of a limited number of spheres moving in perfect circles.

In his *Almagest*, Ptolemy had prepared tables for every-day astronomical calculations. They were limited in scope, inaccurate and inconvenient to use, nonetheless they were the genesis of succeeding generations of astronomical tables. In the ninth century, Muslim astronomers, such as al-Khwārizmī and al-Farghānī, drew upon Greco-Roman texts as a base for their science. They translated the *Almagest*, corrected many of the geographical coordinates in it and improved Ptolemy's astronomical tables. With these new tables it was possible to calculate the setting and rising of the Sun and Moon, deter-

mine the monthly or daily position of planets, and date the phases of the Moon.

With the Muslim conquest of Spain, their scientific methodology and learning was introduced to the Christian West. Scholars from northern Europe flocked to Toledo and Seville, the new centres of learning, where they translated the Arabic texts into Latin and disseminated the knowledge of antiquity to Europe. England's first scientist, Adelard of Bath (c. 1080–c. 1160), visited Toledo, where he learned Arabic and translated al-Khwārizmī's astronomical tables. The Italian known as Gerard of Cremona (1114–1187) translated over seventy Greek and Arabic science texts, including Ptolemy's *Almagest,* while a resident of Toledo.

An important part in the development of navigational astronomy was played by Alfonso X (known as 'Alfonso the Wise'), who ruled as king of León and Castile in the thirteenth century. During his reign he stimulated the cultural life of his kingdoms by patronage of schools in Seville and Salamanca. He compiled the legal knowledge of his time, and produced scientific and historical works. Alfonso is best known today for his accomplishments in astronomy, especially for bringing together fifty scholars and astronomers to translate Arabic works into Castilian. Through their efforts a new set of astronomical tables, called the *Alfonsine Tables*, were completed in 1252. These were later to be revised by Nicholas of Cusa, and again by Johannes Müller, because of their inaccuracies. Although they suffered from the fact that they were based on the Ptolemaic geocentric universe, and were cumbersome to use, requiring a great deal of time to make the computations, they were the most accurate yet in predicting the position of planets.

The primary purpose of these astronomical tables, in the Muslim world as well as the Latin world, was not for use in navigation. At this time, Astrology, Astronomy and Mathematics were linked together as one. Much of the desire for better tables was for their use in Astrology, prompted by the belief that destiny could be predicted through studying the influence of stars and their patterns. There were also religious reasons for better tables: knowing the date of the beginning of Ramadan, or of Easter, depended on an accurate lunar calendar. But in these improved tables were the scientific elements necessary to resolve astronomic problems of navigation.

As mariners extended their voyages south along the west coast of Africa toward the equator, new challenges in navigation arose. The Pole Star, so important in their navigation on account of its ease of use, slowly slipped toward the horizon, rendering it impractical to determine latitude. There was no equivalent star in the southern hemisphere to take its place. The methods of navigation, which had previously served mariners so well, no longer sufficed, and they were obliged to turn to measuring the altitude of the Sun to determine latitude.

While living in Salamanca, Spain, Abraham ben Zacuto (1452–1515), the noted Jewish astronomer and historian, made further corrections and improvements to the revised *Alfonsine Tables*. In 1481, his work entitled *Almanach perpetuum* was translated into Castilian. With these new tables, navigators could determine latitude from the Sun at any time of the day, without having to wait for its meridian passage, and could calculate the position of the planets, including the Sun and Moon. When Spain expelled its Jews, Zacuto went to Portugal, where under King John II he continued his astronomical work. Spanish and Portuguese explorers benefited from Zacuto's revised tables: Christopher Columbus used them on his 1492 voyage, as did Vasco da Gama when he undertook his voyage around the Cape of Good Hope to Calicut, India, in 1498. Putting these tables into practical use required calculations that were still too elaborate and complicated for even the literate and highly trained navigator, and were well beyond the ability of the ordinary sailor. The tables of ephemerides provided by Za-

cuto needed to be simplified. Navigators were better served by manuals such as the *Regimento do astrolabio & do quadrante* (Regiment of the Astrolabe and Quadrant) by Pedro Nuñes. The latter treatise, compiled from Zacuto's *Almanach perpetuum,* contained rules for obtaining latitude by observation of the height of the Sun, and a calendar giving the Sun's declination and position in the Zodiac for a full four years, including leap year. This became the prototype for future Portuguese manuals of the sixteenth century.

After the death of Copernicus, the German astronomer Erasmus Reinhold (1511–1553) recalculated Copernicus's tables to produce a new set of tables that were published in 1551. Since they were dedicated to Albert, Duke of Prussia, they

151. Tables of Declination of the Sun by Abraham ben Zacuto 1491

Basing his work on the Alphonsine astronomical tables, completed in 1252, Abraham ben Samuel Zacuto was able to produce the first scientifically accurate means of calculating latitude from the Sun. Originally written in Hebrew, they were translated into Spanish as *Tratado breve en las influencias del cielo.* Christopher Columbus used these tables, and Zacuto's treatise on solar and lunar eclipses, on his voyages.

JEWISH THEOLOGICAL SEMINARY OF AMERICA, NEW YORK CITY

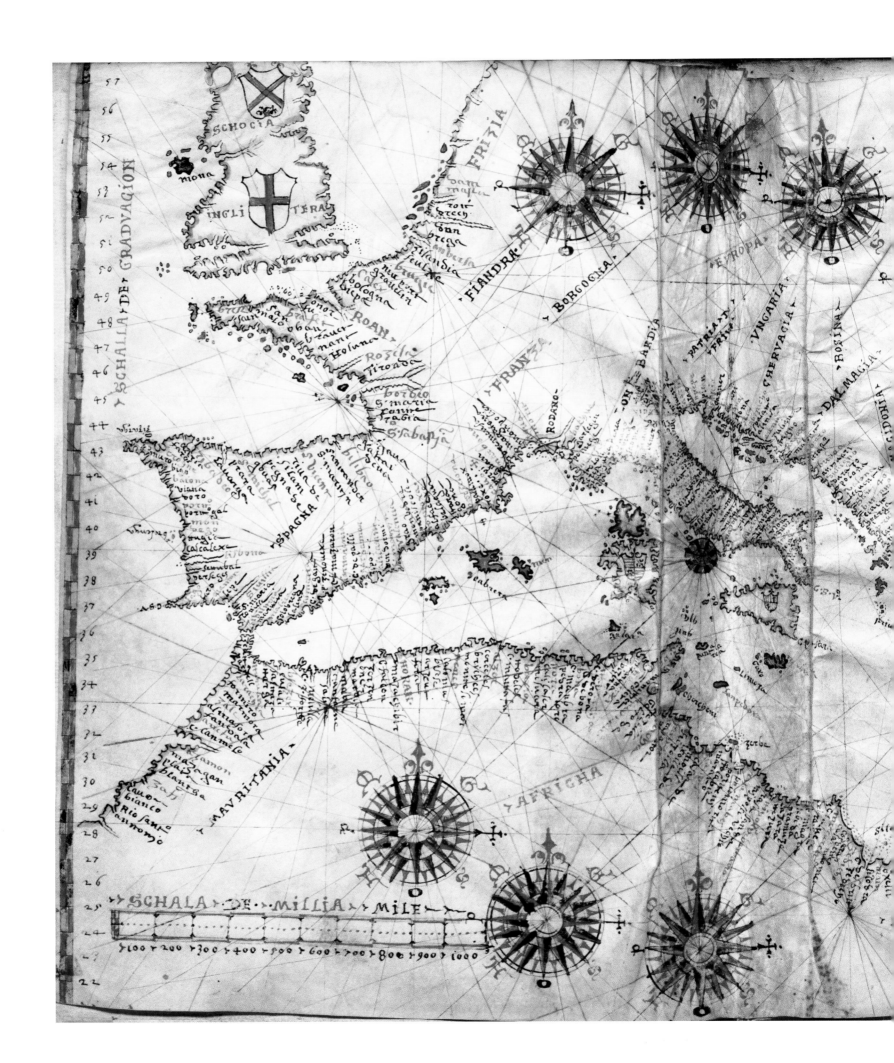

152. & 153. The Portolan Chart and Compass Rose by Battista Testarossa, 1557

In 2007 a newly discovered navigational manuscript came to light. Virtually unnoticed as it reposed on the shelf at the Royal Geographical Society in London, its contents were thoroughly studied, and the results published later in the same year.

Written primarily in Italian in 1557 by Battista Testarossa, and entitled *Brieve Compendio de larte del Navegar*, it is like other manuals of the time on navigation and maritime science in that it wholly encompasses the subjects of cosmography of the world, astronomy and navigation, in theoretical, as well as practical instruction. In the theoretical discussion on longitude, Testarossa proposes using lunar eclipses as a means of determining relative longitude. He also recognizes the relationship of time to longitude. He puts forth a method on how longitude could be determined using a set of seven sand-clocks: a larger one which runs for 24 hours, and six smaller ones which run for one hour, 1/2 hour, 1/4 hour, 1/8 hour, 1/16, and 1/24 hour. In effect, he created a 'sand glass chronometer'.

Included is a portolan chart on vellum, created especially for this manuscript. But this chart of the Mediterranean Sea and a portion of the eastern shore of the Atlantic contains several features significantly different from most portolan charts of the time. It is drawn to direction bearings on the compass rose of true north and south, rather than 'skewed' to compass bearings of magnetic north as was the common practice. This is now the standard system (with magnetic north shown secondarily) on present-day nautical charts. And a latitude scale of the Mediterranean Sea is placed on the chart for the first time. This, along with longitude tables in the text, would enable mariners to provide exact coordinates of important locations – thus improving cartography and aiding the mariner.

At the end of the work, Testarossa pays homage to the great navigators of generations previous to his own – Christopher Columbus, Magellan, John and Sebastian Cabot – 'to dignify the memory and the honour to men who practised 'excellence in navigation'.

ROYAL GEOGRAPHICAL SOCIETY

are called the *Prussian Tables*. They helped promote the fame of Copernicus throughout Europe, and served as the basis for the calendar reform by Pope Gregory XIII (1502–1585). However, the calculations were still defective. Tycho Brahe, after a lifetime of work in which he produced the first new catalogue of stars since the time of Ptolemy, created a new set of ephemerides that gave daily positions of the Sun and Moon for the year 1599. He sent a manuscript copy of these tables to his patron, Emperor Rudolph II (1552–1612), but Brahe died before they could be published.

It remained to Kepler to complete Brahe's tables. Incorporating his own tabulations with those of Brahe, Kepler finally brought the *Rudolphine Tables* to publication in 1627. These were the most accurate yet, keeping the planetary positions to within a margin of error of only 10 seconds of arc, compared with earlier tables that had errors of up to 5 degrees.

THE MYSTERY OF MAGNETISM

An art the sailors have that cannot deceive
By virtue of the magnet, an ugly brown stone
To which iron voluntarily attaches itself.
Touching the needle with it, they fix the
Needle in a straw and float it on water,
Whereupon it turns infallibly to the
North Star without a doubt.

GUYOT DE PROVINS, C. 1200

The ability of an ugly black stone – the lodestone – to attract iron was known since classical antiquity, but at that time it was never conceived that it could be used to impart geographic direction. Knowledge about magnetism advanced with the realization that when iron was rubbed with the lodestone (a naturally occurring magnetic rock) it retained the attractive power of the lodestone. Finally, it was discovered that the magnet, or magnetized iron, when allowed to move freely, pointed toward the north.

Ever since the days of Saint Jerome in the fourth century, the Virgin Mary has been associated with the Pole Star, which stands steadfast and true in the heavens. Mary was the patron saint of navigators, and the Virgin of Good Winds who sailors prayed to, invoking her blessing before the start of each voyage:

Ave Maris stella
Dei mater alma
Atque semper Virgo
Felix coeli porta

Alexander Neckham and the thirteenth-century French monk and scholar, Pierre de Maricourt (Petrus Peregrinus), as well as the British scientist, Roger Bacon (c. 1214 – 1294), all were careful to differentiate the *Stella Maris* (Star of Sea) from

154. The Virgin of the Navigators by Alejo Fernández, c. 1535
The Virgin Mary, Virgin of Navigators and Virgin of Good Winds is seen here watching over and guarding a fleet of ships. It is believed that Christopher Columbus is among the navigators shown.

COPYRIGHT © PATRIMONIO NACIONAL, MADRID

the *Stella Nautica*, the Pole Star. Neckham speaks of the Virgin Mary as Star of the Sea and Queen of the Poles. These scientific authorities in the Middle Ages believed that the needle pointed not to *Polaris*, but to the celestial pole in the heavens; that *Polaris* just happened to circle nearby was considered a happy coincidence. Some ascribed the reason the needle pointed to the North Star as due to a 'mystic sympathy'. Others thought it pointed to a terrestrial north, rather than a celestial (heavenly) north.

By the end of the twelfth century the magnetic compass was already in regular use by the mariners of Europe, and scholars began the scientific study of magnetism. The first person in the West to explore the mysterious properties of magnetism was Alexander Neckham. In his *De naturis rerum* (1190), intended to be a manual of scientific knowledge of the time, Neckham included a brief discourse on the magnetic compass. He remarked how 'when sailors are in cloudy weather [and] can no longer profit by the light of the sun, or when the world is wrapped up in the darkness of the shades of night, and they are ignorant to what point of the compass their ship's course is directed, they touch a magnet with a needle, which [the needle] whirls around in a circle and when its motion ceases, its point looks direct to the north'. Neckham again mentions the magnetic compass in another of his treatises, *De Utensilibus* (c.

155. Fluid compass by Richard Eden, 1579

Pierre de Maricourt's 1269 treatise on magnetism was plagiarized in its entirety by the Italian professor Jean Taisnier in 1508. As evidence of its considered importance it was translated into English in 1572 by Richard Eden. In this page Eden describes and illustrates a simple fluid compass, where a lodestone is laid on a light board on the surface of the water. 'By virtue of the lodestone', he says, '[it] shall it be easy to discern which of the points answers to the Arctic pole, and to the Antarctic pole'.

THE BRITISH LIBRARY, LONDON

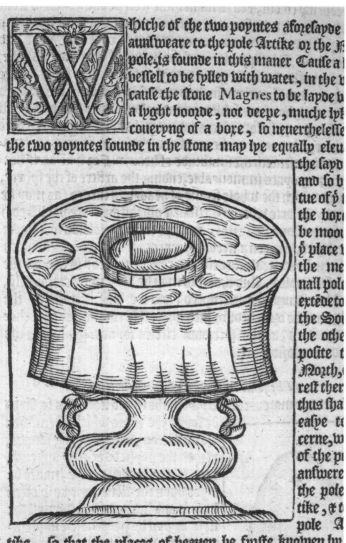

1180), in which he says that sailors use a needle 'to direct their course when the polar star is concealed through the troubled state of the atmosphere'.

Jacques de Vitry, a contemporary writing in 1218 says, in much the same words: 'An iron needle, after having been in contact with the lodestone, turns itself always towards the northern star, which, like the axis of the firmament, remains immovable, while the others [stars] follow their course, so that it is very necessary to those who navigate the sea'. The poem quoted above by Guyot de Provins, c. 1200, celebrates the ability of a needle magnetized by the lodestone to point to the polar star, and in an anonymous French love song (also c. 1200) the poet compares his lady's love with the constancy of the polar star.

The ability of the magnetic needle to point north was accepted without question, but why it pointed north had to wait another four centuries for an answer.

The study of magnetism took another step forward with the work of Pierre de Maricourt. In 1269 this French monk wrote the first scientific treatise, *Epistolae de Magnete*, on the magnetic compass. Maricourt described two types of compass: the dry compass in which the needle is balanced on a pin and allowed to turn freely in the air; and the floating compass where the magnetic element is placed on a card and floated in liquid.

He explained the properties of different kinds of lodestones and outlined the laws by which magnets attract and repel each other. He found that a magnet had two poles, accounting for these forces, and gave them the names of *North Pole* and *South Pole*. Maricourt believed the magnetic needle pointed heavenward toward the Pole Star, rather than to some earthbound force. He said, 'Some ignorant men were of the opinion that the virtue of the magnetic stone commeth not of heaven, but rather of the nature of the place it is engendered, saying that the mines thereof are found in the North, and that therefore ever one part of the stone centres itself toward the north. But these are ignorant that this stone is also found in other places'.

Those who affirmed the 'Point Attractive' resided in the Earth attributed it to a huge mountain of rock of magnetic stone, and it was shown on charts until the beginning of the seventeenth century. When navigators experienced a variation in the direction the needle pointed, they attributed it to there being not one, but two or three attractive points, or mountains of magnetic stone on the Earth. Fully three centuries later, the British scientist, Leonard Digges concluded, 'the attractive point does not reside in the heavens'. But he also goes on to say 'it is no question for great mariners to meddle with, no more than the findings of longitude'.

In 1581 Robert Norman, the English navigator and instrument maker, published *The New Attractive*, containing his observations on the magnetic compass. In Norman's experiments with the compass, he found that the compass needle pointed to the Earth's magnetic North Pole only because the compass

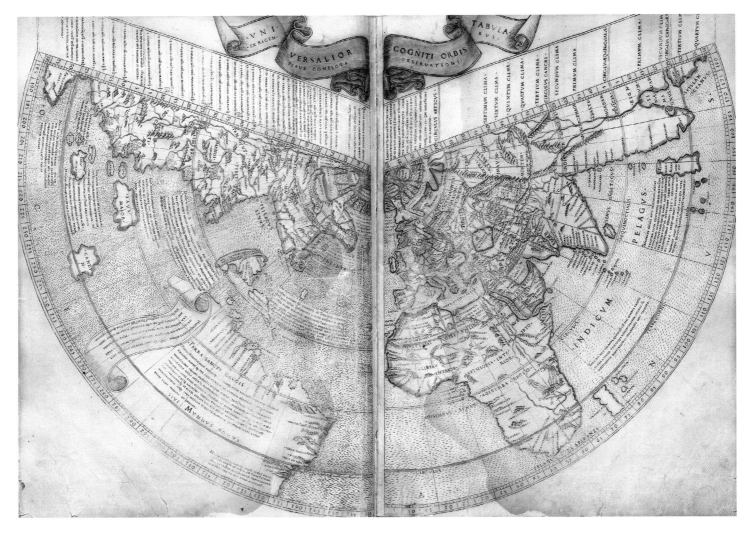

156. World Map by Johannes Ruysch, 1508

On his 1508 map, Johannes Ruysch places a magnetic rock near the North Pole, and ascribes its discovery to the English Friar, Nicholas of Lynn, who made a voyage toward the north in 1355. An inscription on the map reads: 'At the arctic pole there is a high magnetic rock, thirty-three German miles in circumference. A surging sea surrounds this rock, and around it are four islands, two of which are inhabited'. This legend of a magnetic mountain dragging vessels to it with a certain doom appears in the second century AD with Ptolemy, and is later expounded in Arab legend. These same four islands, and the polar magnetic rock, continue to be shown as late as the mid-seventeenth century on the maps of Gerard Mercator.

THE NATIONAL LIBRARY OF FINLAND, HELSINKI

card, with its needle, was constrained in the horizontal plane. It was constructed that way for a very good reason; taken in conjunction with nautical charts, the most useful application of the compass was for direction finding – for pointing north. Norman's experiments showed that if the needle was mounted so as to allow it to swing in a vertical plane it did not align itself with magnetic north, instead, it pointed downward toward the centre of the Earth, aligning itself with the Earth's magnetic lines of force. This 'newe discovered secret and sub-till propertie, concerning of the needle' he called the 'mag-netic dip' (inclination) and the instrument he constructed in this new manner was called the magnetic dip compass.

With his publication in 1581 of *A Discourse of the Variation of the Compass or Magneticall Needle*, William Borough (1536–1599) brought to light another piece of the mystery of magnetism. A scientific navigator of the Elizabethan era, Borough took measurements of variation of the compass in the same place over a period of years, and noted that magnetic north was not permanently fixed in position, but was slowly shifting toward the north – the variation varied. It was an observation for which he had no explanation, but felt that perhaps it depended upon longitude. What he had accomplished, however, was to introduce the notion there was a time factor as well as a geographic factor to magnetic variation.

Twenty-five years after Robert Norman's publication, a general concept of the world distribution of magnetism was postulated by William Gilbert (1540–1603) in his *De Magnete* (On the Magnet). Gilbert was strongly influenced by the work of Pierre de Maricourt, and gave him credit for his study of magnetism. Rather than speculating on the nature of magnetic phenomenon, he took upon himself to understand its principles by experimental study. Gilbert was the first to conceive of the terrestrial globe being a great magnet; he said it accounted for the action of the compass in pointing toward north, and he described the importance of this magnetism in practical problems of navigation. He was also aware that the compass needle did not point to true or geographic north, and believed this was because the Earth was not a perfect sphere. If it were, he concluded, then the magnetic and geographic Norths would coincide.

Scientists attempted to utilize the phenomenon of magnetic variation for tasks other than correcting their compass bearings. João de Lisboa, a Portuguese navigator and author of a treatise on the mariner's compass (*Tratado da Agulha de Marear*), in 1514 tried to establish a relationship between magnetic variation and longitude. Pedro Nuñes, in his *De arte atque ratione navigandi* (1546), also promoted the use of magnetic variation as a means of determining longitude. Mariners had noticed that in the vicinity of the Azores there was no magnetic variation, their compasses deflecting neither to the east or the west of true north. Extrapolating from this observation, Nuñes pronounced that the Azores meridian of longitude had zero degrees of variation. Believing that there was a direct correlation between longitude and the amount of magnetic variation east or west of this meridian, he suggested it could be used to determine longitude.

In the early sixteenth century, Nuñes, and other Portuguese navigators such as João de Castro and Francisco Faleiro, devised 'Shadow Instruments' combining the compass with a plate marked with north–south and east–west lines and a gnomon at its centre. The mid-point of shadows of equal length (equal altitudes of the Sun) before and after meridian passage of the Sun at noon showed true or geographic north. A comparison with the north-pointing compass indicated the amount of magnetic variation. The French pilot, Jean Rotz (c. 1505–1560), also produced a treatise (1542) on magnetic variation and created an elaborate instrument he called a *Cadrans*

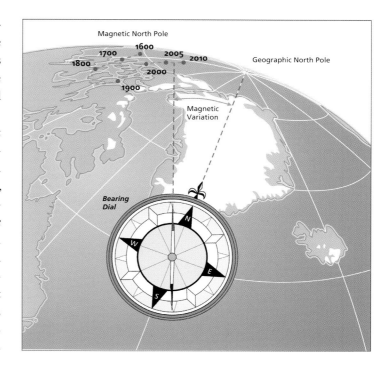

157. Magnetic phenomenon

Magnetic variation varies in different parts of the world according to regional influences. The closer one approaches the Magnetic North Pole, the greater is the amount of difference between Magnetic North and Geographic North. The location of the Magnetic North Pole is subject to yearly change as the result of fluctuations in the flow of electrical current in the Earth's molten core.

158. A detail from a World Map by Edmond Halley, 1730

Edmund Halley, 1730 By the beginning of the eighteenth century magnetic variation and longitude were finally shown to be totally independent of each other. With Edmund Halley's chart *A New and Correct Chart Shewing the Variations of the Compass*, published in 1701, a full and accurate plotting of lines of magnetic variation in the Atlantic Ocean was available. This knowledge enabled the navigator to make the appropriate correction to the ship's course.

JUHA NURMINEN COLLECTION

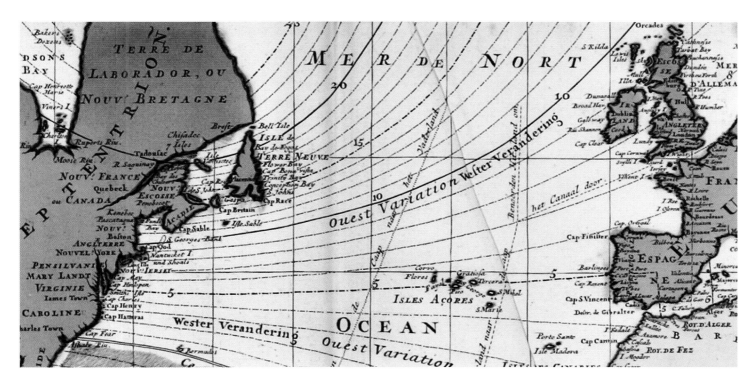

159. Magnetic Dip Compass designed by William Gilbert, 1600

In his study on magnetism and the behaviour of compass needles, William Gilbert noted that when the compass needle was free to rotate in a vertical plane, it dipped below the horizon at different angles. Gilbert thought this characteristic might be useful in navigation to determine latitude.

THE MASTER AND FELLOWS OF CONVILLE GAIUS COLLEGE, CAMBRIDGE

Differential (Differential Sun-dial) to measure it. Like the Portuguese 'Shadow Instruments' Rotz's dial compared the Sun's line of meridian passage with the angle of the magnetic needle. He too believed in a north-south 'true' meridian through the Azores and its potential for determining longitude by magnetic variation.

Unfortunately, Rotz did not have access to the works on navigation and hydrography written by the Portuguese author and mariner, João de Castro. In 1538 de Castro made a voyage to India during which he took careful observations of magnetic variation, and concluded there was no correlation between variation and longitude. Mariners continued their attempts to correlate the amount of easterly or westerly variation of the compass with longitude. But the complex pattern of variation over the Earth's surface made the correlation unreliable, and the method was finally discarded.

Navigators also endeavoured to use magnetic dip (inclination) to determine latitude. In 1535, Francisco Faleiro, a Portu-

guese instrument maker, published a book in which he stated his belief that there was a relationship between the angle of inclination of the dip compass and latitude. But the theory did not hold up against actual observations, namely on account of the assumption there was great symmetry and regularity in variation east and west of the 'true meridian' through the Azores. The idea that magnetic dip, or inclination of the dip compass, could be used to determine latitude lingered on into the seventeenth century. In 1602 William Gilbert, in conjunction with Thomas Blundeville, Edward Wright, and Henry Biggs – all highly regarded English scientists – published a pamphlet in which they proposed that the dip compass could be used to find latitude at sea when the sky was overcast. 'How agreeable, how helpful, how divine!' Gilbert said, 'Sailors when tossed about on the waves with continuous cloudy weather, and unable by means of the celestial luminaries to learn anything about the place or the region in which they are, with a very slight effort and with a small instrument are comforted, and learn the latitude of the place'.

There was found to be some degree of relationship between the dip (inclination) of the needle with latitude, but the results of such a practice were too varied and unreliable to be of any practical use. In general, their theory was reasonable, for at the Earth's magnetic equator (half-way between the north and south magnetic poles) the dip of the compass is 0°; approaching the magnetic North Pole it increases positively to 90°, while conversely, at the magnetic pole in the Southern Hemisphere, the dip is negative at 90 degrees. Unfortunately, these horizontal lines of magnetic force (see diagram) are not straight lines in perfect conjunction with parallels of latitude.

The idea of linking the dip compass with finding longitude while at sea continued to hold the minds of scientists, who put forth various methods to this purpose. As late as 1670, Henry Bond, in his *Longitude Found*, said 'the variation and dip of the needle depend on the same motion of the magnetic poles in their revolution'. In combination with a theoretical table of magnetic elements he founded a method – later to be discarded – for finding longitude at sea with the dip compass.

Although efforts in this direction proved fruitless, ultimately the magnetic dip compass showed itself to be of some value. When trapped for three years between 1829 and 1833 in the Arctic ice while searching for the Northwest Passage, Captain James Ross (1800–1862) made use of his time by taking frequent observations with the dip compass. In 1831 he was able to calculate the exact position of the Magnetic North Pole; a discovery perhaps of greater scientific significance than the discovery of the sought-after passage. 'This is the place', he said, 'that nature has chosen as the centre of one of her great and dark powers'.

The Log

At the end of the Middle Ages dead reckoning became an important means of keeping track of a ship's position at sea. This was accomplished by navigators making careful records of course and speed, with estimates of leeway caused by wind on the beam, and of the drift caused by currents and tide. An experienced navigator can estimate his ship's speed by looking at the height of the bow wave and listening to the sound of the wake. Columbus probably did so. But more accurate methods were needed. The oldest means of measuring a ship's speed with any hope of accuracy was to drop a piece of wood from the bow and use a sand clock to time the flotsam as it floated between two marks on the rail. A more sophisticated development was the chip log, which came into use at the beginning of the seventeenth century (1607). It consists of a 'chip', a piece of board with a shape of a quarter circle, attached at its three corners to a 500-foot line. When the chip is dropped into the sea it stands vertically and perpendicularly to the ship's direction of motion, and remains stationary in the water, pulling out the line. Ballast is fixed along the rim of the chip to insure it falls in the correct position. Knots are tied in the line at intervals of seven fathoms (42 feet). Each pair of sand glass and log, and the spacing of the knots, is tuned by individual experimentation. Speed is measured by dropping the chip from the stern and letting the line run out for half a minute. The cord is attached to the upper corner of the chip by a peg, which pulls free when the cord is tugged firmly. This capsizes the chip, enabling the navigator to pull it back onboard ship after taking the reading. The higher the speed, the more knots run out during the measurement. Their number indicates the speed. Thus the knot became the unit of speed in many languages. The chip log is fairly accurate up to speeds of about fifteen knots and that was sufficient in the era of sailing ships.

A 'traverse board' was used to help the navigator with his dead reckoning. This pegboard is marked with a wind rose provided with eight holes along each compass point, and with a rectangular square-ruled section. Each half hour of the four-hour watch a peg would be put into a hole on the wind rose to indicate the course made good during that half an hour. Another peg would be inserted into the square-ruled board to indicate the speed made good, and each pair of pegs being connected by a thread. This enabled the officer of the watch to keep a record of course and speed that the navigator could read at a glance.

Trials to develop a log that would continuously and more easily give the speed were made from the sixteenth century, but the first log of that kind was not patented until 1802 by Thomas Massey. It was based on a small rotator dragged in the water. The motion was transmitted to a recording mechanism on the rail. In 1861 Thomas Walker patented a more developed design that gave both the speed and distance travelled. It became the practice to read the log at every change of course. A similar concept was Forbes' log, which has a small rotator fixed on the underwater part of the hull. With power-driven ships it also became possible to measure speed by calibrating the rotation frequency of the ship's propeller. The dynamic pressure of the water streaming along the hull could also be used for measuring speed by employing a Pitot tube projecting into the water (Pitometer log). Different applications of electromagnetic phenomena (electromagnetic and thermoelectric devices) in the flowing water also got their use in measuring the speed.

All these methods give the speed of the vessel in relation to water. Modern systems of satellite navigation that indicate the geographic position of the ship are also able to measure the present speed, and distance covered in a given time, relative to the sea floor.

160. Chip Log, 19th century

The wooden chip thrown into the water pulled the line off the reel. The amount of line discharged over a certain period of time indicated the speed of the ship.

JOHN NURMINEN FOUNDATION

161. The Chip Log in use by Richard Andree, 1875

The man with a sandglass is reading half a minute's time for the line to discharge from the reel. The knots on the line released indicate the speed of the ship.

KIELER STADT- UND SCHIFFAHRTSMUSEUM, KIEL

162. Patent Log, 19th century

The patent log consisted of two main parts, a propeller and a gauge. The propeller was towed by the ship, and the amount of its rotation was transmitted by the cable to the gauge fixed on the rail. The speed of the ship was read off the dial. A model developed later gave both the speed and the distance that the ship travelled.

JOHN NURMINEN FOUNDATION

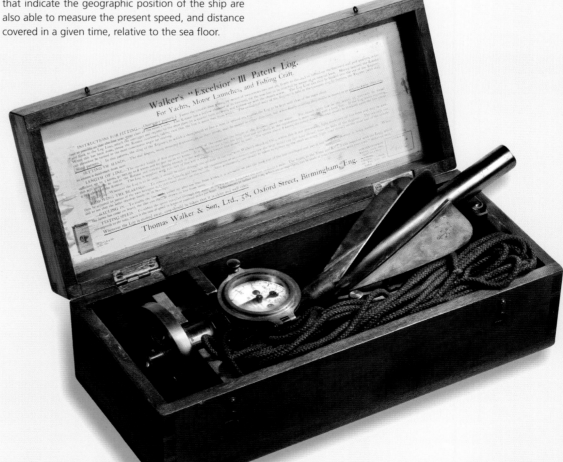

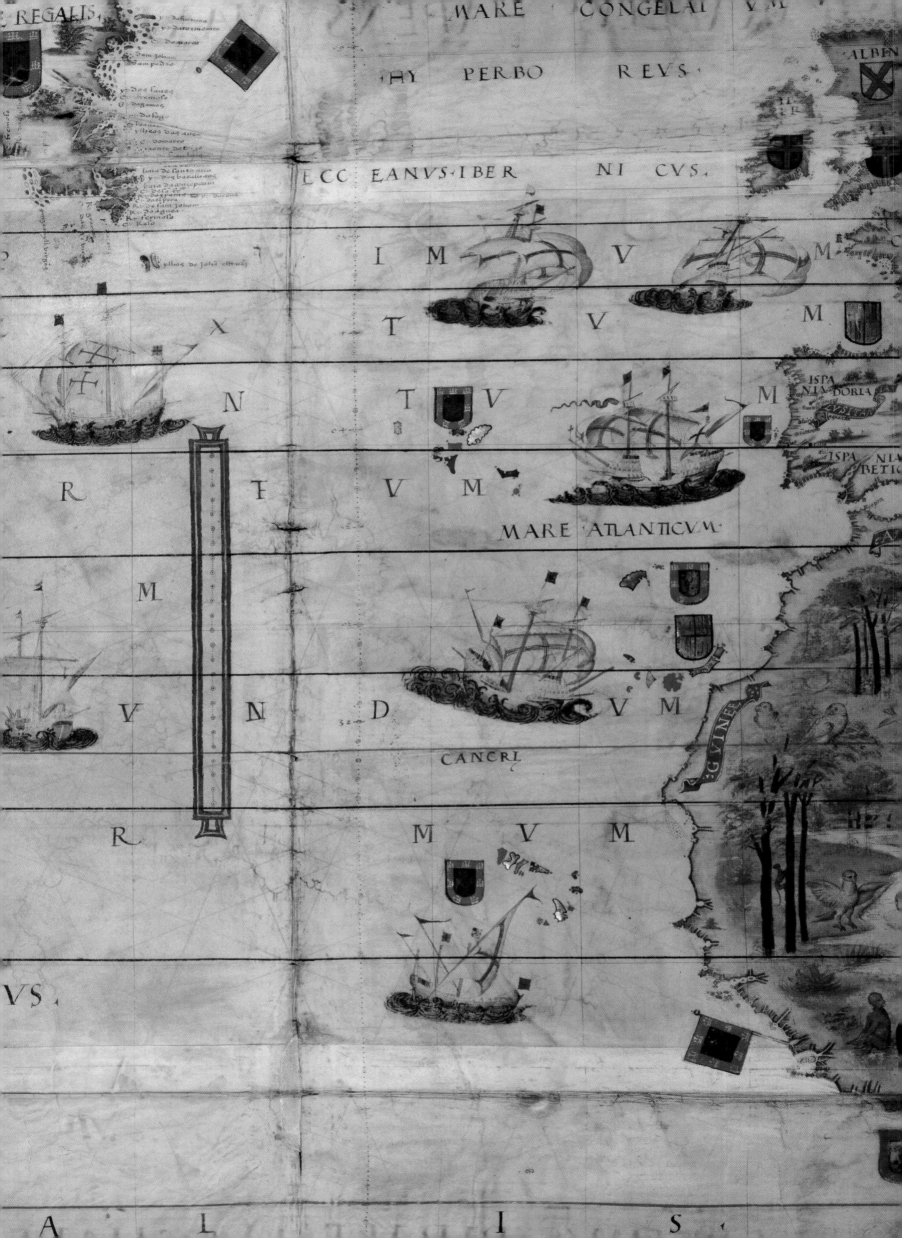

IBERIAN VENTURES
IN THE ATLANTIC

BEYOND THE PILLARS OF HERCULES

Genoa's mariners led the way in leaving the confines of a familiar Mediterranean to sail beyond the Pillars of Hercules into a virtually unknown Atlantic Ocean. In 1278, Lancelot Malocello, a Genoese nobleman, became the first Christian to brave the perils of this limitless sea. Whether he intended to visit the Fortunate Islands (Canaries), or attempted a passage around Africa to India, or simply tried to define the extent and depth of this unexplored watery realm, is not known. He was followed thirteen years later by two galleys, the *Allegranza* and the *St. Antonio*, belonging to another Genoese, Tedisio Doria. This time the object of the expedition was clearly stated: the vessels were to double the Cape of Good Hope and reach India to engage in trade. This voyage marks the first attempt by any European to circumnavigate Africa for the tripartite quest of oceanic discovery, religious expansion and commercial gain. By the mid-fourteenth century, French mariners were also making expeditions into the Atlantic. But these were all isolated, sporadic voyages, the result of private enterprise rather than expeditions initiated by any monarch as a national goal

163. Atlantic Sea by Lopo Homem, 1519

As decreed by the Gods, the Greek hero, Hercules, was assigned twelve labours requiring enormous strength and dexterity. The eleventh task was to retrieve the golden apples from the Hesperides at the far western corner of the world. Blocked from his goal by the mountain that was once Atlas at the western end of the Mediterranean, Hercules split the mountain in half. One part remained as Mount Hacho in Ceuta, Africa, and the other as the Rock of Gibraltar. To the Ancients, these two mountain halves – the Pillars of Hercules – marked the utmost limit of the habitable world. To pass beyond these promontories at the Straits of Gibraltar, out into the Atlantic, was to venture forth into the realm of the unknown.

BIBLIOTHÈQUE NATIONALE DE FRANCE, PARIS

164. The Ferrer Voyage to the Canary Islands from Abraham Cresques' Mappemundi, 1375

On 10 August 1346, a galley captained by Jacme Ferrer left Majorca and coasted the African mainland to sail past Cape Nam, the dividing line between the known world and the unknown. Ferrer's objective was to find the River of Gold, thought to be the Western or Black Nile. To the right of Ferrer's vessel is the legend: 'Cape Finisterre in western Africa. Here, Africa begins and it ends at Alexandria and Babylon.' Calling Cape Bojador the Finisterre of Africa is an apt comparison, for both are subject to quick and vicious storms, shallow water and short, steep waves, holding the promise of danger, or even doom.

BIBLIOTHÈQUE NATIONAL DE FRANCE, PARIS

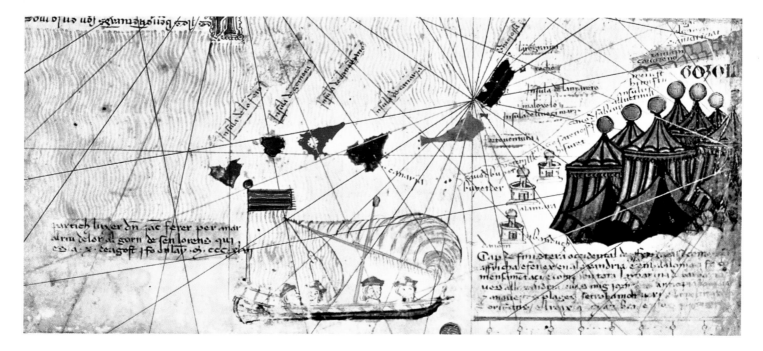

165. An Army on board from *Le Canarien* by Fr. Pierre Boutier and Jehan Le Verrier, c. 1420–1430

Le Canarien presents a detailed narrative of the French and Castilian conquest of the Canary Islands in 1400 by Jean de Béthencourt (1360–1422) and Gadifer de La Salle (c. 1340–1422). In *Le Canarien*, one learns the social dynamics of contact between differing cultures, the struggle for dominance and ownership between France and Castile, as well as the conflicts between the European and indigenous population, with the attempts of subjugation and Christianization.

THE BRITISH LIBRARY, LONDON

166. Prince Henry with Young Afonso V by Nuno Conçalves, 15th century

Prince Henry 'The Navigator', promoted voyages to explore the African coast in search of gold and to find the legendary Christian Kingdom of Prester John. The expeditions initiated by Prince Henry were extended by his successors all the way to India, and helped raise Portugal to a world power.

MUSEU NACIONAL DE ARTE ANTIGA, LISBON

and planned programme of trade and expansion.

It is to the two great Iberian powers of Portugal and Spain that credit must go for pushing the boundaries of the unknown to a new and distant horizon. The name most associated with early exploration of the Atlantic is the Infante Dom Henrique of Portugal – Prince Henry the Navigator.

LINKING THE ATLANTIC WITH THE INDIAN OCEAN

Prince Henry the Navigator

At an early age, Prince Henry (1394–1460), third son of King John I of Portugal, launched the western world into the Age of Discovery, and commenced the heroic age of Portugal. Ceuta, on the Moroccan coast of Africa, was strategically important. For centuries it was a crucial waypoint in the gold trade, and its conquest would give Portugal control over the trade with trans-Saharan caravans that transported goods from the Far East. But once Portugal captured Ceuta, it ceased to be the terminus of an overland trade route. It was this that brought Prince Henry to conceive another way to gain control of the African gold and ivory trade, by promoting voyages along the west coast of Africa, thereby circumventing the Muslim trade routes across the Sahara.

He set in motion a plan to explore the coast of Africa beyond Cape Nam (28° 47' N latitude), the farthest point reached by Spanish navigators, and a coast which was then considered unnavigable. In ten years he sent out fifteen expeditions southward along the coast, each voyage advancing a little farther. Their objective was to seek the source of gold in Guinea, and engage in the trade of gold, ivory and slaves there, coupled with the desire to locate the legendary kingdom of Prester John to enlist his aid in the fight to destroy the Muslim infidels. Still accustomed to following the coast for their navigation, mariners feared leaving sight of shore and having to rely on the compass.

Prince Henry knew nothing concerning the navigation of that coast, but information gained from Moors, and Ptolemy's latitude tables, convinced him that beyond Cape Bojador, on the western bulge of Africa, land continued all the way down to the equator. In 1434, Gil Eannes sailed from the Algarve and made the then unprecedented journey as far as Cape Bojador. Fear of the *Mar Tenebroso* (Sea of Darkness), the unknown, combined with treacherous waters, violent storms and thick fogs discouraged his crew from any attempt to proceed further.

In his voyage the following year (1435), Eannes sailed beyond Cape Bojador for a further 250 miles. It was a momentous occasion in the history of navigation; for over a thousand years no other ships had been able to make headway against that cape's cruel combination of wind, current and reef. In the past ten years fifteen expeditions under Prince Henry had tried, and failed. During this phase of exploration along the west coast of Africa, trade and geographic information replaced crusader and missionary goals as the primary motive.

Finding they could survive the hazards of the unknown seas, Portuguese mariners pressed on. They rounded Cape Verde in 1445, passed Dakar and Guinea, and finally reached Sierra Leone, only 10° above the equator. It was now clear that the south coast of the province of Guinea, which had never

167. Portuguese voyages

Vasco da Gama's pioneer voyage around the Cape of Good Hope and across the Indian Ocean to Calicut, India, in 1497–99 was a turning point in mankind's knowledge of the cosmography of the world. The Indian Ocean was shown not to be an enclosed sea, as Ptolemy believed. Well-established trade routes, which heretofore involved long and arduous Silk Road caravan travels, and several middle-man merchants, had now been shortened by a direct sea-route to the source of spices and access to commercial markets of the Far East.

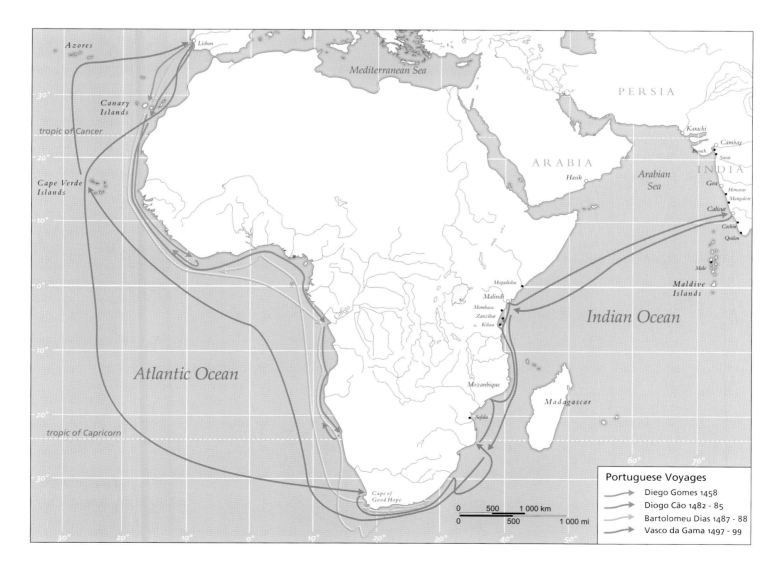

Portuguese Voyages
Diego Gomes 1458
Diogo Cão 1482 - 85
Bartolomeu Dias 1487 - 88
Vasco da Gama 1497 - 99

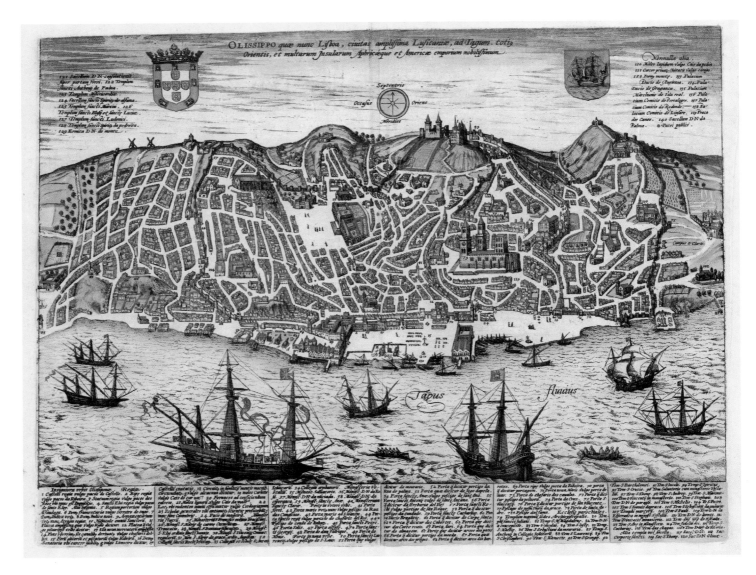

168. Lisbon by Georg Braun and Frans Hogenberg, 1598

During the Age of Discovery, many of the great Portuguese expeditions, including that of Vasco da Gama, departed from Lisbon. By the end of the sixteenth century, Lisbon was the European hub of commerce with the Far East.

JUHA NURMINEN COLLECTION

previously been reached, and of which no knowledge existed of its lands and peoples, was accessible.

On the return voyages, the Portuguese navigators discovered that by making a wide, sweeping arc far west and north into the Atlantic, they could avoid the contrary currents along the coast and gain the prevailing westerly winds needed to speed them homeward. As a result of this detour, the Atlantic archipelagos of the Canaries and Madeira were rediscovered. These island groups, all visited centuries before by Carthaginian and Arab sailors, and more recently by Genoese and French mariners, appeared on charts as early as the 1339 on a portolan by Angelino Dulcert, but it remained for Portuguese mariners to fix their location, firmly establish their identity, and claim ownership by colonization.

Prince Henry died in 1460, having transformed European expansion and trade from the old land-routes to new sea-routes in the Southern Ocean. He had not lived to achieve the goal of doubling *Cabo de Buena Esperanza* (Cape of Good Hope) at the southern extremity of Africa, but it is fair to speculate that in his last years he was beginning to think about a navigable route leading from the Atlantic Ocean all the way to India, the source of spices.

King John II of Portugal

Under King John II (1455–1495), successor to the programme of exploration initiated by Prince Henry, the goal became redefined: to reach India by a sea-route from the Atlantic Ocean. But first, it was necessary to determine how far south the continent of Africa extended, and once it was reached, to see whether the waters of the Atlantic continued into the Indian Ocean.

According to Ptolemy, the Indian Ocean was a completely enclosed inland sea. If this were true, then unless a strait could be found piercing that land called *Terra Incognita*, there would be no way that India and the Far East could be reached by sea from the Atlantic Ocean. Arab maps, on the other hand, showed a navigable passage between the two oceans. Al-Bīrūnī

(973–c.1050), one of the greatest of Muslim geographers of the Middle Ages, expressed his belief that the Southern Sea (Indian Ocean) communicated with the Atlantic, 'although,' he wrote, 'no one has been able to confirm it by sight.'

Scientific advisors to King John concluded that such a passage existed. When it was shown that Cape Bojador could safely be doubled, voyages were extended still farther south. Diogo Cão (d. c. 1486) made two attempts, one in 1482 and the other in 1485–1486, to establish the landmass of Africa, but was unable to double *Promontorium Prassum* described by Ptolemy as the most southern point of the known world. King John chose Bartolomeu Dias next to explore and chart the western coast of Africa to its most southerly point and determine what lay beyond. Dias left Portugal in 1487 and passed south of his goal, Promontorium Prassum, without ever catching a glimpse of it. Dias turned back towards Portugal, and it was only then that he finally saw for himself the cape that had remained hidden from men's eyes for so many centuries. He gave Ptolemy's Promontorium Prassum a new name – *Cabo Tormentoso* (Stormy Cape) – on account of the dangers and storms he encountered there. According to the historian Barros, King John renamed it *Cabo da Boa Esperança* – the Cape of Good Hope – because it promised the hope that the search for a sea-route to India was finally within grasp. In successfully passing *Promontorium Prassum*, Dias finally proved the possibility of a navigable passage from the Atlantic into the Indian Ocean.

King John II then gave to Pêro da Covilhão and Afonso de Paiva the mission to discover where the spices came from. Covilhão and Paiva left Lisbon in May 1487. In their travels, they learned from sailors and Arab traders that the whole coast to the west could be navigated. The King's caravels could sail to Guinea and around the Cape of Good Hope and be confident they could continue to navigate up the eastern coast of Africa to Sofala. From there they could easily reach India, for it was an open sea all the way, with the route well known and not difficult.

Now it remained to initiate an expedition to sail all the way to India in a single voyage. For this, the scientific knowledge already existed. Step by step, as geographical information expanded, progress had also been made in astronomy and navigation. Abraham ben Zacuto's astronomical tables, the *Almanach perpetuum,* were made available by mathematicians and navigation advisors to King John II; from them, latitude could be determined by observations of the Sun and Pole Star. Also, the *Regimento do Estrolabioe do Quadrante & Tractado da Spera do Mundo* (Regiment of the Astrolabe and Quadrant) contained a list of sixty latitudes of known places on the African coast as far as the equator. The Planispheric astrolabe had been transformed into an instrument, the sea astrolabe, or mariner's ring that performed better at sea. With names of particular places and ports written directly on the altitude scale, it eliminated the need to read degrees of altitude in order to find a port.

The primary purpose of the astrolabes and quadrants was not for navigation, since dead reckoning was still the means for set-

169. Portrait of Vasco da Gama by an unknown artist, 15th century
Vasco da Gama, Portuguese explorer and governor of the military Order of Christ, commanded the first ships to sail directly from Europe to India. His accomplishment initiated European dominion in the Indian Ocean and Asia Minor over Muslim commerce, and was responsible for Portugal's success as a colonizing power.
MUSEU NACIONAL DE ARTE ANTIGA, LISBON

ting the course and of determining position. Rather, they were used to correct charts with the proper latitude of prominent landmarks along the way, and of the destination, thus enabling sovereignty rights for to be established newly discovered lands.

In his book on cosmography and navigation, called *Esmeraldo de Situ Orbis* (c. 1505), Duarte Pacheco Pereira provided the Portuguese with rules for the use of the astrolabe in navigation. Pereira was a mariner, a navigator and a chronicler of voyages of discovery. His *Esmeraldo* is first and foremost a guide to navigation. Rules for calculating latitude from altitude of the Sun were certainly known before Pereira put them in written form sometime around 1505–1508, but his real achievement lay in presenting them with the utmost of simplicity and clarity, that made them easily understood by the average navigator.

Vasco da Gama

In the last remaining years of his reign, King John began to plan for the grand expedition to India, but he died before much progress was made. His successor, King Manuel I (1469–

From the Quadrant to the Cross-Staff

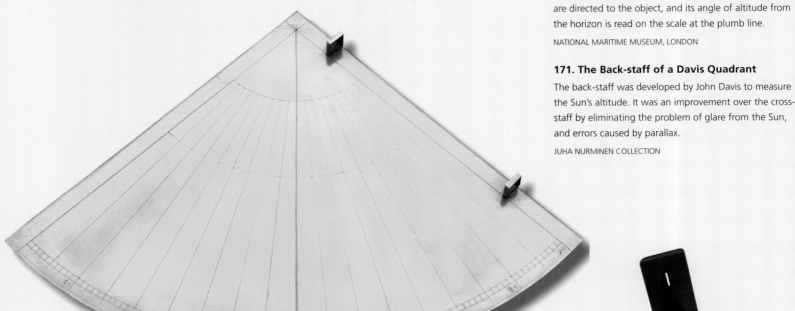

170. A Mariner's Quadrant, c. 1600

This type of quadrant was used by mariners in the seventeenth century. The pointers on the right-hand side are directed to the object, and its angle of altitude from the horizon is read on the scale at the plumb line.

NATIONAL MARITIME MUSEUM, LONDON

171. The Back-staff of a Davis Quadrant

The back-staff was developed by John Davis to measure the Sun's altitude. It was an improvement over the cross-staff by eliminating the problem of glare from the Sun, and errors caused by parallax.

JUHA NURMINEN COLLECTION

A forerunner of the marine quadrant first came into use in Europe as a sundial at the beginning of the thirteenth century, and the first marine quadrants appeared in the middle of the fifteenth century. Functionally they were similar to marine astrolabes, and comprised a piece of board a quarter of a circle in shape with a weighted line hanging from its corner. The upper side of the quarter was pointed towards a star or the Sun and the weighted 'lead line' indicated the altitude of the celestial body where it crossed a graduated scale inscribed on the quarter of the circle. Scales and curves were drawn on the board for determination of the time on the basis of the altitude observation. Jacob ben Mahir developed a combination of the quadrant and an astrolabe called the new quadrant at the end of the thirteenth century, adding to the value of the instrument for computation. With the publication in 1477 of the first modern edition of Ptolemy's *Geographia*, latitude sailing employing the quadrant became commonplace. The early marine quadrants, however, suffered from the same defect as did marine astrolabes in that they were not easy to use on the deck of a rolling ship.

In antiquity, several instruments had been developed to measure the angular distances between celestial bodies and the horizon. Using the natural horizon as the basis for observation made great sense at sea, but these early instruments had been too clumsy to be used on board ship. At the beginning of the fourteenth century Levi ben Gerson introduced the cross-staff or Jacob's staff to measure the altitude of celestial bodies, and the angles between them. With its simple design and lighter weight it was easier to use at sea.

Cross-staffs consist of two parts: a straight stick of about 1 m (3 feet) in length on which a second, and shorter, stick with a hole in its centre stick can be slid.

The observer places his eye at one end of the staff and points it towards the sky, sighting simultaneously along the top and bottom of the transversal slide, which is moved on the staff towards the eye or away from it until the upper end touches the star, and the lower end rests on the horizon. The angle subtended by the slide, and hence the altitude of the star, is indicated by a scale inscribed on the staff. The instrument was usually equipped with three cross bars of different lengths: one for measurements of the Pole Star relatively low on the horizon; one for the Sun in northern seas; another use when sailing close to the Equator, where the Sun would be near the zenith.

The need to look at the Sun was a serious defect in the cross staff, and there was a danger of parallax error if the observer's eye were not in exactly the right position. To eliminate these problems, an English captain by the name of John Davis (1543–1605), introduced in 1594 a simple back-staff, sometimes called Davis's Quadrant. It had two scaled and curved bars protruding in opposite directions from a staff. The shorter one had

a moveable peg to cast a shadow. There was a fixed horizon slit at one end of the bar, and on the other there was the longer curved bar with a moveable pointing slit. At noon the observer stood with his back towards the Sun with the short bar pointing perpendicularly down and with the long one vertically up. By adjusting the device, the shadow of the peg was superimposed on the horizon slit. The pointing slit was moved until the observer saw the horizon through both slits. The noon altitude of the Sun was computed by adding the two angles read on the scales of the two curved bars.

Another instrument using similar principles was the nocturnal, which was used to correct for the parallax of Polaris after its altitude had been measured by other means. It could also be used for checking the local time on board the ship.

A simple device known by its Arabic name, *kamal* (completeness), was used by the Arabs and Chinese during many centuries for estimating latitude. It is rectangular piece of board with a long side of about 5

cem (2 inches). A chord passes through the centre of the board and is knotted at appropriate intervals. In use, one end of the chord is kept between the teeth or close to one eye and the chord is pulled tight. The long side of the board is placed on the horizon and the board is moved either towards or away from the eye until the upper side touches the star. The knots on the chord provide the scale giving the altitude of the star, usually in multiples of 1.5 degrees. This gradation is consistent with an older tradition of measuring the altitude by using the width of fingers at the end of an outstretched arm. The ratio between the width of any individual's finger and the length of their arm is a fairly constantly 1.5 degrees, which also corresponds to three apparent diameters of a full Moon. The Kamal is useful when the object being observed is close to the horizon, as it is in the Bay of Bengal, where the latitude of Polaris at Aden is seen at an altitude of about 10 degrees, and at the tip of the Indian subcontinent a little less. The kamal was less useful in the Mediterranean.

172. Arbalestrille by Jacques de Vaulx, 1583

These instructions from the sixteenth century show how to make the scale bar of a cross-staff, and its use.

BIBLIOTHÈQUE NATIONALE DE FRANCE, PARIS

173. The Frontispiece of *Introduction to Geography* by Peter Apian, 1533

The picture shows angles between the Moon and stars being measured to determine geographical longitude.

THE NATIONAL LIBRARY OF FINLAND, HELSINKI

1521), eager to gain direct access to the spice-trade, continued the next phase of exploration and conquest. Vasco da Gama was selected as Captain-Major of the fleet.

Opinions differ on how much navigational instruction Vasco da Gama received preparation for to his voyage. Much of his instruction, if not most, was provided by the chart and report sent by Covilhão to King John II, and handed down to his

174. *São Gabriel* by Björn Landström, 1961

The *São Gabriel*, flagship of Vasco da Gama's fleet, and captained by da Gama, was a carrack of 178 tons and 27 metres in length. This type of vessel was commonly used in the fifteenth and sixteenth centuries, for its large size could well handle the difficult conditions encountered in open seas, and had sufficient capacity to hold all the provisions necessary for long voyages. The red cross on a white ground, emblazoned on the lower course sails, was the symbol of the Order of Christ, of which da Gama was a member. Founded in 1319, the Order of Christ was a Portuguese military order originating in the Templars, whose goal was to protect Christian interests in the Holy Land.

JUHA NURMINEN COLLECTION

successor, King Manuel. As well, Bartolomeu Dias provided first-hand information from the voyages he had made in that direction. Other books and maps supplied included a copy of Ptolemy's *Geographia*, and a *roteiro* of sailing instructions.

Included among the instruments on the expedition were a large wooden astrolabe, smaller astrolabes of metal and, in all probability, several quadrants, which were still the favoured instruments for taking altitude measurements. Navigation tools common to any voyage included a number of compasses, hourglasses and sounding leads. In order to improve on the accuracy of his dead reckoning, it is possible a rope (*catena a poppa*) was towed to determine the amount of leeway, the sideways slippage made by the ship through the water when the wind was blowing on the ship's beam or quarter.

On 7 July 1497 Vasco da Gama hoisted anchor and set sail from the Tagus River. This was to be the longest voyage yet to be taken by any Portuguese mariner – a dangerous and fearful voyage into the unknown. The passage south along the coast

of Africa was by now familiar, but at the Cape Verde Islands da Gama made a radical departure from the route taken by his predecessors. Rather than turning east into the Gulf of Guinea and following its coast, he continued to hold his course due south. We can safely assume that Dias advised him to do this to avoid having to battle the combined forces of adverse winds and dangerous currents he knew they would meet later along the west coast of Africa.

Favourable Southeast Trade Winds easily propelled the small fleet south until they reached the prevailing westerly winds. Then da Gama turned his ships eastward directly toward the Cape of Good Hope, and on 4 November they sighted land. Four days later, after ninety-six continuous days of sailing during which they covered 3800 miles, the ships anchored at a bay da Gama named St. Helena. The route thrust upon him by nature's design, and which he so bravely endured, proved to be the most effective one possible, and is still in use by sailors today.

As the Portuguese fleet approached the Cape of Good Hope the relative ease of the first part of the voyage changed as they struggled to make progress against an adverse wind and the swift-flowing Benguela Current. Farther east, the full force of the Agulhas Current was against them, and they soon found out how formidable it was. After three days of tacking back and forth, they found they were right back where they had started.

Now a new foe began to take its toll. Scurvy, caused by vitamin deficiency, began to affect the crew, causing swollen hands, bleeding from swollen gums and loss of teeth. In their weakened condition the sailors were unable to carry out even the simplest of duties, placing an extra burden on those who were well. Even so, the Portuguese fleet continued to make progress up the Swahili coast of Africa. Upon reaching Mozambique, at the southwest limit of the Indian Ocean trade, they now felt the certainty of success and the hope of a speedy conclusion to their voyage.

When sailing along the western and eastern coasts of Africa, da Gama had a fair idea of the geography, and knew what to expect. But the only information he had about the Indian Ocean was the report from Pêro da Corvilhão that Arab traders crossed it from Sofala and other African ports. To sail directly across the open Indian Ocean, da Gama needed to have a pilot who knew the patterns of winds and currents of these waters, and a knowledge of the shores they were about to visit. This he found at the port of Malindi. Practically nothing is known of the name and qualifications of the pilot he hired, other than that he was a native of Gujarat, and a sailing master or teacher.

The voyage from Malindi to the west coast of India was trouble-free and rapidly accomplished. The summer monsoon season, with its southwest winds, was most favourable for their passage, and the Portuguese fleet sailed 600 leagues in only twenty-three days. For the first time since they had left the Cape Verde Islands nine months ago, the North Star was again visible above the horizon. The pilot's navigation abilities were good, for he led them to a landfall only seven miles north-northwest of Calicut.

'This is the land you have been seeking,
This is India rising before you;
Unless you desire yet more of the world,
Your long task is accomplished.'
Rejoicing to see he knew the country
Da Gama contained himself no longer
But knelt on deck, arms raised towards the sky,
And gave his heartfelt thanks to God on high.

OS LUSIADAS BY LUIS VAZ DE CAMÕES
EXCERPT FROM CANTO VI

Vasco da Gama sent a message to the ruler of Calicut, the *Zamorin* or 'Lord of the Sea,' informing him that he was an ambassador from the King of Portugal. At first the meeting between the two was friendly, but when local merchants perceived that the purpose of the Portuguese fleet was to circumvent their centuries-old monopoly in the spice trade by establishing a direct sea route to Lisbon from India, the cordial atmosphere quickly degenerated. Misunderstandings, the result of differences in customs and attitudes between two far different cultures, led to antagonism, which deepened to an outright hostility. Late in August 1498, having accomplished what had been instructed of him – to 'discover' Calicut, India – the Portuguese fleet returned home. Sometime at the end of August or beginning of September, the first voyage all the way to Calicut and back was concluded.

The expedition was by no means the resounding commercial success that had been hoped for, since the quantity of spices and precious stones brought back was scant. As for the diplomatic negotiation with an Oriental sovereign, also part of da Gama's instructions, the failure was obvious. But to his credit, da Gama had proved what before was only conjecture, that the ships of Portugal could reach India by a sea-route.

Within six months of da Gama's return to Portugal, a fleet of thirteen heavily armed ships, with a thousand men, was dispatched to Africa and the Malabar Coast of India to establish trading posts. Pedro Álvares Cabral (1467–1520) was appointed Captain of the armada, with Bartolomeu Dias aboard as advisor. No doubt Vasco da Gama thoroughly briefed Cabral before his departure.

Taking the same route that proved so effective for da Gama, Cabral's fleet steered far to the west and then south after leaving the Cape Verde Islands. Whether by accident of wind and current, or by secret design to find if somewhere in the western Atlantic there was land he could claim for Portugal, Cabral sighted

Overleaf

175. Armada of Cabral, from *Livro de Lizuarte de Abreu*, c. 1550–1564

The expedition of Pedro Álvares Cabral to India was a comercially successful venture, and established treaties for direct trade with the Far East. But these achievements came at a tremendous cost of lives and ships. Of the thirteen ships that left the Tagus River, only seven returned. Four ships went down off the Cape of Good Hope, including one that took with it the life of Bartolomeu Dias.

THE PIERPONT MORGAN LIBRARY, NEW YORK

Amdre   guoncaluez   diguo   diaz

Vasquo de Taide

Nuno   Leytaol

Ras dem jrao do   Luis Pixis

Sanchoxe de Touar
daxou e puserao lho fogo

17

VARES·CABRAL·ANO·DE·ɾOO·

Nicolao   coelho

Jaõ·ɾiz

Pedralnez   cabral·

Symaõ   demjrao Bõ

Duqus de figuejro

Bertolameu Diaz

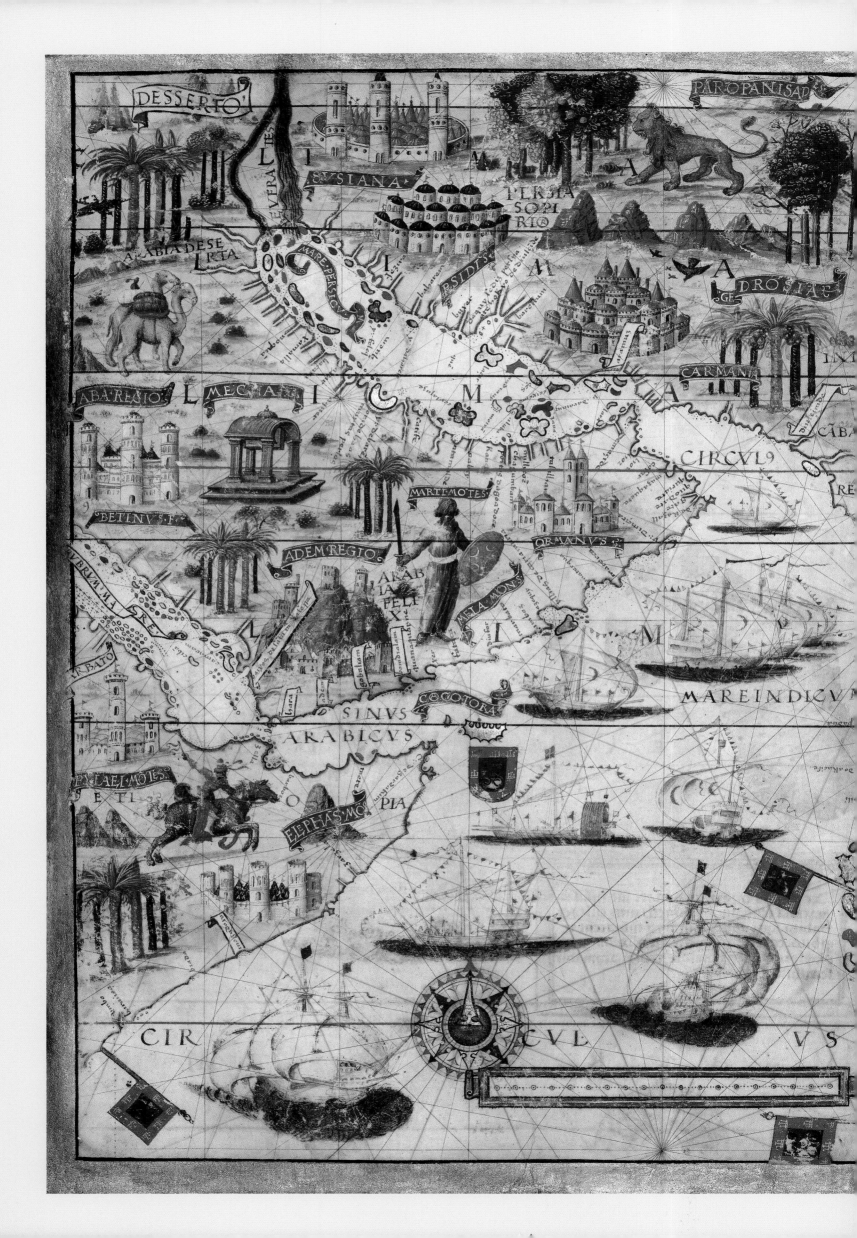

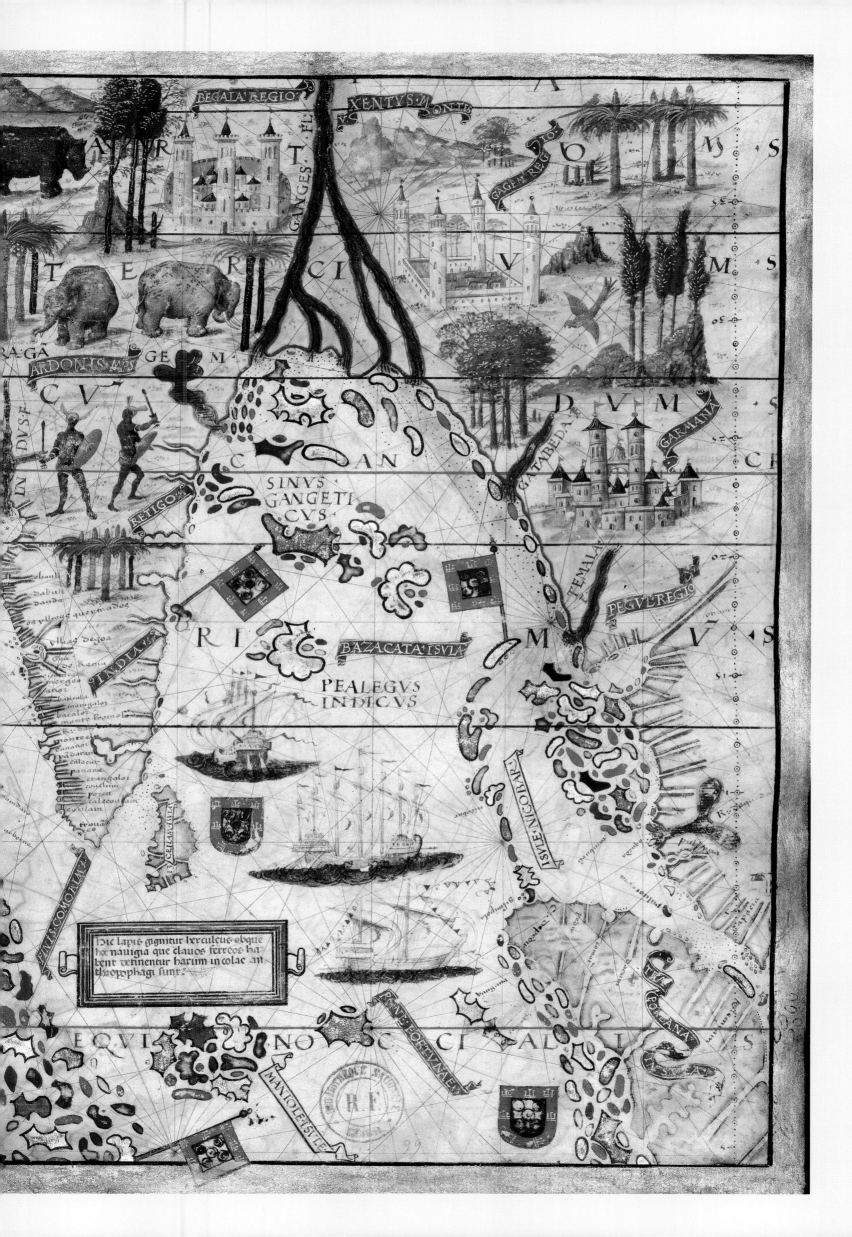

BEGALA REGIO

XENTYS MONTE

GAGAR REGIO

ASVR

TERCI

VM

GANGES FLV

ARDONIS MBS

GE M

GARMANA

CVS

DVM

GATABEDA

INDVS FL

SINVS
GANGETI
CVS

RETIGO

FEMALA

PEGVI REGIO

INDIA

RI

BAZACATA ISVLA

M

VS

PEALEGVS
INDICVS

CEILAN ISVLA

ISVLE NICOBAR

FALS COMORIM

Hic lapis gignitur herculeus obque
hoc nauigia que clauos ferreos ha-
bent retinentur harum in colac an
thropophagi sunt.

EQVI

NO

C

AL

I

RANE FORTVNAE

MANIOLE ISVLE

RF

177. Tapestry of Arzila, 1471

Under King Manuel of Portugal, Vasco da Gama reached Calicut, India in 1498, culminating Portugal's efforts to reach the source of spices by a direct sea-route. King Manuel became known as 'Lord of the navigation, conquest, and commerce of Ethiopia, Arabia, Persia, and India,' and as the 'King of the Spices.' Portugal's remarkable achievements were glorified in literature, such as the epic poem, *Os Lusiadas*, by Luís Camões, and by the Tapestry of Arzila, depicting the Portuguese arrival in India. The Arzila tapestry served as a metaphor for the enormous wealth, and power of King Manuel.

PORTUGUESE INSTITUTE OF ARCHITECTURAL HERITAGE

Previous pages

176. Indian and Arabian Oceans by Lopo Homem, 1519

By 1519 Portuguese dominion in the Indian Ocean included the Malabar Coast of India and Malacca, and had extended its ventures in trade to Siam, the Moluccas, and China. As the result of Portuguese navigation the coastline is accurately depicted, but the interior lands are filled with illustrations stemming from the cartographer's imagination.

BIBLIOTHÈQUE NATIONALE DE FRANCE, PARIS

the mainland of South America on 22 April 1500. He spent twelve days exploring the coast of Brazil, then turned his ships eastward and continued his voyage to the Cape of Good Hope and the original destination of India. But first, he sent one of his ships back to Lisbon to inform the king of his discovery and claim the land for his sovereign. Cabral reached Calicut in September of 1500 and effected treaties to facilitate direct trade. The factories he set up were the nascence of a Portuguese empire in

the Indian Ocean. To consolidate his gains, King Manuel began plans for another expedition to the Indies. Initially Cabral was to be the leader for this new voyage, but political intrigues in the court, in which no doubt da Gama played a role, changed the king's mind, and da Gama was selected instead.

The goal of this, da Gama's second voyage, was to establish trade in the Indian Ocean, and to do so it was necessary to destroy the monopoly in the spice trade held by Arab and Hindu merchants. He was given instructions to devastate Arab shipping, and to wreak retribution on anyone who defied the Portuguese presence. Against any who dared try, da Gama's malevolent spirit erupted into the vilest of acts, extracting the utmost vengeance. Having made the rulers of the Malabar Coast of India fearful of Portuguese power, he filled the holds of his ships with a cargo of spices, pearls and precious stone, and sailed for home.

All of Portugal greeted him with adulation, and King Manuel made him 'Admiral of the Seas of India'. He then remained at home until 1524 when King Manuel's successor, King John III (1502–1557), sent him on what was to become his final voyage to India. Vasco da Gama was 'to rebuild morale and battle the corruption that had weakened Portugal's position there', but he had little time to achieve success; with in three months of his arrival he became ill and died.

With the transit of the Indian Ocean now accomplished, and a regular trade established with India, Portugal finally gained a manifold profit on her investments. Whereas previously it was Muslim merchants in the Indian Ocean, and the Venetians in the eastern Mediterranean, who were masters of the spice trade, Portugal now usurped the prize. Yearly, Portugal sent out fleets of twenty-five and thirty large vessels, and after over four thousand leagues of perilous travel and navigation, they returned with three to four million pounds of spices and drugs, plus silks, pearls and precious stones desired by all of Europe. Portugal protected her interests with armed ships and fortified settlements at strategic points.

WESTWARD, ACROSS THE ATLANTIC OCEAN

Christopher Columbus: Admiral of the Ocean Sea

Christopher Columbus's early years are shrouded in controversy. Based mainly on philological grounds, his birthplace has variously been identified as Portugal, Burgundy, Majorca, Catalonia, or the island of Chios in the Aegean that at the time was a Genoese colony. Columbus himself said he was the first-born son of a poor wool weaver in Genoa in 1451.

During his youth, Columbus worked for his father in the weaving shop, and learned the import-export trade. As a merchant, he made voyages to Genoese colonies throughout the Mediterranean where he gained a familiarity with ships and of the sea. His marriage to a Portuguese noblewoman gave Columbus Portuguese citizenship. After a brief residence in Madeira, in 1473 he went to Lisbon, which had a large Genoese colony, and where his younger brother, Bartolomeo, made his living as a chart maker. Columbus's Portuguese citizenship gave him the right to extend his trade voyages to Portuguese overseas possessions. From 1479 onward, he travelled the Atlantic to ports along the west coast of Africa, the Canary and Madeira archipelagoes, and northward to Bristol in England and Galway in Ireland. Historians are still debating whether he sailed as far as Iceland.

Throughout his extensive journeying Columbus most likely was occupied with his business ventures, rather than acting as a pilot or navigator. Nonetheless, his observant eye and keen mind took in and stored information on the handling of ships, ocean currents, sea surfaces and wind patterns of the Atlantic Ocean – all of which were to serve him well in his forthcoming voyages. At some time during his career, Columbus conceived the idea of engaging in direct trade with Asia by sailing west across the Atlantic.

In addition to the practical experience gained through decades of sailing, Columbus read all he could in search of support for this new plan. Lisbon was the most important port in Europe, and its libraries held all the books on cosmography, philosophy and the sciences Columbus needed to pursue his studies. He also drew upon travel literature for backing, a genre of books popular at the time, the two most influential being *The Travels of Sir John Mandeville* and Marco Polo's *Il milione*.

Whether Sir John Mandeville was an English knight of the fourteenth century, or a French cleric who composed this book in 1357, is unresolved. Whoever the author was, he skillfully wove together the accounts of others into a single narrative, as though they were a journal of his own extensive travels. Mandeville's sources included all the most important pilgrimage accounts of the medieval period of travels to Arabia, Central Asia, North Africa and the Far East. Although much in these writings was of a semi-realistic nature, they brought to a Western audience a first-hand account of the marvellous and wealthy civilization that lay beyond that of their own familiar Mediterranean.

The most famous of medieval European travellers was Marco Polo. His vivid description of Asia and China from the journey he made there in 1271–1295 with his father and uncle, Niccolò and Maffeo, was more complete than was Mandeville's *Travels*, and filled with realistic details. Polo's narrative was primarily told from the standpoint of a merchant, and emphasized the fabulous wealth of Cathay where 'they have gold in the greatest abundance, its sources being inexhaustible'. Of particular interest to Columbus was Polo's statement that the island of *Cipango* (Japan) lay 1500 miles east of Cathay, and that interposed between the two were thousands more islands scattered in the ocean. It seemed to Columbus that these could provide an intermediate waypoint between Europe and Asia, effectively shortening an arduous and lengthy voyage. He carefully annotated passages in a Latin edition copy of Polo's book that he possessed. Thus was the desire stimulated, and the necessity reinforced, of finding a shorter route by sea than that used by the Portuguese, to find the silk and gold of China and the spices of India.

Support for the feasibility of this project was to be found in the geographic and cosmologic lore by authors from classical antiquity. In his *De caelo* (On the Heavens), Aristotle said 'those who imagine that the region around the Pillars of Hercules joins on to the regions of India ... are not, it would seem, suggesting anything utterly incredible.' The words and wisdom of that great authority were carried down through the centuries to be repeated by the great English scholastic philosopher and scientist, Roger Bacon in his *Opus majus*.

As early as the third century BC, the noted astronomer and mathematician, Eratosthenes, had calculated the circumference of the Earth. He arrived at a figure of 250,000 stadia (24,662 miles), a figure surprisingly close to the Earth's true circumference of roughly 25,000 miles. Posidonius of Rhodes (c. 131–51 BC) made his own estimate of the circumference of the Earth and arrived at a figure of 240,000 stadia, a result remarkably near the findings of Eratosthenes. But Strabo, in his *Geographia*, mistakenly reported the Posidonius findings as 180,000 stadia; in spite of being wrong, this figure became accepted as the true measure of the world – a world 28% smaller in circumference than Eratosthenes' calculation. This erroneous figure made the ocean correspondingly small in a smaller world. It was accepted by Ptolemy, handed down through the ages, and embraced by Columbus.

Dead Reckoning

Until the fifteenth century, navigators had scant need to fix their precise position at sea by latitude and longitude. Voyages were short and principally followed the coast; ships were rarely out of sight of land for more than a few hours or days at a time. Navigation relied upon a pilot's knowledge of the coasts, with recognition of its headlands, capes, rivers and towns. Simplified sailing directions aided his memory and provided distances from port to port. But when navigators entered the uncharted regions of the open ocean they needed to know their position at sea, and

be able to plot courses over the waters, in order to be sure of returning home again.

Although astronomers and mathematicians in the very early history of navigation had developed the means to determine positions on the surface of the earth by coordinates of latitude and longitude, they could not be used practically at sea. Mariners also did not have the necessary reference information about the locations of ports, islands, capes or shorelines. Therefore they used the simple method called dead reckoning. The etymology of the word 'dead' is not

179. Sandglass as drawn by Gregorio Dati, 15th century

The hourglass, or sandglass as it also known, appears not to have been developed until the eleventh century, when it was used in conjunction with the magnetic compass and portolan chart for navigation. However, it is not until the fourteenth century that there is definite evidence of its existence. As a reliable means of measuring time at sea it provided time for the ship's log, the change of watch of the helmsman, and as an important tool in dead reckoning helped to supply the ship's approximate location on a chart.

THE NATIONAL LIBRARY OF FINLAND, HELSINKI

178. Wind-rose by Jacques de Vaulx, 1583

Keeping a dead reckoning of the distance travelled on any particular course (rhumb line), navigators were able to determine without requiring any sort of instrument whether the ship's position was increased or decreased by a degree of latitude. Sailing directions provided the number of leagues one had to sail on any rhumb line to raise or lower a degree of latitude.

BIBLIOTHÈQUE NATIONALE DE FRANCE, PARIS

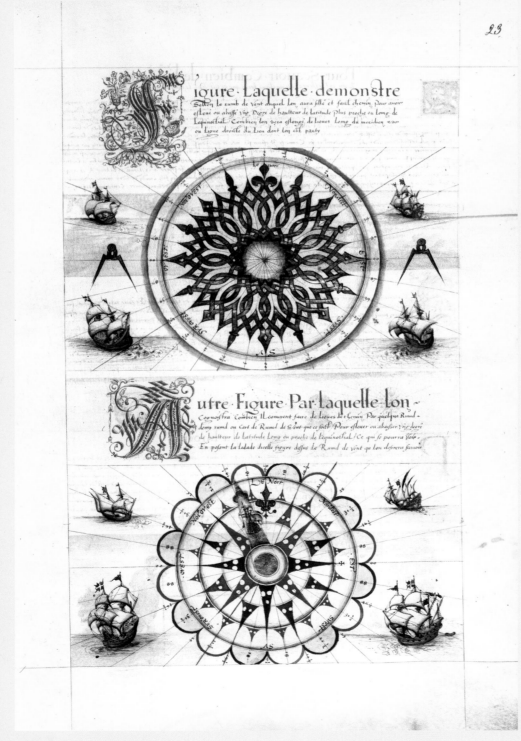

firmly established. According to some, it is a contraction of the word 'deduced', originally written as 'ded' then changed to 'dead'. Others maintain that 'dead' was the first use of the word, and it referred not to death but to something that is dead in the water, that is, not moving. Thus, the reckoning produced a 'set' position. 'Ded' may have been the common spelling of 'dead' before English orthography was established.

But there is no confusion about the practice and function of dead reckoning. In contrast to celestial navigation, which uses the stars or other heavenly bodies to determine a vessel's position, or pilotage,

180. Traverse board, c. 1850

The helmsman, who frequently was not literate and could not keep a log-journal, used a traverse board to keep track of the progress of the ship during a voyage. Every half an hour of the four-hour watch, a peg was placed in the appropriate hole of the compass dial to indicate direction sailed. Each hole in the line of holes radiating along the compass points represented one half hour of the watch. A later development of the traverse board included rows of horizontal and vertical lines, which similarly recorded with pegs the estimated speed of the ship.

NATIONAL MARITIME MUSEUM, LONDON

181. Diagram illustrating how many leagues required to sail on each point to raise a degree of latitude by John Davis, provided after 1959

In his *Seaman's Secrets* of 1595 a more schematic diagram than Jacques de Vaulx's wind-rose for showing how far one had to sail in any direction in order to raise a degree of latitude. English distances are calculated at three nautical miles to the league; thus, there are 20 leagues to one degree of latitude (60 ÷ 3 = 20).

MAGDALENE COLLEGE, THE PEPYS LIBRARY, CAMBRIDGE

with knowledge of the coast, dead reckoning establishes an approximate position of a vessel, relative to a known starting point, based on a continuous record of direction and distance. The magnetic compass was used to indicate the direction, or course, the vessel was steered. Distance was calculated from time, measured by a sandglass, and the speed of the vessel through the water was calculated by a chip log, or was estimated. Time, speed and distance are all interrelated; by knowing any two of these three variables, the third could be determined.

It would seem that such a simple device as the sandglass for keeping time had a long history dating back to the Greco-Roman world. However, its development appears to be fairly recent, and in direct response to the need to keep time at sea. Although specific evidence is lacking for when the sandglass first came into use, it appeared as a timekeeper most likely at the beginning of the twelfth century, in conjunction with the introduction of the magnetic compass to Europe and the use of portolans, or sea charts. Unlike a clock, which keeps continuous time, the sandglass keeps intervals of time.

To measure speed through the water, a length of line was tied with knots at regular intervals; customarily, the distance between knots was every seven fathoms (42 feet). A 'chip' or log of wood was attached to the end of the line, which was placed overboard, and the line allowed to run out freely. After a measured period of time the number of knots was noted, each representing one nautical mile of 6000 feet, hence the term of 'knots' for the speed of a ship in one hour's sailing.

Additional refinements, such as factoring in the amount of leeway (the side-slippage a ship makes in its forward movement through the water due to the pressure of a beam wind), and the effects of the current, improved the accuracy of dead reckoning. Knowing the amount of leeway was accomplished easily by trailing a line overboard and noting the angle of difference between the ship's apparent direction (the course) and its actual direction (course over the ground) as shown by the line. The effects of ocean currents were much more difficult to determine, for they could neither be seen nor measured, although their effects could be estimated by their influence on the height and shape of the ocean waves. Not all navigators possessed this skill, and as the general set (direction) and velocity of currents were virtually uncharted, errors could occur in the estimation of position by as much as 30 miles in one day.

Nevertheless, when followed diligently and recorded regularly, dead reckoning is a reliable means of navigation, sufficient to mark progress across the seas, to plot position on a chart, and determine a future course to an intended landfall. In practice, the navigator drew a break-line which depicted the ship's track. The endpoint of this line showed his corresponding position. Two of the greatest navigators in the fifteenth century, Christopher Columbus and John Cabot, practised dead reckoning successfully on their epic voyages of discovery.

Small errors, however, are cumulative when continued over ocean voyages of great distance, with the potential to cause the ship's demise. Chief among the

possible causes of error in dead reckoning was magnetic variation over the Earth's surface, which at first was not taken into proper account – its importance not comprehended, or worse, ignored. Once navigators understood the difference between magnetic north and true or geographic north, careful recording of the amount of magnetic variation of the compass, with a corresponding correction to the course, significantly reduced this type of error.

Even with today's sophisticated navigational instruments and the means to obtain a precise position fix by satellite (GPS), the prudent mariner will still keep a concurrent dead reckoning of his passage.

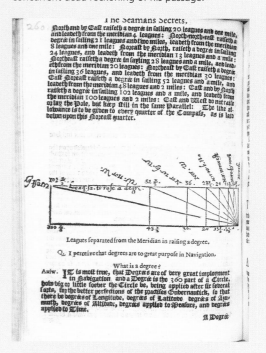

182. Isabella I, Queen of Castile by Spanish school, c. 1490–1492

As Queen of Castile, Isabella (1451–1504) was the first Spanish female monarch. Her marriage to Ferdinand II of Aragon unified the country, and established a centralized power. Pope Alexander VI named the couple 'the Catholic Monarchs' on account of their intense religious convictions. Under Isabella's rule, Spain reconquered Granada from Muslim rule. That same year (1492) saw the reversal of her initial rejection of Columbus's plan, and the giving of her patronage.

THE BRIDGEMAN ART LIBRARY

183. Portrait of a Man called Christopher Columbus by Sebastiano del Piombo, 1519

Although Columbus had attained widespread acclaim throughout the Christian world and in the Court of Castile for his discoveries, no portrait of the Admiral was made during his lifetime. All the alleged portraits of Columbus, of which there were 71 by the end of the nineteenth century, were based upon very brief descriptions made by his contemporary historians. The painting here, dated 1519, is attributed to Sebastiano del Piombo (Sebastiano Luciani) a highly regarded painter in Rome, and student of Michelangelo. Known for his highly observant ability, Piombo has depicted Columbus with an intelligent mien, one given to introspection, and reflecting his own deep personal struggles.

THE METROPOLITAN MUSEUM OF ART, NEW YORK

Church writings also sustained Columbus's beliefs in the success of his proposed voyage. Aeneas Silvius Piccolomini (1405–1464), who rose to the station of pope and chose the name of Pope Pius II, is mostly known for his unsuccessful attempts to promote crusades against the Turks after the fall of Constantinople in 1453. But Pope Pius also compiled a his-

tory of the world, *Historia rerum ubique gestarum,* published in Rome in 1475. Christopher Columbus had a copy of this book in his personal library, and the marginal notations in it are attributed to him. On the question of a spherical Earth, Pope Pius carefully reviewed all the major historians and philosophers of antiquity – Solinus, Strabo, Pliny, Aristotle, Ptolemy – and came to the conclusion: 'on the form of the world almost all are in agreement that it is round.' But whether the Earth was circumnavigable, Pope Pius did not believe it to be possible, yet he cautiously admitted that the feat might eventually be accomplished.

One of the most important cosmological works of the fifteenth century was the *Imago mundi* published in 1483 by Pierre d'Ailly, a reforming Cardinal of Touraine. D'Ailly drew from many classical sources, including Pliny and Ptolemy. Ptolemy had estimated that the Eurasian and African landmasses, the *oikumene,* extended 180° from the western edge of Europe, or 190° if measured from the Canaries, to its eastern limit in Asia. Its north-south limits ran from 63° North latitude to 16 $5/_2$° South latitude. D'Ailly quoted frequently, and often verbatim, from Roger Bacon. Perhaps influenced by a remark of the Roman philosopher Seneca the younger (c. 3 BC–AD 65) in his *Quaestiones naturales,* that 'the sea between Spain and India could be crossed in a few days, if one had a good wind to drive the ship', Bacon amplified Aristotle's remark about the Atlantic Ocean, and wrote 'between Spain and India there was a *mare parvum* (a short sea distance)'. Consequently, d'Ailly extended Ptolemy's size of the terrestrial landmass from 180° to that of 225°, thus reducing the gap of water between Europe and Asia to only 135° of the circumference of the Earth.

Not only had Pierre d'Ailly extended the landmass covering most of the globe, leaving relatively little space for the ocean, but he was also erroneous in his belief that each degree of longitude at the equator was 56 $^2/_3$ nautical miles in length. This figure he got from al-Farghānī (Alfraganus), one of the great Arab scholars and astronomers of the early ninth century. For the first time since Eratosthenes, al-Farghānī had measured the actual length of a degree of longitude, but the scale he used was the Arab nautical mile, which was longer than the Italian mile. D'Ailly, and subsequently, Columbus, who formulated many of his geographical theories from d'Ailly's *Imago Mundi*, converted the Arab miles into Roman miles; in so doing they reduced the Earth's circumference at the equator by 25% of its true value of 24,901 miles.

The Florentine cosmographer Paolo del Pozzo Toscanelli (1397–1428), reputedly the foremost philosopher at the time, further contributed to Columbus's misconception about the width of the Atlantic. In a letter written in June of 1474 to Fernan Martinez de Roriz, Canon at Lisbon, and an intimate friend of the King of Portugal, Toscanelli expressed his cosmographic views. He sent a copy of the same letter the following month to Columbus in which he stated that the distance between Lisbon and the great city of Quinsay, the capital of China, to be 6500 miles. At one third of the circumference of the Earth at that latitude, this diminished by 1600 miles d'Ailly's estimation of the width of the Atlantic. Toscanelli accompanied his letter with a map in which the intervening ocean between the city of Lisbon and the city of Quinsay was divided into 26 equal spaces, each space representing 250 miles. He placed the island of Antilia – an island of legend only, but its existence still believed – halfway between Europe and Japan. With Antilia as a 'stepping-stone' to rest and reprovision, the greatest distance to be sailed would be the 2500 miles between Antilia and Japan. Thus, concludes Toscanelli, '... the spaces of the sea to be crossed in the unknown parts are not great.'

In his letter, Toscanelli said: 'This great country is worth seeking by the Latins, not only because great wealth may be obtained from it, gold and silver, all sorts of gems, and spices, which never reach us; but also on account of its learned men, philosophers, and expert astrologers, and by what skill and art so powerful and magnificent a province is governed, as well as how their wars are conducted.'

Firmly convinced he had sufficient theoretical arguments in favour of this new kind of navigation, Columbus sought backing for it. He recognized that there were extreme financial and military risks in such a venture if undertaken by a merchant company, so he turned to partnership with a monarchy to provide royal financing and protection.

Columbus approached King Afonso V of Portugal, but Afonso had no interest in any exploration by sea because all

of his efforts, energies and finances were then directed toward the war he was waging to win the thrones of Castile and of Aragon, a war that ended disastrously for him. Columbus renewed his proposal when Afonso was succeeded by King John II, but Diogo Cão's successful voyage of 1482, when he nearly reached Africa's southernmost cape, discouraged King John from taking an interest in Columbus's less promising proposal. He did, however, send Columbus to a royal commission of cosmographers for their opinion, but they concluded his proposal was based on the 'imaginary things' that Marco Polo wrote about Cathay and the island of *Cipango* (Japan). They declined any support.

Columbus next turned to Spain, hoping to convince King Ferdinand and Queen Isabella of his navigation scheme. In reviewing his proposal, the Spanish cosmographers rejected it on the grounds that the proportion of land to water over the

184. A page from the *Imago mundi* by Pierre d'Ailly, 15th century

Two books, the *Imago mundi* by Pierre d'Ailly and *Historia rerum* (c. 1470) by Pope Pius II helped Columbus formulate many of his geographical theories and cosmological design of the world. In this page from Columbus's personal copy of *Imago mundi*, one can see in his marginal notations how carefully and fully he studied it.

CATEDRAL DE SEVILLA, BIBLIOTECA COLOMBINA

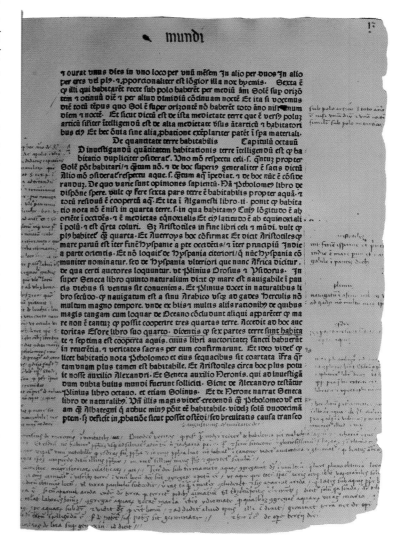

globe was not yet determined. Only when the full distance between the eastern and western extremes of the *oikumene* was known, would it be possible to determine the extent of the ocean between its two shores, and then decide on the feasibility of navigating it. Columbus's response to this argument was that Portuguese voyages of exploration had shown the Eurasian landmass to be larger than the ancient authorities had supposed; this must change the accepted relationship between land and water, for according to Ptolemy, the rest of the globe not occupied by the *oikumene* was sea, without intervening land. With the extent of the sea now diminished by an increased size in land, a voyage from Spain to Japan, he said, is a possibility.

During the many delays in his stay at the Spanish court from 1486 to 1488, Columbus sent his brother Bartolomeo as emissary to seek support from King Henry VII of England.

185. A Reconstruction of Toscanelli's World Map

No original survives of the map Toscanelli provided to Columbus, but in this reconstructed version, it is apparent that he took the known coastline of Europe and Africa from Portolan maps of the time and married it to a coastline of Asia and Japan as described by Marco Polo. In the intervening blank space in the middle of the ocean he positioned the mythical island of Antilia. Reinforcing his idea that this island could be used as a way to shorten the voyage Toscanelli conveniently placed it in the same line of latitude as the Canary Islands and Japan. The name Antilia later became applied to the West Indian Islands as the Antilles, as first shown on the Cantino map of 1500.

According to the chronicler Oviedo, the disheartening message Bartolomeo brought back was that King Henry thought 'it was the most ridiculous idea he had ever heard of and there was no way England would be involved in such a scheme'. Fortune seemed at last to smile for Columbus when in 1488 King John II invited him to return to Portugal, to resubmit his proposal. But Bartolomeu Dias arrived in Lisbon at the same time, announcing he had reached the Cape of Good Hope, and thus could cross the Indian Ocean to sail to India. Any chance of Portuguese backing for Columbus's alternative plan immediately vanished.

At this point, the consensus of opinion amongst the Spanish cosmographers was reversed, to favour Columbus's ambition. Although there were some who continued to question Columbus's estimation of the size of the globe, and some even who still believed the Western Sea (Atlantic) was infinite and unnavigable, the official decision was that Columbus 'was knowledgeable and well spoken and he supported his ideas with sound reasoning'. The consideration that may finally have induced the Catholic sovereigns of Spain to endorse Columbus's plan was Portugal's expanding territory and control of the sea. The 'narrow Atlantic' believed in by Columbus could redress the balance of power, by enabling them to be the first to establish direct maritime trade with the fabulous wealth of Cathay. He also suggested that west of the Azores there might be other lands, yet undiscovered, which could be added to the Spanish realm. Then too, with the whole of the Iberian Penin-

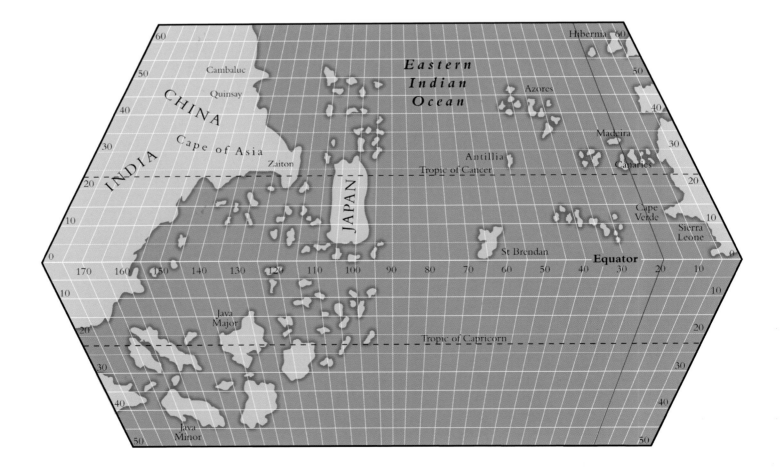

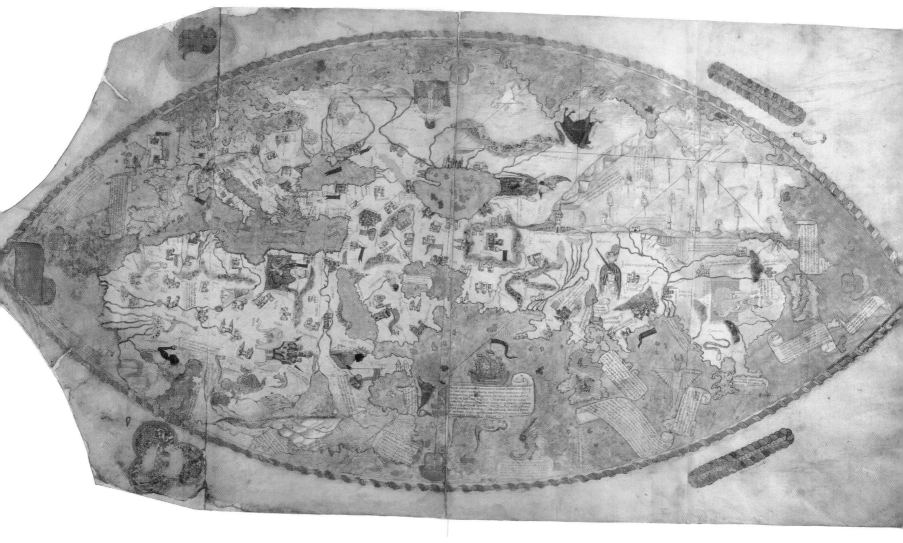

186. Genoese World Map, 1457

The Genoese World Map shows the geographic information available to Columbus before his voyages. Other than the island archipelagos lying in the eastern Atlantic, no land intervenes between Europe and Asia. As greater numbers of voyages were made in the Atlantic during the fifteenth century, cartographers were required to harmonize the new discoveries and an expanding geography of the world with traditionally held world views. This anonymously compiled world map of the Genoese cartographic school exhibits Classical, Arab and Christian influences. Medieval in appearance, it is nonetheless a portolan or sea-chart, having conventional compass rhumb lines and a barred distance scale for navigation. An approximate translation of the title reads: *This is the true description of the world of the cosmographers, accommodated to the marine [sea-chart], from which frivolous tales have been removed.*

BIBLIOTECA NAZIONALE CENTRALE DI FIRENZE

sula regained to the Christian religion by the fall of Granada in 1492, the last of the Moorish stronghold in Andalusia, the Catholic monarchs may have set their crusading sights toward a new goal: repulsing Islam overseas and spreading of Christianity around the world.

King Ferdinand and Queen Isabella agreed to organize an expedition, provide some of the vessels and men, and enter into a two-part commercial contract with Columbus called the Capitulations of Santa Fe de la Vega de Granada. The first part, signed 17 April, spelled out Columbus's privileges and obligations. The second part, signed 30 April, delineated his titles. If the voyage were successful, in return for his willingness to expose himself to dangers in the service of his sovereigns, Columbus would be made Admiral of the Ocean Sea. In addition to this title, which was usually reserved for the nobility and would be hereditary, he would receive military and governing powers, plus monetary rewards. These were extravagant concessions, and some at court expressed their concerns. If trade actually developed from this enterprise, Columbus could receive fifty-five per cent of the profits – five per cent over what the monarchs themselves would gain! Such generosity might be attributed to a spillover from the celebration and general euphoria present after the recent fall of Granada. It might also just be possible that the Catholic monarchs never really expected a successful outcome to Columbus's venture, and promised whatever he asked, believing they would not have to make good on his excessive demands.

On 3 August 1492 Columbus weighed anchor from the port of Palos, Spain, and sailed to the Canary Islands, the departure point for his voyage across the Atlantic. Columbus knew that for the first part of the voyage the prevailing winds and currents would favourably propel his small fleet westward. Furthermore, an east–west passage at this latitude would be shorter than if he embarked from a port closer to the equator. In full anticipation of reaching the Far East, Columbus brought with him gifts and a letter addressed to the Great Khan, emperor of the vast wealth of Cathay, plus an Arabic-speaking Spaniard to act as a translator upon their reaching India.

Of all the navigational tools brought along for the journey, none was more important than the magnetic compass. In long voyages, it was usual to bring a number of instruments because some were bound to be damaged, lost or shown to be inaccurate. But confusion was caused by Columbus bringing compasses made in different workshops, some Genoese and others Flemish, with different designs. The former had the compass card aligned with true north, whereas the Flemish compasses had the needle set on the card at one-half point (5.6°) east to account for the magnetic variation in their region. They worked fine within the limited area for which the compass card was adjusted, but on longer voyages during which magnetic variation changed, this was no longer practical. As the voyage progressed Columbus noted changes in readings between the two types of compass, but attributed them to the different sorts of lodestones used to magnetize the needles. Although he could not account for the changes as he made his way across the ocean, the recording of them in his journal makes Columbus among the first to report the phenomenon of magnetic variation.

To measure the altitudes of the Sun and *Polaris*, the North Star, to determine latitude, Columbus used the astrolabe and quadrant. The cross-staff was certainly known at the time, but Spanish navigators seldom used it. Columbus's skills in celestial navigation were quite deficient and early attempts to determine his position were grossly in error, particularly when he tried to establish his position with readings from the Sun. It was easier to use *Polaris* to determine latitude, since its altitude (with minor corrections) is equal to the latitude of the observer. Although Columbus had the rule books with which to make the necessary corrections by noting the position of the guard stars (two of the bright stars in *Ursa minor*) relative to *Polaris*, he was not always able to get good results.

Columbus cannot be faulted altogether for his deficiencies in celestial navigation. Aboard a ship tossing and pitching about in seas, these instruments were difficult to use. As for the North Star, it is not very bright to begin with, being only one-fifteenth the brightness of *Sirius*, the brightest star in the night sky. In southern latitudes, where it appears lower down on the horizon, its brightness is even further diminished since

187. Columbus's Ships (16 September 1492 in the Sargasso Sea) by Björn Landström, 1961

Numerous paintings and replicas have been made of the *Santa María*, flagship of the fleet of three vessels on Columbus's 1492 voyage. But they are all conjectural, based on contemporary ships of her type, since neither her remains nor blueprints are available. She was a nao, a type more suited to Mediterranean, rather than Atlantic sailing, somewhat over 80 feet in length, and square-rigged. The *Pinta* was a caravel, and square-rigged like the *Santa María*. The *Niña* started out with lateen sails, but in the Canary Islands she was re-rigged with square sails like the other ships, making her better suited for the anticipated down-wind sailing.

COURTESY OF OLOF LANDSTRÖM

Above right
188. Columbus's voyages

There is considerable controversy about which island in the New World was landfall made by Columbus on his first voyage. Shown here, it is Watling Island, the Indian island of Guahahani in the central Bahamas. But based on a reconstruction of Columbus's route from navigational data in his journal, as many as nine other islands have been proposed. The problem is that his navigation was almost entirely by dead reckoning. Although he was excellent in this, by necessity errors were created by currents of unknown direction and strength, leeway made by the vessel and by unknown magnetic variation of the compass. Although small to begin with, the cumulative effects over a long distance render the determination of a definitive path and landfall all but impossible. The 2.67 Genoese nautical miles to a league is generally accepted as the length of league used by Columbus, but there is no certainty in this.

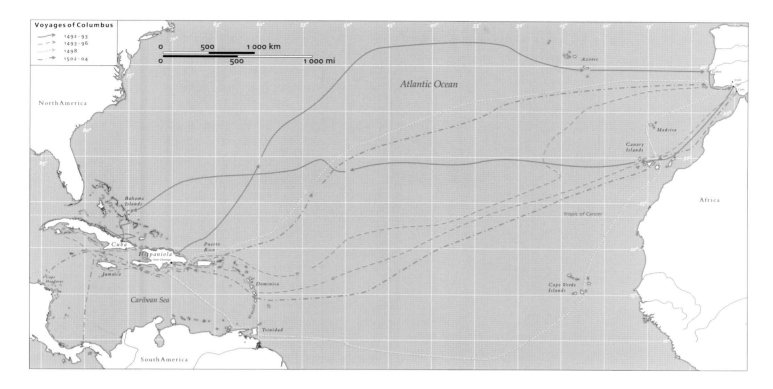

it is viewed through a thicker layer of the Earth's atmosphere.

Where Columbus's true genius as a navigator lay was his ability in dead reckoning.

With the aid of an *ampoletta*, or half-hour sandglass, to mark the time, a compass to indicate direction and a rough means of estimating speed, he determined the distance travelled and established a geographic position. He must have further refined this by factoring in the leeway of the vessel. The lead line for measuring depths was an indispensable item aboard any ship. He could not have known the effect of the currents, for they had yet to be quantified. With this simple procedure Columbus safely sailed out of sight of land for thirty days, and over 3000 miles of uncharted seas to bring his vessels safely to harbour.

On the morning of 12 October 1492 Columbus made landfall in the Bahamas. After taking possession of the discovery for Spain, Columbus sailed from island to island seeking the land of the Great Khan. Failing to find it, he sailed south to explore a portion of the north coast of *Colba* (Cuba) and *La Isla Española* (Hispaniola, now occupied by Haiti and the Dominican Republic). On Hispaniola he founded a small settlement – the first European settlement on the American continent since that of the Vikings five hundred years earlier. Then, feeling he had accomplished all he could, Columbus turned the bow of his vessels homeward bringing the triumphant announcement that he had reached inhabited outer islands; believing them to lie off the coast of India, he called them the Indies.

For the return passage, Columbus sailed in an east-northeast direction until he reached the latitude of the Azores, which brought him back to what had been the farthest edge of the charted Atlantic. This course brought the North Star much

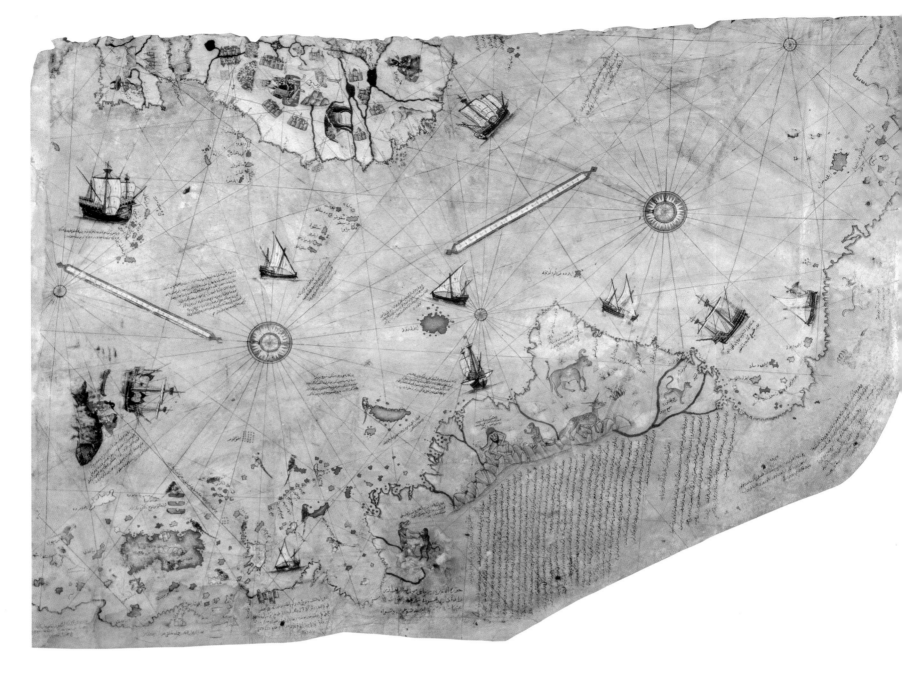

189. World map by Piri Re'is, 1513

From the eleventh century onwards, in their battles fought for Islam, Turkish naval activity contributed to the knowledge of geography and nautical science. In his many years of fighting against the Spanish, Genoese and Venetial navies, the Turkish Piri Re'is accumulated extensive first-hand hydrographic information. Piri Re'is produced many Isolario maps and charts, but he is best known for his world map of 1513 showing the Atlantic Ocean, with the adjacent coasts of Europe, Africa and the New World.

TOPKAPI PALACE MUSEUM, ISTANBUL

higher and brighter in the sky, and Columbus was able to correctly fix his latitude. Though still 1200 miles west of the islands, he knew their latitude and had only to 'run his easting down' to gain them.

He had not brought back any gold, but with the promise of wealth seemingly near, a second voyage, this time with a much larger fleet of seventeen ships, set out the following year (1493). Having noted on his first voyage how the coast of Cuba trended far to the west, on his second voyage Columbus wished to explore further in that direction. In addition, the programme now included establishing permanent trading colonies, and converting the Indians to Christianity.

On this voyage as well, Columbus failed to realize his ambition of reaching Cathay and India, but it did not deter the king and queen from approving a third expedition in 1498 to explore land that lay to the south of the islands he had already discovered. From the Cape Verde Islands he shaped his course southwest toward the parallel of the equator, and then headed due west. Columbus reached the island he named Trinidad, and sailed along the north shore of Venezuela's Orinoco River delta.

Upon exiting the Gulf of Paria, through a strait he called *Boca del Drago* (the Dragon's mouth), Columbus was astonished by the 'amount of fresh water striving to reach the sea'. No land was large enough, he said, to serve as the source for rivers that could pour forth such a quantity of fresh water, 'unless this be a continent', and his convictions wavered about having already arrived at the Indies, that is, India. Within his grasp was the realization that this newly found land that lay to the south was not Asia, but an entirely 'new world', interposed between Europe and Asia.

The sources which helped shape Columbus's concepts of the *Orbis Terrarum* – Ptolemy and other authorities from classical antiquity, and the report of the merchant-traveller, Marco Polo – could not explain the existence of this new land. Nor did biblical theology, proclaiming the unity of all land not covered by the sea, provide an answer.

Columbus still believed that Cuba was part of the Asiatic mainland. If so, then this newly found land should be continuous with it. Finally, he concluded he had reached the Terrestrial Paradise which 'is at the end of the east'. The four great rivers that spring forth from the fountain in the Terrestrial Paradise, explained in Columbus's mind the amount of fresh water in the Gulf of Paria. Still, he could not entirely let go of the idea that here was a 'new world' separate and distinct from the *Orbis Terrarum*, the Island of the Earth.

He would have liked to explore further, but the supplies his ships were carrying to Española (Hispaniola) to make it self-supporting, were quickly dwindling, and he needed to proceed directly there. Columbus had just traversed an ocean, with dead reckoning as the only means to determine longitude, had explored a land that before now was totally unknown to the world, and was about to sail through uncharted waters to Santo Domingo on Española. He now set a compass course northwest by west directly toward Santo Domingo. It is a tribute to his superb navigational skill that with all the geographic uncertainties – not the least of which were the conflicting and confusing concepts of the cosmography of the Earth – that he unerringly determined the correct course, and reached his intended destination.

Even after his fourth voyage (1502–04), when Columbus found that the present-day lands of Honduras, Nicaragua, Costa Rica and Panama blocked any further sailing westward, and confirmed the presence of a new continent, he returned to his firm convictions he had reached Asia. The native inhabitants at the Isthmus of Panama, which he called the province of Ciguare, told him it was only a thin strip of land of ten days journey, and beyond it the ocean lay again. He believed this to be the Malay Peninsula, and in a letter (7 July 1503) to the Catholic monarchs Columbus wrote, 'From there it is only ten days journey to the river Ganges.' Bad weather, hostilities with the Indians, and damaged or lost ships and men, finally took their toll. Broken in spirit and suffering physically, Christopher Columbus returned to Spain to end his sailing career.

The importance of Columbus's momentous achievements in the history of navigation can hardly be overestimated, for they led to an entire rethinking of the cosmography of the Earth, and the start of an unprecedented era of empire building. The general distribution of land and water over the Earth's surface, as understood by the Ancients, was shown to be in error. An entire new continent, which heretofore had not been expected, was shown to exist.

Transformation of the Orbis Terrarum

Columbus remained firm in his belief that the lands he had reached were an eastern extension of Asia. He was confident that Hispaniola must be Japan, since it was situated in the same position as *Cipangu* (Japan) described by Marco Polo. Not all Spanish scholars agreed. Antonio de Nebrija (c. 1444–1522), a leading Spanish philologist, humanist and educator, wrote that 'the land found by the Catholic Kings 45° west of the Canaries is incorrectly termed India by some'. And Rodrigo de Santaella, founder of the University of Seville, said 'those who believe that the islands recently discovered by the Catholic Kings were in India were mistaken'.

The newly discovered lands were called the Indies, but it did not resolve the problem of where on the globe they were located. Thoughts of obtaining wealth (primarily gold) from these lands, wherever they may be, and the opportunity of converting the population of heathens to Christianity, overshadowed any geographical concerns.

In the short span of fifty years, Columbus's remarkable accomplishment enabled Spain to extend her overseas possessions to include most of the Caribbean, large portions of the North and South American continents, and parts of Africa. In contrast to Portugal's colonies, which were limited mainly to islands and coastal regions, Spain penetrated well inland to establish permanent settlements. Expeditions from Spain and Portugal continued to set forth almost yearly to explore further the new lands, and to seek some way to penetrate this newfound barrier to Asia.

In 1506, Spain commissioned the navigators and explorers Juan Díaz de Solis (1471–1516) and Vicente Yáñez Pinzón (1463–1523) 'to discover [in the Caribbean] a channel or open sea'. They discovered the Yucatan Peninsula and the Bay of Campeche, but found no strait or river leading to an open sea. Voyages by Juan Ponce de León (1512) and Francisco Hernando de Córdova (1513) rapidly delineated the geography of the Gulf of Mexico. In 1518 Juan de Grijalva explored both sides of the Yucatan Peninsula and sailed northward along the coast of Mexico as far as the Rio Grande River. This left only the northern shore of the Gulf of Mexico where a way might be found to India and Cathay. Starting at Ponce de León's 'island' of Florida, Alonso Alvarez de Piñeda in 1519 sailed westward until he reached the northern limit of exploration by Grijalva, thus putting an end to the hope of finding a sea-path from the Gulf of Mexico to Cathay. It was not a navigator, but a Spanish planter, Vasco Nuñez de Balboa (1475–1519), living on the island of Hispaniola, who was the first European to behold the Pacific Ocean. Balboa led an overland expedition at the Isthmus of Panama and on 25 September 1513, he looked upon the great Sea of the South – the Pacific Ocean; an event ensuring that his name and deed would be remembered forever.

In 1500 Pedro Álvares Cabral had been the first modern European to sight the Brazilian coast, but as he indicated in one of his letters he was uncertain whether Brazil was a large land or an island. This uncertainty was ended by Amerigo Vespucci (1454–1512), an Italian by birth, when he made two expeditions to the coast of South America. The first, in 1499–1500, was under the auspices of the Spanish crown. He

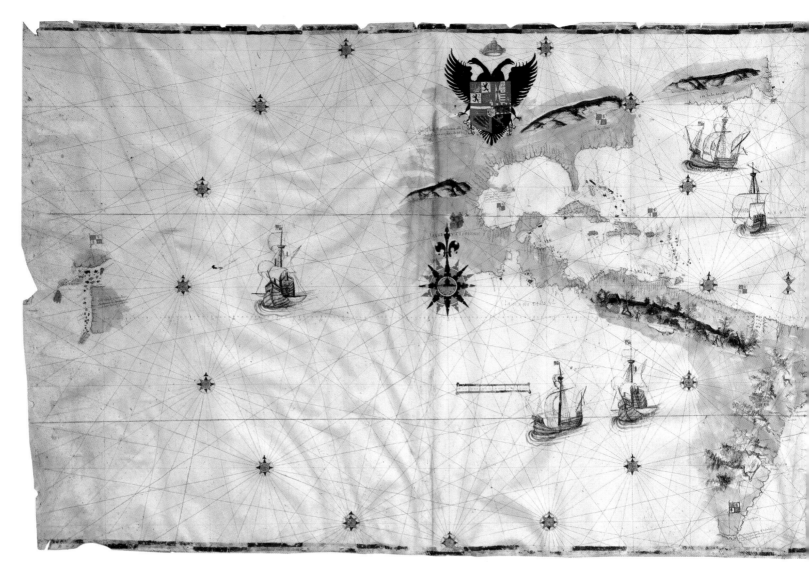

190. Map of the World by Giovanni Vespucci, 1526

A Florentine by birth, Amerigo Vespucci was in Seville in 1491 as a banking agent of the Medici family. While there, he wrote several accounts of four Atlantic voyages that reputedly he had made, and became a friend of Columbus. In 1499 and 1500, Vespucci made two voyages, during which he explored the Caribbean and Atlantic coasts of what is now called South America. Upon his return, he was convinced that he had recognized a new world, one which was not part of Asia, as Columbus had thought. Vespucci accordingly named it *Mundus Novus* (New World) in a pamphlet he wrote in 1504. This pamphlet reached the cosmographer, Martin Waldseemüller, who, on his world map of 1507, named it *Mundus Novus* AMERICA as credit to Amerigo Vespucci. In 1526, Giovanni Vespucci produced this version of his map. It was intended to be wrapped around a cylinder, for the Philippine Islands and New Guinea are shown on both the far west and far east of the map.

COURTESY THE HISPANIC SOCIETY OF AMERICA, NEW YORK

made landfall at Cape Agostinho in Brazil, and sailed along its northern coast to the Caribbean and the Bahamas before returning home. His second expedition was for King Manuel I of Portugal, in which he was to seek a strait through the land leading into the Indian Ocean. From his landfall at Cape São Roque in Brazil, Vespucci sailed south the entire length of the continent until he reached the Strait of Magellan. After his return, a pamphlet recounting the voyage, and allegedly written by Vespucci, was published in 1504. In it, the extensive coastline of the Americas was for the first time referred to as a *Mundus Novus* – a New World.

Vespucci's exploration finally ended the old Ptolemaic cosmography. Ptolemy had asserted the southern hemisphere was covered with water, but Vespucci had shown that a landmass extended into far southern latitudes. The *oikumene* of Ptolemy comprised a single, continuous land, extending from Europe at the western edge to Asia in the east. Now, it was shown that there was a new block of land, a new continent, interposed between the two shores of the *oikumene*.

Having exhausted any hope of finding a strait through the middle of the American continents, exploration was now directed towards discovering a way around the southern extremity of this new land, in the same manner as a way had been found to sail around the southernmost cape of Africa to reach the Indian Ocean. In 1511–12 Diego Ribero (d. 1533), with João de Lisboa as pilot, made an attempt under the flag of Portugal, but failed to reach the 'back side' of that continent. In de Solis's third and last voyage, his fleet ascended the Rio de la Plata, whereupon stepping ashore he and all his crew were killed, roasted and eaten. Not until the expedition of Ferdinand Magellan in 1519 was the passage found to an ocean beyond the southern continent, and the route to the East Indies and Cathay discovered.

With the publication of *Historia General y Natural de las Indias Occidentales* (General and Natural History of the West Indies) by Gonzalo Fernández de Oviedo y Valdéz in 1535, it was finally accepted that the American continent and the Indies

was not attached to Asia. 'Rather it is more likely', Oviedo says, 'that the mainland [*Terra Firma*] of these Indies is another half of the world, as big, or perhaps even greater than Asia, Africa and Europe.'

DIVIDING THE OCEAN SEA: THE TREATY OF TORDESILLAS

Throughout the period of exploration, ownership of the newly 'discovered' island archipelagos was continually in dispute. In an effort to re-establish the peace that had once existed, Spain and Portugal agreed upon the Treaty of Alcáçovas in 1479–1480, which established the right of King Afonso V of Portugal, and Prince John his son, to possession of all the lands, trade and barter in Guinea, as well as the archipelagos of Madeira, Azores and the Cape Verde Islands. It repeated the rights given to Portugal in earlier papal bulls to possess lands in the Ocean Sea extending from Cape Bojador, along the African coast, through all Guinea, and beyond toward the southern and eastern shore. The conjecture was entertained as early as 1452 that Portuguese ships would eventually double the Cape of Good Hope to reach India. King Ferdinand and Queen Isabella of the Kingdom of Castile received all the Canary Islands. This treaty dividing the Atlantic islands between the Iberian powers was affirmed in the papal bull *Aeterni Regis*

issued by Pope Sixtus IV (1414–1484) in 1481.

When Christopher Columbus returned from his epic voyage of 1492–93, contrary winds had prevented him from going directly to Spain to give a report of his voyage. He landed first in Portugal, where he had an audience with King John II. Upon hearing Columbus's narration of his successful voyage, and the newly discovered lands he had reached in 'the islands of India', King John exclaimed that these discoveries properly belonged to Portugal, and not to Spain! He justified this claim on the recently signed Treaty of Alcáçovas with Spain and its confirmation in the bull *Aeterni Regis*. To King John it little mattered that Columbus reached the Indies by sailing in the wrong direction.

Shortly thereafter, when Columbus had his audience with the Catholic Monarchs of Spain and related his discoveries and the meeting with King John, they hastened to assure their ownership of the new lands in the western Atlantic. Ferdinand and Isabella inveighed upon Pope Alexander VI, himself a Spaniard, to grant ownership of the lands reached by Columbus to the Spanish Crown, in the same manner as previous popes granted ownership to Portugal over those islands in the Atlantic and along the coast of Africa that they had discovered. His Holiness was quick to comply, and on 3 May 1493 issued the bull *Inter caetera divini maiestate, beneplacita opera*.

In a sweeping gesture of munificence, his *Inter caetera* gave to Castile full sovereignty and unlimited power over all the

Ships of the Age of Discovery

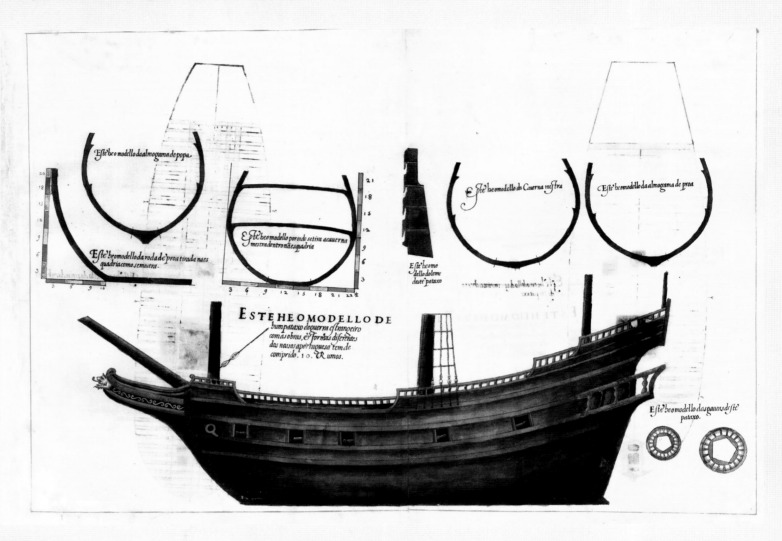

Este heo modello da almogama de popa.

Este heo modello da voda de proa tirada nas quadria como semestra.

Este heo modello porõde setim acauerna mestra dentro nãe squadria

Este heo modello doteme deste pataxo

Este heo modello da Cauerna mestra

Este heo modello da almogama de proa

ESTE HEO MODELLO DE bum pataxo de guerra esfragoeiro com as obras, & formas diferêntes dos naxos aportuguesa tem de comprido. 10. Rumos.

Este heo modello das gauxos deste pataxo.

CARAVEL

The Portuguese developed the ocean-going caravel from their fishing vessels. It was small and rather light but still strong enough to survive on the Atlantic, and it turned out to be an ideal exploration ship during the early years of the Age of Discovery. At the beginning of the fifteenth century Prince Henry the Navigator sent caravels southward along the African coast because they had a shallow enough draft to sail near the coast. During the return voyage against the wind they had to be able to tack and for this reason they were rigged with two or three lateen sails. These ships were known as caravela latina.

From the caravel derived the ocean-going three-masted caravela redonda, where a lateen sail on the mizzenmast was complementary to the square sails. Caravels were longer, lighter and faster than were other contemporary large vessels, and also much more streamlined. They were rather broad beamed in the bow, which had rounded frames, and had a shallow hull. Aft there was a transom stern on which was built a castle for defence against borders, but there was no forecastle. The caravel carried a crew of anything from six to 100, depending on the type of ship and the duration of the voyage.

These agile sailing ships turned out to be so seaworthy and reliable that almost every seafaring nation

in Europe used them by the end of the fifteenth century; they were a particular favourite of Spanish and Portuguese explorers. With such ships, Bartolomeu Dias rounded the Cape of Good Hope, and Vasco da Gama found the seaway to India. The *Niña* and the *Pinta* of Columbus's first voyage were also caravels. *Pinta* had been rigged with square sails in Palos, but the *Niña* was equipped with three lateen sails, which Columbus replaced with square sails at the Canary Islands because he had no intention of tacking against the wind. The ease with which its rig could be converted was an advantage of the caravel.

Towards the end of the sixteenth century the popularity of the caravel decreased markedly, when a need developed for larger cargo capacity to bring home booty from the new world.

CARRACK

Until the end of the fourteenth century, ships could be classed by their geographic origin, but this distinction was eliminated when the northern cog and the southern round ship evolved into the carrack, which the Portuguese called by the name *nau* – in Spanish *nao* – simply meaning 'ship'. Carracks, or naus, became the standard freighters all over Europe in the fifteenth century; they were first proper European

191. Caravel by Manuel Fernandes, 1671

The caravels were light and agile sailing ships; because of their shallow draught they were suitable for the early explorations. The caravels were especially popular among the Spanish and Portuguese explorers.

BIBLIOTECA DA AJUDA, LISBON

ocean-going ships because they were large enough to be stable in a seaway. Their hulls were wide and bulky and their sterns rounded, and large carracks had several decks for accommodation and armament. They were the first of the three-masted sailing ship types and were to be the forerunner of later ship designs. The fore and main masts were rigged with square sails and the mizzenmast with a lateen sail. If there was a need to equip the vessel with a fourth mast, called the bonaventure mast, a lateen sail was also used. The sail area, and consequently also the ship's speed, could be increased with another square sail, the topsail, which was set above the mainsail.

During the sixteenth century and in the first part of the seventeenth century almost all Spanish and Portuguese trading journeys to India and China were made with carracks. All five ships in Ferdinand Magellan's 'Armada de Moluccas' were carracks, and

192. Cadamosto's Caravels by Björn Landström, 1964

Alvise Cadamosto was an experienced seaman and explorer in the service of Henry the Navigator. He was the first European to set foot on Cape Verde. His report from the Gambia River suggests that he did not use the astrolabe or the quadrant to navigate. He did make careful observations of the stars, however, and noted, for example, the rise of the Southern Cross above the horizon, deducing his latitude from it. The ships in his expedition were typical caravels with lateen sails.

COURTESY OF OLOF LANDSTRÖM

Columbus's famous flagship *Santa Maria* was probably a small carrack. Columbus was not very pleased with her because of her deep draft, slow sailing and poor manoeuverability compared to the *Pinta* and the *Niña*. He wrote in his logbook that *Santa Maria* measured 80 'toneladas,' which means that she could carry 80 tons of wine.

To increase their defensibility against boarding by pirates, carracks were provided with high castles fore and aft, which had the unfortunate effect of making them so top heavy that there could be a risk of capsizing in strong winds. The castles were built as separate parts of the ship, often with stairs leading up to them, and were subjected to such stress in a rolling seaway that they could become structurally weak. Because the forecastle of the carrack extended forward of the stem, it could turn the ship away from the wind in a hard blow.

Until the end of the fifteenth century, merchant vessels and war ships were fairly similar. The latter were quite simply merchantmen armed with small and light naval guns, which at first were mounted on the upper deck. The carrack was the first sailing ship type to carry heavier guns on battery decks under the weather deck, with closable, top-hinged gun ports on both sides making it possible to direct gunfire low down on the enemy vessel's sides. In 1510 King Henry VIII of England built the 32 m-long carrack *Mary Rose* for military purposes. Because of her small size, her gun ports were situated too close to the waterline, and she capsized and sank when water entered through her ports. The wreck of *Mary Rose* remains on display at a museum in Portsmouth, England.

GALLEON

The poor performance of carracks in a seaway led to the development of a new, slimmer but still roomy ship design known as the galleon. The first stages of this ship type are uncertain, but possibly it was developed in Spain. It spread fast all over Europe and was used from the sixteenth century until the end of the seventeenth century. Although originally it was a war ship, and fought in great naval battles, the galleon turned out to be fast with excellent sailing capabilities and large cargo-carrying capacity. It was used to carry treasure from Asia and America to Europe.

The fore deck of the galleon was made lower and the hull somewhat longer and narrower, which improved manoeuvrability and increased speed. The forecastle was kept smaller, and aft of the stem, to reduce the effect of wind on the hull forward, and also to make it easier to handle the 'blind sail' beneath the bowsprit, so-called because it obstructed the view forward. Instead of the rounded stern of the carrack, the galleon was constructed with a narrower and straighter stern, which also better carried the weight of the aft castle. The stern was decorated with paintings, and with gilded and painted sculptures and pillars. In the final stage there were so many of them that they affected the stability of the vessel. Aft there was an open balcony, the gallery. This feature was new to the galleon, but galleries were to remain on ships until the nineteenth century.

The galleon usually had four masts with topmasts, and above the mainmast's topsail was a third sail, the topgallant sail. Lateen sails were carried in the mizzen and bonaventure masts. Towards the end of the sixteenth century a vertical lever for operating the long rudder bar (whipstaff) was introduced. This enabled the helmsman to see the sails when he was steering. When staying, this was especially important, because in a major change of course the vessel was turned by the sails.

Galleons varied considerably in size and shape. They were also easy to convert; during their lifespan they could be rebuilt many times for different purposes in war and trade. As warships they were quite heavily armed, with two battery decks and several smaller decks. They were strong and well protected, but not very seaworthy in rough weather. Using the riches brought home from America, Spain built many large warships to protect her merchant vessels. In England Sir John Hawkins (1532–1595) developed a lighter and faster version of the galleon. With such vessels Queen Elizabeth's fleet was able to prevent the Spanish invasion of England in 1588.

The first remarkable galleon was Sir Francis Drake's flagship, *Golden Hind*, on which he circumnavigated the world. Another famous galleon, the *Mayflower*, brought the Pilgrim Fathers to America in 1620. The small *Mayflower* had a crew of 25 and was able to carry some 100 passengers. The largest, most expensive and most richly decorated galleon of the seventeenth century was the pride of the Swedish Navy, the *Vasa*, which sank due to poor stability at the very beginning of her maiden voyage from Stockholm.

193. Carrack by Björn Landström, 1961

The carrack, which was used both for warfare and for trading, was the first European large, ocean-going ship. Characteristics of the carrack included high-raised structures, called castles, at the bow and stern of the vessel, and three masts. On the fore mast and main mast it carried square sails, and on the mizzen mast a lateen sail, which meant that it could combine the benefits of both sail types.

COURTESY OF OLOF LANDSTRÖM

Don Fernando e doña Ysabel

por la graçia de Dios Rey e reyna de Castilla de Leon de Aragon de Seçilia de Granada de Toledo de Valençia de Galisia de Mallorcas de Seuilla de Çerdeña de Cordoua de Corçega de Murçia de Jahen del Algarbe de Algezira de Gibraltar e de las yslas de Canaria Conde e Condesa de Barçelona e Señores de Vizcaya e de Molina Duques de Athenas e de Neopatria Condes de Rosellon e de Çerdaña marqueses de Oristan e de Goçiano en vno con el prinçipe don Juan nuestro muy caro e muy amado hijo primero eredero de los dichos nuestros Reynos e Señorios Por quanto por don enrrique enrriques nuestro mayordomo mayor e don gutierre de cardenas comendador mayor de leon e nuestro contador mayor y el doctor Rodrigo maldonado todos del nuestro consejo fue tratado asentado e capitulado por nos y en nuestro nonbre e por virtud de nuestro poder con el serenisimo don Juan por la graçia de Dios Rey de Portugal e de los Algarbes de aquende e de allende el mar en africa Señor de Guinea nuestro muy caro e muy amado hermano e con ... de Sosa Señor de Usagres e berenguel e don Juan de Sosa su hijo almotaçen mayor del dicho serenisimo Rey nuestro hermano e Ayres de Almada corregidor de los fechos çeuiles de su corte e del su desenbargo todos del consejo del dicho serenisimo Rey e por ... mano en su nonbre e por virtud de su poder sus enbaxadores ... años vinieron sobre la diferençia de lo que a nos y al dicho serenisimo Rey nuestro hermano pertenesçe de lo que hasta siete dias deste mes de Junio en que estamos de la ... es ... e ... esta por descubrir en el mar oçeano en la qual dicha capitulaçion los dichos nuestros procuradores entre otras cosas prometieron que dentro de çierto ... la capitulaçion e contenido en ella otorgariamos e firmariamos e jurariamos e ratificariamos e aprouariamos la dicha capitulaçion por nuestras personas e nos queriendo ... cunplir e guardar todo lo que en nuestro nonbre fue asentado e capitulado e otorgado açerca de lo suso dicho mandamos traer ante nos la dicha escriptura de la dicha capitulaçion ... asiento para la ver e ... e el tenor della de verbo ...

En el nonbre de Dios

todo poderoso padre e hijo e espiritu santo tres personas realmente distintas e vna sola esençia diuina Manifiesto e notorio sea a todos quantos este publico ynstrumento vieren como en la villa de tordesillas a siete dias del mes de Junio año del nasçimiento de nuestro señor Jhesu Christo de mill e quatroçientos e nouenta e quatro años en presençia de nos los secretarios e escriuanos e notarios publicos de yuso escriptos estando presentes los honrrados don enrrique enrriques mayordomo mayor de los muy altos e muy poderosos prinçipes los señores don fernando e doña ysabel por la graçia de Dios Rey e reyna de Castilla de Leon de Aragon de Seçilia de Granada etç. e don gutierre de cardenas contador mayor de los dichos Señores Rey e Reyna e el doctor Rodrigo maldonado todos del consejo de los dichos Señores Rey e Reyna de Castilla e de Leon e de Aragon e de Seçilia e de Granada etç. sus procuradores bastantes de la vna parte e los honrrados don Ruy de Sosa Señor de Usagres e berenguel e don Juan de Sosa su hijo almotaçen mayor del muy alto e muy exçelente ...

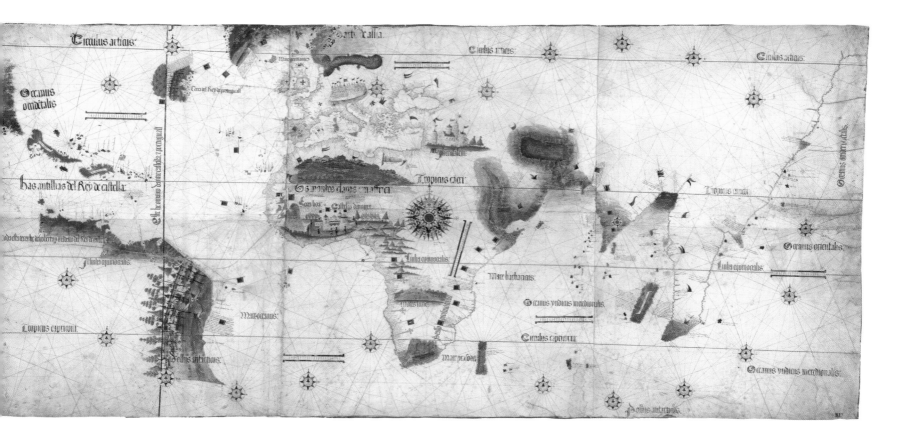

195. Carta del Cantino, 1502

The earliest, and arguably the most attractive, depiction of the new boundary line created by the 1497 Treaty of Tordesillas is the nautical chart entitled *Carta de navigat per Isole nouam tr[ovate] in le parte de India* (Chart for the navigation of the islands lately discovered in the parts of India), and dated 1502. More simply called the 'Cantino World Map', it reflects recent achievements of Portuguese mariners – Vasco da Gama, Pedro Álvarez Cabral and Gaspar Córte-Real – as well as the discoveries of Columbus for his Spanish sovereigns. At roughly 47.5°-west longitude in this detail of the western hemisphere, a prominent vertical line, clearly labelled, shows the demarcation of ownership of the world as agreed upon by Castile and Portugal. Bold lettering west of the line proclaims that the Antilles belong to the King of Spain, while the flag of Castile is planted among the islands. Cuba, the queen of the Antilles, is named after Queen Isabella, the Catholic monarch, while the second largest island of the archipelago is called Hispaniola. To this day, Portuguese is the language spoken in the area of Brazil that falls east of the line of demarcation, while it is Spanish in all lands west of the line.

BIBLIOTECA ESTENSE UNIVERSITARIA DI MODENA

194. A page from the Treaty of Tordesillas, 1494

In an attempt to resolve disputes over ownership of lands newly discovered in the Atlantic Ocean, the Treaty of Tordesillas (1497) divided the entire Atlantic Ocean with a vertical line between Spain and Portugal. But when mariners of both sovereign nations reached the Pacific Ocean on the opposite side of the Earth, the vertical line no longer had relevance. Both powers laid claim to the Moluccas (Spice Islands), and desired the fabulous wealth to be gained from them. Regardless of the difficulties between these two nations, they had effectively sealed off the seas south of the Canary Islands, preventing incursion by the vessels of any other nation.

INSTITUTO DOS ARQUIVOS NACIONAIS, TORRE DO TOMBO, LISBON

lands discovered and yet to be discovered in the New World by Columbus, or any other Spanish mariner. In quick succession, Alexander VI issued three more bulls, each a modification of the original *Inter caetera* intended to resolve issues of conflict between Spain and Portugal. In the last of these bulls, King John's tenuous claim to the Indies that he might have had from previous bulls and treaties was completely abrogated.

By then, both Spain and Portugal had come to the realization that calling upon the Vatican to help mark their respective spheres of discovery and ownership was unsatisfactory. None of the papal divisions were totally acceptable; either they gave away too much land to one power, or took away dominion from a power whose ownership had already been established. For the sake of peace and concord they decided to resolve their differences by treaty, independent of the papacy. On 7 June 1494, in the small Spanish town of Tordesillas, they finally reached an agreement. A straight line was to be drawn:

> '... *from the Arctic Pole to the Antarctic Pole … at a distance of 370 leagues from the islands of Cape Verde to the West … all discoveries, going by the Eastern side [of the line] belong to the King of Portugal and his successors. And all the rest … going by the Western side, belong to the King and Queen of Castile.'*

For the first time, a political line, placed by papal bull, and by the mutual consent of the two great Iberian powers, divided the Ocean Sea.

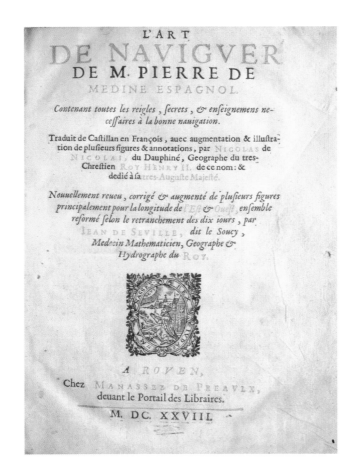

196. The New World by Nicolas de Nicolay, 1554

Nicolas de Nicolay, both artist and spy, became 'géographe du Roy' (Court Geographer) to the King of Spain. He travelled far and wide, and built up an extensive collection of cartographic material. In 1550, Nicolay translated Pedro de Medina's *Arte de Nauegar* from the original Spanish into French. Subsequently, it was published in several editions, including this Lyon edition of 1576.

JUHA NURMINEN COLLECTION

197. Frontispiece of *L'art de Navigner de M. Pierre de Medine Espagnol* by Pedro de Medina, 1628

Pedro de Medina's treatise, *Arte del Navigar,* published in 1545, was a principle force contributing to the art of celestial navigation. It contained all the regulations and lessons, including figures and tables of the Sun and Moon, necessary to good navigation. Enormously successful during its time, it was translated from the original Spanish to many languages, including Italian and French.

JUHA NURMINEN COLLECTION

198. Portuguese Carracks off a Rocky Coast by Joachim Patinir, 16th century

One of the very few contemporary paintings of sixteenth-century ships is Joachim Patinir's depiction of ten vessels, including a caravel, three galleys and a rowing barge. Reportedly, the largest ship is the *Santa Catarina*, a Portuguese carrack in the East Indies trade. In 1603, the Dutch East India Company (VOC) captured the ship, along with its valuable cargo of musk. In the hard competition between nations for foreign trade, this was a common practice.

NATIONAL MARITIME MUSEUM, LONDON

The difficulty with this grand plan was in reaching agreement on whose measurements of distance to use. In the fifteenth and sixteenth centuries each nation employed a different estimation of the circumference of the Earth for determining the number of leagues in a degree. Portuguese navigators arrived at 17 ½ leagues in a degree, whereas Spain accepted a smaller measurement of 16 ⅔ leagues in a degree. There was also the question of where the measurement would begin, since the wording in the treaty was sufficiently vague that the distance to the final line of demarcation could vary by as much as 463 nautical miles.

With the voyage of Magellan in 1519–1522 a southwest passage around Cape Horn to the Orient was finally achieved, making the region accessible to Spain as well as to Portugal. Each nation keeping within its proscribed domain – Portugal sailing eastward of the line, and Spain westward of it – they had arrived at the same place on the opposite side of the world. Both powers laid claim to the Moluccas and to the fabulous wealth to be gained from them. The question now arose whether the division of the Ocean Sea extended to the opposite side of the Earth to the Pacific. No one knew with any certainty whose territory the Moluccas fell within. The need for a clear definition of boundaries became urgent. Without agreement on the longitude of the demarcation line, its counter-meridian would remain unknown. The emphasis on negotiations now shifted to the determination of ownership of new islands, in a new ocean.

In 1524, in the city of Vitoria, both sides reached a tentative agreement to set the line of demarcation and to determine ownership of the Molucca Islands. The arrangement was the same as that proposed earlier to clarify the line of demarcation, but in addition to the authorities on geography and navigation, there were to be three lawyers appointed by each side. They were to receive the proofs, documents and witnesses, and make a judgment about possession. Officials from both courts were also present. They continued discussions for two years, but reached no decision.

Eventually the Pacific question was laid to rest when Spanish conquest and settlement of lands in Mexico and South America gained for her abundant treasure, mostly in silver, some of which was traded for Chinese silk and gold at Manila in the Philippines. Portugal had her trade routes around the Cape of Good Hope to India and Malacca. From her colonies along the African coast, Portugal extracted wealth from gold mines, the sale of ivory and through the trade of black slaves. From Malacca, and the Spice Islands, she derived enormous profits in the trade of spices.

In the closing decades of the sixteenth century the maritime supremacy enjoyed by Spain and Portugal began to wane. Explorations of discovery by the nations of northern Europe created new powers in the Ocean Sea, and merchants from the

independent provinces of the Netherlands and from England were able to seize a share of wealth from the Spice Islands, India and the West Indies.

FROM THE ART OF NAVIGATION TO A TECHNICAL SCIENCE

Casa de Minas e Guinea (Portugal)

Prince Henry's programme of overseas expansion into unfamiliar seas and to unknown lands created new technical requirements. Charts had to be created incorporating the geography of newly explored coasts. Portuguese pilots had to be trained in the art of oceanic navigation to replace the Genoese or Catalan pilots first employed. Manuals of celestial navigation, and sailing directions (roteiros) describing the best routes to be followed, comprehensive observations of entry to ports, wind, weather, and current patterns all had to be compiled and published.

For these purposes, 'Mestre Jacome de Malhorca' was brought to the Portuguese court in 1419 by Prince Henry as 'a man expert in the art of navigation and in the making of charts and instruments, and to teach his expertise (*sciencia*) to Portuguese practitioners of that art'. Jacome, or Jafuda Cresques (c. 1350–1427), was the son of Abraham Cresques who was a well-known cartographer in Majorca, and creator of the Catalan Atlas. His son inherited his father's abilities in cartography, and was granted the title of *Magister cartorum navigandi* at the court of Afonso V of Portugal. But his role as coordinator of Portugal's discoveries and nautical sciences is not entirely clear.

Duarte, heir to the throne of King John I of Portugal, and brother of Prince Henry the Navigator, created an organization known as the *Casa de Mina e Guiné* (House of Mines and Guinea). This became the official centre for Portuguese cartography and navigation relating to Prince Henry and his successors. When Portuguese trade extended beyond Africa to Goa, and the Malabar Coast of India following the voyage of Vasco da Gama in 1497–98, the name of Casa de Mina e Guiné was changed to *Casa de India* to incorporate the expanded empire. Eventually, it controlled the colonization of Brazil.

The Casa de India coordinated all functions related to trade with Portugal's far-flung colonial network. The navy that had been created in the previous century by King Diníz I (1279–1325) was equipped by the Casa to defend Portugal's mines on the Guinea coast, convey supplies to a series of strategically located forts, and protect Portugal's chain of coastal factories reaching to India, and eventually beyond to Malacca and the Spice Islands. The Casa administered all matters of commerce from India to Lisbon: it oversaw the construction of ships, prepared fleets with the necessary equipment, regulated the load-

199. An English Nocturnal, unsigned, 18th century

To indicate the approximate time at night, an instrument called the nocturnal measured the orientation of axis of the Little Dipper as it appeared to rotate in a counter-clockwise direction around the North Star. An almanac provided the orientation at midnight for every night of the year. In effect, the nocturnal was a kind of night-time 'sundial'.

MUSEUM OF THE HISTORY OF SCIENCE, UNIVERSITY OF OXFORD

ing and unloading of merchandise, and collected all taxes.

As Portugal's school of navigation it included a chief cosmographer, whose function was to draw charts based on the new geographic information from these voyages and to keep them updated. In addition, the cosmographer organized the sailing directions for the navigators and gave instructions to the pilots. In 1529, the chief cosmographer, and keeper of maps and instruments was Pedro Nuñes.

Casa de la Contratación (Spain)

When Spain's realm expanded into the New World, it required a similar structured organization to control all commerce, and a school of navigation to assure safe passage to the new lands. In 1503, the *Casa de la Contratación* (House of Commerce) was established in Seville. Using Portugal's Casa de India as a model, the Catholic monarchs of Spain, Ferdinand and Isabella, created the Casa de la Contratación to 'stimulate, direct, and control traffic with the New World'. The essence of its being was to assure a complete monopoly of business with America.

The Casa de la Contratación grew into a complex organization, with royal officials responsible for all fiscal duties relating to expeditions. Its revenue came from a concession on licensing, the collection of fees, fines and taxes on merchandise imported from America, as well as goods exported to there from Spain. This was supplemented by taxes on ship registry, size and tonnage. Goods brought into Spain for re-exportation to Chile and Peru were subject to additional taxes. It handled insurance protection on transported merchandise, and adjusted claims on the fleet and merchandise on outgoing and returning ships. The judicial branch handled lawsuits relating to commerce and navigation, and even had its own jail.

In 1508 Ferdinand created a school of navigation as part of the Casa de la Contratación. It had a *Pilot-major* whose duty was to train pilots and test their proficiency. Amerigo Vespucci was appointed as the first Pilot-major. Other renowned Pilot-majors were Sebastian Cabot, who held that post for thirty years, and Diego Ribero, who navigated Vasco da Gama and Albuquerque to India. Only the most distinguished navigators were admitted to this post, selected for their theoretical knowledge of navigation and for having demonstrated practical abilities in successful expeditions. The Casa was expanded in 1552 by the creation of a *Cathedra* (professor's chair) of the Art of Navigation and Cosmography, and again in 1583 by the founding of the Academy of Mathematics in Madrid.

Pilots and masters of ships were taught the sciences of astronomy and mathematics, and the practical aspects of navigation in a systematic manner. Upon completion of the course they had to pass an examination and receive a certificate of competence. Ursula Lamb, present-day authority on

the Spanish maritime empire, succinctly enumerated what was expected of the pilots: 'they had to prove familiarity with the route they proposed to sail, with the harbours and coasts along the way and at the destination, be able to set a course by a chart, steer a compass course, determine the latitude of their position, and they were required to keep a dead-reckoning track of their voyage. They had to show a familiarity with astronomical tables and their use, and to show an understanding of the construction, principle and use of instruments (quadrant, astrolabe, cross-staff, and compass).'

The Pilot-major also supervised the *Padrón real*, a master chart used as the standard reference for the production of all other charts issued to pilots and navigators. As new geographic information arrived, the Padrón real was updated. Similar Padróns existed for nautical instruments. Other instruments were compared to these to assure uniformity and accuracy.

By 1525, the organization had grown too complex for the Pilot-major to handle these multiple tasks, and the responsibility was divided among separate individuals. In addition to a Pilot-major, who still oversaw the teaching and examination of pilots, there was a separate cosmographer in charge of charts (but the Pilot-major retained responsibility for the Padrón real), and another cosmographer in charge of instruments. From 1552 until 1707 there was a teaching chair for cosmography.

When Pedro de Medina assumed the post of Pilot-major in 1545, his knowledge in all aspects of the science of navigation was so extensive, and his practical experience in sailing so great, that his duties virtually encompassed what previously was handled by a group of experts. Medina taught navigation and mathematics to pilots, and supervised their examination. Two of his treatises, *Arte de navegar* (1545) and *Regimiento de navegación* (1552), became the standard teaching texts.

The Casa de la Contratación remained in existence until 1790, when changes in administrative structure, increased costs of transportation of goods, foreign competition, and internal rivalries between Seville and Cádiz contributed to its demise. By this time another nation, England, with a newly acquired science of navigation based on advances in astronomy and mathematics, was becoming masters of the sea.

Pedro Nuñes

The studies and written works of Pedro Nuñes (1502–1578) significantly contributed to the science of navigation, and helped propel Portugal into mastery of the sea and a major world power. Nuñes obtained his degree in medicine from the University of Lisbon in 1525, and within seven years he held the chair of logic, chair of moral philosophy, and chair of metaphysics. In 1529, Nuñes became chief cosmographer and keeper of maps and instruments for King Sebastian of Portugal (1554–1578). Eight years later he was appointed to

200. The Battle of Lepanto, 7 October 1571, by H. Letter, late 16th century

One of the most decisive naval battles to be fought anywhere on the globe took place on 7 October 1571 at Lepanto in the Ionian Sea off western Greece. In three hours the fleet of the Holy League, a coalition of Christian sea powers made up of the Republic of Venice, the Papal States, the Republic of Genoa, the Duchy of Savoy and the Knights of Malta, virtually destroyed the Ottoman Navy which lost 240 ships, leaving thirty thousand men dead or wounded. The victory put a stop to the western expansion of Islam, and was the last major sea battle to be fought entirely by oared galleys.

NATIONAL MARITIME MUSEUM, LONDON

the chair of mathematics at the University of Coimbra, a post 'specifically created to provide instruction in the technical requirements for navigation'.

Nuñes was the first to show that, when plotted on a plane chart, even though the rhumb line of a ship's course cut across meridians at a constant angle, the line curved toward the Pole as the result of converging meridians. This created another problem for navigators. In their dead-reckoning it was necessary to take into account the diminishing number of leagues between one degree of meridian and another at different latitudes, and how to determine the correct distances. With his knowledge of spherical trigonometry, Nuñes solved this difficulty with an instrument of his own devising. It consisted of a quadrant with a silk thread, moveable bead, and scales on the two straight sides. With proper positioning of the thread and bead, plus some simple mathematics, navigators could determine the number of leagues travelled.

Nuñes also devised a means to measure the amount of magnetic variation (sometimes called declination) and its effect on the compass needle. He created an instrument consisting of a disc with a gnomon and a magnetic needle at its centre. To keep it level at sea it was suspended by cords or set in gimbals. With the needle set at the meridian, pairs of azimuth readings were taken of Sun shadows before noon and afternoon, i.e. the horizontal component of direction to the Sun, measured in degrees clockwise around the horizon, starting at North, and simultaneous astrolabe readings were made of the Sun's elevation. The two azimuths of the Sun were averaged, and compared with the position of the needle. A more direct, and simpler, method of comparing the azimuth of the Sun at meridian passage with the azimuth of the compass needle pointing to magnetic north was impossible because an astrolabe lacked the accuracy needed such a measurement.

Nuñes's work directly influenced English scientists, such as Dr John Dee, William Borough and Thomas Digges. Eager to learn the 'new navigation,' they realized from Nuñes's work that any substantial improvement in the methods of navigation, by necessity, would have to come from a study of astronomy, and the use of mathematical tables.

Pedro de Medina

Although Nuñes led the way in this new navigation, it was the Spanish cosmographer, Pedro de Medina (1493–c. 1567), who made it accessible to mariners, not only in Spain, but throughout the maritime world. Medina was a self-taught scholar in mathematics and astronomy who rose to the exalted position of Pilot-major of Spain's Casa de la Contratación. He was not an inventor of instruments or creator of mathematical solutions to problems, like Nuñes; his ability lay in explaining in a clear and simple manner the nature of the Earth and the heavens and its application to nautical science.

Medina's most important works on navigation are *Arte de navegar* (1545) and two editions of *Regimiento de navegación* (1552 and 1563). Over twenty foreign editions evidence the widespread and prolonged popularity of his treatises, with translations into English, Italian and Flemish continuing until the beginning of the

seventeenth century. Medina's navigation manuals were 'intended for unskilled navigators', but they were equally used by the most accomplished practitioners in the art of navigation: William Barentsz carried a copy of the Dutch translation on his third voyage from Spitzbergen to Nova Zembla in 1596; an English translation was on board the *Golden Hind* with Francis Drake in his circumnavigation in 1577–80; and it was used by Martin Frobisher in his search for the Northwest Passage in 1576.

In addition to his scholarly writings, Pedro de Medina had a royal warrant, in connection with the Casa de Contratación, to draw charts, prepare sailing directions, and make instruments – all of which he had the right to sell. Although he never actually made any instruments, he examined for accuracy those made and sold by others. On several occasions, he was called upon as an authority on cosmography to help settle the dispute between Spain and Portugal on possession of the

Philippines and other Pacific islands, according to the line of demarcation set by the Treaty of Tordesillas.

As equally successful as were Medina's treatises, was the nautical manual *Breve compendio de la sphera y de la arte de navegar* (A short compendium on the sphere and the art of navigation), written by Martin Cortés de Albacar (1532–1589) and published in 1551. Cortés was a mathematician, geographer, and professor of navigation in Cádiz. He represented his book, as 'the first practical text of everything a navigator should know.' It was more comprehensive than Medina's work, and consisted of three parts: part one was on the composition of the world and the universal principles of the art of navigation; part two on movements of the Sun and Moon and the effects they produce; part three on the construction and use of instruments and rules of the art of navigation.

HEMISPHERIV AB AEQVINOCTIALI LINEA, AD CIRCVLV POLI ARCTICI.

IMAGE OF THE WORLD
IN WORD AND LINE

LEADING THEORISTS FOR A NEW DISCOVERY

At the beginning of the sixteenth century England had little interest in expeditions to the New World; attempts to reach the Far East by a northwest route had thus far proved unsuccessful. By the mid-sixteenth century it became apparent that her lack of scientific knowledge in navigation and curtailed voyages of exploration seriously hampered her attempts at world trade. If English mariners were to plot their way confidently through unknown seas, and wrest their share of profit from trade on the far side of the world, they had to learn the 'new navigation'. This depended on a thorough knowledge of astronomy, coupled with the application of mathematics. Prompted by the writings of Robert Thorne and other noted geographers urging explorations of far northern routes, there was renewed interest in a northern passage to Cathay which had lain dormant since the voyages of John (1450–1498) and Sebastian Cabot (c. 1476–1557).

Petrus Martyr

Petrus Martyr d'Anghiera (c. 1457–1526), eminent cartographer and humanist at the Spanish court, if not the very first person to conceive of a northern passage leading from the Atlantic Ocean to the Pacific Ocean, was certainly one of the early and influential writers about such a route. In his *De Orbe Novo* (The New World) published in 1515 Martyr told

201. Arctic Regions by Gerard and Cornelis de Jode, 1593

Gerard de Jode, from Nijmegen, Netherlands, settled in Antwerp in c. 1550 as an engraver and publisher of maps. He never hesitated to contact the leading experts of his time on astronomy, mathematics and navigation; John Dee, for example, inspired him to incorporate the four major islands from the voyage of Nicholas of Lynn, into the Arctic Ocean.

JUHA NURMINEN COLLECTION

of the exciting new discoveries made in the Western Atlantic by Sebastian Cabot. Martyr noted that Cabot 'had discovered a new continent, lying where he had not expected to find another land but that of Cathay'. As Cabot sailed along this coast he described 'a course of waters toward the west, but same running more soft and gently than the swift waters that the Spaniards found in the navigation southward'. Both Cabot and Martyr believed that this course of waters 'betokened a passage of water through the continent'.

Robert Thorne

Twelve years later, Robert Thorne, a Bristol merchant living in Seville, Spain, took up very similar ideas to those of Petrus Martyr. In a 1527 letter to King Henry VIII of England, and to Dr Edward Leigh (Ley) the Kings's ambassador to Spain, titled *A Declaration of the Indies*, Robert Thorne promoted the idea of voyages of discovery to seek a northern passage to the Moluccas, and extolled the advantages this achievement would bring to English tradesmen. He believed the peoples of the Far East might want England's corn and seeds if made available to them, as much as the English wished their spices and stones.

Thorne's conclusion from studying the Spanish charts available to him was that it was possible to sail directly over the North Pole to Asia. Not only would such a route eliminate contact and potential battle with Spanish or Portuguese vessels, but would cut the distance of the voyage in half. Although navigation under the Pole was commonly thought to be difficult, dangerous, and even impossible, Thorne contended that the opposite is true; 'these seas are navigable and may be passed through without any danger on account of the perpetual clearness of the day without darkness of the night'. He believed this constancy of light would also enable English mariners to discover strange lands, coasts and countries that might otherwise be passed for fear of danger in sailing close by them in the darkness of night.

After passing the Pole, they could choose to sail to China, the East Indies or Malacca, and return to England by way of the Cape of Good Hope, thus encompassing the whole world. It was not so much a matter, he believed, of transgressing upon, or usurping what rightfully belonged to the Emperor of Spain and King of Portugal; rather, that on the way toward the Spice Islands, other lands, 'no lesse riche of golde and spicerie', might be discovered. It was, Thorne thought, a matter that could be obtained at the King's pleasure, involving very little cost, danger, or work to the King or any of his subjects. 'The effort would be almost nothing compared to the infinite profit and perpetual glory'.

Roger Barlow

Roger Barlow (d. 1554) was another successful and wealthy merchant of Bristol whose business kept him for ten years in Seville where he managed his trade. While there he saw a manual for Spanish seamen written in 1519 by Martín Fernández de Enciso, an astronomer in the court of Charles V. Entitled *Suma de Geográfia*, this manual contained all that was known at the time about the art and science of navigation, including a description of the nautical instruments, the mathematics necessary for their use, and some tables showing solar declination. Barlow realized how important it would be for English maritime expansion to have the same information. English mariners could have the ability to navigate, as did the Portuguese and Spanish, and not have to rely upon pilots from these countries to guide them. With this in mind, Barlow translated Enciso's work, and in 1541 presented it to King Henry VIII, with the title *A Brief Summe of Geographie*.

Like Thorne, Barlow also believed that a passage directly over the North Pole was not only possible, but quite practical. To Barlow, the advantage of a trans-Polar route to Cathay was 'in shortening [the navigation] half the waie, for the other [Spain and Portugal] must saile by great circuites and compasses, and thes [the English] shal saile by streit wais and lines'.

Sir Humphrey Gilbert

The theme of a Northwest Passage was once again taken up – this time by Sir Humphrey Gilbert (c.1539–1583). Gilbert believed that simply by 'entering a wide passage between Baccalaos [Newfoundland] and Canada, one would sail into an immense sea leading into the fabled Strait of Anian'. From there it would be but 'a short sail to Japan, China and the Moluccas, where there would be a lucrative trade in goods'. As a further incentive, he added that English goods could be sold at a great profit in the Far East. Additionally, he saw in this venture the possibility of settling these most distant lands with England's most unwanted peoples – its poor and its criminal elements.

In a petition to Queen Elizabeth I in 1565 Gilbert made an audacious proposal, in which he was willing 'to make tryall thereof ... at his owne costs and charges' to attempt the voyage. All that he asked in return for his efforts and expenses was 'a monopoly of trade through the passage for his lifetime, and a 25% cut of the customs duties on all goods brought through it to England'. These terms were scarcely considered by the Queen. His words, however, had some effect, for they helped persuade a group of Merchant adventurers of London to organize and finance the voyages of Martin Frobisher to find the elusive Northwest Passage.

William Bourne

William Bourne (c. 1535–1582) also contributed to the growing interest in the 'new navigation' in England. As a gunner and mathematician by profession, Bourne had a deep interest in England's maritime ventures. His *A Regiment for the Sea*, first published in 1574, was a complete English seaman's manual. Bourne wrote this work as a critical response to an earlier English translation (1561) of a Spanish sea-manual. In his book, Bourne described five possible ways English vessels could reach Cathay. By 1580, of these five possible routes to Asia, two had already been accomplished. For the remaining three – the Northwest Passage, Northeast Passage, and a route directly over the North Pole – their only affirmation lay in the classic concept of distribution of water and Earth, a concept which gathered in validity in a progression of new maps throughout the centuries; a concept which continued undiminished in force in spite of repeated failures to complete a passage to the Indies by a northern route.

Of the way across the top of North America – the Northwest Passage – to Cathay, Bourne was cautious about Martin Frobisher's claim that he had found the strait leading to the Pacific. 'It is doubtful', he says, 'that Frobisher Strait is really the long sought passage into the East Ocean Sea [Pacific] it; might well only be a bay or gulf'. Nonetheless, he was not altogether willing to completely deny the possibility, and remarked that there 'may be a passage thereabout ... between the northern part of America and such lands lying toward the North Pole'.

Bourne favored the route directly over the North Pole to Cathay, as had Thorne and Barlow. In both the previous works, the northern route was deemed not only to be the shortest possible way to the Far East, but the only quarter of the globe not under control of the Spanish or Portuguese, and thus still open to exploration by English mariners. Its greatest disadvantage was that the cosmography of this region was the least known, and open to greatest conjecture. Geographers of the Ancients believed that the Arctic was a congealed (frozen) sea, which prevented anyone from entering, a belief still widely held during Bourne's time, but he discounted this, saying that in the high Arctic latitudes the great salt sea is known not to freeze. He reasoned that ice is formed in the shallow water of rivers and sounds, and when broken up in the springtime is driven out into the sea by currents.

Bourne also had an answer for the concern expressed by Gilbert and others about the extreme cold in the arctic. Like the Dutch geographer, Peter Plancius, Bourne believed that the closer one got to the Pole, the warmer it would become, not colder. The perpetual Sun would not only make the climate more temperate, but also dispel the darkness, and drive away fear. Ever cautious, he says, 'It is possible that in my discourse it is mere foolyshnesse and a thinge unpossible for it to bee done, and yet notwithstanding no man can tell before that it is put in experience'.

Bourne's *Regiment for the Sea* was so successful that there were eleven editions printed in English, the last being in 1631. It was translated into Dutch, with three more editions, and then into Spanish, which completed the circle from where the 'new navigation' began.

Dr John Dee

Of all the learned persons in Elizabethan England, arguably none was more influential in furthering England's maritime ventures than Dr John Dee (1527–1608). His power was due not so much to his writings, but to the direct, personal instruction he gave to those mariners who set forth on their voyages of discovery. Dee's friends included the most eminent geographers, cartographers and scientists of his time; with them he discussed the cosmography of the world – in particular, concepts of an open waterway in far northern latitudes by which the Far East

202. Portrait of John Dee, by an unknown artist, 16th century

One of the great intellectual giants of the Elizabethan Era, Dr John Dee was a preeminent mathematician, respected astronomer and a leading expert in navigation. As consultant on navigation and cartography to the Muscovy Company, more than any single individual, he led the way for England to become a major world power.

ASHMOLEAN MUSEUM, OXFORD

203. Frontpiece of *General and rare memorials pertayning to the Perfect Arte of navigation* by John Dee and Gulielmus Canterus, 1577

Only one of four books on navigation written by Dr John Dee was ever published. In this, his second volume, Dee is more concerned with geography and exploration than the science of navigation, although he does discourse on his invention, the paradoxal compass. He realized that England's economic growth and power lay in colonial expansion, and the key to its success was the sea. Here, on the title page to his *General and rare memorials pertaining to the Perfect Arte of Navigation*, English ships are setting out to explore and assert British claims to new territories; seated at the helm of a ship is Queen Elizabeth as Imperial navigator.

THE BRITISH LIBRARY, LONDON

Plotting the Tides

Tides occur in all oceans, in contrast to currents which are limited to specific regions. That tides are affected by astronomical events was realized as early as the fourth century BC by Pytheas of Massalia (380–310 BC) when he voyaged to northern waters. He noted the tides of the ocean, and reported that they increased as the Moon became full, and diminished as it waned. Although not entirely correct, he was the first to perceive that the tides were produced and regulated by the Moon. Posidonius of Rhodes (c. 135–51 BC), from his observations during a journey to Spain, not only acquired a distinct knowledge of the diurnal occurrence of the tides, but also the effects of the different positions of the Sun and Moon relative to the Earth.

Exactly how the Moon acted to exert its influence on tides was much more difficult than stating the pos-

204. A detail from *Historia ecclesiastica gentis Anglorum*, c. 1375–1406 from the original work by Venerabilis Bede of the 8th century

Dedicated to a life of monasticism in Northumbria, England, Bede translated over forty books in every field of knowledge. Influenced by Pliny's *Natural History*, Bede described major events within each year, including astronomical phenomena, such as motions of the planets, occurrences of eclipses and timing of the tides. In his *De Temporum Ratione*, although principally a work on the calendar, Bede also clearly described the relationship between the phases of the Moon and the stages of the tide.

THE BRITISH LIBRARY, LONDON

205. Tide diagram by Guillaume Brouscon, 1548

This ingenious diagram by Guillaume Brouscon made it possible for the Breton sailor, or any other sailor, regardless of language, to comprehend at a glance the time of ebb and flow of tide on an hourly basis, of any port relative to an 'established' port, as long as the day of the Moon is known. The chart is oriented with west at the top; the two compass roses, however, are each oriented in a manner most convenient for a clear reading of the tide lines.

BIBLIOTHEQUE NATIONALE DE FRANCE, PARIS

tulate. Like most of the scientific knowledge of the ancients, information on the tides was transmitted to the Latin west through Arabic treatises. The most influential of these works was the writings of Ab Ma'shar (Albumasar) (AD 787–886), a Persian astronomer and mathematician. Like Aristotle, Albumasar believed that the motions of the Sun, Moon, stars and planets regulated events on Earth. In his *Kitab al-mudkhal al-kabir ila 'ilm ahkam an-nujjum*, written in Baghdad in AD 848, Albumasar devoted six chapters to the tides and their causation. He gave eight reasons for the tidal inequalities, as caused by the position and motions of the Sun and Moon relative to the Earth. The physical explanation on how the Moon, and to a lesser extent, the Sun, affected tides he attributed to a sympathetic vibration – a natural attraction – wherein there was a bond *(nexus)* between the dragging Essence (the Moon and Sun) and the dragged Substance (the tides). The tides moved in sympathetic conjunction with its watery sister, the Moon. He came tantalizingly close to a concept of gravitational force.

His treatise on astrology and the scientific theory of natural things was translated in 1133 from the

Arabic into Latin by John of Seville as *Introductorium in Astronmiam*, and again in 1140 by the polymath monk, Hermann of Carinthia, who also wrote treatises on the astrolabe. These works were widely read and influential in the thinking on astronomy during the Middle Ages. Not until the seventeenth century, with an understanding of the principles of fluid mechanics, and of gravitational forces, was a scientific explanation on the cause of tides provided.

Throughout most of the world the predominant type of tides experienced are semi-diurnal, with two high tides and two low tides in 24 hours. The primary influence on the vertical movement of the Earth's waters is the gravitational effect of the Moon pulling the water toward it. The Sun also exerts a gravitational pull on the water, but to a lesser extent, since it is at a MUCH greater distance from the Earth. The combined effect of the gravitational pull of these two bodies creates a bulge of water, a rising of the ocean's level, on the side of the Earth facing them, and another bulge on the opposite side of the Earth, where the water is trying to move away from the Earth. These two bulges follow the Moon as it revolves around the Earth. Since

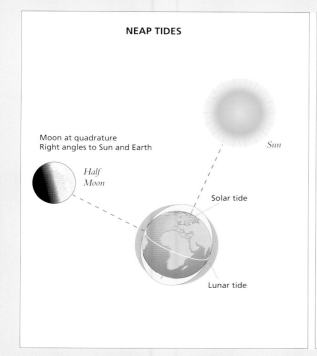

NEAP TIDES

Moon at quadrature
Right angles to Sun and Earth

Half Moon

Sun

Solar tide

Lunar tide

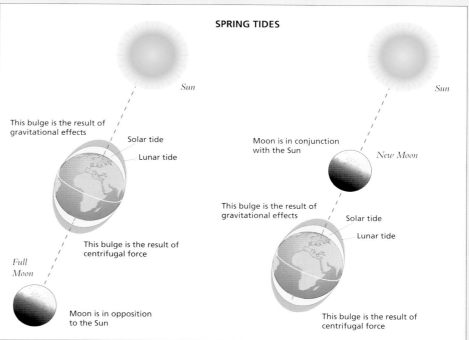

SPRING TIDES

This bulge is the result of gravitational effects

Solar tide

Lunar tide

Sun

Full Moon

This bulge is the result of centrifugal force

Moon is in opposition to the Sun

Moon is in conjunction with the Sun

New Moon

Sun

This bulge is the result of gravitational effects

Solar tide

Lunar tide

This bulge is the result of centrifugal force

---

a lunar day is 48 minutes longer than a solar day of 24 hours, the time interval between two successive high tides is 12 hours and 24 minutes in a 24-hour day.

During a new Moon, when the Sun, Moon, and Earth are in alignment with each other (a condition known as syzygy), and during a full Moon, when the Moon is in opposition to the Sun, tides fuller than normal, called Spring tides, are produced. The word 'spring', here, does not refer to a season, but comes from the German word *springen*, meaning 'to leap up'. When the Moon is at quadrature, that is, when it is at right angles (90°) to the axis between the Sun and the Earth, the result is a tide of minimal range called Neap tide. This is because the gravitational effects of the Sun and the Moon partially counteract each other out. Etymology of the word 'neap', coming from the Old English *nép*, is obscure.

Declination of the Sun north or south of the celestial equator also affects the height of tides. When the Sun is at 0° declination during vernal and autumnal equinoxes (respectively 21 March and 23 September), it exerts a lesser tidal effect. But as the Sun's declination increases toward its maximum at the summer and winter solstices (respectively 21 June and 21 December) there is a corresponding increase in the tidal bulge.

If it were just the relative position of the Sun and Moon as they orbit around the Earth, the wave crest, or bulge, created would be a progressively moving single broad wave pulse circling the Earth. But the major ocean basins are complex in shape and interrupted by landmasses. Acting upon these bodies of water is the Coriolis force, created by rotation of the Earth. This causes a high water crest to move continually in a counter-clockwise direction around a central, or nodal, point. These rotary currents, shifting through all directions of the compass are the major offshore tidal currents. In the open ocean, the tide range is about 2 feet, but it increases near the shore to around 6 to 10 feet on the average. There are notable exceptions, such as the Bay of Fundy on Canada's eastern coast, where due to the configuration of the bay, Spring

tides at the head of the bay can be as high as 52 feet. In contrast, the Mediterranean Sea, Baltic Sea, and Caribbean Sea are relatively tideless. Geographic location and weather patterns can produce local variation in the tides.

In the North Atlantic, tides oscillate around one major node located south of Greenland, creating a crest of water sweeping around the coasts of the Atlantic basin. From any one point on shore, this phenomenon is observed as a reversing current, flooding and ebbing out of the bays, sounds and rivers. As the level of water rises, it is said to flood, and as it recedes, it is ebbing.

Being able to predict the time of rise and fall of tides was of great importance to the navigator. Problems could be created by insufficient water to carry his vessel over a bar blocking the entrance to a harbour, or too shallow water within the harbour itself; safely inside, upon leaving, it was necessary to know when best to set sail. Tidal currents, stronger than the speed of the boat trying to beat against it, can be created as the flow of water is forced through a narrow constriction, accelerating its speed, or when the tidal flow augments that of the natural flow of a river.

In the Middle Ages, mariners relied upon rutters (books of sailing instructions), or their equivalent, such as the Portuguese *roteiro*, for their information on tides. These, however, were of a most general nature, giving simple rules on how to determine on what day there would be a new Moon. Until printed tide tables for each port were produced, mariners either made their own calculations with the aid of prediction devices, or simply waited out the tide by anchoring, and acted on their observations of the tide's strength and direction of its flow.

206. Tides

The effect of the Sun, as the Earth orbits around it, and the Moon's orbit around the Earth both exert an influence on the rise and fall of water, creating the tides. Of the two, the Moon being closer has the greater effect.

207. Careened Ship in Amsterdam harbour by Sunset by Ludolf Backhuysen

Growth of barnacles and seaweed on the bottom of a ship markedly slows its progress, while Toredo worms, these 'termites of the ocean,' voraciously eat their way through the planking, leaving a mere shell of the original wood. In long distance sailing, these twin scourges had to be dealt with. This was accomplished with the help of tides. At a suitable place the ship was anchored at high tide, and when the tide went out, the ship lay on her side with the bottom exposed. This procedure is called careening a ship. The sea-growth was then removed, and a suitable coating applied to repel the worms. Today, marine railways, travel-lifts, and dry-docks replace the practice of careening.

FITZWILLIAM MUSEUM, CAMBRIDGE

Operandi modus huius ſecundi inſtrumenti verus
qdem & certus eſt, quoties annus currens ſiue pro‑
poſitus in arcu limbi inferioris rotæ ab indice X Y
procedendo ſecundum dies ordinem, uſq ad 29
diem Ianuarii, horam 12, Mi.44 ſiue ſtellam lunæ
ſic depictam ✳☽ reperitur. Annus ille cum ſilo (vt
prius dictū eſt) ſignatur, eidemq denuo index X Y
adducitur, qui inuariatus ad operationis ſinem ſic
perdurabit. Si uero poſt primam ſiue radicalem
indicis locationem annus ppoſitus à ſtella prædicta

(ſupputatione ſecundum dierū ordinem facta) uſq ad
indicem X Y occurrat, iam dictæ ſtellæ centrum inſpice, p
huncq ſilū tende, cui ſubducis indicem T. Mox deinceps
ſilum ducatur per ppoſitum ſiue currentem annum, ubi in‑
terſectio ſili cum circulo T diem tantū, aut diem horamq
dabit. Dies ille tandem in limbo Ianuarii requiſitus, cum
ſilo ſignatur, eidemq denuo oſtenſor X Y ſubiungitur, ita
autem rota illa ultimum ſui locum ſortita eſt. Atqui nunc
mihi uideor ſatis ſuperq poſitionem rotæ X Y declaraſſe,
admonens interim, ut ſimilia de rota Z V intelligantur,
qualia de rota X Y prodita ſunt, intereſſe tamen hoc vnum
quod hic conſiderandus erit index Z V, & centrum ſtellæ
iuxta 27 Ian: diem ſignatæ cū charactere draconis ſic ✳☊

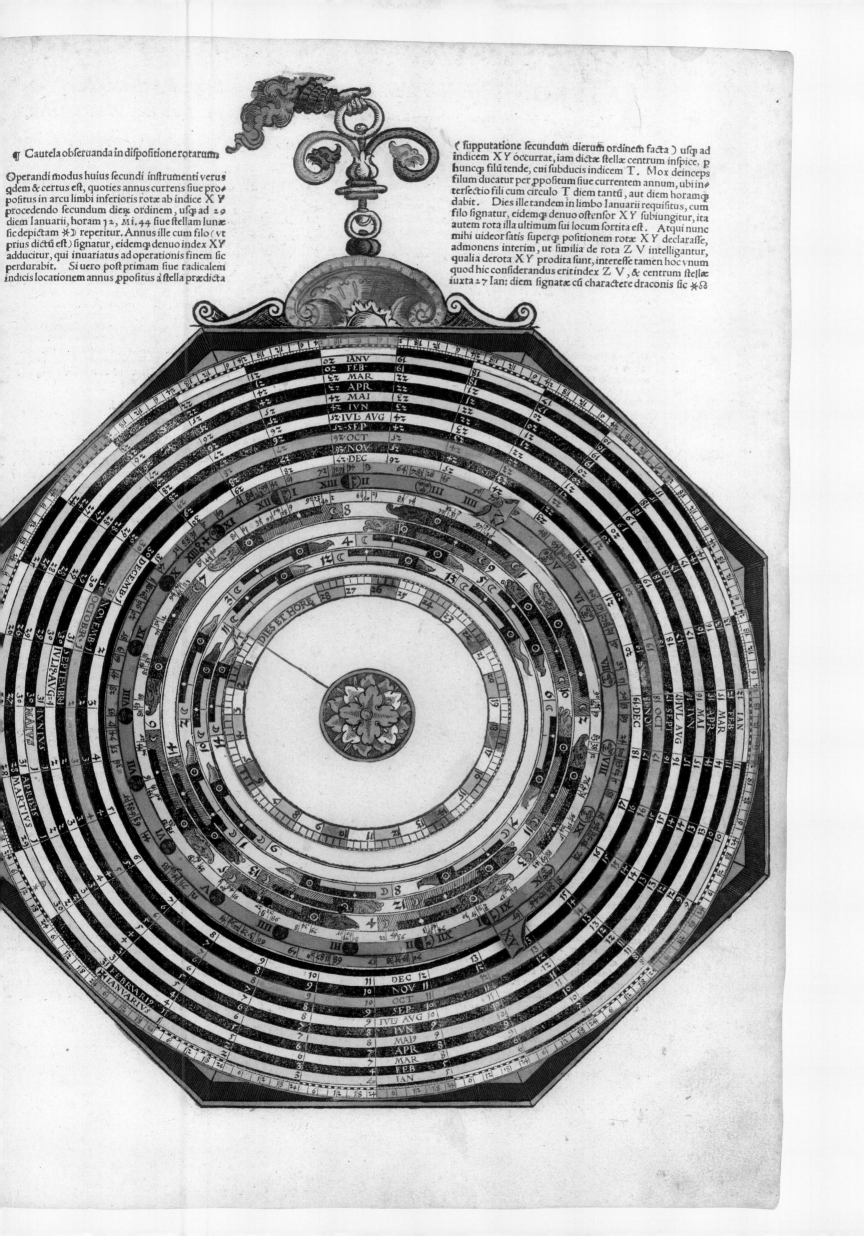

The writings of these theorists promoted voyages of exploration into far northern latitudes of the Atlantic, and extended the bounds of the known world. Topographic detail began to be shown with greater accuracy, while previously erroneous information was deleted or corrected.

THE MEASURERS FOR A NEW COSMOGRAPHY

Transmission into the Latin West of Ptolemy's writings and maps spurred a renewed interest in mathematical geography. While cosmology was primarily a philosophical construct on how the universe worked, cosmography addressed cartographic problems, such as the shape and dimensions of the Earth, measurements and map projections. It aimed to measure mathematically and to map the entire universe – the celestial sphere and the terrestrial sphere. This monumental project necessitated uniting the disciplines of mathematics, astronomy, surveying and cartography. It also required the invention of new or better instruments with which to measure the planets, continents and countryside. In the first half of the sixteenth century, two men – Peter Apian and Gemma Frisius – stand out as major figures toward advancing the goals of cosmography.

Peter Apian

In 1524, Peter Apian (1495–1552), professor of mathematics and astronomy at the University of Ingolstadt in Bavaria, published his mathematical treatise entitled *Cosmographicus liber* (Book of Cosmography). Primarily based on the works of Ptolemy and medieval sources, Apian's work explained to the general public astronomy, geography, climate, weather, cartography, surveying and navigation. Although the first edition was not immensely successful, it did enjoy a modest reputation and led to two other major works: an *Instrument Buch* (Instrument Book), published in 1533, and in 1540 his *Astronomicum Caesareum* (Astronomy fit for an Emperor), which he dedicated to the most important person in Europe in the sixteenth century – Charles V, the Holy Roman Emperor, who at the same time ruled officially as King Charles I of Spain.

Five years after the first appearance of Apian's *Cosmographicus liber*, a second edition was brought out by Gemma Frisius. After subsequent additions to the book it soared in popularity, and was translated into several languages, with forty-five editions in the next eighty-five years. Part of the book's success was due to its practical and utilitarian treatment of the mathematical sciences and cosmography. Navigators, surveyors, instrument makers and cartographers all saw in it practical applications to their own discipline. Also contributing to the book's triumph were descriptions of the known world, particularly its discussion of newly discovered lands in the western hemisphere.

Apian's *Astronomicum* was more elaborate and sumptuous than his *Cosmographicus liber*. In it, he presented ideas on how to use solar eclipses, as well as lunar distances, to determine longitude. Astronomical and nautical almanacs were already available, and contained tables predicting the lunar orbit that allowed the prediction of the angular measure between the Moon and certain very bright stars. With the use of a nautical almanac, and the measured local distance against the difference at a selected reference, it was possible to calculate the longitude. These methods, however, were impractical for use at sea, and the instruments available, principally the cross-staff, were not sufficiently accurate for the measurement required.

211. The Nautical squere, *Quadratum nauticum* by Gemma Frisius, 1556

Among the instruments invented by Gemma Frisius was a new cross-staff, and a *quadratum nauticum* (Nautical quadrant), with which Gemma said a navigator could find the difference of longitude between two places, and also the difference of their latitudes. But without a clock, the instrument and method was useless.

MUSEUM OF THE HISTORY OF SCIENCE, UNIVERSITY OF OXFORD

210. Universal astrolabe by Anthoine Mestrel, 1551

Gemma improved upon the planispheric astrolabe with a stereographic projection capable of being used at any latitude. Known as a universal astrolabe, or as he called it, the *astrolabium Catholicum*, it did not need separate latitude plates for its astronomical functions, but could be used anywhere. To perform other navigational calculations, Gemma had another of his 'inventions', the *quadratum nauticum*, engraved on the reverse side, instead of the usual equal-hour diagram or shadow-square placed there.

MUSEUM OF THE HISTORY OF SCIENCE, UNIVERSITY OF OXFORD

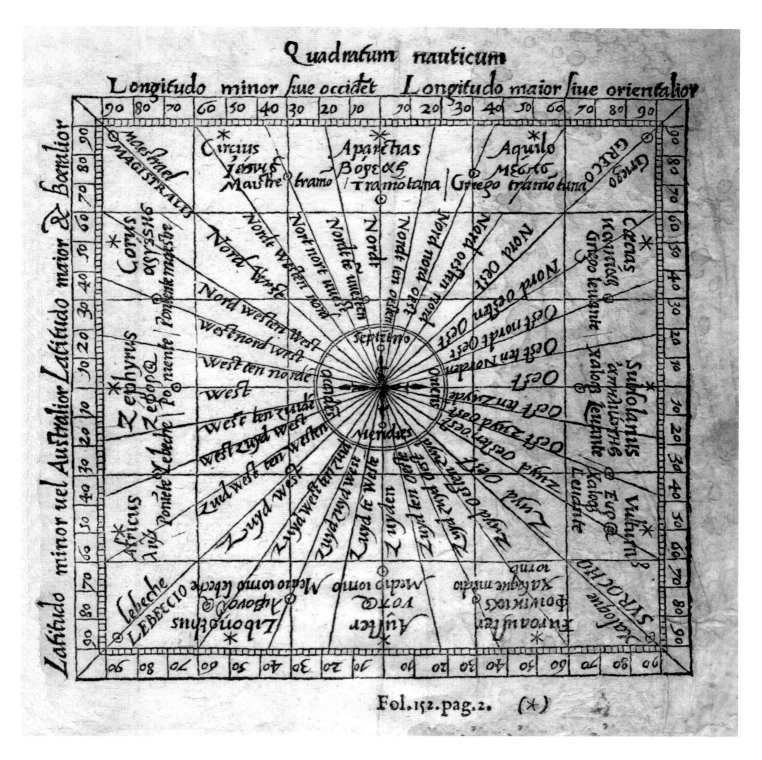

Gemma Frisius

Gemma Frisius (1508–1555) was acknowledged as the leading mathematician, practical as well as theoretical, in the Low Countries. In addition to his mathematical abilities, Gemma's published works on cosmography were already considered the standard textbooks of the time. It was a fortuitous period in history for Gemma, for at this time Flanders and the Netherlands were under the rule of Spain, with King Charles V its monarch. As court cosmographer to Charles V, Gemma had access to all the Spanish maps and its navigational texts, as well as those from the rest of continental Europe under the Emperor's control. *De revolutionibus orbis coelestium* (On the Revo-

lution of the Heavenly Spheres) by Nicolaus Copernicus had just been published (1543), in which he had described his heliocentric hypothesis of the universe. Gemma was among the first to advocate this conception, and praised Copernicus for 'establishing the things sufficient for true finding and interpretation of phenomena'.

A pair of terrestrial and celestial globes he made in 1536 and 1537 in conjunction with his then student, Gerard Mercator, and his world map in 1540, helped Gemma Frisius became an important force in world geography. Depicted on both the terrestrial globe and on the map was a wide and navigable strait north of North America connecting the Atlantic with the Pacif-

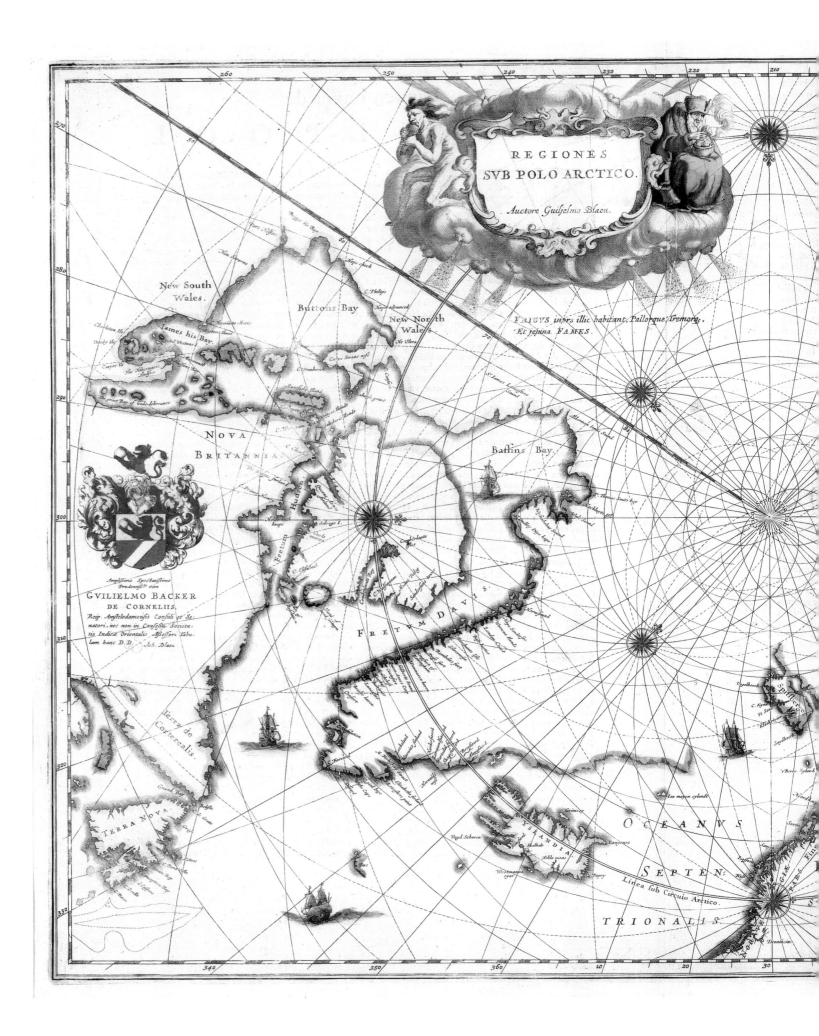

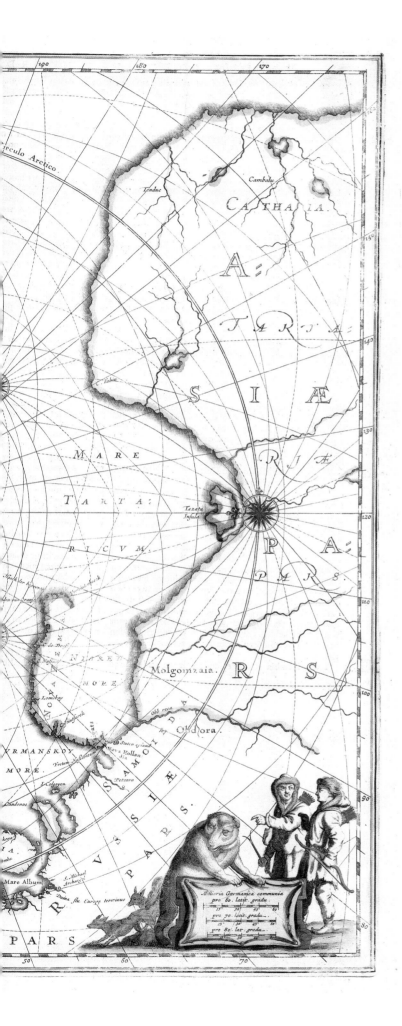

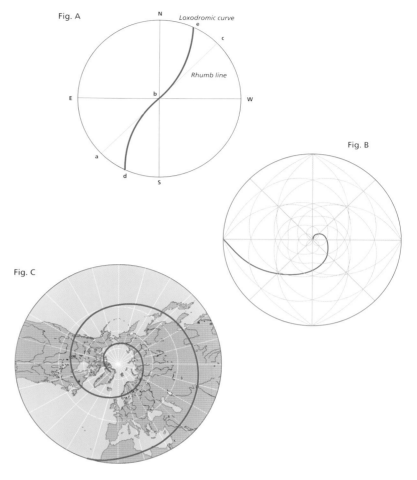

213. Loxodromic curves

Fig. A. In his *Treatise on the Sphere*, Pedro Nuñes showed that when navigators steered a compass course on a rhumb line from point b. to point c., instead of arriving at point c., as anticipated, they actually reached point e. due to converging meridians. This curved line was later to be called a loxodromic curve.

Fig. B. The more elaborate diagram made by Pedro Nuñes is a polar view of the same loxodromic curve.

Fig. C. Gerard Mercator corrected the curve established by Nuñes, showing that it was actually a helical line, as he showed superimposed on a globe.

212. Regions under the Arctic Pole by Willem Blaeu, c. 1640

On his 1640 map, *Regiones Sub Polo Artico* (Regions under the Arctic Pole), Willem Blaeu transposed John Dee's helical lines onto the surface of a map, thereby showing the navigator their practical relevance to navigation, especially in the polar regions.

JOHN NURMINEN FOUNDATION

ic Ocean. Gemma did not believe, as did other cosmographers of the time, that the recently discovered lands of Newfoundland and Labrador were a part of the polar extension of Asia. His geographical concept of a wide passage north of North America was adopted by other mapmakers, and had a strong influence on the leading theorists in England, such as John Dee who was then a student of Frisius, and Humphrey Gilbert.

The same time Gemma produced his globe he published a three-part book entitled *De principiis astronomiae et cosmographiae*; Part one described and defined all the terms used by geographers and navigators: longitude, latitude, meridian and

upt kan verstaen wozden/als boren in de Erem
n oostelijcker is geseydt/dat een Stierman
e van Peru op alsulcke twee verschepden tijden
plaets na de Son willende peplen(en dese tafe
Declinatie sonder 't voozschzeven insicht te ge
n) al wel ende recht peplende/daer dooz 10 minu
hil soude vinden in de hooghte.

Het vijfde Exempel.

schepen bp een zijnde/schepden upt dese Landen
aert oostwaert/en komt na sijn rekeninghe op
September in 't eerste Jaer na 't Schzickel-jaer
der zijde des Aertrijcks/ick neem 180 graden in
verschepden van Engelauts-eynde/vindt in dese
de Declinatie des Sons op dien dagh 1 graed
. Het ander Schip vaert westwaert/en komt
op de voozschzeven plaets na zijne reeckeninge
den 26. maer op den 25 September/en vindt de
te in dese Tafelen vooz dien dagh een graed 4
/verschillen alsoo in de tijt een dagh/en volgens
eclinatie 24 minuten/'t welck ontstaet upt dese
: Het eerste ghevaren tegens den opganck des
o graden/heeft sijn tijdt 12 uren verkozt. Het
varen met de Son 180 graden/heeft sijn tijdt
erlanght/en daer dooz een nacht minder gehadt
erste. Dewijle dan de Declinatie op die tijdt in
el 24 minuten toeneemt/soo moet die ootwaert
is/12 minuten Declinatie minder/en die west
varen is/12 minuten meerder reeckenen als de
uptwijsen/en sullen so bepde eenderlep declina
eten 1 graed 16 minuten behouden.

cht en twintighste Hooftstuck.

en de Polus-hooghte sal vinden by de Sonne.

e hooghte van den Polus te vinden bp de Zon/
taet vooznamelijck een saecke aen te mercken/te
ghp zijt benoozden ofte bezupden de Zon/dat
on staet noozdwaert ofte zupdwaert van u/dat
licht ghemerckt/als men op 't Aertrijck wat
verschepden van de Linie ost van de Zon: maer
de Son na bp ober het hooft gaet/soo en kan
upt het ooghe niet wel sien. Stelt daerom een
vooz u/dat ghp siet waer het zupden ende nooz
eemt dan u Astrolabium/ende hangt hem alsoo
e kant recht staet nae het zupden/ende den an
r't noozden/soo suldp seer nau/ja op een hapz
de Son wanneerse op 't hooghste komt/staet
ert ofte zupdwaert van 't Zenith. Wildp dan
te van den Polus soecken/soo wanneer ghp zijt
de Son/dat is/als de Son zupdwaert van u
neemt eerst de jupste hooghte/ende bp soo verre
atie der Sonnen is noozdelijck/soo treckse af
ebonden hooghte/'t gene dat oberblijft is de
van den Equinoctiael in 't zupden/die getroc
o (als in 't voozgaende Capittel is geleert) so
hp de hooghte van den Noozder Polus.
Exempel.

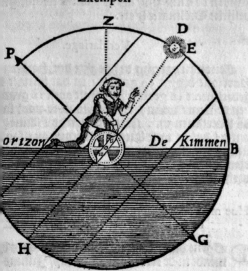

In dese Figuer zp P. den Noozder ende G. den zupder
pool/E. H. den Equinoctiael/A.B. den Horizont/Z. het
Zenith/ende D. de Son. Laet de hooghte der Sonne
B. D. boben den Horizont zijn 60 graden/de noozdelijcke
Declinatie E. D. acht graden. Soo ghp dan D. E. acht
graden treckt van B. D. de hooghte der Sonne/soo sal u
ober blijven B. E. 25/dat is de hooghte des Equinoctiael
die getogen upt 90. blijft 38. de hooghte van den noozder
Polus A. P. als in 't verbolgh van 't vier-en-twintigste
hooft-stuck is bewesen.

Is de Declinatie zupdelijck/so voegtse bp de gen
hooghte/indien dat dan 't samen-gevoegde getal m
is als 90/soo wijset u aen de hooghte van de Lini
zupden/die ghetrocken upt 90 als boven/wijst
hooghte van den Noozder Polus.

Exempel.

De hooghte der Sonne zp D.B. 40 graden/die zup
lijcke Declinatie der Sonne E.D. 20 graden/so men a
deert E.D. 20 graden bp D.B. 40/komt vooz E. B. 60 gra
den de hooghte des Equinoctiaels/die getrocken upt 90/
als E. G. de wijde tusschen den Equinoctiael en den

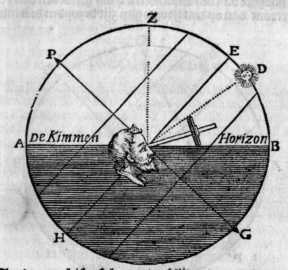

Zupder-pool/soo sal u 30 over blijven vooz G. B. dat is:
soo veele den Zupd-Pool is gesoncken onder den Hori
zont/ende gelijck booren is geleert en bewesen: soo veele
als den eenen Pole is onder den Horizont/effen soo veel
is den anderen daer boven: Soo sal dan hier den Noozd
Pool P. 30 graden verheven wesen.

Maer indien de hoogte der Sonnen t'samen gevoeght
met de declinatie/meerder uptbzenght als 90 graden/
daer upt sult ghp verstaen/dat den Equinoctiael is be

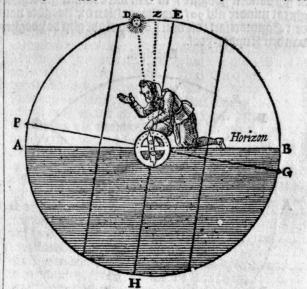

noozden u hooft/effen soo veele/als het voozsz. te samen
gevoeghde getal meerder is als 90. Ende de volgende sal
den Zupder-Pool oock soo veel verheven wesen.
(♃ 3) Exempel!

214. Mariner's astrolabe

The navigator held the mariner's astrolabe by the ring,
and looked through the sights toward a celestial body. He
then read the angle of the body from a scale on the rim.
The weight at the bottom stabilized the instrument in
wind and rough seas.

NATIONAL MARITIME MUSEUM, LONDON

**215. Instruction on how to use the astrolabe by
Pieter Goos, 1671.**

JUHA NURMINEN COLLECTION

From the Astrolabe
to the Sextant

The theory of the astrolabe was developed by
Apollonius and Hipparchus in the pre-Christian era,
and the instrument was widely employed in the Islamic
world from the ninth century to determine local time
and the cardinal points of the compass, both of which
were needed to establish the time of prayer and the
direction to Mecca. The instrument was developed
further by the Arabs, and became important in the
Christian West at the beginning of the thriteenth century. It was used until the end of the middle ages.

In its final shape the astrolabe was a versatile device. In principle it comprised a circular disk hanging
from a ring attached to its rim. Suspension of the instrument from this ring provided vertical and horizontal null points. A pointer bar (alidade) with eye slits at
its opposite ends pivoted about the centre of the disk,
so that a sighting could be made on a celestial body,
or on a natural feature such as a mountain. The altitude of the star, or of the mountain peak, was then
read on a graduated scale at the rim of the disk. There
were also two moveable scales on the periphery of
the disk. These were used to determine the days of a
year and the position of the Sun on the ecliptic. As a
measuring instrument the astrolabe gave an accuracy
of about one tenth of a degree.

The reverse side of the astrolabe was a geometrical
computing device that could be used to determine the
rising and setting times and directions (azimuths) of celestial bodies at a place of known latitude. It was based
on the idea of the celestial globe with its circles projected from the South Pole on the disk. For this purpose

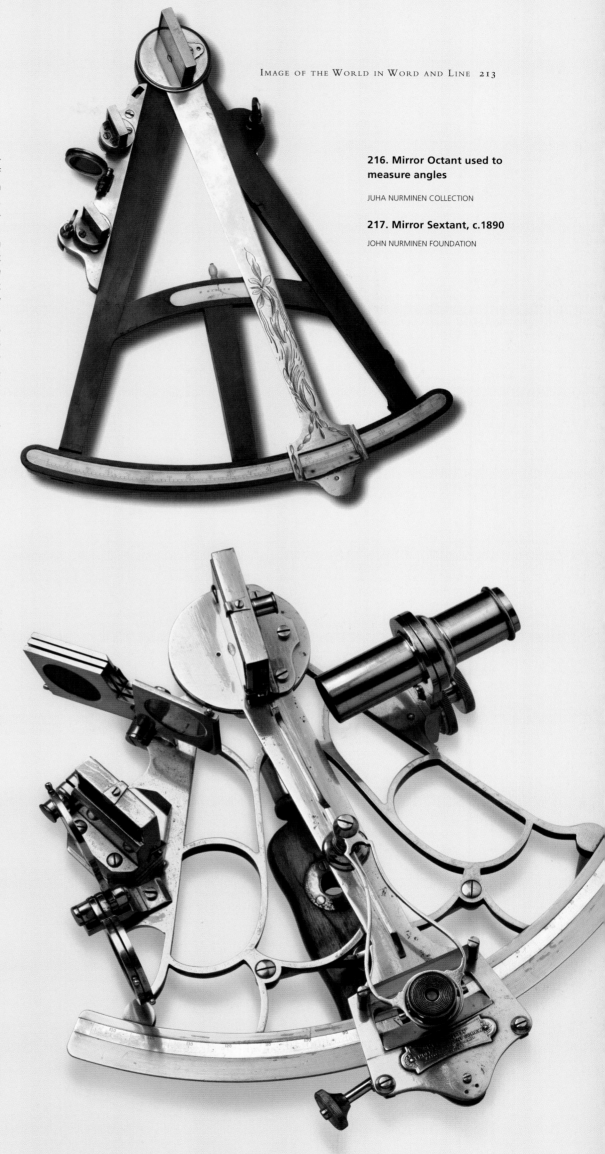

216. Mirror Octant used to measure angles

JUHA NURMINEN COLLECTION

217. Mirror Sextant, c.1890

JOHN NURMINEN FOUNDATION

the instrument was provided with a set of interchange-able disks for different latitudes, or *climae*. On top of these disks, a web-like disk (rete) was placed on which the most prominent stars, the zodiac, and, sometimes, important cities were depicted. The web disk was piv-oted on the centre of the astrolabe.

An astrolabe independent of latitude was devised in Toledo, Spain, by Ibn Al-Zarqali (or Arzachel) in about the middle of the twelfth century. The *Astrolabum catholicum* (universal astrolabe) probably was the most sophisticated development of that instrument built by Gemma Frisius in the middle of the sixteenth century.

For use at sea, a simpler form of astrolabe, a mariner's astrolabe, was used for measuring the altitudes of stars or the Sun. It usually had nothing but a graduated circle and a pointer in order to make it less sensitive to gusts of wind, and was given extra weight at its bottom to in-crease its stability. But the astrolabe was never satisfac-tory for taking altitudes at sea, and mariners discovered that they could obtain more accurate measurements by sighting on the horizon. Instruments had been used in the ancient world for measuring the angular distance between the horizon and a celestial body, and in the late middle ages instruments, the cross-staff and back-staff, were developed for use at sea, where the horizon is usually clear. They continued to serve the navigator in measuring angles well into modern times.

These instruments, however, also had their limita-tions, as it was difficult to measure the altitude of a celestial body while simultaneously sighting on the horizon. At the beginning of the eighteenth century Robert Hooke invented a method of bringing the ob-ject and the horizon together into the field of view by using three mirrors. One of the mirrors was piv-oted to move an image of the celestial body down until it appeared to be on the horizon, and the dou-ble angle of turn was read on a graduated sector in order to gain the altitude.

The sector on Hooke's instrument was one eighth of a full circle, and consequently the device was called an *octant*. The next step was based on much the same principle. It was a mirror quadrant independent-ly submitted in 1731 by John Hadley of Great Britain and Thomas Godfrey of the United States. The mod-ern mirror sextant was developed on it by about 1757 by John Bird and John Campbell. As indicated by its name, the sector of that instrument is one sixth of full circle and it can be employed to measure angular dis-tances of up to 120 degrees. The sextant is equipped with a magnifying monocular in order to enhance the accuracy of observation. When a vernier calliper is fit-ted, employing a sliding gradicule that multiplies the divisions of the main scale, an accuracy better than one minute of arc can be obtained. It also has a set of filters to reduce the glare of the Sun and Moon.

With these instruments, and with the development of marine chronometres that provided navigators with the time at the prime meridian, it became possible to determine a ship's geographic position with an accu-racy that was adequate for navigational purposes. The sextant was also useful for measuring angles between the Moon and surrounding stars. The method of de-termining time at a reference meridian by measuring the position of the Moon in relation to the fixed stars, known as lunar distances, had been completed after much effort at the end of the eighteenth century, and offered another independent method of checking the position at sea.

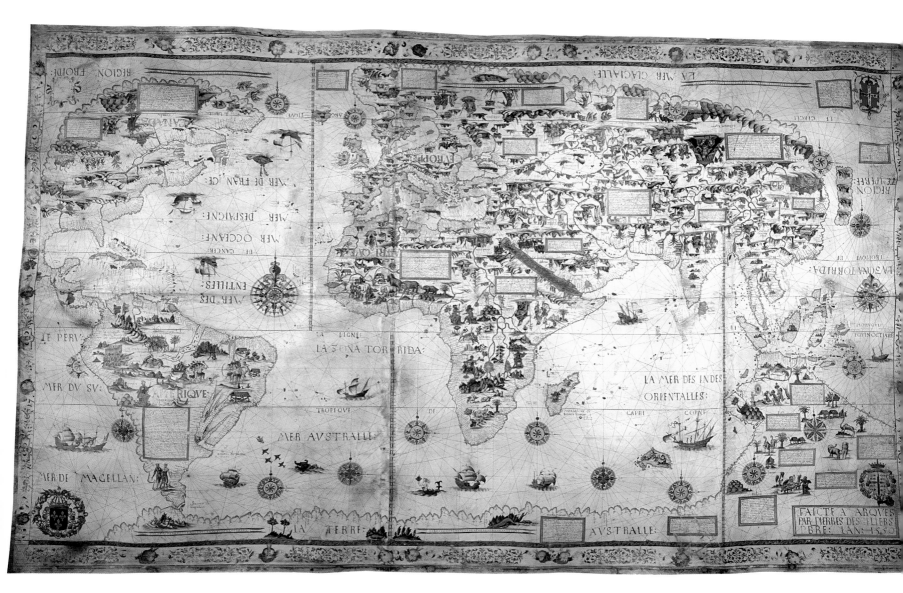

218. Map of the World by Pierre Desceliers, 1550

Pierre Desceliers has been called 'the father of French hydrography'. He started out as a priest at Arques, France, and taught mathematics to his brethren in Dieppe; there he became the leading figure of the Dieppe school of cartography. Descelier's world map summarizes the geographical discoveries of previous years. These manuscript nautical charts were kept more up to date than printed maps. As a medieval miniaturist, he embellished his map with anecdotal pictures, such as depicting the French explorer, Jacques Cartier, approaching Indians during his three voyages between 1534 and 1542.

THE BRITISH LIBRARY, LONDON

etc; the part two gave practical instructions on how best to use the globe; part three included information on the world and on islands and other places recently discovered.

In his book *De uso globe* (1530), Gemma was the first person to correctly solve the problem of how to calculate longitude by carrying a clock to sea set at a selected reference meridian, such as Greenwich, England, now provides. Local time would be established by observing the altitude of the Sun at noon. Since the Earth rotates 15 degrees in an hour, the difference between the standard reference time and local time would provide longitude.

With an accurate timepiece and an astrolabe, he wrote, 'I would be able to find the longitude of places, even if I was dragged off unawares across a thousand miles'. Jean-Baptiste Morin (1583–1656) did not believe that Gemma's method would work, remarking, 'I do not know if the Devil will succeed in making a longitude timekeeper, but it I folly for man to try'.

Gemma's method for determining longitude was superior to Apian's suggestions for using eclipses of the Sun or lunar distances; the former were not frequent enough, and lunar tables were not yet satisfactorily accurate. Gemma's method was correct, but it remained only a theoretical solution for the next 250 years until a portable clock could be constructed that would be sufficiently accurate when taken to sea. Only then could longitude be determined and the art of navigation finally become a science.

As voyages of discovery created a rapidly expanding world, the need was generated for improved charts. Through the disciplines of geography and mathematics, a new science of navigation emerged that allowed mariners to extend their ventures still farther, and with greater confidence.

The navigator plots a compass direction on his sea chart as a straight line, called the rhumb line. It cuts across all lines of longitude at a constant angle. Throughout most of the sixteenth century, mariner's sea charts were plotted on a square grid with meridians of longitude and parallels of latitude straight parallel lines, ignoring convergence of meridians of longitude at the poles. These charts, variously called plane, plain or platte-form charts, since they transposed the curved surface of a globe onto a flat plane, were the cause of navigation errors in east-west distances. When mariners attempted to sail this rhumb line drawn on their plane charts, even though they adhered to the compass course, the ship did not end up at the desired destination. The problem became more extreme the closer they got to the polar regions where the meridians of longitude converge to a single point.

By 1520, the Portuguese pilot João de Lisboa, in his *Livro da Marinharia*, recognized the difficulty created for navigators by converging meridians, and proposed making a plane chart in the shape of a quarter section of the globe, showing the lines of longitude converging toward the pole. Such a chart was actually made, but it appears to have been for diplomatic use at the Conference of Badajoz (1524) when Portugal and Spain were attempting to resolve the demarcation of their respective territories, rather than intended for navigational purposes.

Although the work by Pedro Nuñes at the University of Coimbra in Portugal was abstract and theoretical in nature, his goal was to enable the navigator to plot a compass course on a nautical chart and arrive at the desired destination. In his *Tratado da Sphera* (Treatise on the Sphere) published in 1537, Nuñes showed how rhumb lines of the navigator, although they appeared straight on their sea charts, actually produced a curved line when plotted on a globe. This error could be avoided simply by using a globe to plot a course, rather than a plane chart, but a globe is impractical for use aboard a ship.

Nuñes diagrammed the difference between the presumed course (a straight rhumb line) and the course actually travelled, which is curved. He referred to this curved line by various phrases, such as *hua certa maneira de linhas* curves (a certain kind of curved lines). At a later date, loxodromic curve (from the Greek *loxos*, slanted, and *drome*, path) became the name for this sinuous line. In order to counteract the loxodromic curve the navigator has to make continual, small corrections in his compass headings.

Gerard Mercator

Born in 1512 in the small Flemish town of Rupelmonde, Gerard Mercator earned his academic degree in the study of philosophy at the University of Louvain, in Brussels. Under the tutelage of Gemma, Mercator's interests expanded to include mathematical geography, mapmaking, copperplate engraving, and the construction of nautical instruments. The terrestrial globe he constructed with Gemma, on which recently discovered islands and lands were shown, had as an additional purpose the glorification of mathematics.

Mercator also felt the need to address the problem of loxodromic curves initiated by his predecessors. Correcting Nuñes's curve, Mercator showed it actually to be a helical line, which he placed on a globe he made in 1541. This led to the development of a new map of the world, created and published in 1569, which finally solved a navigation problem that until this time had beset mariners. In his new projection of the Earth's surface (technically called an isogonic, or conformal, cylindrical projection), Mercator kept all the meridian lines parallel and equidistant to each other without converging at the pole. To compensate for the greater space between the lines of longitude near the pole, he proportionately increased the distances between lines of latitude from the equator toward the pole.

The solution to keeping the bearings and rhumb lines, without distorting the angles, lay in keeping the scale the same in both dimensions; that is, at any given point on the map, the vertical scale along the meridians has to be the same as the horizontal scale along the parallels of latitude. Although this produced a map where the relative sizes and shapes of landmasses were markedly enlarged as they become closer to the polar region, Mercator's projection had one distinct advantage over all other projections: it allowed the navigator to plot a ship's course as a straight line and a constant angle, no matter how it cut across the meridians. For ease of navigation with sea charts it has not been improved upon to this day.

When Mercator produced his map with the new projection, the mathematics necessary to produce the proper spacing of the latitude parallels were not available to him; he had arrived at his solution with only a compass and protractor. It took another three decades before Edward Wright (c. 1558–1615), a professor of mathematics at Cambridge, geographer and designer of navigational instruments, worked out the trigonometric tables for Mercator's projection. The invention of logarithms, necessary to create this projection mathematically, and the calculus and differential geometry to derive the equations, did not occur until fifty years later.

The map that was to change the future of cartography and navigation so profoundly received scant attention when it was published; Mercator's approach was too advanced for popular

Overleaf

219. Map of the World by Gerard Mercator, 1569

Mercator used his new projection plan, where all meridian and longitude lines are straight and at right-angles to each other, for the very first time in this wall map, published in 1569. He had arrived at it by intuition, and couldn't explain it mathematically; that was Edward Wright's task at the end of the same century. Expressly conceived for use in marine navigation, it enabled navigators to plot their course on a plane chart without error. It was so successful that, to this day, it continues to be used on navigation charts.

BIBLIOTHEQUE NATIONALE DE FRANCE, PARIS

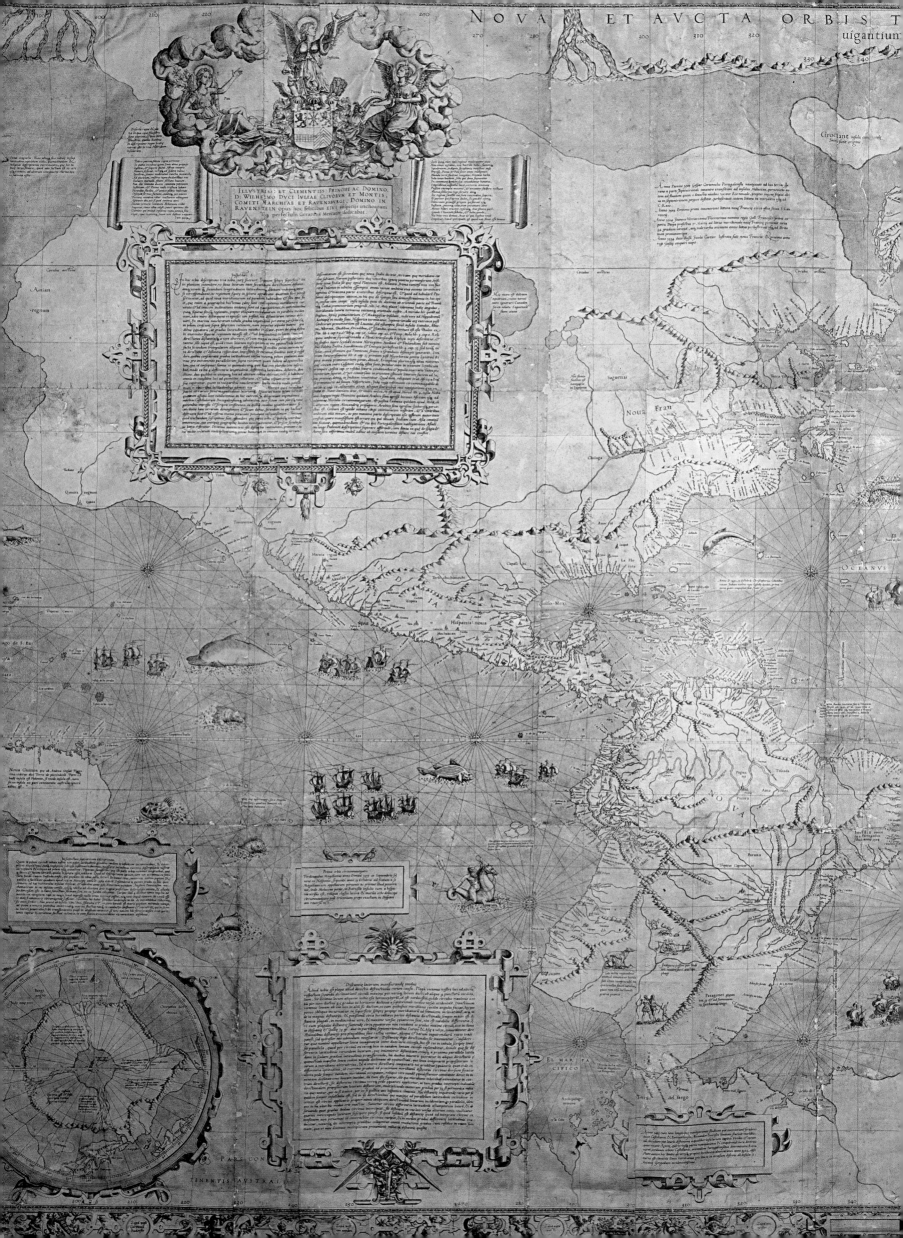

acceptance. Another of his maps, showing the polar regions, and emphasizing the feasibility of a Northwest Passage and a Northeast Passage to the Orient, attracted far more interest. Waghenaer's atlas, *De Spieghel der Zeevaerdt* (Seafarer's Mirror) of 1584, the first actual sea-atlas, continued using the old plane chart projection. In 1661, with the publication of Robert Dudley's atlas, *Dell' Arcano del Mare* (Secrets of the Sea), the first sea-atlas was produced with charts of the entire world based on the Mercator projection. But it was not until the eighteenth century that this most important projection plan for navigation began to be used consistently.

If Mercator's sole contribution to mapmaking were limited to his revolutionary invention of a new projection plan, his eminence in cartography would be unshakeable. But he also initiated another idea new to cartography – that of binding together a collection of loose maps into a single book. Similar books were already being produced in Italy, but they were made using manuscript maps of different sizes, and were not unified with a text into a cohesive whole in a printed format. Mercator coined the term 'atlas' for this map-book form, and in 1569 he began to put together an *Atlas* intended to 'describe the creation and history of the world'.

Before his *Atlas* was published, the Flemish scholar and geographer, Abraham Ortelius, a contemporary and friendly rival of Mercator, produced his atlas in 1570, entitled *Theatrum Orbis Terrarum* (Theatre of the World). It embodied the goals of Mercator, who had advised and encouraged him in his *Theatrum* project. Ortelius drew heavily upon Mercator's 1569 world map, and to his credit acknowledged his mentor for the source and support. For the first time, there was a comprehensive collection of maps all presented in a uniform size, style and accompanied by a text as an integral and necessary part of the compilation. In the construction of these maps, Ortelius incorporated information from the most distinguished of thirty-three cartographers and eighty-seven leading authorities on geography.

Theatrum Orbis Terrarum not only changed the direction cartography henceforth would take, by releasing it from the bonds of a Ptolemaic geographic tradition, it also helped shift the principal site of map production from Italy to the Netherlands. Continually updated, corrected and revised by Ortelius, his *Theatrum* went through thirty-one editions. From the initial 70 maps it contained, the *Theatrum* expanded to a 167 maps in 1612; but by this time, it became supplanted by the works of other cartographers whose maps included more accurate details from recent discoveries.

When the Flemish artist, engraver and cartographer, Jodocus Hondius (1563–1612), moved to Amsterdam, he purchased the plates of Mercator's unfinished *Atlas* from his grandson. Along with additional maps of his own, Hondius published this 'new' *Atlas* in 1606. It quickly became successful and helped to renew Mercator's somewhat fallen stature which had become overshadowed by Ortelius's *Theatrum Orbis Terrarum*.

220. Portrait of Gerard Mercator, 1630

In a cartographic context, Gerard Mercator was one of the most important people in the sixteenth century. He modernized mapmaking by freeing it from outdated, classical precedents, and was the first person to use the term 'atlas'. Because of his wide travels and Protestant faith, this scientist was accused of heresy by the inquisition. Although he managed to avoid the death penalty, he endured seven months in prison.

JUHA NURMINEN COLLECTION

221. Title page from *Certaine Errors in Navigation Detected and Corrected* by Edward Wright, 1610

The importance of mathematics and astronomy as the foundation for a new navigation is emphasized on the title page of Edward Wright's *Certaine Errors in Navigation*. Depicted are an armillary sphere, an astrolabe, the astronomical rings of Gemma Frisius, a cross-staff and other tools, plus a book (likely an almanac). The Sun, Moon and stars in the heavens surmount all, while the small insert map at the bottom is in the Mercator projection; an improved cartography is the result of a thorough knowledge of mathematics and astronomy.

THE NATIONAL LIBRARY OF FINLAND, HELSINKI

The art of navigation had been in use for thousands of years, yet, as Edward Wright stated, to that point it was far from the perfection desired. Even experienced and judicial mariners, in sailing from the West Indies to the Azores, found that when they navigated by their charts, their course was in error by as much as 150 or 200 leagues (390–520 nautical miles). Ordinary charts, Wright said 'are in many places much like an inextricable labyrinth of error, out of which

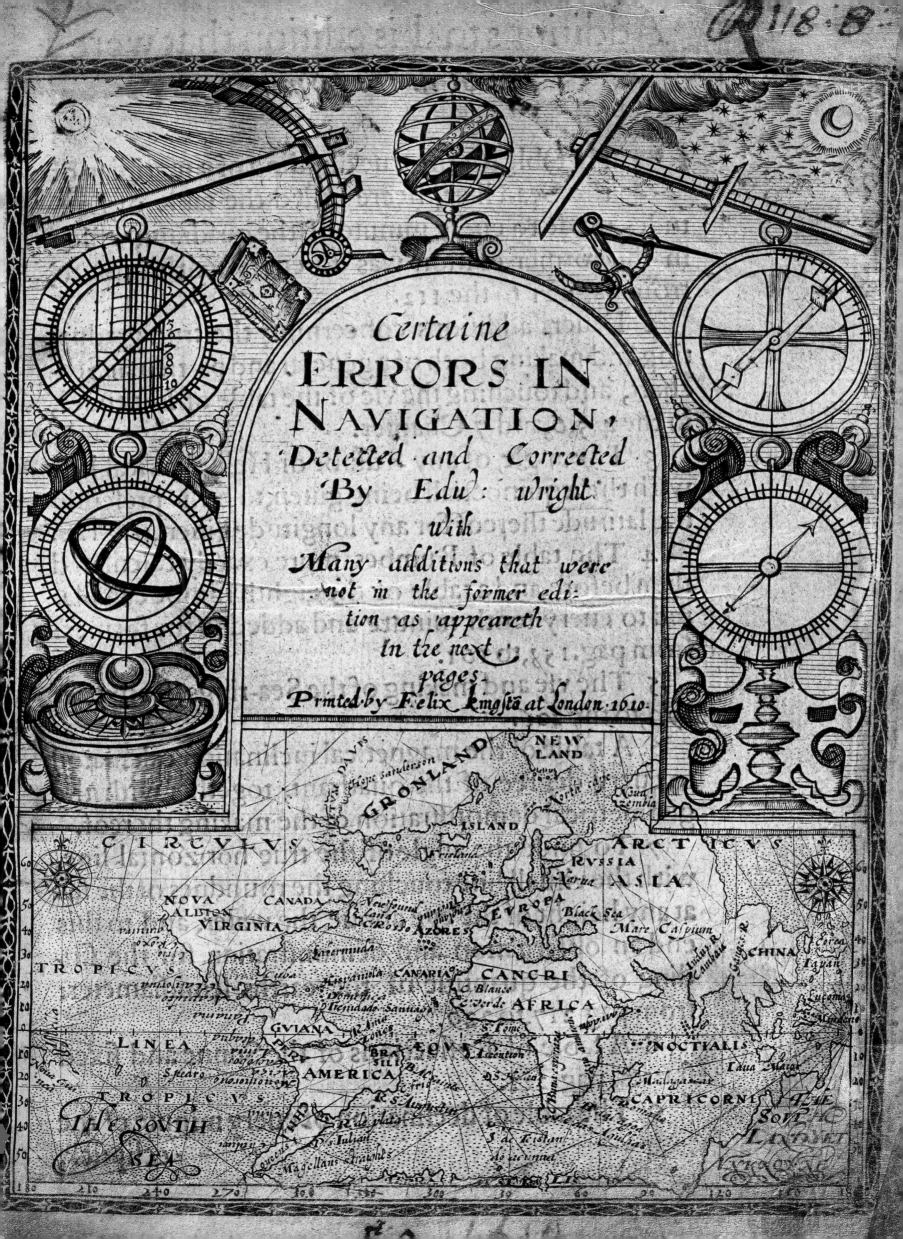

Certaine
ERRORS IN
NAVIGATION,
Detected and Corrected
By Edw: wright
with
Many additions that were
not in the former edi-
tion, as appeareth
in the next
pages.
Printed by Felix kingstā at London. 1610.

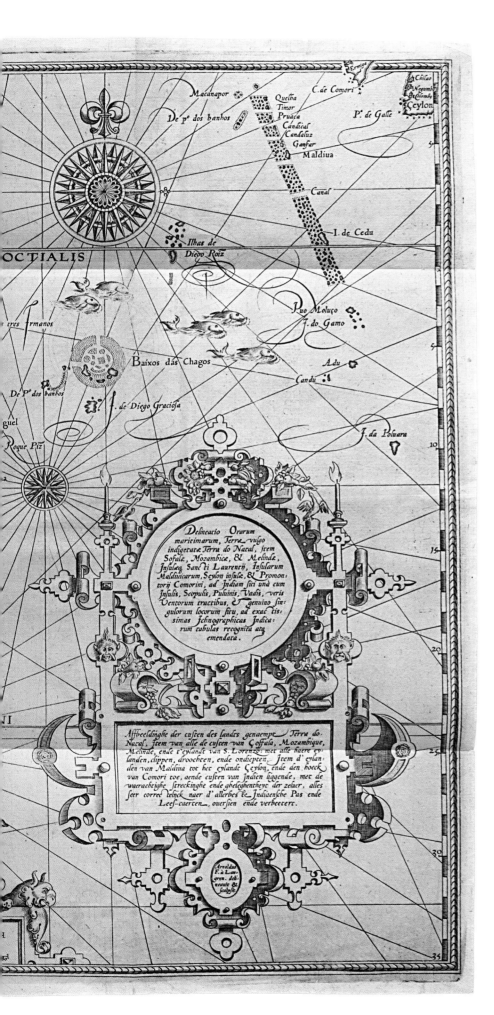

222. Eastern Coast of Africa and Madagascar by Jan Huygen van Linschoten, 1638

Linschoten was secretary to the Portuguese archbishop in Goa between 1583 and 1588. When he returned to Holland in 1592 he started to write his travel reports, primarily about the East and West Indies. He had them illustrated by the engravers, Jan and Baptista van Doetecum, and they were published in Amsterdam in 1596 and in following years.

JUHA NURMINEN COLLECTION

it will be very hard for a man easily to unwinde [release] himself'.

Wright modified and improved Mercator's system to reduce errors in the common sea-chart, and make the chart agree in courses, heights and distances with the globe. He published the results in 1599 in his *The Correction of Certain Errors in Navigation*. The following year, Wright added proper astronomical tables and instructions to the book, and published it as *Certaine Errors in Navigation, detected and corrected*.

While calculating the mathematical formulations for the Mercator projection, Wright shared this information with Hondius, who then hurried into print the first large wall-map of the world (1595–98) based on a Mercator projection. Wright felt his intellectual efforts had been trespassed upon; nonetheless, he credited Hondius with advancing this important innovation in cartography, and by one of those strange quirks of history, it is Edward Wright who is generally known for creating this sixteenth-century cartographic landmark. He published *his* map 'A Chart of the World on Mercator's Projection' in 1600, with a geography based on a globe by Emery Molyneus in 1592.

Second in importance to proper navigation, and the cause of errors, said Wright, was the compass, and he discussed the problems of magnetic variation. After the chart and compass, the cross-staff was the instrument that produced the most navigational errors. By not considering the height of the eye above the water, it neglected the effects of parallax, and other errors were created by not regarding the apparent diametre of the Sun. Wright described how these errors could be reduced. Miscalculations also proceeded from inaccurate tables of declination of the Sun and fixed stars. In his new tables of ephemerides, Wright not only corrected previous errors, but also described how to use the tables, and then provided an example, taking the mariner step by step through the process.

Wright's *Certain Errors in Navigation* did much to advance England's role as a leader among nations in maritime affairs.

Lighthouses and Seamarks

From the very beginning of maritime commerce the need was recognized for navigation aids to warn of dangers along the coastlines and serve as a guide for safe entry to important harbours.

The earliest and most simple form of beacon was a fire built on top of a hill or cliff. The first regularly maintained beacon may well have been built sometime between 1700 and 1250 BC at a promontory of land called Sigeum at the Hellespont, close to the ancient city of Troy. It is subject to debate as to whether this served as an aid to navigation at the entrance to this important seaway, or as a monument for the supposed location of the tomb of Achilles. Most likely, light-structures were built in the earliest historical epochs, but the first recorded lighthouse was built shortly after the founding of Alexandria, Egypt, by Alexander the Great in 331 BC.

In antiquity, Alexandria was one of the busiest ports in the Mediterranean, serving frequent trade with Ostia, the harbour city of ancient Rome. But prevailing winds, and silt from the Nile River deposited far out to sea, made navigation difficult. Alexandria's low-lying, featureless shore necessitated a man-made structure to guide sailors to its port. Ptolemy I Soter, who took command after the death of Alexander the Great, conceived and initiated the construction of a tower on the island of Pharos, seaward of the centre of the city. Construction started at the beginning of the third century BC, and was completed around 280–279 BC From various accounts, it was a monumental edifice built in three tiers and standing well over 400 feet high, all surmounted with sculptures of Greek deities. In its uppermost tier a bonfire was kindled to serve as a beacon; focused by a mirror of polished bronze it helped project the light far out to sea.

This lighthouse served as the model for many others to follow. It stood for over 1500 years, guiding mariners safely to the port of Alexandria. But throughout its history, the Mediterranean was subject to many earthquakes and in 1303 a major earthquake brought about its final destruction. In November 2005, French diving archeologists discovered the foundation of the Pharos lighthouse, and attempts are underway to gain the necessary finances to restore it.

Often, the most prominent landmark to guide mariners to a harbour is the tall steeple of the city's church, but this beacon is of no use at night. Spurred by the Hansa trade and herring fishery, lighthouses were erected in the Baltic Sea as early as the eleventh century. Throughout the Middle Ages, a network of lighthouses spread throughout the Baltic Sea, eventually reaching the Neva River when St. Petersburg, Russia, was founded.

Lighthouses need more than merely be seen; as an effective aid to navigation they must also identify their unique location. Differentiation by shape and colour serve for daytime recognition, while at night a specific pattern of light flashes, interrupted by a period of darkness, clearly identifies each lighthouse. This pattern of flashes and eclipse (darkness) is known as the light's 'characteristic', and the rate of the interval of darkness is called the 'period'. Over the course of centuries many fuels have been used for the light source: wood, coal, whale oil, seal fat, kerosene, and diesel-fuelled generators to create electricity for the incandescent bulb. The invention of a multiprism lens by Augustin Fresnel in 1822 enabled the collecting and directing of the light source to become more effective. Because of its efficiency, the Fresnel lens, when set high enough to compensate for the curvature of the Earth, can make a 1000-watt light bulb visible up to 21 miles out to sea.

Shifting sandbars, changing river channels and rocks hidden beneath the water's surface require, a different form of navigational aid. To indicate these dangers, some sort of floating marker or buoy is required. When they came into use for the first time is uncertain, but in the earliest set of sailing directions, *Lo compasso de navigare*, written about 1230, mention is made of a buoy in the Guadalquivir River to aid mariners in approaching Seville, Spain. Within a few decades of this, buoys were in use in northern European waters, guiding mariners to the important commercial centres of Amsterdam and Kampen in the Netherlands. These buoys were mostly hollow wooden casks, anchored with chain to stone. Every harbour area had its own system of marking, and maintenance was handled by individual port authorities.

A system of lateral buoys, marking the boundary of a channel, was adopted by the Russians in the Gulf of Finland in the early eighteenth century. Red or white buoys indicated whether they were to be kept to port or starboard of the ship as it approached a harbour from the sea, or moved up the river. This system of

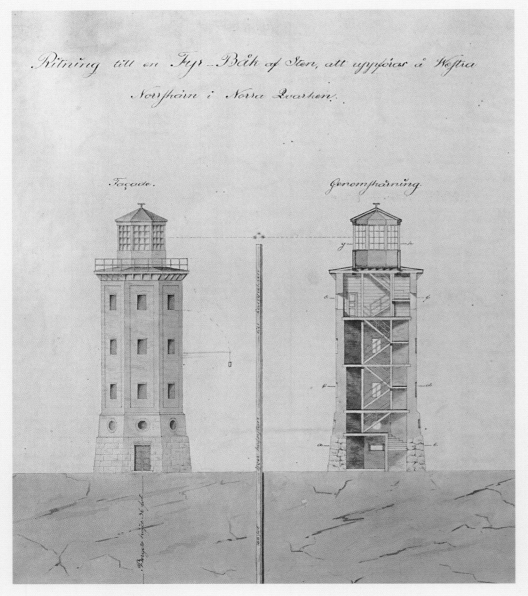

223. The Drawing of Norrskär Lighthouse by E. Lohrmann, 1843

Norrskär lighthouse, which is situated in the northern Merenkurkku Strait, was completed in 1843. It was the last manned lighthouse in Finland, not becoming automatic until 1984. Its tower is 21 m high. The German-Finnish architect Ernst Lohrmann (1803–1870) who made this drawing, was superintendentin 1841 (until 1867) after C.L Engel.

THE MARITIME MUSEUM OF FINLAND

lateral markings is used throughout the world today, although in different regions there is a different colour coding. Differing shapes also help to distinguish the port from the starboard buoys in a lateral system. At night, a light mounted on buoys shows their location; their colour and regularity of flashes distinguish one buoy one from another.

In those regions where dense fog is a frequent occurrence and obscures visualization of the buoy, sound-emitting devices are added in the form of a bell, gong or whistle to help the mariner locate the buoy. These sound buoys all depend upon the motion of the sea to swing the clapper against a bell or a gong. In the case of a whistle buoy, sound is produced by the compression of air in a column, like in a pipe organ.

Another system, that of cardinal buoys, addresses the problem of ships approaching a danger from all directions when there is no clear reference for which way to safely pass. Of Russian origin, these buoys are placed at the four cardinal points of the compass; top-marks indicate their position relative to the danger. The earliest form of these marks was woven baskets, but in common with other nations they have been supplanted by the use of triangles. Cardinal buoys must be used in conjunction with a nautical chart and a mariner's compass. Safe-water buoys are usually mid-channel markers in major shipping lanes, and have safe water all around them. Isolated danger buoys are solitary buoys placed, as their name implies, to mark a danger, such as a shipwreck.

In shallow water, or channels of lesser importance to commercial traffic, spar buoys are used to mark a channel. As their name implies, these are poles attached to the sea bottom in the same manner as other buoys. They may indicate direction either by the lateral system or the cardinal system. In shallow water, such as at the eastern end of the Gulf of Finland, they must be taken ashore over the winter, otherwise the freezing of the water and movement of the ice would wrench them from their assigned position. In waters where there is a large tidal range, such as in the Bay of Fundy, at low tide they may lie down on their side, rendering them useless as a marker.

Cairns, a man-made loose pile or pyramid of stones, can be found all over the world and have been erected for a variety of reasons, including as an aid to navigation. They are particularly well suited for this purpose in the Gulf of Finland with many thousands of islands and skerries, often separated by only a narrow band of water. With their visibility enhanced by whitewashing, they help distinguish one island from another and serve to guide the way. The cairn has been in use here since the Middle Ages, and perhaps even earlier by the Vikings to mark their trade routes. High wooden towers, poles, or even tall brush, surmounted by an attention-grabbing feature, were also in early use.

It wasn't until the beginning of the sixteenth century that governments began to take over the maintenance of buoys and organize some sort of standardization. Presently, the International Association of Lighthouse Authorities (founded in 1957), has established a world buoyage lateral system. It indicates the general direction to be taken and limits of safe water when a ship approaches a harbour, river or other waterway from seaward and in well-defined channels.

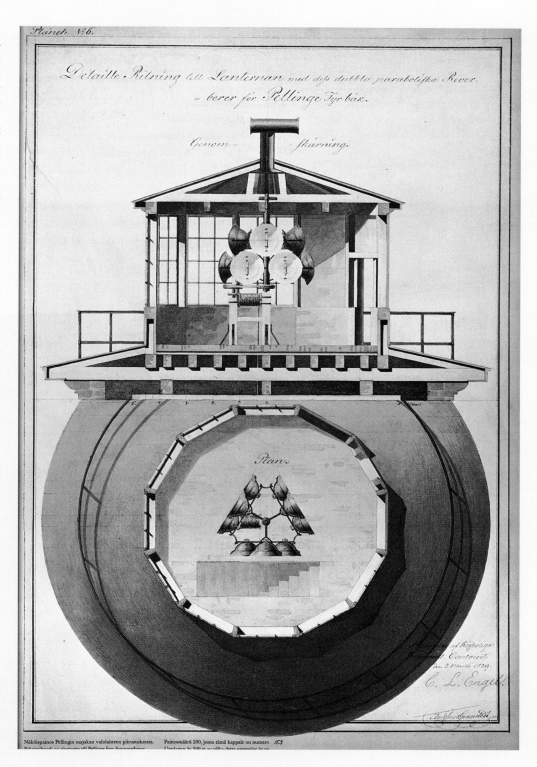

224. The Lightning System Drawing of Pellinki Lighthouse by Carl Ludvig Engel, 1829

Lighthouses are a necessity in the treacherous waters of the Finnish coast. The Pellinki lighthouse was built on the island of Glosholmen in the Gulf of Finland in 1832. It was based on designs made by Carl Ludwig Engel (1778–1849) in 1829. The lighthouse was 36 m high, with the tower itself, 25 m. This image shows the lighting system of the lighthouse, with nine lamps and nine parabolic reflectors. The revolving system was rotated by a weight-operated clockwork mechanism. The location of the lighthouse poorly chosen, however, and it was replaced by another on Söderskär Island in 1862.

THE MARITIME MUSEUM OF FINLAND

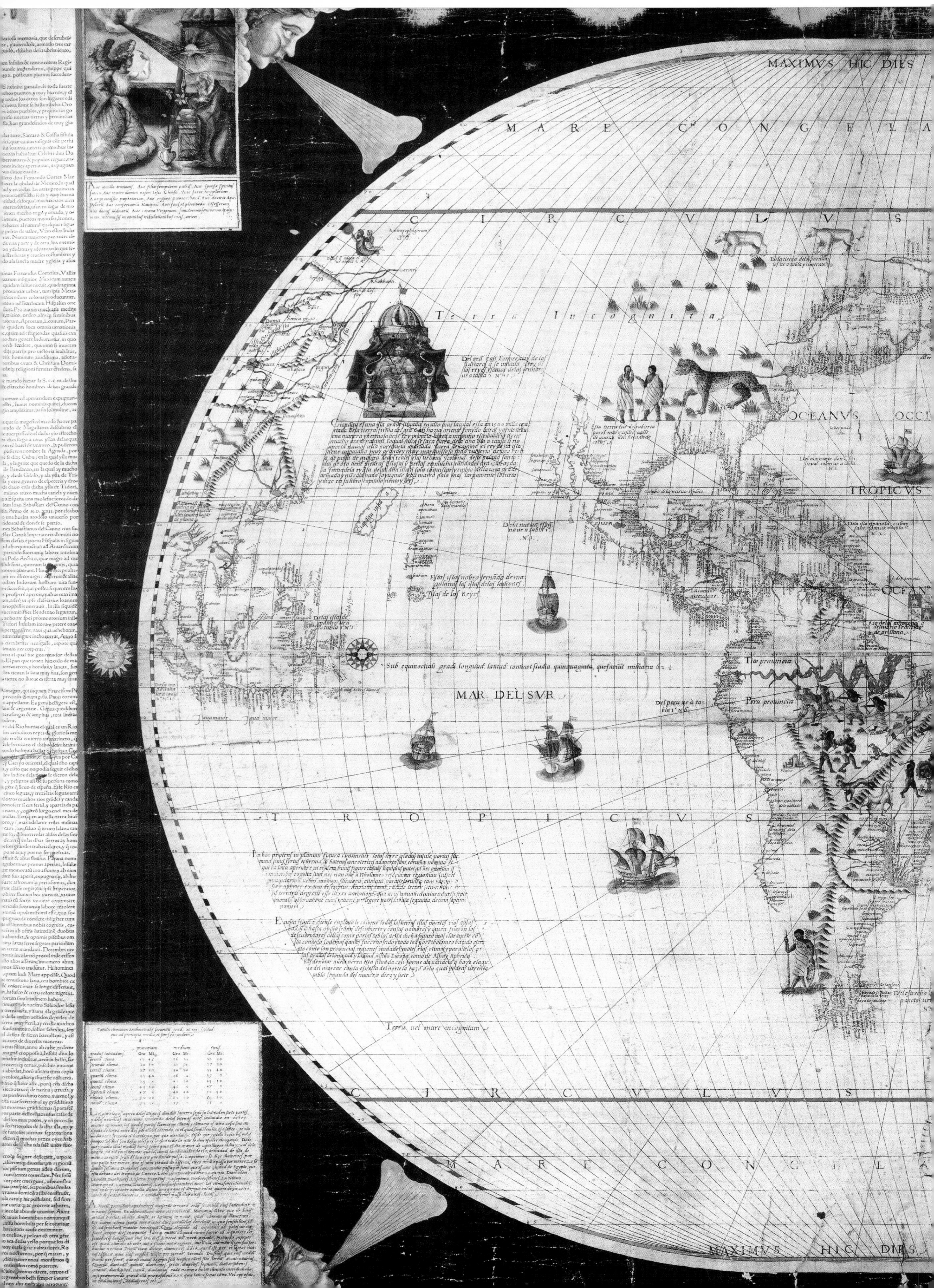

MARE CONGELA

CIRCVLVS

Terra Incognita

OCEANVS OCCI

TROPICVS

OCEAN

MAR DEL SVR

Islas de los Reyes

Sub equinoctiali graci longitud latitud continet stadia quinquaginta, quefaciut millaria ...

Tiv prouincia

Peru prouincia

TROPICVS

Terra uel mare incognitum

CIRCVLVS

MARE CONGELA

MAXIMVS HIC DIES

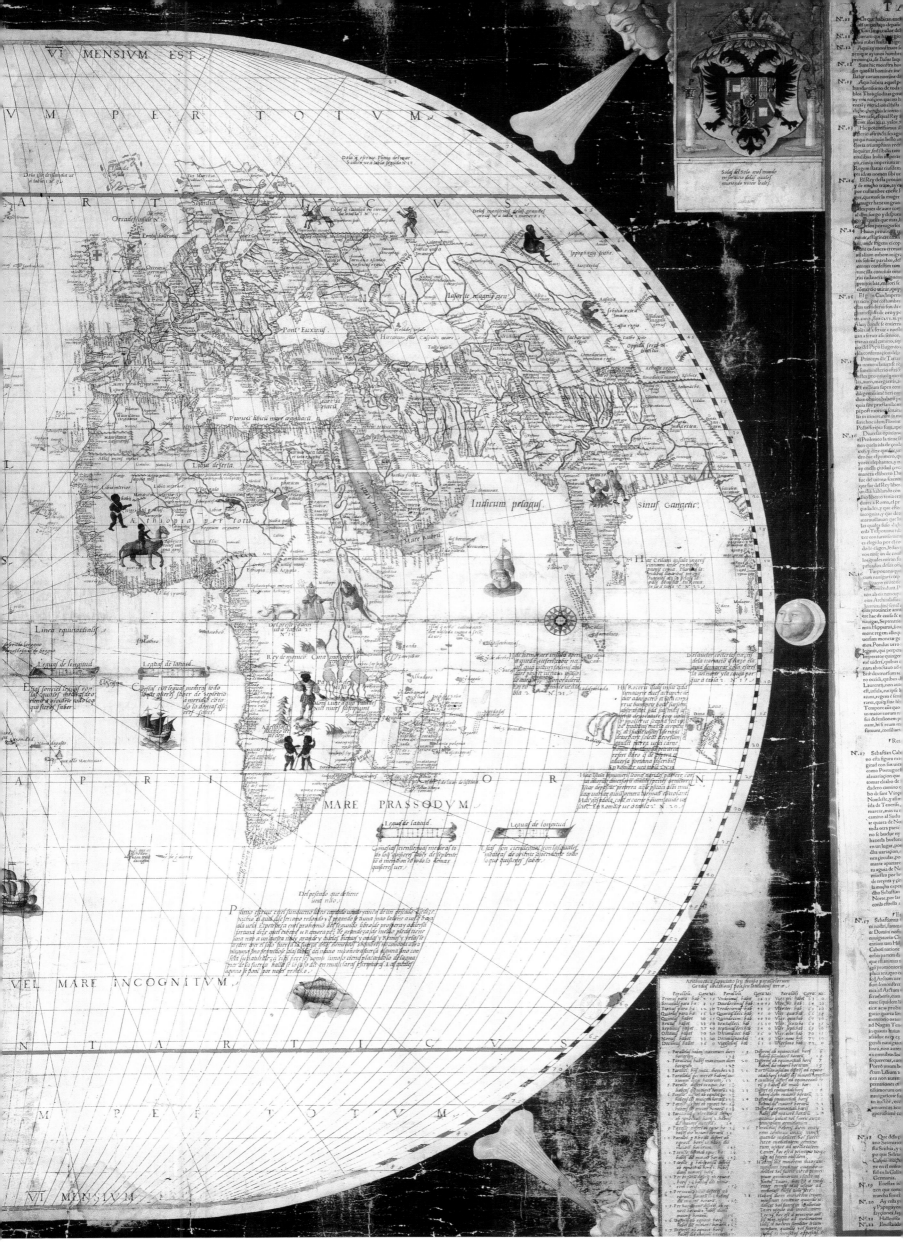

thay had to lie somewhere in this middle section of the North American continent, and persuaded a group of silk merchants and Florentine bankers resident in Lyons, France, to finance an expedition in 1524 under the French flag.

In accordance with his plans, Verrazzano approached the American coast at about 34° N, placing him near Cape Fear, the most southerly of Carolina's three capes. From there, he headed south a short distance before returning to his search northward, most likely realizing he had already come as close to potentially hostile Spanish ships as he dared. As he sailed along the outer banks of Carolina he saw open water extending all the way to the horizon on the far side of a narrow strip of land. In his letter to Francis I, Verrazzano says 'here is an isthmus a mile in width and about 200 long, in which from the ship we could see *el mare oriental...*[this sea] is the same which flows around the shores of India, China and Cataya.' In his eagerness to be the first to have discovered what so many others before had failed to do, he made the mistake of assuming there were no further impediments to the Orient. He did not take the trouble to find out that the water beyond the isthmus, which he named *Verrazzania*, was no more than a few miles wide, and was bounded on the far side by the low-lying mainland shore of North America. Instead, he continued his explorations, following the shore northward, until he dropped anchor in New York outer harbour. With the ship's boat he explored New York's Upper Bay, and left without exploring or naming what is now called Hudson River. Verrazzano continued to follow the coast until he reached the northern end of Newfoundland, then turned back to France.

Upon his return, he gave a full account of the trip to King Francis I, saying: 'My intention on this voyage was to reach Cathay and the extreme eastern coast of Asia, but I did not expect to find such an obstacle of new land as I have found'. What he found contradicted the belief of the Ancients that the eastern and western shores of the *oikumene* were washed by the same Ocean Sea, uninterrupted by any intervening land. The voyage of Verrazzano, and that of Estevão Gomes (d. 1538) who also searched the coast of North America for a Northwest Passage in 1525, had established that a new continent unbroken by any strait or passage leading to the Pacific extended from the southern tip of Patagonia to within 1,200 miles of the North Pole.

This only left the far north open for exploration by the countries seeking a way around Spanish and Portuguese prescriptive claims to commerce with India and the Far East. As the wealth and power of Spain and Portugal increased from their trade in the New World and Far East, so too did the desires and pressures mount in France and England to become equal commercial participants. True, there was profit to be made by ships returning with cod, timber and furs; still, it was not the same as a hold filled with gold, silver, silks, spices and ivory.

Before France could send expeditions toward the northwest, the major impediment toward travel in the Atlantic, created by

227. Portrait of Giovanni da Verrazzano by Francesco Allegrini, 1767

English, Portuguese and French expeditions all showed that there was no passage from the Atlantic Ocean to the Pacific Ocean in the far northern latitudes of the New World. To the south, Spanish searches equally met with failure. This left only the middle section of the North American continent to explore for a possible route to Cathay. Giovanni da Verrazzano, a Florentine by birth, but sailing under the French flag for Francis I, set out in 1524 to sail this remaining section of coast. Although he was no more successful than the others before him, he did finally prove that this landmass intervening between Europe and the east coast of Asia extended all the way from within 1200 miles of the North Pole to Patagonia, without a strait or passage leading to the Pacific Ocean.

THE PIERPOINT MORGAN LIBRARY, NEW YORK

228. Northwest Passage Searches

Every possible inlet and strait along the eastern coast of North America was investigated for a way to pass through the continent, enter the Pacific and reach the Orient. Endless failures did not diminish the attempts, they only strengthened the resolve to find the Northwest Passage. To the dismay of Jacques Cartier, the wide Gulf of St. Lawrence narrowed down to a river, and finally to impassable rapids; in repeated voyages, John Davis and William Baffin each found their endeavours blocked by solid ice; attempted passages in more southerly latitudes were equally disappointing. The most promising course appeared to be the bay now named after Henry Hudson. Once beyond the narrow opening, water opened up to an apparently limitless horizon. All general signs: the disposition of ice; the great tides, known to exist only in open oceans, and the direction from which they flowed; the presence of whales; even the colour of water, all pointed toward success, until eventually all hope was given up of a passage by this route.

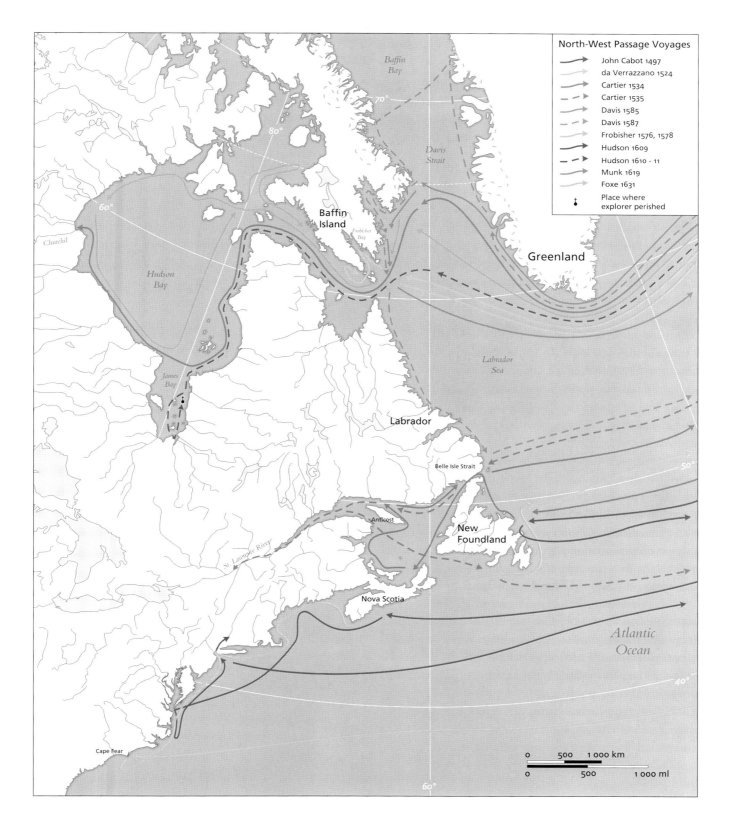

North-West Passage Voyages

→	John Cabot 1497
→	da Verrazzano 1524
→	Cartier 1534
⇢	Cartier 1535
→	Davis 1585
⇢	Davis 1587
→	Frobisher 1576, 1578
→	Hudson 1609
⇢	Hudson 1610 - 11
→	Munk 1619
→	Foxe 1631
⚓	Place where explorer perished

division of the ocean between Spain and Portugal, had to be removed. Francis I convinced the present pope, Clement VII, to rule that Spain's territorial claim 'applied to lands already discovered', not those discovered by later explorers. In the eyes of France, the new edict was sufficient to establish her rights to search for a Northwest Passage.

With the support of the French crown, and approval from the Vatican, Jacques Cartier (1491–1557) of St. Malo made three voyages, in 1534, 1535 and 1541–42, 'to the kingdom of *Terres Neufves* (Newfoundland), to discover certain isles and countries where there is said to be found a vast quantity of gold and other rich things'. Cartier thoroughly explored the Gulf of St. Lawrence and its river as far as navigation permit-

ted. But the route to China was never found, nor was the mythical kingdom of Saguenay that was to have been France's counterpart to Spain's riches from Mexico and Peru. With the succession to the French throne of Henry II, who saw little use in American exploration, France abandoned further efforts in that direction.

Undiminished Hopes

Rather than dispelling belief in the existence of a North-west Passage, Cartier's disappointment reinforced all the more strongly in the minds of Englishmen that it had to lie in the

... settled in ...

400 miles, for almost ...

longitude, very neere, East & west, &

of 70. $\frac{2}{3}$

And from Colgoyeve to Vaygatz, 2[0]

Degrees difference (onely in Longitude), [of]

of Latitude also: /   79 78

And from Vaygatz to the Promontory

degrees difference of Longitude, (the whole &

betwene ~~two~~ two its

shortest distance ~~and~~ also East & West III in

Ende likewise of 70) ~~make~~ are 1200 miles; [the]

from Wardhowse to Tabin

ma totalis, 600 Leagues, or 1800 miles English

course, Allowing in a Discovery Voyage, for

with an other but 40. miles English, yt is evident

from Wardhowse to Tabin the course may be [sayled]

Eastrly in 36. dayes. But by Gods Help yt may be

finished in much shorter time: bothe by Help of winde pr[o]

perous & light continuall. for the tyme requisite thereto ...

When you are past Tabin, or come to the Lon[gi]

tude of 142 (as yo Charte showeth), or [of] two, three

4 or 5, degrees farder, Easterly, yt is probable [that]

you fall finde the Lande on your right hand, wain

much Sowtherly & Eastward. In wch course you

are like enogh to fall into the mowth of the famous

River Oechardes, or some other of some other name,

wch (yet) I sometime to pas by the renowmed Cit[y]

of Cambalu, & that mowth to be in Latitude abo[ut]

50

230. Portrait of Martin Frobisher by Cornelis Ketel, 16th century

A former buccaneer, the English navigator and hydrographer, Martin Frobisher, made three journeys between 1576 and 1578 to the waters of Baffin Island. On his first voyage, in search of the Northwest Passage, Frobisher believed he had found gold on Baffin Island. He went back the next year and collected 200 tons of black ore, which he brought back to England. Frobisher left on his third journey with a fleet of fifteen vessels intending to create England's first permanent settlement in North America, and transport the ore back to England. Ultimately, the ore was proved to be worthless, the colony failed before it even started, and Frobisher had not found the Northwest Passage. His name can be seen in many charts later in the misplaced channel in south Greenland.

THE BODLEIAN LIBRARY, UNIVERSITY OF OXFORD

229. First page of instructions for *Voyages of Discovery* given by Dr John Dee for Arthur Pet and Charles Jackman on their 1580 Voyage

In his instructions to Arthur Pet and Charles Jackman for their voyage to discover of the Northeast Passage, Dee calculated each segment of the distances from Wardhaus (Vardø) to Cape Tabin (Taymyr) and arrived at a total distance of 1800 nautical miles. According to Dee, if they made 50 nautical miles in one days' sailing, then the most lengthy and difficult part of the voyage would be completed in only thirty-six days. This might, he said, be achieved even faster if they had good winds. Furthermore, the sailing and navigation would be easier because of the perpetual light both day and night.

THE BRITISH LIBRARY, LONDON

high Arctic waters above Canada. In all the searches for a sea-route between western Europe and Asia it was never a question of whether the passage to Asia existed, but always where it was to be found. The concept of a strait or sea linking the two oceans was waiting to be validated, rather than discovered.

Prompted by the writings of Robert Thorne, and by Sir Humphrey Gilbert's *Discourse of a Discoverie for a New Passage to Cataia* (1566), a group of merchant adventurers was formed in London to finance an expedition led by Martin Frobisher (1535–1594). Preparations were thorough to assure success. Frobisher possessed a large array of the best navigation instruments available, including a sea-astrolabe, cross-staff, eighteen hourglasses, and twenty compasses of varying kinds. He also possessed English and Spanish navigation books, including Pedro de Medina's *L'Arte del Navegar* (1545), Niccolò Zeno's chart (1558), and Mercator's 1569 general map. A number of blank, ruled, charts were supplied on which to record observations and discoveries. Dr John Dee and the accomplished navigator Stephen Borough instructed Frobisher on the rules of geometry, navigation and cosmography.

Frobisher sailed westward in June of 1576, arriving by the end of July at the southern end of Baffin Island, then called *Meta Incognita*. He explored its coast and sailed a considerable distance into a deep inlet. He was unable to investigate the full length of the bay, but felt assured that to the west, beyond the two headlands at its far end, lay the open sea. Believing he had found the Northwest Passage to Cathay and the East Indies, Frobisher named this body of water Frobisher Strait, likening it to its southern counterpart, Magellan Strait, leading to the Pacific Ocean. In reality, Frobisher Bay is closed at its western end; Frobisher had not found the strait to the Orient on this expedition, or during his two subsequent voyages, in 1577 and 1578.

A decade after Frobisher's disappointments, the search for a Northwest Passage was taken up by John Davis (c. 1550–1605). Influential friends were granted a charter, and formed a company called 'Divers Worshipfull Merchants of London and the West Country', to seek out a passage to China. With the bark *Sunshine* of London and the bark *Moonshine* of Dartmouth, he set out from Dartmouth, England, on 7 June 1585.

As the two ships approached the east coast of Greenland a thick fog hid any view of land, and Davis became concerned, for he heard a 'great roaring of the sea', like waves breaking on a shore. When the fog broke up the next day, land appeared before them, but it was scarcely a sight to bring any measure of joy to their hearts; deformed, rock-strewn mountains, their tops covered with snow, appeared above the fog, and solid ice extending a full league into the sea clung to the shore. On account of the irksome noise of the ice and the utter barrenness of the land, Davis named this eastern coast of Greenland the 'Land of Desolation'.

All attempts to sail the *Sunshine* and *Moonshine* north along this forbidding coast were thwarted by strong northerly winds and the solid ice that nearly encompassed them. The only pas-

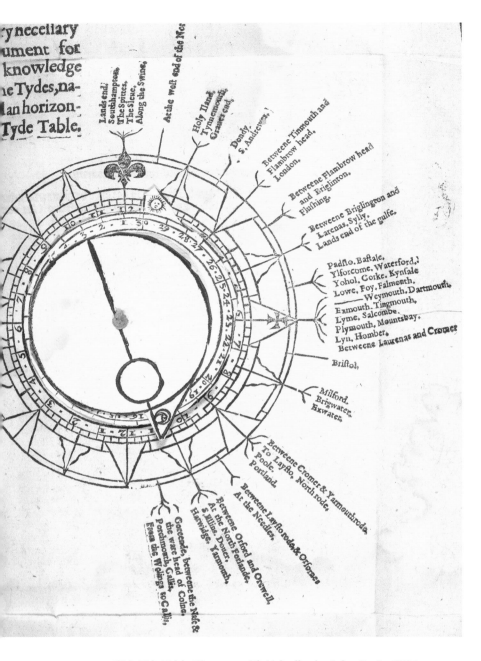

231. Tide Table Diagram with Volvelles by John Davis, 1657

Captain John Davis was one of those rare individuals whose sailing skills were equally matched with knowledge of the theoretical science of navigation. In his book *The Seamans Secrets* (1595) Davis showed, with the use of volvelles (moveable discs of paper) how to calculate the tides around England. This not only made it a good teaching device, but an instrument of practical usage as well.

MAGDALENE COLLEGE, THE PEPYS LIBRARY CAMBRIDGE

sage left open lay to the south. Davis coasted the land as it trended south, west, and then northwest, until finally at the latitude of 64° 15'N he headed into shore. Here, in the middle of a group of islands, the two ships dropped anchor. Davis had reached the entrance of a fjord, where the Danish city of Godthaab (now called Nuuk) is situated.

After two days, rest the expedition continued northwest until once again they raised land at the latitude of 66° 40'N on the east coast of Baffin Island. Reaching the entrance to Cumberland Sound, the two ships headed in and followed its northern shore for a distance of 180 nautical miles. Expectations were high that this indeed was the long sought-after passage, for the water had the colour, nature and quality of an open ocean. Like Frobisher, Davis did not sail his newly discovered sound until reaching its utmost limit, and like Frobisher, Davis allowed himself to believe he had found the Northwest Passage before he fully corroborated it. With this much accomplished, and the promise of a successful completion apparently so near, he turned the *Sunshine* and *Moonshine* homeward.

Immediately upon returning to London, he began seeking the support and funds for a second voyage. In a letter to Sir Francis Knight he wrote: 'The north-west passage is a matter nothing doubtful, but at any tyme almost to be passed, the sea navigable, voyd of yse, the ayre tolerable, and the waters very depe'. Within six months he had gathered the necessary funds to outfit four ships in a way that ensured a greater chance of success in 1586 than he had had in his previous voyage.

Off the west coast of Ireland Davis divided the fleet. One part was to search north on the east side of Greenland to see if a way could be found past the impenetrable wall of ice that had stopped him the previous year, while he would explore the strait on the west side of Greenland. Davis fell in with land at the southern end of Greenland, but the amount of ice and snow prevented him from landing. After many storms he finally doubled Cape Farewell, and made landfall on the west coast of Greenland where he had been the previous year.

On 11 July, with a fair wind, the small fleet raised sail and coasted north to the latitude of 63° 8'. Whereas in the previous year Davis found the sea clear of ice and the water warm, now the largest island of floating ice he had ever seen blocked his way. Davis headed west across the strait to Baffin Island, and made landfall at approximately the same place as the year before. Then he sailed south until he came to the entrance to Cumberland Sound. This is the place he believed last year would yield the way to the Northwest Passage, and in his journal now he says 'here we had great hope of a through passage'. For whatever reason, Davis apparently changed his mind about Cumberland Sound leading to the Pacific Ocean, and sailed across its mouth without attempting to explore to its end. Maintaining a southerly course, he also passed Frobisher Strait without entering. We might assume he already knew this sound to be a false lead, and so he did not bother with it. With winter approaching, Davis shaped his course back to England.

Once again he had failed to find a Northwest Passage, but the quantity of fish he found off the coast of Labrador and Newfoundland, some of which he brought back to England with him, held promise that profit might yet be gained in another expedition. In 1587 he set out in three ships. Two of them were to be employed strictly for fishing, thus allowing the Company of Merchant Adventurers to defray some of the costs of the expedition, and perhaps even reap a little profit, while Davis would continue his search for the Northwest Passage in the third, the pinnace *Ellen*.

Like the first voyage, the beginning was troublesome. The *Ellen*'s tiller broke, causing loss of control over her helm, and the ship was leaking badly. But rather than return to England in disgrace, all aboard agreed to live and die together, committing themselves to the ship. After affecting repairs at sea Davis sailed the *Ellen* north along the western coast of Greenland until he reached 72° 12'N latitude. At this, the most northerly point reached in all three of his voyages, the Sun at night remained 5 degrees above the horizon. Winds from the north prevented sailing any farther in that direction and he headed west, coasting along the southern edge of the margins of Arctic ice. Once again he found himself at the mouth of Cumberland Gulf, but this time he did not fail to explore it fully, sailing all the way to the bottom of the sound, and in doing so disproved what before he had believed was a through passage to the Pacific.

As he sailed by the entrance to what later would be called Hudson Bay, Davis noted with awe 'the sea falling down into the gulfe with a mighty overfal, and roring, and with divers circular motione like whirlepooles, in such sort, as forcible streames passe thorow the arches of bridges'. Safely escaping the great banks of ice being ejected from the bay, he coasted south to 54° latitude on the coast of Labrador. By this time the men had had their fill of sailing with the constant dangers of swift currents, ice and cold, and Davis assented to return to England.

The failure of this, his third attempt to find the Northwest Passage, did not diminish Davis's determination, but merchants were no longer willing to spend their money on expeditions to Arctic regions. In 1588 Spain sent its great armada against England, and maritime energies were diverted to national survival.

England was just awakening to the realization that the knowledge of her mariners in open ocean navigation was woefully inadequate. The use of dead reckoning to locate position, the lead line to determine depth, and knowledge of the tides, was sufficient for her inshore fisheries, but longer, offshore passages to the New World required the ability to calculate exact positions by astronomical observation and mathematical reasoning when well out of sight of land. No longer content to rely on Portuguese and Spanish navigational texts, English authors began to produce their own treatises, such as Robert Recorde's *The Castle of Knowledge* (1556), William Bourne's *A Regiment for the Sea* (1574), and a *Discourse of a Discoverie for a New Passage to Cataia* (1576) by Humphrey Gilbert.

Davis took a notable part in the development of this learning; his expertise in the theoretical science of navigation matched his sailing skills, and sets him apart from most other explorers of the time. He wrote two treatises on navigation: *The Seamans Secrets*, first published in 1595, and *The Worlde's Hydrographicall Discripion*, published that same year. The first part of *The Seamans Secrets* contained practical information for the seaman: it described the use of the compass, its errors caused by magnetic variation, and how to measure and correct for this variation; how to take measurement of the altitude of the Sun and Pole Star to calculate latitude; and the necessity of keeping track of the ship's course that it may be correctly plotted on a chart. He urged seamen to keep an accurate account of the ship's progress in a logbook; noting daily the distance run, latitude calculated, the course steered, direction and strength of the wind, and magnetic variation.

In the second part of *The Seamans Secrets* Davis discussed more theoretical issues, such as the problem that a fixed compass heading, or rhumb line, when laid down as a straight line on their chart, was actually an ever-tightening spiral when projected on a globe. He also wrote on the practice of great circle sailing. It would be safe to assume that Dr John Dee's work on the 'paradoxall' compass played a considerable role in Davis's education on this subject.

Davis considered the cross-staff to be superior to the quadrant and astrolabe for measuring the altitude of a celestial body, but it had several drawbacks. It was difficult to align the lower tip of the transverse bar with the horizon, while at the same time sighting the Sun with its upper tip. There was also the problem of having to look directly at the Sun, which is harmful to the eyes. Davis invented an instrument, called the back-staff, which solved these problems. Sometimes named the Davis quadrant, or as the French call it, the English quadrant, the back-staff remained in use for nearly a century.

Davis also devised a means of predicting tides that was more elaborate and more flexible than contemporary prediction diagrams. As its name implies, his 'horizontal tide-table' was primarily designed to determine the time of high or low tide at various locations. In his *Worlde's Hydrographicall Discription* Davis gave 'proof' that the Northwest Passage was undoubtedly there, waiting only to be discovered. Although none of the three voyages he had undertaken to find that passage had been successful, his belief in its existence was not diminished. In a letter to his good friend Sanderson, he wrote 'The passage is most probable, the execution easie'.

After Davis's 1587 voyage, his days of Arctic exploration were over. It did not, however, end Davis's sailing career. For his navigational skills he was hired as pilot by the Dutch East India Company on voyages around the Cape of Good Hope. And in 1604 Davis was engaged by the newly founded English East India Company as pilot on their first fleet to discover and trade with Cathay and Japan. At his accession to the English throne, King James I had brought to an end

233. Queen Elizabeth I by an unknown artist, 1585–1590

Elizabeth I (1533–1603), the last Tudor monarch the Queen of England and Ireland from 1558 to her death. At this time England had become Protestant and had Catholic enemies. Spain especially was furious with British privateers, such as Francis Drake, who had the backing of Queen Elizabeth leading to a confrontation between Britain and Spain. The destruction of the invincible Spanish Armada was the basis of Britain's rule of the seas.

NATIONAL PORTRAIT GALLERY, LONDON

232. Greenwich Hospital from the North Bank of the Thames by Canaletto, c.1752

Countries on the path to becoming colonial powers built observatories to advance the techniques of navigation, especially position finding. France founded an observatory in Paris in 1667, while Great Britain built one in 1675 on the orders of King Charles II at Greenwich, east of London on the south bank of the Thames. The famous observatory can be seen through the tree-tops in the distance, left of the tower on the right. It was designed by the astronomer, mathematician and famous architect Sir Christopher Wren. There had been royal palaces at Greenwich for centuries; in the background in the centre of the picture, between the two towers, is the Queen's House built for Queen Anna in 1616–1638 and designed by the architect Inigo Jones. The largest complex of palaces was completed in 1751 to serve as a navy hospital. The building has also housed an academy of navigation. Today, the National Maritime Museum is at Greenwich and the observatory itself is a museum. Since 1833, a red ball has been dropped every day at 1 pm from the top of the pole above the observatory. Ships use the time-ball to check their chronometers. The observatory has played a key role in developing methods of determining geographical longitude. In addition, observations were made for lunar tables, and the accuracy of John Harrison's maritime chronometers was studied at Greenwich.

NATIONAL MARITIME MUSEUM, LONDON

234. Logbook of Charles Wilde on the *Buritto* from England to Madras 1649–1651 and back 1651–1652

Until the middle of the sixteenth century no official record was kept of a vessel's progress throughout its voyage. In 1553 Sebastian Cabot initiated a list of rules and regulations for the newly formed Muscovy Company, about to set out in search of the Northeast Passage. Every captain was to fully note on a regularly scheduled basis the speed and compass direction of his vessel, give weather conditions, describe state of the sea, and calculate latitude. As seen in this page from the logbook of Charles Wilde during his voyage from England to Madras in 1649–1651, Wilde followed the standard set by Cabot. Additionally, he illustrated his logbook with a plan, or bird's-eye view of the coast, and a horizon profile of the land as a mariner would see it when approaching from the sea. This aided in identification to assure a proper landfall.

THE BRITISH LIBRARY, LONDON

235. The Kara Sea by Hugh Smyth, 1580

Mindful of the instructions given by William Burrough for a careful mapping of the route to Cathay, Hugh Smyth, who accompanied Arthur Pet on his expedition, made this sketch of the geography of Nova Zembla, Vaygach Island and the mainland. On it he showed the position of rocks, depths in fathoms, and the nature of the sea-floor (here, red ooze) as brought up by the lead-line. He indicated that the current on the south shore of Nova Zembla sets to the north-northwest and south-southeast depending on the state of the tide. The most important feature of the landscape on the map is the 'Infinite Ice', labelled in two places in the Kara Sea.

THE BRITISH LIBRARY, LONDON

the long war between England and Spain, making possible this commercial use of the southern routes to Asia by an English company. Ironically, Davis's life ended not in some desolate, ice-bound Arctic region, but in the Far East while on a second voyage for the East India Company, where Japanese pirates killed him.

BEYOND BLEAK RUSSIA'S NORTHERNMOST CONFINES

At the same time that expeditions set forth to find a passage north of Canada, leading to the Pacific, explorations for a route by sailing directly over the North Pole, or toward the east, over the top of Russia and Siberia, were being sought just as assiduously.

The greatest obstacle to a northeast route was that the geography of the region was almost totally unknown. According to the Roman geographer, Pomponius Mela (c. AD 40) the region of Scythia covered the whole of the Eurasian landmass, extending to what we now think of as northern

Russia. A circumfluent ocean theoretically made a passage north of Scythia possible. Pliny, who quoted extensively from Mela, said the entire coast of Scythia was most inhospitable: in the far north, extending all the way to the Tabin [Tamarus] Promontory, are vast areas of solitude and isolation, alternating with tribes of Scythian Anthropophagi – men who feed on human flesh – and the haunts of multitudes of wild beasts. 'Everything in this country', he says, 'is ferocious, beginning with men'.

By the mid-sixteenth century, the Anthropophagi of the Ancient's lore was replaced with an identifiable group of natives – the Samoyedes – who lived north and northeast of the White Sea. Clearly, the dangers mariners faced when they advanced beyond Norway's North Cape, was not limited to elements of the sea: wind, wave, and ice. Landing their ships ashore for need of repair, or for reprovisioning, could lead to a death more horrible than a watery grave in the icy sea.

Sebastian Cabot, back in England after his residence in Spain, believed that a sea-route north of Russia to Cathay was possible, and convinced London merchants that by entering upon this new and strange navigation they would be able

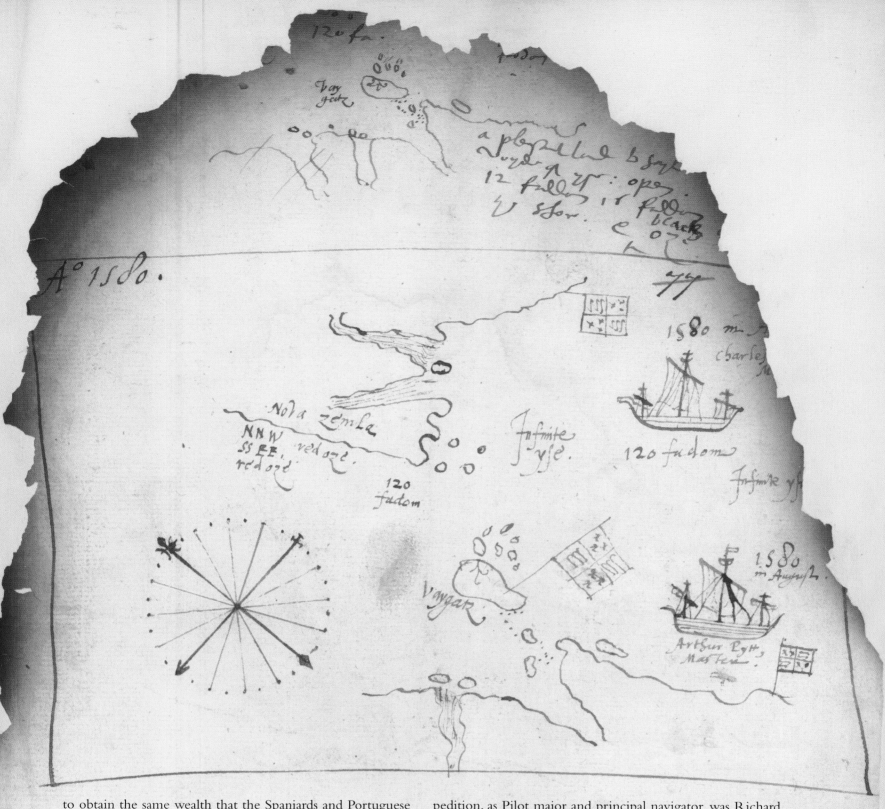

to obtain the same wealth that the Spaniards and Portuguese received from their discoveries. To initiate this new venture, over one hundred merchants united into 'The Mystery and Company of the Merchant Adventurers of the City of London...for the discovery of Cathay, and divers other regions, dominions and places unknown'. The Merchant Adventurers of England came to be known by a much shorter name: The Muscovy Company.

Hugh Willoughby

In 1553 the Muscovy Company prepared three ships 'for the search and discovery of the northern part of the world, to open a way and passage to our men for travel to new and unknown kingdoms'. All were put under the command of Sir Hugh Willoughby (d. 1554), a man well connected at the court of King Henry VIII. Second in command on the ex-

pedition, as Pilot major and principal navigator, was Richard Chancellor (d. c. 1555).

In order to prevent dissention that might hinder the voyage, Sebastian Cabot drew up a list of thirty-three rules and regulations defining the duties of the officers, and proscribing the behaviour of the sailors to one another aboard the ships, as well as toward those people they might encounter in their travels. Item number seven of Cabot's ordinances stated that the Master and Pilot of every ship should keep a written record on a daily basis, in which 'the navigation of every day and night, with compass headings, and observation of the lands, tides, elements, altitude of the Sun course of the Moon and stars' be described. This was the first time in the history of navigation that a daily record such as this was required. Previously, information concerning a voyage was scant, if present at all, and written in the form of a personal journal, or as a letter from the mariner to his sovereign. The same care and thought was given to the vessels on which the expedition depended.

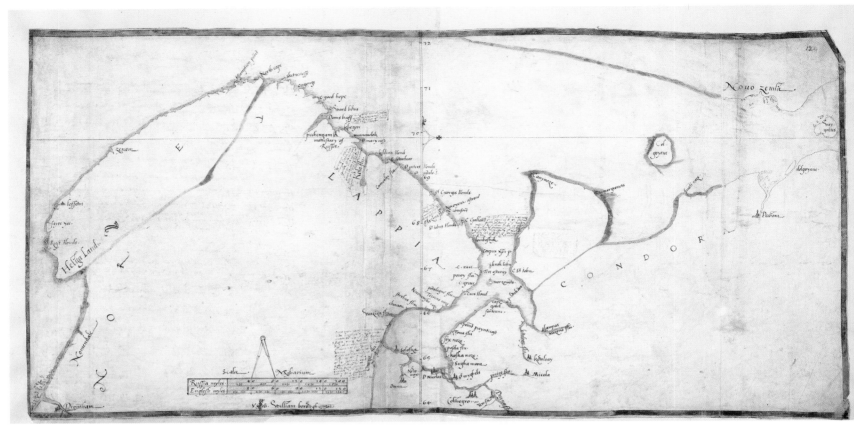

236. Chart of the Northern navigation by William Borough, c. 1578

An important component of the expeditions sponsored by the Muscovy Company in search of the Northeast Passage was a thorough and detailed mapping of the coast. Stephen Borough, an accomplished navigator, instructed his younger brother William on the rules of geometry, navigation and cosmography. Together, they made many voyages in the Arctic Seas along the coasts of Norway and Lapland. In 1578, William Borough drew up this sea chart extending eastward to Vaygach Strait. The western portion of the route was already well known, as evidenced by the depiction of harbours and many place-names as far as St. Nicholas on the White Sea. East of that, detailed geographic information still waits to be filled in. The English knew that the River Ob flowed into the Kara Sea on the Far side of Vaygach Strait, but beyond, all was speculation.

THE BRITISH LIBRARY, LONDON

Until now, no English ship had sailed farther east than the Norwegian town of Vardø (70° 21'N latitude, and 031° 5.58'E longitude) on the northeast coast of Finnmark.

Summer was far spent when two of the three ships (*Bona Confidentia* and *Bona Esperanza*) took shelter behind a rocky island in a broad bay to wait for a favourable wind. But fully a week passed, and Willoughby then thought it best to overwinter there, 'seeing the yeare farre spent, & also evill wether, as frost, snow, and haile, as though it had beene the deep of winter' was already upon them. He could not have selected a more inhospitable spot to spend the winter than this bleak and barren part of the Lapland coast.

Winter deepened, becoming unbearably cold to the unfortunate English sailors who had no concept of what an Arctic winter could be like. Gradually, the days shortened, until finally, the pale, weary Sun, incapable of providing even the scantest warmth, dropped below the horizon to disappear altogether. After 25 November, perpetual darkness, even at midday, was upon them. Willoughby saw his ships locked in the ice, and covered with drifting snow. He watched in horror as his crew died one by one. By the end of winter of 1554 the two ships were crushed in the ice, and sixty-five men, including Willoughby, starved and froze to death in this cruel and uncaring country.

Richard Chancellor

Chancellor, with only a single ship – the *Edward Bonaventure* (along with her pinnace and ship's boat) – had to assume all the responsibility for the expedition. A foreboding about the voyage, and a melancholy from which he had suffered at the beginning of the voyage, was deepened by the loss of his commander. The presumed loss of the other two ships emphasized the perilous nature of this venture. Stretching out before him lay the even greater uncertainties of an uncharted, trackless sea. Chancellor was well prepared for the task; he was well trained as a practical seaman, having sailed to Greece and France in earlier voyages. He also was a skilled maker of navigational instruments, improving upon earlier models by providing them with greater scale divisions, thus allowing for greater accuracy of reading. On the theoretical and academic side, he learned his navigation and mathematics from a master, John Dee, who was a close personal friend as well as his mentor. The two had held many conferences together, in which they worked out tables of ephemerides to be used during the voyage.

Chancellor was not a man to be defeated by fear of danger. It was not in his nature. Nor would he dishonour himself, by quitting, he wrote in his journal that he would 'either bring that to pass which was intended, or else to die the death'. With his superb navigational skills, aided by good fortune, Chancellor brought the *Edward Bonaventure*, her pinnace and ship's boat, safely to harbour at the small settlement of Nenocksa on the White Sea near the westernmost branch of the Dvina River. Nothing more could be done this year toward reaching Cathay, but there was the possibility of opening trade relations with Tsar Ivan IV, Ivan Vassilovitch, also known by the sobriquet 'Ivan the Terrible'. Leaving the *Bonaventure* at anchor, Chancellor sailed the pinnace upriver as far as the town of Kholmogory, arriving there in October. In what was already a 'horrible and extreme winter', he then endured the hardships of a 1500 mile journey by sled to reach Moscow, the chief city of Muscovie and the seat of the 'God Emperor', the Tsar of all Russia.

With the arrival of spring, Chancellor and his companions left Moscow to return to England. The news he brought back to the investors of the Merchant Adventurers of London was not a propitious beginning for the newly formed company – there were no tremendous profits. He had not reached Cathay. He had not even 'discovered' a northern route to Russia. But he was able to give the Merchant Adventurers of London a letter from the Tsar signed and sealed in Muscovy in February 1554, stating his desire to enter into a commercial relationship with England. This document, for the first time, opened a direct route by sea for English trade with Russia. Actually, it gained two routes: one, north of Norway and Finland into the White Sea; the other, through the Baltic Sea and Gulf of Finland, which previously had been denied by the strength of the Hanseatic League.

The prospect of trade with Russia was potentially profitable for the London Merchants, who commissioned Chancellor to undertake another voyage to Muscovy in 1555. But the ultimate goal of reaching Cathay was not forgotten. Item number fifteen of the Muscovy Company's Articles read: 'It is to be had in minde, that you use all wayes and meanes possible to learne howe men may passe from Russia, either by land or by sea, to Cathaia'. Chancellor succeeded in strengthening the ties with Tsar Ivan, who granted the Muscovy Company a royal charter not only giving it access to trade, but also granting 'full and free authority' to sail any of its ships to whatever part of the world they wished and the right to conquer any of the cities, towns, castles, Islands or Mainland they discovered, – bold proclamations, indeed, for a fledgling company, and a nation just starting on a new venture to raise her maritime skills and power.

Stephen Borough

In the spring of 1556, the Muscovy Company sent Stephen Borough (1525–1584) to continue the search for the Northeast Passage by sailing to the River Ob on Russia's bleak northern coast – a voyage that would take him 900 miles farther east than had been accomplished by Chancellor in 1553. The English knew that the River Ob flowed into the Kara Sea, located at the far boundary of the Russian northern shore, but beyond, all was speculation. There were rumours that the sea beyond the Ob was a warm sea, and once this was reached, it should be an easy sail eastward, then south into the Oriental (Pacific) Ocean.

The boat selected for this voyage was a mere pinnace, a ship's boat of about 20 tons. Experience had shown how severe the weather could be in these far northern latitudes, and the Company reasoned that, when bad weather arose, a small boat, which needed very little water under her keel, could sail close to the coast and take refuge in harbours inaccessible to a larger ship. Stephen Borough, with his younger brother William (1536–1599) and a crew of eight men, set out in the pinnace *Searchthrift*, and made good progress until they approached Nova Zembla. All attempts to pass into the Kara Sea by Vaygach Strait to find the River Ob were thwarted by howling winds, terrible seas and blocked by monstrous heaps of ice. Finally, on 22 August, Borough turned the *Searchthrift* homeward. Although Borough never made it to the River Ob, his attempt did provide England with its first real knowledge of this ice-chocked place.

Pet and Jackman

Despite these failures, the Muscovy Company organized another expedition for the elusive Northeast Passage. The persuasions of Anthony Jenkinson, and the already partially completed voyage by Stephen Borough, combined with the Company's obligations to its investors, must have had much to do with this decision.

Two barks, the *George* and the *William*, respectively captained by Arthur Pet and Charles Jackman, were sent to search and discover a passage by sea to Cathay. William Borough, recognized both for his sailing experience in 1556–57 and for his published works (including maps), was Director of the expedition. The long list of instructions he gave to the two mariners was of a practical nature, while Dr John Dee again provided the theoretical and mathematical guidance on navigation. Borough's chief interest lay in mapmaking, and for this he gave detailed instructions to the two explorers on how to measure and record the form of the coast. They were also to observe the tides and currents: the direction of the tide, its velocity, the range between high and low waters, and when they occurred.

To aid them in their search, the Muscovy Company provided Pet and Jackman with three maps. The first was a

Northeast Passage

→	Willoughby & Chancellor 1553 - 54
→	Borough 1556 - 57
→	Pet & Jackman 1580
→	Barentsz 1596 - 97 van Heemskerck
→	Hudson 1608
♠	Place where explorer perished

237. Northeast Passage Searches

Attempts to reach Cathay by sailing directly over the North Pole, or eastward over the top of Nova Zembla proved to be impossible on account of solid ice, while frigid cold and the constant threat of swirling ice in Vaygach Strait crushing their frail craft, thwarted all efforts to enter the Kara Sea by that way.

238. Map of the Far North by Theodore de Bry and Gerrit de Veer, 1601

This chart was produced to show the last voyage of William Barentsz, when he discovered Bear Island and Spitzbergen. In addition to the new geographical knowledge resulting from Barentsz's voyages, the map also reflects the recent voyages made by Martin Frobisher in 1576 and 1578, and John Davis in 1585, by naming the straits after their discoverers. The only part of the Spitzbergen and Nova Zembla coast displayed is that which had been explored. The most northerly cape of the Siberian coast, Cape Tabin, was generally believed to jut into the icy waters of the Arctic as far north as 78 degrees. Doubling this was the final impediment to sailing through the Strait of Anian and out into the Pacific. Here, however, in common with other Dutch cartographers, Cape Tabin is placed much farther south at 74° N latitude, thus affirming the ease with which the passage to Cathay could be made. In a polar projection chart such as this, north is not at the top of the page, but is a single point at the centre. Hence the multiple fleur-de-lys, indicating north, changes its orientation in each of the three wind-roses, to point toward the Arctic Pole.

JOHN NURMINEN FOUNDATION

chart drawn by Borough and based on his own experience. It showed the intended route not as a rhumb (straight) line, but as a series of curved lines in a spiral, as devised by Dee. These were the compass courses required to reach their destination, and compensated for the projection plan on the charts they had. Dee prepared the second chart for the expedition, showing the north coast of Siberia quite differently than that prepared by Borough. According to Dee's interpretation of the available evidence, neither the Ob promontory, nor Cape Tabin, extended any farther than 70°N latitude, and left no question as to whether the Kara Sea was a land-locked bay. It showed that once past Vaygach, there was a wide passage all the way to Cape Tabin, where Pet and Jackman could then turn southward. Lastly, there was a blank chart upon which the two navigators could fill in the geography and discoveries according to their observations.

Dr Dee and Gerard Mercator had maintained a friendship since their student days in Louvain, and continued with discussions on the geography of the far north. Like Dee, Mercator believed that Cathay was easily reached by a Northeast Passage. But where he disagreed with Dee was the extent of Cape Tabin into high latitudes. Mercator concluded that

the promontory of Tabin reached 77° 36'N latitude, and past Vaygach, the Scythian Sea was an almost completely enclosed bay with Cape Tabin its eastern boundary. Mercator did not deny the existence of a strait at the far eastern end of the Kara Sea leading into the Pacific Ocean, but confined it on his map to a very narrow opening. The dangers in attempting to round the cape, as Mercator perceived, were the vast quantities of ice in the bay, which already had prevented Borough from entering it. Furthermore, he felt that rounding Cape Tabin would bring Pet and Jackman too close to the magnetic pole, causing their compass to fluctuate violently, rendering it useless for navigation. On 30 May 1580, the *George* and the *William* left Harwich on the east coast of England, and with fair winds they doubled Norway's North Cape without incident. Afterward the two ships became separated. Pet reached Vaygach Island in the *George*, and followed its coast south. Contrary winds and ever-present ice required continual changes of course, but the *George* finally sailed 4 or 5 leagues (12 or 15 nautical miles) through the strait south of Vaygach Island. Ice, which before was only a hindrance to movement, now entirely blocked the way from sailing any farther into the Kara Sea, and they were forced to conclude

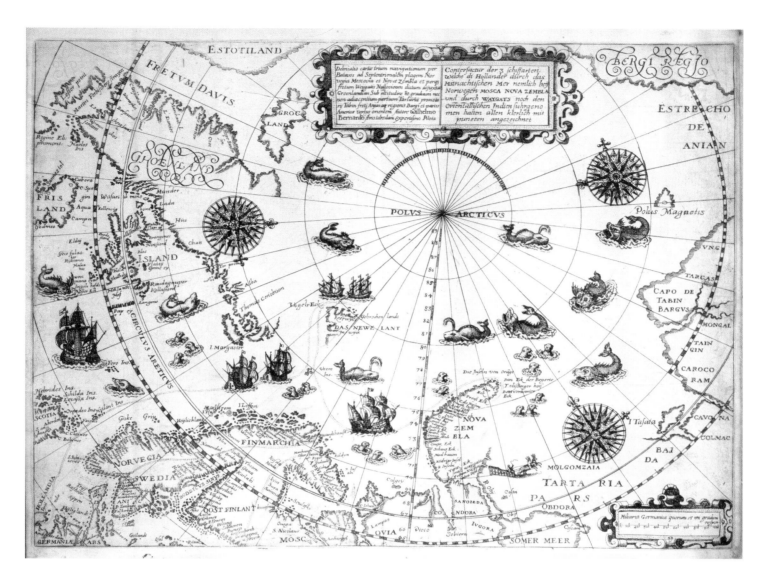

that the great masses of ice swirling around in the Kara Sea were an insurmountable barrier to reaching Cathay.

With a long list of failures and deaths since Hugh Willoughby was first sent in search of a northern route across the top of Siberia to Cathay, the Muscovy Company abandoned their efforts in that direction. The company of English merchants continued to fund ships and voyages, but limited their travels to northern ports on the White Sea, remaining content for the while with the established trade with Russia.

Willem Barentsz

Emboldened by the successes in their White Sea trade with Russia, Dutch merchants determined to extend their trade by sailing farther east. In 1594 the Dutch fitted out two vessels, captained by Cornelius Nai and Brandt Tetgales, for an expedition to Cathay in northern seas. Before the voyage got underway, a third ship was added to the fleet, commanded by Willem Barentsz (1550–1597). Although the objective was the same for all three vessels – to reach Cathay and India by northern seas – the route to be taken by Barentsz differed from the others.

Upon the advice of Peter Plancius, a clergyman and scholar with much scientific enthusiasm, Barentsz was to enter the Kara Sea by sailing north, around the northern tip of Nova Zembla. All three mariners were to sail in company until they reached Kil'din in Lapland, where they would separate and go their individual ways. The Nai and Tetgales portion of the expedition, south of Nova Zembla, was a failure. Barentsz's ship, however, the *Mercury* of Amsterdam, benefited from favourable winds and weather. Having sailed over 400 miles in five days, it came to 20 miles off Nova Zembla at 73° 25'N latitude. Following the west coast of Nova Zembla northward, Barentsz made observations of the wildlife found there, and noted any good anchorages for ships. Along the way he kept a careful record of distances run, compass headings, depths and the type of bottom found with the sounding lead, winds, and general weather conditions. To determine his latitude, Barentsz used two types of instruments: the cross-staff and the mariner's, or sea, astrolabe.

An extensive sheet of ice greeted Barentsz when he reached the Islands of Orange at the northern end of Nova Zembla. Thereafter, it was a constant struggle, with innumerable changes of course, to try and find a way around, or through, any openings of the ice. Finally on 1 August Barentsz accepted the impossibility of driving the *Mercury* and her exhausted crew any farther, and agreed to turn back.

The goal of sailing to Cathay was not realized, yet the promise of success was so tantalizingly close, the Amsterdam merchants determined they would prepare a second expedition. This time the fleet was made larger, consisting of seven vessels, and all who participated in the previous expedition took part again. To ensure success, all the vessels carried twice the normal complement of men and provisions – enough to last for more than one and a half years. Such was the confidence that a route could be found, that this time it was more than an exploratory voyage; the holds of the ships were filled with merchandise and money to initiate trade with China and other countries visited along the way.

All the ships were to proceed to Vaygach Strait and make a concentrated effort to sail through into the Kara Sea. Unlike the previous summer, when the strait displayed itself in a benign manner, this time ice quickly shut them in and stopped any progress. Feeling they had done their best and could do no more, six of the ships abandoned their attempt, and steered for home. Barentsz decided to continue, and steered north to reach the Kara Sea by sailing around the north end of Nova Zembla. But for all his perseverance, he was defeated. With a worn out and near rebellious crew, and winter fast approaching, Barentsz capitulated to the wishes of the others and returned to Amsterdam.

Peter Plancius believed that Barentsz had not sailed far enough north before turning east, reasoning that ice forms only along the shore and not in the open polar sea. With his support, Barentsz was able to convince the merchants to finance a trans-polar expedition. They provided two ships, which were commanded by Jan Corneliszoon Rijp and Jacob van Heemskerck; Barentsz was employed only as chief pilot, apparently to prevent him attempting another impractical passage through Vaygach Strait. The small fleet made rapid progress, and by 1 June they were already above the Arctic Circle and experiencing the midnight Sun. But once they reached 74° N, ice

began to appear and plague their progress. They managed to sail through it, but the farther they went, the thicker the ice became. When land was sighted, the men were given the opportunity to row ashore in the ship's boats to stretch their legs and explore the island. To this desolate plateau rising to a group of three mountains on its western shore Barentsz gave the name of Bear Island, and the solitary hill at its southern extremity he appropriately named Mount Misery. He calculated the latitude of the island with remarkable accuracy as 74° 30'N, off by only 52 seconds of arc (0.9 nautical miles).

From Bear Island the two ships continued sailing north, and at latitude 79° 30'N they again saw land. Because of the vast quantities of floating ice, and the large size of the island, they first thought this new land to be Greenland, and named it *Nieuland* (New Land). Actually, they were well to the eastward of Greenland at the island now called Spitzbergen. Ice prevented them from circumnavigating it, but they did explore a large portion of its western shore and a small portion of its northern coast. Unable to extricate themselves from the ice closing in on them, they were forced to return to Bear Island. There the two ships divided, with Jan Corneliszoon Rijp making a renewed attempt to sail northward in the expectation that somewhere under 80° latitude there would be a passage through to the east side of Nieuland. Blocked by ice, he returned to Holland.

Barentsz sailed south, and headed for the northeast corner of Nova Zembla. Here too ice prevented sailing any farther, and when his vessel was totally enclosed with ice he and his men were obliged to overwinter. Driftwood found on the shore enabled the men to build a small hut, and provided fuel to give a bit of heat throughout the winter. They endured ten months confined in the cruel climate of Nova Zembla, but of the seventeen men, only two died – most likely of scurvy. Their ship did not fare as well; not only was it damaged and made unseaworthy, but also it proved impossible to set free from the crushing grip of ice. Two small, open ship's boats were their only chance for survival, and in these they set forth

239. View on Norskøyene on Spitsbergen by Franz Wilhelm Schiertz, 1879

Although Viking or Russian sailors may have visited Spitsbergen as early as the twelfth century, its discovery is attributed to Willem Barentz in 1569. When Barentsz first reached Spitsbergen he believed that it was Greenland, and called it by that name. Only that portion north of 80° latitude did he call *Nieuland*. It wasn't until 1613 that the name of Spitsbergen was ascribed to it by the publisher Hessel Gerritsz. Dutch cartographers, however, called it Nieuland, which later was changed by the English King James to Newland. Today, under Norwegian sovereignty it is called Svalbard, literally meaning 'cold edge.'

THE NATIONAL MUSEUM OF ART, ARCHITECTURE AHN DESIGN, OSLO

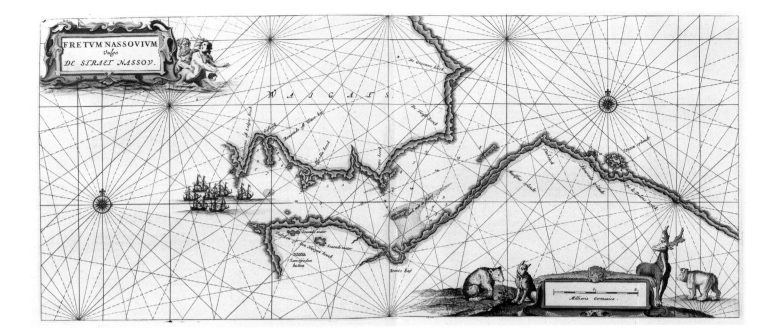

to sail and row homeward. Perceiving he had not long to live, Barentsz's last thoughts were of the well-being of others, and he gave to van Heemskerck directions for the course he must steer. On the seventh day, Barentsz died, a victim perhaps not so much of the harsh climate, as from the undeniable defeat of his cherished dream of sailing to Cathay.

For a short while, the Dutch benefited from the whaling stations on Spitzbergen, and the trade in walrus ivory. The failure of Barentsz's voyage ended their attempts to find a Northeast Passage, and efforts were re-directed southward toward the Spice Islands in the Pacific. The formation in 1602 of the Dutch East India Company led to the rapid development of commercial routes around the Cape of Good Hope to Ceylon, the East Indies and Japan.

FAILURES UNENDING

Henry Hudson

Despite its many attempts to find the Northeast Passage, all ending in death and failure, the possibility of success in such a venture seemed so much within grasp, and if accomplished, the rewards to be so great, that the Muscovy Company of England decided to renew its efforts. They hired Henry Hudson (c. 1550–1611) to seek the shortest, the fastest, and hence most profitable, route to Cathay.

On this, the first of Henry Hudson's four voyages of exploration, he attempted to sail directly over the North Pole, a route believed possible, but as yet untried. Hudson left England on 1 May 1607 in his frail bark, the *Hope-well*. From Barentsz's earlier expedition to Spitzbergen, Hudson knew precisely what to expect when he arrived there. Sailing north, he explored Spitzbergen's great bays and sounds, grasping for any evidence

240. The Strait of Nassau by Joan Blaeu, 1662

Yugur Shar, the strait between Waygatch Island and the Russian mainland, leading to the Kara Sea, is seen here as charted during the Barentsz expeditions in 1594–1596.

THE NATIONAL LIBRARY OF FINLAND, HELSINKI

241. The Whale Fishery and Killing the Bears by John Harris, 1780

In the sixteenth to eighteenth centuries, Spitzbergen was the whaling centre for Dutch, English, French and Norwegian fleets. It has been estimated that the Dutch alone took over 60,000 whales from here for their meat, baleen, and especially the valuable oil boiled down from the blubber. So lucrative was the whaling industry at Spitzbergen that it was called the 'Northern Goldfield'.

JOHN NURMINEN FOUNDATION

that might support the theory by Thorne and Plancius of an open Polar ocean. Ultimately, he came to within 577 nautical miles of the North Pole, to 80° 23' N latitude – a navigational record that would not be exceeded for the next 100 years. 'This I am sure now', Hudson wrote, 'that between 78° 30' and 82° there is no passage by this way. But I think this land may be profitable to those that will adventure it'.

The following year Hudson again set out under the auspices of the Muscovy Company to explore the Arctic. This time he planned to investigate two routes to the Kara Sea: the sea north of Nova Zembla, and the deep indentation at the southern end of Nova Zembla, Costing Sarch, to determine whether it was a strait or river through the main body of Nova Zembla. Upon reaching the Kara Sea he intended to pass north of the River Ob and from there, by following the coast of Siberia, be able to round Cape Tabin, the final impediment to sailing into the Pacific Ocean.

Hudson left England on 22 April 1608, once again in the *Hope-well*, and headed north along the coast of Norway. When

The WHALE FISHERY and KILLING the BEARS.

The Whale *from which the* Bone *is* Taken.

The Whale Louse.

A Spear.

A Herpoon.

The Fin Fish.

The Sea Unicorn.

The Morse.

242. The Henry Hudson Map by Theodore de Bry and Hessel Gerritsz, 1613

The map drawn by Hudson on his voyage in 1610–1611 survived the mutiny, and upon return of the vessel *Discovery* to England, was sent to Peter Plancius in Holland, where it was engraved and published by Hessel Gerritsz. Hudson recognized and corrected many errors of Greenland's geography on earlier maps, and in spite of its several shortcomings in topographic details it was far more accurate than those of any other contemporary cartographers. The lack of land at the western side of Hudson Bay implied that it was the passage to China and Japan, and kept alive the search for the Northwest Passage for the next 150 years.

JOHN NURMINEN FOUNDATION

he tried using the Costing Sarch to gain access to the Kara Sea, the strength of the current he encountered there, both on the flood and ebb tide, encouraged hope that it would be kept clear of ice. But again Hudson was to be disappointed. Had he succeeded in pushing his way through the ice, he would have found that Costing Sarch was only a deep bay, and not a strait leading to the Kara Sea.

Henry Hudson once again attempted to find a northern route to the Orient, this time sailing under the Dutch flag. Before 1579, the Netherlands were a diverse group of provinces lacking any national unity, held together only by geography and common language, and owing a feudal obligation to the Habsburg emperor Charles V (1500-1558), and to his successor, Philip II of Spain. William of Orange (1533-1584) led a revolt against Spain's tyranny and religious intolerance, with the result that, at the Union of Utrecht in 1579, seven of the provinces united and proclaimed their political and religious freedom from Spain. An independent state was formed, called the Republic of the Seven United Provinces.

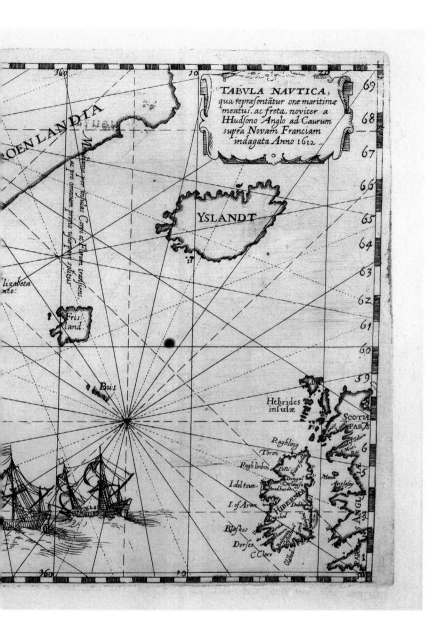

This Republic was to become the cornerstone of the Dutch Republic.

Until 1580, Dutch ships were able to engage in trade, carrying spices from the port of Lisbon to the rest of Europe. But with the death in 1580 of Henry of Portugal (1512-1580), the Burgundian Cardinal, and great-uncle of King Sebastian of Portugal, and the seizure of the Portuguese crown by Philip II of Spain (1527-1598), the entire political situation changed. With Portugal under Spanish authority, Dutch ships could no longer enter Lisbon. They were forced to venture farther afield, sailing directly to the Far East.

The United East India Company, *De Verenigde Oost-Indische Compagnie,* which was formed in 1602, sought the Northeast Passage. They contacted the English navigator Henry Hudson, whose earlier explorations in 1607 and 1608 to reach Cathay by sailing directly over the North Pole were well known.

Hudson's contract stipulated that he was 'to think of discovering no other route or passage, except the route around the north or northeast, above Nova Zembla'. On 25 March 1609

he set sail from Amsterdam. But when his ship had barely reached North Cape, Norway, there was a threatened mutiny and Hudson turned west to cross the Atlantic Ocean to search for a passage to Cathay in that direction. Two possibilities remained open: either through the strait with its 'furious overfall', described by John Davis, or through the strait Davis called Lumley's Inlet, now known as Frobisher Bay.

It was conceivable too, that in latitudes south of 40°N latitude there might be a strait, sound or river leading to a Western Sea from Chesapeake Bay. From there, perhaps by travelling through the Great Lakes, it might be possible to pass into the Pacific Ocean. This idea was expressed in a letter to Hudson by his acquaintance, Captain John Smith (1580–1631), founder of the Virginia colony at Jamestown.

Hudson tried several times to enter the Chesapeake, but gave up efforts in that direction and continued his exploration northward. The large river that now bears his name seemed a likely possibility for reaching the Pacific. Hudson sailed it as far as was navigable, but with the realization that this could not be the elusive passage, he turned homeward.

Returning again into English service, Hudson obtained financial backing from an independent group of London Merchant Adventurers, and set out in 1610 to continue the search north of 60°N latitude. He headed directly for the strait with its 'furious overfall' .Now called Hudson Strait, the passage was a constant battle against swift currents and threat of destruction from the ever-present ice. Hudson was in despair, thinking he would never get out of the ice, but would perish there. Finally, he broke through to enter the bay, and by all indications – the open sea that lay ahead and the direction of the tides – success had finally been attained. Instead of continuing west to bring the voyage to a successful conclusion, or returning to England prematurely like Frobisher and Davis before he had established his discovery beyond doubt, Hudson proceeded to sail as far south as was physically possible. Being already too late in the year to attempt a return voyage, the expedition over-wintered in James Bay.

The following spring, with a crew much diminished in number due to starvation and disease, he set out to return to England. Before they left Hudson Bay there was a mutiny and Hudson with eleven others were put out in the ship's pinnace, and left to drift into oblivion. Those who survived the two years of Arctic hardships finally made it back to England, bringing with them the false news that the Northwest Passage had finally 'been found'.

The probability of their being an outlet to Hudson Bay in the north or west, leading to the Pacific, was so firmly held that in the following decades many other mariners sought to be its first discoverer. In 1613, Sir Thomas Button (d. 1634) was confident he would prove the existence of this passage; as an afterthought, he might also be able to rescue the abandoned Henry Hudson and his men. He did neither. In an expedition two years later, Robert Bylot, who had sailed with Hudson on

Ocean Perils

243. A Bathing Party, HMS *Clio* by Thomas Somerscales, c.1902

The mood conveyed in this painting of a ship in the doldrums is one of peacefulness and relaxation. The crew is taking the opportunity to enjoy a bathing party in the water. In reality, however, the situation is fraught with anxiety and is one of increasing despair. As the ship hangs motionless in the water, baking in the hot Sun, its planks dry out; the sails slat back and forth taking more of a beating than when under the constant pressure of wind in a storm; food and water supplies diminish; and minor problems and frustrations among the crew magnify into dangerous conflicts.

N.R. OMELL GALLERY, LONDON

244. *La Favorite*: under sail for Bourbon [Réunion Island] at the approach of the second hurricane, 1833–1839

A hurricane presents the ultimate challenge to vessel and man. When Captain Cyrille-Pierre-Théodore Laplace was sent by France in 1829 to explore the Indian and Pacific Oceans to gather information in order to improve and promote overseas trade, he was unfortunate enough to encounter two ferocious hurricanes. His vessel, *La Favorite*, shown here, survived both storms, and Laplace was able to sail *La Favorite* to the intended destination.

LINDA HALL LIBRARY OF SCIENCE, ENGINEERING AND TECHNOLOGY, KANSAS CITY

Storms pose one of the greatest threats to mariners. Huge waves washing over the deck, rigging torn apart, sails blown to shreds, and masts and yardarms splintered into useless sticks, generate a struggle for survival – perhaps even cause the vessel to sink. Violent winds may drive a ship helplessly onto shore, with the certainty of destruction. Rare is the ocean voyager who has not at one time or another had to endure the wrath or suffer losses from severe storms.

No storm at sea is greater than the fury unleashed by a 'tropical cyclone'. The nomenclature of tropical cyclones varies throughout the globe. Spawned in warm, tropical or subtropical waters, the hurricane is a regionally specific name for a strong tropical cyclone. In the North Atlantic Ocean, and in the northeast Pacific Ocean east of the international date line (roughly at or near 180°, opposite the Prime Meridian of 0° longitude), and in the south Pacific Ocean east of 160° E longitude, these storms are called hurricanes. In the southwest Indian Ocean this type of storm retains its generic name of tropical cyclone. In the western Pacific they are termed typhoons, derived from the Cantonese *t'ai fung*, meaning a 'great wind'.

In order for tropical cyclones to form, many conditions are required, the two most important being the formation of an intense low-pressure system and warm ocean water with a temperature of at least 80° Fahrenheit. A rapidly cooling atmosphere that is potentially unstable and a minimum distance from the equator of at least 300 miles in order for the Coriolis effect to maintain the low-pressure disturbance are further causes. There must be sustained winds of 74 mph (33 m/s, 64 knots) to qualify being called a hurricane.

Christopher Columbus was fortunate enough not to have encountered any major hurricanes during his transatlantic voyages, but he quickly gained knowledge of the conditions causing them. While in Santo Domingo in 1502, he warned Spanish admirals to postpone departure of a fleet of treasure vessels returning to Spain. As a result of his unheeded advice, the flotilla sailed directly into a hurricane, sending twenty-four ships, hundreds of men and a fortune in gold to the bottom of the sea.

The history of European exploration and settlement in North America has been altered by hurricanes. From their centre in Mexico, Spanish colonists spread north and east along the Gulf Coast toward a land called Florida. Settlements at the eastern end of the Gulf of Mexico were important to serve as a barrier against English and French incursions southward into what Spain considered her domain. Colonies in Florida were also necessary to protect Spanish treasure fleets from piracy as they left the Caribbean for Spain.

An attempt made by Don Tristán de Luna y Arellano in 1559 to create a Spanish colony in Florida was prevented by a hurricane destroying almost all of his fleet. And in 1564, when French Huguenots (Protestants, Lutherans) established a fledging colony in what is now Pensacola, Florida, a hurricane destroyed French vessels coming to the aid of the settlement, and could not avert its destruction and massacre by the Spanish.

In the Pacific Ocean, typhoons have also had an effect on world history. Kublai Khan, military leader of the Mongol Empire (1260–94), and founder and first Emperor (1279–94) of the Chinese Yuan Dynasty, attempted in 1274 to expand the Mongol Empire through the conquest of Japan. His fleet was turned away by the intervention of a typhoon. Seven years later he made another attempt, this time with a fleet of 1170 ships and an army of 100,000 Mongols. Most of the fleet was destroyed by a typhoon. In honour of this fortuitous typhoon that saved Japan from its first foreign invasion, the Japanese named it *kamikaze*, translated as divine wind.

Ocean storms need not attain the strength of a hurricane to cause savage effects on ships. In the battle of Sevastopol during the Crimean War (1854–56), an intense early winter storm struck the French and British fleets bringing supplies. This famous storm resulted in the sinking of twenty-one British vessels and severe French losses, prompting the British Admiralty and French Marine to jointly create a weather network to forecast future storms and provide warnings. From this, the Beaufort wind scale categorizing the force of winds, was developed in 1806.

The absence of any wind is equally abhorred by sailors, and can be just as destructive. With sails hanging limp and lifeless, the ship remains motionless for days, weeks and even months at a time. During this period of waiting for a breeze to spring up, supplies of water and food gradually diminish, along with the morale and discipline of the men. The ship's planking dries and shrinks, requiring constant caulking. A passage slowed by calms can also mean a severe economic loss to investors in trade ships.

By necessity, mariners of northern Europe on their spice-trade voyages had to pass through two broad bands of calms to reach their goal. At the latitude of roughly 35°N to 30°N the winds are predominantly very light, and the weather is hot and dry. The same occurs in the southern hemisphere in the same latitude range. These bands of calm are known respectively as the calm of Cancer and the calm of Capricorn, but seamen call them the Horse Latitudes, believed to be named such because when becalmed for a long time, sailors threw the horses (carried as cargo to the West Indies) overboard in order to conserve a dwindling water supply. Both bands of calms shift north and south with the corresponding shift in the declination of the Sun.

The equatorial region presents another belt of calms. Sailors call this place the Doldrums; meteorologists have several names for it: equatorial trough, meteorological equator, and the inter-tropical convergence zone. Lying between the northeast trade winds in the northern hemisphere, and the southeast trades in the southern hemisphere, it is a nearly continuous trough of atmospheric low pressure, with light and variable winds. It can also give rise to sudden storms, which, if conditions are right, develop into tropical cyclones. Like the calms of the Horse Latitudes, the Doldrums shift with the season.

Another hazard to sailing vessels is the waterspout, a form of tornado that occurs over water. They are characterized by a sharply defined column of rising warm air and water vapour reaching to, and connected with a cumuliform cloud. Generally, they form in the subtropics during the warm season, but they are not limited to this area or time. Unlike hurricanes that cover an area of hundreds of miles, waterspout diametres are measured in metres, ranging from only a few metres to a hundred metres. Also, unlike hurricanes, waterspouts are short-lived. But to a slow-moving ship, unable to get out of the way, their wind speed reaching up to 195 mph can be just as destructive as a hurricane.

John Davis, while exploring the shore north of Gilbert Sound in Greenland during his voyage in 1586, witnessed a waterspout. In his journal, Davis wrote:

'...myself espied a very strange sight...which was a mighty whirlewinde taking up the water in a very great quantity furiously, mounting it into the ayre ...since it was in the course that it should passe, we were constrained that night to take by our lodging under the rocks'.

Odysseus, in his epic voyage (Homer's *Odyssey*, Book XII), chose to lose some of his sailors to the horrible six-headed monster of Scylla than to risk the destruction of his entire ship to the other monster Charybdis, who, in a narrow channel of water, sucks down black water and spouts it forth forming an enormous whirlpool. Traditionally, this whirlpool, caused by the meeting of currents, has been placed at the Strait of Messina off the coast of Sicily. Recent scholarship suggests that a more likely location is off Cape Skilla in northwest Greece.

Equally well known for the strength of its currents and dangerous whirlpool is the Moskenes Maelstrom, off the coast of Norway. Called the Charybdis of the north, this whirlpool is the result of the differences between rising and falling tides. Half way between the tides, the current changes direction. When this occurs, whirlpools form, and currents attain speeds of up to six knots. Authors in the seventeenth and eighteenth century described this whirlpool in terms no less fantastic than those of Homer. While the Maelstrom may not 'drag ships under, smashing them to smithereens against the sea bed', mariners treat this dangerous bit of sea with care and respect.

245. A View of Cape Stephens in Cook´s Straits with Waterspout by William Hodges, 1776

In this, his second voyage (1772–1775), Captain James Cook was sent by the British Admiralty to search for the postulated continent of *Terra Australis Incognita* (Antartica). Accompanying him in the *Resolution* was William Hodges as the official artist on this expedition. At the strait (now bearing Cook's name) separating New Zealand's North Island from the South Island, at Cape Stephens they witnessed a waterspout which Hodges captured in oils. A waterspout may be likened to a tornado over land, but rather than the wind funnelling down from clouds to touch the Earth, the wind reaches upward from the water's surface toward the clouds.

NATIONAL MARITIME MUSEUM, LONDON

246. Tropical Cyclones

At sea level in the northern hemisphere, winds circulate in a counter-clockwise direction (clockwise in the southern hemisphere) toward the centre of a low-pressure system; there, they ascend to the upper atmosphere where the water vapour is cooled and condensed, and heat that has been absorbed from the ocean released. The 'eye wall' in the very centre of the storm is the result of cool air sinking; it is here that the dense wall of thunderstorms and the strongest winds are found. In the northern hemisphere, upper-level outflow of air spills out in a clockwise spiral.

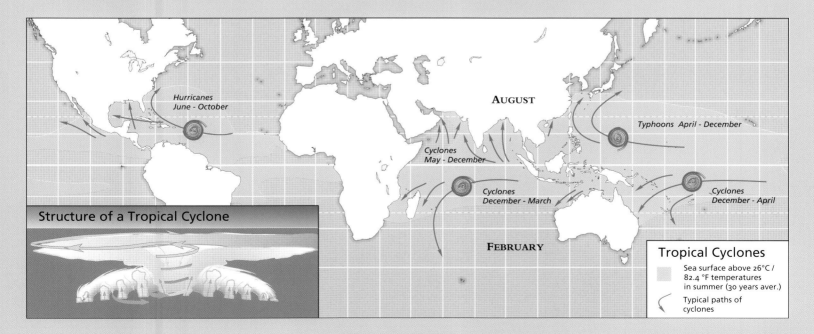

Hurricanes
June - October

AUGUST

Typhoons April - December

Cyclones
May - December

Cyclones
December - March

Cyclones
December - April

FEBRUARY

Structure of a Tropical Cyclone

Tropical Cyclones

Sea surface above 26°C / 82.4 °F temperatures in summer (30 years aver.)

Typical paths of cyclones

the 1610–11 voyage, fared no better.

Following these failures, Captain Jens Munk (1579–1628) was commissioned in 1619 by Christian IV, King of Denmark and Norway, to find the Northwest Passage. Having succeeded on entering Hudson Bay, he sailed to the southwest coast to look for any possible exit there, and then was forced to overwinter at the estuary of the Churchill River on the western shore of the bay. Of the sixty-four sailors that started out with the expedition, only Munk and two others survived the deadly outbreak of scurvy, to return home. These three, weakened by disease and starvation, in an amazing achievement of seafaring managed to sail one of the vessels across the Atlantic to Norway, and back to Copenhagen. The map Munk prepared of his expedition was the first to depict this vast inland sea in its entirety; he gave it the name of *Novum Mare Christian*.

English efforts to find a Northwest Passage through Hudson Bay were continued with the voyages of Captain Thomas James (c. 1593–1635) in the *Mary*, from Bristol, and Captain Luke Foxe (1586–1635) in the *Charles*, from London. Both were commissioned by King Charles I of England (1600–1649), and both left in the same year of 1631. Captain Zachariah Gillam, in the ketch *Nonsuch*, went into Baffin's Bay where he sailed as far as 75°N latitude. From there, he entered Hudson Bay and explored it as far south as 51°N latitude. By now, any further exploration in Hudson Bay was judged to be fruitless.

FROM DOCTRINE AND DISCOVERY
TO A PLACE ON THE MAP

By the close of the sixteenth century, the Dutch Republic was a major sea power with a wide and complex trade network; her vessels carried Baltic grain, herring from the coasts of England, Scotland and Greenland, and wine, silver and salt from Spain and France. Dutch mariners needed better sailing instructions than those currently available, which were generally of modest size, and contained crudely drawn woodcuts that allowed for scant hydrographic detail. Certain moments in history are favoured by a simultaneous combination of events that bring forth an innovative work. Such is the case with the publication in 1584–85 of a sea-atlas, *De Spieghel der Zeevaerdt* (The Mariner's Mirror), at Leiden in the province south of Holland.

Lucas Janszoon Waghenaer

Born in Enkhuizen, a small fishing port on the Zuider Zee in the Province of North Holland, Lucas Janszoon Waghenaer (c. 1533–1606) grew up surrounded by talk about the sea and of shipping. In his youth he became a seaman and an accomplished pilot, serving in that capacity until he retired. He knew from personal experience the importance of having good charts and reliable sailing directions. In a manner unprecedented, he joined an atlas of sea charts with a manual of sailing instructions to provide in a single work all the information a navigator required to sail the coasts and waters of northern and western Europe. The generous size of the book allowed the charts to be sufficiently large to show offshore details – rocks, shoals and any other navigational hazards – as well as aids to navigation such as buoys, beacons and anchorages. For the first time tidal data was given on charts, and soundings were shown, specified in fathoms.

To further assist the pilot in identifying his position, Waghenaer placed on the chart profile views of the coast, as one would observe them in approaching from the sea. Elaborate cartouches, colourful sea monsters and ships in full sail decorated the unessential spaces. As well, a number of symbols indicated shipwrecks, submerged rocks, towns and bridges, which to this day are still employed.

To avoid confusion and error, all the charts were drawn to the same scale, and the same symbols used consistently throughout the charts. These were arranged in the logical progression for making a voyage. At the beginning of the sequence of charts, Waghenaer placed a general chart of northwest Europe to be used for overall planning. This, he followed with more detailed charts: two of the Netherlands, seven of France, and nine of Spain and Portugal. The port of Cádiz was the southernmost extent of the collection. To these he later added twenty-two charts extending the atlas northward from the Netherlands to include the North Sea, Norwegian Sea and the Baltic Sea. Each map was marked with three scales indicating the number of leagues to a degree: 20 to an English degree, 17½ to a French degree, and 15 leagues to a Dutch degree. In keeping with this very systematic approach, the back of each chart contained a verbal commentary, the sailing directions which completed all the information needed for navigation in unfamiliar waters.

As an accomplished pilot and hydrographer, Waghenaer realized the necessity for a mariner to know the principles and practices of navigation. In his own words: 'that which any man...exerciseth, searcheth out and observeth himselfe, sticketh faster in memory than that which he learneth from others'. Therefore, at the beginning of his book he included thirty-six pages of instructions on all matters relating to navigation, some of which had never before been printed. These included: a diagram showing how to find out the new Moon without a calendar or ephemerides, a listing of the fixed stars and their use, declination of the Sun and the use thereof, how to find the tides of all coasts, and how the navigator should make and use his own personal chart.

He provided tables of the altitudes or latitudes of the pole of the most famous places, points and capes, and instructions on the way to find the height of the pole by the stars that are visible between the tropic of Cancer and the tropic of Capricorn. Bound within the book was a volvelle, a construction of

247. Preparing the winter quarters at Churchill River on the western shore of Hudson Bay, 1619–20

Jens Munk's arrival in Hudson Bay was so late in the year that he was forced to overwinter on its western shore near the mouth of what is now called Churchill River. Lack of vitamin C caused such a severe outbreak of scurvy that by spring there were only three survivors. Incredibly, Munk and the two others sailed one of the vessels back to Norway.

UNIVERSITY LIBRARY OF TROMSÖ

moveable paper discs that allowed the navigator to make his own calculations. Waghenaer gave instructions on the finding of the latitude and how to make the latitude graduations on a cross-staff. And an elaborate wind-rose showed the number of leagues that must be sailed for each rhumb to raise a degree. In short, Waghenaer created in his *De Spieghel der Zeevaerdt* a veritable encyclopedia of navigational knowledge, both theoretical and practical.

Prompted by Dutch envoys in London that an edition be printed in Latin, the *lingua franca* for all geographic works in the international market, Waghenaer's *De Spieghel* was translated and published in Latin in 1586. English pilots, however, less familiar with Latin, needed a translation into their own tongue. For this, new plates were engraved, copied from the originals and complete in all details – including coastal profiles, soundings, anchorages, and all other hydrographic and cartographic detail – even as to ornamentation. Only two changes were made: place names were turned into their English forms, and the engraved pattern used to depict water was removed. In the original Dutch plates that had been engraved by the van Doetecum brothers, who also engraved many of the important maps of Plancius, a purely decorative, overall pattern of wave-

lets filled in the watery segments of the map. In the English edition the sea was purposely left blank. This way the navigator could make any corrections he might find, and add his own observations on the location of rocks, depths, and other information, thereby continually keeping the chart up to date. The English edition published under the title of *The Mariners Mirrour* in 1588 was extremely successful. The charts were so popular that Waghenaer's anglicized name of 'Waggoner' came to be a generic name referring to any sea-atlas.

In 1592 Waghenaer produced a second pilot book entitled *Thresoor der Zeevaert* (Treatise on the Art of Navigation). The style in all respects remained the same as in *De Spieghel*, with

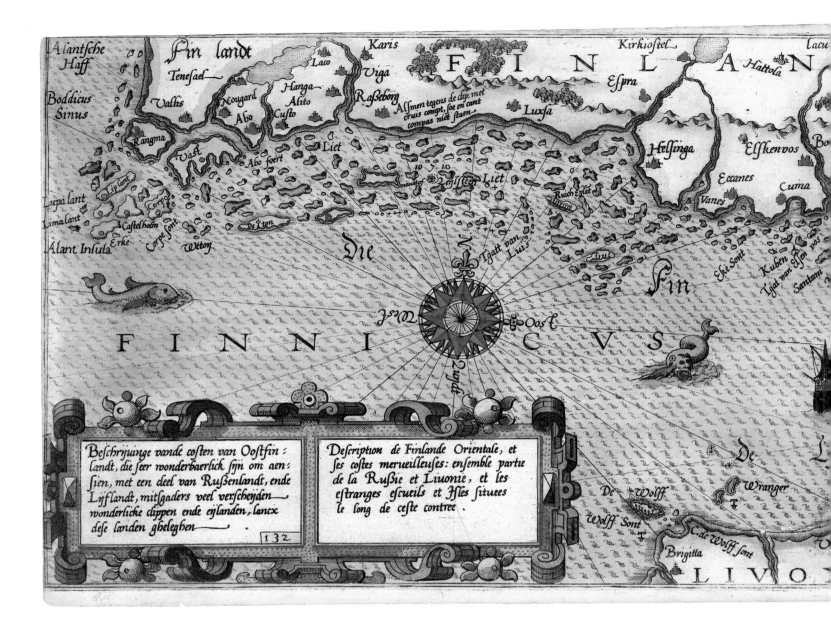

carefully delineated coastal drawings and detailed harbour plans, but they were modified somewhat to fit a smaller format. Where new information had become available since the printing of *De Spieghel*, he incorporated corrections and additions into the earlier charts. Waghenaer also added new charts, extending the original coverage to include the White Sea as far as Nova Zembla, the Straits of Gibraltar, and Andalusia as far as Malaga.

Peter Plancius

Peter Plancius (1552–1622) had been born and raised in Flanders, but he was forced to seek refuge in the Dutch Republic to avoid religious persecution. There, as one of the leaders of the Calvinist party and minister of the Reformed Church of Amsterdam, he pursued his interests in cosmography and astronomy and became a recognized authority on geography. His studies earned him the role of official cartographer for the Dutch East India Company. Peter Plancius had provided charts to aid Barentsz in his quest in northern waters, and now he turned his attention to providing the same material for Dutch mariners in southern waters.

In 1597, the first Dutch ship returned from a voyage to India,

and in the following year, expeditions to the East increased to twenty-two ships. After the formation of the Dutch East India Company in 1602, the number of ships sailing to the East Indies in a single year had become a torrent of eighty-nine ships. Plancius helped plan these southern voyages and instructed its navigators on how to measure star positions with an astrolabe, and how to chart the southern sky. Waghenaer's sea-atlas, which had previously served Dutch mariners so well, now was seriously deficient, for its charts terminated at the Straits of Gibraltar. In addition for coastal charts in extended latitudes, Dutch pilots needed the ability to set their course on the high seas, out of sight of land, and where the sky presented a totally unfamiliar picture.

With the secrets gained from Spanish and Portuguese navigators, and with the help of English mariners who by their skill and experience furthered the science of navigation, Plancius set up a school of navigation in Enkhuysen. The Dutch translation in 1580 of Michel Coignet's (1549–1623), *Nieuwe Onderwysinghe op de principaelste puncten der Zeewert*, and of William Bourne's *A Regiment for the Sea* in 1594, had made them readily accessible to Plancius. Also at his disposal was the navigation manual, *L'arte del Navegar* (Art of Navigation) by Pedro de Medina, who in service of the Casa de Contratación taught mathematics and navigation to Spanish pilots. As well

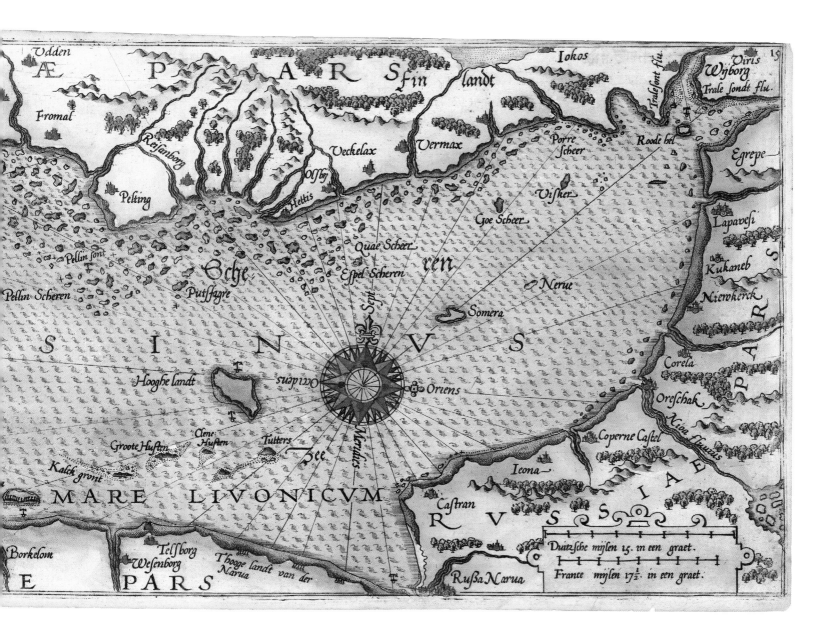

248. The Gulf of Finland by Lucas Janszoon Waghenaer, 1598

In 1592, Waghenaer published his second atlas, which was entitled *Thresoor der Zeevaert*. It shows, for example, the route from Vyborg in the eastern part of the Gulf of Finland to the Aland Sea, west of the Gulf. The Finnish coast was considered strange and its rocky waters and islands peculiar, as is mentioned in the cartouche of the map. According to Waghenaer, Utö was a large island with a mast that had a barrel in its top. He also mentions that near *Seylstein* along the route to Turku, the compass needle merely spins and will not settle until the ship is at least a mile away from it.

JUHA NURMINEN COLLECTION

249. Frontispiece of *De Spieghel der Zeevaerdt* by Lucas Janszoon Waghenaer, 1586

The engraving depicts various contemporary navigational aids, including the quadrant, the mariner's astrolabe and the cross-staff.

THE NATIONAL LIBRARY OF FINLAND, HELSINKI

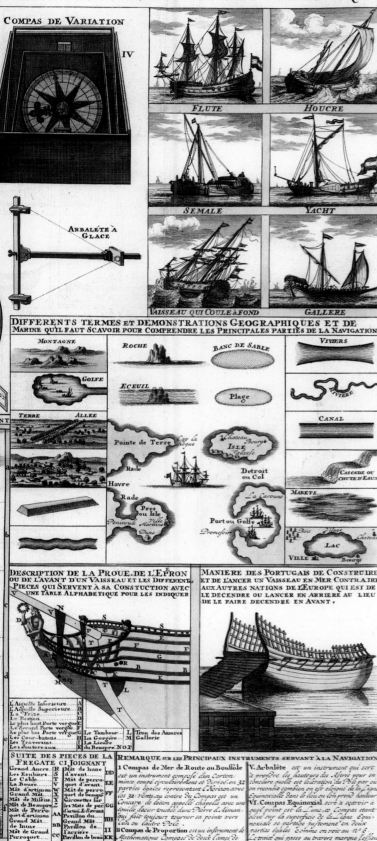

250. Highly-detailed instructive broadsheet by Henri Abraham Châtelain, 1705-1720

This broadsheet provides a host of information on ship building, navigational devices, various types of ship and even groupings in naval battle. Ship types on the top row at left and right, a wind-rose in the middle (III), scale rulers on both sides of it, the main compass of a ship (I) and a compass used to determine variation (IV). Below, variations of the Jacob's staff used for measuring declination, a sundial (VI), a backstaff (VII), a nocturnal used to determine the precise position of the celestial pole with the help of the North Star and to determine local time based on the attitude of the Little Bear (VIII). In the middle there are battle and convoy groupings, and at right definitions of geographical terms. The pictures at the bottom show the structure of a frigate and the names of its masts, yards, rigging and hull sections.

JUHA NURMINEN COLLECTION

as instructing navigators on the use of astrolabe and cross-staff, he taught them how to measure and record magnetic variation from true north, believing, as did other theorists of the day, that longitude could be determined from the variation (declination) of the magnetic compass. The training Plancius's school provided to Dutch mariners allowed the Dutch Republic to become a serious commercial rival to Spain.

In his capacity as official cartographer, Plancius took this information brought back to him and incorporated it into his charts and globes. As one of the founders of both the Dutch East India Company and, in 1621, the Dutch West India Company, he had a personal financial stake in the creation of accurate charts. These charts, with their increasing latitudes were drawn using Mercator's new projection plan and published by the printer Cornelis Claesz. From them, Plancius also made manuscript copies, and provided sailing instructions for use on the second Dutch expedition to the East Indies in 1598. In all, Plancius produced over a hundred individual maps, and greatly influenced the work of other cartographers at the end of the sixteenth century.

The Dutch Flute

At the beginning of the seventeenth century a new and remarkable type of merchant vessel appeared on the seas. It was the Dutch flute, which came to hold a key position in the success of the Dutch foreign trade, as they were to sail on the European sea-trades for more than 200 years. When other nations focused on building warships, the Dutch designed a cargo vessel, which was very economic to build and operate. Dutch shipbuilding was in a league of its own compared to other seafaring nations. Amsterdam became the most important port in Europe, and on some occasions more than one hundred vessels were in the port simultaneously.

The flute had a spacious cargo hold, which was larger than in other ships at the time. In addition to that, it had such a shallow draft that it could sail on rivers and call at the small ports. It had a rather flat bottom and was a relatively long and narrow ship. The lower part of the hull was round and wide, but above the waterline the sides turned inwards, which created a narrow weather deck and pointed bow; the castle to aft was also narrow and high. The purpose of this design was to avoid the toll in the Sound, which was determined by the amidships dimensions of the vessel. When the taxation system changed in 1669, the weather deck of the flute became wider.

The construction of flutes was to a great extent standardized, and mechanized by the use of wind-powered sawmills. Pine was widely used as a building material because it was cheap, plentiful and easily worked. However, it was not as strong as oak, and Dutch flutes required regular maintenance and repair.

The flute turned out to have good sailing qualities even though it was not very fast. It had three masts, of which the fore mast and the main mast usually had two square sails and the mizzenmast a lateen sail. Because of its simple rigging the flute was easy to handle at sea and did not demand a large crew. In England there were complaints that the Dutch only required a third of the crew used on English ships of corresponding size. A reason for this was that the English merchantmen had three masts and carried

251. Whaling in Spitsbergen by Fredrik Martensen, 1675

The flute was often used for whaling in Arctic waters. These vessels were equipped with stronger masts and the planking in the bow was strengthened to withstand ice. This picture shows whalers at Spitsbergen towards the end of the seventeenth century.

JUHA NURMINEN COLLECTION

252. Model of a Flute

The Dutch flute carried cargo in short routes on the North European sea lanes. It was a reliable and safe ship type, and the building and operating costs were low. The flute was three-masted, and the handling of the simple rig demanded only a handful of men. In its large hold many types of cargo could be carried.

JOHN NURMINEN FOUNDATION

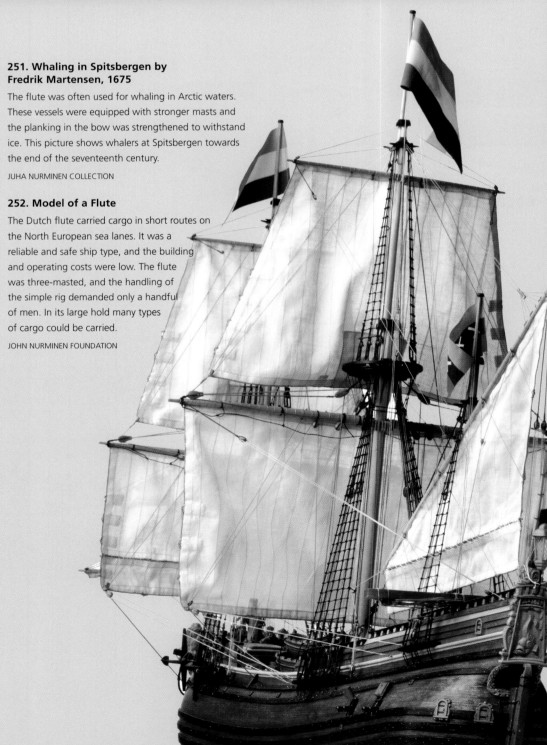

FRETI DANICI OR SVNDT ACCVRATISS DELINEATIO.

253. The Öresund by Georg Braun and Frans Hogenberg, 1588

This image depicts Öresund (the sound between Denmark and Sweden) as seen from the Kronborg castle and the town of Helsingör, looking toward the lighthouse on the Kullen headland, Helsingborg, Landskrona, Malmö (Elbogen) and the island of Ven with Uraniborg. The Kronborg Castle is situated at the narrowest point of the sound. The castle was built to enforce the collection of Sound Dues from all ships that entered or left the Baltic, at the behest of the Danish King (Erik of Pomerania). The Sound Dues were one of the most important income sources for the Danish Crown for several centuries. The picture of the sound is from *Civitates Orbis Terrarum* from 1588. It was the first atlas containing over 350 bird's-eye views and plans of the world's major cities.

JOHN NURMINEN FOUNDATION

topgallant sails. They were more like warships, as they could carry up to 28 guns on deck.

The commercial success of the Netherlands underlined the enormous benefits of the flute and it soon became the most important type of freighter in Europe. It was designed for carrying large amounts of cargo at a low cost and no extra money was spent on decoration. In their holds they could carry virtually any cargo. Some flutes were designed for carrying wood and were able to load logs longer than the vessel itself due to a door in the stern. The grain carriers had watertight cargo holds, enabling stowage of the cargo in bulk rather than in barrels or sacks.

Stronger and larger flutes with a battery deck were built for dangerous routes. However, the use of guns demanded larger crews, which increased costs. The guns also took valuable cargo space and therefore most of the flutes had little or no armament. Such vessels were popular targets for pirates.

Flutes were also used in whaling. The Dutch began whaling in the beginning of the seventeenth century, immediately after Willem Barentsz and Jan Corneliszoon Rijp had reported a huge number of whales in the Arctic Ocean when they discovered Spitsbergen during their search for the Northeast passage. Flutes were converted to whalers and davits were installed on the poop deck for handling the whaleboats. The bow was ice strengthened with double planking as the vessels operated in Arctic conditions. On the other side of the world exploration voyages were also made with flutes. When in 1642 the Dutchman Abel Tasman discovered New Zealand, one of the vessels in his fleet, the *Zeehaen*, was a flute and the other, the *Heemskerck*, was a yacht.

Another Dutch merchantman was the pinnace, which was identical to the flute with one exception: It was smaller and was armed. It had a transom stern in warship-style and the navy used it for scouting and escorting. As it was faster than the flute it was also used on some merchant trades.

THE WORLD ENCOMPASSED

'. . . it is not the beginning, but the continuing of the same,
until it is thoroughly finished, that yieldeth the true glory'.

SIR FRANCIS DRAKE

When the Treaty of Tordesillas was drawn up in 1494 between Spain and Portugal dividing the world into two sovereign zones by a vertical line running from the Arctic Pole to the Antarctic Pole, it was never explicitly stated, or even implied, that this line extended a full 360 degrees of the Earth's circumference, and thus had a counter-meridian on the other side of the Earth. Despite unresolved problems in determining where that line should be drawn in the Atlantic, both sides honoured the agreement they entered into. The emerging question was on whose side the Moluccas in the Indonesian archipelago lay within. The huge value of the spice trade made inevitable half a century of conflict over their control.

Spanish cosmographers, such as Martín Fernández de Enciso (b. c. 1570), supported Spain's claim that the Moluccas were within the Spanish sphere and could be reached by continually sailing west, and across the Pacific. By adopting the figure of 16 ⅔ leagues, instead of 17½ leagues as the measure of a degree, Enciso markedly reduced Portugal's portion of the world. Portolan maps made by the Portuguese cartographers, Jorge and Pedro Reinel, also clearly placed the Moluccas within the Spanish sphere.

CIRCUMNAVIGATION SUCCEEDED

Ferdinand Magellan

Portuguese by birth, Magellan (c. 1480–1521) had served under King Manuel I and voyaged to the Malabar Coast of India and Malacca on the west coast of the Malay Peninsula. But disputes with the king led him to offer his services to the young King Charles I of Spain. In King Charles, Magellan found a receptive audience, for he was able to bring to Spain his first-hand knowledge about the closely guarded Portuguese route to Malacca. In Ferdinand Magellan, Charles found an opportunity to challenge the lead taken by the Portuguese in developing trade routes to the Far East, and commissioned him to command an expedition.

Magellan chose for his scientific officer and co-commander Rodriguo (Rui) Faleiro, a Portuguese mathematician and astronomer, knowledgeable in nautical sciences. Although Magellan was clearly to be leader in the expedition, Faleiro would be in charge of scientific matters. In preparation for the journey Faleiro attended to the collection of charts, navigational tables, astrolabes and compasses. His most important

contribution was his *Regimento*, a thirty-chapter treatise he had published sometime between 1516 and 1519. In it he outlined three main methods on how to determine longitude: by measuring the conjunction of the Moon with planets; by observing lunar distances; and by correlating the amount of magnetic variation of the compass with longitude. But before the voyage began, his increasing bouts of insanity, and unresolved disputes with Magellan, caused him to be dismissed.

In his stead, the Spanish astronomer, Andrès de San Martin, accompanied the expedition as pilot. But Faleiro's collected charts and navigations tools, and particularly his *Regimento*, remained with the fleet. This was critical to the success of the mission in order to provide the exact location of the Moluccas, and prove Spain's sovereignty over them.

In the few intervening years since Columbus had sailed westward across the Atlantic, much had been learned about the coastline of the New World. Amerigo Vespucci's 1501 voyage along the coast of South America as far as Patagonia had, at the very least, shown Brazil to be a continent, dispelling any notion of it being an island. Vespucci's lack of description of major geographic landmarks, however, throws an element of uncertainty about the extent of his exploration.

The same misconceptions about the size of the world, which had given Christopher Columbus a false hope of reaching Asia, were shared by Magellan. Ptolemy's estimate of the Earth's circumference, derived from Strabo's erroneous interpretation of earlier and correct calculations by Eratosthenes and Posidonius, reduced its size by twenty-eight per cent. Marco Polo's overestimate of the distance between Asia and Japan also lessened the breadth of the Pacific Ocean. In a letter written to Magellan by Francisco Serrão, a close and personal friend, he estimated the distance between Malacca and the Moluccas in excess of their true value. In doing so, it placed them farther east and within the Spanish zone. The weight of all this 'evidence' shrank the

255. Portrait of Ferdinand Magellan by an unknown artist, 1848

The Portuguese navigator, Ferdinand Magellan, sailed under the flag of Spain to find a new route to the Moluccas (Spice Islands) and prove that they lay in Spain's half of the world, as defined by the Treaty of Tordesillas (1494). In November 1520 he found between Patagonia and Tierra del Fuego the desired passage leading from the Atlantic to the Pacific Ocean. It took thirty-seven days after entering the Strait now bearing his name before he emerged at its far end. Magellan was the first to lead a circumnavigation of the globe. Unfortunately, he never lived to see the completion, for he was killed in the Philippines and it was Juan Sebastián del Cano who piloted the *Victoria* back to Spain.

MUSEO NAVAL, MADRID

254. A Detail from Hessel Gerritsz's map, 1622

BIBLIOTHÈQUE NATIONALE DE FRANCE, PARIS

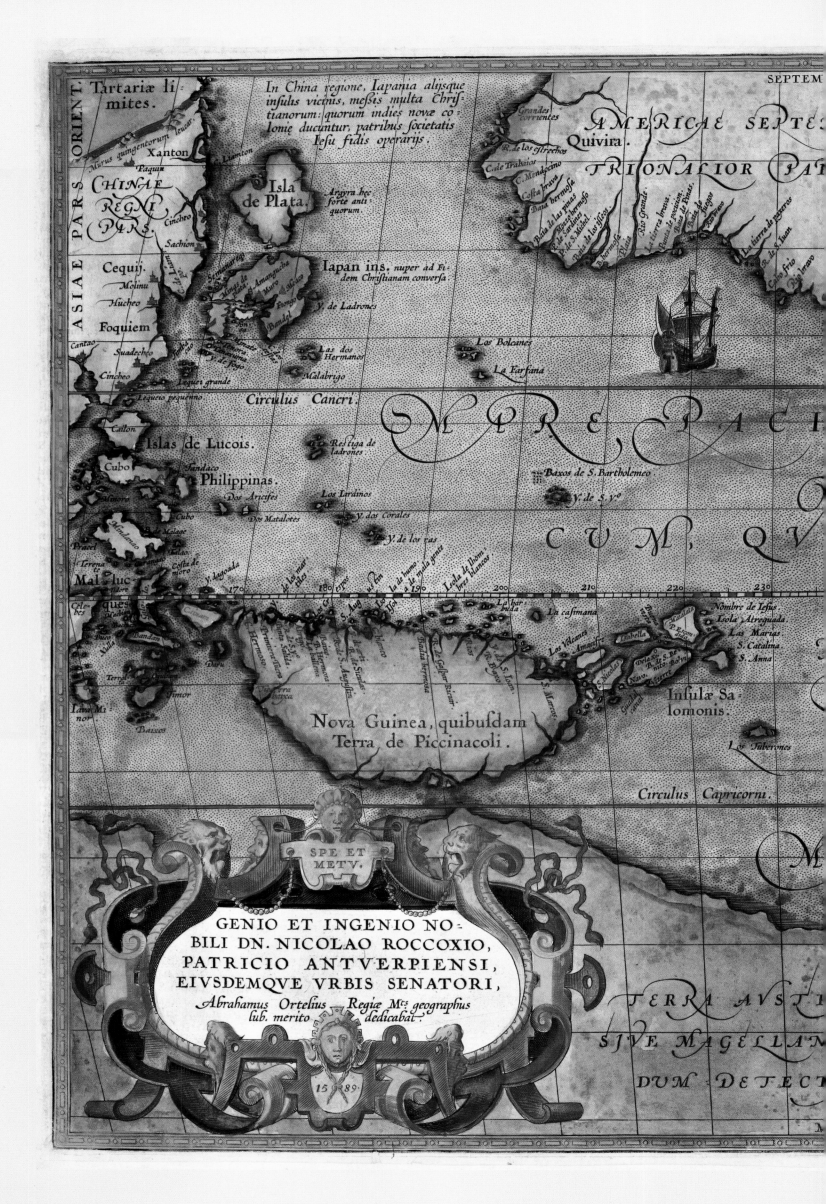

ASIAE PARS ORIENT. Tartariæ li-
mites.

In China regione, Iapania alijsque
insulis vicinis, messis multa Chris-
tianorum: quorum indies novæ co-
loniæ ducuntur, patribus societatis
Iesu fidis operarijs.

AMERICÆ SEPTE:

Quivira

TRIONALIOR PAR

Murus quingentorum leucar.

Xanton
Paquin
CHINÆ
REGNI
PARS.

Cequij.
Molinu
Hucheo

Foquiem

Cantao
Suadecheo
Cincheo

Isla
de Plata.

Iapan ins. nuper ad Fi-
dem Christianam conversa.

Y. de Ladrones

Argyra hęc
forte anti-
quorum.

Grandes
corrientes
R. de los estrechos
C. de Trabaios
C. Mendocino
Costa brava
Baia hermosa
Baia de las pinas
P. de Sardines
P. de S. Michel
Baia de Los Vises
Baia hermosa
P. hermosa
Rio grande
La tierra brava
La punta de piedra
Baia de S. Pedro
C. fegoro
La tierra de pageros
R. de S. Iuan
Cabo frio
Rio bravo

Las dos
Hermanos

Los Bolcanes

La Farfana

Lequet grande
Lequeio pequenno

Circulus Cancri.

MARE PACIF

Cailon
Islas de Lucois.

Restiga de
ladrones

Baxos de S. Bartholemeo.

CVM QV

Cubo
Sandaco
Philippinas.
Dos Arcifes

Saluoro
Cubo

Mindanao
Bate Malage

Praçel
Terena

Mal-luc

Dos Matalotes

Los Lardinos

Y. dos Corales

Y. de los ras

de las mar
tilles

170   180   190   200   210   220   230

Y. de S. Vº

Celebes

Nombre de Iesus
Isola Atreguada
Las Marias
S. Catalina
S. Anna

La casimana
Los Volcanes
Amactre

Isabella

Nova Guinea, quibusdam
Terra de Piccinacoli.

Insulæ Sa-
lomonis.

Los Tuberones

Circulus Capricorni.

SPE ET
METV.

GENIO ET INGENIO NO-
BILI DN. NICOLAO ROCCOXIO,
PATRICIO ANTVERPIENSI,
EIVSDEMQVE VRBIS SENATORI,
Abrahamus Ortelius   Regiæ Mtis geographus
lub. merito   dedicabat.

TERRA AVSTR

SIVE MAGELLAN

DVM DETECT

15 89

MARIS PACIFICI,

(quod vulgò Mar del Zur)

cum regionibus circumiacentibus, insulisque in eodem
passim sparsis, novissima descriptio.

MARIS ATLANTICI,

SIVE MAR DEL NORT

PARS.

Bermuda

Cuba

Spagnola

Iamaica

S. Ioan

La Trinidad

Noua Hispania.

Messico

Caribana.

Cartagena

Quito.

V V L G O

Circulus Aequinoctialis.

AMERICAE

MERIDIONA=

LIOR PARS.

Peru.

Charcas.

M A = N Y =

Prima ego velivolis ambivi cursibus Orbem,
Magellane novo te duce ducta freto.
Ambivi, meritoq; vocor VICTORIA: sunt mi
Vela, alæ; precium, gloria, pugna, mare.

Chili.

Patagones.

D E L

Z V R.

Archipe=
lagus in=
sularum.

Fretum Magella
nicum.

Mar
del Nort.

Cum privilegijs Imp. & Reg. Maiestatum,
nec non Cancellariæ Brabantiæ, ad decennium.

Tierra del Fuego.

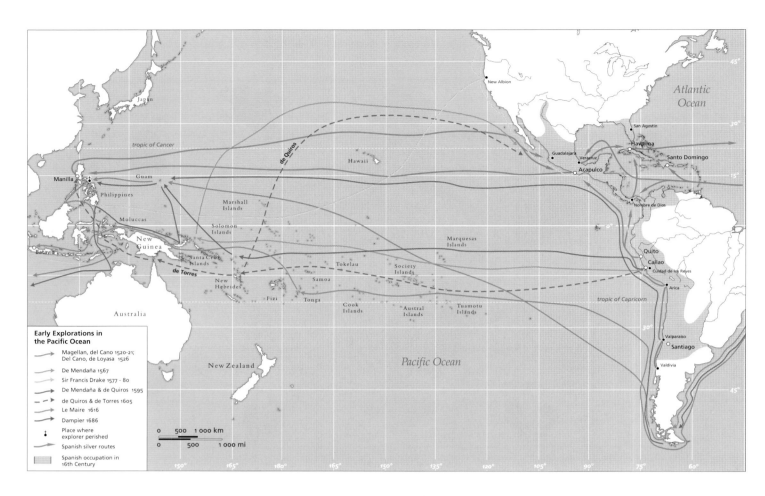

Early Explorations in the Pacific Ocean

Magellan, del Cano 1520-21;
Del Cano, de Loyasa 1526

De Mendaña 1567

Sir Francis Drake 1577 - 80

De Mendaña & de Quirós 1595

de Quirós & de Torres 1605

Le Maire 1616

Dampier 1686

Place where explorer perished

Spanish silver routes

Spanish occupation in 16th Century

0   500   1 000 km

0   500   1 000 mi

260. Early Explorations in the Pacific Ocean

The first voyage initiated expressly in search of Australis Incognita was led by Pedro Sarmiento de Gamboa (1532–1592), a Spanish historian, mathematician, astronomer, and explorer. He believed it to lie west of Tierra del Fuego, and that it extended as far north as the equator. In 1605, Pedro Fernándes de Quirós (1565–1614) and Luis Váez de Torres (1565–1610) left Peru to find the great austral continent. Torres proved the insularity of New Guinea by sailing through the strait that now bears his name.

As voyages across the Pacific Ocean increased in number, Spanish navigators began to understand the patterns of winds and currents there. In the central Pacific, winds and currents are predominantly from the east, like they are in the Atlantic basin. They learned that in the Pacific, as in the Atlantic, it was necessary to sail far to the north to pick up the prevailing Westerlies to speed their voyage homeward.

Sir Francis Drake

The Treaty of Tordesillas between Spain and Portugal, confirmed and supported by papal bulls, supposedly prevented the English from competing with these two nations for routes to the Far East. England now looked for new markets for its goods, and colonies for its growing population; equally strong was her desire to partake in the treasures gained by Spain and Portugal in their overseas expansion. Protestant England did not recognize papal authority, and envious of the great wealth being accumulated by Spain and Portugal, determined to seek its own fortunes. A group of private investors, all High Court officials, perhaps including even Queen Elizabeth, and an experienced sailor by the name of Francis Drake (1540–1596), financed an expedition to sail into the Pacific Ocean. It would pass through the Strait of Magellan, and reconnoiter the west coast of South America and beyond.

Before his epic voyage of 1577–1580, which made Drake the first Englishman to circumnavigate the world, he already had strong piloting skills and navigational abilities. In the Caribbean Sea, Drake raided Spanish ships as they transported gold, silver and other treasure homeward. Cruising along the coast of Panama in 1572, he sacked the village of Nombre de Dios where the Spaniards stored Peruvian gold before shipping it back home. Soon afterward, from a mountaintop on the Isthmus of Panama (then called Darien) Drake viewed the great South Sea, the Pacific Ocean, which sparked his desire to sail there in an English ship.

Although it never appeared in the official charter, the purpose of the Drake expedition was three-fold: to found colonies and set up trading posts on the unoccupied coast of Chile; to gain a foothold at the Isthmus of Panama in order to give England access to the Pacific by a route much shorter and less dangerous, even with the short overland travel, than by sailing all the way around the southern tip of South America; and to disrupt Spanish strength by raiding its ships and ports.

England was not officially at war with Spain, nor could she at this time afford to be so, although there were portents that such a conflict was not far off. Queen Elizabeth could, however, strike a clandestine blow against Spain without an outright declaration of war through privateering, a form of legalized, government-sanctioned piracy. In reprisal for the Spanish destruction of an English trading fleet at San Juan de Uola, Drake was commissioned as a privateer and authorized to arm his ship, attack ships of other countries and seize their cargo.

With the galleon *Pelican* as flagship of a fleet of five ships, and a crew of about 180 men, Drake sailed from Plymouth, England, in December 1577. To assure success of the expedition, secrecy was essential to prevent Spain from learning about Drake's intent to attack its power in the Pacific, mounting a diplomatic protest in London, and perhaps even sending forces to reinforce her colonists. The destination, as far as the crew had been told, was Alexandria, Egypt, for the purpose of trade. But as the fleet passed the Strait of Gibraltar without entering, and continued to sail southward toward the Cape Verde Islands, it became evident to the men that they had been deceived. By the time they reached Brazil and were sailing down its coast mutiny was brewing. For the sake of the success of the expedition, Drake had the main perpetrator tried and beheaded at Port San Julian, Patagonia. A month later yet another mutiny appeared in the offing, but this time he quelled it by discourse, rather than action, exhorting everyone, common sailors and gentlemen alike, to work together in common accord.

When Drake captured a Portuguese vessel off the Cape Verde Islands he retained its pilot, Nuño da Silva, aboard the *Pelican* for his knowledge of winds and currents in the southern Atlantic Ocean and piloting abilities along the coast of Brazil. In spite of the conflict of national loyalties, Drake found in him a friend with whom he could exchange ideas and knowledge, and da Silva was retained throughout much of the voyage. With his help, Drake's fleet traversed the Strait of Magellan in only sixteen days, a feat that had taken his predecessor over a month to accomplish. To mark this success, and to honour one of the patrons of the expedition, Drake changed the name of his ship from *Pelican* to the *Golden Hind*.

But whereas the great South Sea showed itself to be gentle and yielding to Magellan, to Drake it showed a more tempestuous side. Upon entering it, a violent storm blew the *Golden Hind* southward – far enough for Drake to view an open sea south of Tierra del Fuego.

With only a single ship, for one had been lost, one had returned to England, and two others Drake had scuttled so as to focus his efforts, he sailed up the coast of Chile and Peru, attacking Spanish settlements and ships. He met with little resistance, for the Spanish were caught by surprise and totally unprepared. His greatest prize was the capture and plunder of the ship

261. Portrait of Sir Francis Drake by an unknown artist, c. 1580

The Elizabethan naval commander, Sir Francis Drake, spent his early career as privateer, slave trader and civil engineer. In later years, he is well known for his role in the defeat of the Spanish Armada. Yet there is much about the exploits of this sixteenth-century explorer that remain unanswered: exactly where he landed on the California coast of North America, to which he gave the name New Albion, is in question; the most northerly latitude he reached, before turning back is disputed; and the true goal of his circumnavigation, as designated by Queen Elizabeth, remains undisclosed.

NATIONAL PORTRAIT GALLERY, LONDON

Nuestra Señora de la Concepción, nicknamed the *Cacafuego*.

He then continued northwards. It is uncertain exactly how far up the west coast of North America Drake sailed, but the general opinion is that he reached what is now called the Strait of Juan de Fuca at the border between the present-day United States and Canada. Then he turned back south and stayed for over a month somewhere in the vicinity of present-day San Francisco, California. He claimed the surrounding region for England, and named it *Nova Albion* (New England).

The *Golden Hind* completed her navigation by sailing westward across the Pacific to the Philippines, the Moluccas, and

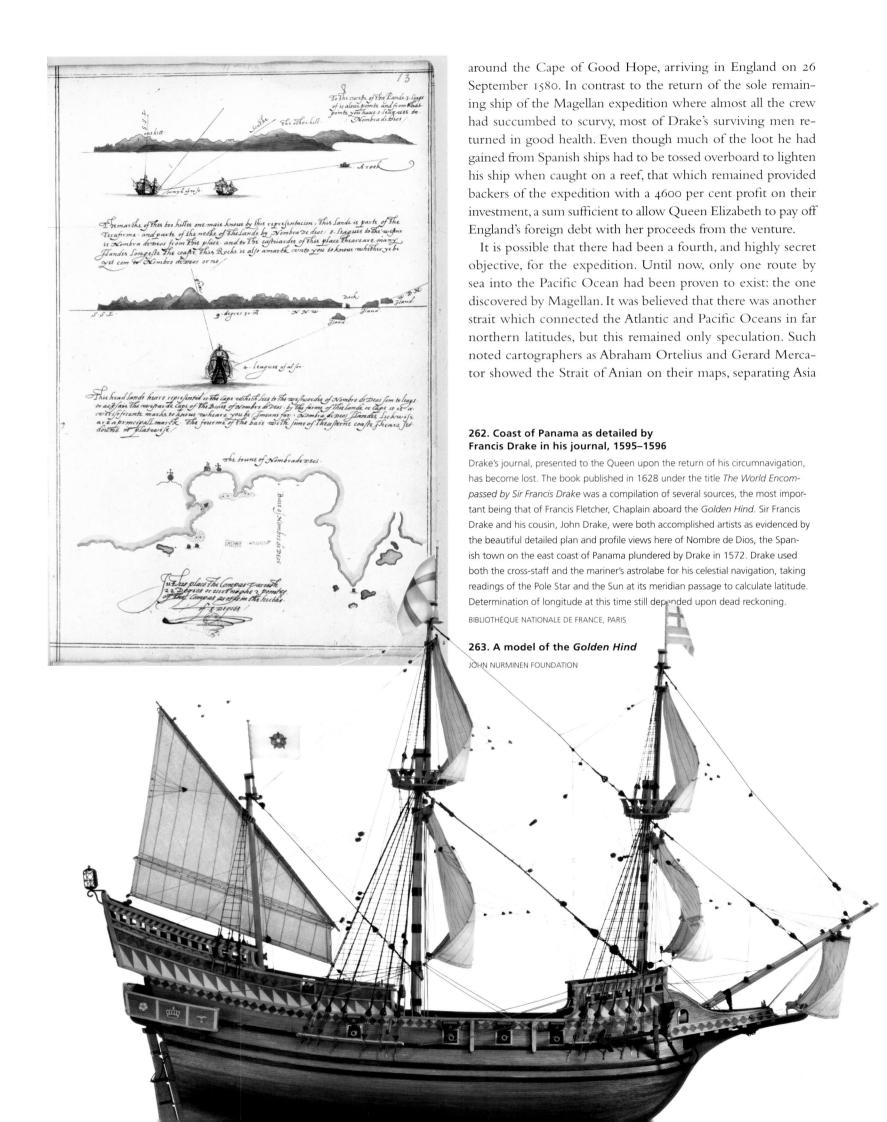

around the Cape of Good Hope, arriving in England on 26 September 1580. In contrast to the return of the sole remaining ship of the Magellan expedition where almost all the crew had succumbed to scurvy, most of Drake's surviving men returned in good health. Even though much of the loot he had gained from Spanish ships had to be tossed overboard to lighten his ship when caught on a reef, that which remained provided backers of the expedition with a 4600 per cent profit on their investment, a sum sufficient to allow Queen Elizabeth to pay off England's foreign debt with her proceeds from the venture.

It is possible that there had been a fourth, and highly secret objective, for the expedition. Until now, only one route by sea into the Pacific Ocean had been proven to exist: the one discovered by Magellan. It was believed that there was another strait which connected the Atlantic and Pacific Oceans in far northern latitudes, but this remained only speculation. Such noted cartographers as Abraham Ortelius and Gerard Mercator showed the Strait of Anian on their maps, separating Asia

262. Coast of Panama as detailed by Francis Drake in his journal, 1595–1596

Drake's journal, presented to the Queen upon the return of his circumnavigation, has become lost. The book published in 1628 under the title *The World Encompassed by Sir Francis Drake* was a compilation of several sources, the most important being that of Francis Fletcher, Chaplain aboard the *Golden Hind*. Sir Francis Drake and his cousin, John Drake, were both accomplished artists as evidenced by the beautiful detailed plan and profile views here of Nombre de Dios, the Spanish town on the east coast of Panama plundered by Drake in 1572. Drake used both the cross-staff and the mariner's astrolabe for his celestial navigation, taking readings of the Pole Star and the Sun at its meridian passage to calculate latitude. Determination of longitude at this time still depended upon dead reckoning.

BIBLIOTHÈQUE NATIONALE DE FRANCE, PARIS

263. A model of the *Golden Hind*

JOHN NURMINEN FOUNDATION

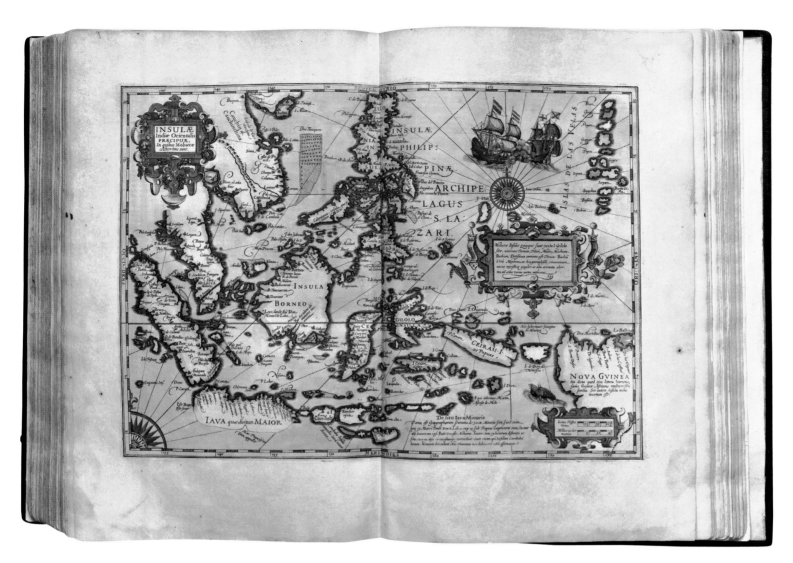

264. East India Archipelago by Gerard Mercator and Henricus Hondius, 1630

With the help of maps he brought from Spain, Peter Plancius drew a chart of the East India archipelago. It was published c. 1593, and later copied in part by Henricus Hondius. While the original was decorated with pictures of clove and nutmeg, Hondius instead inserted texts about the ruthless battles by the Spanish, Portuguese, Dutch and English to gain control of the spice trade from the Moluccas (Spice Islands).

JUHA NURMINEN COLLECTION

from the northwest of North America (now Alaska). Dr John Dee, the encyclopedic cosmographer and advisor to Queen Elizabeth in matters of policy, strongly believed in the existence of the Strait of Anian. Whether the western end of a Northwest Passage or the eastern end of a Northeast Passage led into the Pacific Ocean through the Strait of Anian was yet to be proved.

It may be conjectured that the goal of Sir Francis Drake's expedition was to seek the as-yet-undiscovered Strait of Anian and provide absolute confirmation of its existence. If Drake was successful in finding the Pacific end of the northwest or northeast passage, England would have a shorter and easier route to the Moluccas and riches of the Far East. In support of this surmised goal, it may also be possible, as Mercator believed, that the real purpose of the Pet and Jackman expedition sent by the Muscovy Company in 1580 in search of the Northeast Passage was to rendezvous with Drake in the Pacific and escort his ships back to England.

Drake's circumnavigation did not resolve the question of the Strait of Anian, but it did reveal that the landmass of Tierra del Fuego was not connected to the hypothetical Southern Continent, Terra Australis. A passage was now known to exist between the southern tip of South America at Cape Horn,

and Antarctica, connecting the Atlantic and Pacific Oceans. From 1616 onward, when Willem Corneliszoon Schouten (1567–1625) captained the *Eendracht* through it, this would become the favoured passage between the two oceans, and is called Drake Passage.

Knighted by Queen Elizabeth for his circumnavigation, Sir Francis Drake's incursion into the Pacific Ocean through the Strait of Magellan demonstrated to Spain that she was about to lose control of this sea-lane, until now claimed exclusively as her own, and that the Pacific Ocean could no longer be considered a 'Spanish Lake'. In 1586–88, Thomas Cavendish (1560–1592) became the third person to circumnavigate the globe when he successfully duplicated Drakes' route. Like

265. English Ships and the Spanish Armada, August 1588 by an unknown artist, 16th century

In 1587 the 'Invincible' Armada of Spain and Portugal was sent by His Most Catholic Majesty Philip II, with the blessing of Pope Pius V, to end the Protestant rule of Elizabeth I, Queen of England, and re-convert the country to Catholicism. Before it even had a chance to rendezvous, Sir Francis Drake made a pre-emptive strike at Cadiz, Spain, where the fleet was assembling, delaying its sailing until 1588. When the whole English fleet encountered the Armada in the English Channel, Lord Howard of Effingham, Lord Admiral of England, was in overall command, but Drake, Sir John Hawkins and Sir Martin Frobisher being the more experienced naval commanders, were in tactical control. At the final battle off Gravelines, which is now in France but was then part of Flanders, the Armada was dispersed and forced to return to Spain. The prevailing southwest wind obliged the Armada to direct its course north of Scotland and Ireland into the North Atlantic, where the weather caused more disastrous loss to ships and men than cannonballs and musket fire ever accomplished. A serious error on the part of the navigators who had failed to take into account the effect of the Gulf Stream brought them too close to the Irish coast, and over two dozen vessels were driven onto the rocks by the most northerly hurricane ever to be recorded. Lack of knowledge of just how cold and stormy these waters can be, even under 'fair' conditions, resulted in the loss of more lives.

NATIONAL MARITIME MUSEUM, LONDON

Drake, he also raided Spanish ships and ports in the Pacific, but he made no major new discoveries. When Spain was eventually stung into mounting an attack on England, Drake played an important part in the defeat of the great Spanish Armada, first by raiding the Portuguese coast in 1587, and when finally the armada sailed in 1588, by taking a subordinate command in the English fleet that put to sea from Plymouth to meet it.

FOREIGN TRADE EXPANDED

Dutch East India Company

The Dutch were no more inclined to respect the provisions of the treaty of Tordesillas than were the English. William Barentsz (1550–1597), Oliver Brunel and Balthasar de Moucheron (a wealthy merchant from Antwerp in Zealand), had opened up the sea-lands beyond Norway's North Cape, and into the Arctic. Other than a limited trade with Russia by way of the White Sea, however, little commercial success resulted from these expeditions. After initial, unsuccessful attempts to reach the Far East by sailing north of Russia and Siberia, Dutch ventures turned toward challenging Portuguese domination in the lucrative Asian trade by sailing southeast, around the Cape of Good Hope.

Crucial to any success in reaching the Indies was knowledge of the route and general instructions on navigational hazards. Detailed sailing instructions in the form of roteiros (rutters), were jealously guarded by the Portuguese and unavailable to Dutch mariners – that is, until Jan Huyghen van Linschoten (c. 1563–1611), a native of Enkhuizen, Holland, was appointed Secretary to the Archbishop of the Portuguese colony of Goa. That gave him access to all the charts and secret nautical information of the Portuguese. When he returned to Holland, Linschoten published his 'pirated' set of sailing instructions in 1595. Entitled *Reys-gheschrift vande navigatien der Portugaloysers in Orienten* (Travel Accounts of Portuguese Navigation in the Orient), it contained the detailed charts and practical information necessary for Dutch mariners to navigate between Portugal and the Indies, as well as between India, China and Japan.

266. The Island of Goa by Jan Huyghen van Linschoten, 1638

In 1510, the Portuguese fleet, commanded by Afonso de Albuquerque, entered Goa. Initially, Albuquerque was defeated by the native inhabitants, but he returned with reinforcements and took control of Goa, ordering the massacre of its Muslim inhabitants. He destroyed the monopoly in the spice trade held by Arab and Hindu merchants. The Portuguese colony of Goa, on the west coast of India, became the centre of commerce in the Indian Ocean from where Portugal controlled the spice trade. At its height, Goa was referred to as the 'Rome of the Orient'.

JUHA NURMINEN COLLECTION

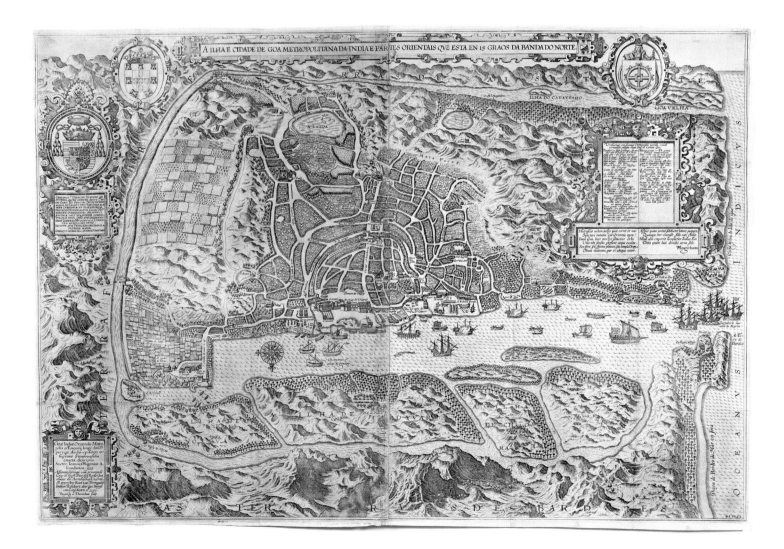

That year a Dutch company, the *Compagnie van Verre* (Company of the Foreign Parts) was formed, and three years later it sent out a commercial fleet of four ships to the Indies under the command of Cornelis de Houtman (c. 1565–1599). Aboard each vessel was a set of sailing instructions, called the *Reysgeschrift*, containing Linschoten's sailing instructions. The fleet reached the Javanese port of Bantam by way of the Cape of Good Hope, thus inaugurating a new era in Dutch enterprise and colonial expansion. Holland was now able to trade goods directly from her settlements on the islands of the Malay Archipelago. De Houtman's success caused Dutch ships to flock to the Indies, and by 1601 there were no less than fifteen Dutch commercial ventures backing voyages to the Far East. But these expeditions faced two major problems. First, they had to be prepared to battle with Portuguese vessels en route, and then with Malay pirates once they reached their destination. Second, since these were private, independent ventures, they were in competition with one another, which reduced their profits.

Both problems were solved by the unification of many small, rival companies into a single corporate body: *De Verenigde Oost-Indische Compagnie* (United East India Company) – or VOC. In 1602, the States-General of Holland granted the VOC a twenty-one-year charter, giving the company a monopoly on trade with the East via either of two routes: east, around the southern tip of Africa, or west, around South America by the Strait of Magellan. The charter also gave the VOC far-reaching powers, including the right to wage war and conclude peace in that part of the world.

In the first year of its founding, the Dutch East India Company sent a fleet of four ships to Asia and the coast of China. They established trading factories in Java, Sumatra and the Spice Islands, and gained a monopoly there in nutmeg and mace. Factories were also established off the coast of Japan as well as on mainland China (Canton). With the voyage of Joris van Spilbergen (1602), the Dutch began to compete with the Portuguese in the cinnamon trade in Ceylon (now Sri Lanka). Within half a century the VOC had completely displaced the Portuguese from this coastal region and gained a monopoly in cinnamon. Dutch outposts extended to include colonies at the Cape of Good Hope, Persia (now Iran), Malacca (Melaka, now in Malaysia), Siam (now Thailand) and parts of southern India.

The VOC became the world's richest private company. It created an enormous commercial enterprise, controlling trade in the Far East for two centuries. A large measure of its success came from complete management over every aspect of the enterprise: they designed, built and maintained their own ships in their own shipyards, made their own sea charts, trained their own pilots, and even made their own navigational instruments; overseas, they created settlements and fortifications to maintain their supremacy.

Dutch West India Company

Encouraged and emboldened by its recent triumph in achieving its independence from Spain (1609), the Netherlands sought to press their advantage by attacking Spanish ships as they returned from their colonies in the New World. When the Dutch West India Company, a counterpart to the Dutch East India Company, was formed in 1621, its charter gave it a monopoly of trade in the Atlantic Ocean with all countries west of the Cape of Good Hope, and east of the Strait of Magellan. The Charter also gave it authority to protect trade by granting the right to wage war on Spanish colonies and to prey on Spanish ships in the New World. With such raids, the Dutch hoped they would cripple Spanish power by preventing her from shipping significant resources of gold and silver. Opposing interests in the Netherlands, however, prevented any concentrated, united effort in this direction.

English East India Company

Linschoten's sailing instructions opened the way to the East for English merchants just as it did for the Dutch. In 1600, Queen Elizabeth I granted a royal charter establish-

267. Attack on Portuguese Galleons in the Bay of Goa, 30 September 1639 by Hendrick van Anthonissen, 1658

The decline of Goa, Portugal's capital of Eastern trade, began with the coming of the Dutch in the first half of the seventeenth century. Although they destroyed Portuguese power in the East, Goa still remained in Portuguese hands, but much lessened in importance. Depicted here is an attack by Dutch vessels on Portuguese galleons in the bay of Goa.

RIJKSMUSEUM, AMSTERDAM

ing the Honourable East India Company, and giving it a trade monopoly in the East Indies. Like the Dutch East India Company, it too was a private, commercial venture ruled by influential London merchants, with shares in the company widely sold.

Initially, the trade centred in India, rather than the East Indies. The company created strongholds in India in direct competition with Portuguese bases in Goa and Bombay. Later, it established bases in Surat, Madras, Bombay and Calcutta, almost totally displacing Portuguese domination. Eventually, it virtually ruled all of India. Although it made some inroads into the spice trade in the Indies, the British East India Company could not displace the Dutch monopoly there, and shifted its focus to South Asia and China.

Commercial rivalry between the United Dutch Provinces and England produced intense jealousy, resulting in frequent and major sea battles between the two nations lasting over a hundred years. In the North Sea, the conflict was over the large fleet of Dutch fishing vessels that took the herring England considered to be in her waters. In the Spice Islands

Overleaf

269. Chart depicting the first Dutch voyage to the East Indies by Theodore De Bry, 1599–1628

In 1595, with a fleet of four vessels, the captains Cornelis de Houtman and Pieter Dircksz led the first Dutch voyage to the East Indies. The newly formed Dutch East India Company that soon followed, displaced the Portuguese in the Spice Islands, and became the largest trading company in the world. It had a monopoly on trade in the East, as well as the exclusive right to make charts there. During their voyages, captains of the ships made rough sketches of their routes; brought back to Amsterdam, these were refined and illustrated in detail by professional cartographers.

COURTESY OF BERNARD J. SHAPERO RARE BOOKS, LONDON

268. Moluccas by Joan Blaeu, 1662

This west-orientated chart of the northern Moluccas was published in 1635 by the Dutch East India Company's cartographer Willem Janszoon Blaeu. His son Joan inherited the copperplate. The biggest among the islands was named by Marco Polo, today Halmahera. The Moluccas were small but very important Islands, as there could be found the most desirable and rarest spices: nutmeg and cloves. The spices were initially loaded on to smaller vessels and carried to a 'spice centre' at Jakarta, from where they were carried to Europe on larger ships.

THE NATIONAL LIBRARY OF FINLAND, HELSINKI

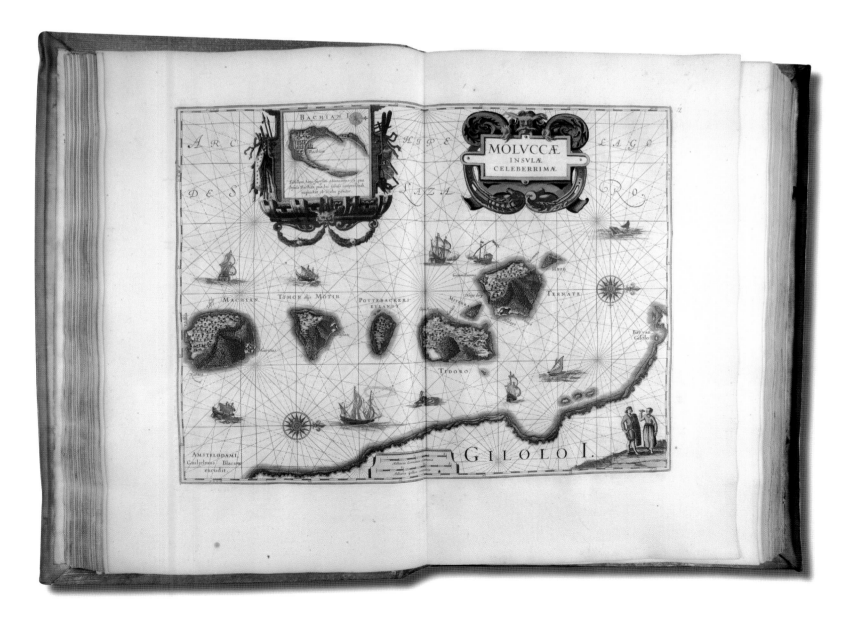

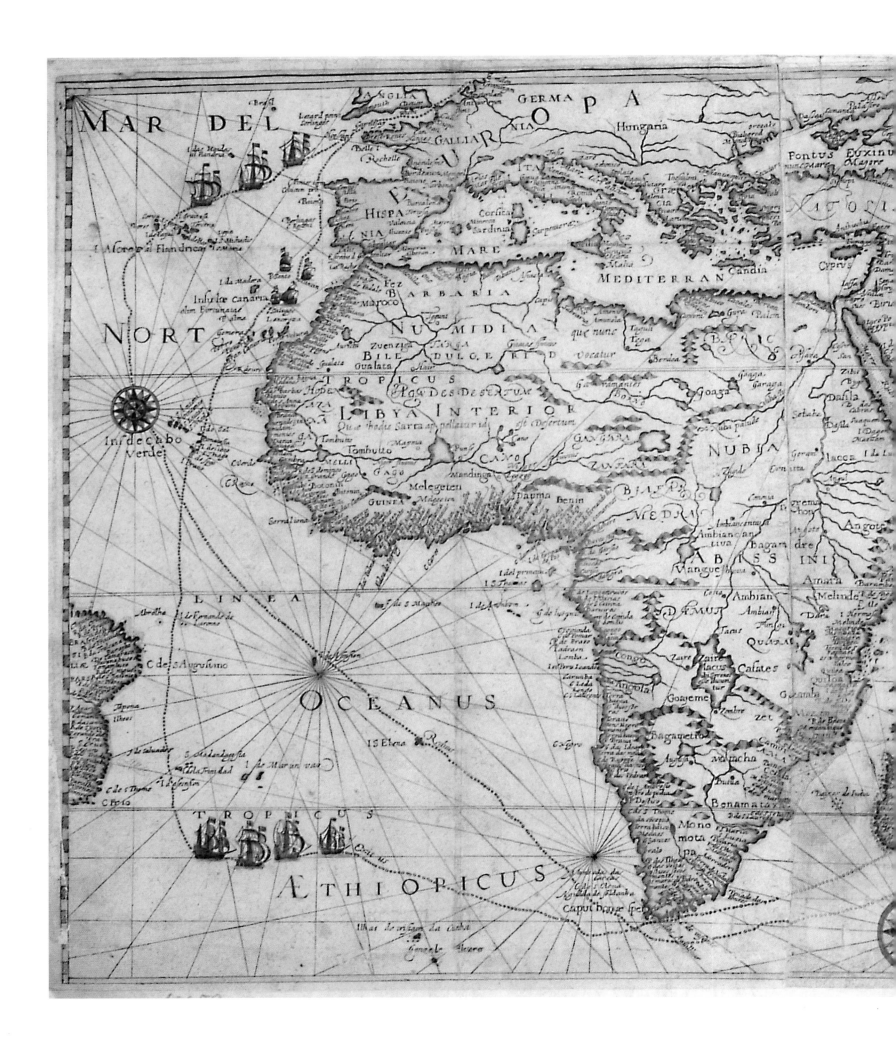

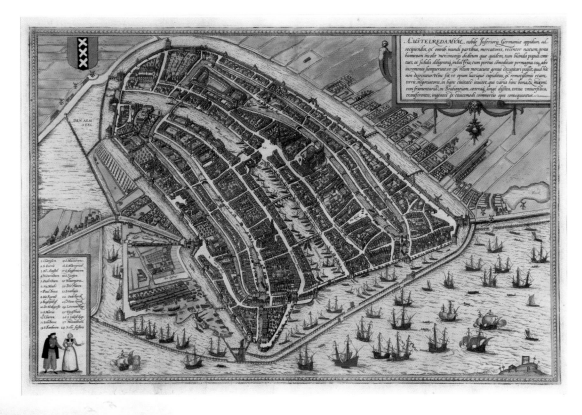

270. Amsterdam by Georg Braun and Frans Hogenberg, 1572

Amsterdam, Holland's largest city, flourished in the fourteenth century as the centre of trade with cities of the Hanseatic League. The city entered its 'Golden Age' in the seventeenth city with the formation of the Dutch East India Company (VOC); overseas possessions and a monopoly of trade in spices in the Far East made it one of the wealthiest cities in the world. Ships sailed from Amsterdam to ports in the Baltic Sea, North America, Africa, Indonesia and Brazil. The goods brought back were then shipped from Amsterdam to the rest of Europe.

JUHA NURMINEN COLLECTION

271. The Return of the Dutch East India Fleet, 1 May 1597; the *Hollandia*, *Mauritius* and *Duyfken* in Harbour at Amsterdam by Andries van Eertvelt, 17th century

The first trading expedition to the East Indies was led by Cornelis de Houtman. The voyage was not profitable and only three of the original four ships arrived home. The return of these ships had a major influence on the Dutch commerce and trade. New voyages were planned, which led to the birth of Dutch East India Company.

NATIONAL MARITIME MUSEUM, LONDON

it was over the cloves and nutmeg. And in the waters of the far north, the competition was waged in the whaling industry where Holland's activities overshadowed the English.

EXPLORATION CONTINUED

Le Maire and Willem Corneliszoon Schouten

Isaac Le Maire (1558–1624), a wealthy Amsterdam merchant, and a director in the Dutch East India Company for two years, was stimulated by what de Quirós had written about his 1605 voyage in search of Terra Australis, and especially his frequent mention of gold. He decided to initiate an expedition of his own to the great Southern Ocean (Pacific). He turned for advice to Willem Corneliszoon Schouten, a prominent navigator who, having already made three voyages to the East Indies, had extensive knowledge of South Seas islands. Le Maire asked Schouten whether he thought there was a passage leading from the Atlantic to the Pacific other than that which Magellan had discovered. And if so, whether he believed that there were lands south of such a passage that might provide riches as great as those from either the East Indies or West Indies. That land he had in mind was Australis Incognita.

Schouten believed that such a passage did exist south of the Strait of Magellan. He based this on Magellan's suspicion that Tierra del Fuego was an island not a continent, and that water existed beyond it. This supposition had been confirmed by Drake's report that, following his transit of the Strait of Magellan during his circumnavigation in 1577–80, he had sighted the southern tip of Tierra del Fuego when he was blown about a hundred miles south by a storm. As for the possibility there were riches to be found in land south of Tierra del Fuego, Schouten supported that idea as well.

Together they formed an enterprise recorded as The Australian Company, and which came to be known as the 'Gold-seekers.' However, there is some ambiguity about the two men's real intentions. It is possible they were using the name only to allay suspicion on the part of the Dutch East India Company (VOC), and that their true destination was the Indies where they would obtain gold from trade in spices. The charter of the VOC prohibited any Netherlands subjects, other than those of the Company, from reaching the Indies eastward by way of the Cape of Good Hope or westward through the Strait of Magellan. It did not preclude anyone from discovering countries in the south by a new route. If Le Maire did find another strait south of that which Magellan had discovered, he would thereby circumvent the restraints in the VOC charter.

East Indiamen

The mariners of northern Europe, especially the Dutch and the English, soon followed the Portuguese around Africa to join in the trade of Asia. The Portuguese established a dominant position in the spice trade, establishing garrisons in the Spice Islands. The Dutch, however, established themselves in South Africa, Sri Lanka, Malaya and Indonesia, and held most of their positions throughout the seventeeth and eighteenth centuries. The Netherlands rose to be the richest nation in Europe and the dominating power in foreign trade. It has been estimated that in 1665 the Dutch owned three quarters of all the vessels in the world, counting for a total of 16,000 ships. Their merchant navy was eight to ten times greater than that of France.

The mightiest enterprise in the Netherlands was the Dutch East India Company (Verenigde Oostindische Compagnie), which was established in 1602. Its success was mainly based upon the ability of the numerous Netherlands shipyards to build vessels in serial production at advantageous prices. The company sent some thirty vessels a year on voyages to East India, and were able to lower their freights so much that they could undersell their competitors in the sea routes to Asia.

When the Dutch arrived in Asia, they first made dangerous and long voyages from Europe and back, but soon they developed a system which could be compared to the 'hub-and-spoke' system in modern logistics. Fast yachts, tailor-made for Asian circumstances, collected cargoes from several ports in feeder traffic to the 'hub' in Batavia (now called Jakarta). From there, ocean-going deep-sea vessels ('retourshepen') made the ocean crossing with the valuable goods to Europe.

These Dutch East Indiamen were three-masted full-rigged ships with a transom stern. They carried topgallant sails above the topsails in the fore and main masts and a gaff sail in the mizzenmast. They usually had two decks, although the largest vessels had three and they were decorated in the contemporary baroque style to overawe both friend and foe. A large cargo hold was essential, but the Indiamen were also required to accommodate soldiers, sailors, craftsmen and passengers. Further space had to be reserved for guns and ammunition both for offensive and defensive purposes. The ships needed to be as fast as possible without compromising sea-keeping qualities, and the shallow coastal waters of the Netherlands limited their draft.

English merchants had established the Honourable East India Company in 1600, two years before their Dutch rivals, but it was not until after the Anglo-Dutch wars in the middle of the seventeenth century that the English company came to equal, and then to surpass, the Dutch one. It established itself strongly in India, and came to dominate trade with China. The port of London soon became a competitor to Antwerp as the most important port in Europe. During the following 250 years the Company's East Indiamen made some 4600 voyages from London.

English East Indiamen were much like the Dutch *retourschepen*, even if they were not as large, at least during the first half of the seventeenth century. They were strongly constructed, three-masted, full-rigged ships. When England took the lead as a shipbuilding nation, this was first noticed in the hull form of the vessels. By the end of the eighteenth century, the high aft castle began to disappear and the midship deck line became nearly horizontal. This hull form became common during the sailing vessels of the following century.

The ships looked like floating palaces, profusely decorated both fore and aft. Below deck they were spacious and finished to a high standard for officers and important passengers. The comfort of the ratings was poor and ordinary passengers endured extreme overcrowding. Their quarters were close and dark; there was not always enough fresh air, as the hatches had to be kept closed in rough weather; it was sometimes impossible even to keep a candle burning.

The vessels designed for the East Asian companies' Asian trades were actually combined warships, freighters and passenger vessels. They were floating warehouses and so large that they were often mistaken for warships. They were heavily armed because they had to counter pirates and enemies. A large crew was needed to handle the guns, but the valuable cargo ensured that the companies could accept the additional costs.

Most of the English East Indiamen were built in England, with the company establishing its own shipyard in Deptford in 1609. However, soon the company realised that it was cheaper to charter ships than to own them. In India smaller vessels were built for the local trades. There it was possible to use tropical hard wood such as teak as building material, which protected the bottom better from sea worms than the British oak. From the middle of the eighteenth century, it became common to use copper plating to protect the underwater hull.

Voyages to Asia and back were measured in years with these large freighters, but it did not matter as long as the company had a monopoly on the trade with India and China. When the company lost this advantage in 1813 and 1833 respectively, it needed faster ships to compete with the others. First the East Indiamen were replaced by Blackwell frigates, and then by fast sailing clippers.

272. Two Dutch Merchant Ships Under Sail Near the Shore in a Moderate Breeze by Willem van de Velde the Elder, 1649

The vessels of the East India Companies were strongly armed as they carried valuable merchandise from Asia to Europe. They were the largest freighters of their time. Space was needed for cargo, passengers and soldiers. These impressive and splendid ships ruled the oceans and reflected the power and wealth of their owners.

NATIONAL MARITIME MUSEUM, LONDON

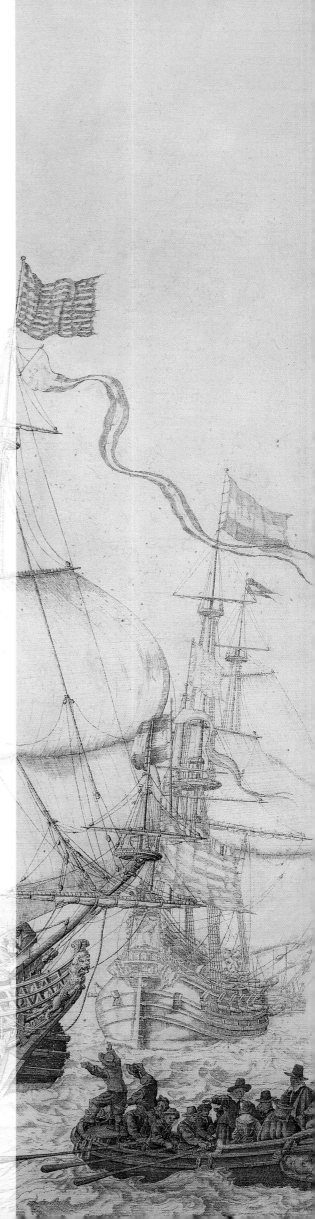

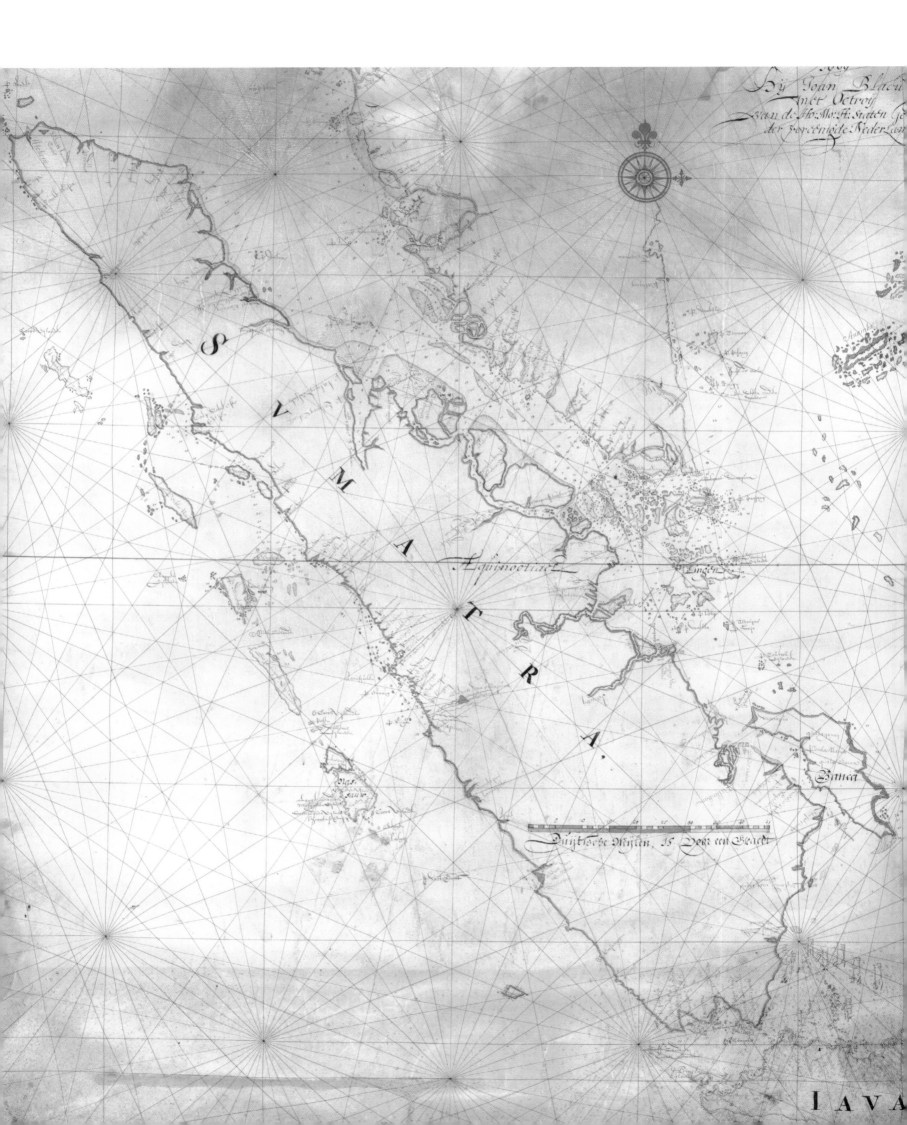

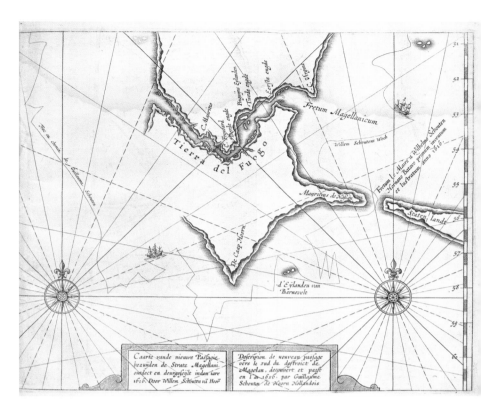

274. Spice pots, 16th and 17th centuries

Spices were the principal import from Southeast Asia. They were transported in purpose-made earthenware pots such as these, which are from Burma and Siam (modern Thailand).

JUHA NURMINEN COLLECTION

275. Description of a new passage south of the Strait of Magellan by Willem Corneliszoon Schouten, 1619

This map shows the route of the Willem Schouten expedition along the tip of South America. In his logbook, dated 29 January 1616, Schouten writes: 'It is noon and we are sailing in variable winds. We are approaching a land of mountains and snow, and its cape is the shape of v and come down to the sea. We name it Hoorn and it's in 57°, 48'. The Weather is calming down and we are sailing with the north wind and western currents during the night, the sea is swelling a little restless'.

JUHA NURMINEN COLLECTION

Previous page
273. Sumatra by Joan Blaeu, 1669

The Dutch East India Company used Sunda Strait, between the Indonesian islands of Sumatra and Java, as their gateway to the Spice Islands, thereby circumventing the Portuguese controlled Strait of Malacca. Accurate charting of Sunda Strait, with its strong tidal currents, shifting sand banks, and shallow water at its eastern end, was required for safe navigation.

MARITIEM MUSEUM ROTTERDAM

Le Maire and Schouten outfitted two ships for the expedition: the *Eendracht* (Unity), with Willem Schouten as Captain; and the *Hoorn*, a slightly smaller ship, skippered by Willem's brother, Jan Schouten. Isaac Le Maire's son, Jacob, accompanied them. They left from Texel in North Holland in June of 1615, crossed the Atlantic, and reached Port Desire in Patagonia in December. There, they careened the boats to clean their bottom before proceeding on the voyage. Unfortunately, while burning a fire of dry reeds under the *Hoorn* to clean its bottom of barnacles and weed, the ship accidentally caught on fire and was destroyed.

In January, Schouten proved the existence of an alternative passage. Although the discovery justifiably should have been given Schouten's name, it was named after Le Maire, and remains so today. To port side (their left) as they entered the strait, land they saw received the name of Staaten Landt. This, they thought, might be part of Terra Australis, but they did not stop to explore it. The southernmost tip of the continent they named *Kaap Hoorn* (Cape Horn), after the ship that was accidentally destroyed; Hoorn also happened to be Schouten's birthplace in North Holland. They now entered the great Southern Ocean, where they passed through several island groups, stopping occasionally for food and water. Jacob Le Maire wanted to continue sailing south and westward in search of Terra Australis, but was convinced by Schouten to sail instead along the northern coast of New Guinea.

At the end of October the expedition came to an end at Batavia (now Jakarta), the main settlement of the Dutch East India Company in the Far East. There, the *Eendracht* was seized by the VOC on the grounds of their having trespassed upon the Company's prohibitions. Captain Schouten and Le Maire, along with others, were sent back to the Netherlands. Le Maire never made it home. He died along the way chiefly of

From a Sandglass to the Chronometer

The sundial and water clock were invented more than five millennia ago but they were not fit for seafaring. The first timepiece suitable for use in a ship – the sand clock – was invented probably in Europe before the beginning of the fourteenth century. It is still called a sand clock, even though crushed eggshells that do not scratch the glass and make it opaque have replaced the sand. Shipboard time was measured by using a sandglass that ran for half an hour, and it was the duty of the youngest on watch to turn and announce the glass. From the beginning of the seventeenth century a half-minute glass was used when measuring the ship's speed with a chip log.

During the era of the great discoveries, when voyages took several months, it became necessary to have an independent method for checking time. This was provided by the rotation of the Earth. The sky turns about the celestial pole once in 24 hours and provides a natural clock, but the time it indicates is sidereal time. The sidereal day is about four minutes shorter than is the solar day, and the sidereal month a full two hours shorter. Navigators learnt how to check the hour of the night against the position of either the Little Bear (Little Dipper) or the Great Bear (Big Dipper), and how to correct for sidereal drift. Simultaneously they could check the local time that kept changing on a long voyage with the changing longitude.

At the end of the Middle Ages an instrument was devised – the nocturnal – for finding the necessary correction between sidereal and solar time. It consisted of two circular disks with different diametres and a hole at their common centre. The days of a year are engraved at the rim of the outer disk, the hours of a day on the inner one. The navigator holds the nocturnal parallel to the equatorial plane and aims it towards the Pole Star by looking through the hole. An arm on the nocturnal is turned and brought to alignment either with the Pointer stars of the Little Bear or with the pair of stars at the right end of the Great Bear. By bringing the noon mark into coincidence with the day the local time can be read on the scale. The nocturnal also gives the correction for the altitude of the Pole Star that had been measured by other means.

Thus it was possible to find the local time at sea without a clock, but an accurate clock was the best way of knowing the time at a reference longitude, for example at the port of origin. This was navigationally important because the time difference between local time and the time at a reference longitude is the same as the angular difference between the longitude of the reference meridian and that of the ship. The first mechanical clocks were driven by weights, and they were used for regulating church bells from the end of the thirteenth century. In the following century clocks driven by a spring were invented. These would have been better suited for shipboard use, but their accuracy was poor. This was much improved with the patenting of a mechanical pendulum by Christiaan Huygens in 1656, but it was found that early pendula were too sensitive to disturbances for use on board ship. Robert Hooke and Huygens competed to develop an oscillator based on a spring that was alternatively wound and unwound, and by the middle of the 1670s the spring regulator was developed. By the 1720s the best pendulum clocks erred less than one second per month. The spring clocks that might be used on ship, however, still left much to be desired.

The first accurate marine clock was developed in England by John Harrison (1693–1776), who was a skilful mechanic. He invented several improvements to clock work, including self-lubricating bearings made of greasy lignum vitae wood, bi-metallic compensators to deal with changes of temperature, and the frictionless escapement. By combining his inventions he constructed four different sea clocks between 1735 and 1759. The first one was tested on a voyage to Lisbon and functioned well. The project progressed slowly, however, mainly because Harrison always wanted to improve his designs. Finally in 1762 and 1763, H4, his fourth clock which in design and construction differed completely from its predecessors, proved its excellence on a voyage from England to Jamaica and back. After nearly five months at sea, the clock error was less than two minutes, which was equivalent to half a degree. That satisfied the requirement for a prize that had been offered by the British Parliament as long ago as 1714. A copy of H4 (also called K1) was ordered from Lacrum Kendall a watchmaker, and served Captain James Cook as 'our faithful guide on his second and third voyages to the Pacific in 1772 to 1775 and 1776 to 1779 when Cook was killed, the expedition returning home in 1780.

Great Britain tried to keep Harrison's sea clock secret from rivals. The Admiralty gave an order that, if a ship had to be abandoned, its logbook and the clock were not to be left on board. Despite this care, however, in 1766 a sea clock was developed in France by Pierre Le Roy (1717–1785). It is his clock that must be considered as the model for the marine chronometer. Soon an industry was created for their production, and they became irreplaceable tools for finding geographic positions and for mapping previously unknown corners of the world. It became a global practice to provide ships at port with an optical time signal from a nearby observatory for correcting the time of the bridge chronometer.

Together with the mirror sextant, the chronometer completely changed navigation. Not until the advent of the radio was it otherwise possible to provide ships at sea with the time of the reference meridian, and even then, because of uncertainties of radio communication, the new technology did not make the chronometer obsolete. It was not until the late in the twentieth century that satellite navigation reduced the role of the ship's chronometer.

276. Sandglass, 18th century

JUHA NURMINEN COLLECTION

277. British chronometer, 19th century

JOHN NURMINEN FOUNDATION

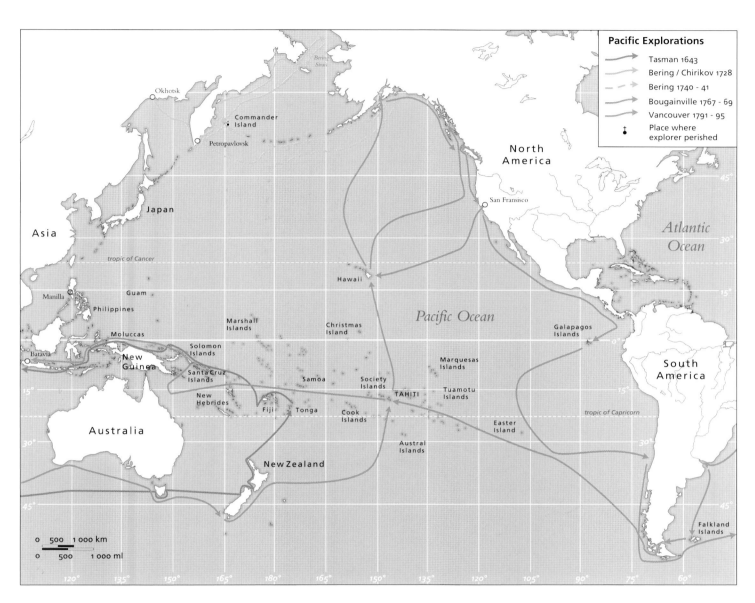

278. Pacific Explorations

'grief and vexation on account of the disastrous end of an enterprise which had been so successful till the arrest of the ship and cargo'. Belief in the southern continent of Terra Australis continued in spite of these failures. Not until circumnavigation of the globe in far southern latitudes by Captain James Cook (1772–75), was this fantasy sufficiently disproved.

The Great South-Land Revealed

At the beginning of the seventeenth century, through the combination of plan and accident, portions of the Terra Australis Incognita of Aristotle, the great southern continent, began to take shape as what we now call Australia. Dutch fleets on the way to Batavia and the Moluccas led this phase of expansion of geographic knowledge in the eastern portion of the Indian Ocean and the Pacific. On one of his many voyages (c. 1606–1618) to the East Indies in the service of the Dutch East India Company, Willem Janszoon, skipper of the vessel *Duyfken* (the Little Dove), sailed along the southern coast of New Guinea, and then headed south. He reached the west

coast of present-day Cape York Peninsula and explored 192 miles of its coastline, making Janszoon the first documented discoverer of Australia. He also would have discovered the western entrance to the Torres Strait, separating New Guinea from Australia, had he not mistakenly believed it to be only a long bay.

Over the course of the next three and a half decades portions of this great South-land were touched by others, but they were discontinuous stretches of what was known then only as a large landmass south of Indonesia, and failed to yield a comprehensive picture of its extent. Dirk Hartog (1580–1621) and Frederik de Houtman (c. 1571–1627) both landed on the west coast of Australia, respectively in 1616 and 1619. And in 1623 Jan Carstenszoon extended the exploration begun by Janszoon by reaching the extreme south of the Gulf of Carpentaria on Australia's northeast coast. The first to sight Australia's south coast was Pieter Nuyts (1598-1655) in the *Gulde Zeepaard* (the Golden Seahorse), as a result of being carried too far south by

279. Portrait of Abel Tasman, his wife and daughter by Jacob Gerritsz Cuyp, 1637

After the painting was completed, Abel Tasman left Holland for Batavia (now Jakarta), bound to the East India service for ten years. Tasman is shown standing with his hand outstretched, holding navigational dividers against the table-mounted globe. This infers the importance of exploration within his life. Navigational instruments hang on the wall behind the globe.

NATIONAL LIBRARY OF AUSTRALIA, CANBERRA

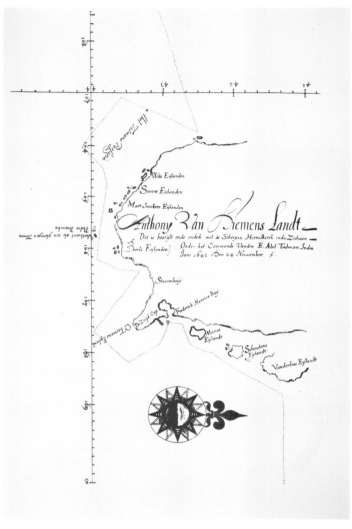

the strong winds of the Southern Ocean. Nuyts and François Thijssen, the captain of the *Gulde Zeepaard*, followed that southern shore for 960 miles.

Abel Janszoon Tasman

With the objective of extending Dutch commerce, Anton van Diemen, Governor-general of Batavia, commissioned Abel Tasman (c. 1603–1659) and Frans Jacobszoon Visscher, as pilot-major and hydrographer, to explore the waters around the great South Land, Australia. Van Diemen hoped that Tasman and Visscher would make new discoveries, and chart the remaining unknown part of the globe, but the commercial objective of finding lands or islands that would be profitable for the Company was uppermost in importance. Their orders were to determine whether a passage south of the western and southern coasts of Australia could be found leading into the South Sea – the Pacific Ocean. Such a passage, if found, would provide a short and convenient way to the gold-bearing country of Chile, and extend the Dutch East India Company's operations of trade to South America.

This new route would also make it possible for Dutch vessels to waylay Spanish silver ships sailing between Manila and Acapulco, Mexico, which never expecting the Dutch to come from this direction would be easy prey to piracy. If no passage existed west of Australia, then they were to look for a channel in the region of New Guinea and the Solomon Islands. After-

280. Map of Anthony van Diemen's Land from Abel Tasman's Journal, 1642

Those sections of the coast Tasman and Visscher had actually sailed are charted with admirable accuracy. They used Tenerife in the Canaries (16.5° west of Greenwich) as their prime meridian, taking the average of their several longitude findings to 'fix' the longitude of places. In their charting, substantial errors arose from lack of true information, which was supplanted by supposition. The land they named Van Diemen's Land (Tasmania) was not circumnavigated; not having established its insularity, it was appended to that part of the south coast of Australia already known through the exploration by Pieter Nuyts. Originally the Great South-land was named t' Eendracht, after Dirk Hartog's vessel in which he first landed on an island off Australia's west coast. This name was later changed to New Holland, and finally attained the present name of Australia on the map produced by Matthew Flinders in 1814. It would not be until 1770, with the voyage of Captain James Cook, that the east coast of Australia would finally be charted.

JOHN NURMINEN FOUNDATION

281. Portrait of William Dampier by Thomas Murray, 1697–1678

William Dampier's early career at sea was mainly as a buccaneer. When not engaged in piratical plundering, his enquiring mind noted the general pattern of winds and their distribution over the world's oceans. He distinguished the difference between tidal currents and ocean currents, and correctly deduced that equatorial currents were the cause of trade winds. Dampier's observations and insights were studied by future generations of scientists and navigators, including Captain James Cook.

NATIONAL PORTRAIT GALLERY, LONDON

was connected with the great South-land, or if a passage existed between them. With this second voyage, Tasman accomplished the charting of 2560 miles of the entire northwest coast of Australia previously unknown to the Dutch. But the dangers of these waters, with its multitude of hidden, and dangerous, coral reefs, kept this commercially promising region free of further exploration until the mid-eighteenth century.

William Dampier

At the end of the seventeenth century it was still a remarkable achievement for any man to circumnavigate the globe; William Dampier (1652–1715) did it thrice over, sailing more than 200,000 miles during his lifetime. In his voyages, Dampier visited all five continents and covered regions of the world that were largely unknown to Europeans.

Most of Dampier's life at sea was as a buccaneer, a polite synonym for pirate, who let circumstances of the moment rather than any planned intent dictate his travels and actions. At the start of his first circumnavigation (1681–1691), Dampier seized a 36-gun Danish vessel off the Cape Verde Islands. In the seventeenth century, any ship, regardless of national origin, allegiances or treaties, was fair game for any other – every vessel was a predator, and every vessel was prey. He went on to range the west coast of the Americas from Cape Horn to Acapulco, plundering Spanish ships and settlements. Eventually Dampier made his way across the Pacific to Guam, the Philippines and Australia, which had come to be called New Holland. After three years of wandering around Southeast Asia in various ships he returned to London.

The subsequent publication of his journal, entitled *A New Voyage Round the World* (1697–1709), was an immediate success, and brought him fame as a travel writer. Dampier's vivid and detailed descriptions of all he encountered opened the eyes of the general public to the far-off regions of the world. His was an enquiring mind, and throughout his voyages around the world he took careful notes of the places he visited, their geography, botany, zoology, and the customs and culture of the indigenous peoples.

Future navigators benefited from Dampier's geographic surveys and charts. His observations included the local weather patterns, tides, and pattern of winds and currents. With the production of his 'Chart of the General and Coasting Winds in the Great South Ocean (Pacific)', for the first time the world had a fully integrated pattern of the direction and extent of the trade-wind systems around the Earth, with their limits at the Variables, and how these wind systems were related to the major currents of the ocean.

ward, they were to proceed to the west coast of New Guinea and ascertain whether it was connected to Australia.

Tasman and Visscher left Batavia in August of 1642 with the yacht *Heemskerk* and a storehouse ship, the flute *Zeehaan*. They named the first new land sighted *Anthoonij van Diemen's landt* (now called Tasmania) in honour of the man who commissioned the expedition. When it was apparent this land would yield no spices or other riches, they continued sailing eastward. The next landfall was the west coast of a new land, now called the South Island of the two main islands of New Zealand. As they proceeded north, they entered what appeared to be their objective, a channel or strait into the South Sea. But a tide running from the southeast convinced them it was only a large bay, and thus they did not discover the strait into the Pacific that would later be found by James Cook in 1770.

In effect, Tasman and Visscher had circumnavigated Australia, albeit for a greater part of the voyage thousands of miles off the coast, and had established definitely that the South-land, Australia, was a new land, and not part of Terra Australis Incognita. Important as this geographic discovery was, it brought them no approval for their efforts. They had not succeeded in finding a channel into the South Sea, had failed to set up new trading posts that would bring profits to the Company, and found no new sources of pepper and spices. Nonetheless, they were commissioned to make a second voyage the following year.

This time, although the objective remained the same, that is to find a passage leading into the South Sea and a way to Chile to form trade connections, the area of search shifted northward. They were to determine whether New Guinea

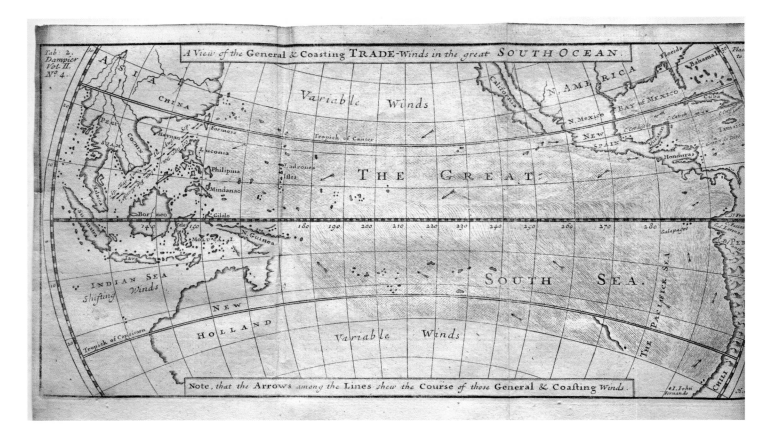

282. A View of the General & Coasting Trade-Winds in the Great South Ocean by William Dampier, 1729

Dampier's scientific endeavours in winds and currents culminated with his chart of the general and coasting winds in the Great South Ocean. He clearly delineated the region of calms, and the doldrums, as well as the Intertropical Convergence Zone north of the equator. Dampier showed the shift in direction of winds along coasts, and was the first to delineate the seasonal variation of the monsoons in the Indian Ocean. With this chart, mariners had a comprehensive picture of winds in the currents in the Pacific Ocean, as well as those in the Atlantic Ocean.

JUHA NURMINEN COLLECTION

George Anson

Aiming to strike a blow to Spanish domination in the Pacific Ocean the British Admiralty dispatched two fleets in 1740. One, under command of Vice-admiral Edward Vernon, was sent to the Caribbean to gain control of the Atlantic side of Panama. This would facilitate the movement of men and supplies across the isthmus from the Atlantic to the Pacific. At the same time, another smaller fleet was sent around Cape Horn to attack Spanish possessions in the Pacific; the commander of this small squadron, consisting of six warships with the HMS *Centurian* as flagship, was an experienced sailor in the Royal Navy, George Anson (1697–1762).

In crossing the Atlantic, Anson's ships were caught in the Doldrums and many of the men became sick and died – primarily of scurvy, the scourge of sailors. They arrived at Cape Horn later than planned, and experienced the worst of its stormy weather. Mountainous seas, violent tidal currents and sudden squalls accompanied by rain, hail and snow made progress painfully slow. Two of the ships gave up the struggle and returned to England.

More pleasing circumstances were expected when they finally entered the Pacific; instead, their miseries and sufferings only rose to a higher pitch. One disaster after another beset them. In battling the constant storms the fleet became separated, and scurvy again took its toll. Aboard the *Centurian*, almost all those aboard were afflicted to some degree, and in the month of April alone, forty-three died of it. Another ship was lost to shipwreck off the coast of Chile.

The *Centurian* made it to Juan Fernandez Island, and later the other two ships arrived there. But their condition was so deplorable that one had to be burned. By now, most of the crew was dead or dying, but those who survived regained their strength, nourished by fresh food and the island's natural vegetation.

Undaunted by all these disasters, Anson proceeded to carry out his orders to maraud Spanish shipping and settlements. He captured merchant ships, and managed to inflict damage at the Spanish port of Paita on the Peruvian coast. He also learned to his dismay that the Caribbean plan for Darien had been a total disaster. There was yet one more goal that Anson would try to achieve, that is to seize a Spanish galleon on its route from Acapulco to Manilla in the Philippines. By now, the pattern of wind systems in the Pacific Ocean was generally known. Accordingly, Anson shaped his course westward at 13° N, where the Northeast Trade Winds would carry him across the Pacific. But what was not known at this time is that the belt of trade winds shifts north and south with the change of seasons as the Sun moves between the north and south hemisphere. Once again the two ships were caught in the doldrums, and what should have been a seven- or eight-week crossing turned out to take 114 days. Fever and scurvy took the lives of more men, and one more ship, not having enough crew to sail her, had to be destroyed.

Finally, the ever-present tide of bad luck turned, and one of the richest Spanish galleons, the *Nuestra Señora de Covadonga,* was captured. After a circumnavigation which took three years and nine months, Anson and his crew returned to England where he was welcomed as a hero and became an extremely wealthy man with his share of the prize money.

The homecoming was not an unalloyed victory, for of the 1939 officers and crew that started out, 1051 died on the voyage – mostly of scurvy – while 700 deserted or returned home on two of the ships. Although the general medical profession did not know that it was the lack of Ascorbic Acid (Vitamin C) that caused this disease, as early as 1593, Sir Richard Hawkins, in a voyage to the South Pacific, recognized the treatment. 'That which I have seen most fruitfull for this sickness', he said, 'is sower [sour] oranges and lemons'. And in 1636 John Woodall published his findings that the use of fresh vegetables and citrus fruits would prevent scurvy. In 1747, three years after the completion of Anson's voyage, James Lind came to the same conclusion after controlled studies. He presented his results to the British Admiralty, but it wasn't until 1795 that lemon or lime juice was finally mandatory for all sailors.

The voyage of George Anson marked the end of an era in oceanic voyaging. Privateering and buccaneering were replaced with new goals: exploration of the last remaining uncharted regions of the world, and the gaining of scientific knowledge.

acquire a new commercial empire in the South Atlantic and Pacific. When an attempt to form a settlement in the Falkland Islands, known to the French as Îles Malouines failed, Louis-Antoine de Bougainville (1729–1811) expanded his horizon to more distant shores with a plan to circumnavigate the world. In late 1776 he set sail from Nantes in a frigate *La Boudeuse,* followed in early 1777 by a store ship, the flute *L'Étoile.* Their route took them through the Strait of Magellan and across the Pacific. Upon landing in Tahiti, although he was not the first European to visit there, Bougainville claimed it for France. Arriving back in France in the spring of 1779, Bougainville became the first Frenchman to circumnavigate the globe. It is remarkable that he returned with all but 9 men of the original 330 crew and officers.

Perhaps the most significant advance in the history of navigation made by this voyage was the addition to the ship's roster of persons whose role was that of scientific investigation of natural phenomena. The expedition carried Philibert Commerson, a botanist and naturalist, Louis-Antoine Starot de Saint-Germain as writer and historian, and an astronomer, Pierre-Antoine Véron, to make accurate longitude determinations.

Bougainville discovered or located very few new islands. But in the two months spent traversing the Strait of Magellan, he had mapped it in detail, making it safer for future navigators. Through systematic observations of longitude, he helped fix the location of many island groups discovered by Spanish explorers two hundred years earlier, but whose exact location was still unknown. And his successful claim for France of Tahiti, which was as much within the Spanish zone of Tordesillas as were the Falkland Islands, effectively ended the influence of that treaty.

Louis-Antoine de Bougainville

The French had been as active as the British in establishing a commercial empire in North America, Africa and Asia, but the Seven Years War between France and Britain, which ended with the signing of the Treaty of Paris in 1763, deprived France of her colonies in North America, and reduced her position in India. In the following years the French government sought to

283. The Capture of the *Nuestra Senora de Cavadonga* by HMS *Centurion*, 20 June 1743 by Samuel Scott, c. 1743

The second half of the sixteenth century were chaotic times in Europe, with most nations engaged in open hostilities. Privateering was simply considered a form of commercial enterprise. George Anson's capture of the Spanish treasure galleon, *Nuestra Señora de Covadonga*, helped to finance the expedition, and on a personal level made him a wealthy man.

NATIONAL MARITIME MUSEUM, LONDON

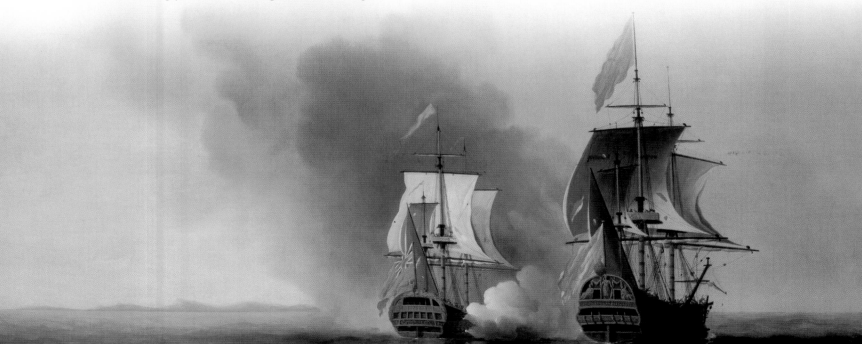

ENDEAVOURS EXTENDED

The breezes blew, the white foam flew,
The furrow follow'd free:
We were the first that ever burst
Into that silent sea.
SAMUEL TAYLOR COLERIDGE,

THE RIME OF THE ANCYENT MARINERE

THE CHALLENGE OF LONGITUDE

Since antiquity, latitude was easily calculated by measuring the angular height of a star or the Sun above the horizon, but for longitude, with its vertical lines (called meridians) which pass through both poles, measurement was much more difficult. It was general knowledge that time and longitude were interdependent: in twenty-four hours the Earth rotates 360 degrees, and every hour of rotation is a 15-degree change in longitude. Hipparchus, one of the greatest Hellenistic astronomers, intensively studied the longitude problem. He was the first to suggest using eclipses of the Moon to get an accurate reading of time at two places. From this it would be a matter of course to determine the longitude of the places of observation. But his system was difficult to put into practice, and eclipses of the Moon occur infrequently. For nearly two millennia the problem remained unsolved.

Without clocks that could keep accurate diurnal time and remain functional at sea, scientists turned to using other astronomical events as markers of time. One of the most important astronomers of the fifteenth century was Johannes Müller of Königsberg, called Regiomontanus. While engaged in making observations of the Moon Müller came to the conclusion that its rapid movement across a background of stars could be used to determine longitude at sea. If mariners were provided with tables giving the distance of the Moon from certain fixed stars they could compare reference time (local time of the reference longitude) with local time of the ship's position, and thus determine longitude. This solution was a logical development from Hipparchus's use of lunar eclipses. The theories of both men, however, could not be put into practice until the position of the Moon could be predicted with sufficient accuracy and until instruments were developed that were able to give precise measurements.

In spite of the problems inherent in using lunar distances to determine longitude, this approach continued to interest scholars. In 1514 Johannes Werner (1468–1528), a follower of

284. Ship caught in a storm on the rocky coast in Normandy by Julius Hintz

All mariners dread having their vessel driven by the wind toward a nearby shore. Called a 'lee shore', it is extremely difficult under sail to 'claw' one's way off against the wind, and results in an almost certain destruction of the vessel, and death of its crew.

PETER TAMM COLLECTION, HAMBURG

Regiomontanus, repeated the idea of using lunar distances for calculating longitude. The idea of measuring the angular distance between the Moon and a fixed star was again taken up by Peter Apian, professor of mathematics and astronomy at the University of Ingolstadt in Bavaria. Still, the lack of lunar tables of sufficient accuracy thwarted all efforts to the finding of longitude. Furthermore, Apian did not take into account the problem of parallax of the Moon; that is, the apparent shift in the position of the Moon against the background of stars caused by the difference in the observer's position. Gemma Frisius, a professor of mathematics and medicine at the University of Louvain at Brabant in modern Belgium, and contemporary of Apian, corrected this defect in a published version of Apian's *Cosmographicus liber* (1529). But determining longitude by lunar distances remained a problem until instruments with sufficient accuracy were developed.

Gemma Frisius's interest in practical navigation also led him to publish *A New Way to Find the Longitude* (1530), in which he demonstrated the value of creating a clock with sufficient accuracy, and rugged enough to be taken to sea, that mariners would be able to determine the difference between reference time and local time. The time difference would then be translated into longitude. This solution ultimately proved to be the correct one, although it was beyond the technology of the sixteenth century. Establishing longitude at sea continued to elude navigators even as late as the middle of the eighteenth century. Samuel de Champlain (1567–1635), who explored much of Atlantic Canada and founded France's first permanent colony in North America, believed 'God did not intend that man should ever be able to determine longitude at sea'.

When the great Italian astronomer Galileo Galilei (1564–1642) turned his telescope to the sky he discovered the four principal moons of Jupiter. He proposed that their occultations and eclipses could be used to find longitude. The advantage of using the Jovian moons, instead of the Earth's own Moon, was their high frequency of occurrence. However, Galileo's scheme, like that of Regiomontanus, suffered from the same lack of an accurate published almanac, to which was added the significantly greater difficulty of making observations while at sea.

With a stake in their maritime enterprises, the major countries of Europe began to offer financial rewards to the inventor of a reliable method for finding longitude at sea. The first nation to offer a prize was Spain in 1567 under Phillip II. Galileo put forward his idea of using the moons of Jupiter to determine longitude, and supplied tables that could accurately predict their position. But his method received scant enthusiasm in the Spanish court, and when he turned to Holland, which also offered a prize, his ideas were similarly dismissed.

French mathematicians and astronomers entered the race. Jean-Baptiste Morin (1583–1556) proposed to the minister of King Louis XIII the same system of lunar distances suggested a century earlier by Gemma Frisius. Like Gemma, Morin made allowances for parallax of the Moon and recognized the need for instruments that could measure celestial bodies with greater precision. Where the two men differed was in the emphasis Gemma had placed on inventing a clock that would be accurate when taken to sea.

In 1731 the Englishman John Hadley (1682–1744) and American Thomas Godfrey (1704–1749) presented in the Royal Society in London their independently made inventions: mirror quadrants. The instrument called Hadley's quadrant, which in fact was an octant, finally solved the need for an instrument capable of measuring angular distances with sufficient precision. Both inventors had applied Robert Hooke's idea of using mirrors in their instruments. The instrument also had the advantage of observing angles in any plane, thus making it useful not only for altitude measurements, but also for measurement of the distances between the Moon and a fixed star. Reverend Nevil Maskelyne (1732–1811) published in 1767 a *Nautical Almanac* which was based on the extensive and long-lasting astronomical work by Tobias Mayer of Göttingen and James Bradley of Greenwich. This almanac contained accurate lunar tables which finally took care of the need for more accurate astronomical timetables. During a voyage by Maskelyne in 1769 to measure a transit of Venus, he developed 'simplified' instructions for calculating longitude by lunar distances. These were published in *The British Mariners Guide*. Simplified they may have been, but allowing for the time needed to make the observations, and for working the calculations, including the corrections for parallax and refraction, his method still took four hours to complete.

As voyages increased in number, and mariners entered uncharted regions of the globe, the need to determine longitude accurately correspondingly increased. Ships had foundered before upon entering the English Channel, but no shipwreck in these waters exceeded in the number of deaths, nor brought such dangers to public attention, than the disaster that occurred on 22 October 1707.

Sir Cloudesley Shovell (c. 1650–1707), a distinguished and accomplished sea-officer, was bringing a fleet of fifteen warships, plus six of lesser rank, back to England after a successful attack on Toulon, France. On that morning they came into soundings, with 90 fathom of water. Hazy weather prevented the taking of observations, but Sir Cloudesley believed they had cleared the Isle of Ushant off the west coast of Brittany, and the way was clear for them to enter the Channel. He set course East by North, and at 8 o'clock that evening, to their great surprise and alarm, found they were upon the Scilly Islands at the southwest corner of England, and several of the ships made the signal of distress. Within minutes, the 'Bishop and Clerks' rocks, westward of the Scilly Islands, claimed the *Association,* flagship of the fleet. It sunk with the loss of 800 men, including Sir Cloudesley. Three other ships of the fleet also sank there, bringing the death toll to 2000 souls.

The catastrophe resulting from this mistaken position was as much an error of latitude determination as it was of longitude, for they were nearly 120 nautical miles farther north than supposed, and 100 nautical miles out in the reckoning of longitude. The problem was further compounded by inaccurate charts which placed the Scilly Islands 14–20 miles north of their actual position, leading the officers to think they had more sea-room than actually existed.

To prevent similar disasters from happening again, in 1714 the government of Great Britain offered a prize of £20,000

285. Portrait of Sir Cloudesley Shovell by Michael Dahl, 1702–1705

Sir Cloudesley Shovell is remembered as Commander of the fleet that was disastrously lost when upon entering the English Channel it struck rocks off the Scilly Islands. This awakened England's realization that a better means of navigating, other than by dead reckoning, was required. As a result accurate clocks were developed by which longitude could accurately be determined at sea.

NATIONAL MARITIME MUSEUM, LONDON

286. Northeast Coast of Asia from Nova Zembla to Japan by Pieter Goos, 1666

In the seventeenth century, lack of reliable timekeeping instruments made the calculation of longitude difficult. Pieter Goos misjudged the distance between Nova Zembla and Japan by as much as eighty degrees of longitude, thus resulting in this distorted map of eastern Asia.

COURTESY OF BERNARD J. SHAPERO RARE BOOKS, LONDON

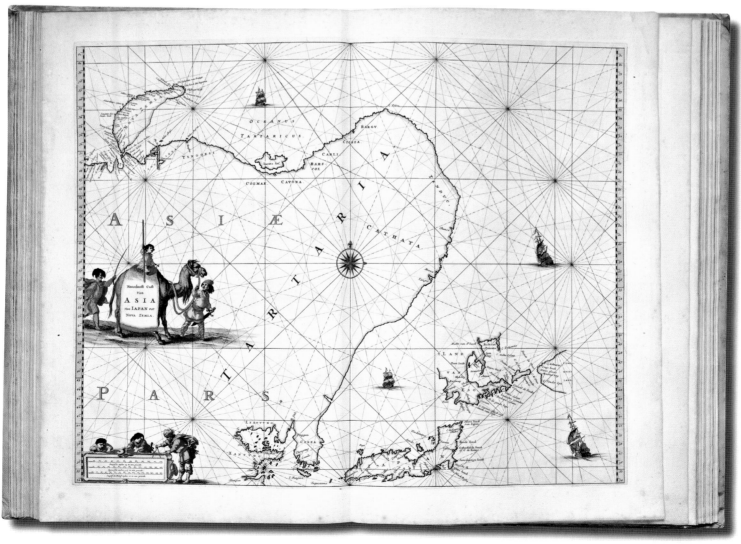

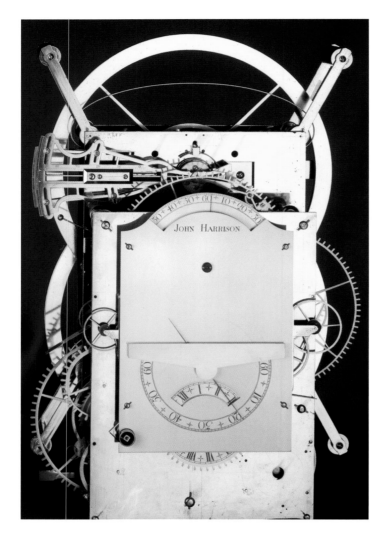

287. H3, Marine timekeeper designed by John Harrison, 1757

Although John Harrison's marine timekeeper, H3, failed to reach the required accuracy, and thus was unsuccessful in winning the Board of Longitude prize, it did incorporate several innovations of practical use today. More importantly, it led Harrison to totally rethink his approach to making an accurate timepiece.

NATIONAL MARITIME MUSEUM, LONDON

288. H4, Marine timekeeper designed by John Harrison, 1759

John Harrison's H4 timepiece proved to be the ultimate solution in obtaining longitude of a ship while at sea. Based on a watch made by John Jefferys, it proved to be astonishingly accurate. James Cook was full of praise for his K1 watch (a copy of the H4) that he used in charting the southern Pacific Ocean.

NATIONAL MARITIME MUSEUM, LONDON

to anyone who could provide a solution to finding longitude at sea. To qualify for the reward, calculations had to be accurate within half a degree of a great circle. This equals two minutes of time (1/30th of an hour) of longitude. To administer and judge the longitude prize, a Board of Longitude was organized.

Attention turned to creating a clock that would meet the challenge. By the beginning of the eighteenth century, watchmakers knew the physical principles and had the technical skill to make an accurate timepiece. A timepiece was now needed that was rugged enough to endure the abusive conditions of motion, moisture and temperature changes while at sea, and still maintain sufficient accuracy. John Harrison (1693–1776), a well-established English clockmaker, had made improvements in clock design by inventing one that needed no oil for lubrication. In the mid 1720s, working with his younger brother, James, he solved the problem of the effects of temperature on a long pendulum which causes it to gain or lose time with its change in length. He accomplished this by making the pendulum with alternate rods of brass and steel. This achieved an accuracy of one second in a month. Although far exceeding the timekeeping accuracy required by the Board of Longitude, a pendulum clock was impractical for use at sea.

Harrison solved the problem of erratic pendulum motion on a tossing ship with a spring-driven clock. A pair of counterbalancing springs made the clock independent of gravity; any change in motion of one spring was balanced by the other spring. Designated H1, it was presented to the Board of Longitude in 1735, and tested on a voyage to Lisbon in 1736. Harrison went through successive models of H2 and H3, each correcting deficiencies of the previous model. H3 improvements included a new anti-friction device, and a bimetallic strip to compensate for the effects of temperature on the balance spring.

At this point, Harrison changed his design approach entirely, and shifted to a model resembling a very large pocket watch. His son William (1728–1815) took H4, as it was called, on a voyage to Jamaica in 1762. In 81 days it was found to be only

5.1 seconds slow, which was equal to 0.02 degrees on a great circle. After returning home, almost five months later, the error was less than two minutes of time, corresponding to half a degree. Another test made on a voyage two years later also showed this timepiece to meet the requirements of accuracy for the Board of Longitude. But continual wrangling between the Board and Harrison prevented his being awarded the prize money in full. There were additional demands for Harrison to make two copies of H4 to be tested. They would be submitted to the Royal Observatory, where Nevil Maskelyne, appointed as Astronomer Royal in 1765, would check the accuracy and reliability of the watches. This was a setback for Harrison, for Maskelyne did not believe that any timepiece could be more reliable for finding longitude than using lunar distance measurement.

John Harrison, with William, produced H5, one of the copies of H4, while another English watchmaker, Larcum Kendall, produced the other copy of H4, designated as K1.

On his second circumnavigation voyage (1772–1775) Captain James Cook carried K1 with him to evaluate its accuracy and reliability, comparing it to the calculations made for longitude by lunar distances. He found it exceeded all expectations and learned to trust it completely, calling it a faithful guide through all the vicissitudes of climates.

In 1778, the London clockmaker, John Arnold (1735–1799), simplified John Harrison's K1 timepiece and reduced its cost by leaving out some of the more expensive parts. Nonetheless, it performed exceeding well in trials at the Royal Observatory. Arnold called his precise timekeeper a 'chronometer'. At last seamen were able to bring the local time of a reference meridian (the Royal Observatory at Greenwich, for English mariners) aboard ship; local noon could be taken by celestial observation, and the distance between the two times used to determine longitude. This became the preferred method of calculating longitude, and the challenge of longitude was successfully met.

NEW HORIZONS

Tabin Promontorium (Cape Tabin) had been described by geographers of ancient Greece, and although its exact position was unknown, throughout the centuries cartographers continued to show it on their maps at the northeastern extremity of Asia. In the search by English and Dutch navigators for a Northeast Passage, ice-choked seas north of Siberia were an impenetrable barrier to reaching Cape Tabin and fixing its location. That there was a sea-route beyond Cape Tabin and through the fabled 'Strait of Anian' into the Pacific Ocean, still remained to be determined.

289. Detail of World map by Louis Renard, 1715

In this decorative corner of Louis Renard's world map, Neptunus is seen with his consort Amphitrite, a sea-goddess, and other symbols of maritime life. Renard became known for depicting on his world map the isogonic lines of magnetic variation, published by Edmond Halley in 1700.

JUHA NURMINEN COLLECTION

Semyon Ivanov Dezhnev

In 1647, the Russian merchant and navigator, Semyon Dezhnev (c. 1605–1673), along with Fedor Alexeyev, set out to explore eastward of the Kolyma River in northeastern Siberia. The objective was twofold: to collect payment from the native people in tribute to the Tsar; and to gain wealth in trade from the furs, valuable walrus-ivory and silver reported to be abundant in the region east of the Kolyma River.

Fifty men set out in four kochs, single-masted wooden sailing ships specially designed for sailing in ice conditions of the Arctic Seas, but the expedition did not reach far beyond the Kolyma River. The following year (1648) they made another attempt, this time they passed Cape Tabin, and sailed out into an open sea. Dezhnev and Alexeyev became the first navigators to go from the Arctic Ocean into the Pacific. They established that Asia and North America were not connected, but separated by a body of water – the Strait of Anian (now called the Bering Strait). European knowledge of this important geographical discovery remained in obscurity for nearly a century because official reports had lain hidden and unread in departmental archives. Dezhnev himself did not realize

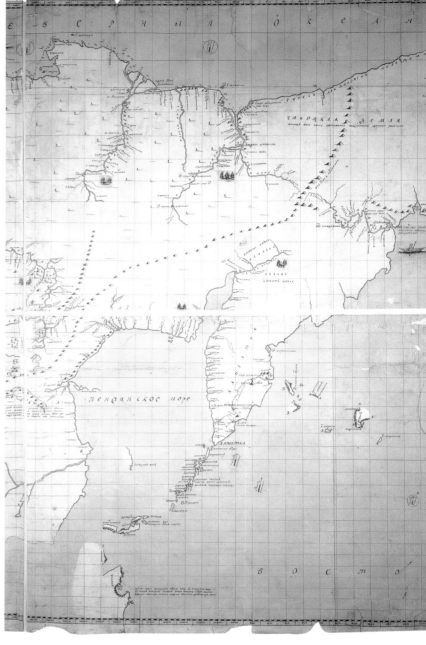

290. A Portrait of Catherine II as Legislator in the Temple of the Goddess of Justice by Dmitry Levitzky, early 1780s

Catherine the Great ruled as Empress of Russia from 1762 until 1796. During her reign she enlarged the territory of Russia, instituted many reforms, and extended Russian power, prestige and influence in European affairs. Catherine continued to promote the maritime expeditions initiated by Tsar Peter the Great.

THE TRETYAKOV GALLERY, MOSCOW

291. Kamchatka peninsula by Ivan Elagin, 1746

This forms part of a summary map of Russian discoveries in the Arctic and Pacific Oceans. It was drawn by the marine officer, Ivan Elagin, in 1746 after Vitus Berings's second expedition to Kamchatka peninsula in the Russian Far East, and to Alaska in 1740–41. Alexei Chirikov was second in command of the expedition aboard the vessel *Svjatoj Pavel* (St Paul).

RUSSIAN STATE ARCHIVES OF MILITARY HISTORY, MOSCOW

the full significance of his discovery or just how close he had come to approaching North America, believing that his greatest achievement was in finding a large walrus rookery.

Vitus Bering / Alexei Chirikov

Tsar Peter the Great, who ruled Russia from 1694 to 1725, was determined to transform his medieval country into a modern European power. In the last year of his life (1725), he authorized an expedition for exploration of the North Pacific with the objective of planting a Russian colony in North America. He selected as leader Vitus Jonassen Bering (1681–1741), a Dane who was serving in the Russian navy, and provided Martin Spanberg (c. 1695–1761) and Alexei Chirikov (1703–1748) as his assistants. This would come to be called the 'First Kamchatka Expedition' (1725–1730).

Their voyage by sea closely followed along the eastern shore of Siberia toward the far eastern corner of Asia. In one month, to the exact day, all sight of land was left behind as they broke out into the Chukchi Sea. At 65° N latitude, they had doubled the Chukchi Peninsula, as Dezhnev had done eighty years earlier but from the other direction.

Having felt he had accomplished the instructions given

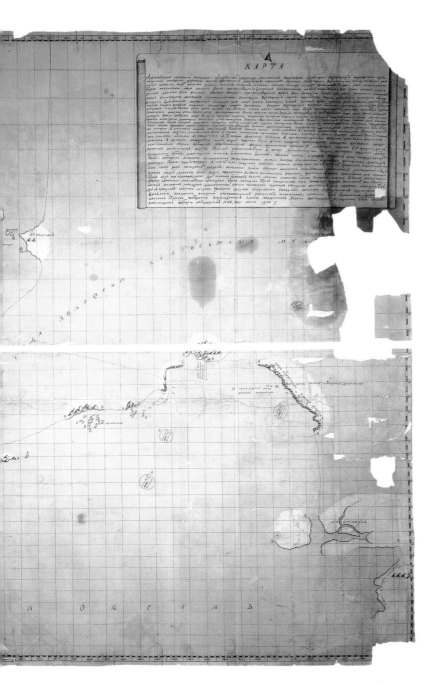

their way separately to the mainland of Alaska, discovering various Aleutian Islands along the way. The voyage of Bering and Chirikov initiated Russian colonial expansion in North America. Eager to exploit a new rich source of furs, traders began to migrate to Alaska, and by the beginning of the nineteenth century, Russia had an American colony, with its capital in Sitka.

Catherine the Great, who became Empress in 1762, pushed further the northern expeditions. Through the Academy of Sciences she gave elaborate instructions to the captains and scientists of future expeditions, requiring them to describe in detail the peoples they met and the natural history of the places visited.

James Cook

Throughout the history of navigation some men, such as Christopher Columbus, had great practical skill in navigation; others, like Magellan, pushed the bounds of their discoveries to lands farther than any others before them; while some, like Dampier, were keen observers, who went beyond extending geographic knowledge by describing the natural history and peoples of the regions visited. Captain James Cook (1728–1779) was the embodiment of all these skills, united to a degree unmatched by any navigator either before or since.

The Royal Society of London, England's oldest organization for scientific research founded in 1660, in conjunction with the British Admiralty, commissioned Lt James Cook to command an expedition to circle the globe. The purpose of the voyage was twofold: one was to observe the planet Venus as it passed in front of the Sun (called the transit of Venus), which was predicted to occur in 1769; and the other was to search for the great southern continent, the Terra Australis Incognita. As an officer in the Royal Navy, Cook had demonstrated his proficiency in celestial navigation on a voyage in 1766–67 to chart Canada's Gulf and River of St. Lawrence. He used a solar eclipse to provide an accurate position fix on the Newfoundland coast as a reference standard for his surveying. Through a network of shore triangulation he produced accurate and beautiful charts. Cook's major strengths were geography and astronomy, but he was also learned in other sciences.

Observation of the transit of Venus would provide an accurate estimate of the longitude at the observation points, but was primarily intended as a means of advancing astronomy. Using the observations made at several different locations the distance of Venus from the Sun could be accurately calculated, and the distances to other planets worked out. To assist him, Cook was accompanied by John Green (c. 1685–1757) who was an assistant at the Greenwich observatory to the Astronomer Royal, the same Nevil Maskelyne who devised a simplified method for finding longitude at sea through lunar distances. The scientific team was also to include two botanists who were to collect and classify as many new species as they could. Joseph Banks (1743–

him by the Tsar, Bering decided to return to Kamchatka. But Chirikov argued that they should either continue sailing eastward until 'The Great Land,' as America was called, was reached, or sail westward as far as the Kolyma River, thus establishing with certainty a Northeast Passage. Spanberg was more inclined to agree with Bering, feeling they could not survive a winter in these latitudes. After sailing to 67° N, close enough in the narrow strait where they would have seen the American coast if only the weather had not been so foggy, they turned their vessel homeward.

If officials in Imperial Russia had any reason for dissatisfaction with the results of this expedition, it did not prevent them from approving a second expedition proposed by Bering. Called the Great Nordic Expedition of 1738–42, it was on a much larger scale, with the purpose of exploring the sea between Asia and America, and to map the west coast of America. They made

Dangerous Ground

The world's oceans are strewn with the perils of solitary rocks, shoals, reefs, low-lying atolls and bold capes: at best they challenge the navigator's abilities and endurance to the utmost; at worst, they condemn the ship and its unfortunate souls to their doom.

The approach to land is always filled with apprehension by mariners, and a careful watch has to be kept for possible hidden rocks. Even beyond the coast, far from the shore, there are no assurances that the water is deep and safe for navigation. Offshore shoals and coral reefs in uncharted water are difficult to anticipate. The shape and height of ocean waves could provide warning of a sudden shoaling of the water, calling for caution. If conditions are right with the Sun, changes in the colour of the water may indicate a change in depth. The thin white line of waves breaking on rocks or coral may alert one to impending peril. But at night, this might be mistaken for no more than the glint of moonlight on wave crests.

In 1580, Sir Francis Drake, England's best-known privateer, struck a coral reef in the Indonesian Archipelago. He lightened his ship, the *Golden Hind*, by dumping cargo. She was lifted off the reef by a favourable shift in the wind, and Drake successfully completed his voyage to become the first Englishman to circumnavigate the globe.

On a trading voyage to Indonesia in 1619 the Dutch sea captain, Frederik de Houtman (c. 1571–1627), discovered a low-lying group of islands about 60 miles off the western coast of Australia. Predominantly coral based, they are fringed with bars and reefs. Houtman successfully navigated his way through this maze of reefs and low-lying islands which were subsequently given the name of Houtman Abrolhos. Even though this archipelago was charted, and the very word Abrolhos, a contraction of the Portuguese phrase meaning 'keep your eyes open', gave warning to sailors to beware of danger, it has claimed many ships. The most notorious shipwreck here was the *Batavia*, a Dutch East India Company ship on its maiden voyage in 1628 to the town of Batavia (present-day Jakarta) in Indonesia. Its captain, believing he was still hundreds of miles from the charted shores of Terra Australis Incognita (Unknown Southern Land) was not prepared for imminent danger. At night and while under full sail, he ran up on the reef. Before this devastating event occurred, mutiny was already brewing. But the disaster brought out all that is base in the human spirit: avarice, treachery, deceit, jealousy, rape and murder.

The *Batavia* was the first but not the last of many ships to be wrecked on these reefs. A century later, another Dutch East India ship, the *Zeewijk* struck on the southernmost reefs of the Abrolhos group in 1727. Its survivors, acting more admirably than those of the *Batavia*, constructed a small ship from the wreckage, and in an amazing feat of navigation successfully sailed to Java.

Treacherous reefs can claim even the most wary and competent of navigators. Captain James Cook sailed on his first voyage of discovery in 1770 on HM Barque *Endeavour*. His superior skills in navigation were not enough to prevent running aground on the Great Barrier Reef off the east coast of Australia. By lightening of the ship, he was able to get off on the next high tide.

In the North Atlantic, both Giovanni di Verrazzano and Estevão Gomes noted the dangerous sandbanks and shoals lying off the east coast of North America during their voyages in 1524. In 1609, Henry Hudson found his ship, the *Half Moon*, caught on the reefs off Nantucket Island, with their shallow, irregular bottom, and their swift, erratic currents. Dangerously close to the breaking waves, he anchored and waited for a favourable tide and better weather. By 'the great mercy of God', he said, 'we got clear of the flats'.

Sailors were not only threatened by shoaling water; the configuration of the land creates special conditions that may be perilous. Before completion of the Panama and Suez Canals, for Europe's mariners to

reach India and the Far East they had to sail the great southern oceans and double the Cape of Good Hope or Cape Horn. Under the direction of Prince Henry of Portugal, and his successor, King John II, Portugal's navigators ventured south along the west coast of Africa. At its southernmost tip, the Cape of Good Hope, they met with the treacherous conditions created by collision of two swiftly moving currents – the warm water Algulhas Current, sweeping south out of the Indian Ocean, and the icy Benguela Current rushing north out of the Antarctic. Tremendous turbulence is created where the two oceans meet. When strong weather fronts and large low-pressure systems bringing gale-force winds from the west and southwest encounter these currents off the cape, they create monster-sized waves.

292. The Straits of Magellan – The Land of Patagonia by Captain John Narbrough, 1670

293. A Shipwreck by Hjalmar Münsterhjelm, 1881

Dangerous shallows, cape-ends and narrows are found in all seas. This rare illumination depicts the Magellan Straight, which can be very dangerous to ships. The painting shows the rough waters in the islands of the Gulf of Finland, which are very difficult to navigate. There are more than 10,000 islands in the Gulf, with even an even greater number of treacherous underwater rocks.

THE BRITISH LIBRARY, LONDON.

JUHA NURMINEN COLLECTION

Such is the fury created here by the combined forces of wind, current and land configuration, that when Bartolomeu Dias doubled this cape in 1487, he named it *Cabo Tormentoso*. In his voyage to India ten years later, Vasco da Gama spent three days tacking back and forth off the cape attempting to best the swift-flowing Alguhas Current, only to find that at the end of his struggle he was right back where he started.

The alternative was a route to the southwest, around Cape Horn, which at 56° S latitude is 1260 miles farther south than the Cape of Good Hope. Those who venture here are forced to battle the Antarctic Circumpolar Current (West Wind Drift) that unhindered circles the globe. Between the southern tip of the South American Continent and the Antarctic Peninsula this current is forced to squeeze through the relatively narrow Drake Passage, causing it to accelerate in velocity. This increase in speed as the result of constricted passageways is known as 'channeling' and affects winds in the same manner as it does currents.

Prevailing westerly winds in these latitudes, channeled through Drake Passage, can reach a velocity of 100 knots. This speed is partially the result of another effect, 'cornering'. When the wind hits the Andes Mountains it is blocked by their 2½ mile height, and forced to turn southward until it can flow freely again. At the point of turning it augments the existing prevailing flow of wind, with the resultant effect of accelerated velocity. The dynamics of channelling and cornering are found wherever current or wind meets with an obstruction, whether they be smaller capes, headlands or around the ends of islands, but

nowhere are they as powerful as at Cape Horn.

Waves and swells gain in height as their fetch – the distance they can travel uninterrupted – increases. With nothing to stop the huge waves that roll around the globe in far southern latitudes they present a formidable struggle for ships under sail. Another form of channeling, vertical channeling, as it were, exists at Cape Horn. After crossing the deeps of the Pacific Ocean, the waves and swells hit the shallower waters of the continental shelf, causing them to increase in size, to where they reach a height of 45–60 feet.

Passing from the Atlantic Ocean into the Pacific Ocean through the protected channels between Tierra del Fuego and Patagonia presents another set of challenges. The winds here are tempestuous and fickle; sudden squalls with blinding snow, sleet or rain alternate with extensive periods of calm and dense fog. In the narrow channels of the Strait of Magellan and Beagle Channel, mariners are either beating against wind, with ships that are notable for their lack of manoeuvarability or forced to lie becalmed and at the mercy of erratic currents.

Another danger awaits the mariner in these passageways. Dense, cold air from the snow- and ice-covered mountaintops, can suddenly and without warning rush down the slopes. Called willawaws, these katabatic (from the Greek word *katabatos*, meaning descending) winds can strike with velocities in excess of 100 miles per hour, laying the unsuspecting ship on its beam ends in a matter of seconds. When Charles Darwin voyaged here, he said that 'death, instead of life seemed the predominant spirit'.

294. A Portrait of Captain James Cook by John Webber, c.1780

Captain James Cook was the greatest explorer of the eighteenth century. During his three circumnavigations of the world from 1768 through 1780, he delineated the bounds of the Pacific Ocean from the Arctic Circle to the Antarctic Circle, and discovered Hawaii. Cook helped turn exploration into a science: he expanded knowledge about the geography, hydrography and natural history of the Pacific Ocean; he observed and recorded the ethnology of its native peoples. Cook is credited with conquering scurvy, the dreadful disease that took its toll on all earlier expeditions; there were no deaths from scurvy on any of Cook's three voyages. Such was Cook's exemplary behaviour to the indigenous peoples he encountered on the various islands, that they revered him as a god.

MUSEUM OF NEW ZEALAND TE PAPA TONGAREWA, WELLINGTON

295. South Channel of Orleans, Quebec, charted by James Cook, c. 1759–1760

In preparation for an impending attack on Quebec City, the capital of New France, the British Admiralty sent a young navigator, James Cook, later known for his explorations in the Pacific Ocean, to chart the St. Lawrence River. Cook surveyed large portions of the river, including a dangerous channel south of *Île de Orléans*. His careful charting, including soundings, and the placement of buoys, allowed an armada of over 200 ships to advance upon the city of Quebec and successfully attack it.

THE BRITISH LIBRARY, LONDON

1820) was a fellow of the Royal Society, and Dr Carl Solander had studied under the famed Carolus Linneaus (1707–1778), developer of the system of naming species by binary names, which we still use. The natural history artist Sydney Parkinson (1745–1771), and the landscape painter Alexander Buchan (1829–1907), were to draw the collected specimens, and record through paintings the events of the voyage.

Once the observation of Venus was completed, the principal objective of the expedition was to resolve the issue of the Great Southern Continent. Alexander Dalrymple (1737–1808), who was also a Fellow of the Royal Society, and first hydrographer of the British Admiralty, was firmly convinced of its existence. Believing it to be a vast and fertile land with a wealth of resources, he wanted to be the first to discover it, and gain possession for England before it was claimed by any other nation.

Instructions given by the Admiralty to Cook were virtually unchanged for all three voyages. He was to 'explore diligently the coasts he might discover; carefully observing the true situation thereof both in Latitude and Longitude, the Variation of the Needle, bearings of head Lands, height, direction and course of the Tides and Currents, Depths and Soundings of the Sea ...and also surveying and making Charts, and taking views of such Bays, Harbours and parts of the coast as may be useful in navigation'.

The ship selected for the expedition was a three-masted barque, formerly a collier, by the name of *Earl of Pembroke*. Though only 106 feet long, the ship was strongly built, and admirably suited for sailing close inshore for the survey work ahead of her. She was re-outfitted and commissioned as HM barque *Endeavour*.

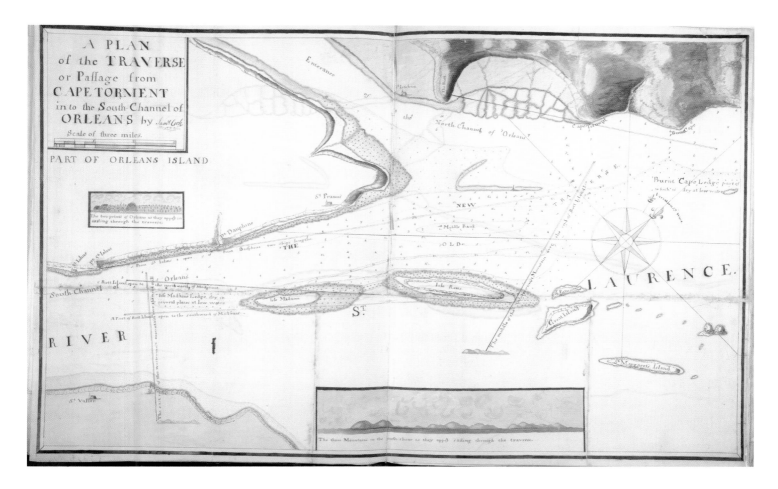

The viewing station selected for Cook's expedition was the island of Tahiti in the South Pacific, which had been discovered by Samuel Wallis in 1767, and named King George III's Island, the year before Bougainville claimed it for France. The *Endeavour* left England on 26 August 1768, crossed the Atlantic, and after a stop at Rio de Janeiro to replenish supplies, passed through the Le Maire Strait and rounded Cape Horn to enter the Pacific. Cook headed directly for Tahiti, and arrived there twelve weeks ahead of the astronomical event, and with time to build a fort and observatory for viewing the transit of Venus.

The observations of Venus were disappointing, despite the favourable conditions on the day of the transit. Separate observations taken by Cook, Green and Solander all differed by an amount exceeding any anticipated margin of error. It was necessary to observe the point of contact when Venus first entered in front of the Sun and the point at which it exited. But the hazy corona around Venus made this difficult to ascertain with any precision. Observers in other parts of the world encountered the same problem.

Having accomplished as much he could, Cook made a circumnavigation of Tahiti to survey and map it, and then continued across the Pacific to follow through on the other goal of the voyage, that of finding the southern continent of Terra Australis. From Tahiti, he took with him a native named Tupaia, who was familiar with the geography of the western Pacific and the system of Polynesian navigation. With his help Cook reached New Zealand.

Although the chronometer had already been invented by this time, Cook did not have one on board. To fix the latitude and longitude of the islands he discovered, Cook used the system of lunar distances, measuring the Moon's angular distance from a suitable star. The instrument he used was Hadley's quadrant, and calculations were obtained from tables in the newly published *Nautical Almanac*.

From Tahiti, Cook shaped his course southward to the latitude of 40° S, considered to be the probable location of any southern continent. When no landmass was encountered, he turned northward, and then west, until he reached the east coast of the land discovered by Tasman in 1642. Tasman called it Staaten Landt, believing it might be the same Staaten Landt off Cape Horn seen by Le Maire and Schouten during their voyage in 1616, and who thought it might be attached to Terra Australis. Cook's circumnavigation of the north and south islands of New Zealand laid to rest the misconception that it was part of the southern continent, and in six month's time he charted the entire coastline of New Zealand, and found the strait between the two islands, now called Cook Strait, which Tasman and Visscher had missed, thinking it to be only a large bay.

Cook intended next to determine whether Tasmania, Van Dieman's Land, was part of Terra Australis, but before he could reach it, gales forced the *Endeavour* northward. At a point on the southeast coast of Australia (New Holland) he sighted land. He was unable to settle with certainty the geographic question of Van Dieman's Land, but from the way the mainland coast of Australia trended toward the southwest, and knowing the position of Van Dieman's Land, he conjectured that the two were not connected. Turning northward, Cook worked his way up the east coast of Australia – the first European upon those shores – surveying and charting 2000 miles of coastline as he went along. At 34° S latitude, the *Endeavour* dropped anchor in a shallow bay, which Cook named

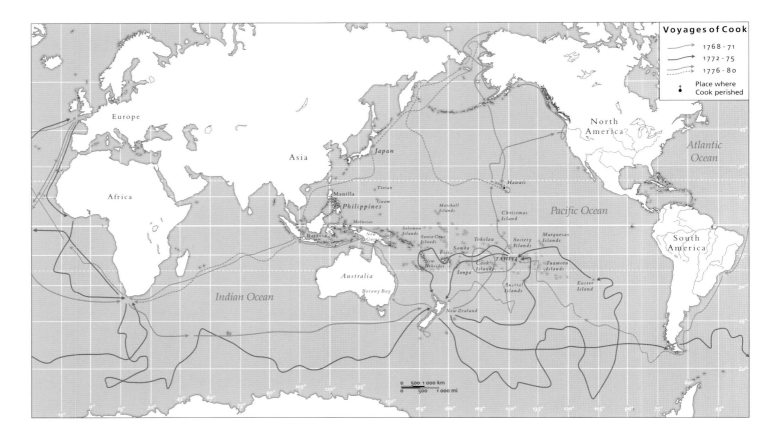

296. Voyages of Captain James Cook

Botany Bay on account of the vast quantities of new plants collected there by Banks and Solander. Upon his return to England, Banks was to propose that an English colony should be planted there.

After leaving Botany Bay, the *Endeavour* was almost lost when she grounded on the uncharted Great Barrier Reef off the northeastern coast of Australia. But Cook was able to clear the ship off, and after making repairs he eventually continued the voyage northward to Papua and New Guinea, a region already charted by Portuguese and Dutch navigators. With his assignment completed, he headed homeward, passing through the strait between New Guinea and New Holland, which Cook knew had been discovered by Luis Vaez de Torres in 1604, and sailed along the southern coast of Java to Batavia. There he carried out a major overhaul of the *Endeavour* before crossing the Indian Ocean.

At this point in the voyage, for the first time in the history of long-distance seafaring, not a single man had been lost to scurvy. Fresh vegetables obtained along the way, and Cook's insistence that citrus fruit and sauerkraut be fed to the crew, had prevented what had previously been an inevitable scourge among sailors. But the return to England was not without its casualties. Malaria and other fevers caught in the pestilential Batavia, and other assorted diseases, claimed several lives, including those of the Polynesian navigator, Tupaia, and Banks's Finnish secretary. The surviving crew made it back to England in July 1771 in a weakened condition, after a three-year voyage.

Within a year of his return to England, Cook embarked on a second circumnavigation with orders to explore to the southward of Tierra del Fuego and Australia, and finally put an end to all diversity of opinion about the existence of a Terra Australis. It had already been determined from Cook's previous voyage, and the explorations of others preceding him, that no southern lands of any great extent existed northward of 40° S latitude. It was Cook's intent, therefore, to circle the globe 'weaving in and out of the sixtieth parallel'.

As before, any discovery was to be thoroughly charted, with its latitude and longitude accurately fixed. For this purpose, Cook was provided with the newest and best instruments, including three timepieces made by John Arnold, England's finest watchmaker. The Board of Longitude also commissioned the watchmaker, Larcum Kendall, to make a pocket-watch version of Harrison's latest marine timekeeper, H4. Called K1, it too was taken along for evaluation.

The expedition comprised two ships, HM sloop *Resolution*, commanded by Cook, and HM barque *Adventure*, commanded by Tobias Furneaux. Taking careful note of the seasons, Cook set his departure so as to arrive in the far southern latitudes during favourable summer weather. Since the prevailing winds in these high latitudes would be westerly, the course of circumnavigation was around the Cape of Good Hope and toward the east.

As intended, Cook circled much of the globe near 60° S latitude; on three occasions he brought the *Resolution* below the Antarctic Circle (66° 30' S), making him the first to accomplish this feat. In February of 1744, he penetrated to

297. A Grey-headed Kingfisher by George Foster

This painting of a kingfisher is a good example of the observations made in natural history on expeditions. It is from the Cape Verde islands, visited during Captain James Cook's second voyage (1772–1775) to explore the southern continent.

THE NATURAL HISTORY MUSEUM, LONDON

298. Dusky Bay New Zealand by James Cook, c.1759–1760

Captain James Cook circumnavigated New Zealand, and charted 2400 miles of its coastline, in just six months (October 1769–March 1770).

THE BRITISH LIBRARY, LONDON

Overleaf:

299. Chart of the N.W. Coast of America and the N.E. Coast of Asia, Explored in the Year's 1778 and 1779 by Henry Roberts and James Cook, 1794

A chart of Captain Cook's last explorations along the North American coast into Bering Strait which confirmed the existence of a strait between Asia and Alaska.

JUHA NURMINEN COLLECTION

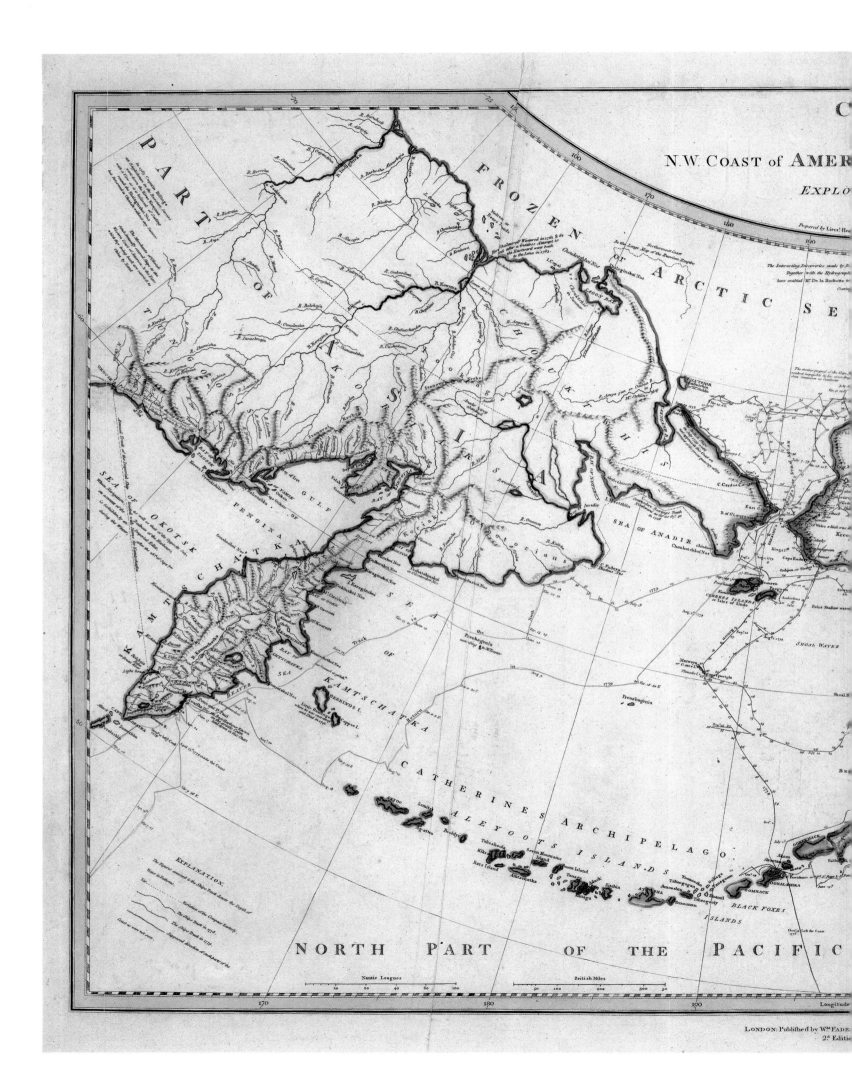

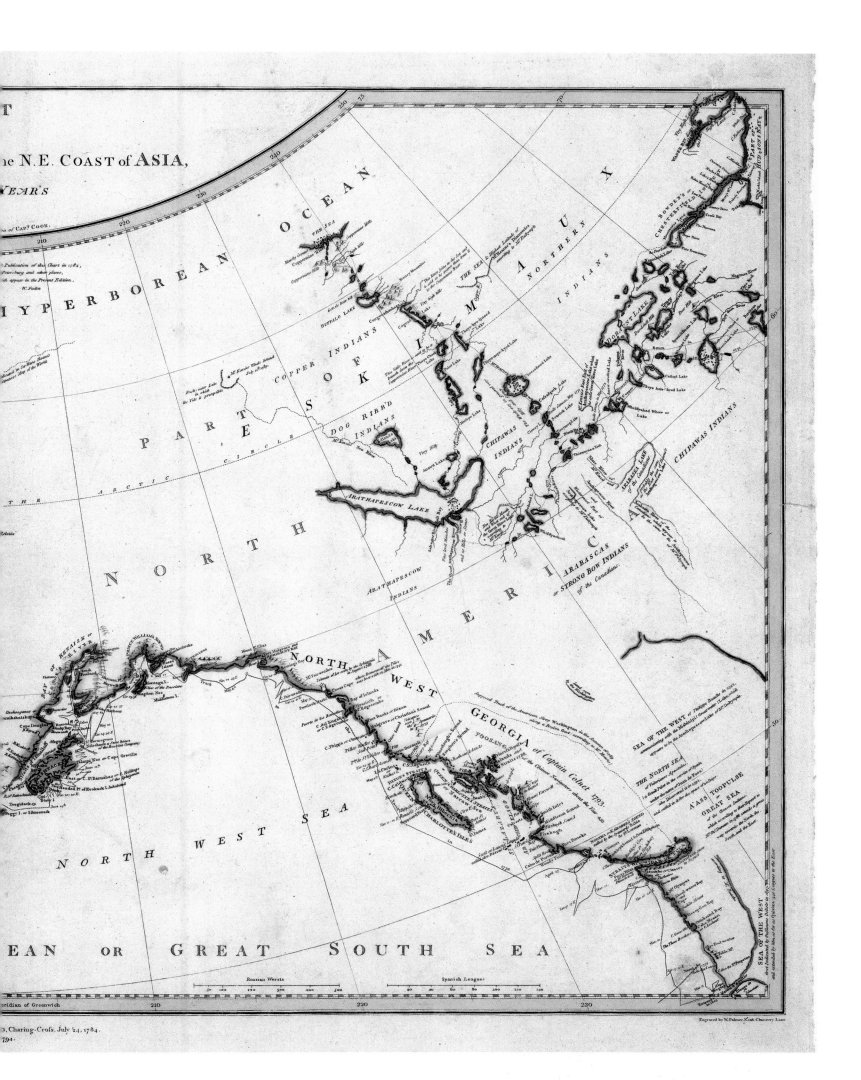

the N.E. COAST of ASIA,

YEARS

HYPERBOREAN OCEAN

NORTHERN INDIANS

ESKIMEAUX

PART OF

NORTH AMERICA

ARATHAPESCOW LAKE

ARATHAPESCOW INDIANS

COPPER INDIANS

DOG RIB'D INDIANS

CHIPAWAS INDIANS

CHIPAWAS INDIANS

ARABASCAS or STRONG BOW INDIANS of the Canadians

NORTH WEST SEA

NORTH WEST

GEORGIA of Captain Colnet 1793.

CHARLOTTE'S ISLES

NORTH WEST SEA

EAN   OR   GREAT   SOUTH   SEA

Engraved by W. Palmer, N.128. Chancery Lane

300. The Ice Islands by William Hodges, 1777

The *Resolution* is dwarfed by this large iceberg, which stopped her during Cook's second voyage in January 1773. The crew is hunting and taking in ice to fill up the fresh-water storage tanks.

JUHA NURMINEN COLLECTION

301. Model of HMS *Resolution*

Resolution, James Cook's flagship during his second and third voyages, was launched at Whitby in 1770 as a North Sea collier, the *Marquis of Granby*. Her lower deck length was 110 feet 8½ inches (33.7 m), maximum beam was 35 feet 3½ inches (11.0 m), and she had a draft of 13 feet 1½ inches (4.0 m). The *Marquis of Granby* was purchased in 1772 by the Royal Navy and commissioned as the *Drake*. At the naval yard in Deptford the *Drake* underwent an extensive refit before the first expedition. Before the *Drake* sailed, the King and the Earl of Sandwich advised that the vessel be renamed so as not to offend the Spanish. And so she departed from Plymouth in 1772 as the *Resolution*.

JOHN NURMINEN FOUNDATION

Joseph Billings' and Gavril Sarychev's travel account

In 1785, Empress Catherine II sent Joseph Billings (c. 1758–1806) and Gavril Sarychev (1763–1831) to explore the coasts of eastern Siberia and western Alaska and the Aleutian Islands. Because of his experience, Billings became the expedition's leader. He was one of the officers on James Cook's final voyage. Billings' and Sarychev's nine-year voyage resulted in several excellent maps and ethnographical accounts. Later, Gavril Sarychev continued his careful charting work in the Baltic Sea.

302. A Yakut shaman with his drum

303. A 'reindeer Tungushian' in summer attire

304. View of a port on the Jassatshnaja River on the coast in the Kolyma River area

JUHA NURMINEN COLLECTION

EEN JAKUTISCHE SCHAMAN.

EENE RENDIERTUNGUZIN IN HARE ZOMERKLEEDING.

Exploration Ships in the Pacific and the Antarctic

Lieutenant James Cook made his first expedition, between 1768 and 1771, with the 29-metre barque *Endeavour*. Formerly the *Earl of Pembroke*, she was built in 1764 in Whitby for the English East Coast coal trade supplying London. Displacing 366 tons, *Endeavour* was constructed to be a workhorse, carrying as much cargo as possible at a low cost. In the eighteenth century the term barque did not describe the ship's rigging, but was a common name for a blunt-bowed smallish cargo vessel. *Endeavour* was a three-masted ship, rigged with three square sails on the fore and main masts; in the eighteenth century the practice of using a topgallant sail above the topsail had became common. On her mizzenmast *Endeavour* carried a square sail above a gaff sail. The blunt bow and the broad beam made her hull quite box-shaped, but she was sturdily built and very seaworthy in rough seas, although her fastest logged speed was only 8 knots. Her large hold was needed so that the provisions and scientific equipment for a long journey could be loaded, and the shallow draft of the East-Coast collier was useful as it permitted exploration of coastal waters, reducing the risk of damage from grounding, and increasing the chance of refloating her should she go aground. When *Endeavour* ran onto the Great Barrier Reef, the crew were able to save her and, after two months' repair, were able to continue the voyage.

Prior to Cook's first voyage the *Endeavour* was docked and converted to an exploration ship at Deptford on the River Thames to accommodate 94 scientists and crew. The space below deck was completely rebuilt. Decks and cabins were added, storage space expanded, and the rig was totally renewed to withstand the storms on the oceans. Another layer of planking was added to protect the bottom from tropical sea worms.

Cook was a practical seaman. He understood the importance of serving his men fruits and vegetables, especially pickled cabbage, and of keeping the ship clean.

When the first expedition returned to England, Cook immediately started preparations for the next (1772–75). For his second voyage, Cook wanted two vessels to provide mutual support in the event of another grounding. *Endeavour* was sold to France and renamed *La Liberte*, but Cook chose vessels of the same type as the *Endeavour*, chartering the *Resolution* and the *Adventure*, both colliers built in 1770. The flagship *Resolution* was a little bigger than the *Adventure*, but each had a larger hold and more space between decks than had *Endeavour*, providing the crew with more light and fresh air in the damp climate. They were equipped with state-of-the-art navigational aids, ice anchors, and an apparatus for distilling fresh water from seawater. In 1773 Cook made history when he was the first European to cross the Antarctic Circle, but he never sighted the Antarctic.

For his third and last voyage (1776–80), Cook employed the smaller collier *Discovery* as companion to his flagship *Resolution*. The purpose of the voyage was to discover the Northwest Passage between the Atlantic and the Pacific, but arctic ice stopped the expedition at Bering Sound. Cook died in 1779 at Hawaii after he was attacked by the inhabitants, and the *Resolution* returned home without him.

BEAGLE

The designation of sailing ships by the layout of their rig began in the early nineteenth century. A two-masted ship with square sails on both masts was called a brigantine. They were small and agile vessels, easier to handle than large ones and in the Royal Navy they were often used for scouting and coastal defence.

The naturalist Charles Darwin made the brigantine *Beagle* famous. She was in no way a remarkable ship, just one of some 100 ships of the Cherokee class, which had been built for the Royal Navy. Their hulls were painted black and there was hardly any decoration. They were not popular among crews, who give them the nickname of 'coffin brigs': twenty-six of them sank. For the expedition *Beagle* was converted to a barque by adding a mizzenmast to make her easier to manoeuvre, which was needed for working in shallow coastal waters. The deck was raised by 18 inches to enlarge the space below, and four of her ten guns were removed.

The first expedition (1826–30) brought *Beagle* to South American waters. It was not a successful voyage and the conditions were poor on board. The crew suffered from diseases and short rations, and bad weather affected the passengers. The captain

of the ship became so depressed that he committed suicide and his second, Robert FitzRoy, brought the ship home.

It was the second expedition of 1831–36 that made the *Beagle* famous. Under command of Captain FitzRoy, the purpose of the second voyage was to chart the South American coast. In addition to that, the longitude of important locations was to be established by chronometers of which up to twenty-two were carried on board. The scientists and the crew comprised seventy-four persons, among them the young student Charles Darwin. The observations of this voyage formed the basis of Darwin's theories about evolution, although the *Origin of Species* was not to be published until 1859.

Six months after her return, *Beagle* again set sail, now heading for Australia. Returning to England in 1843, she was employed for a while with the Coast Guard, and then sold in 1870. Her beyond this fate is unknown.

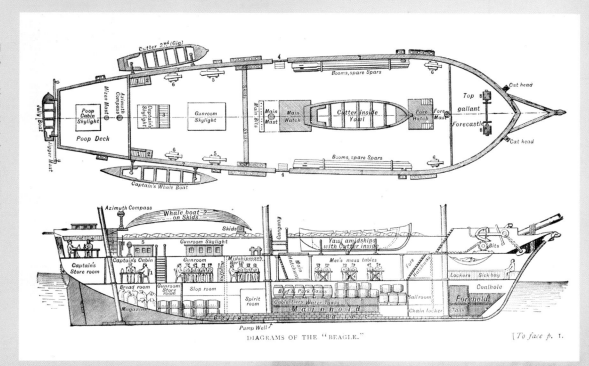

305. HMS *Beagle* in the Murray Narrows, Beagle Channel by Conrad Martens, 19th century

All is tranquil and attractive in appearance in this painting by Conrad Martins of HMS *Beagle* in the Strait of Magellan. In absolute contrast, Charles Darwin, the naturalist aboard the *Beagle* wrote: 'The atmosphere ...in this climate, where gale succeeds gale, with rain, hail, and sleet, seems blacker than anywhere else. In the Strait of Magellan, looking due southward from Port Famine, the distant channels between the mountains appeared from their gloominess to lead beyond the confines of this world'.

THE BRIDGEMAN ART LIBRARY

306. Diagrams of HMS *Beagle*

The cross-section of the *Beagle* shows how confined space was on ships and how the crew's supplies were stowed. The ship had several boats, including whalers and skilled carpenters made more of these small boats when required during a voyage. When Robert FitzRoy became Beagle's master, he made a number of improvements such as raising her sides.

THE NATURAL HISTORY MUSEUM, LONDON

71° 10' S latitude, roughly 1 100 miles from the South Pole. He also continued mapping in the Pacific Ocean further to the northward, adding Tonga, Fiji, the New Hebrides, Easter Island and New Hebrides. From the cultural and linguistic similarities he observed in all these island peoples, who stretched across the western Pacific from New Zealand to Easter Island, and encompassed an area one-fourth the circumference of the globe, he surmised they had a common ancestry.

As before, he used a Hadley's quadrant and the system of lunar distances to measure longitude, but now he could confirm them with his pocket chronometer (K1) which exceeded all expectations, showing it to be remarkably accurate and trustworthy. The Board of Longitude was at last brought to recognize that Harrison had a right to the prize offered by parliament for a reliable means of finding longitude at sea. By comparison, the timepieces made by Arnold did poorly, owing, as Cook stated, to the 'vicissitudes of climate'.

After a voyage lasting three years and covering 70,000 miles, Cook returned to England. On this journey he lost only four men, and none to scurvy. Most importantly, with his circuit of the southern ocean, he proved there was no possibility of a southern continent, Terra Australis Incognita, 'unless', as he said, 'it was near the pole, and out of the reach of navigation'.

All attempts at finding the Northwest Passage from its Atlantic side had previously ended in failure. The British Admiralty decided to search for its entrance from the Pacific, and commissioned Cook to lead yet a third expedition, which was ordered to sail north and east from the Bering Strait to find a northern passage by sea from the Pacific to the Atlantic Ocean. Two ships, the *Resolution*, commanded by Cook, and the *Discovery*, commanded by Charles Clerke (1741–1779), set out in 1776 to achieve this goal. This time, Cook carried a simplified version of Kendall's K1, the K3, but it did not perform as well as the K1.

Passing through the Pacific, the expedition discovered many of the Hawaiian Islands, which Cook named the Sandwich Islands, after the Earl of Sandwich. The expedition reached the shores of North America near the to what is now Oregon border, and followed the coast northward along present day Canada and Alaska. As the land continued to trend toward the northwest, the likelihood of finding an entrance to a passage leading to the Atlantic seemed less and less probable. After passing through the strait into the Bering Sea, they reached Icy Cape on the North American Shore, and across to North

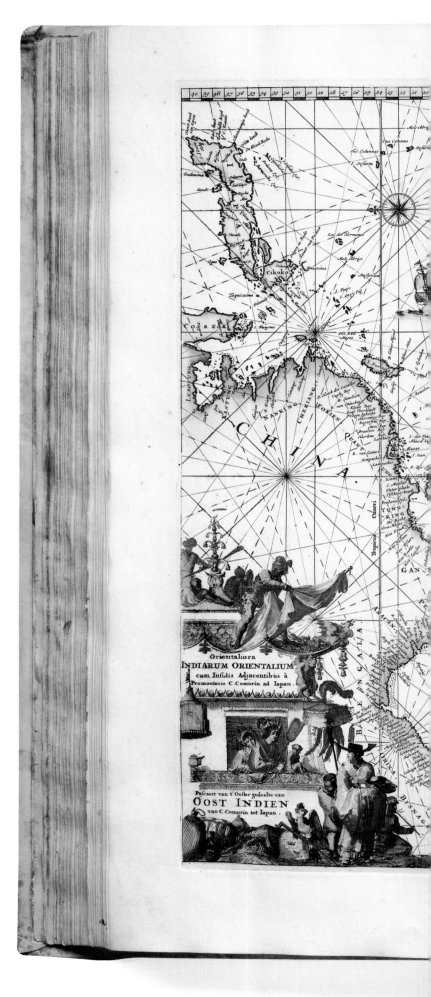

307. Map of the North Sea by Louis Renard, 1715

Lucas Janszoon Waghenaer's first sea atlas (1584–1585) set the standard for sea atlases by other cartographers, and became a tradition lasting until the end of the eighteenth century. In this Renard map, reefs, shallows and anchorages are all marked with appropriate symbols, following the style of Waghenaer.

JUHA NURMINEN COLLECTION

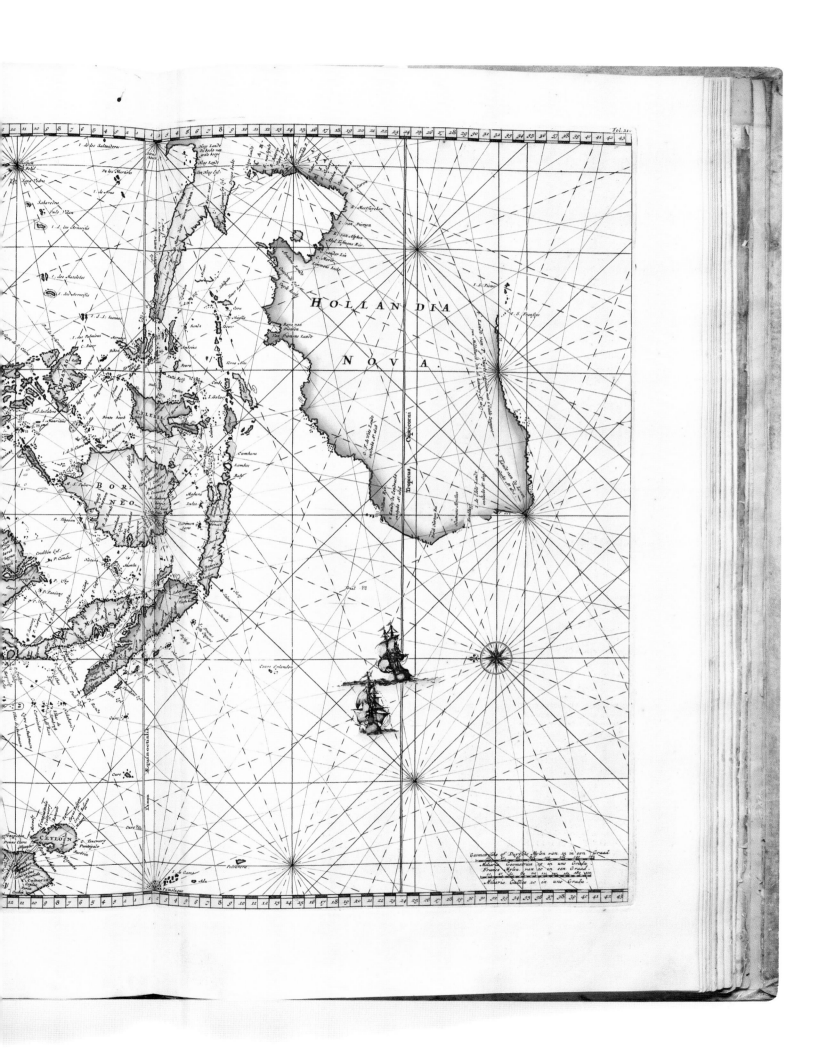

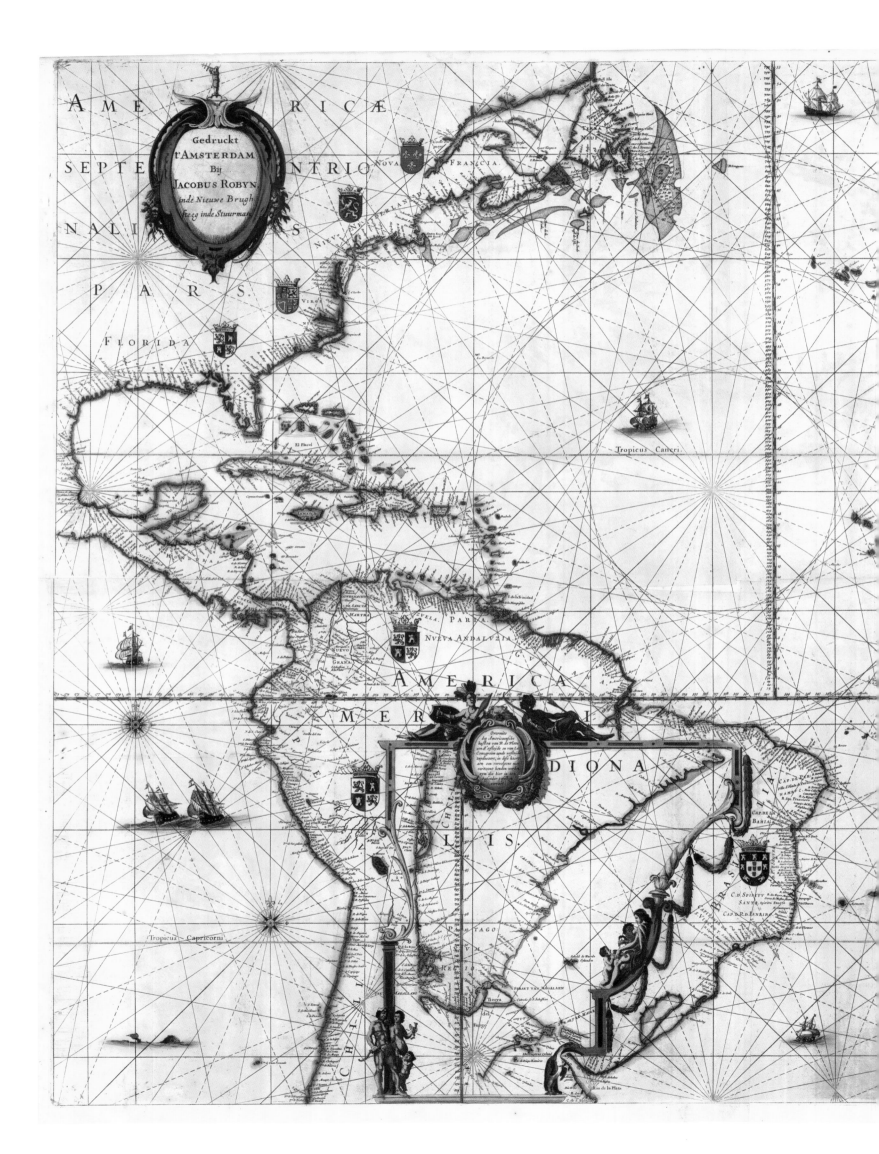

309. Drawing from Willem Blaeu's *The Light of Navigation* by David Winckeboons, 1612

Willem Blaeu published his *The Light of Navigation* in 1608, which is a seafaring guide similar to The Mariner's Mirror. His book used an improved way to present hydrographical information and provided more accurate guidance for coastal sailing to make navigation easier. His work was translated into several languages in addition to English (1612) and it was popular among many generations of seafarers. The drawing is of a teacher providing instruction in the use of navigational aids.

JUHA NURMINEN COLLECTION

308. Map of the West Indies by Jacobus Robijn, c.1674

The atlas of sea charts Willem Blaeu published in c. 1629 contained an important chart of the Atlantic Ocean, based on the Mercator projection. It became the prototype for other cartographer's maps of the Atlantic, such as Jacobus Robijn's map, published c. 1674.

COURTESY OF MAP HOUSE OF LONDON

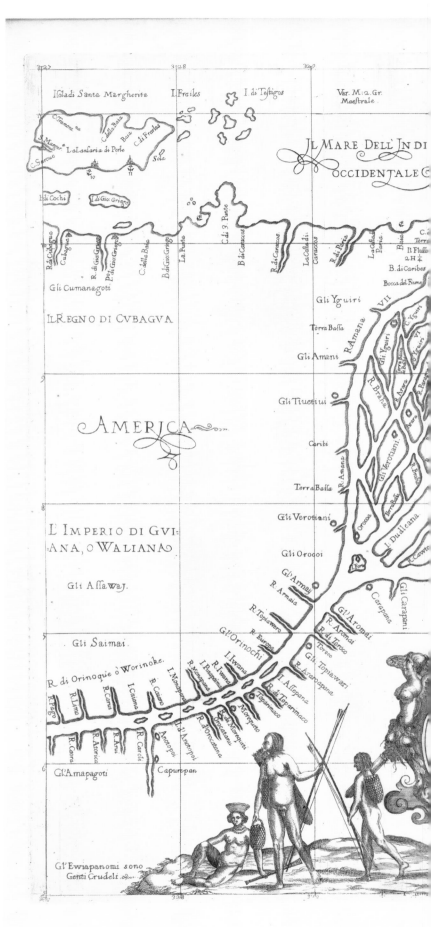

310. Portrait of Sir Robert Dudley by an unknown artist

Robert Dudley was the illegitimate son of the 1st Earl of Leicester and Lady Douglas Sheffield. At the age of fourteen he joined the British navy during the Spanish Armada. Dudley was married three times and moved to Italy where he became a naval advisor to Ferdinand I, Grand Duke of Tuscany.

JUHA NURMINEN COLLECTION

311. Map of Trinidad and Guyana by Robert Dudley, 1647

The twenty-one-year year old British nobleman, Robert Dudley, led an expedition in 1594 to Guyana. In 1647 he published *Dell' Arcano del Mare* (Secrets of the Sea), a monumental work on navigation, shipbuilding, and sea charts. His *Dell' Arcano del Mare* was a first in many ways: it was the earliest printed sea atlas to cover the entire world; the first to be made by an Englishman; and the first to be designed using the Mercator projection plan. It took eight years of work to complete the copper plates

THE NATIONAL LIBRARY OF FINLAND, HELSINKI

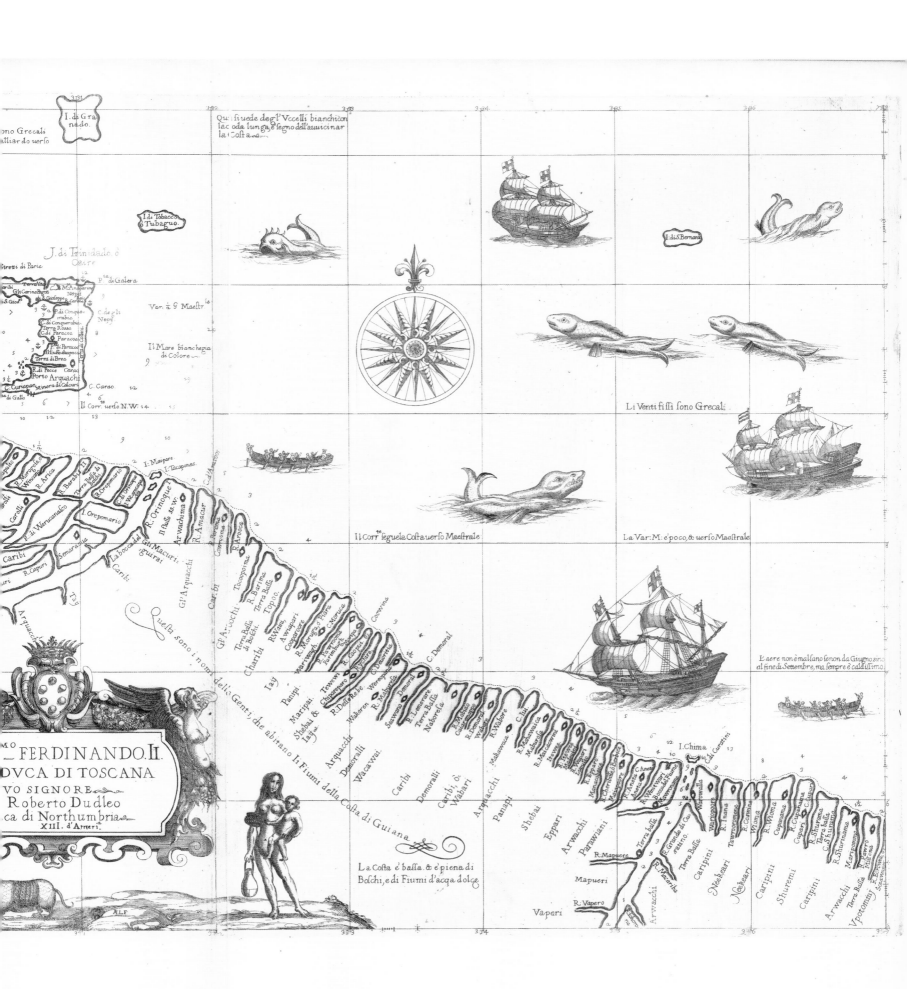

I. di Granado.

ono Grecali
alliar do uerso

Quefti uede deg l' Vccelli bianchi con
la coda lunga, è fegno dell' auuicinar
la Cofta a ...

I. di Tobacco,
ò Tubaguo.

J. di Trinidado, ò
Obare

P.te di Galera

Var. à 9 Maeftr

Il Mare bianchegia
di Colore
9

Il Corr uerſo N.W. 14

I. di S. Bernard

Li Venti fiffi fono Grecali

Il Corr feguela Cofta uerfo Maeftrale

La Var: M: e'poco, & uerſo Maeftrale

Queſti ſono i nomi delle Genti, che abitano Li Fiumi della Cofta di Guiana

L' aere non è mal ſano ſenon da Giugno ſin
al fine di Settembre, ma ſempre è caldiffimo

FERDINANDO. II.
DVCA DI TOSCANA
VO SIGNORE
Roberto Dudleo
ca di Northumbria
XIII. d' Ameri.

La Cofta e' baffa, & e' piena di
Bofchi, e di Fiumi d' acqua dolce

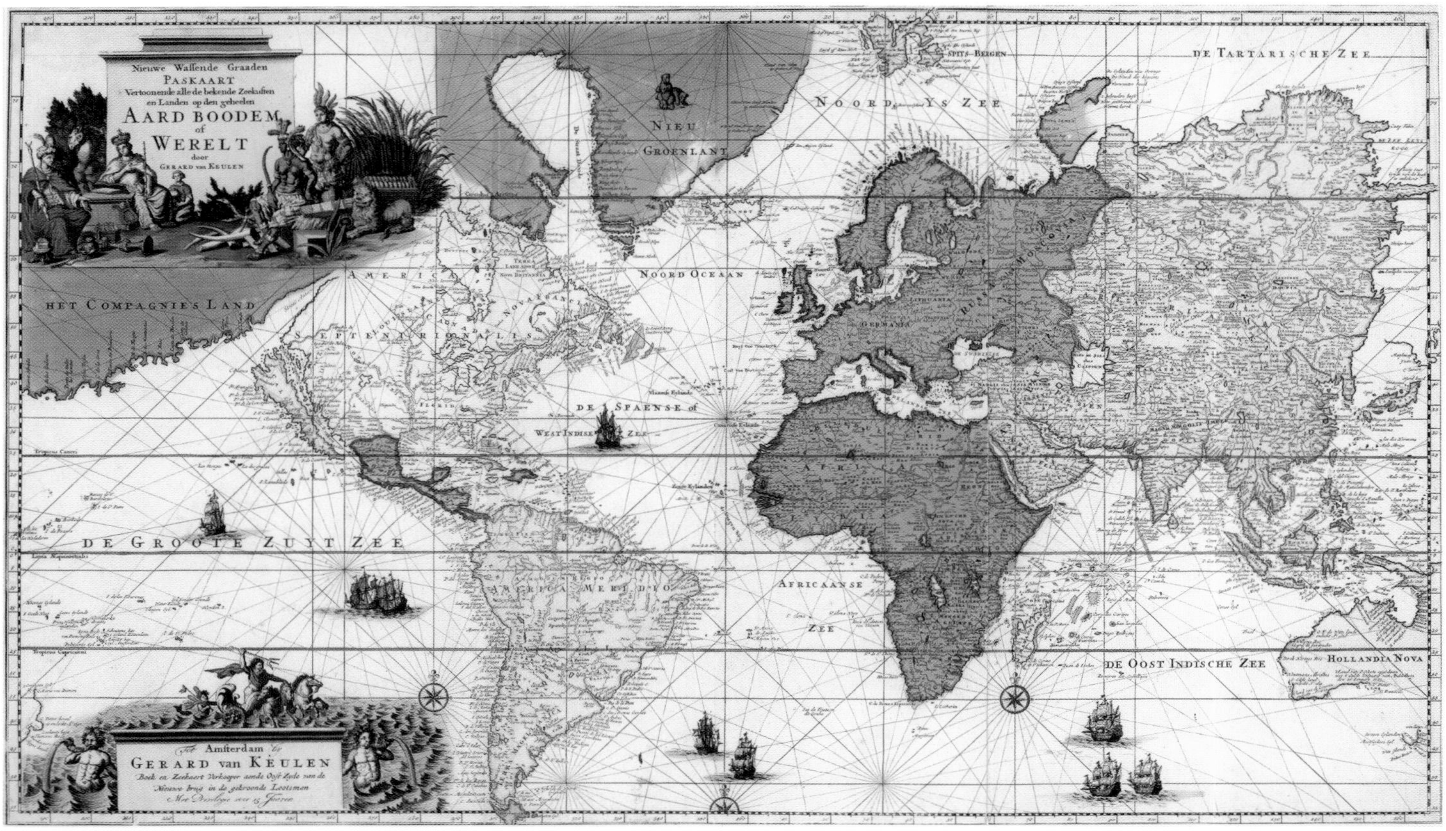

312. A World Map by Gerard van Keulen, c. 1710–1720

The van Keulen family opened their book- and map-house business in 1678. Over the years it became one of the leading publishers of sea charts and continued to operate for over 200 years. In this Mercator projection map California is seen as an island. This error was common through almost a century in contemporary maps.

JUHA NURMINEN COLLECTION

Cape on the Russian side. Besieged by ice, the latitude of 70° 44' was the farthest north they could reach. Cook then headed back south to the Sandwich Islands, thinking to try again the following summer. He discovered two more of the Hawaiian Islands, Maui and Hawaii (*Owhyhee*), and was killed there in a skirmish with the native people. King George III is said to have cried when he heard the news of Cook's horrible death.

Captain Charles Clerke, who had sailed with Cook on his two earlier circumnavigations, took over command of the *Resolution*. That summer he headed back north in search of the Northwest Passage, but enjoyed no greater success than had Cook. He headed over to the Siberian side of Bering Strait, but before he could reach Kamchatka, he died of tuberculosis. The next in command, John Gore, brought the expedition home to Britain. The elusive Northwest Passage was not found, but James Cook's third and last voyage did result in the first correct maps of the Bering Strait.

In his pamphlet published in 1780, Robert Brooke paid tribute to Cook, declaring 'The ocean may be his grave, but the whole globe is his monument'. He had set a new standard for ocean cartography, and for the management of ships on distant voyages. His care for the health and happiness of his crews

was fundamental to his success, and his humanity was equally reflected in his treatment of the indigenous peoples of the Pacific. Cook's voyages mark a shift from earlier explorations with their purpose of extending dominion, to the new goal of enlarging scientific knowledge. The study of oceanography, natural history and ethnography, pioneered by Cook, became the dominant theme in future voyages by others.

The work started by Captain Cook was to be continued by Joseph Billings, who had accompanied him on his third voyage. Subsequently he entered the Russian service, and in 1785 Empress Catherine II of Russia commissioned him to command an expedition to explore the coasts of Siberia and Alaska. Billings's deputy was the Russian officer, Gavril Sarychev, a navigator and hydrographer. In a voyage lasting nine years, they produced accurate maps of the Chukotka Peninsula in eastern Siberia, the west coast of Alaska, and the Aleutian Islands.

THE SEA ON PAPER

Gerard Mercator revolutionized the design of charts for mariners when he introduced a grid system allowing mariners to plot their course as a straight line, or rhumb line, on a chart. Although a great advance for those making long-distance voyages, they lacked the detailed information needed to approach shore safely and enter a harbour. This deficiency was rectified when the Dutch chartmaker, Lucas Janszoon Waghenaer, published the first sea-atlas, called *Spieghel der Zeevaerdt* in 1584. In a single book, it contained a bound collection of all the charts, filled with hydrographic detail, plus profile views of the land, along with the sailing directions needed to sail from North Cape, Norway, to Cádiz, Spain. It initiated the development, and set the pattern, for all pilot books that followed. His charts, however, lacked any latitude and longitude scales. The achievement of the next generation of chartmakers was to combine Mercator's science and Waghenaer's practicality.

The Dutch chartmaker, Willem Jansz Blaeu (1571–1638), followed the pattern set by Waghenaer with his publication in 1608 of *Het Licht de Zee-vaert* (The Light of Navigation). The many successive editions, in many languages, of Blaeu's work kept his charts more up to date than those of Waghenaer. Throughout the middle years of the seventeenth century, Amsterdam boasted a number of prolific mapmakers and chartmakers. Abraham Goos (c. 1590–1643), and his son, Pieter Goos (active between 1650 and 1678), both produced sea-atlases and pilot-guides. Pieter Goos's *Zee-Spiegel* (Surface of the Sea) was the first pilot book to cover waters beyond European navigation.

Hendrick Doncker, active in the years 1655 to 1699, broke from the practice common at the time by many chartmakers of copying from other chartmakers. His charts were completely original, and were noted for their accuracy and continual updating. Dutch chartmaking reached its apogee with the sea-atlases and pilot books produced by Johannes Van Keulen (1654–1715) and his descendents. As the founder of a publishing house in Amsterdam producing marine atlases, Johannes van Keulen continued the trend begun by Pieter Goos and Doncker of producing books and sailing directions for waters outside of Europe. His *Zee-Atlas* continued evolving with the addition of new charts, and was published for nearly one hundred years. The *Zee-Atlas* was followed by the *Nieuwe Groote Lichtende Zee-Fakkel* (the New and Great Illuminating Sea Torch) in 1681–

313. The Gulf of Finland by Aleksey Ivanovich Nagayev, 1794

Russian sea charting started during the era of Peter the Great. Foreign mapmakers were invited from the Netherlands and France to help Russia begin its own chart making. In 1715 the Naval Academy of St. Petersburg was established, initiating Russian sea charting. Nagayev's Atlas of the Baltic Sea, created in 1757, was the greatest of its time, and remained in print into the nineteenth century. Maps were greatly protected for the information they contained. Old copper plates were often sold, or even stolen, with their faults as well as their virtues, transferred to new charts.

JUHA NURMINEN COLLECTION

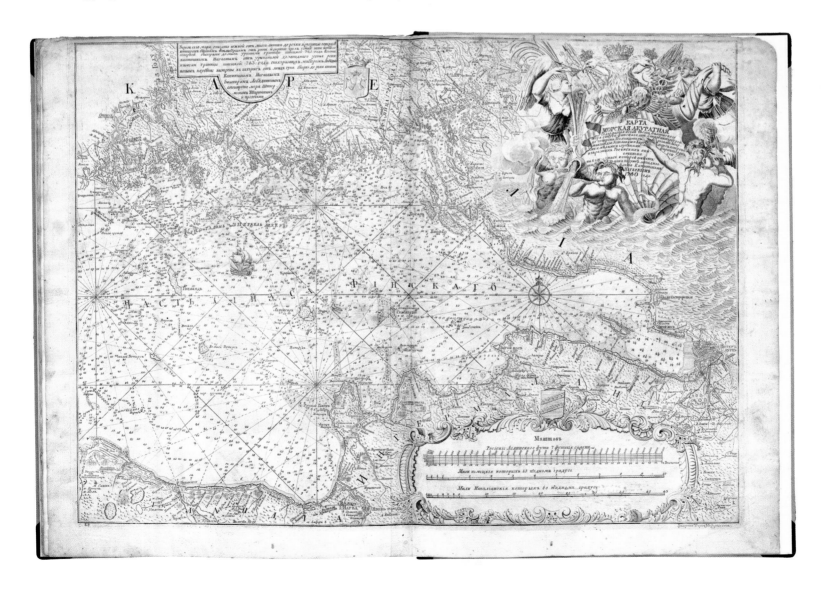

Painted by T.Whitcombe.   Bailey sculp?

DESTRUCTION of the DANISH FLEET before COPENHAGEN, April 2ᵈ 1801.

Plate I.

Published June 1 1804 at 48 Strand, for J.Jenkins's Naval Achievements

314. The Destruction of the Danish Fleet off Copenhagen on 2 April 1801 by Thomas Whitcombe, 1837

Horatio Nelson played a decisive role in three major battles: Abukir Bay in Egypt in 1798, the Battle of Copenhagen in 1801 and in Trafalgar in 1805. The painting depicts ships lining up in the Copenhagen battle. During the battle, the commander of the British fleet issued an order to retreat. Nelson's appraisal of the situation was different, however, and he refused the order. Thanks to his determination and obstinacy, the British beat the Danish in this famous battle.

JUHA NURMINEN COLLECTION

1682. These texts and charts far exceeded in quality all others preceding them, and effectively eliminated all competitors in the publication of sea-atlases and pilot books.

At the end of the seventeenth century, England and France, with their expansion in maritime activities, began to free themselves from a reliance on Dutch chartmakers. One of the earliest innovators in the printing of marine charts was Sir Robert Dudley (1574–1649), an Englishman forced into exile to live in Florence, Italy. His monumental atlas, *Dell'Arcano del Mare* (Secrets of the Sea), published in 1646–7, was the first sea atlas to cover the entire known world, and the first to use the Mercator projection with clearly marked lines of latitude and longitude on all the charts. Dudley's approach to chartmaking was a scientific one, incorporating depth soundings, winds and currents.

John Seller (c. 1630–1697), another important figure in the early history of chart publication in England, published a wide range of books on navigation and made a variety of navigation tools and instruments. His first and most important work was a sea-atlas, *The English Pilot*, which eventually covered the world. Seller combined detailed navigational information (rocks, shoals and soundings) with comprehensive geographical details within the interior of the land, into a visually beautiful chart.

By the eighteenth century, these private entrepreneurs in publishing were beginning to face competition from the hydrographic departments of government agencies. In 1667 King Louis XIV (the Sun King) of France, and Jean-Baptiste Colbert the king's Secretary of State and a major force in the development of the French merchant marine and navy, established an observatory in Paris. Its first director was the Italian cosmographer Giovanni Domenico Cassini (1625–1712). Using the method suggested by Galileo, Cassini was the first astronomer to successfully make measurements of longitude by using eclipses of the satellites of the Moon. An atlas of the sea charts, called *Le Neptune François,* which was published in 1693 by Nicolas Sanson and Alex Hubert Jaillot, with Cassini, established France as a leader in cartography.

Not until late in the eighteenth century did Britain come to the fore in chartmaking.

In the 1770's Lieutenant Joseph-Frederick Wallet Des Barres while serving in the British Army in North America, surveyed the Bay of Fundy, Nova Scotia, and Gulf and River of St. Lawrence. Other surveyors continued the work of Des Barres until the entire east coast of North America was surveyed. These were published in *The Atlantic Neptune*. In all, there were 158 charts, and for the first time a separate sheet was included showing the conventional symbols used.

In 1795 the British Admiralty established a Hydrographic Office, with Alexander Dalrymple appointed as the first Hydrographer. He organized the Admiralty Chart Committee and the first of its charts was produced. Their reputation was quickly established as the most accurate and reliable charts available. When Sir Francis Beaufort took over as Hydrographer, he expanded the survey to cover all coastlines throughout the world, and in greater detail than had previously been shown. Innovations included delineating the high and low tide lines on the coasts, depth of waters as established by soundings, a five-fathom curve, buoys, and compass roses with true direction, and magnetic north indicated with an arrow to one side. British Admiralty charts set the standard for all others to follow.

One of the first monuments Peter the Great constructed in his new Imperial capital at St. Petersburg was an Admiralty building. To the Admiralty he gave everything concerned with the management of a fleet at sea, including hydrographic and cartographic research. Under the command of Captain Aleksey Ivanovich Nagayev (1704–1781) an atlas was published in 1757 containing fifteen charts of the Baltic Sea which for the first time made use of isobaths, lines connecting equal depths, to

315. A portrait of Rear-Admiral Sir Horatio Nelson by Lemuel Francis Abbott, 1800

The most significant battle of the Napoleonic Wars was the Battle of Trafalgar, fought on 21 October 1805 at Cape Trafalgar in southwest Spain. The decisive victory of Britain against the allied forces of the French and Spanish fleets confirmed the Royal Navy as supreme naval power, and made Vice-Admiral Lord Nelson, the British commander, Britain's greatest naval hero.

NATIONAL MARITIME MUSEUM, LONDON

delineate the limits of shoals. In the last quarter of the century the navigator and hydrographer, Gavril Andrejevich Sarychev (1763–1831), mapped much of Russia's far eastern and northern coastline, as well as many of the Aleutian Islands and other islands in the Bering Sea. These advances in charting and cartography reflect Russia's rise in importance in the world.

At first, America depended on charts purchased from British publishers, but after the Revolutionary War (1774–76) it began to achieve cartographic, as well as political independence. Under President Thomas Jefferson, the United States Coast Survey was formed in 1807, making it the oldest scientific organization in the country. In a series of systematic studies begun in 1845, the Coast Survey charted all physical features of near and far offshore waters. Today, the office of the Coast Survey is a component of the National Oceanic and Atmospheric Administration (NOAA) in the Department of Commerce, Washington DC. Its historical map and chart collection, dating from the late 1700s to the present day, contains over 20,000 maps and charts.

FRONTIERS UNLIMITED

*The only true voyage of discovery is
not to go to new places,
but to have other eyes.*

MARCEL PROUST
REMEMBRANCE OF THINGS PAST

NEW GOALS: SCIENTIFIC VENTURES

Through his descriptions of the native people, their culture, the land's plants and animals, Captain James Cook created a new world order. Following the pattern set by Cook, expeditions in the nineteenth century shifted their aims. To some extent, all sea voyages contained a certain amount of information gathering, particularly for navigational purposes, but until Cook's expedition in 1768 to measure the transit of Venus, scientific enquiry was not a primary objective. The nineteenth century saw a marked increase in the number of expeditions for the express purpose of gathering information on the physical sciences, natural history, and customs and manners of other cultures.

Meteorology

As Hydrographer of the British Admiralty for twenty-five years, Sir Francis Beaufort (1774–1857) did much to further advances in navigation. He enlarged and improved charting of the oceans by that institution, supported research by oceanog-

raphers, hydrographers and geographers, and commissioned others in their voyages of exploration. He is best remembered, however, for developing the scale for wind force now named after him. It had become clear from the Royal Navy's loss of ships due to storms that a classification of winds, with proscribed regulations regarding the handling of ships in various strengths of wind, was needed to forestall such events. By the beginning of the eighteenth century a twelve-point scale of winds, describing them as calm, breeze, fresh breeze, etc. up to storm, had already been devised. In 1805, Beaufort enlarged the scale to thirteen in number, and quantified each wind according to the amount of sail a fully rigged frigate could carry under each wind. In 1838, the Royal Navy made the observation and recording of winds using the Beaufort Force numbers mandatory aboard its ships. The wind equivalents first set by Beaufort evolved over time to reflect changes in ship design; canvas-carrying equivalents for wind force were eventually replaced by appearance of the sea-state, and wind speed was expressed in miles per hour.

Captain Robert FitzRoy (1805–1865) was the first to receive sailing orders to take wind observations using the Beaufort wind

316. The Corvette *La Recherche*, near Beeren Island, 7 August 1838 by Auguste Mayer, 1852

French scientists aboard the corvette, *La Recherche*, investigated natural sciences and anthropology in their journey to lands in far northern latitudes. Results of the expedition, named after the vessel upon which it sailed, were published in sixteen volumes, with an additional five volumes of illustration.

JUHA NURMINEN COLLECTION

317. A portrait of Sir Francis Beaufort by Stephen Pearce, 1850

Francis Beaufort (1774–1857), born in Ireland, became an officer in the British
Royal Navy and for a quarter of a century was the Admiralty hydrographer. He
invented the wind force scale in 1805, used to estimate wind speed by observing
the effect of wind at sea or on land. The Beaufort scale was revised several times,
but has been discontinued now by most countries. Thanks to his powerful office,
Beaufort was influential in formulating programmes for British expeditions. It was
Beaufort who chose Charles Darwin to be the close assistant of Captain FitzRoy,
whom he had trained, on the first voyage of the Beagle in 1831–1836.

NATIONAL PORTRAIT GALLERY, LONDON

318. Ship in a Gale by Benjamin Olsen, 1923

The barque is sailing in a gale and the wind speed is 39–46 mph (8 in a
Beaufort scale).

JUHA NURMINEN COLLECTION

**319. Portrait of Robert FitzRoy
by an unknown artist**

Vice-Admiral Robert FitzRoy, a navigator, meteorologist, and marine surveyor, was captain of the HMS *Beagle*, made famous by the inclusion of Charles Darwin as naturalist on the voyage. He was given command of the *Beagle* after his predecessor took his own life. Because FitzRoy also later killed himself, the *Beagle* was said to be a cursed ship.

ALEXANDER TURNBULL LIBRARY, WELLINGTON

**320. A Barometer designed by
Robert FitzRoy, c. 1870**

After *Beagle*'s famous voyage, FitzRoy founded the British Meteorological Office in 1854. He pioneered weather forecasts and newspapers started to print his daily prognoses. In the 1870s, he developed a barometer – named after him – which included a thermometer and a hygrometer. These devices were installed in weather stations on the eastern coast of the Atlantic and they provided data on atmospheric pressure from measurements taken at the same time to the central office in England where more comprehensive forecasts were made. The data could be collected quickly thanks to the electric telegraph that had been much improved since the 1840s. Similar activity was soon also started in Russia, France, Italy and Portugal.

JOHN NURMINEN FOUNDATION

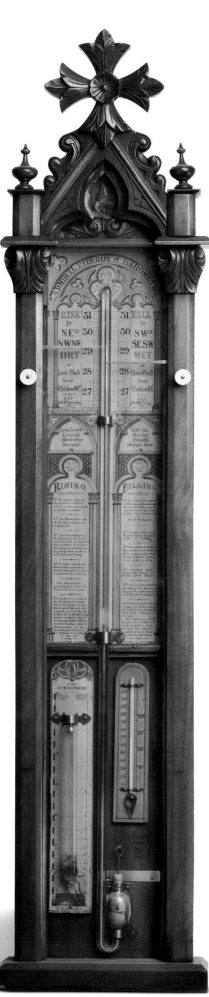

scale. He was sent on a hydrographic and surveying expedition with the HMS *Beagle* to continue the work of a previous survey made with that same vessel, to chart Tierra del Fuego, Patagonia, the South American Coasts and some islands in the Pacific. On this voyage of 1831–1836, FitzRoy pursued his studies of the scientific forecasting of weather. He devised an instrument, called the 'storm glass', a type of barometer which contained a liquid mixture of ingredients in a sealed glass container. By observing the clarity, or lack thereof, of the fluid, and the kind of precipitant in it, one could predict the weather on a short-term basis. The basic premise for its workability was the effect on the fluid of temperature and pressure. Exactly how pressure exerted its influence is not fully understood.

Upon his return, FitzRoy was given the newly created post of Head of Meteorology at the Board of Trade in England. He continued to work on several different types of 'true' barometers which continued to be used into the twentieth century. Upon his recommendation they, along with instructions for interpreting the results, were set up in ports to create a network of weather stations. With the recent development of the first wireless telegraph by Guglielmo Marconi in 1897, ships at sea were able to send in their accumulated data in a timely manner. Mariners at sea, as well as those in harbour about to set out, could now be prepared for potential heavy weather.

Oceanography

Voyages in ever increasing numbers ranged over all the seas of the world, and governments began to commission expeditions to gather data and research samples in a systematic and organized manner. Oceanography encompassed a wide range of subjects, including geological study of the ocean floor, chemistry of the ocean's waters, its marine biology, and the interaction between the atmosphere and the ocean. Among these studies was hydrography, the measurement and description of the physical characteristics of bodies of water and their boundaries. The principle purpose was for improved

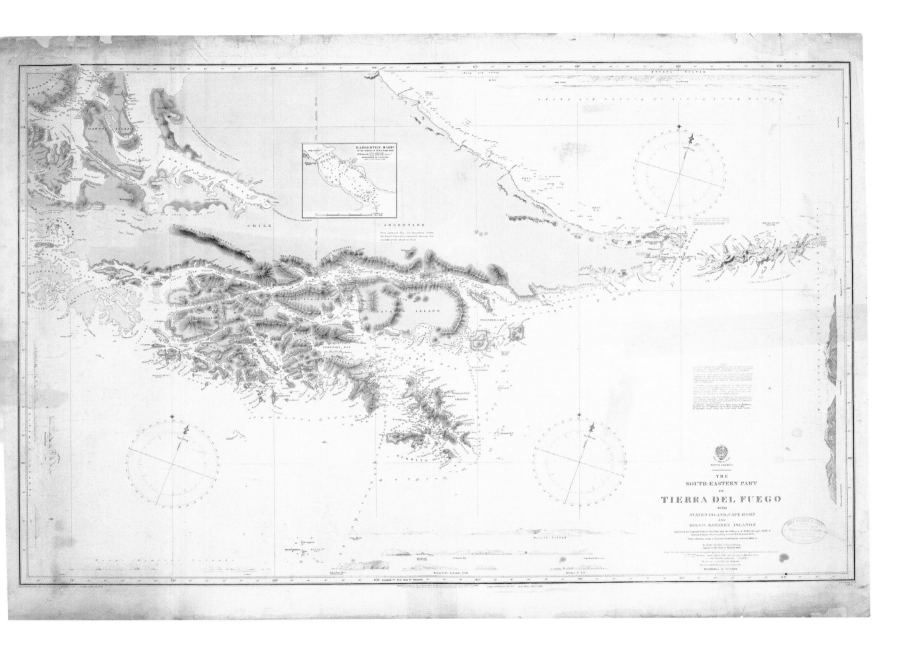

321. The South-Eastern Part of Tierra del Fuego with Staten Island, Cape Horn and Diego Ramirez Islands by Robert FitzRoy and E. N. Kendal, 1892

In 1831, the British Admiralty sent the survey vessel, HMS *Beagle* to survey the coast of South America. Robert FitzRoy, became captain of the *Beagle* to map Patagonia and Tierra del Fuego. British Admiralty charts have become the standard of reference throughout the world for thoroughness and accuracy.

JOHN NURMINEN FOUNDATION

and more complete information to aid marine navigation and nautical charting.

In 1830 a depot of Charts and Instruments was established for the US Navy Department. It began nautical chart production in 1835, original hydrographic work in 1838, and four years later Lieutenant Matthew Fontaine Maury (1806–1873) became its first superintendent. His interest in plotting the migratory patterns of whales led him to study the data from thousands of ship logs and charts going back to the very start of the navy. From them, Maury collated all the observations on weather, winds and ocean currents. With his *Wind and Current Chart of the North Atlantic*, published in 1852, Maury showed the best routes for ships to travel by taking advantage of the prevailing winds and the direction and strength of surface ocean currents, thereby shortening the voyage. He called these ways 'paths of the seas'. The publication in 1855 of his *The Physical Geography of the Seas and its Meteorology* was the first extensive book to be published on Oceanography. His uniform system of recording data has been adopted by other nations in developing charts for the major trade routes. Maury's work has earned for him the nicknames of 'Scientist of the Seas', and the 'Father of Naval Oceanography'.

The British government furnished a three-masted, square-rigged ship, HMS *Challenger,* for an extensive expedition of scientific observations. Its main task was to determine what plant and animal life could live below 300 fathoms (1800 feet);

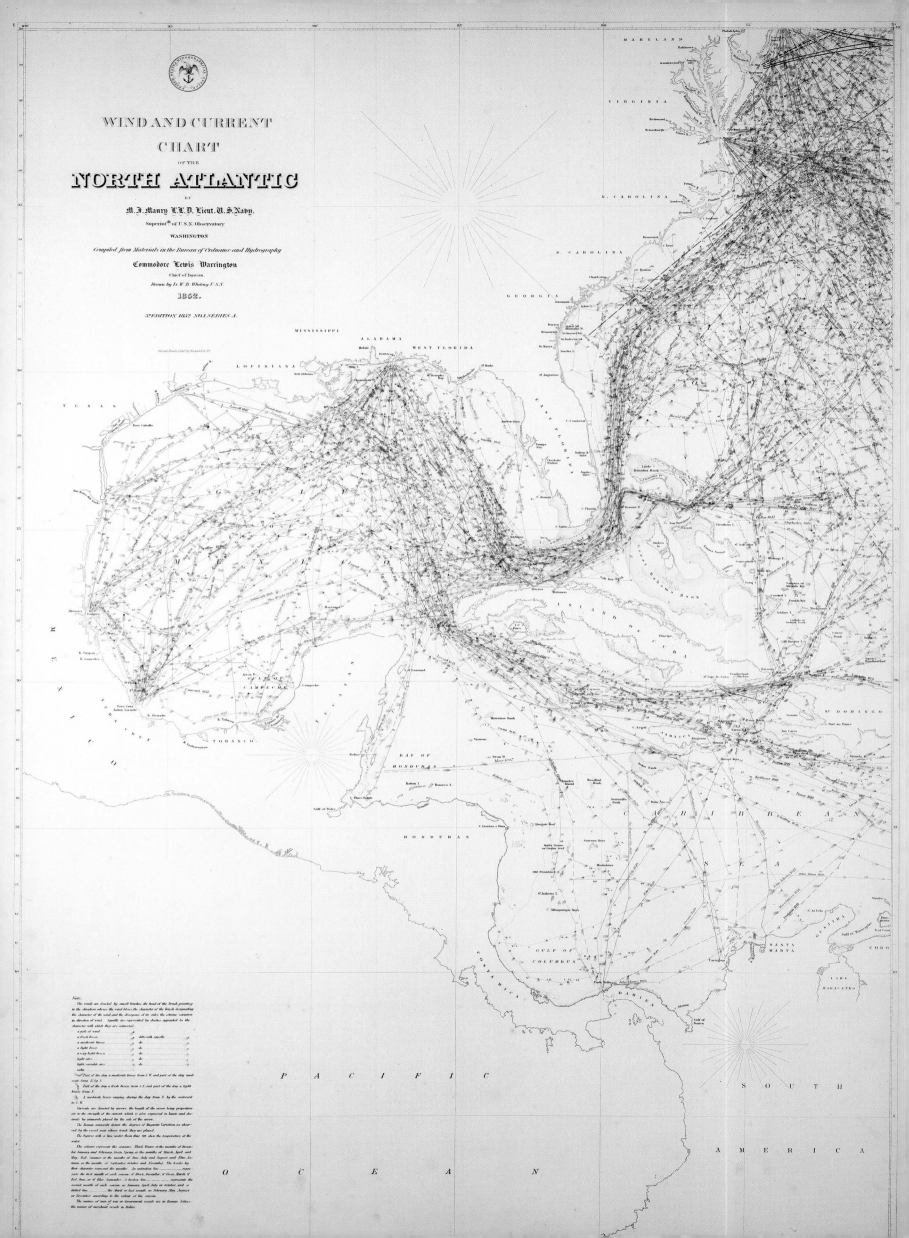

WIND AND CURRENT
CHART
OF THE
NORTH ATLANTIC
BY
M. F. Maury LL.D. Lieut. U.S. Navy.
Superint of U.S.N. Observatory
WASHINGTON
Compiled from Materials in the Bureau of Ordnance and Hydrography
Commodore Lewis Warrington
Chief of Bureau.
Drawn by Lt. W.B. Whiting U.S.N.
1852.
3ᵈ EDITION 1852 NO.1 SERIES A.

322. Wind and Current Chart of the North Atlantic by Matthew Fontaine Maury, 1852

Tracks of the vessels from which Lieutenant Maury extracted his information are shown in this detail section of his North Atlantic Chart. The tracks, along with the wind and current observations are colour-coded for different seasons of the year. The 'shuttlecock' symbol represents wind and the head points in the direction from which it blows. Length of the lines radiating outward from the head is an indication of its strength. Similarly, the arrow-shaped symbol indicates direction and strength of ocean currents. Maury's charts also included observations of water temperature and compass variation.

NATIONAL MARITIME MUSEUM, LONDON

323. *Lophius naresii*, an unknown angler

This fierce-looking angler was found in the depths of the ocean during HMS *Challenger*'s voyage in Nares Harbour of the Admiralty Islands.

COURTESY OF DARTMOUTH COLLEGE, HANNOVER

324. Examining the contents of a trawl on HMS *Challenger*

HMS *Challenger* had several different trawls and nets on board to catch, for example, fish for scientific study. They could be lowered to a maximum depth of approximately 3600 metres.

THE NATIONAL LIBRARY OF FINLAND, HELSINKI

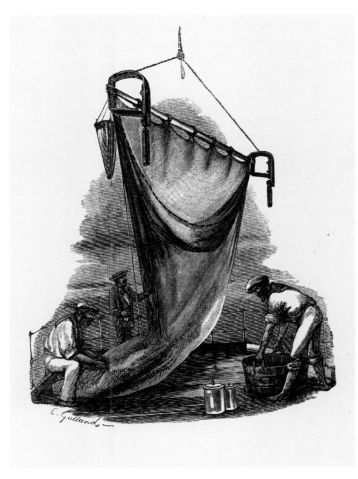

for this, the *Challenger* was equipped with trawls and dredges to gather samples, and modified to make room for a staff of naturalists, chemists, physicists, and an official artist. Specially designed workrooms and laboratories were provided to carry out their work. Charles Wyville Thomson (1830–1882), Professor of Natural History at Edinburgh University, was leader of the expedition, with Captain George Nares (1831–1915) as commander of the vessel. In her voyage lasting from 1872 to 1876, the *Challenger* sailed 68,890 nautical miles, from the limits of drift ice in the North Atlantic polar seas to below the Antarctic Circle. As near as possible, it stopped at equal intervals to take depth soundings and make observations of salinity, temperature and water density at different depths. Flora and fauna were collected and examined, ocean surface currents were noted, and at a few places, records were made of the direction and rate of subsurface currents. Geology and topography of the ocean floor was charted.

When completed, over forty charts were produced and the published reports, between 1855 and 1895, occupied fifty volumes. As the first world-wide oceanographic study, the expedition provided important information for the fishing industry, shipping, and the laying of telegraph cables. Other nations were stimulated to set out their expeditions. Today, there are about 250 institutions established for the study of the ocean.

21st 11.30 a.m. Cast off from the Jetty, in Portsmouth Harbour, and with steam commenced our voyage of Scientific exploration and circumnavigation. For a wonder the sun shone out just as we started and remained out as we discharged our Pilot and a few friends, to the Tug which had accompanied us out as far as Spithead — These good people did their best to enliven our departure — and we were greated with three cheers as they shoved off — and immediately afterwards we proceeded for the Needles. The lively propensities of the ship were soon to be developed, for even before we reached the Needles — signs of motion were observable, and made me anxious to get everything secured as quickly as possible — precautions which were soon to be found necessary, as a falling Barometer and awkward looking sunset gave every indication of a gale from the Sea. In the first watch it became thick — and plenty of drizzle. at 7.30 a.m. we got a glimpse of the Start Light abeam — and lost

22nd sight of him 2 hours afterwards.

The 22nd opened with a fine
bright sunshine — the wind having
hauled gradually from West
round to the Southward
a moderate breeze. to which
we made all Plain Sail
Except Royals and F. Jib.
altering course to W½S. to keep
get good Westing in case of falling

in with the expected SW. gale — At Midnight the wind and sea
began to increase — and necessitated a gradual shortening of sail
until 4 a.m. found us under Topsails on the Cap and Courses — There
was a nasty confused sea — and the Ship was uncommonly uneasy
rolling 22° to Starboard and 4° to Port, with a few hints that she could
and would ultimately do more — The Barometer still fell steadily
and the ship was kept rap full on the Port Tack to make Westing in

23rd case of a ship to the SW. — A lively day promised — under close reefed
Topsails and gaff sails with heads hauled in — a fresh gale from
the SSW. the ship rolling 35° to leeward — During the day
the Bar. fell and the wind rose. Done in the hope

24th of getting wind from NW. but "Breas wouldn't "
The wind never getting farther round than from
SSW. SW. to WSW. a heavy sea running and ship knocking about a great
deal. The first night in a gale of wind always produces a few "mishaps"
fortunately ours were confined to those at which one could well
afford to laugh — nothing more serious happening than the "gutting" of
one or two cabins and the tendency to fly, of a patent wire wire
sounding reel — which found its way down into the Cockpit very close
to the Paymaster's head.

Salpa &c.

Petimbuabo &c

326. The Lane-snapper and the Tobaccopipe-fish by Mark Catesby, 1743

Catesby's *Natural History of Carolina, Florida and Bahama Islands* was the first published account of the flora and fauna of North America.

JUHA NURMINEN COLLECTION

325. First page from the Journal of HMS *Challenger*, 1872 - A Personal Diary of Aldrich Pelham, 1872

Although an official logbook was kept during expeditions, it was very common for men to keep personal journals. On the British scientific expedition, with Captain Nares as commander of the *Challenger*, Lieutenant Aldrich kept his journal both in good and bad weather, and included watercolours of the most exciting events.

ROYAL GEOGRAPHICAL SOCIETY

Natural History

The study of natural history and the collecting of specimens was an important part of all these nineteenth-century scientific circumnavigations. Botanists, ornithologists, ichthyologists, herpetologists and men from almost every other field of the biological and physical sciences were aboard the ships. Most of the names of these naturalists, and their accomplishments, have dropped into obscurity. Two individuals, however, are still well remembered by the general public. Baron Alexander von Humboldt (1769–1859), a Prussian naturalist and explorer took part in many expeditions to Central and South America in the years between 1799 and 1805. During his exploration of the coasts, rivers and inland geography, Humboldt collected plant, animal and mineral specimens, and performed many scientific observations, including terrestrial magnetism. He discovered the cold current off the west coast of South America that runs from the southern tip of Chile to northern Peru. That current, now named after him, is one of the most productive marine ecosystems in the world. Humboldt's main emphasis lay not in the collection and graphic depiction of material, but in the incorporation of all the sciences into a unified and generalized physical world.

When Captain Robert FitzRoy undertook the task of hydrographic charting of the South American coast, and the making of longitude corrections using calibrated chronometers checked against astronomical observation and geographi-

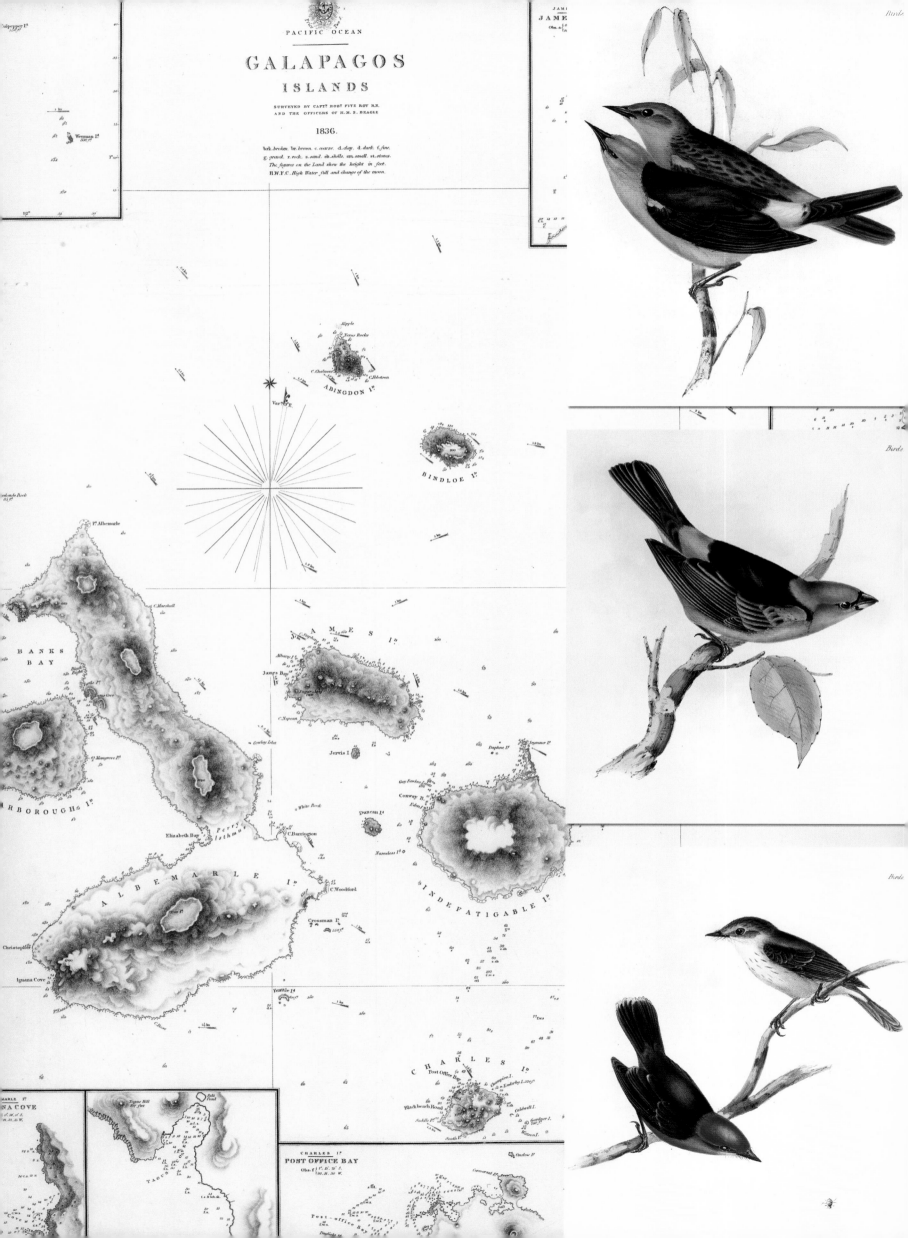

Mammalia Pl. 10.

Delphinus Fitz-Royi

Beagle's voyage 1832–1836

As the naturalist on board the *Beagle* during its 1832–1836 voyage, Darwin noticed how species on the Galapagos Islands had adapted to the varying environments of the islands. He began to doubt the permanence of species and the possibility that this variation may have to do with natural selection.

327. Admirality Chart of the Galapagos Islands by Robert FitzRoy and E. N. Kendal, 1836

JOHN NURMINEN FOUNDATION

Inset, above
328. *Xanthornus flaviceps* by John Gould, 1840

Inset, middle
329. *Tanagra Darwini* by John Gould, 1840

Inset, below
330. *Pyrocephalus nanus* by John Gould, 1840

Right above
331. *Delphinus Fitz-Royi* by Richard Owen, 1840

Right
332. *Reithrodon Chinshilloides* by Richard Owen, 1840

JUHA NURMINEN COLLECTION

Mammalia Pl. 27.

Reithrodon Chinchilloides

The Clipper

The fame of the greyhounds of the sea, the beautiful clipper ships that raced around the world bringing high-value cargoes to Europe and Eastern America, is second to none. Premium prices were paid for the cargoes of the first tea clippers home each year from China, and their captains could count on generous bonuses, each new record clipping the time the perishable cargo was exposed to possible spoilage in the ship's hold. Fast sea transports had been unknown until the beginning of the nineteenth century, but the changing world and industrialization offered new possibilities and also new demands. The great impulse for the technical revolution in sea transportation came from the high-value, low bulk cargoes connected with the gold rushes in California in 1848 and Australia in 1850, and the opening of competition in the tea trade due to the ending of the British Navigation Act in 1849. Due to their high speed, the clippers may be regarded as predecessors to our 'ro-ro-' and passenger ferries, as they were designed to carry valuable cargo and passengers as fast as possible.

Typically, the clipper ship was a slim hulled and fast, wooden or composite built, three-masted full-rigged sailing ship with square sails in all masts. Composite building, using lighter and stronger iron frames while retaining wooden planks that could be covered with sheet copper antifouling, made it possible to build longer, finer and faster ships. The length of the clipper was larger in relation to the beam than in any earlier large sailing vessel type. The hull lines were extremely slim fore and aft and the sail area very large. In addition to square sails the vessels carried staysails and in following wind could set additional studdingsails on booms on both sides of the square sails.

Sailing a clipper was not an easy task. The clipper was relatively small and agile, but because of the huge sail area they carried they could be difficult to handle, especially for a master who had been used to slow and more stable ships. For example the famous *Cutty Sark* is about 65-m long, with the height of the main mast from deck level to the top a full 46 m. It is estimated that her huge sail area corresponded to an engine output of 3000 horsepower (hp). Clippers could have rather poor stability because of the large rig. When encountering a fierce squall it was bad practise to put the helm up, because the speed increased, and, because the yards might be braced more fore and aft than those of other ships, the sails could get the full weight of the squall abeam. The rail of the ship might get so far under water that the helm lost its power. Due to the large angle of the heel, the yards might not come down even if the halliards were to be let fly, with the probable consequence of damage to mast and rigging, or even the foundering of the ship. Only a few captains could get the most out of their ships.

The fineness aft of the clipper ship made them exceptionally manoeuvrable. It is told that when beating against the wind up the Shanghai River the captain of the *Titania*, instead of going through stays to change tacks, made one tack bow first and the other stern first. But the stern of a clipper was often so slim that the ship could take green seas aboard aft when changing course in rough seas. It was therefore common to wear such ships round in stormy weather.

The English Blackwell-frigates, and other small and fast vessel types such as the Baltimore clipper, are regarded as the prototypes of the true clipper ship. The first generation of these ships was built in the US. The *Rainbow*, which was built in New York in 1845, is considered the first real clipper. The most famous of the American clippers was *Flying Cloud*. She was one of the fastest sailing ships of all time and it is told that she reached a speed in excess of 18 knots. Twice she made a record-breaking voyage in 89 days from New York to San Francisco via Cape Horn.

An economic recession in 1857, and the American Civil War between 1861 and 1865, caused American shipbuilding to stagnate, a development of which British shipyards took advantage. The second-generation clippers were British-built of composite construction and saw their glory days on the tea trade.

The climax of the clipper era was the race in 1866. The clipper *Fiery Cross* left Foochow in China fully loaded with tea on 29 May, while *Ariel*, *Taeping* and *Serica* set sails the following day. After a dramatic voyage, *Ariel* and *Taeping* sailed abreast up the English Channel and both vessels docked in London on the evening of 6 September within 20 minutes of each other!

The heydays of the clipper lasted only a few decades from the mid 1800s. In 1838 the steam-powered *Sirius* and *Great Western* made their first Atlantic crossings, and by the 1880s sailing ships came to be used only for cargoes that did not require either speed or predictability, such as bulk grain, and coal to feed the bunkers of the steam packets. During the same period steam-powered ocean-going ships also became practical. One of the most prestigious routes in the age of the clipper ship ended with the inauguration of the Suez Canal in 1869. Thereafter, these graceful beauties of the seas were condemned to less and less important routes before they were broken up.

333. *Onward the Lightning* by Montague Dawson

This is the British clipper *Lighting* in a strong, following wind. The heyday of the clippers lasted just a few decades at the end of the nineteenth century, but the legend of these slim-hulled and fast-sailing vessels remain. The clippers often raced when they carried tea, spices, silk and porcelain from Asia to Europe. With the development of engine-powered ships the clippers were gradually transferred to secondary trades, such as carrying coal or guano.

PETER TAMM COLLECTION

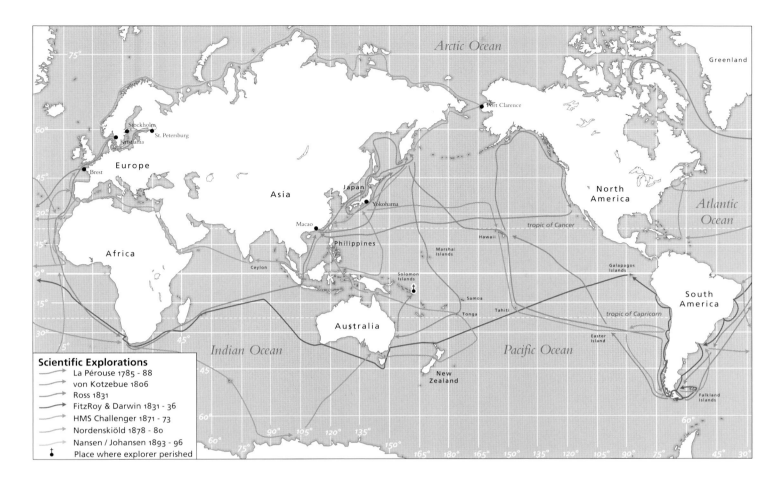

Scientific Explorations

- La Pérouse 1785 - 88
- von Kotzebue 1806
- Ross 1831
- FitzRoy & Darwin 1831 - 36
- HMS Challenger 1871 - 73
- Nordenskiöld 1878 - 80
- Nansen / Johansen 1893 - 96
- Place where explorer perished

334. Scientific Explorations

As the nineteenth century opened, the general distribution of land and water over the Earth's surface had been determined, and charted with a fair degree of accuracy. The only new lands left to explore were pushed to the farthest reaches of the Arctic and Antarctic regions. The goals of oceanic voyages shifted to scientific expeditions for the study oceanography, natural history, ethnology and geodesy.

cal points, he had no idea it would not be his name, but the name of the vessel and the young naturalist brought aboard that would bring everlasting fame. That vessel was the HMS *Beagle*, and the naturalist was Charles Darwin (1809–1882).

The idea there was some sort of change, a natural progression, leading to more complex and 'perfect' animals and plants had been proposed as early as 1809 by the French naturalist Jean-Baptiste de Lamarck. He did not call it 'evolution', but thought of it rather as 'transformation' of species over a long period of time. That there were certain 'natural laws' wherein a gradual process could be responsible for great changes was also put forth by the British geologist, Sir Charles Lyell, in his *Principles of Geology* (1830–33). The works of both these men greatly influenced the young Darwin. His accomplishment on this voyage, which lasted from 1831 to 1836, was in discovering what that mechanism of change was. It centred on natural selection. He wrote: 'it at once struck me that ... favourable variations would tend to be preserved and unfavourable ones to be destroyed'. This eventually resulted in one of the most important works in the history of biological science, *On the Origin of Species*.

Ship Magnetism

In the sixteenth and seventeenth centuries the nature of terrestrial magnetism and its effects on the magnetic compass had come to be understood. Attempts to correlate the amount of variation of the compass with longitude were finally abandoned when the pattern of variation over the Earth's surface showed this relationship to be unreliable. Likewise, endeavours to use magnetic dip (inclination of the compass needle in the vertical plane) as a means of establishing latitude also proved unsound. It took until the end of the seventeenth century before a full and systematic study of magnetic variation was undertaken. A milestone was the full charting of lines of magnetic variation by Edmond Halley (1656–1742) in 1701. With his data navigators could make the appropriate correction to the ship's course.

While advances were being made in an understanding of terrestrial magnetism and its effect on the ship's compass, another problem of magnetism was slowly taking shape. A gradual transition in ship construction techniques began to have

Overleaf

335. HMS *Trush* by W. Fred Mitchell, 1890

Launched in 1889, the iron-hulled gunboat of the British Navy was equipped with a steam engine, as well as masts and sails. Iron structures became increasingly common in the nineteenth century, and required new means to compensate for compass deviation.

JUHA NURMINEN COLLECTION

W.Fred.Mitchell. 1892.

336. A Portrait of Edmond Halley by Sir Godfrey Kneller, c. 1721

Although Edmond Halley is best known to the general public for the comet named after him, he was highly influential in the advancement of navigation. A mathematician, meteorologist and geophysicist, as well as an astronomer, Halley published a study on the trade winds and the monsoons, and drew the first map with contour lines, or isogons, indicating equal magnetic variation. He made a celestial map of the southern hemisphere and numerous observations of the position of the Moon relative to stars.

NATIONAL MARITIME MUSEUM, LONDON

its effect on the compass in as early as 1670. In England, in addition to the usual fastenings of iron bolts, nails and other minor fittings, lodging knees and hanging knees made of iron began to replace the traditional wooden knees used to support the beams of the ship. By 1707, France too began building with iron knees (*courbes de fer*). These, along with diagonal bracing of iron, materially strengthened the ship's structure. Toward the end of the eighteenth century as the quantity of good ship-building wood declined, the trend of using iron in

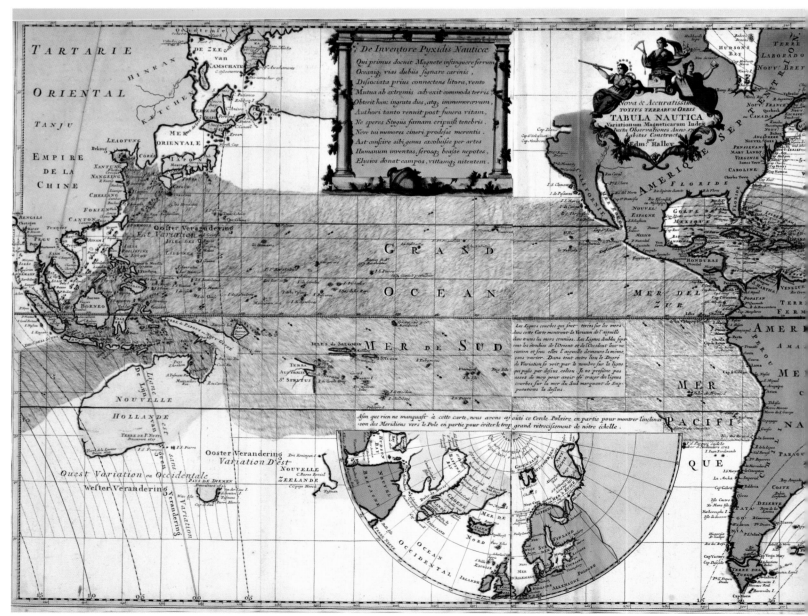

ship construction increased correspondingly. Magnetic compasses reacted to all this ferrous metal, and also to the canons in men-of-war, giving an incorrect reading of magnetic north. This type of error, where the needle is deflected by influences in its proximity is called deviation, a term coined by John Ross (1777–1856) when he encountered the problem on his search for the Northwest Passage in 1818.

The English naval captain, Matthew Flinders (1774–1814), noted abnormal behaviour of the compass needle on the voyages he made between 1801 and 1803 to make a detailed survey of the entire coastline of Australia. At this time the southern coast of Australia had not yet been charted. During the course of his survey work, during which he took over 2500 compass bearings, he found that not only did metal aboard the ship cause deviation of the compass, but that the deviation changed according to the position of the compass on the ship, and with the heading of the vessel. Additionally, compass deviation was proportionate to the magnetic dip, differing at different latitudes.

To correct for deviation, Flinders proposed that a length of iron bar be let into the deck, with its upper end level with the compass card in the binnacle. It corrected compass errors when the ship changed her magnetic latitude, and the iron bar came to be called a Flinders bar. It was many years, however, before seamen incorporated the Flinders bar in their vessels.

337. The New World Map by Edmond Halley and Joshua Ottens, 1730

Under the joint monarchs of King William III and Queen Mary II of England, Edmund Halley (1656–1742) was commissioned to make extensive observations of terrestrial magnetism to improve knowledge of variation of the compass. Halley made two voyages between 1698 and 1700 in which he covered the Atlantic Ocean from 52° north to 52° south. A sufficient number of observations were taken that they could be connected into lines of equal variation, or isogonic lines. Halley published the results in 1701 in a *General Chart of the Variation of the Compass*. The following year, he extended these lines to include the Indian Ocean. Lines of magnetic variation of the Pacific Ocean, however, still remained uncharted.

JUHA NURMINEN COLLECTION

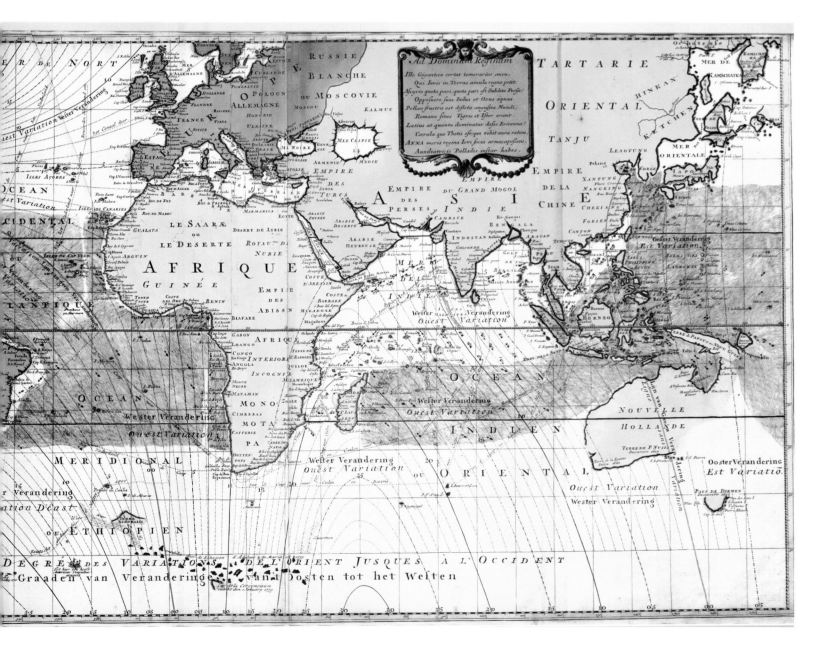

As the quality of iron improved and its costs diminished, more and more parts– masts, booms, yards, bowsprit– of the traditional wood ship were replaced with iron until finally, even the decks and sides of the ship were made of plates of wrought iron and ultimately ships made of steel. This advance in construction provided the ultimate in structural rigidity of the hull, and those great Man of War ships and vessels of the Dutch and English East India trade which had once been sovereign of the seas gave way to a new era of iron vessels propelled by steam and fossil fuel.

With the advent of iron-hulled vessels, yet another cause for anomalous behaviour of the compass needle arose – the very ship, itself, acted as a permanent, giant magnet. Correcting the compass for deviation by judiciously placed magnets near the compass did not solve the problem, for the built-in magnetism of a ship changed while at sea. The pounding of waves and vibrations of the hull caused by engine and propellers were the cause of this. Furthermore, polarity of the iron plates of a ship changed with changes in magnetic latitude.

Until the cause of this compass error – by as much as 50 degrees – was realized, there ensued disastrous endings to some voyages. Such was the case of the frigate HMS *Apollo*, leading a convoy of merchant ships in 1803. Thinking to be safely off the coast of Portugal by 180 miles, she instead piled into the coast, taking with her forty other vessels to their destruction. She was not the only vessel to suffer such a fate by relying on what previously had been the navigator's most trusted instrument. Sailing from Rio de Janeiro in 1830, the HMS *Thetis*,

338. The Compass Binnacle from the 20th century

The increasing use of iron in shipbuilding, which affected the compass, meant that special attention had to be paid to correcting for deviation. To counteract this effect, Matthew Flinders (1774–1814) developed a system, in which iron bars (Flinders bar) were fixed to the compass, being placed in the binnacle in a vertical position. Flinders was also the first to circumnavigate the southern continent, which he named Australia. He was later imprisoned by the French on Mauritius in 1803, but returned to England after seven years' captivity.

JOHN NURMINEN FOUNDATION

339. A Portrait of William Scoresby Junior

William Scoresby, Junior, an English priest, accompanied his father, William Scoresby, Senior, on several voyages to the Arctic as a mariner, pioneer scientist and explorer. In 1856 he travelled to Australia to study terrestrial magnetism.

THE NATIONAL LIBRARY OF FINLAND, HELSINKI

ran full speed into a vertical cliff, sinking to the bottom with a cargo of over a million dollars in silver and other treasures, and the loss of twenty-five souls. In the ensuing years, with an increasing number of iron-hulled vessels, such incidents increased alarmingly, until in the mid 1830s the Admiralty finally took notice, began to study the problem, and sought a means to correct the deviation of the compass needle.

The English Arctic explorer and scientist, William Scoresby (1789–1857), whose father, an Arctic whaler also named William Scoresby, had an abiding interest on the subject of magnetism and its effects on the marine compass. Scoresby (junior) came up with the final solution to the problem of compass errors resulting from these multiple, individual changes in the ship's magnetic state. Rather than trying to correct the ship's compass, he proposed that a second compass should be carried and placed as far away from the hull as possible, at the highest point of the mast. This secondary compass, relatively unaffected by the changes affecting the main compass, would serve as a standard of reference. It let one know the amount of deviation of the main compass, and thus allowed the navigator to make the necessary correction to the ship's course.

Scoresby also suggested that the magnetic needle of the compass card be made of laminated, hard-steel, for it would hold its magnetism longer than other needles. He, and the mathematician, Archibald Smith, promoted the use of multiple needles placed in a precise, mathematically formulated pattern on either side of the pivot point. These reduced the tendency that a single needle had of aligning itself with the direction of the ship's roll. Large, iron balls placed on either side of the compass, a system developed later, took care of compass errors caused by non-ferromagnetic influences, such as electrical currents, on the vessel.

340. Louis XVI giving instructions for La Pérouse for his voyage of exploration around the world, in the presence of marquess de Castries, Marine Minister, 29 June 1785 by Nicolas André Monsiau

In 1785, King Louis XVI of France commissioned a voyage of exploration to be led by Jean-François de Galaup, Comte de La Pérouse. The expedition was France's most ambitious maritime endeavour; during its circumnavigation of the world every field of science was to be studied. Additionally, La Pérouse was to explore the northwest coast of Asia and America with the goal of establishing a fur trade there. King Louis personally gave final instructions, specifying the itinerary and the objectives. The artist, Nicolas André Monsiau, captured the moment in this painting. La Pérouse wrote that if they lived up to the expectations 'this voyage will certainly be remembered by posterity and our names will linger on over the centuries long after those of Cook and Magellan'.

RÉUNION DES MUSÉES NATIONAUX, PARIS

THE ICE-CHOKED SEAS

Wouldst thou, – so the helmsman answered,
Learn the secret of the sea?
Only those who brave its dangers
Can comprehend its mystery!

HENRY WADSWORTH LONGFELLOW
THE SECRET OF THE SEA

The three voyages of circumnavigation by James Cook changed the way Europeans viewed the world. He encompassed the whole of the Pacific Ocean to within the far limits of both polar latitudes, and accurately fixed with latitude and longitude the proper location of places. Cook's voyages placed what previously were fragmented and obscure geographic bodies into a coherent, integrated whole. The mariners who followed Cook continued to push the boundary of exploration toward those few last remaining, unknown and distant parts of the globe.

By the 1820s the greater portion of the Earth's oceans had been explored; what remained, for the most part, lay in those areas surrounding the poles. The harsh climate was forbidding to any colonization, while the bitter cold and ice-chocked seas made sailing difficult and dangerous. A shortness of season further hampered voyages of exploration. And in the Arctic waters north of Canada, extreme magnetic variation rendered the compass practically useless as a guide.

Still, there were reasons to endure the hardships and make the effort to fill in these last blank places on the map. Profit was to be made from whaling and valuable ivory of walrus tusks in the Barentsz Sea north of Norway and Russia. In the far northern Pacific Ocean, whaling and a fur trade of sea otter pelts were strong incentives. In the southern Pacific and far southern latitudes of the Atlantic, whaling and sealing were profitable enterprises. Fur seals were sought for their pelts, and elephant seals for the oil rendered from their blubber to be used for lamp fuel.

Beyond economic reasons, there was also the quest to fulfill those goals as yet unattained by any mariner – to sail as close to the very top and bottom of the Earth as possible, and finally to connect the two oceans by sailing through a Northwest Passage and a Northeast Passage.

341. Sea Anemones and other Jelly Fishes

Adam Johann Ritter von Krusenstern led the first Russian circumnavigation in 1803–1806. The expedition included his ship the *Nadezhda* (Hope) and Yuri F. Lisiansky's *Neva*. Both seafarers conducted hydrographic research during the voyage for the purpose of chart-making. The expedition also made natural-historical observations and produced illustrations. The latter include this drawing of a *Portuguese man-of-war*, a large sailing siphonophore with long stinging tentacles that reach far into the depths.

JUHA NURMINEN COLLECTION

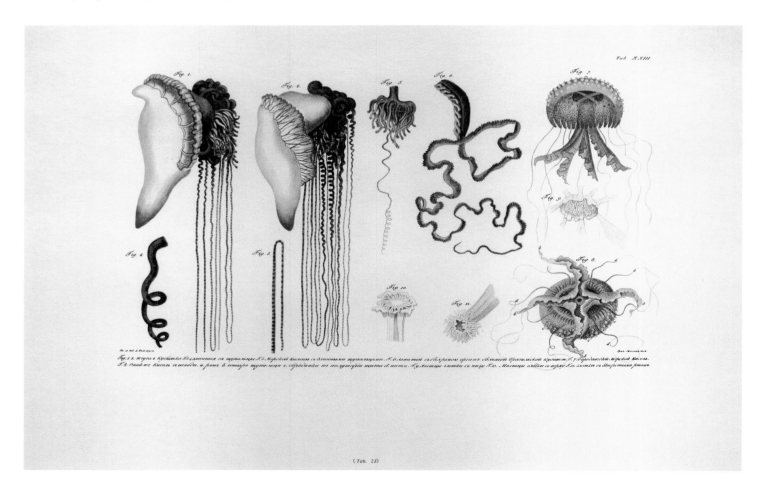

342. *Fram* in Winter by Wally Herbert, 1989

Explorer Fridtjof Nansen's vessel, *Fram,* was the best polar ship of its time, designed to be surrounded by the ice and move with its flow. The greatest cause of death to the crew in expeditions was not shipwreck or battle, but scurvy. Men did not die because of it on Cook's, Nordenskiöld's and Nansen's voyages, however: they understood the preventing effect of fresh food, like vegetables and fruits and were wise enough to adopt the nutrition habits of the indigenous people. And so whenever they stopped at land they supplemented their diet with the same foods the local inhabitants ate.

JOHN NURMINEN FOUNDATION

Arctic Seas

Cook's accomplishments in the Pacific Ocean had far over-shadowed earlier French explorations there. In an effort to expand France's role in trade in the Pacific and expand her territorial possessions, King Louis XVI commissioned a new voyage of exploration to circumnavigate the globe. Jean François Galaup, Comte de La Pérouse (1741–1788), a captain with thirty years of experience in the French Navy, was given command of the expedition and captain of the *Boussole*. A second ship, the *Astrolabe* was commanded by Paul Antoine de Langle.

In addition to exploration this was to be a major scientific expedition, and carried nine scientists, two surveyors and cartographers. La Pérouse was instructed to explore the coasts near the Bering Strait. France wanted to form her own market in the fur trade already established by Russia between the northwest coast of America and China. The expedition sailed from Brest in 1785, and after rounding Cape Horn headed toward the Russian coast. North of Japan, La Pérouse found the strait (now named after him) leading into the Okhotsk Sea. Sailing through the Kuril Islands the expedition reached Kamchatka Peninsula of eastern Russia. Having completed its main mission of surveying the Asian coast in these waters, the expedition headed south.

Since the voyages of Bering and Chirikov in the mid-eighteenth century, Russia continued to explore the waters of the North Pacific. By 1776, the last of the unexplored islands of the Aleutian Archipelago were discovered in an expedition (1770–1776) by Captain Pyotr Krenitsyn and Lieutenant-Commander Mikhail Levashov. With the voyages of Grigory Shelekhov and Alexander Baranov in 1783–1786, Alaska and the Aleutian Islands were annexed to Imperial Russia. Shelekhov founded the first Russian settlement in North America on Kodiak Island in 1798, resulting in the formation of the mercantile Russian-American Company. It received a charter by Tsar Paul giving it a complete monopoly over all Russian enterprises in North America. The company controlled all exploration, trade and settlement in the North Pacific. Baranov founded New Archangel, now called Sitka, which became the capital of Russian America.

Stimulated by this territorial expansion and by the economic benefits gained in the fur trade Russia initiated its first circumnavigation of the globe. Under the patronage of Tsar Alexander I, Ivan Fyodorovich Kruzenshtern (1770–1846), Lieutenant-Commander in the Russian Navy, was given command of the sloop *Nadezhda* (Hope). A second vessel, the sloop *Neva* was commanded by Lieutenant-Commander Yury Lisyansky. The expedition was to set up sea routes for Russian trade between its Baltic Sea ports and its colonies in America, and between the Russian-American Company and Japan and China.

Both ships left Kronstadt in the Gulf of Finland in 1803 and sailed around Cape Horn to reach the Pacific Ocean. Here, the two ships became separated. Kruzenshtern, with the *Nadezhda*, headed for Kamchatka, where along the way he explored the coast of the island of Sakhalin that lies in the Sea of Okhotsk between Japan and Russia. Lisyansky, with the *Neva*, sailed to Russian America, and explored the Aleutian Islands. Both men made charts and wrote detailed geographical descriptions of the lands they visited. After three years, each safely returned home to Russia. Sea routes to advance Russian trade had been established. All of present-day Alaska and the coast of British Columbia as far as the northern end of Vancouver Island was Russian territory. Its colonies extended southward to the very limits of Spanish territory near present-day San Francisco.

Otto von Kotzebue (1787–1846), a Baltic German navigator in the Russian service, had sailed with Kruzenshtern on his 1803–1806 voyage. In 1815, he was given command of his own expedition with the instruction to explore the less known parts of the Pacific and explore and map the interior of the northwest region of North America. Hope was entertained that, in following the coastline of the Bering Sea beyond where Cook had sailed, there might be a channel across the Arctic north leading to the Baffin Sea in the North Atlantic. A deep inlet (now named after Kotzebue) on Alaska's north coast in the Chukchi Sea, just above the Arctic Circle, held promise of success. But when followed through to the end, it turned out to be only a deep sound. A western entrance to the Northwest Passage would have to wait for some future discoverer. By 1867, when Russia sold Alaska to the United States, it had sent more than 250 expeditions into the North Pacific.

Searches begun in the sixteenth century by English and Dutch explorers to reach the North Pole by ship lay at rest until the middle of the nineteenth century; beyond Spitzbergen ships either were crushed by pressure in the pack ice or forced to retreat. With the exception of a failed attempt in 1827 by two English Arctic explorers, William Edward Parry (1790–1855) and James Clark Ross (1800–1862), it was not taken up again until the Finnish born explorer and scientist, Adolf Erik Nordenskiöld (1832–1901), tried three times to reach the North Pole. On the third attempt in 1868, with the ship *Sophia,* he managed to reach 81° 42' N, the highest latitude yet attained in the northern hemisphere, but concluded it was not possible to attain the North Pole by ship.

Fridtjof Nansen (1861–1930), a Norwegian zoologist, oceanographer, philanthropist and writer also proposed to sail over the North Pole. He knew from the experience of others the problems a frozen sea imposed. Nansen conceived a bold, inventive plan; he would purposely let his ship become frozen into the pack ice and let it drift with the ice across the North Pole. The wreckage of a ship from an 1881 expedition that had been abandoned north of Siberia and found much later on the southwest coast of Greenland led Nansen to conjecture that ocean currents had caused the ice, with the ship, to drift this considerable distance.

Rather than modify an existing vessel to meet the demands of Arctic voyaging, Nansen had one designed and built specially for this venture. Its hull was rounded in shape, allowing it when squeezed by the ice to rise up and ride on top. It was built with oak timbers three feet thick, covered with iron sheeting, and designed so that all exterior fittings could be removed to prevent the ice from getting a grip. On 26 June, 1893, Nansen's ship, the *Fram* (meaning 'onward' in Norwegian), embarked from Norway and headed for the New Siberian Islands in the Russian Arctic Sea. Just north of 78° N latitude they reached solid pack ice. The *Fram* was tethered to it to begin its westward journey, a trip Nansen anticipated would take three years.

During this time he maintained a regular schedule of scientific observations. Very deep soundings, by as much as 2000 fathoms, disproved the prevailing theory that the Arctic Ocean was a shallow body of water. Temperature recordings were also much higher than expected, overturning the belief that the polar basin was very cold.

As predicted, the *Fram* continued to drift west and north across the Arctic Sea, locked in the ice. When it reached what appeared would be its most northerly point, Nansen, with one accompanying person, left the ship to attempt to reach the North Pole by kayaks, sledges and dogs. Seventeen men were left on the *Fram* while it slowly continued its westward drift.

With winter weather fast approaching, at 86° 13' N latitude Nansen and his companion turned back, and spent the winter on Franz Joseph Land. By chance encounter with a British expedition the following spring (1896), they were returned to Norway. At almost the same time, the ice released its hold on the *Fram*, and with her remaining crew she was sailed back home, safely arriving with no loss of life three years and three months after her departure. The vessel had reached 85° 55' N latitude, and a record unbroken until 1958 when the US atomic submarine *Nautilus* went under the North Pole. The 'voyage' of the *Fram* validated Nansen's conjecture about the existence of sea currents in the Arctic Sea.

Antarctic Seas

In the pursuit of fur seals and new sailing grounds in Antarctic seas, the Anglo-Scots sealer and navigator, Captain James

Weddell (1787–1834) explored the region between the South Orkney Islands and South Sandwich Islands. He made accurate observations there, and charts of the region, but by 1821 the stocks of seals had already been seriously depleted in these waters, convincing him that he must go still farther south. On 20 February 1825, Weddell eventually reached the latitude of 74° 34' S latitude and 30° 12' W longitude – 204 miles beyond James Cook's achievement.

To aid the American whaling and sealing industries in these waters, in 1836 the United States sponsored its first scientific voyage for exploring and surveying. Particular emphasis was placed on charting the region beyond Patagonia and Tierra del Fuego. Officially titled the United States Exploring Expedition, it was more commonly known as the Charles Wilkes (1798–1877) expedition, after Captain Wilkes who commanded it. Two war sloops, a brig, a storeship and two tenders carried the team of scientists, including naturalists, geologists and artists.

Between 1838 and 1842 the expedition circumnavigated the globe, and sailed over 87,000 miles, gathering data and charting the oceans. On this expedition a large part of the coastline of the continent of Antarctica was charted and mapped for the first time. The results of the expedition were published, and over the years eventually filled eighteen volumes and eleven atlases of charts.

England's accomplishments in Antarctica, and burgeoning interest by the United States in that same region, prompted France to send expeditions to assure her place in the southern seas. Serving in the French Navy, Captain Jules Dumont

d'Urville (1790–1842) set out in 1837 in two ships, the *Astrolabe* and the *Zélée,* to the South Shetland Islands with the plan to proceed south 'as far as the ice permitted'. A reward was offered to the crew if they exceeded Weddell's accomplishment by reaching 75° S latitude.

Dumont d'Urville had already shown his abilities as a navigator while engaged in hydrographic and botanical research in two earlier voyages throughout the Pacific Ocean in 1822–25 and 1826–1829. His mapping of the islands, seemingly scattered at random across that immense ocean, was so thorough and complete that they now were organized into three major groups of Melanesia, Polynesia and Micronesia. Throughout the voyage Dumont d'Urville documented the magnetism of the Earth, and systematically gathered the temperature of the ocean at different depths.

His third voyage (1837–40) was to far southern latitudes with the express purpose of determining the position of the south magnetic pole. On the third of three attempts to reach Antarctica he finally gained firm ground and planted the flag

343. *Astrolabe* caught in the ice by Auguste Mayer, 1842

In order to free Dumont d'Urville's ship, the *Astrolabe*, when it was caught in the ice, the men pushed the ice floes aside by hand with pickaxes and warped their way forward by trying the *Astrolabe* to large floes. It took five days to free themselves from the ice and into an open channel. Dumont d'Urville said: 'Nothing anywhere in the world could be more gloomy and more repulsive than the aspect of these desolate regions.'

TREASURES OF THE NOAA LIBRARY COLLECTION, WASHINGTON D.C.

344. Launching the *James Caird*, 1916

Ernest Henry Shackleton, and five members of his expedition, managed to sail 800 miles in the *James Caird*, a 23-foot lifeboat, to the Elephant Islands during the Antarctic winter in 1916. Because of the rough conditions, this voyage in the *James Caird* is one of the most incredible navigational achievements in the history of seafaring.

ROYAL GEOGRAPHICAL SOCIETY

of France. He ascertained he was near the magnetic pole, for the compass was swinging wildly. Unknown to Dumont d'Urville, Charles Wilkes was exploring the same region at the same time. Dumont d'Urville encountered the vessel *Porpoise* commanded by Wilkes, but neither Captain made any attempt to communicate with the other. Both later laid claim to being first discoverer of the continent of Antarctica.

From his previous voyages in the Arctic, James Clark Ross was already well experienced as a navigator in icy waters, and an expert in magnetism. In 1839, he turned his attention in the other direction and commanded an Antarctic expedition in two ships, the *Erebus* and the *Terror,* to the South Magnetic Pole. He sailed to within 200 miles of the geographic South Pole before a solid barrier of ice stopped him. Unable to penetrate farther he turned north, writing: 'we might with equal chance of success try to sail through the cliffs of Dover, as to penetrate such a mass'. Throughout his voyage Ross charted much of the Antarctica coastline.

The best known figure of British polar expeditions is Ernest Henry Shackleton (1874–1922), an Anglo-Irish explorer whose goal was to reach both the magnetic and geographic South Pole. In the 1907–1909 Nimrod Expedition, named after his ship, *Nimrod*, Shackleton sailed to the Ross Ice Shelf. From there, by sledge the expedition reached the South Magnetic Pole (which at that time lay at 71° 36' S) and later came to within 97 miles of the Geographic South Pole. His next expedition, known as the Imperial Trans-Antarctica Expedition, set out in 1914 to explore the Weddell Sea, and then cross the Antarctic Continent to Ross Island on the other side of the continent. But his ship, the *Endurance*, became trapped in the pack ice of the Weddell Sea where it drifted for nine months until eventually it was crushed by the ice.

Twenty-eight men floated on the ice in the ship's three lifeboats until they reached Elephant Island at the edge of the Antarctic Peninsula. Twenty-two of the men remained on Elephant Island, while Shackleton and five others set out toward South Georgia Island to seek help at the whaling stations there. In one of the most remarkable feats of small boat navigation, the 22½-foot open boat, *James Caird*, sailed in one of the Earth's most inhospitable oceans, with its bitter cold and the wind driven fury of monstrous waves. The only navigation tools they had were a sextant and a compass. At that, the almost perpetually cloud-covered sky permitted the navigator, Frank Worsley, only four sightings to plot their position during the entire trip. If the calculations were off, and they missed South Georgia Island, the entire ocean of the Southern Atlantic would be before them with no chance of sailing back against the persistent westerly winds and Antarctic Circumpolar Current. After seventeen days, they landed on the south side of the island. A Chilean ship, the *Yelcho* was dispatched to pick up the men on Elephant Island.

Connecting the Two Oceans

The untimely death of Henry Hudson in 1611 by a mutinous crew prevented him from following through on what he believed to be the passage through North America leading from the Atlantic to the Pacific Ocean. William Baffin (1584–1622), an English explorer the equal of John Davis in scientific navigation, also attempted it in 1615. He acted as pilot, and Robert Bylot, who had sailed with Hudson on that fateful voyage, was captain; the ship was Henry Hudson's ship, the *Discovery*. They entered Hudson Strait and explored the northwestern portion of that bay. When they found themselves blocked by land and were in shoal water, 'very thick pestered with ice,' they headed homeward. Explorations of Hudson Bay, particularly its northwestern portion which seemingly held great promise, finally proved there was no passage by this way. Baffin still believed a passage existed, but if it was to be found it would have to be in the north of Davis Strait.

The following year, in the same ship, and with Bylot remaining as captain, Baffin sailed up Davis Strait and into the bay, now named after him, until blocked by ice. They reached 78° N, 250 miles farther than Davis was able to sail. In his report upon returning, Baffin concluded that in that great bay (Baffin Bay) 'there is no passage, nor hope of passage in the north of Davis Strait'.

Although William Baffin failed to find the passage, he did much to advance the science of navigation. On his 1615 voyage in Hudson Bay he was the first person to use lunar observations taken at sea to determine longitude. His measurements of latitude, and notes on the tide, were extremely accurate, benefiting future explorers, and his readings of magnetic variation aided in the construction of the first chart of magnetic variation printed in 1701.

Two centuries passed before the elusive Northwest Passage was again sought. This time William Edward Parry, one of the most successful Arctic explorers in the first half of the nineteenth century, made three voyages. John Ross had sailed past Lancas-

ter Sound in Baffin Bay in 1818, believing it was a dead-end. Parry did not share that opinion, and in 1819 set out from England to Davis Strait and Lancaster Sound. He was proven right when he sailed through the Sound, threaded his way through tortuous channels packed with ice and reached Melville Island. Ice in Melville Sound prevented any further travel.

The news caused great excitement upon his return, for at 110° W longitude Parry had made it most of the way to the Beaufort Sea. It seemed now that the passage was easily within grasp and the two oceans would finally be linked. Unfortunately, his next two voyages (1821–22 and 1824–1825) in which he took a more southerly route were failures.

The threat of Russia being the first to navigate the Northwest Passage by sailing from west to east, and thus able to claim sovereignty over Arctic Canada, prompted England to continue her pursuits with more fervour. In 1818 the British Admiralty sent John Franklin (1786–1847) to explore the Arctic Sea. In the mistaken belief that the polar cap was an open sea he tried to reach the Bering Strait by sailing from Spitzbergen over the North Pole. Solid ice north of Spitzbergen quickly caused this expedition to turn back. An entirely different approach was planned for Franklin's next expedition. Under sail, Parry would seek the passage from Baffin Bay, while Franklin would explore the Arctic coast from the landward side; the intent was that the two would be able to meet. From 1819

345. *Gjøa* by Lauritz Haaland

Roald Amundsen's voyage along the Northwest Passage was successful because he managed to find a winding, navigable route. It would have not been possible on a large ship, but Amundsen's agile *Gjøa* proved its abilities in the narrow and icy paths. The picture shows *Gjøa* in the heavy winds of the North Atlantic.

NORSK SJØFARTSMUSEUM, OSLO

to 1822, Franklin traversed the North American mainland by foot and canoe, exploring and charting a major portion of the southern contours of the Northwest Passage. John Franklin's fourth expedition (1845) in the Canadian Arctic was his last, fated to a frozen death when his ships, the *Erebus* and *Terror* became locked in the ice, never to escape.

After 400 years of failed attempts to sail through north of North America – a goal that had its basis in a philosophical construct of the world postulated by Aristotle in the fourth century BC – the existence of a Northwest Passage was finally validated by the Norwegian explorer, Roald Amundsen (1872–1928). Amundsen's voyage was foremost one of discovery; the collection of scientific information was of little consequence in his plans. He did, however, study magnetism and became an expert in the subject. With this knowledge he intended to update the findings on magnetic variation and the position of the Magnetic North Pole made by John Ross, and his nephew James Clark Ross, seventy years earlier.

On 16 June 1903, Amundsen and seven others set off in the ship *Gjøa* to Greenland to pick up supplies, and head into the Canadian Arctic. That September they reached the farthest point sailed by John Franklin and found safe haven in which they spent two winters exploring over land and ice. In the spring of 1905 they started out again, and met a ship that was sailing east from the Pacific end of the passage. Amundsen now knew the completion of his journey was assured. But it took one more winter's stay before he could reach the Pacific Ocean, and in October of 1906 the *Gjøa* sailed into San Francisco Bay.

A number of factors contributed to Amundsen's success where others had failed. He thoroughly studied the routes taken by previous explorers, and learned from their failures as

346. *Vega* under Aurora Borealis by Adolf Bock, 1927

Vega could not have navigated the North-East Passage without steam power. In the early part of the voyage, the expedition was supported by the ships *Lena* and *Yenisey*, one of which transported coal. Thanks to its steam-driven propulsion, *Vega* could proceed at considerable speed even in ice. Even the sloop that sounded the shallow waters ahead of *Vega* had steam propulsion.

STATENS SJÖHISTORISKA MUSEUM, STOCKHOLM

347. Photograph of Adolf Erik Nordenskiöld

Nordenskiöld was not only an explorer but also the founder of the science of cartography. With proceeds from the book he wrote on *Vega's* voyage along the Northeast Passage, he added to his considerable collection of maps, with the help of which he wrote his monument of cartographic history, the Facsimile Atlas. Today, his collection of maps is in the Finnish national library and is on the UNESCO World Heritage List.

NORDISKA MUSEETS ARKIV, STOCKHOLM

348. Ship and Pocket Chronometers used during A. E. Nordenskiöld's Expeditions in 1878–1879

Chronometers were trusted on the *Vega*. Its Russian charts, especially their longitudes, of the Siberian coast underwent considerable revision based on the position fixing done during the ship's voyages. Despite considerable variation in temperature and humidity, *Vega's* chronometers performed well. When the ship traversed the Northeast Passage, Greenwich Time had been accepted as the universal standard time. The crew checked their time via telegraph from Tromsö. When *Vega* arrived in Yokohama more than a year after it had first left port, its main chronometer, a Frodham 3194, was checked against a chronometer in Tromsö; it was only a little over five minutes late.

KUNGLIGA VETENSKAPSAKADEMIEN, STOCKHOLM

well as their successes. For the most part, the path he intended to take was that pioneered by John Franklin, so it was already well charted. In the time spent overwintering, Amundsen became friends with the native Inuit and learned their techniques for Arctic survival. His ship, *Gjøa* was a small fishing craft, only 69 feet long, and of shallow draft, which made it relatively easy to manoeuvre through the narrow leads in pack ice. It also had a small diesel auxiliary engine that could be used when contrary wind and current made sail impractical. And finally, Amundsen was favoured by an unusually warm Arctic summer; narrow channels and sounds that had been frozen over before were now open.

After accomplishing what no other mariner before him had been able to do – sail the entire length of the Northwest Passage – Amundsen turned his attention to another goal, that of being the first to reach the geographic South Pole. In 1910 he set out from Norway to the Ross Ice Shelf in Nanson's old ship the *Fram*, probably the strongest wooden ship ever built. From there, by sledges and dogs he arrived at the South Pole on 14 December 1911, one month before a British expedition under the direction of Robert Falcon Scott, with the same goal.

349. A Chart of the Hydrological Department of the Russian Maritime Ministry depicting The Northern Arctic Sea, 1874

A chart from the Hydrographic Department of the Russian Admiralty, on which A.E. Nordenskiöld marked the route he sailed on his vessel *Vega*. On 19 August 1878, the *Vega* dropped anchor off Cape Chelyuskin, the most northerly point of the Eurasian continent. To correct any error on the chart, Nordenskiöld confirmed his position by astronomical observation the following day.

JOHN NURMINEN FOUNDATION

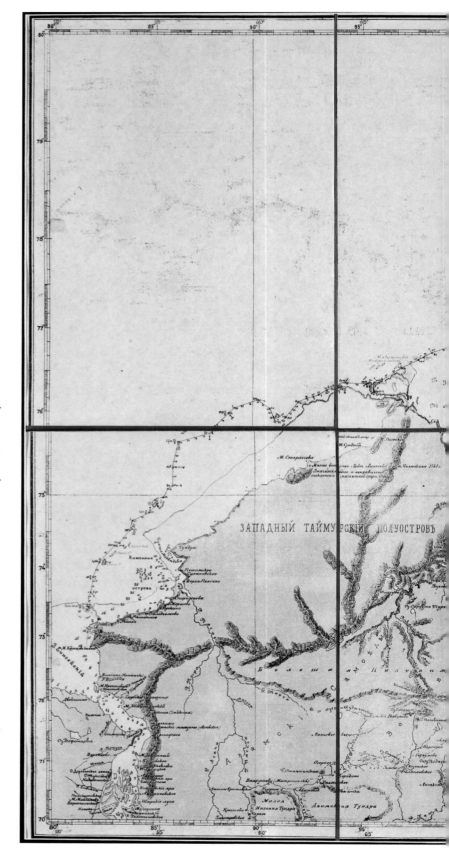

The search for a navigable passage over the top of Russia and Siberia to the Pacific, the Northeast Passage, was sought just as assiduously as its counterpart, the Northwest Passage. The many attempts to sail it made by English and Dutch explorers during the sixteenth century had been unsuccessful. The farthest east they managed to reach was Nova Zembla, beyond which they could not push their way through the dense pack ice that awaited them in the Kara Sea. At the eastern end of the passage, Russian expeditions, most notably the Great Nordic Expedition of 1734–1743, led by Vitus Bering (1680–1741), made some progress. The northern coast of Siberia, out to the Bering Sea, was successfully sailed and charted. But the ice of the Kara Sea in the middle section of the Northeast Passage continued to remain an impenetrable barrier to the completion of any passage.

After his highly successful Arctic ventures to Spitzbergen and to Greenland, Nordenskiöld decided he too would take up the quest to open the Northeast Passage. With the vessel *Pröven,* Nordenskiöld embarked from Tromsö, Norway in 1875. He sailed east, through the White Sea, into the Kara Sea, and all across the top of Russia, as far as the mouth of the Yenisei River at 80° E longitude. From there, Nordenskiöld rowed a small boat 1000 miles up river to central Russia where he opened commercial ties between Sweden and Russia.

What was once an impossible task, penetrating the Kara Sea, was now shown to be feasible. The last remaining segment of the passage along the northern coast of Siberia and into the Pacific Ocean had already been completed by Russian navigators. It remained now only to be brought to completion in a single voyage.

Many advances in technology occurred in the 321 years since Hugh Willoughby and Richard Chancellor sought the passage. It was a new era of fully powered steam vessels. Ships under sail alone lacked manoeuvrability in narrow straits and could not contend with the constant, rapid dodging of ice floes required in these high latitudes. For this expedition, Nordenskiöld's vessel, the *Vega,* was built as a steam-auxiliary in Germany specifically for Arctic conditions. Chronometers set to Greenwich Mean Time, by now accepted as the basic universal time, were available as an accurate timepiece for determining longitude. When he reached Yokohama, Nordenskiöld was able to check the accuracy of his chronometer by the recently developed telegraph, and thus ascertained his calculations of longitude throughout the long voyage were correct. The sextant, successor to the octant and quadrant, allowed greater precision in measuring the angular height of a celestial body to determine position. Taken together, navigational measurements and charting reached higher standards of accuracy, and allowed Nordenskiöld achieve his goal of being the first to sail the Northeast Passage.

In preparation of the voyage, Nordenskiöld thoroughly studied accounts of earlier voyages, and collected all available historical literature and maps. He concluded the reason those be-

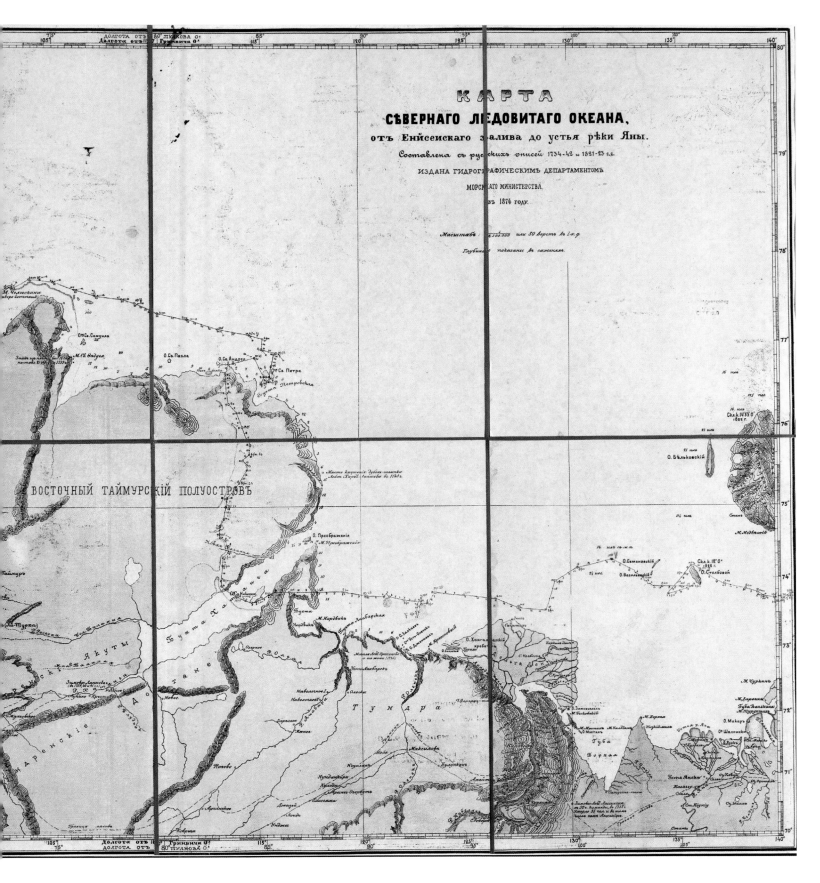

fore him had failed was that they had sailed too far out from the mainland, in the belief they would find there an open polar sea. He planned instead to hug the shore as closely as possible thinking the water there would be warmed by the northward flowing rivers which poured forth from the interior of Russia.

On 22 June 1878, four ships left from Karlskrona, Sweden; three of them were support vessels carrying coal and supplies for the *Vega*. Additionally, their holds contained cargo for the new trade established at the Yenisei. Nordenskiöld was in command of the entire *Vega* expedition, while a Swedish naval

lieutenant, Louis Palander (1842–1920) was master of the *Vega* and responsible for the navigation. An extensive complement of scientists accompanied the expedition, for it was to be as much an examination of natural and physical conditions as it was a geographic exploration.

They were only 120 miles from the Bering Strait which separates Siberia from Alaska, when the ships became frozen into the drift ice, and were forced to remain there for ten months of the winter. In the spring of 1879 the ice released its grip and the *Vega* continued her journey, completing the first transit of

Vega and the First Cargo Steamers

Nordenskiöld's research ship *Vega* was completed in 1873 in Bremerhaven, Germany, for the Swedish company Ishavet, at a time when engine power was taking over from sail. This barque-rigged steamer retained the slim exterior of a sailing vessel, including a clipper bow and some small deckhouses. The hull was built of oak and proved to be strong enough to withstand the ice of the Arctic Sea. Built as a whaler, the *Vega* had a gross tonnage of 357 registered tons and a length overall of 43.4 m, making her quite a small ship even in her day; a typical seagoing cargo steamer of the period was built of iron or steel and had a gross registred tonnage of several thousand.

The introduction of the marine steam engine was revolutionary in many ways. Although sailing clippers were fast, and had a large cargo capacity, they were totally depending on the winds. The earliest use of steam propulsion was for tugs to help sailing vessels enter harbour. Scheduled liner traffic was out of the question in the age of sail. With the development in the 1880s of the triple expansion compound steam engine, reliability was increased, and the cost of operation was reduced to the point where it became practicable to build large ocean-going steamers. The leading seafaring nations soon established a global network of liner traffic.

A milestone in the development of steam navigation was the replacement of fragile paddle wheels with robust and efficient screw propellers, radically improving their manoeuvrability and reliability. In ideal conditions, using the propeller's direction of rotation to his advantage, a skilful master could berth his ship without assistance from a tug. It is even easier to handle a twin-screw vessel, but such machinery was very rare in ordinary freighters.

The *Vega* was not particularly progressive technically, but in Nordenskiöld's opinion she was suitable for sailing through the Northeast Passage. The compound steam engine had a modest output of 60 hp and its fuel consumption was 10 cubic feet of coal an hour. A lot of coal was needed, and therefore sails were used to save fuel. According to the seller, *Vega* sailed and manoeuvred exceptionally well and could reach a speed of 9 to 10 knots using her sails alone. A typical cargo steamer of those days could not perform better.

The combination of steam and sail for ship's propulsion reflected the seaman's suspicion of engine power, but was also a sensible compensation for the poor reliability of the earliest steam engines. If the engine stopped, it was always possible to continue by sail. The reliability of steam engines increased enough by the end of the nineteenth century that freighters were no longer rigged as sailing vessels, although they sometimes could hoist a few auxiliary sails.

The accommodation on *Vega* was all situated below deck. The only superstructure was a small deckhouse on the poop deck for the companionways to the gunroom and the machinery spaces. The engine room was situated aft and the boiler room in the adjacent compartment towards the bow. The officers' compartment was situated above the engine room and the ratings' quarters were on the 'tween deck in the fore part of the vessel. The petty officers had their

cabins aft of the crew's space.

The open bridge was situated aft, above the small deckhouse. So that the helmsman could see the sails when she was making way under sail, the helm was located aft, directly above the rudder. To meet the needs of the exploration voyage, the lower hold was filled with iron tanks to strengthen the hull against the ice pressure; in these were stowed provisions, water and coal. On the large open deck a steam sloop was stowed and on a grating above deck the ship carried two lifeboats.

The basic freight steamer had a different general arrangement. The superstructure was situated amidships, leaving space for cargo holds and hatches fore and aft. The booms in the two masts were not installed for sails but for handling cargo. The deep cargo holds had 'tween decks for the stowage of general cargo. The bridge was in the fore part of the superstructure and long into the twentieth century was open. Aft of the bridge was a small chart house for navigation. The helmsman stood on the bridge and followed orders from the officer on watch, or from

351. Drawing of Louis Palander

Shipmaster Louis Palander had full charge of navigation on *Vega*, a task in which he was very successful. *Vega* was the first ship to circumnavigate Eurasia. The ship and its crew returned to Stockholm in 1880, more than a year after they had first set sail.

JUHA NURMINEN COLLECTION

350. Model of *Vega*

The *Vega* was built at Bremerhaven in 1873 as a whaler for Arctic waters, but was bought in 1877 for Nordenskiöld's expedition to the Northeast Passage. It was rigged as a barque although it had a 60 hp steam engine. In the early days of steam the sail was regarded as a reliable and economic complement for propulsion.

JOHN NURMINEN FOUNDATION

the captain. When he turned the helm, the force was transferred mechanically to the rudder by lines. The master controlled the engine with a telegraph, which could be rotated to indicate a certain speed forward or astern, and which transmitted that order to the engine room where it was executed by the engineers controlling the main steam valves. It only became possible to control the engines directly from the bridge in the 1960s.

Before *Vega* left for her exploration voyage the ship was docked and repaired at the navy yard in Karlskrona, at which time the interior was converted to suit the needs of the expedition. The *Vega* left the shipyard on 22 June 1878 with a carefully selected crew of nineteen men from the elite of the Swedish navy. A few days later the scientists boarded the ship in Göteborg.

The master of the *Vega* was the young lieutenant Louis Palander, who skilfully manoeuvred his ship through unknown waters. Of great use was the sloop, which sounded the depth before the *Vega* to find a navigable channel. In this way the expedition could maintain a higher average speed. It also prevented disastrous groundings, which could have endangered the whole expedition.

Determination of the ship's exact position was of the utmost importance for the cartographic purposes of the expedition. The chronometers that were supplied were not state-of-the art, but they could be synchronized to Greenwich time using telegraph. At the start of the expedition the exact time was acquired from the Stockholm Observatory via the telegraph in Tromsö. As this was before the age of wireless telegraphy, the next time the chronometers could be calibrated was when the vessel arrived at Yokohama.

On 24 April 1880 when the ship returned to Sweden after the long voyage, there was a big celebration. Asia had been circumnavigated for the first time in history. However, *Vega* was soon again on duty as a whaler, and in 1903 she sank off Greenland after being damaged by ice.

Nordenskiöld's successful expedition showed that steam power could be used in Arctic conditions. Later, more powerful steam engines made it possible to break the ice in the Baltic Sea and in other regions – even in the Northeast Passage. In the path of *Vega* follow powerful icebreakers, assisting ice-strengthened cargo vessels tailor made for Arctic conditions. But to date, the Northeast Passage remains impracticable for general sea transportation.

the Northeast Passage. Nordenskiöld's first port in the Pacific Ocean was Port Clarence, Alaska. From there he sailed to Yokohama, Japan, Canton (China), Ceylon (now Sri Lanka), and through the Suez Canal into the Mediterranean and the Atlantic, triumphantly returning to Stockholm on 24 April 1880.

This navigational feat made Nordenskiöld and Palander not only the first to sail the Northeast Passage and prove that with a strong vessel it was possible for others as well, but the first mariners to make a complete circumnavigation of Eurasia. Articles and journals latewritten by them and the scientists aboard the expedition, made significant advances in the fields of geography, cartography, hydrography, marine surveying, magnetism, paleontology, mineralogy and biology. As a final note to the careful preparatory planning, they returned without a single loss of life or vessel. In reward, Nordenskiöld was made a baron and Palander was knighted as Palander af Vega.

FIRST CIRCUMNAVIGATION SINGLE-HANDED

Having lost his ship and family, Captain Joshua Slocum (1844–1909) could no longer find a position as a ship's master in the 1890s. Fortunately, a friend offered him a ship, which was in bad need of repair. It proved to be an old sloop that had lain covered in a field for seven years. Slocum was forced to build the vessel almost anew, but it was not the first ship that he had built. After a year's hard work, *Spray* was ready.

Slocum gives no reason as to why he set off on his journey around the world. It had been done often before, but never by a single sailor alone. His predecessors had looked for new lands and new routes or sought to conquer others; Slocum was the first to circumnavigate the Earth for pleasure. Of course, a solo circumnavigator has to sail a small boat because large ships cannot be handled alone. Slocum also proved that an able seaman can sail around the Earth using simple methods and tools.

When he set sail from Boston harbour in April 1895, he had more than twenty years' experience as a ship's master, a tin clock bought at Yarmouth, which cost a dollar and a half except that he got it for a dollar because its glass was shattered, a compass and a sounding line. With incomprehensible accuracy he sailed directly to his destinations – the Azores, Marquesas Islands, Christmas Island, Mauritius and St. Helen – using only these simple aids of navigation.

He asked for his position from ships he encountered but for the most part they only confirmed his own calculations. His sloop *Spray* had an astounding ability to stay on course. In twenty three days he sailed from Thursday Island to Cocos Islands, a distance of 2700 miles. During all that time he spent only three hours at the helm, including his entry into the harbour at his destination. He simply tied the helm to hold *Spray* and she kept her course.

When at sea, Slocum always took great care to enter a daily fix of his position on his chart. 'The Southern Cross I saw every night abeam. The Sun every morning came up astern; every evening it went down ahead. I wished for no other compass to guide me, for these were true. If I doubted my reckoning after a long time at sea I verified it by reading the clock aloft made by the Great Architect, and it was right'.

In his book *Sailing Alone Around the World* he is already halfway through the story, approaching the Marquesas Islands, when he discloses that he did also bring a sextant '... the sky being beautifully clear and the Moon being "in distance" with the Sun, I threw up my sextant for sights. I found from the result of three observations, after a long wrestling with lunar tables, that her longitude by observation agreed within five miles of that by dead reckoning'.

He was convinced he had his position right and expected to see land in a few hours. And he did: he saw Nuka Hiva, the southernmost island of the Marquesas. This made even Slocum embarrassed of boasting about his seamanship and writes: 'I hope I am making it clear that I do not lay claim to cleverness or to slavish calculations in my reckonings. I think I have already stated that I kept my longitude, at least, mostly by intuition. A rotator log always towed astern, but so much has to be allowed for currents and for drift, which the log never shows, that it is only an approximation, after all, to be corrected by one's own judgement from data of a thousand voyages; and even then the master of the ship, if he be wise, cries out for the lead and the lookout'.

He cannot keep himself from writing about his great astronomical experience, however. Before calculating the position mentioned above, his first measurement of elevation had placed him hundreds of miles further west than dead reckoning suggested'. I knew that this could not be correct. In about an hour's time I took another set of observations with the utmost care; the mean result of these was about the same as that of the first set. I asked myself why, with my boasted self-dependence, I had not done at least better than this. Then I went in search of a discrepancy in the tables, and I found it. In the tables I found that the column of figures from which I had got an important logarithm was in error'. People are usually good at what they enjoy doing. Slocum loved navigation; 'The work of the lunarian, though seldom practised in these days of chronometers, is beautifully edifying, and there is nothing in the realm of navigation that lifts one's heart up more in adoration'.

The solitary sailor had benefits larger crews lack. Never before had his crew been so undivided or so sharp-eyed. As he approached the Cocos Islands, their proximity was announced by a white tern, which the islanders called the 'Cocos Island's pilot'. After sailing for more than two weeks in the Cocos Islands, Slocum saw a formation of clouds dead ahead, motionless while other clouds sped across the sky. As the *Spray* advanced, a dark shape rose from beneath the cloud at midnight: Rodriguez Island. On another occasion, Slocum was awakened in the morning by the cries of a rare gannet,' which I recognized at once as a call to go to deck'. As he clambered on deck, he saw St. Helen some 20 miles ahead.

In Slocum's opinion the dangers of his voyage had nothing to do with navigation. That, as we now know, was easy. After passing Gibraltar, he would have been captured by a pirate felucca had he not been saved by a sudden storm. Without the carpet tacks he had received as a gift and spread on the deck, the Fuegians that had crept into his boat at night would have killed him and looted his boat. When he drifted on to sands off the coast of Uruguay, it was not navigational error but because he was sailing by eye in the middle of the night, so close to the coast. Sailing from Juan Fernández to Samoa, the *Spray* hit a whale but the only damage suffered was by Slocum himself, who was doused by the whale's tail as it struck the water. On St. Helen, a goat he had been given ate everything it possibly could, including his Caribbean charts.

Slocum's story is excellent proof of what a person with self-confidence can do, as long as he is not too self-impor-

tant. Slocum always saw the amusing side in everything, himself included. He received a grand welcome in ports around the world. He also had time to enjoy his stopovers, sometimes staying in a port for quite some time. It was a different time then, although Slocum did find fault in the crew of an overtaking transport that was too busy to wish him a good morning: ' There are no poetry-enshrined freighters on the sea now; it is a prosy life when we have no time to bid one another good morning'.

His story is an object lesson of how navigation has changed over the centuries. It used to be a tour-de-force of human ability. It required both thorough knowledge and intuition, as Slocum proved. Today, the skill has become a technical one thanks to automated equipment. Navigation is no longer the ability to combine observations of various phenomena and information and draw conclusions on them. This is why it is so important to write the history of navigation now, since anything too new and revolutionary can no longer be expected.

352. *Spray* by Lars-Erik Malmlund, 1984

JUHA NURMINEN COLLECTION

THE ELECTRONIC AGE

The same challenges faced by Phoenician mariners when they first ventured forth from the Mediterranean Sea out into the Atlantic Ocean 2 700 years ago, still confront today's navigators. But advances in electronics and the use of computers now solve these problems with greater speed and accuracy.

The magnetic compass, long established as a means for determining direction, has also progressed with the development of the gyrocompass. As its name implies, the gyrocompass is essentially a gyroscope, a spinning wheel. The only direction it can point to is true north, rather than magnetic north, thereby making it totally independent of influences of the earth's magnetic field, and unaffected by a metal ship.

It took many centuries of advances in astronomy, accurate time-keeping devices, and improved instruments for measurement before navigators were able to plot their latitude and longitude with any degree of accuracy. But even with sextant and chronometer it was still time consuming and involved a significant amount of mathematical calculations. The use of pocket calculators to do the computation shortened this procedure. Even so, the ability to take celestial sightings for navigation was wholly dependent upon weather conditions; a cloud-filled sky, obliterating the view of astronomical bodies during the day or at night, and heavy seas creating error in the sighting, made position fixing impossible.

The technology for keeping accurate time, so essential in navigation to determine longitude, has seen many advances. The wire telegraph was supplanted by radio (wireless telegraphy) for checking the time, allowing ships to receive time signals when at sea. Radio broadcasts presently provide a continuous count of time in seconds, based on superbly precise atomic clocks. This gives the navigator exact Greenwich Mean Time (the reference standard), now called Universal Time Coordinated (UTC).

Measuring the depth of water by dropping a weighted length of line overboard has been replaced by acoustic soundings. SONAR (Sound Navigation and Ranging) using sound through the water to navigate or detect other vessels came into use in the early 1920's. When used to determine depth it is called echo-sounding. These instruments, called fathometers, send a pulse of sound through the water and 'listens' for reflections of the pulse. The time from emission to reception is measured and converted into distance. Early fathometers were capable of measuring depths ranging from 100 to 4,716 fathoms. It took another two decades, however, before they were sufficiently accurate for shallow water. Side-scan sonar creates images of large areas of the sea floor; used for mapping it allows for three-dimensional bathymetry.

During World War II, the systems of Decca RADAR (Radio Detection and Ranging), an outgrowth of the gramophone and records company of Great Britain, and LORAN (Long Range Navigation) developed in the United States, enable navigators to determine position at sea independent of any weather restrictions. These systems are based on the principle of timed differences of the receipt of signals broadcast from multiple, land-based radio stations. When they were commonly in use, nautical charts had an overlaid grid of lines expanding outward from the stations and labeled with the time differences. Decca and LORAN receivers displayed the specific time differences which the navigator then related to the grid on his chart. Where the lines from each station intersected was the position of the vessel. Later, the receiver automatically converted this to latitude and longitude. However, radio-based navigation has limitations in coverage, and is affected by atmospheric effects and magnetic storms from solar flares.

Radio waves of radar are also used to detect and determine the distance or speed of objects. As used in marine navigation, it enables one to visualize land and other objects, such as ships, which would ordinarily be hidden from sight by fog, smoke, clouds, or at night. A transmitter rotating 360° continuously sends out signals which when reflected from the object are displayed on a screen as a two-dimensional image, along with a range of distance and time. Sophisticated radars can tag and

353. Stormy Ocean. Adolf Bock, 1923.

keep track of ships in a busy shipping channel, display their future track based on present speed and direction, and determine the time and position of potential collision. The feasibility of radar was first demonstrated in 1904 and is still a primary tool today of navigation on ships.

Satellites orbiting the earth allow the navigator to determine his position anywhere on earth with a speed and accuracy never before achieved. GPS (Global Positioning System) has made Decca and LORAN virtually obsolete. In GPS, more than twenty-four satellites circle the earth each day at an altitude of 20 000 kilometers (12 600 miles), broadcasting precisely timed radio signals to receivers. They are positioned in such a manner that at any one time at least four of them are above the horizon. The GPS receiver measures the distance to at least four satellites and calculates the correct latitude, longitude and elevation. Accuracy of the determined position is within two meters (six feet), but with the aid of other techniques can be improved to an accuracy of within one cm (half an inch). In effect, GPS is a modified LORAN, ground based system. And like LORAN, is also affected by changes in atmospheric conditions, especially when a satellite is at a low angle for observation, thereby increasing the distance the signal must pass through the ionosphere. In the near future, Russia will expand its now operating independent satellite navigation system called GLONASS (Global Navigation Satellite System), soon to be followed by other satellite navigations systems of the European Union, China, and France.

The orbit of Geostationary satellites is synchronized with the Earth's rotation on its axis, so that they hover continuously over the same spot. Positioned at a higher altitude than the other satellites, these satellites are able to view the whole earth rather than just one segment. They collect data and provide imagery that is transmitted to stations on the earth. Instruments monitor storms, hurricanes, ice fields, and provide a host of other meteorological information. Major currents of the ocean are continuously checked. The procedure for defining these currents is no different than that used by Benjamin Franklin — by measuring their temperature — but today, instead of a thermometer being placed in the water, satellite infrared imagery and altimetry, combined with color enhancement by computer, measure and show the current's location. With this information at hand, commercial shipping has improved route choices, can avoid hazardous weather, and shorten voyage duration.

Nautical charts containing data accumulated over the centuries are now in digital form and viewable on a computer, with software programs allowing one to overlay any set of parameters desired. GPS signals can be interfaced with these programs to show the ship's position and track directly on the chart.

Great as all these improvements in navigation throughout the centuries have been, sometimes painfully achieved through disastrous occurrence, to guide the mariner safely over the seas, one element has remained unchanging. It all finally comes down to each man's judgement, gained through experience and the use of his senses — of what he sees, hears, and feels — when traversing the paths of the sea.

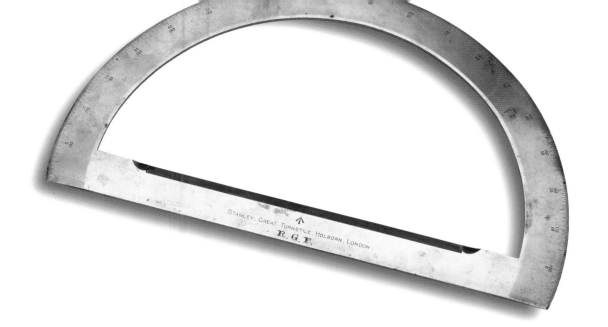

APPENDICES

PICTURE LIST

1. **Reefing the Foresail**. John Stobart. *American Maritime Paintings of John Stobart by John Stobart and Robert Davis,* copyright © 1991 by M.H.P. Enterprises, Inc. (Used by permission of Dutton, a division of Penguin Group (USA) Inc.).

2. **Jacques de Vaulx**. Frontispiece, *Les Premières oeuvres.* 1583. (Bibliothèque nationale de France, Paris. MS. Français 150, fol. 1).

3. **An English Ship in a Gale Trying to Claw off a Lee Shore**. Willem van de Velde, the Younger. 1672. (National Maritime Museum, London. BHC0900).

4. **Maidens Lighthouse**. Alpo Tuurnala, 2006. (Donald S. Johnson).

5. **Vincenzo Maria Coronelli** (1650–1718). Frontispiece, *Gli argonauti pro ultra.* 17th century. (Juha Nurminen Collection).

6. **Terrestrial globe**. J. & G. Cary. London, Beginning of the 19th century. (Juha Nurminen Collection)

THE DAWN OF NAVIGATION

7. **HMS *Resolution* and *Adventure* with Fishing Craft in Matavi Bay**. William Hodges (1744–1797). 1776. (National Maritime Museum, London. BHC1932).

8. **James Cook** (1728–1779). »The Society Islands«. *Charts and Maps made during the Voyage of Discovery in the South Pacific Ocean, by Captain James Cook, commander of the Endeavour, in 1769 and 1770.* (The British Library, London. Add. 21593 C).

9. **Polynesian Migration**. Jari Patanen, 2007.

10. **Antonio Pigafetta** (c.1491–1534). Islands of the Lateen Sails. »Isles des Larrons«. *Navigation de l`Inde supérieure.* 16th century. (Bibliothèque nationale de France, Paris. MS. Français 24224, f. 20 v).

11. **Native Watercraft of the Island of Anamocka.** *Journal or Description drawn up by Abel Jansz. Tasman of the Discovery of the Unknown South-Land in 1642.* Facsimile. Los Angeles, 1965. (Juha Nurminen Collection).

12. **Carolinian Star Compass**. Stewart Gray, 2007.

13. **Sailing toward a Star**. Stewart Gray, 2007.

14. **Navigation Chart from the Marshall Islands**. *Anthoropology Artifact Catalogue No. E398227.* (Department of Anthropology, Smithsonian Institution, Maryland).

15. **Singalesian outrigger**. Björn Landström (1917–2002). *Tie Intiaan. Löytöretkistä maitse ja meritse alkaen Puntin retkikunnasta v. 1493 eKr. päätyen Hyväntoivonniemen löytämiseen v. 1488 jKr.* Helsinki, 1964. (Courtesy of Olof Landström).

16. **Inuit kayak**. *I.N.J. Historia navigationis Martini Forbisseri angli praetoris sive capitanei, a.c. 1577.* Hamburg, 1675. (Juha Nurminen Collection).

17. **Ship carving in Virgin Islands**. Nicolaes Witsen (1641–1717). *Aeloude en hedendaegsche scheeps-bouw en bestier: waer in wijtloopigh wert verhandelt, de wijze van scheeps-timmeren, by Grieken en Romeynen ... beneffens evenmatige grootheden van schepen onses tijts, ontleet in alle hare deelen...* Amsterdam, 1671. (Juha Nurminen Collection).

18. **Kayak**. Wilhelm A. Graah (1793–1863). *Undersögelses reise till. Östgusten af Grönland.* Copenhagen, 1832. (Juha Nurminen Collection).

19. **Queen Hatshepsut's ship**. Björn Landström. *Laiva. Katsaus laivan historian alkukantaisesta lautasta atomikäyttöiseen sukellusveneeseen.* Helsinki, 1961. (Courtesy of Olof Landström).

THE SEAFARER'S NATURAL WORLD

20. **Sea Painting**. Johannes Holst (1880–1965). 1913. (Peter Tamm Collection, Hamburg).

21. **The Earth in its Orbit, Equinoxes and Solstices**. Jari Patanen, 2007.

22. **Ocean Winds**. Jari Patanen, 2007.

23. **Ocean Surface Currents**. Jari Patanen, 2007.

24. **Savannah, Moonlight over the Savannah River in 1850**. John Stobart. *American Maritime Paintings of John Stobart by John Stobart and Robert Davis,* copyright © 1991 by M.H.P. Enterprises. (Used by permission of Dutton, a division of Penguin Group (USA) Inc.).

25. **Low Tide, Sunset**. Eugène Boudin (1824–1898). (Association Peindre en Normandie, Conseil Régional de Basse-Normandie).

26. **Coordinates in Celestial and Terrestrial Spheres**. Jari Patanen, 2007.

27. **Louis Renard** (fl.c. 1702–1707). »Indiarum Occidentalium Tractus Littorales cum Insulis Caribicis«. *Atlas de la navigation, et du commerce qui se fait dans toutes les parties du monde.* Amsterdam, 1715. (Juha Nurminen Collection).

28. **Johannes Covens** (1697–1772) – **Cornelis Mortier** (1661–1711). Celestial map. »Planisphaerium coeleste«. c. 1759. (Juha Nurminen Collection).

29. **Precession of Equinoxes**. Jari Patanen, 2007.

30. **Parhelion**. Figura admirandi meteori. Joan Blaeu (c. 1599–1673). *Atlas Maior Sive Cosmographia Blaviana.* Amsterdam, 1665. (The National Library of Finland, Helsinki).

31. **Aurora Borealis**. Fridtjof Nansen (1861–1930). *Farthest North.* 1897. (John Nurminen Foundation).

32. **Optical Phenomena of Unequal Refraction**. William Scoresby Junior (1789–1857). *Journal of a Voyage to the Northern Whale-Fishery...* Edinburgh, 1823. (Juha Nurminen Collection).

ANCIENT SAILING ROUTES AND PERIPLI

33. **Gregorio Dati** (1362–1425). *La Sfera.* 15th century. (The National Library of Finland, Helsinki).

34. **Queen Hatshepsut**. Photographed by Jürgen Liepe. (Egyptian Museum, Cairo).

35. **Queen Hatshepsut's Ship leaving from Punt, redrawn from the original mural carving from Deir-el-Bahri**. Björn Landström. *Tie Intiaan. Löytöretkistä maitse ja meritse alkaen Puntin retkikunnasta v. 1493 eKr. päätyen Hyväntoivonniemen löytämiseen v. 1488 jKr.* Helsinki, 1964. (Courtesy of Olof Landström).

36. **Realm of Phoenicians**. Jari Patanen, 2007.

37. **Amphora, c. 350 BC**. (Juha Nurminen Collection).

38. **Kyrenian ship**. Kari Jaakkola, 2000. (John Nurminen Foundation).

39. **Sebastian Münster** (1489–1552). Map of the Nordic Countries. »Schonlandia XIII nova tabula«. Basel, 1540. (John Nurminen Foundation).

40. **Periplus of Scylax**. Attributed to Scylax of Caryanda (fl. 6th century BC). c. 1200. (Bibliothèque nationale de France, Paris. MS. Sup.Grec 443, p.1).

41. **The Sea Battle of Salamis**. Wilhelm von Kaulbach (1805–1874). c. 1858. Photographer Blauel/Gnamm – Artothek. (Bayer. Staatsgemäldesammlungen).

42. **Ancient Peripli**. Jari Patanen, 2007.

43. **Alexandria Harbour**. Stewart Gray, 2007.

44. **Lighthouse of Pharos**. Stewart Gray, 2007.

45. **Georg Braun** (1541–1622) – **Frans Hogenberg** (1535–1590). »Ostia«. *Civitates Orbis Terrarum* Vol. IV.

95. **Bartolomeo dalli Sonetti**. Khios and adjacent mainland. *Isolario*. Venice, 1485. (National Maritime Museum, London. F1641, P/21 ,46).

96. **16th century manuscript showing the teaching of astronomy using an astrolabe**. (© Courtesy of University Library Istanbul/MuslimHeritage.com).

97. **Astrolabe with Geared Calendar**. Muhammad b. Abi Bakr. Isfahan, 1222. (Museum of the History of Science, University of Oxford.150526).

98. **Astrolabe**. Jacques de Vaulx. *Les Premières oeuvres*. 1583. (Bibliothèque nationale de France, Paris. MS. Français 150, fol. 15).

99. **Arab dhows in the harbour of Aden**. Björn Landström. *Tie Intiaan. Löytöretkistä maitse ja meritse alkaen Puntin retkikunnasta v. 1493 eKr. päätyen Hyväntoivonniemen löytämiseen v. 1488 jKr*. Helsinki, 1964. (Courtesy of Olof Landström).

100. **Arab Dhow**. Stewart Gray, 2007.

101. **Arab Ocean Trade Routes**. Jari Patanen, 2007.

102. **Arab compass**. From: David A. King. A Survey of the Scientific Manuscript in the Egyptian National Library. (ARCE/ Catalog 5; Winona Lake, Ind: American Research Center in Egypt/ Eisenbrauns, 1986). P1 XCVII cp.317)).

103. **Kamal (latitude hook)**. Stewart Gray, 2007.

EARLY NAVIGATION IN NORTHERN WATERS

104. **Mappa Cottoniana**. Second quarter of 11th century. (The British Library, London. Cotton MS. Tiberius B.V., fol. 56v.).

105. **Abraham Ortelius** (1527–1598) – **Andreas (Velleius) Vedel** (1542–1616). »Islandia Illvstris. Ac Potent Regi Fredericoll Daniae, Norvegiae, Slavorum, Gothormqve regi, etc principi svo Slementissimo». 1590. (Juha Nurminen Collection).

106. **Saint Brendan and the Whale**. *Navigatio Sancti Brendani Abbatis*. c.1460. (Universitätsbibliothek, Heidelberg. Cod. Pal. Germ. 60, fol. 179v.).

107. **Athanasius Kircher** (1602–1680). Ocean currents and volcanoes. »Systema Ideale Quo Exprimitur Aquarum per Canales hyrdagogos subterraneos…». *Mundus subterraneus in XII Libros digestus ; Quo Divinum Subterrestris Mundi Opificium, mira Ergasteriorum Naturæ in eo distributio, […] Universæ denique Naturæ Majestas & divitiæ summa rerum varietate exponuntur. Abditorum effectuum causæ acri indagine inquisitæ demonstrantur ; […] Tomus I. Ad Alexandrum VII. Pont. Opt. Max*. Amsterdam, 1678. (The National Library of Finland, Helsinki).

108. **Benjamin Franklin** (1706–1790). »A Chart of the Gulf Stream». 1782 (NOAA Central Library, Washington D.C.).

109. **J. Forest**. Globe Terrestre, c. 1880. (Juha Nurminen Collection).

110. **Early Maritime Ventures in Northern Waters**. Jari Patanen, 2007.

111. **The North Cape**. Peder Balke (1804–1887). 1840. (National Gallery, Oslo).

112. **Jan Huygen van Linschoten** (1562–1611). North Cape, Norway. 1601. (University Library of Tromsö).

113. **Joan Blaeu**. Adult walrus with her pup. »Nova Zembla», backside of the map. *Atlas Maior* Vol. I. 1662. (John Nurminen Foundation).

114. **Guthlac Roll**. East Anglia, c. 1210. (The British Library, London, Harley Roll Y. 6, roundel 4).

115. **The Rutter of the Sea**. Pierre Garcie (c. 1430–1503). 1521. (The British Library, London, X.635/83).

116. **Sounding Weights**. (Courtesy of John Peter Oleson).

117. **Lucas Janszoon Waghenaer** (1533–1606). The Coast of England. »Zee Caerte van Engelants eijndt, Alsoe hem tselfde Landt verthoont beginnede van Sorlinges tot Pleijmondt. doer Lucas Iansz Waghenaer van Enchuijsen». *De Spieghel der Zeevaerdt*. 1584. (The National Library of Finland, Helsinki).

VIKING ROUTES AND THE LONG DISTANCE NAVIGATION

118. **A detail from the Bayeux Tapestry**. 11th century. (Musée de la tapisserie de Bayeux).

119. **Jón Gudmonson** (1574–1658). »Gronlandia Iona Gudmundi Islandi». c. 1640. (Det Kongelige Bibliotek, Copenhagen. DKB gl. kgl. Saml. 2881 4, 11r).

120. **Viking Routes and Colonization**. Jari Patanen, 2007.

121. **Viking 'Sun Compass' (placed in present-day compass card)**. Stewart Gray, 2007 (Sun Compass used by courtesy of Søren Thirslund)

122. **A page from *Flateyjarbók***. 14th century. Photographed by Jóhanna Ólafsdóttir. (Stofnun Árna Magnússonar í íslenskum fræðum, Reykjavik. MS GKS 1005, fol. Bl 079r).

123. **Abraham Ortelius**. A Map of the Northern Regions. »Septentrionales Regiones. Septentrionalivm Regionvm Descrip.» Antwerpen, 1598. (John Nurminen Foundation).

124. **Monsoon Winds**. Jari Patanen, 2007.

125. **Global Wind Patterns**. Jari Patanen, 2007.

126. **Rainbow**. Ivan Aivazovsky (1817–1900). 1873. (The Tretyakov Gallery, Moscow).

127. **Picture Stone from Gotland**. (© Christer Åhlin/The Museum of National Antiquities, Stockholm. 11521).

128. **King's Mirror, the Viking View of the World**. Stewart Gray, 2007.

129. **The Gokstad ship**. Photographer Eirik I. Johnsen. (© Museum of Cultural History, University of Oslo. Cf23957).

130. **Prow of the Oseberg ship**. Photographer Eirik I. Johnsen (© Museum of Cultural History, University of Oslo. Cf22279_A_C5000).

131. **Gerard Mercator** (1512–1594). Polar map from »Nova Et Aucta Orbis Terrae Descriptio Ad Usum Navigantium emendatè accommodata…». Duysburg, 1569. (Maritiem Museum Rotterdam. Atlas51).

132. **A Knarr**. Björn Landström. *Laiva. Katsaus laivan historian alkukantaisesta lautasta atomikäyttöiseen sukellusveneeseen*. Helsinki, 1961. (Courtsesy of Olof Landström).

133. **Viking Ship**. Björn Landström. *Tie Intiaan. Löytöretkistä maitse ja meritse alkaen Puntin retkikunnasta v. 1493 eKr. päätyen Hyväntoivonniemen löytämiseen v. 1488 jKr*. Helsinki, 1964. (Courtsesy of Olof Landström).

134. **Maelstrom**. Relationes Curiosae. Eberhard Werner Happel (1647–1690). 1708. (John Nurminen Foundation).

135. **Faded mural of Zheng He**. Photographer Michael Yamashita.

136. **Sailing routes of Zheng He**. Jari Patanen, 2007.

137. **The Ship of Zheng He**. Stewart Gray, 2007.

138. **Zheng He's name**. Jue Feng. 2007.

ADVANCES IN SCIENCE

139. **Tycho Brahe in his observatory**. Effigies Tychonis Brahe O.F., Aedificii et instrumentorum astronomicorum structoris… Joan Blaeu. *Atlas Maior* Vol. I. Amsterdam, 1662. (The National Library of Finland, Helsinki).

140. **Regiomontanus** (1436–1476). Epitome of Almagest. 1491. (Master and Fellows of Trinity College, Cambridge. MS VI.15.50).

141. **Andreas Cellarius** (fl. 1656–1702). A Ptolemaic Depiction of the World's Structure. »Scenographia Systematis Mundani Ptolemaici». *Harmonia Macrocosmica*. Amsterdam, 1660. (Juha Nurminen Collection).

142. **Andreas Cellarius** – **Pieter Schenk** (1645–1715)

– **Gerard Valk** (c. 1650–1726). A Depiction of the Copernican System. »Scenographica Systematis Copernicani«. 1708. (Juha Nurminen Collection).

143. Compass. Gregorio Dati. *La Sfera.* 15th century. (The National Library of Finland, Helsinki).

144. An Example of a British compass. 19th century. (John Nurminen Foundation).

145. Lodestone made in St. Petersburg. c. 1790. (Juha Nurminen Collection).

146. Deviation graph. Caple ship *Putsaari*, Kantvik, 29 May 2006. (The Finnish Navy).

147. The Compass binnacle. 20th century. (John Nurminen Foundation).

148. Galileo Galilei. Justus Sustermans (1597–1681). c. 1639. (National Maritime Museum, London. BHC2700).

149. The Phases of the Moon. Galileo Galilei (1564–1642). *Sidereus Nuncius.* 1610. (By Concession of the Ministero per i Beni e le Attività Culturali della Repubblica Italiana. Biblioteca Nazionale Centrale di Firenze. Gal. 48. 9r.).

150. Telescope. 19th century. (Juha Nurminen Collection).

151. Tables of declination of the Sun. Abraham ben Zacuto (c. 1450–1510). *Hibur ha-galod.* Middle East, 1491;179-. (Courtesy of The Library of The Jewish Theological Seminary, New York. MS 2602, fol. 82v-83r).

152. Battista Testarossa. Portolan chart. *Brieve Compendio de larte del Navegar.* 1557. (Royal Geographical Society).

153. Battista Testarossa. Compass rose. *Brieve Compendio de larte del Navegar.* 1557. (Royal Geographical Society).

154. The Virgin of the Navigators. Alejo Fernández. c. 1535. (Copyright © Patrimonio Nacional, Madrid. N° inv. 10020581).

155. Fluid compass. Richard Eden (c. 1521–1576). *A Very Necessary and Profitable book Concerning Navigation, compiled in Latin by Joannnes Taisnier.* 1579. (The British Library, London, 51.c.1).

156. Johannes Ruysch (d. 1553). »Universalior Cogniti Orbis Tabula. Ex recentibus confecta observationisbus.«. *Geographia.* Roma, 1507–1508. (The National Library of Finland, Helsinki).

157. Magnetic phenomenon. Jari Patanen, 2007.

158. Edmond Halley (1656–1742) – **Joshua Ottens** (1704–1765). »Nova Et Accuratissima Totius Terrarum Orbis Tabula Nautica...«. Amsterdam, 1730. (Juha Nurminen Collection).

159. Magnetic Dip Compass. William Gilbert. 1600.

(The Master and Fellows of Conville Gaius College, Cambridge).

160. Chip log. 19th century. (John Nurminen Foundation).

161. The chip log in use. Richard Andree. 1875. (Kieler Stadt- und Schiffahrtsmuseum, Kiel).

162. Patent log. 19th century. (John Nurminen Foundation).

IBERIAN VENTURES IN THE ATLANTIC

163. Lopo Homem (d. 1565). Atlantic Sea. *Atlas Miller.* 1519. (Bibliothèque nationale de France, Paris. GE DD 683 RES).

164. Abraham Cresques (d. 1387). The Ferrer Voyage to the Canary Islands. *Mappemundi, the Catalan Atlas of the Year 1375.* Facsimile. Zurich, 1978. (Bibliothèque nationale de France, Paris).

165. An Army on board from *Le Canarien*. Fr. Pierre Boutier – Jehan le Verrier. c. 1420–1430. (The British Library, London, Eg. 2709, fol. 2).

166. Prince Henry with the young Afonso V. Nuno Gonçalves (1450–72). 15th century. (Museu Nacional de Arte Antiga. Divisão de Documentação Fotográfica–Instituto Português de Museus, Lisbon. 01.03.19).

167. Portuguese voyages. Jari Patanen, 2007.

168. Georg Braun – Frans Hogenberg. Lisbon. »Olissippo, quae nunc Lisboa, civitas amplissima Lusitaniae...«. *Civitates Orbis Terrarum* Vol. I. Cologne, 1598. (Juha Nurminen Collection).

169. Portrait of Vasco da Gama. Unknown artist. 15th century. (Museu Nacional de Arte Antiga. Divisão de Documentação Fotográfica–Instituto Português de Museus, Lisbon. 473/11/40).

170. A Mariner's quadrant. c. 1600. (National Maritime Museum, London. F2110).

171. The Back-staff of a Davis Quadrant. (Juha Nurminen Collection).

172. Arbalestrille. Jacques de Vaulx. *Les Premières oeuvres.* 1583. (Bibliothèque nationale de France, Paris, Ms. Français 150, f 16).

173. Peter Apian (1495–1552). Frontispiece, *Introductio geographica.* Ingolstadt, 1533. (The National Library of Finland, Helsinki).

174. *São Gabriel*. Björn Landström. 1961. (Juha Nurminen Collection).

175. Armada of Cabral. *Livro de Lizuarte de Abreu.* c.1550–1564. (The Pierpont Morgan Library, New York. MS M.525, Par 2, fol.16v-17).

176. Lopo Homem. Indian and Arabian Oceans. »Oceano Índico, Arábia, Índia »1519. (Bibliothèque nationale de France, Paris).

177. Tapestry of Arzila. 1471. (Portuguese Institute of Architectural Heritage, Lisbon).

178. Wind-rose. Rose de Vents. Jacques de Vaulx. *Les Premières oeuvres.* 1583. (Bibliothèque nationale de France, Paris. MS Françe 150, fol.23).

179. Sandglass. Gregorio Dati. 15th century. (The National Library of Finland, Helsinki).

180. Traverse board. c. 1850. (National Maritime Museum, London. F4621).

181. Diagram illustrating how many leagues required to sail on each point to raise a degree of latitude. John Davis (1543–1605). *Seamans Secret.* 1657. (Magdalene College, The Pepys Library, Cambridge).

182. Isabella I, Queen of Castile. Spanish school. c.1490–1492. Prado, Madrid. (The Bridgeman Art Library. IND 244310).

183. Portrait of a Man, called Christopher Columbus. Sebastiano del Piombo (c.1485–1547). 1519. Photograph ©1979 The Metropolitan Museum of Art. (The Metropolitan Museum of Art. Gift of J. Pierpoint Morgan, 1900.00.18.2).

184. A Page from the *Imago Mundi*. Pierre d'Ailly (1351–1420). *Imago mundi.* (Catedral de Sevilla. Biblioteca Colombina).

185. A Reconstruction of Toscanelli's World Map. Stewart Gray, 2007.

186. Genovese World Map. 1457. (By concession of the Ministero per i Beni e le Attività Culturali della Repubblica Italiana. Biblioteca Nazionale Centrale di Firenze. Portolano 1).

187. Columbus's ships, 16th September 1492 in Sargasso sea. Björn Landström. *Kolumbus. Valtameren Amiraali Don Cristóbal Colón ja hänen läntisen meritien kautta Intiaan tekemänsä matkat.* Helsinki, 1966. (Courtesy of Olof Landström).

188. Columbus's voyages. Jari Patanen, 2007.

189. Piri Re'is (1466–1554). World map. 1513. (Topkapi Palace Museum, Istanbul).

190. Giovanni Vespucci (fl. 1512–1526). Map of the World. Mapa mundi. 1526. (Courtesy of The Hispanic Society of America, New York. K42).

191. Caravel. Manuel Fernandes. *Livro des Traças de Carpintaria.* 1671. (Biblioteca da Ajuda, Lisboa. 54-XIV-21, fol. 113).

192. Cadamosto's caravels. Björn Landström. *Tie Intiaan. Löytöretkistä maitse ja meritse alkaen Puntin retkikunnasta v. 1493 eKr. päätyen Hyväntoivonniemen löytämiseen v. 1488 jKr.* Helsinki, 1964. (Courtesy of Olof Landström).

193. **Carrack.** Björn Landström. *Laiva. Katsaus laivan historian alkukantaisesta lautasta atomikäyttöiseen sukellusveneeseen.* Helsinki, 1961. (Courtesy of Olof Landström).

194. **A page from the Treaty of Tordesillas.** 1494. (Instituto dos Arquivos Nacionais/Torre do Tombo, Lisbon.Gaveta 17, mç. 2, n.° 24).

195. **Carta del Cantino.** »Carta da navigar per le isole novamente trovate in la parte de l'India«.1502. (Biblioteca Estense Universitaria di Modena).

196. **Nicolas de Nicolay.** The New World. »Novveau Monde«. *L'Art de naviguer.* Lyon, 1554. (Juha Nurminen Collection).

197. **Pedro de Medina** (1493–c. 1567). Frontispiece, *L'art de Navigner de M. Pierre de Medine Espagnol. Contenant toutes les reigles, secrets, & enseignemens necessaires á la bonne navigation.*, Rouen, 1628. (Juha Nurminen Collection).

198. **Portuguese Carracks off a Rocky Coast.** Joachim Patinir (c.1485–1524). 16th century. (National Maritime Museum, London. BHC0705).

199. **An English Nocturnal, unsigned, 18th century.** (Museum of the History of Science, University of Oxford. 150493).

200. **The Battle of Lepanto, 7 October 1571.** H. Letter. Late 16th century. (National Maritime Museum, London. BHC0261).

IMAGE OF THE WORLD IN WORD AND LINE

201. **Gerard de Jode** (1509–1591) – **Cornelis de Jode** (1568–1600). Arctic Regions. »Hemispheriu(m) ab Aequinoctiali Linea, ad Circulu(m) Poli Arctici«. Antwerpen, 1593. (Juha Nurminen Collection).

202. **Portrait of John Dee.** Unknown artist. 16th century. (Ashmolean Museum, Oxford)

203. **John Dee** (1527–c. 1608) – Gulielmus Canterus (1542–1575). Frontispiece, *General and rare memorials pertayning to the Perfect Arte of navigation…*London, 1577. (The British Library, London, 48.h.18).

204. **A detail from Historia ecclesiastica gentis Anglorum, from the original work by Venarabilis Bede of the 8th century.** c. 1375–1406. (The British Library, London, Arundel 74, fol. 2v).

205. **Tide diagram.** Cadran des marées pour les côtes françaises. Guillaume Brouscon. 1548. (Bibliotheque nationale de France, Paris. MS. Français 25374, fol. 25).

206. **Tides.** Jari Patanen, 2007.

207. **Careened ship in Amsterdam harbour by Sunset.** Ludolf Backhuysen (1630–1708). (Fitzwilliam Museum, Cambridge).

208. **Peter Apian** (1495–1552). Cordiform World Map. »Carta Cosmographica, con los nombres, propriedad, y virtud delos vientos«. Antwerp, 1575. (Juha Nurminen Collection).

209. **Volvelles.** Peter Apian. *Astronomicum Caesareum.* 1540. (Courtesy of the John Carter Brown Library at Brown University).

210. **Universal astrolabe.** Anthoine Mestrel. Paris, 1551. (Museum of the History of Science, University of Oxford. 151754).

211. **The Nautical square, Quadratum nauticum.** Gemma Frisius (1508–1555). *De Astrolabo catholico.* Antwerp, 1556. (Museum of the History of Science, University of Oxford. Catalogue no. 3, fig. 39).

212. **Willem Janszoon Blaeu** (1571–1638). Regions under the Arctic Pole. »Regiones Svb Polo Arctico«. Amsterdam, c. 1640. (John Nurminen Foundation).

213. **Loxodromic Curves.** Jari Patanen, 2007.

214. **Mariner's astrolabe.** (National Maritime Museum, London. F3502).

215. **Instruction on how to use the astrolabe.** *Eerste deel de Nieuwe groote zee-spiegel.* Pieter Goos (c. 1616–1675). Amsterdam, 1671. (Juha Nurminen Collection).

216. **Mirror Octant used to measure angles.** 19th century. (Juha Nurminen Collection).

217. **Mirror Sextant.** c. 1890. (John Nurminen Foundation).

218. **Pierre Desceliers** (c. 1500–1558). Map of the World. 1550. (The British Library, London. Add. 24065)

219. **Gerard Mercator.** Map of the World. »Nova et aucta orbis terrae description ad usum navigantium emendate accomodate«. Dyusburgin, 1569. (Bibliotheque nationale de France, Paris. GE A 1064).

220. **Portrait of Gerard Mercator.** Gerard Mercator – Henricus Hondius (1597–1651). *Atlas sive Cosmographiae Meditationes de Fabrica Mundi Et Fabricati Figura. Primum à Gerardo Mercatore inchoatae, deindè a Iudoco Hondio Piae memoriae ad finem perductae, Iam verò multis in locis emendatae, et de novo in lucem editae. Edito Decima. Sumptibus et typis aeneis Henrici Hondij.* Amsterdam, 1630. (Juha Nurminen Collection).

221. **Edward Wright.** Title page, *Certaine Errors in Navigation Detected and Corrected.* London, 1610. (The National Library of Finland, Helsinki).

222. **Jan Huyghen van Linschoten** (1563–1611). Eastern Coast of Africa and Madagascar. *Histoire de la navigation.* Amsterdam, 1638. (Juha Nurminen Collection).

223. **The Drawing of Norrskär Lighthouse.** E. Lohrmann (1803–1870). 1843. Facsimile. (The Maritime Museum of Finland).

224. **The Lightning System Drawing of Pellinki Lighthouse.** Carl Ludvig Engel (1778–1849). 1829. Facsimile. (The Maritime Museum of Finland).

BY ICY SEA TO THE MIGHTY KINGDOM OF CATHAY

225. **Juan de la Cosa** (d. 1509). Chart of the World. »Mapa del Mundo«. 1500. (Museo Naval, Madrid).

226. **Sebastian Cabot** (c. 1484–1557). Map of the World. 1544. (Bibliothéque nationale de France, Paris).

227. **Portrait of Giovanni da Verrazzano.** Francesco Allegrini. *Viaggio fatto nel 1524 all' America settentrionale.* 1767. (The Pierpoint Morgan Library, New York. MA 776).

228. **Northwest Passage Searches.** Jari Patanen 2007

229. **First page of instructions for a** *Voyages of Discovery* **given by Dr John Dee for Arthur Pet and Martin Jackson on their 1580 Voyage.** John Dee. (The British Library, London. Cotton Otho E. VIII).

230. **Portrait of Martin Frobisher.** Cornelis Ketel (1548–1616). 16th century. (The Bodleian Library, University of Oxford).

231. **Tide Table Diagram with Volvelles.** John Davis. *Seamans Secret.*1657. (Magdalene College, The Pepys Library, Cambridge).

232. **Greenwich Hospital from the North Bank of the Thames.** Canaletto or Giovanni Antonio Canal (1697–1768). c. 1752. (The National Maritime Museum, London. BHC1827).

233. **Queen Elizabeth I.** Unknown artist. 1585–1590. (National Portrait Gallery, London. NPG 2471).

234. **Logbook of Charles Wilde on the** *Buritto* **from England to Madras 1649–1651 and back 1651–1652.** (The British Library, London, MS. Sloane 3231, p. 1).

235. **Hugh Smyth.** The Kara Sea. 1580. (The British Library, London. Cotton Otho E.VIII, fol. 78).

236. **William Borough** (1536–99). Chart of the Northern navigation. London, c. 1578. (The British Library, London. Royal 18 D III, fol.123v–124).

237. **Northeast Passage Searches.** Jari Patanen, 2007.

238. **Theodore de Bry** (1528–1598) – **Gerrit de Veer** (fl.1594–1599). Map of the Far North. »Deliniatio cartae trium navigationum per Batavos ad Septentrionalem plagem Norvegia Moscovia et Nova Zembia«. Amsterdam, 1601. (John Nurminen Foundation).

239. **View on Norskøyene on Spitzbergen.** Franz Wilhelm Schiertz (1813–1887). (The National

Museum of Art, Architecture and Design, Oslo. NG.M.00763)

240. Joan Blaeu (c. 1599–1673). The Strait of Nassau. »Fretum Waigats, sive nassavicvm«. *Atlas Maior* Vol. I. 1662. (The National Library of Finland, Helsinki)

241. The Whale Fishery and Killing the Bears. John Harris. London 1780. (John Nurminen Foundation).

242. Theodore de Bry – Hessel Gerritsz (1581–1632). The Henry Hudson Map. »Tabula Nautica, qua repraesenta tur orae maritimae meatus, ac freta….«. Frankfurt am Main, 1613. (John Nurminen Foundation).

243. A Bathing Party, HMS *Clio*. Thomas Somerscales (1842–1927). c. 1902. (N.R. Omell Gallery, London)

244. *La Favorite*: under sail for Bourbon (Reunion Island) at the approach of the second hurricane. From: Cyrille Pierre Theodore Laplace. *Voyage Autour du Monde par les Mers de l'Inde et de Chine, exécuté sur la corvette de l'Etat la Favorite pendant les années 1830, 1831 et 1832.* Paris, 1833–1839. (Linda Hall Library of Science, Engineering & Technology, Kansas City).

245. A View of Cape Stephens in Cook's Straits with Waterspout. William Hodges. 1776. (National Maritime Museum, London. BHC1906).

246. Tropical Cyclones. Jari Patanen, 2007.

247. Preparing the winter quarters at Churchill River on the western shore of Hudson Bay. 1619–1620. (University Library of Tromsö).

248. Lucas Jansz(oon) Waghenaer (1533–1606). The Gulf of Finland. »Bechrijuinge vande costen van Oostsinf:landt, die seer woondrbaerlik sijn om aen:… «. Amsterdam, 1596–1598. (Juha Nurminen Collection).

249. Lucas Janszoon Waghenaer (1533–1606). Frontispiece, *De Spieghel der Zeevaerdt.* 1586. (The National Library of Finland, Helsinki).

250. Highly-detailed instructive broadsheet. Nouvelle carte pour conduire a la connoissance de la marine et a demontrer la plus part des instrumens… Henri Abraham Chatelain (1684–1743). *Atlas historique… vol 7.* Amsterdam 1705–1720 (2 ed. 1732–1739). (Juha Nurminen Collection).

251. Whaling in Spitsbergen. Hvalfangst ved Spitsbergen. Fredrik Martensen.1675. (John Nurminen Foundation).

252. Model of a Flute. (John Nurminen Foundation).

253. Georg Braun (1541–1622) **– Frans Hogenberg** (1535–1590). The Öresund. »Freti Danici Or Sundt accuratiss. delineatio«. *Civitates Orbis Terrarum* Vol. IV. 1588. (John Nurminen Foundation).

THE WORLD ENCOMPASSED

254. Hessel Gerritsz. »Mar del Sur, Mar Pacifico«. 1622. (Bibliothèque nationale de France, Paris. GE SH ARCH 30).

255. Portrait of Ferdinand Magellan. Unknown artist. (Museo Naval, Madrid).

256. Jean de Dinteville and Georges de Selve ('The Ambassadors'). Hans Holbein the Younger (1497–1543). 1533. (The National Gallery, London. NG1314).

257. Gerard Mercator – Henricus Hondius. Strait of Magellan. »Exquisita & magno aliquot mentium periculo lustrata et iam retecta Freti Magellanici Facies«. *Atlas sive Cosmographiae Meditationes de Fabrica Mundi Et Fabricati Figura. Primum à Gerardo Mercatore inchoatae, deindè a Iudoco Hondio Piae memoriae ad finem perductae, Iam verò multis in locis emendatae, et de novo in lucem editae. Edito Decima. Sumptibus et typis aeneis Henrici Hondij.* Amsterdam, 1630. (Juha Nurminen Collection).

258. Abraham Ortelius. The Pacific. »Maris Pacifici (quod vulgò Mar del Zur) cum regionibus circumiacentibus, infulisque in eodem pafsim fparsis, nocifsima descriptio«. *Theatre De L'Univers, Contenant Les Cartes De Tout Le Monde. Avec Une Brieve Declaration D'Icelles. Par Abraham Ortelius. Le tout reveu, amendé, & augmenté de plusieurs Cartes & declarations par le mesme autheur. M.D.LXXXVII.* 1587. *Christoffer Plati.,* Antwerp, 1587. (Juha Nurminen Collection).

259. Battista Agnese (1514–1564). World Map with Route of Magellan. c. 1544. (Library of Congress, Washington D.C.).

260. Early Explorations in the Pacific Ocean. Jari Patanen, 2007.

261. Portrait of Sir Francis Drake. Unknown artist. c.1580. (National Portrait Gallery, London. NPG 4032).

262. Francis Drake (c.1540–1596). Coast of Panama. *Journal de bord de la dernière campagne de Francis Drake.* 1595–1596. (Bibliothèque nationale de France, Paris, MS. Anglais 51, fol.13).

263. A model of the *Golden Hind*. (John Nurminen Foundation).

264. Gerard Mercator – Henricus Hondius. East India Archipelago. »Insulae Indiae Orientalis praecipuae, in quibus Moluccae celeberrimae sunt «, *Atlas sive Cosmographiae Meditationes de Fabrica Mundi Et Fabricati Figura. Primum à Gerardo Mercatore inchoatae, deindè a Iudoco Hondio Piae memoriae ad finem perductae, Iam verò multis in locis emendatae, et de novo in lucem editae. Edito Decima. Sumptibus et typis aeneis Henrici Hondij..* Amsterdam, 1630. (Juha Nurminen Collection).

265. English Ships and the Spanish Armada, August 1588. Unknown artist. 16th century. (National Maritime Museum, London. BHC0262).

266. Jan Huyghen van Linschoten (1563–1611). The Island of Goa. »A Ilhae cidade de Goa«. *Histoire de la navigation.* Amsterdam, 1638. (Juha Nurminen Collection).

267. Attack on Portuguese galleons in the Bay of Goa, 30 September 1639. Hendrick van Anthonissen (1605–1660). 1658. (Rijksmuseum, Amsterdam. SK-A-2126).

268. Joan Blaeu. Moluccas. »Insulae Moluccae. celeberrima«. *Atlas Maior* Vol. X.1662. (The National Library of Finland, Helsinki).

269. Theodore de Bry (1528–1598). Chart depicting the first Dutch voyage to the East Indies. »Descriptio Hydrographica accommodata ad battavorum navagatione in Javam insula… «. Frankfurt, 1599–1628. (Bernard J. Shapero Rare Books, London).

270. Georg Braun (1541–1622) **– Frans Hogenberg** (1535–1590). Amsterdam. »Amstelredamvm«. *Civitates Orbis Terrarum* Vol. I. 1572. (Juha Nurminen Collection).

271. The Return of the Dutch East India Fleet, 1 May 1597; the *Hollandia*, *Mauritius* and *Duyfken* in Harbour at Amsterdam. Andries van Eertvelt (1590–1652). 17th century. (National Maritime Museum, London. BHC0748).

272. Two Dutch merchant ships under sail near the shore in a moderate breeze. Willem van de Velde the Elder (1611–1693).1649. (National Maritime Museum, London. BHC0860).

273. Joan Blaeu. »Sumatra«. 1669. (Maritiem Museum Rotterdam).

274. Spice pots, 16th and 17th centuries. (Juha Nurminen Collection).

275. Willem Corneliszoon Schouten (c. 1580–1625). Description of a new passage south of the Strait of Magellan. »Caarte vande nieuwe passagie bezuijden de Strate Magellani…«. *Journal van de reyse ghedaen door Willem Cornelisz Schouten 1615–1617.* Amsterdam, 1619. (Juha Nurminen Collection).

276. Sandglass. 18th century (Juha Nurminen Collection).

277. British Chronometer. 19th century. (John Nurminen Foundation).

278. Pacific Explorations. Jari Patanen, 2007.

279. Portrait of Abel Tasman, his wife and daughter. Jacob Gerritsz Cuyp (1594–1650). 1637. (National Library of Australia, Canberra. PIC T267 NK3).

280. Map of Anthony van Diemen's Land. *Journal or Description drawn up by Abel Jansz. Tasman of the Discovery of the Unknown South-Land in 1642.* Facsimile. Los Angeles, 1965. (Juha Nurminen Collection).

281. **Portrait of William Dampier.** Thomas Murray (1663–1735). c. 1697–1698. (National Portrait Gallery, London. NPG 538).

282. **William Dampier** (1651–1715). »A View of the General & Coasting Trade -Winds in the great South Ocean». *A Collection of Voyages.* Vol. I–IV. London, 1729. (Juha Nurminen Collection).

283. **The Capture of the *Nuestra Senora de Cavadonga* by HMS *Centurion*, 20 June 1743.** Samuel Scott (1702–1770). c. 1743. (National Maritime Museum, London. BHC 0360).

ENDEAVOURS EXTENDED

284. **Ship caught in a storm on the rocky coast in Normandy.** Julius Hintz (1805–1862). (Peter Tamm Collection, Hamburg).

285. **Portrait of Sir Cloudisley Shovell.** Michael Dahl (1659–1743). c. 1702–05. (National Maritime Museum, London. BHC 3025).

286. **Pieter Goos** (c. 1616–1675). Northeast Coast of Asia from Nova Zembla to Japan. »Noordoost Cust van Asia van Iapan tot Nova Zemla». 1666. (Bernard J. Shapero Rare Books, London).

287. **H3, Marine timekeeper.** John Harrison (1693–1776). 1757. (National Maritime Museum, London. D6789_1).

288. **H4, Marine timekeeper.** John Harrison. 1759. (National Maritime Museum, London. D9661).

289. **Louis Renard.** »Nova totiusterrarum orbis tabula ex officina...» *Atlas de la navigation, et du commerce qui se fait dans toutes les parties du monde.* Amsterdam, 1715. (Juha Nurminen Collection).

290. **A Portrait of Catherine II as Legislator in the Temple of the Goddess of Justice.** Dmitry Levitzky (1735–1822) Early 1780s. (The Tretyakov Gallery, Moscow).

291. **Ivan Elagin.** Kamchatka peninsula. »Karta. Do Tabol'ska s atlasa rosiskago, a ot Tabol'ska s raznych opisaniev i vajažev kamtsaÐkoj ÐkspediÐii kart ... maja 1746». (Russian State Archives of Military History, Moscow)

292. **John Narbrough** (1640–1688). »Straits of Magellan. The Land of Patagona, etc. The draught of Magellan Straits, drawn by Captain John Narbrough, anno 1670, on board His Majesti's Shipp Sweepstaks, as I pased and repased the Straits...». 1670. (The British Library, London, Maps.K.Top.124.84).

293. **Shipwreck.** Hjalmar Munsterhjelm (1840–1905). (Juha Nurminen Collection).

294. **A Portrait of Captain James Cook.** John Webber (1751–1793). c. 1780. (Museum of New Zealand Te Papa Tongarewa, Wellington. 1960-0013-1)

295. **James Cook.** »South Channel of Orleans, Quebec». *Charts and Maps illustrating the Voyages and Surveys of Captain James Cook and other discoverers.* c. 1759–1760. (The British Library, London, Add. 31360, No. 14).

296. **Voyages of Captain James Cook.** Jari Patanen, 2007.

297. **A Grey-headed kingfisher,** *halcyon leucocephala.* George Foster (1754–1794). 1772–1775. (The Natural History Museum, London. 5060).

298. **James Cook.** »Dusky Bay New Zealand». *Sixty-seven Charts and maps illustrating the voyages and surveys of Capt. James Cook, R.N., and other discoverers.* c. 1760–1780. (The British Library, London, Add. 31360, fol. 56).

299. **James Cook – Henry Roberts.** »Chart of the N.W. Coast of America and the N.E. Coast of Asia, Explored in the Year's 1778 and 1779. Prepared by ... Henry Roberts,...». *A Voyage to the Pasific Ocean... for makind discoveries in the northern hemisphere... Performed under the direction of Captains Cook, Clerke, and Gore ... in the years 1776, 1777, 1778, 1779 and 1780.* London William Faden, 2 ed. 1794. (Juha Nurminen Collection).

300. **The Ice Islands.** William Hodges. *A Voyage towards the South Pole, and round the World. Performed in His Majesty's Ships the Resolution and Adventure, in the Years 1772,1773,1774, and 1775. Written by James Cook, Commander of the Resolution.* Vol I. London, 1777. (Juha Nurminen Collection).

301. **Model of HMS** *Resolution* (John Nurminen Foundation).

302. **A Yakut shaman with his drum.** Een jakutische schaman. *Reis in het Noordoostelijke Siberie, en op de ljszee en den Noordostelijken Oceaan, door Gawrila Sarytschew, Eerste deel.* Amsterdam, 1808. (Juha Nurminen Collection).

303. **A 'reindeer Tungushian' in summer attire.** Enne rendiertunguzin in hary zomerkleeding. *Reis in het Noordoostelijke Siberie, en op de ljszee en den Noordoostelijken Oceaan, door Gawrila Sarytschew, Eerste deel.* Amsterdam, 1808. (Juha Nurminen Collection).

304. **A View of the port on the Jassatshnaja River on the coast in the Kolyma river area.** *Reis in het Noordoostelijke Siberie, en op de ljszee en den Noordoostelijken Oceaan, door Gawrila Sarytschew, Eerste deel.* Amsterdam, 1808. (Juha Nurminen Collection).

305. **HMS** *Beagle* **in the Murray Narrows, Beagle Channel.** Conrad Martens (1801–1878). 19th century. Down House, Kent. (The Bridgeman Art Library. BAL 4367).

306. **Diagrams of HMS** *Beagle.* *A Naturalists Voyage Round the World by Charles Darwin.* 1912. (The Natural History Museum, London. 11718).

307. **Louis Renard.** The Map of the North Sea. »Mare Germanicum ac Tractus Maritimus retro Hiberiniam et Scotiam.» *Atlas de la navigation, et du commerce qui se fait dans toutes les parties du monde.* Amsterdam, 1715. (Juha Nurminen Collection).

308. **Jacobus Robijn** (1649–c. 1710). The map of the West Indies. »West Indische Paskaert...». c. 1674. (Map House, London).

309. **Drawing from Willem Blaeu's** *The Light of Navigation.* David Winckeboons (c. 1617–1670). Amsterdam, 1612. (Juha Nurminen Collection).

310. **A Portrait of Sir Robert Dudley.** Unknown artist. *The Voyage of Robert Dudley...to the West Indies 1594–1595...Ed. George F. Warner.* London, 1894. (Juha Nurminen Collection).

311. **Robert Dudley** (1574–1649). Map of Trinidad and Guyana. »Al Sermo Ferdinando .II. Grandvca di Toscanasvo Signore Don Roberto Dudleo Duca di Northumbria XIII. D'America.». *Dell'Arcano del Mare.* 1647. (The National Library of Finland, Helsinki).

312. **Gerard van Keulen** (1678–1727). A World Map. »Nieuwe Wassende Graaden paskaart vertoonende alle de bekende Zeekusten en Landen op den geheelen aard boodem of werelt». c. 1710–1720. (Juha Nurminen Collection).

313. **Aleksey Ivanovich Nagayev** (1704–1781). The Gulf of Finland. »Chast' sinusa Finskago». *Atlas usego Baltiiskago moray.* St. Petersburg, 1757. (John Nurminen Foundation).

314. **Destruction of the Danish Fleet: before Copenhagen, 2 April 1801.** Thomas Whitcombe. *The Naval Achievements of Great Britain From the Year 1793 to 1817.* London, 1837–1838. (Juha Nurminen Collection).

315. **A Portrait of Rear-Admiral Sir Horatio Nelson.** Lemuel Francis Abbott (1760–1803). 1800. (National Maritime Museum, London. BHC2889).

FRONTIERS UNLIMITED

316. **The Corvette** *La Recherche*, **near Beeren Island, 7 August 1838.** Auguste Mayer. *Voyages en Scandinavie en Laponie au Spizberg et aux Feröe Pendant les années 1838, 1839 et 1849 Sur la Corvette la Recherche...M. Paul Gaimard.* 1852. (Juha Nurminen Collection).

317. **A Portrait of Sir Francis Beaufort.** Stephen Pearce. 1850. (National Portrait Gallery, London. NPG 918).

318. **Ship in a Gale.** Benjamin Olsen (1873–1935). 1923. (John Nurminen Foundation).

319. **A Portrait of Robert FitzRoy.** Unknown artist. (Alexander Turnbull Library, Wellington, N.Z. B-015-008).

320. **Barometer designed by Robert FitzRoy.** 1870. (John Nurminen Foundation).

321. **Robert FitzRoy** (1805–1865) – E. N. Kendal »The South-Eastern Part of Tierra del Fuego with Staten Island, Cape Horn and Diego Ramirez Islands». 1892. (John Nurminen Foundation).

322. **Matthew Fontaine Maury** (1806–1873). »Wind and Current Chart of the North Atlantic». 1852. (National Maritime Museum, London. STK298:3/6,1).

323. *Lophius naresii*, **an unknown angler.** © Dr. David C. Bossard. Reproduced from *The Report on the Shore Fishes procured during the voyage of H.M.S. Challenger in the Years 1873–1876, by Albert Günther.* 1879. (Courtesy of Dartmouth College, Hanover, NH. Used by Permission).

324. **Examining contents of Trawl on HMS** *Challenger. Report on the Scientific Results of the Voyage of H.M.S Challenger during the years 1873–76.* Narrative, Vol. I. First Part, Chapter IV. Edinburgh, 1880–95. (The National Library of Finland, Helsinki).

325. **First page from the Journal of HMS** *Challenger* **1872 – a personal diary.** Aldrich Pelham (1844–1930). 1872. (Royal Geographical Society).

326. **The Lane-snapper and the Tobaccopipe-fish.** Mark Catesby (1679–1749). *Natural History of Carolina, Florida and the Bahama Islands.* 1743. (Juha Nurminen Collection).

327. **Robert FitzRoy – E.N. Kendal.** »Galapagos Islands. The Hydrographic Office of the Admiralty Pacific Ocean». 1836. (John Nurminen Foundation).

328. *Xanthornus flaviceps.* John Gould (1804–1881). *The Zoology of the voyage of HMS Beagle, under the command of captain FitzRoy, R.N., during the years 1832 to 1836.* Part III. Birds. (Juha Nurminen Collection).

329. *Tanagra Darwini.* John Gould. *The Zoology of the voyage of HMS Beagle, under the command of captain FitzRoy, R.N., during the years 1832 to 1836.* Part III. Birds. (Juha Nurminen Collection).

330. *Pyrocephalus nanus.* John Gould. *The Zoology of the voyage of HMS Beagle, under the command of captain FitzRoy, R.N., during the years 1832 to 1836.* Part III. Birds. (Juha Nurminen Collection).

331. *Delphinus Fitz-Royi.* Richard Owen (1804–1892). *The Zoology of the voyage of HMS Beagle, under the command of captain FitzRoy, R.N., during the years 1832 to 1836.* Part I. Fossil *Mammalia.* (Juha Nurminen Collection).

332. *Reithrodon Chinshilloides.* Richard Owen. *The Zoology of the voyage of HMS Beagle, under the command of captain FitzRoy, R.N., during the years 1832 to 1836.* Part I. Fossil Mammalia. (Juha Nurminen Collection).

333. **Onward the** *Lightning.* Montague Dawson (1895–1973). (Peter Tamm Collection).

334. **Scientific Explorations.** Jari Patanen, 2007.

335. **HMS** *Thrush.* W. Fred. Mitchell. 1890. (Juha Nurminen Collection).

336. **A Portrait of Edmond Halley.** Sir Godfrey Kneller (1646–1723). c. 1721. (National Maritime Museum, London. BHC2734).

337. **Edmond Halley** (1656–1742) – **Joshua Ottens** (1704–1765). The New World map. »Nova Et Accuratissima Totius Terrarum Orbis Tabula Nautica... ». Amsterdam, 1730. (Juha Nurminen Collection).

338. **The Compass binnacle.** 20th century. (John Nurminen Foundation).

339. **Portrait of William Scoresby junior.** (The National Library of Finland, Helsinki)

340. **Louis XVI giving instructions for La Pérouse for his Voyage of Exploration Around the World, in the presence of marquess de Castries, Marine Minister, 29 June 1785.** Nicolas André Monsiau (1754–1837). Versailles, château de Versailles et de Trianon. © Photo RMN/ © Gérad Blot. (Réunion des Musées Nationaux, Paris).

341. **Sea Anemones and other Jelly Fishes.** *Atlas to Krusenstern's Voyage Round the World 1803–1806.* Moscow, 1813. Facsimile. (Juha Nurminen Collection).

342. *Fram* **in Winter.** Wally Herbert. 1989. (John Nurminen Foundation).

343. **Astrolabe caught in the ice.** L'Astrolabe arretee par un glacon avant sa sortie de la banquise, 9 Fevrier 1838. Auguste Mayer (1805-1890). *Voyage au pole Sud et dans l'Oceanie sur les corvettes l'Astrolabe et Zelee, execute par ordre du roi pendant les annees 1837, 1838, 1839, 1840, sous le commandement de M. J. Dumont d'Urville … Atlas hydrographique par M.C.A. Vincendon-Dumoulin...* Plate 24. Paris, 1842. (Treasures of the NOAA Library Collection, Washington D.C.).

344. **Launching the** *James Caird.* Photographed by Frank Hurley. 1916. (Royal Geographical Society).

345. **Gjøa.** Lauritz Haaland (1855–1938). (Norsk Sjöfartsmuseum, Oslo).

346. *Vega* **under Aurora Borealis.** Adolf Bock (1890–1968). 1927. (Statens sjöhistoriska museum, Stockholm).

347. **Photograph of Adolf Erik Nordenskiöld.** Photographed by Louis Palander. (Nordiska Museets Arkiv, Stockholm).

348. **Ship and pocket chronometers used on A. E. Nordenskiöld's expedition.** Charles Frodsham. Cronometer no. 3194 Box Watch. London, 1857. Chronometer no. 8873 Deck Watch, London, 1859. (Kungliga Vetenskapsakademien, Stockholm).

349. **A Chart of the Hydrological Departement of the Russian Maritime Ministry, depicting the Northern Arctic Sea.** »Karta Severnago Ledovitago Okeana, ot Yenyseiskago Zaliva do ustya reki Yany. Sostavlena s russkikh opisei 1734–42 i 1821–23 g.g». St Petersburg, 1874. Facsimile. (John Nurminen Foundation).

350. **Model of** *Vega.* (John Nurminen Foundation).

351. **Drawing of Louis Palander.** *Nordost-Passagen Vid publicistklubbens fest för Nordenskiöld.* Stockholm, 1880. (Juha Nurminen Collection).

352. *Spray.* Lars-Erik Malmlund. 1984. (Juha Nurminen Collection).

353. **Stormy Ocean.** Adolf Bock (1890–1968). 1923. (John Nurminen Foundation).

LITERATURE

Abranson, Erik C. *Sailing Ships of the World,*. Wiltshire, 1992

Abulafia, David (ed). *The Mediterranean in History*. London, 2003

Aczel, Amir D. *The Riddle of the Compass the invention that changed the world*. San Diego, 2001

Ahmad, Nafio. *Muslim Contribution to Geography*. Lahore, 1947

Albuquerque, Luis & Gil Eannes. *Centro de Estudos de Hisória e Cartografia Antiga Série Separatas – 183*. Lisboa, 1985

Alexander, Caroline. *Endurance, Shackletonin legendaarinen Antarktiksen retki*. Helsinki, 1998

Anderson, David. *The Spanish Armada*. London, 1998

Andrews, Kenneth R (ed). *English Privateering Voyages to the West Indies 1588-1595*. The Hakluyt Society, London, 1959

Aristotle,.*Meteorologica*. English translation by H.D.P. Lee Harvard University Press, Cambridge, 1962

Armesto, Felipe-Fernández. *Before Columbus: Exploration and Colonization from the Mediterranean to the Atlantic 1229-1492*. Philadelphia, 1987

Aughton, Peter. *Endeavour, The story of Captain Cook's First Great Epic Voyage*. 2002

Axelson, E (ed). *Diaz and His Successors*. Capetown, 1988

Bagrow, Leo. *History of Cartography*. London, 1985

Ball, Robert W. D. *Nautical Antiques With Value Guide*. Atglen, 1994

Barraclough, Geoffrey (ed). *The Times Atlas of World History*. London, 1989

Barrington, Daines. *The Possibility of Approaching the North Pole Asserted*. 1818

Barrow, John. *A Chronological History of Voyages into the Arctic Regions Undertaken Chiefly for the Purpose of Discovering a North-East, North-West, or polar Passage Between the Atlantic and Pacific: From the Earliest Periods of Scandinavian Navigation, to the Departure of the Recent Expeditions, Under the Orders of Captain Ross and Buchan*. London, 1818

Barrow, John (ed). *The Voyages of Captain Cook*. Hertfordshire, 1999

Bawlf, Samuel. *Sir Francis Drake's Secret Voyage to the Northwest Coast of America, ad 1579*. Salt Spring Island, 2001

Beaglehole, J. C. *The Exploration of the Pacific*. London, 1947

Beaglehole, J.C. *Cook, the Navigator, Proceedings of Royal Society London Lecture delivered, June 3, 1969*. Great Britain, 1969

Beazley, Charles Raymond. *The Dawn of Modern Geography. A History of Exploration and Geographical Science. – 3 Vol*. London, J. Murray, 1897-1906

Beazley, Charles Raymond. *John and Sebastian Cabot: the Discovery of North America*. New York, Burt Franklin (first published 1898)

Bedini, Silvio A. (ed). *The Christopher Columbus Encyclopedia – Vol. I & II*. New York, 1992

Beechey, F.W. *A Voyage of Discovery towards the North Pole Performed in His Majesty's Ships Dorothea and Trent*. London, 1843

Bennet, James A. *The Divided Circle: A History of Instruments for Astronomy, Navigation and Surveying*. Oxford, 1987

Bérez-Mallaína, Pablo E. *Spain's Men of the Sea. Daily Life of the Indies Fleets in the Sixteenth Century*. Baltimore, 2005

Bergreen, Laurence. *Over the Edge of the World: Magellan's Terrifying Circumnavigation of the Globe*. New York, 2004

Berjeau, J. Ph Calcoen. *A Narrative of the Second Voyage of Vasco da Gama to Calicut in 1502*. Antwerp, 1504,. Facsimile reproduction London, 1874

Berthon, Simon & Robinson Andrew. *The Shape of the World The Mapping and discovery of the Earth*, 1991

Biddle, Richard, *A Memoir of Sebastian Cabot; with a Review of the History of Maritime Discovery*. London, 1832

Biggar, Henry Percival. *The precursors of Jacques Cartier, a Collection of Documents…* Ottawa, 1911

Billings, Joseph. *An Account of a Geographical and Astronomical Expedition to Northern parts of Russia*. London, 1802

Binding, Paul. *Imagined Corners Exploring the World's First Atlas*. London, 2003

Blake, John. *The Sea Chart*. London, 2004

Blandford, Percy. *An Illustrated History of Small Boats A History of Oared, Poled and Padled Graft*. Buckinghamshire, 1974

Bligh, William. *A voyage to the South Sea, undertaken by command of His Majesty…1969* (facsimile)

Blundevile, M. *His Exercises, containing six Treatises…* London, 1594

Bohlander, Richard E (ed). *World Explorers and Discoverers*. New York, 1992

Bourne, William. *A Regiment for the Sea: Conteyning most profitable Rules, Mathematical experiences, and perfect knowledge of Nauigation, For all Coastes and Countreys: most needful and necessarie for all Seafaring men and trauellers, as Pilotes, Mariners, Marchants, etc. Exactly devised and made by William Bourne – 1574*, Cambridge, 1963

Boxer, Charles. R. *The Dutch Seaborne Empire 1600-1800*. London, 1965

Boxer, Charles R. *The Portuguese Seaborne Emprie 1415-1825*. New York, 1969

Boxer, Charles R. (ed). *The Tragic History of the Sea" Further Selection from the Tragic History of the Sea 1559-1565*. The Hakluyt Society, London, 1968

Brochado, Costa et al. *Dom Henrique the Navigator*. Lisbon, 1960

Brown, Lloyd A. *Map Making. The Art That Became a Science*. Boston, 1960

Bräunlein, Peter J. *Behaim Martin Legende und Wirklichkeit eines berühmten Nürnbergers*. Bamberg, 1992

Burnell, Arthur Coke (ed). *The Voyage of John Huyghen van Linschoten to the East Indies*. vol. I, The Hakluyt Society. London, 1885

Burney, James. *A Chronological History of Discoveries in the South Sea or Pacific Ocean Part I-V*. London, 1803

Bunbury, Edward Herbert. *A History of Ancient Geography among the Greeks and Romans. – 2 Vol*. New York, 1959

Cameron, Ian. *Magellan and the First Circumnavigation of the World*. London, 1974

Cameron, Ian. *Lodestone and Evening Star: The Epic Voyages of Discovery, 1493BC – A.D. 1896*. New York, 1966

Camoens, Luis de. *The Lusiad, or Portugals Historicall Poem: Written in the Portingall Language and Now newly put into English by Richard Fanshaw Esq*. London, 1655

Campbell, Tony. *Early Maps*. New York, 1981

Campbell, Tony. *The Earliest Printed Maps 1472-1500*. Berceley, 1987

Casson, Lionel. *The Ancient Mariners Seafarers and Sea Fighters of the Mediterranean in Ancient Times*. Princeton, 1991

Catalogue of an Exhibition at the British Museum Sept-Oct. *Prince Henry the Navigator and Portuguese Maritime Enterprise*. Great Britain at The Stellar Press, 1960

Cecil, Jane (ed). *The Voyages of Christopher Columbus*. London, 1930

Chabás, José & Bernand R. Goldstein. *Astronomy in the Iberian Peninsula: Abraham Zacuto and the Transition from Manuscript to Print. Transactions of the American Philosophical Society* Vol. 90, pt. 2. Philadelphia, 2000

Chaucer, Geoffrey. *Chaucer and Messahalla on the Astrolabe Early Science in Oxford*. v. 5. Oxford, 1929

Chierlin, Lars Anders. *Sjömäns daglige assistent eller anvisning uti de nödvändigaste stycken af Navigationsvetenskapen med dertil nödige figurer och tabeller*. Stockholm, 1777

Clancy, Robert & Alan Richardson. *So Came They South*. Silverwater, 1988

Cohn, Ellen R. *Benjamin Franklin, Georges-Louis Le Rouge and the Franklin/Folger Chart of the Gulf Stream*. Imago Mundi Vol. 52, 2000

Cook, James. *A Voyage towards the South Pole, and Round the World*. London, 1777

Cook, James. *A Voyage to the Pacific Ocean. Undertaken, by the Command of His Majesty, for Making Discoveries in the Northern Hemifphere. Performed Under the Direction of Captains Cook, Clerke, and Gore, In His Majesty's Ships the Resolution and Discovery; in the Years 1776, 1777, 1778, and 1780. vol.I-II-III*. London, 1785

Cordingly, David. *Captain James Cook Navigator, The Achievents of Captain James Cook as a Seaman, Navigator and Surveyor*. London, 1990

Cornell Tim & John Matthews. *Atlas of the Roman World*. Oxford, 1987

Coronelli, Vincenzo. *Libro del Globi Venice 1693* (1701) Facsimile. Amsterdam, 1969

Corréa, Gaspar. *The Three Voyages of Vasco da Gama, and his Viceroyalty. From the Lendas de India of Gaspar Corréa. Accompanied by Original documents. Translated from the Portuguese, with Notes and introduction, by E.J. Stanley Reprint of the 1869 edition*. The Hakluyt Society, New York, 1963

Cortesão, Armando. *History of Portuguese Cartography*, Vol. II. Coimbra, 1971

Cortesão, Armando. *The Nautical Chart of 1424 And the Early Discovery and Cartographical Representation of America*. 1954

Cortesão, Armando. *The Mystery of Vasco da Gama Junta de Investigações do Ultramar*. Lisbon Coimbra, 1973

Cortesão, Armando (ed). *The Suma Oriental of Tomé Pires and The Book of Francisco Rodrigues* Vol I-vol II, The Hakluyt Society. London, 1944

Cotter, Charles H. *A History of the Navigator's Sextant*. Glasgow, 1983

Coxe, William. *Account of the Russian Discoveries Between Asia and America. To wich Are Added, the Conquest of Siberia, and the History of the Transactions and Commerce Between Russia and China*. London, 1804

Crane, Nicholas. *Mercator The Man Who Mapped the Planet*. New York, 2002

Crone, G.R. (Translator and Editor). *The Voyages of Cadamosto and other Documents on Western Africa in the Second Half of the Fifteenth Century*. The Hakluyt Society, London, 1937

Cumming, William P & Louis De Vorsey Jr. *The Southeast in Early Maps*. London, 1998

Cuthbertson, Brian. *John Cabot and the Voyage of the Matthew*. Halifax, 1997

Dampier, William. *Collection of Voyages*. Vol. II. London, 1724

Darwin, Charles. *Über den Bau und die Verbreitung der Corallen- Riffe. Charles Darwin*. Stuttgart, 1876

Darwin, Charles. *Journal of Researches into the Natural History and Geology of the Countries Visited During the Voyage of H.M.S. Beagle Round the World, Under the Command of Capt. Fitz Roy*. London, 1890

Daumas, Maurice. *Scientific Instruments of the Seventeenth and Eighteenth Centuries and their Makers*. London, 1989

David, Andrew (ed). *The Charts and Coastal Views of Captain Cook's Voyages The Voyage of the Endeavour 1768-1771*. Vol I. The Hakluyt Society, London, 1988

Davis, John. *The Seamans Secrets. Facsimile Reproduction of 1633 edition*. Published by John Carter Brown Library, New York, 1992

Davis, John. *The Worldes Hydrographical Discription. Facsimile reproduction of 1595 edition in British Museum*. London, 1925

De Jode G. *Speculum Orbis Terrarum*. Antwerpen 1578, Amsterdam, 1965

De Long, George W. *The Voyage of the Jeannette. The Ship and Ice Journals of George W. De Long, Commander of the Polar Expedition of 1879-1881*. VOL. II. Boston, 1884

de Medina, Pedro. *A Navigator's Universe. The Libro de COSMOGRAPHÍA of 1538*. Chicago, 1972

Deacon, Margaret. *Scientists and the Sea, 1650-1900: a Study of Marine Science*. London, 1971

Dee, John. *The Perfect Arte of Navigation. Full title: General and Rare Memorials pertayning to the Perfect Arte of Navigation: Annexed to the Paradoxal Compas, in Playne: Now first published: 24 yeres, after the first invention thereof. Originally published in 1577*. Published in facsimile by Da Capo Press, New York, Amsterdam, 1968

Dekker, Elly & Pieter van der Krokt. *Globes from the Western World*. London, 1993

Digges, Leonard. *A Prognostication Everlasting: corrected and augmented By Thomas Digges / Leonard Digges. First published in 1555 under title: A Prognostication of Right Good Effect A reproduction of the copy in the British Library*. Amsterdam, 1975

Dunn, Samuel. *The Theory and practice of the longitude at sea*. London, 1778

Edgell, John. *Sea Surveys Britain's contribution to hydrography*. London, 1965

Ehrensvärd, Ulla. *History of Nordic Maps – from Myths to Reality*. Helsinki, 2006

Ehrensvärd Ulla, Pellervo Kokkonen, Nurminen Juha. *Mare Balticum–The Baltic 2000 Years*. Helsinki, 1995

Ericsson, Christoffer H., Leena Miekkavaara, Juha Nurminen, Nils-Erik Raurala. *Routes of the Sea*. Mänttä, 1998

Ericsson, Christoffer H., Esko Häkli, Juha Nurminen, Wilhelm Odelberg, Edwin Okhuizen, Leena Pärssinen. *The Northeast Passage from Vikings to Nordenskiöld*. Helsinki, 1992

Enterline, James, Robert Erikson. *Eskimos & Columbus Medieval European Knowledge of America*. Baltimore, 2002

Fleming, Fergus. *Barrow's Boys. A Stirring story of daring, fortitude and outright lunacy*. London, 1998

Flinders, M. *A Voyage to Terra Australis; Undertaken for the Purpose of Completing the Discovery of That Vast Country, and Prosecuted on the Years 1801, 1802, and 1803, in His Majesty's Ship the Investigator, and Subsequently in the Armed Vessel Porpoise and Cumberland Schooner…vol I-II*. 1814

Forster, John Reinhold. *History of the Voyages and Discoveries made in the North*. London, 1786

Franklin, John. *Narrative of a Journey to the Shores of the Polar Sea, in the Years 1819, 20, 21, and 22*. London, 1823

Frost, O.W., Ed. *Bering and Chirikov: The American Voyages and their Impact, Alaska Historical Society*. Anchorage, 1992

Fuson, Robert H. *The Log of Christopher Columbus*. Maine, 1987

Galvin, John (ed). *The First Spanish Entry into San Francisco Bay 1775*. San Francisco, 1971

Gingerich, Owen. *The Book Nobody Read: Chasing the Revolutions of Nicolaus Copernicus, Walker and Company*. New York, N.Y.: 2004

Ginsberg William B. (ed). *Norvegia Regnum The Collection of Maps and Sea Charts of Norway 1602-1827*. 2001

Gibb, H.A.R (ed). *The Travels of IBN Battūta A.D. 1325-1354* Vol I. The Hakluyt Society, London, 1958

Gibbons, Henry K. *The Myth and Mystery of John Cabot*. Martin Cat Pub., 1997

Golder, F.A. *Bering's Voyages vol.1 An Account of the Efforts of the Russians to Determine the Relation of Asia and America*. New York, 1922

Golder, F.A. *Bering's Voyages vol.2 An Account of the Efforts of the Russians to Determine the Relation of Asia and America*. New York, 1925

Golowin, M. *Merisodan historia*. Porvoo, 1925

Gosch, C.C.A. (ed). *Danish Arctic Expeditions, 1605 to 1620. Book I. - The Danish Expeditions to Greenland in 1605, 1606, and 1607; to which is Added Captain James Hall's Voyage to Greenland in 1612*. The Hakluyt Society, London, 1847

Gosch, C.C.A. (ed). *Danish Arctic Expeditions, 1605 to 1620. Book II. - The Expedition of Captain Jens Munk to Hudson's bay in Search of a North-West Passage in 1619-20*. The Hakluyt Society, London, 1847

Gould, Rupert T. *The Marine Chronometer Its History and development*. Woodbridge, 1989

Graham-Gampbell, James (ed). *Cultural Atlas of the Viking World*. Oxfordshire, 1994

Gross, M. Grant. *Oceanography A View of the Earth*. New Jersey, 1987

Gurney, Alan. *Compass A Story of Exploration and Innovation*. New York, 2004

Hakluyt, Richard. *Voyages, Navigations, Traffiques, and Discoueries of the English Nation*. London, George Bishop, Ralfe Newberie and Robert Barker, 1600

The Hakluyt Society. *Select Letters of Christopher Columbus*. London, 1870

The Hakluyt Society. *The Voyage of Semen Dezhnev in 1648*. London, 1981

The Hakluyt Society. *The First Voyage Round the World by Magellan*. London, 1874

The Hakluyt Society. *The Journal of Christopher Columbus and Documents Relating to the Voyages of John Cabot and Caspar Corte Real*. London, 1893

Harland, John. *Seamanship in the age of Sail An Account of Shiphandling*. London, 1985

Harley J.B. & David Woodward (ed), *The History of Cartography vol I. Cartography in prehistoric, Ancient, and Medieval Europe and Mediterranean*, Chicago, 1987

Harley J.B.& David Woodward (ed). *The History of Cartography vol. II, Cartography in the Traditional Islamic and South Asian Societys*. Chicago, 1992

Harley J.B.& David Woodward (ed). *The History of Cartography vol II, Cartography in the Traditional East and South-East Asian Societys*. Chicago, 1994

Harrisse, Henry. *The Discovery of North America: A Critical Documentary, and Historical Investigatio*. London, Henry Stevens and Son, 1892

Harrisse, Henry. *L'atterage de Jean Cabot au continent Américain en 1497*. Goettingue, Imprimerie de l'Université, 1897

Harrisse, Henry. *John Cabot the Discoverer of North America and Sebastian his Son: A chapter of the Maritime History of England under the Tudors, 1496-1557*. London, Benjamin Franklin Stevens, 1896

Haskell, Francis. *History and its Images Art and the Interpretation of the Past*. New Haven, 1993

Hattendorf, John B. *The Boundless Deep…The European Conquest of the Oceans, 1450 to 1840*. Providence, 2003

Henri, Yule. *The Book of Ser Marco Polo The Venetian Concerning the Kingdoms and Marvels of the East*, vol. I. & vol. II. London, 1921

Heaps, Leo. *Log of the Centurion Based on the original papers of captain Philip Saumarez on board HMS Centurion, Lord Anson's flagship during his circumnavigation 1740-44*. London, 1973

Hodgkin, Robert Howard. *A History of the Anglo-Saxons*. Oxford, 1935

Hornborg, Eirik. *Purjehdusmerenkulun historia*. Porvoo, 1965

Howse, Derek. *Greenwich Time and the Discovery of the Longitude*. Oxford, 1980

Howse, Derek & Michael Sanderson. *The Sea Chart An Historical Survey based on the Collections in the National Maritime Museum*. Norwich, 1973

Hues, Robert. *Tractatus de globis et eorum usu. A Treatise descriptive of the Globes*. The Hakluyt Society, London, 1889

Hutchinson, Gillian. *Medieval Ships and Shipping*. London, 1998

Ingstad, Helge. *The Norse Discovery of America, Vol. II. The historical background and the evidence of the Norse settlement discovered in Newfoundland.* Oslo, 1985

Jane, Cecil (Translator and Editor). *The Voyages of Christopher Columbus: Being the Journals of his First and Third, and the Letters Concerning His First and Last Voyages, to which is added the Account of his Second Voyage Written by Andres Bernaldez.* London, 1930

Jane, Cecil (ed*). Select Documents Illustrating the Four Voyages of Columbus* Vol I. The Hakluyt Society, London, 1929

Jane, Cecil (ed). *Select Documents Illustrating the Four Voyages of Columbus* Vol II. The Hakluyt Society, London, 1932

Jourdin, Michel and Monique de La Roncière. *Sea Charts of the Early Explorers: 13th to 17th Century.* Translated by L. le R. Dethan, Thames & Hudson, 1984

Johnson, Donald S. *Charting the Sea of Darkness The Four Voyages of Henry Hudson.* New York, 1995

Johnson, Donald S. *Phantom Islands of the Atlantic.* New York, 1994

Joyner, Tim. *Magellan,* Maine, 1992

Karttunen, Hannu, Jarmo Koistinen, Elena Saltikoff, & Olli Manner. *Ilmakehä ja sää.* Ursan julkaisuja 62, Helsinki, 2002

Kemp, Peter & Richard Ormond. *The Great Age of Sail Maritime Art and Photography.* Oxford, 1986

Kennedy, Gavin. *Captain Bligh the man and his mutinies.* London, 1989

Kerr, Robert. *A General Collection of Voyages and Travels, arranged in systematic order: Forming a Complete History of the Origin and Progress by Sea and Land From the Earliest Ages to the Present Time.* Edinburgh, 1824

Kirby, David. *Östersjöländernas historia 1492-1772.* Stockholm, 1994

Kirby, David & Merja-Liisa Hinkkanen. *The Baltic and the North Seas.* London, 2000

Klencke, Herman. *Alexander von Humboldts Lif och Resor, en Biografisk Minnesvård af Herman Klencke.* Stockholm, 1879

Klint, G. *Pilote de la Mer Baltique.* Paris, 1856

Koeman, Cornelis. *The Sea on Paper, Theatrum Orbis Terrarum.* Amsterdam, 1972

Koeman, Cornelis. *The History of Lucas Janszoon Waghenaer and his Sipegel der Zeevaerdt.* Lausanne, 1964

Koeman, Cornelis. The *Sea on paper The Story of the Van Keulens and their "Sea-torch".* Amsterdam, 1972

Kotzebue, Otto von. *Reise um die Welt in den Jahren 1823, 24, 25 und 26.* Weimar, 1830

Kovach, N. A. *Abel Janszoon Tasmans Journal.* Los Angeles, 1965

Lainema Matti, Nurminen Juha. *Ultima Thule – Arctic Explorations.* Helsinki, 2001

Laivat ja merenkulku. Helsinki, 1998

Lamb, Ursula. *Nautical Scientists and their clients in Iberia (1508-1624): Science from Imperial perspective.* Lisboa, 1984

Lamb, Ursula. *A Navigator's Universe; the Libro de cosmographia of 1538. Translated and with an introduction to Pedro de Medina's work.* University of Chicago Press, 1972

Landström, Björn. *Kolumbus Valtameren Amiraali Don Cristóbal Colón ja hänen läntisen meritien kautta Intiaan tekemänsä matkat.* Helsinki, 1966

Landström, Björn Laiva. *Katsaus laivan historiaan alkukantaisesta lautasta atomikäyttöiseen sukellusveneeseen.* Helsinki, 1961

Landström, Björn. *Tie Intiaan Löytöretkistä maitse ja meritse alkaen Puntin retkikunnasta v. 1493 eKr. päättyen Hyväntoivonniemen löytämiseen v. 1488 jKr.* Helsinki, 1964

Lane, Frederik C. *Venice A Maritime Republic.* Baltimore, 1973

Lang, A. W. *Seekarten der südlichen Nord- und Ostsee.* Hamburg, 1968

Lanman, Jonathan T. *On the Origin of the Portolan Charts, The Hermon Dunlap Smith Center for the History of Cartography Occasional Publication No. 2.* Chicago, 1987

Larner, John. *Marco Polo and the Discovery of the World.* New Haven, 1999

Linchoten, Jan Huygen van. *Histoire de la navigation.* Amsterdam, 1638

Linklater, Eric & John Murray. *The Voyage of the Challenger.* London, 1972

Lockley, Ronald M. *Animal Navigation.* New York, 1967

Logan F. Donald. *The Vikings in History.* London, 1992

Mackenzie, Alexander. *Voyages from Montreal, on the River St. Laurence, Through the Continent of North America, to the Frozen and Pacific Oceans: In the years 1789 and 1793. With a Preliminary Account of the Rise, Progress, and Present State of the Fur Trade of That Country.* London, 1801

Markham, Clements R. (translator, notes, and introduction). *The Journal of Christopher Columbus (during his 1st voyage, 1492-93) and Documents relating to the Voyages of John Cabot and Gaspar Corte Real.* The Hakluyt Society, London, 1893

Markham, Clements (ed). *Early Spanish Voyages to the Strait of Magellan.* The Hakluyt Society, London, 1911

Marcus, G.J. *The Conquest of the North Atlantic.* Oxford University Press, 1981

Marsden, John. *The Fury of the Northmen.* New York, 1993

Maury, Matthew Fontaine. *The Physical Geography of the Sea and its meteorology.* Mineola, 2003

May W. E. *A History of Marine Navigation.* Wiltshire, 1973

McConnell, Anita. *No Sea Too Deep The History of Oceanographic Instruments.* Bristol, 1982

McKie, D., Harcourt Brown, H.W. Robinson. *Annals of Science A Quaterly review of the history of science since the Reneissance,* vol. I. London, 1936

Medina, Pedro de. *The Libro de Cosmographía of 1538 A Navigator's Universe Translation and Introduction by Ursula Lamb Published for The Newberry Library By the University of Chicago Press.* Chicago, 1972

Middleton, W. E. Knowles. *The History of the Barometer.* Wiltshire, 1994

Miller Christy (ed). *The Voyages of Captain Luke Foxe of Hull and Captain Thomas James of Bristol in Search of a North-West Passage in 1631-32* Vol. II. The Hakluyt Society, London, 1894

Correa, Gaspar. *The Three Voyages of Vasco da Gama and His Viceroyalty.* The Hakluyt Society, London, 1869

Milton, Giles. *Big Chief Elizabeth How Englands Adventurers Gambled and Won the new World.* London, 2000

Milton, Giles. *Nathaniels's Nutmeg How One Man's Courage Changed the Course of Histor".* London, 1999

Milton, Giles. *The Riddle and the Kinight In Search of Sir John Mandeville.* London, 2001

Mohn, H.& C. Wille. *The Norwegian North-Atlantic Expedition 1876-1878.* 1882

Mollat du Jourdin, Michel, Monique de la Roncière, M-M Azard, I Raynaud-Nguyen, M-A Vannereau. *Sea Charts of the Early Explorers 13th to 17th Century,* New York, 1984

Monmonier, Mark. *Rhumb Lines and Map Wars A Social History of the Mercator Projection.* Chicago, 2004

Morison, Samuel Eliot. *The European Discovery of America The Northern Voyages a.d. 500-1600.* New York, 1971

Morison, Samuel Eliot. *The Great Explorers The European Discovery of America.* New York, 1978

Morison, Samuel Eliot. *Admiral of the Ocean Sea A Life of Christopher Columbus,* vol. I. Boston, 1942

Murphy, Henry C. *The Voyage of Verrazzano A Chapter in the Early History of Maritime Discovery in America.* New York, 1875

Müller, Gerhard Friedrich. *Bering's Voyages. The Reports From Russia.* Fairbanks, 1986

Månszon, Johan. *Een Siö-book som innehåller Om Sjöfarten i Öster-Sjön Jänväl och Koosar, Landkänningar, Streckningar, Inlopen, Banckar och Grunden.* Stockholm, 1644

Nansen, Fridtjof. *Farthest North Being the Record of a Voyage of Exploration of the Ship Fram 1893-96 and of a Fifteen months' Sleigh Journey By Dr. Nansen and Lieut. Johansen With an Appendix by Otto Sverdrup Captain of the Fram.* Vol. I. London, 1897

Nansen, Fridtjof. *In Northern Mists Arctic Exploration in Early Times.* Vol. I. London, 1911

Nebenzahl, Kenneth. *Maps from the Age of Discovery Columbus to Mercator.* London, 1990

Nebenzahl, Kenneth. *Der Kolumbus Atlas Karten aus der Frühzeit der Entdeckungsreisen.* Braunschweig, 1990

Nichols, Peter. *Evolution's Captain The Dark Fate of the Man Who Sailed Charles Darwin Around the World.* New York, 2003

Nordenskiöld, Adolf Erik. *Facsimile-Atlas till kartografiens äldsta historia Innehållande afbildningar af de viktigaste kartor, tryckta före år 1600.* Stockholm, 1889

Nordenskiöld Adolf Erik. *Periplus. Utkast till sjökortens och sjöböckernas äldsta historia.* Stockholm, 1897

Nordenskiöld, Adolf Erik. *Vegas fård kring Asien och Europa Jemte en historisk återblick på föregående resor längs gamla verldens nordkust. Förra delen.* Stockholm, 1880

Nordenskiöld, Adolf Erik. *Vegas fård kring Asien och Europa Jemte en historisk återblick på föregående resor längs gamla verldens nordkust. Senare delen.* Stockholm, 1881

Nordenskiöld, Adolf Erik. *Nordost-Passagen, Vid Publicistklubbens fest för Nordenskiöld, den 30 april 1880.* Stockholm, 1880

O'Gorman, Edmundo. *The Invention of America.* Indiana University Press, 1961

Paluka, Frank. *The Three Voyages of Captain Cook,.* Pittsburg, 1974

Parry, J. H. *The Discovery of the Sea*. New York, 1974

Parry, William Edward. *Narrative of an Attempt to Reach the North Pole, in Boats Fitted for the Purpose, and Attached to His Majesty's Ship Hecla, in the Year 1827 Under the Command of Captain William Edward Parry.* London, 1828

Parry, William Edward. *Journal of a Voyage for the discovery of a North-West Passage From the Atlantic to the Pacific; Performed in the Years 1819-20, in His Majesty's Ships Hecla and Griper Under the Orders of Captain William Edward Parry.* London, 1821

Parry, William Edward. *Journal of a Second Voyage for the Discovery of a North-West Passage from the Atlantic to the Pacific; Performed in the Years 1821-22-23, in his Majesty's Ships Fury and Hecla, under the orders of Captain William Edward Parry.* London, 1824

Parry, William Edward. *Journal of a Third Voyage for the discovery of a North-West Passage From the Atlantic to the Pacific; Performed in the Years 1824-25, in His Majesty's Ships Hecla and Fury Under the Orders of Captain William Edward Parry.* London, 1826

Pastoureau, Mireille. *Voies Océanes: Del'ancien aux Nouveaux Mondes.* Editions Hervas, 1990

Pelletier, Monique. *Couleurs de la Terre, Des Mappe Mondes Médiévales aux Images Satelitales.* Paris, 1998

Penrose, Boies. *Travel and Discovery in the Renaissance 1420-1620.* London, 1952

Pereira, Duarte. *Pacheco Esmeraldo de Situ Orbis, Lisbon: c. 1505-1508, Translated and edited by George H.T. Kimble.* London: Hakluyt Society, Second Series, No. 74, 1937

Perry, T. M. *The Discovery of Australia The Charts and Maps of the Navigators and Explorers.* Melbourne, 1982

Phipps, Constantine John. *A Voyage Towards the North Pole Undertaken by His Majesty's Command 1773.* London, 1774

Pigafetta, Antonio. *Magellan's Voyage A Narrative Account of the First Circumnavigation*, vol II. New Haven, 1969

Pohl, Friedrich-Wilhelm. *Die Geschichte der navigation.* Hamburg, 1999

Polak, Jean. *Bibliographie Maritime Francaise depuis les temps les plus reculés jusqu'à 1914.* Grenoble, 1976

Polak, Jean & Michele. *Bibliographie Maritime Francaise depuis les temps les plus reculés jusqu'à 1914.* Grenoble, 1983

Postnikov, Alexei. *Russia in maps a history of the geographical study and cartography of the country.* Moscow, 1996

Power, Bernard A. *Climatological Analysis of Old Norse Sailing Directions for North Atlantic Routes*, The Royal Institute of Navigation Journal of Navigation 55: 109-116. 2002

Preston, Diana & Michael. *A Pirate of Exquisite Mind The Life of William Dampier, Explorer…* New York, 2004

Priestley, Herbert Ingram (editor and translator). *The Luna Papers: Documents Relating to the Expedition of Don Tristán de Luna y Arellano for the Conquest of La Florida In 1559-1561*, Vol. I & II. Deland, Florida: Florida State Historical Society, MCMXXVIII

Priestley, Herbert Ingram. *Tristán de Luna - Conquistador of the Old South A Study of Spanish Imperial Strategy.* California, 1936

Ptolemaeus, Claudius. *Cosmographia.* Roma 1478. Amsterdam, 1966

Ptolemaeus, Claudius. *Cosmographia.* Bologna 1477,

Amsterdam, 1963

Pumfrey, Stephen. *Latitude The Magnetic Earth.* Cambridge, 2003

Putman, Robert. *Early Sea Charts.* New York, 1983

Pärssinen, Leena (ed). *Terra Cognita, Maailma tulee tunnetuksi.* Helsinki, 2000

Quinn, David Beers. *England and the Discovery of America, 1431-1620.* New York, 1974

Raisz, Erwin. *Principles of Cartography.* New York, 1962

Randier, Jean. *Marine Navigation Instruments.* London, 1980

Randles, W.G.L. *The Unmaking of the Medieval Christian Cosmos, 1500-1760: From Solid Heavens to Boundless Æther.* Aldershot, 1999

Randles, W.G.L. *Geography, Cartography and Nautical Science in the Renaissance.* 2000

Ravenstein, E.G. (Editor and Translator*). A Journal of the First Voyage of Vasco da Gama, 1497-1499.* The Hakluyt Society, London, 1893

Ravenstein, E. G.(ed). *A Journal of the First Voyage of Vasco da Gama 1497-1499.* The Hakluyt Society, London, 1898

Renfrew, Colin and Zubrow, Ezra B.W. (editors). *The Ancient Mind: Elements of Cognitive Archaeology.* Cambridge University Press, 1999

Rice, A. L. *British Oceanographic Vessels 1800-1950.* London, 1986

Richard, Henry (ed). *The Voyages of the Venetian Brothers, Nicolò & Antonio Zeno, to the Northern Seas, in the XIVth Century Comprising the Latest Known Accounts of the Lost Colony of Greenland; and of the Northmen in America Before Columbus.* The Hakluyt Society, London, 1873

Riley-Smith, Jonathan (ed). *The Atlas of the Crusades.* London, 1990

Roesdahl, Else. *Viikingit.* Helsinki, 1993

Roseman, Christina Horst. *Pytheas of Massalia.* Chicago, 1994

Rosenfeldt, Werner von. *Navigationen eller Styrmans-Konsten Til Ungdomens Nytta med Kongl. Amiralitetet.* Facsimile, 1693

Ross, John. *Appendix Narrative of a Second Voyage in Search of North-West Passage, and of a Residence in the Arctic Regions During the Years 1829, 1830, 1831, 1832, 1833.* London, 1835

Sabine, Edward. *Narrative of an Expedition to the Polar Sea.* London, 1840

Sanderson, Michael. *Sea Battles A Reference Guide.* Devon, 1975

Sarytschew, Gawrila. *Account of a Voyage of Discovery to the North-East of Siberia, the Frozen Ocean and the North-East Sea.* London, 1806

Saunders, Harold N. *All the Astrolabes.* Oxford, 1984

Savours, Ann. *The Search for the North West Passage.* London, 1999

Savours, Ann. *The Voyages of the Discovery The Illustrated History of Scott's Ship.* Kent, 1992

Scammell, G.V. *The World Encompassed The First European Maritime Empires c.800-1650.* London, 1981

Scoresby, William. *Journal of a Voyage to the Northern Whale-fishery Including Researches and Discoveries on the Eastern Coast of West Greenland, Made in the Summer of 1822, in the Ship Baffin of Liverpool.* Edinburgh, 1823

Scoresby, William. *An Account of the Arctic Regions, with*

a *History and Description of the Northern Whale-fishery.* vol. I – vol.II. Edinburgh, 1820

Seller, J & C. Price. *The English Pilot. The Fifth Book.* London 1701. Amsterdam, 1973

Serres Dominic & John Thomas. *Liber Nauticus and Instructor in the Art of Marine Drawing.* London, 1805. Facsimile, London, 1979

Sharp, Andrew. *Ancient Voyagers in Polynesia.* Berkley, 1964

Singer, Dorothea Waley. *Giordano Bruno, His Life and Thought: With Annotated Translation of His Work on The Infinite Universe and Worlds.* New York, 1968

Shirley, Rodney W. *The Mapping of the World Early Printed World Maps 1472-1700.* London, 1984

Skelton, R. A. *Explorers' Maps Chapters in the Cartographic Record of Geographical Discovery.* London, 1970

Skelton, R. A. (ed). *The Journals of Captain James Cook CHARTS AND VIEWS Drawn by Cook and His Officers and Reproduced from the Original Manuscripts.* Woodbridge, 1999

Skelton, R. A., Thomas E. Marston, & George D. Painter. *The Vinland Map and the Tartar Relation.* New Haven, 1965

Slocum, Joshua. *Sailing alone Around The World.* London, 2003

Sobel, Dava. *Longitude The True Story of a Lone Genius Who Solved the Greatest Scientific Problem of his Time.* New York, 1995

Stevens, Henry N. *Ptolemy's Geography A brief account of all the printed editions down to 1730.* Facsimile, Amsterdam, 1908

Stevenson, Edward Luther. *Terrestrial and Celestial Globes their History and Construction Including a Consideration of their Value as Aids in the Study of Geography and Astronomy* vol. I-vol. II. New York, 1971

Stimson, Alan. *The Mariner's Astrolabe. A survey of known, surviving sea astrolabes.* Utrecht, 1988

Stimson, Dorothy. *The Gradual Acceptance of the Copernican Theory of the Universe.* New York, 1917

Suarez, Thomas. *Early Mapping of the Pacific.* Singapore, 2004

Subrahmanym, Sanjay. *The Career and Legend of Vasco da Gama.* Cambridge, 1997

Taylor E. G. R. *The Haven-Finding Art A History of Navigation from Odysseus to Captain Cook.* London, 1958

Taylor, E.G.R. & Richey M.W. *The Geometrical Seaman A book of early nautical instruments.* London, 1962

Temple-Leader, John. *Life of Sir Robert Dudley followed by The Italian Biography of Sir Robert Dudley and Six Additional Plates from the "Arcano Del Mare".* Amsterdam, 1977

Theberge, Albert E. *Technical Papers 1989 ASPRS/ ACSM Annual Convention Surveying and Cartography.* NOAA Central Library Call No. TA501. A638 1989 Vol. 5, 1989

Thrower, Norman J.W (ed). *The Three Voyages of Edmond Halley in the Paramore 1698-1701*, The Hakluyt Society. London, 1981

Thirslund, Søren. *Navigationens historie I-III.* 1998, Helsingør

Thirslund, Søren. *Viking compass guided Norsemen to America.* S. Thirslund & C.L.Vebaek, 1992

Thomas, Stephen D. *The Last Navigator.* London, 1987

Thornton, John. *The English Pilot. The Third Book.* London 1703, Amsterdam, 1970

Throckmorton, Peter (ed). *The Sea Remembers Shipwrecks and Archaeology From Homer's Greece to the rediscovery of the Titanic.* London, 1987

Tibbetts, G. R. *Arab Navigation in the Indian Ocean Before the Coming of the Portuguese.* London, 1971

Tibbetts, G.R. *Arabia in Early Maps a bibliography of maps covering the Peninsula of Arabia.* New York, 1978

Tibbetts, G.R. *The Navigational Theory of the Arabs in the Fifteenth and Sixteenth Centuries, Agrupamento de Estudos de Cartografia Antiga Junta de Investigações do Ultramar.* Lisboa, Coimbra, 1969

Tiele, P.A. (ed). *The Voyage of John Huyghen van Linschoten to the East Indies.* vol. II , The Hakluyt Society. London, 1885

Tollens, Hendrik. *An Arctic Poem Translated by Daniel van Pelt, with preface and historical introduction G.P. Putnam's Sons.* London, 1884

Turner, Gerard L'E. *Antique Scientific Instruments.* Dorset, 1980

Turner, Gerard L'E. *Nineteenth-Century Scientific Instruments.* London, 1983

Turner, Sharon. *The History of the Anglo-Saxons From the Earliest Period to the Norman Conquest.* Paris, 1840

Urness, Carol. *Waldseemüller's Globe and Planisphere of 1507.* Minneapolis, 1999

Urness, Carol. *Portolan Charts.* Minneapolis, 1999

Veer, Gerrit de. *The Three Voyages of William Barents to the Arctic Regions (1594, 1595, and 1596).* The Hakluyt Society, London, 1876

Vilhjálmsson, Thorsteinn. *Time and Travel in Old Norse Society* (Paper given at conference in Reykjavik) Science Institute, University of Iceland Reykjavik, Iceland, 1999

Vorsey, Louis de. *Pioneer Charting of the Gulf Stream: The Contributions of Benjamin Franklin and William Gerard De Brahm,* Imago Mundi, Journal of the International Society for the History of Cartography No. 28 (Second Series, Vol. 2). Kent, England, 1976

Vorsey, Louis de. *Gulf Stream on Eighteenth Century Maps and Charts.* The Map Collector, Issue 15, June 1981

Waghenaer, Lucas Jansz. *Spieghel der Zeevaerdt.* Leyden 1584-1585, Amsterdam, 1964

Wagner, Henry. *Sir Francis Drake's Voyage around the World Its aims and achievements.* San Francisco, 1926

Wakely Andrew. *The Mariner's Compass Rectified.* London, 1757

van den Broecke, Marcel P.R. *Ortelius Atlas Maps an Illustrated Guide.* Goy, 1996

Wallis, Helen (ed). *Carteret's Voyage Round the World 1766-1769 vol. II – vol. II.* The Hakluyt Society, London, 1965

Waters, D.W. *The Rutters of the Sea The Sailing Directions of Pierre Garcie.* New Haven, 1967

Waters, D. W. *The Art of Navigation in England in Elizabethian and Early Stuart Times.* London, 1958

Waugh, Albert E. *Sundials Their Theory and Construction.* New York, 1973

Verne, Jules. *Exploration of the World.* London, 1879

White, Andrew Dickson. *A History of the Warfare of Science with Theology in Christendom.* New York, 1932

Whitfield, Peter. *New Found Lands Maps in the History of Exploration.* New York, 1998

Whitfield, Peter. *The Mapping of the Heavens.* London, 1995

Williams, Glyn. *The Price of all the Oceans The Triumph and Tragedy of Anson's Voyage Round the World.* London, 1999

Williams, J.E.D. *From Sails to Satellites The Origin and Development of Navigational Science.* Oxford, 1994

Williams, Neville. *The Sea Dogs Privateers, Plunder and Piracy in the Elizabethan Age.* New York, 1975

Williams, Richardson. *A General Collection of Voyages and Discoveries Made during the Fifteenth and Sixteenth Centuries.* London, W. Richardson, 1789

Wilson, Derek. *The World Encompassed Drake's Great Voyage 1577-1580.* London, 1977

Wilson, Derek. *The circumnavigators.* New York, 1989

Winter, Heinrich. *Die Katalanische Nao von 1450.* Magdeburg, 1956

Vollmer, John E., Keall, E.J., Nagai-Berthrong, E. *Silk Roads - China Ships An Exhibition of East-West Trade.* Toronto, 1983

Wright, John Kirtland. *The Geographical Lore of the Time of the Crusades: A Study in the History of Medieval Science and Tradition In Western Europe.* New York, 1965

Wroth, Lawrence C. *The Way of a Ship An Essay of the Literature of navigation science.* Portland, 1937

Wroth, Lawrence, C. *Some American Contributions to the Art of Navigation.* Boston, 1947

Yamashita, Michael. *Zheng He.* Vercelli, 2006

Yefimov, A.V.(ed). *Atlas of Geographical Discoveries in Siberia and North-Western America XVII-XVIII Centuries.* Moscow, 1964

Yenne, Bill. *The Atlas of the Solar System.* Greenwich, 1987

INDEX OF NAMES